GERMANS

At the end of the Second World War, mass forced migration and population movement accompanied the collapse of Nazi Germany's occupation and the start of Soviet domination in East-Central Europe. Hugo Service examines the experience of Poland's new territories, exploring the Polish Communist attempt to 'cleanse' these territories in line with a nationalist vision, against the legacy of brutal wartime occupations of Central and Eastern Europe by Nazi Germany and the Soviet Union. The expulsion of over three million Germans was intertwined with the arrival of millions of Polish settlers. Around one million German citizens were categorized as 'native Poles' and urged to adopt a Polish national identity. The most visible traces of German culture were erased. Jewish Holocaust survivors arrived and, for the most part, soon left again. Drawing on two case studies, the book exposes how these events varied by region and locality.

HUGO SERVICE is Departmental Lecturer in Modern European History at the University of Oxford.

NEW STUDIES IN EUROPEAN HISTORY

Edited by

The aim of this series in early modern and modern European history is to publish outstanding works of research, addressed to important themes across a wide geographical range, from southern and central Europe, to Scandinavia and Russia, from the time of the Renaissance to the present. As it develops the series will comprise focused works of wide contextual range and intellectual ambition.

A full list of titles published in the series can be found at:
www.cambridge.org/newstudiesineuropeanhistory

GERMANS TO POLES

Communism, Nationalism and Ethnic Cleansing after the Second World War

HUGO SERVICE

CAMBRIDGE
UNIVERSITY PRESS

University Printing House, Cambridge CB2 8BS, United Kingdom

Cambridge University Press is part of the University of Cambridge.

It furthers the University's mission by disseminating knowledge in the pursuit of education, learning and research at the highest international levels of excellence.

www.cambridge.org
Information on this title: www.cambridge.org/9781107595484

First published 2013
First paperback edition 2015

A catalogue record for this publication is available from the British Library

Library of Congress Cataloguing in Publication data
Service, Hugo, 1981–
Germans to Poles : communism, nationalism and ethnic cleansing after the second World War / Hugo Service.
pages cm. – (New studies in European history)
Includes bibliographical references and index.
ISBN 978-1-107-67148-5 (hardback)
1. Language policy – Poland – History. 2. Language policy – Germany – History. 3. Polish language – Political aspects – History. 4. German language – Poland – History. 5. Germany – World War, 1939–1945 – Language. I. Title.
P119.32.P6S47 2013
306.44′9438 – dc23 2013008430

ISBN 978-1-107-67148-5 Hardback
ISBN 978-1-107-59548-4 Paperback

Additional resources for this publication at www.cambridge.org/service

Contents

Maps

Acknowledgements

I must thank a number of scholars for helping me to write this book. I am indebted most of all to my dad, Robert Service, and to my doctoral supervisor, Richard J. Evans, both of whom have read this book in its earlier and later incarnations and have contributed to its writing in many more ways besides. I am extremely grateful, too, to Timothy Snyder, Christopher Clark, Michael Wildt, Rudolf Muhs and Norman Davies for the enormous help they have given me along the way. I am also very grateful to Jim Bjork, Michael Fleming and Gerhard Wolf for reading draft chapters and to Marek Wierzbicki, Piotr Bajda and Spasimir Domradzki, who read the entire manuscript as part of the 'Recovering Forgotten History' conference which I attended in Wrocław and Kraków in early summer 2012. All of these scholars offered valuable suggestions and criticisms which enabled me to improve the book considerably. Any mistakes and flaws still present in the text are, of course, my own responsibility. I would also like to thank Gertrud Pickhan for hosting me during a pleasant year I spent at the Freie Universität Berlin in 2007–8.

I am greatly indebted to the British Academy, the Alfred Toepfer Stiftung and the German Academic Exchange Service, without whose generous support I simply could not have written this book. I would also like to express my gratitude to the directors and staff of the Polish State Archives in Jelenia Góra, Opole, Wrocław and Katowice and the German Federal Archive in Bayreuth, who allowed and helped me to use the archival documents on which this book is principally based.

On a more personal note, I wish to say thank you to Stefan Baker, his cousin Ewa Krzyżanowska-Łepecka and Artur Jaworski for easing my move to Poland and to Przemek Szymczonek and Asia Bogacz for immersing me in the Polish language and making my time in Poland so enjoyable. I wish also to thank my mum, Adele Biagi, who has always been a source of help and advice. And I want to say a particular thank you to Anita Hurrell, who was there from the very start of this project. Without her practical, emotional and intellectual support I doubt this book would exist.

Abbreviations

APJG	Archiwum Państwowe we Wrocławiu Oddział w Jeleniej Górze
APK	Archiwum Państwowe w Katowicach
APO	Archiwum Państwowe w Opolu
APW	Archiwum Państowe we Wrocławiu
BOD	Bundesarchiv, Bayreuth, Ost-Dokumentation
CuRep	Current Issues Report by
head JGTA	The head of Jelenia Góra Town Administration
JG Chief	Jelenia Góra District's Chief Official
JGDA	Jelenia Góra District Administration
JGDA head S-PD	The head of Jelenia Góra District Administration's Social-Political Department
JGDA S-PD	Jelenia Góra District Administration's Social-Political Department
JG DepChief	Jelenia Góra District's Deputy Chief Official
JGTA	Jelenia Góra Town Administration
JGTA head S-PD	The head of Jelenia Góra Town Administration's Social-Political Department
JGT Pres	Jelenia Góra's Town President
Ltr	Letter
LSRA	Lower Silesia's Regional Administration
LSRA S-DP	The Lower Silesian Regional Administration's Social-Political Department
MoRep	Monthly Report by
O Chief	Opole District's Chief Official
ODA	Opole District Administration
ODA head S-PD	The head of Opole District Administration's Social-Political Department
ODA S-PD	Opole District Administration's Social-Political Department

O DepChief	Opole District's Deputy Chief Official
OTA	Opole Town Administration
OTA head S-PD	The head of Opole Town Administration's Social-Political Department
OTA S-PD	Opole Town Administration's Social-Political Department
OT Pres	Opole's Town President
Rep	Report
SiRep	Situation Report by
SRO	State Repatriation Office
USRA	Upper Silesia's Regional Administration
USRA S-PD	The Upper Silesian Regional Administration's Social-Political Department
VoiInspCom	Silesia Voivodship Inspection Committee (*Komisja Kontrolna Wojewódzka*)
WR	Witness Report, [writer of report], [writer's former place of residence in the prewar German territories east of the Oder-Neisse Line], [date when report was written]
WRs	Witness Reports

Introduction

Strolling around Opole a few years ago, I came across a poster declaring in Polish to passing strangers, 'Learn German!' Seeing an advertisement for a German language course in a twenty-first-century Polish town should be completely unremarkable. Germany is an obvious destination for Polish citizens seeking to study or work abroad, and it is no surprise that German language courses are on offer there. And yet the existence of such a poster was remarkable. At the start of 1945, the vast majority of Opole's inhabitants had spoken German as their first language. Around a year later it became a punishable offence to speak German in public there. This book does not seek to understand how the German language went from being forbidden in Opole after the end of the Second World War to being an attractive language for its residents to learn six decades later. Rather, it aims to understand the changes which took place in the first few years after the war that brought about this drastic turnaround in fortunes for the German language, in Opole and all other towns, cities and villages located in the territories which Poland gained from Germany in 1945. It seeks to understand the radical nationalist transformation which Poland's Communist-controlled regime attempted to impose on these territories in the second half of the 1940s.

These events have penetrated public consciousness in the English-speaking world very little since the late 1940s. Insofar as they have, the focus has always been on one particular element: the mass expulsion of Germans at the end of the Second World War. During the Cold War there were two separate sets of writings about the forced migration of Germans from postwar Polish territory. On one side of the Iron Curtain, West German publications treated the topic as one episode in a larger event: the flight and expulsion of Germans from the whole of East-Central and Eastern Europe in the years 1944–9. West German works tended to conflate the deliberate expulsion of German citizens and ethnic Germans from the eastern half of Europe, which got underway after the 'liberation' by Soviet and Soviet-backed forces, with the panicked flight and evacuation of civilians from the approaching Red Army in late 1944 and early 1945. This fostered the false impression that the wartime experience of flight and expulsion – which was characterized throughout by chaos, suffering and violence – differed little from what German citizens and German-speakers experienced in Poland, Czechoslovakia and elsewhere once the war was over. These West German publications tended to be memoirs or collections of testimonies rather than historical studies, produced by individuals with a direct connection to the events rather than professional historians. Correspondingly, they were of questionable scholarly value. Yet this literature formed an important part of the way in which West German society tried to come to terms with Germany's Nazi past in the first two and a half decades after the war. They helped to establish a firm consensus in West Germany in the 1950s and 1960s that Germans had been among the greatest victims of the Second World War and that these refugees and expellees from 'the East' had endured a fate in the years 1944–9 comparable to that of the Jews in the Holocaust.[1]

The West German government actively encouraged this trend. With the aim of furnishing West Germany with material for negotiations at a future peace conference, Bonn sponsored the collection of German witness testimonies. A selection of them was published as the multivolume *Documentation of the Expulsion of Germans* between 1953 and 1961. Edited and compiled by a team of leading German historians and containing a very large number of valuable historical sources accompanied by scholarly introductions, this documentary collection was the only serious contribution to historical research on this subject in West Germany before the 1980s. Yet despite clear efforts made by a number of the historians involved in

[1] For discussions of West German collective memory of the flight and expulsion of Germans from East-Central and Eastern Europe and the West German victimhood narrative, see Gilad Margalit, *Guilt, Suffering and Memory: Germany Remembers Its Dead of World War II* (Bloomington, Indiana, 2010), especially pp. 200–20; Robert G. Moeller, 'Remembering the War in a Nation of Victims', in Hanna Schissler (ed.), *The Miracle Years. A Cultural History of West Germany, 1949–1968* (Oxford, 2001), pp. 83–109; Bernd Faulenbach, 'Die Vertreibung der Deutschen aus den Gebieten jenseits von Oder und Neiße: Zur wissenschaftlichen und öffentlichen Diskussion in Deutschland', *Aus Politik und Zeitgeschichte*, B51–2, 2002, pp. 44–54; Rainer Schulze, 'Memory and Commemoration of Flight and Expulsion in Germany', in Pertti Ahonen, Gustavo Corni, Jerzy Kochanowski, Rainer Schulze, Tamás Stark and Barbara Stelzl-Marx, *People on the Move: Forced Population Movements in Europe in the Second World War and Its Aftermath* (Oxford, 2008), pp. 145–51; Krzysztof Ruchniewicz, 'Das Problem der Zwangsaussiedlung der Deutschen aus polnischer und deutscher Sicht in Vergangenheit und Gegenwart', *Berichte und Forschungen: Jahrbuch des Bundesinstituts für Kultur und Geschichte der Deutschen im östlichen Europa*, 10, 2002, pp. 8–13.

the project to ensure that the events it examined were understood in their proper context – which included of course the atrocities committed by the German occupiers of East-Central and Eastern Europe during the war – it too focused overwhelmingly on the suffering of Germans at the war's end. Indeed, it played a crucial role in establishing the German victimhood consensus in West German society during the 1950s and 1960s.[2]

This situation changed around the end of the 1960s, when social, generational and political changes brought to the fore voices calling for a reappraisal of the recent past within West German society. From that time onwards, organizations in the Federal Republic claiming to represent German and German-speaking refugees and expellees from East-Central and Eastern Europe were politically marginalized (see the Conclusion for more on the West German expellee movement). Books on the flight and expulsions continued to appear in the 1970s and 1980s, but they now struggled to find recognition in wider West German society.[3] Academic scholarship on the fate of the refugees and expellees did emerge in the Federal Republic at this time, but it was concerned with the integration and assimilation of these people in postwar West Germany rather than with their displacement in the years 1944–9. It was not until the mid 1980s that professional historians in the Federal Republic finally started to take seriously the subject of the mass uprooting of Germans and German speakers from East-Central and Eastern Europe at the end of the war – and to do so in a way which directly challenged the German victimhood consensus which had taken firm root in the country in the intervening decades.[4]

[2] Theodor Schieder et al. (eds.), *Dokumentation der Vertreibung der Deutschen aus Ost-Mitteleuropa* (5 vols. Bonn, 1953–61). For details on the origins, production and objectives of this multivolume documentary collection, see Mathias Beer, 'Der »Neuanfang« der Zeitgeschichte nach 1945. Zum Verhältnis von nationalsozialistischer Umsiedlungs- und Vernichtungspolitik und der Vertreibung der Deutschen aus Ostmitteleuropa', in Winfried Schulze and Otto Gerhard Oerle (eds.), *Deutsche Historiker im Nationalsozialismus* (Frankfurt am Main, 1999), p. 277; Beer, 'Im Spannungsfeld von Politik und Zeitgeschichte. Das Großforschungsprojekt "Dokumentation der Vertreibung der Deutschen aus Ost-Mitteleuropa"', *Vierteljahrshefte für Zeitgeschichte*, 46, 1998, pp. 363–5; Robert G. Moeller, *War Stories: The Search for a Usable Past in the Federal Republic of Germany* (Berkeley and Los Angeles, 2001), pp. 51–87.

[3] The political and social changes of the late 1960s and 1970s also explain why a government-commissioned report on 'expulsion crimes' completed by the German Federal Archive in 1974 was not published until 1989. See *Vertreibung und Vertreibungsverbrechen 1945–1948. Bericht des Bundesarchivs vom 28. Mai 1974. Archivalien und ausgewählte Erlebnisberichte* (Bonn, 1989); Mathias Beer, '"Ein der wissenschaftlichen Forschung sich aufdrängender historischer Zusammenhang". Von den deutschen Schwierigkeiten, "Flucht und Vertreibung" zu kontextualisieren', *Zeitschrift für Geschichtswissenschaft*, 51, 1, 2003, pp. 61–2.

[4] Wolfgang Benz (ed.), *Die Vertreibung der Deutschen aus dem Osten. Ursachen, Ereignisse, Folgen* (Frankfurt am Main, 1985). See also Gerd Becker, *Vertreibung und Aussiedlung der Deutschen aus Polen*

The situation was very different in the other German state. As a potential source of friction between the German Democratic Republic and other members of the Communist bloc, the topic of the expulsion of Germans and ethnic Germans from East-Central and Eastern Europe was almost completely avoided by historians and writers during the four decades that East Germany existed. The subject was taboo in the GDR. Officially, both the displacement of these people and the loss of Germany's prewar eastern territories to Poland were a simple consequence of the crimes committed by the elites of the Nazi Party and the German military. They therefore did not need to be discussed.[5] In Communist Poland, too, the expulsion of Germans was a highly sensitive subject. There was nothing in the way of public discussion. A letter written by Polish Catholic bishops to their counterparts in Germany in 1965 seeking reconciliation over events during and after the war was met with a wave of anti-Catholic propaganda and measures from the Communist authorities. This demonstrated very visibly to Polish society that no public discussion of this subject would be tolerated. On the other hand, academic study of the subject was allowed. In fact, it was in Communist Poland that serious historical scholarship got fully underway, largely unnoticed to the west of the Iron Curtain. Benefiting from access to Polish state archives, historians in Poland produced a number of important studies in the late 1960s and 1970s on the postwar expulsion of Germans from Poland. These works described in impressive detail particularly the more organized phase of the process from 1946 onwards. The works of Stefan Banasiak and Bronisław Pasierb deserve particular mention. Nevertheless, with the partial exception of Banasiak's unpublished study, censorship and self-censorship ensured that all Communist-era Polish studies presented a highly sanitized version of the events, skating over or omitting altogether those aspects which put the Polish authorities and Soviet military in a bad light.[6]

und den ehemals deutschen Ostgebieten. Vorgeschichte, Ursachen und Abläufe (Doctoral dissertation, Justus-Liebig-Universität Gießen, 1988).

[5] For more on the suppression of public discussion and historical writing about this subject in the German Democratic Republic, see Michael Schwartz, 'Tabu und Erinnerung. Zur Vertriebenen-Problematik in Politik und literarischer Öffentlichkeit der DDR', *Zeitschrift für Geschichtswissenschaft*, 2003, 1, pp. 85–101; Schwartz, 'Vertreibung und Vergangenheitspolitik: Ein Versuch über geteilte deutsche Nachkriegsidentitäten', *Deutschland Archiv: Zeitschrift für das vereinigte Deutschland*, 30, 2, 1997, pp. 182–95; Ruchniewicz, 'Zwangsaussiedlung', pp. 13–16.

[6] Stefan Banasiak, *Przesiedlenie Niemców z Polski w latach 1945–50* (unpublished manuscript, Uniwersytet Łódzki, 1968); Bronisław Pasierb, *Migracja ludności niemieckiej z Dolnego Śląska w latach 1944–1947* (Wrocław, Warsaw, Kraków, 1969); Zdzisław Łempiński, *Przesiedlenie ludności niemieckiej z województwa śląsko-dąbrowskiego w latach 1945–1950* (Katowice, 1979); Tadeusz Białecki, *Przesiedlenie ludności niemieckiej z Pomorza Zachodniego po II wojnie światowej* (Poznań, 1969); K. Skubiszewski,

The subject did not gain wider public attention in Poland until the collapse of Communism in 1989. The path had been laid for this in the 1980s by Jan Józef Lipski's 1981 *samizdat* pamphlet 'Two Fatherlands – Two Patriotisms' and Adam Krzemiński's 1988 article 'I Forced Horst Bienek to Migrate' in the officially authorized magazine *Polityka*. Both acknowledged German suffering in Poland at the end of the Second World War.[7] Then, as censorship disappeared and the political atmosphere was transformed by the end of Communist government, Polish historians and journalists began to write critical studies and articles at the start of the 1990s about the postwar Polish authorities' treatment of Germans. This stimulated a lively public debate on the topic. By the mid 1990s, a new generation of German historians also began to take up the subject, as they overcame fears of being accused of pursuing a German nationalist agenda and as they acquired the language skills necessary to make use of sources in suddenly accessible Polish state archives. These historians were at pains to distance themselves from the tendency of their West German forerunners to dwell on the misery of Germans.

Yet this did not cause the German victimhood narrative to disappear in the unified German state. In fact, around the turn of the millennium, this narrative experienced a powerful resurgence in the Federal Republic of Germany – with a wave of new novels, television documentaries, magazine articles, museum exhibitions and works of popular history giving it a prominent place in public discourse once more. Such activities can be understood as part of a public process of redefining German national identity in the wake of the unification of East and West Germany. The 'rediscovery' of the flight and expulsion of Germans from East-Central and Eastern Europe in the last fifteen years happened partly because it was an aspect of the recent past shared by both East and West Germans that could be understood as involving Germans as 'victims' rather than 'perpetrators'. The resurgence of German victimhood, however, also transformed the character of the public debate in Poland. It helped to steer it away from the more critically reflective stance taken in the early to

Wysiedlenie Niemców po II wojnie światowej (Warsaw, 1968); Stanisław Żyromski, *Przesiedlenie ludności niemieckiej z województwa olsztyńskiego poza granice Polski w latach 1945–1950* (Olsztyn, 1969).

[7] For discussions of how the subject of the expulsion of Germans was approached in Communist-era Poland by the regime and by the country's historians, see Włodzimierz Borodziej, 'Historiografia Polska o "wypędzeniu" Niemców', *Studia i Materiały*, 2, 1996, pp. 249–69; Ruchniewicz, 'Zwangsaussiedlung', pp. 16–20; Jerzy Kochanowski, 'Memory and Commemoration of Flight and Expulsion in Poland', in Ahonen et al., *People*, pp. 155–60. A published version of Jan Józef Lipski's essay 'Dwie ojczyzny – dwa patriotyzmy. Uwagi o megalomanii narodowej i ksenofobii Polaków' can be found in Lipski, *Powiedzić sobie wszystko . . . Eseje o sąsiedztwie polsko-niemieckim* (Gliwice 1996), pp. 36–73.

mid 1990s to a far more defensive one in the postmillennium years. On a number of occasions over the past decade, public memorialization of flight and expulsion in Germany has provoked strong condemnation from journalists and politicians in Poland. The controversy has at times been explosive. It has impacted significantly on diplomatic relations between Germany and Poland. The longest-lasting and most intense controversy has revolved around plans devised by Germany's expellee movement, led by the controversial conservative politician Erika Steinbach, to establish a so-called Centre against Expulsions in Berlin. Serious public opposition to this proposal in Poland and heavy criticism from left-leaning politicians in Germany managed to obstruct it for a number of years. But in 2008 the German federal government did approve an alternative plan to create an exhibition and documentary centre in Berlin concerned with flight and expulsion. At the time of writing, the centre had still not been opened.[8]

In the academic sphere things have looked very different. In the last two decades Polish, German and Anglo-American historians have together provided a critical reassessment of events in Poland's new territories at the end of the Second World War. The maltreatment, incarceration and forced migration of German citizens and ethnic Germans in Poland at the war's end has been subjected to a thorough reexamination in an important documentary collection compiled by Polish and German historians and edited by Włodzimierz Borodziej and Hans Lemberg. There have also been many excellent new studies by the Polish historians Bernadetta Nitschke, Edmund Nowak, Stanisław Jankowiak, Piotr Madajczyk, Danuta Berlińska, Jerzy Kochanowski, Leszek Olejnik, Witold Stankowski, Zenon Romanow, Beata Ociepka and, outside Poland,

[8] For discussions of the recent resurgence of German victimhood discourse and the public memorialization of flight and expulsion in Germany, see Margalit, *Guilt*, especially pp. 221–88; Eva Hahn and Hans Henning, *Die Vertreibung im deutschen Erinnern: Legenden, Mythos, Geschichte* (Paderborn, 2010); Helmut Schmitz (ed.), *A Nation of Victims? Representations of German Wartime Suffering from 1945 to the Present* (Amsterdam and New York, 2007). For more on the 1990s public debate in Poland about the expulsions of Germans, see Klaus Bachmann and Jerzy Kranz (eds.), *Przeprosić za wypędzenie? O wysiedleniu Niemców po II wojnie światowej* (Kraków, 1997) and Włodzimierz Borodziej and Artur Hajnicz (eds.), *Kompleks wypędzenia* (Kraków, 1998). For the Polish response to the postmillennium renewal of German victimhood discourse, see Thomas Petersen, *Flucht und Vertreibung aus Sicht der deutschen, polnischen und tschechischen Bevölkerung* (Bonn, 2005); Kochanowski, 'Memory', p. 158. For opposition from German academic historians to the resurgence of German victimhood discourse, see Jürgen Danyel and Philipp Ther (eds.), *Flucht und Vertreibung in europäischer Perspektive*, special issue of *Zeitschrift für Geschichtswissenschaft*, 2003, 1. For the current situation regarding the exhibition and documentary centre to be established in Berlin, see http://www.dhm.de/sfvv/presse.html [last accessed 27.7.2012].

Sebastian Siebel-Achenbach.[9] New light has similarly been shed on the fate of the German citizens in Poland's new territories who were designated by the postwar Polish authorities as 'indigenous Poles' (*autochtoni*) and therefore given the opportunity to avoid expulsion to Germany – in studies by the historians Bernard Linek, Piotr Madajczyk, Grzegorz Strauchold, Andrzej Sakson, Michał Lis, Zenon Romanow, Małgorzata Świder, Richard Blanke, Leszek Belzyt and Andreas Kossert.[10] This has moved us far beyond the important but limited Communist-era studies of Jan Misztal, Zbigniew Kowalski and others.[11]

Another subject addressed by the new studies is the mass influx of Polish settlers into Poland's new territories at the end of the war – studied alongside related topics by the Polish historians Stanisław Ciesielski, Dorota Sula,

[9] Włodzimierz Borodziej and Hans Lemberg (eds.), *Niemcy w Polsce 1945–1950. Wybór Dokumentów* (4 vols., Warsaw, 2000–2001); Bernadetta Nitschke, *Wysiedlenie ludności niemieckiej z Polski w latach 1945–1949* (Zielona Góra, 1999); Edmund Nowak, *Cien Łambinowic* (Opole, 1991); Edmund Nowak, *Obozy na Śląsku Opolskim w systemie powojennych obozów w Polsce (1945–1950). Historia i implikacja* (Opole, 2002); Stanisław Jankowiak, *Wysiedlenie i emigracja ludności niemieckiej w polityce władz polskich w latach 1945–1970* (Warsaw, 2005); Piotr Madajczyk and Danuta Berlińska, *Polska jako państwo narodowe. Historia i Pamięć* (Warsaw and Opole, 2008); Jerzy Kochanowski, *W polskiej niewoli. Niemieccy jeńcy wojenni w Polsce 1945–1950* (Warsaw, 2001); Leszek Olejnik, *Losy volksdeutschów w Polsce po II wojnie światowej* (Warsaw, 2006); Olejnik, *Polityka Narodowościowa Polski w latach 1944–1960* (Łódź, 2003); Witold Stankowski, *Obozy i inne miejsca odosobnienia dla niemieckiej ludności cywilnej w Polsce w latach 1945–1950* (Bydgoszcz, 2002); Zenon Romanow, *Ludność niemiecka na ziemiach zachodnich w latach 1945–1947* (Słupsk, 1992); Beata Ociepka, *Deportacja, wysiedlenie, przesiedlenia – Powojenne migracje z Polski i do Polski* (Poznań, 2001); Sebastian Siebel-Achenbach, *Lower Silesia from Nazi Germany to Communist Poland* (Basingstoke and London, 1994).

[10] Bernard Linek, *Polityka antyniemiecka na Górnym Śląsku w latach 1945–1950* (Opole, 2000); Piotr Madajczyk, *Przyłączenie Śląska Opolskiego do Polski 1945–1948* (Warsaw, 1996); Madaczyk, *Niemcy polscy 1944–1989* (Warsaw, 2001); Grzegorz Strauchold, *Autochtoni polscy, niemieccy czy... Od nacjonalizmu do komunizmu (1945–1999)* (Toruń, 2001) and *Myśl zachodnia i jej realizacja w Polsce Ludowej w latach 1945–1957* (Toruń, 2003); Andrzej Sakson, *Stosunki narodowościowe na Warmii i Mazurach 1945–1997* (Poznan, 1998); Michał Lis, *Ludność rodzima na Śląsku Opolskim po II wojnie światowej (1945–1993)* (Opole, 1993); Zenon Romanow, *Polityka władz polskich wobec ludności rozimej ziem zachodnich i północnych w latach 1945–1960* (Słupsk, 1999); Małgorzata Świder, *Die sogenannte Entgermanisierung im Oppelner Schlesien in den Jahren 1945–1950* (Lauf a.d. Pegnitz, 2002); Richard Blanke, *Polish-Speaking Germans? Language and National Identity among the Masurians since 1871* (Köln, 2001); Leszek Belzyt, *Między Polską i Niemczami. Weryfikacja narodowościowa i jej następstwa na Warmii Mazurach i Powiślu w latach 1945–1960* (Toruń, 1996); Andreas Kossert, *Preußen, Deutsche oder Polen? Die Masuren im Spannungsfeld des ethnischen Nationalismus 1870–1956* (Wiesbaden, 2001).

[11] Jan Misztal, *Weryfikacja narodowościowa na Śląsku Opolskim 1945–1950* (Opole, 1984) and *Weryfikacja narodowościowa na Ziemiach Odzyskanych* (Warsaw, 1990); Zbigniew Kowalski, *Powrót Śląska Opolskiego do Polski. Organizacja władzy ludowej i regulacja problemów narodowościowych w latach 1945–1948* (Opole, 1983); Józef Lubojański, *Polska ludność rodzima na ziemiach zachodnich i północnych. Dzieje polskiej granicy zachodniej* (Warsaw, 1960); Edmund Wojnowski, *Warmia i Mazury w latach 1945–1947. Życie polityczne* (Olsztyn, 1970); Bohdan Jałowiecki and Jan Przewłocki (eds.), *Stosunki polsko-niemieckie. Integracja i rozwój ziem zachodnich i północnych* (Katowice, 1980); Anna Magierska, *Ziemie zachodnie i północne w 1945 roku. Kształtowanie się podstaw polityki integracyjnej państwa polskiego* (Warsaw, 1978).

Czesław Osękowski and others.[12] This has allowed a more sophisticated idea of the Polish resettlement of these territories to emerge than could be provided in circumstances of censorship by the important Communist-era studies of Stefan Banasiak, Krystyna Kersten, Jan Czerniakiewicz, Tomasz Szarota and others.[13] The influx of Polish settlers into the new territories is examined, together with the postwar expulsion of Germans and other important elements of the postwar transformation of Poland's new territories, in excellent studies by the German historians Philipp Ther, Andreas Hofmann, Gregor Thum and Michael G. Esch, by the American historians T. David Curp and Padraic Kenney, and by the British historian Michael Fleming.[14] One of the most recent trends has been to look at these events by focusing on particular localities – as has been done in studies of cities and districts by Gregor Thum, Jan Musekamp, Piotr Madajczyk and Karol Jonca.[15] Another particularly important contribution to the subject has been made by Marcin Zaremba in a study aimed at placing the treatment of perceived 'national minorities' in post-liberation Poland in a broader

[12] Stanisław Ciesielski (ed.), *Przesiedlenie ludności poslkiej z kresów wschodnich do Polski 1944–1947* (Warsaw, 1999); Dorota Sula, *Działalność przesiedleńczo-repatriacyjna Państwowego Urzędu Repatriacyjnego w latach 1944–1951* (Lublin, 2002); Czesław Osękowski, *Społeczeństwo Polski zachodniej i północnej w latach 1945–1956. Procesy integracji i dezintegracji* (Zielona Góra, 1994); W. Geiszczyński, *Państwowy Urząd Repatriacyjny w osadnictwie na Warmii i Mazurach 1945–1950* (Olsztyn, 1999).

[13] Stefan Banasiak, *Działalność osadnicza Państwowego Urzędu Repatriacyjnego na Ziemiach Odzyskanych w latach 1945–1947* (Poznań, 1963); Banasiak, *Osadnictwo na ziemiach zachodnich i północnych w latach 1945–1950* (Warsaw, 1965); Krystyna Kersten, *Repatriacja ludności polskiej po II wojnie światowej* (Warsaw, 1974); Jan Czerniakiewicz, *Repatriacja ludności polskiej z ZSRR 1944–1948* (Warsaw, 1987); Tomasz Szarota, *Osadnictwo miejskie na Dolnym Śląsku w latach 1945–1948* (Wrocław, 1969); Elżbeta Kościk, *Osadnictwo wiejskie w południowych powiatach Dolnego Śląska w latach 1945–1949* (Wrocław, 1992); Henryk Dominiczak, *Proces zasiedlenia województwa zielenogórskiego w latach 1945–1950* (Zielona Góra, 1975); Sylwester Koczkowski, *Osadnictwo polskie w Szczeninie 1945–1950* (Poznań, 1963); Leszek Kosiński, *Procesy ludnościowe na Ziemiach Odzyskanych w latach 1945–1960* (Warsaw, 1963); Arkadiusz Ogrodowczyk, *Nad Odrą i Bałtykiem. Osadnictwo wojskowe na zachodnich i północnich ziemiach Polski po drugiej wojnie światowej* (Warsaw, 1979); Stanisław Łach, *Osadnictwo wiejskie na ziemiach zachodnich i północnych Polski w latach 1945–1950* (Słupsk, 1983).

[14] Philipp Ther, *Deutsche und polnische Vertriebene. Gesellschaft und Vertriebenenpolitik in der SBZ/DDR und in Polen 1945–1956* (Göttingen, 1998); Andreas R. Hofmann, *Die Nachkriegszeit in Schlesien. Gesellschafts- und Bevölkerungspolitik in den polnischen Siedlungsgebieten 1945–1948* (Köln, 2000); Gregor Thum, *Die fremde Stadt. Breslau 1945* (Berlin, 2003); Michael G. Esch, *"Gesunde Verhältnisse": Deutsche und polnische Bevölkerungspolitik in Ostmitteleuropa 1939–1950* (Marburg, 1998); T. David Curp, *A Clean Sweep? The Politics of Ethnic Cleansing in Western Poland, 1945–1960* (Rochester, New York, 2006); Padraic Kenney, *Rebuilding Poland: Workers and Communists, 1945–1950* (Ithaca, New York and London, 1997); Michael Fleming, *Communism, Nationalism and Ethnicity in Poland, 1944–1950* (Abingdon, 2010).

[15] Thum, *Breslau;* Jan Musekamp, *Zwischen Stettin und Szczecin: Metamorphosen einter Stadt von 1945 bis 2005* (Wiesbaden, 2010); Piotr Madajczyk, 'Część Druga. Studium Przypadku: Powiat Kozielski 1945–1948', in Madajczyk and Berlińska, *Polska*, pp. 375–568; Karol Jonca (ed.), *Wyesiedlenie Niemców i osadnictwo ludności polskiej na obszarze Krzyżowa-Świdnica (Kreisau-Schweidnitz) w latach 1945–1948. Wybór dokumentów* (Wrocław, 1997).

social and sociopsychological context.[16] Finally, mention should be made of the role played in challenging Cold War era assumptions about early postwar events in Poland's new territories by historical literature about related events in neighbouring Czechoslovakia and in East-Central and Eastern Europe as a whole. Particularly important contributions have been made in this regard by Tomáš Staněk, Detlef Brandes, Andreas Wiedemann, Ray Douglas and Benjamin Frommer and by the valuable volume of essays edited by Philipp Ther and Ana Siljak.[17]

Taken together, the Polish, German and Anglo-American studies of the past two decades support two broad conclusions about the transformation of Poland's new territories at the end of the Second World War. The first is that the mass expulsion of Germans was neither a simple act of knee-jerk revenge for Nazi German atrocities, nor merely the result of implementing the decisions reached by Britain, America and the Soviet Union at the Yalta and Potsdam conferences in 1945. Both played a role in this very significant case of forced migration. But the expulsion of well over three million Germans from Poland's new territories in the aftermath of the war was, above all, a response to long-term Polish nationalist objectives. As will be outlined in Chapter 2, in the aftermath of the war the Polish Communists made use of part of the nationalist programme of Poland's interwar National Democratic movement in an attempt to win popular support for their fledgling regime. Attempting to achieve certain key objectives contained in this movement's nationalist ideology, the Polish Communists implemented a campaign of ethnic homogenization throughout Poland's postwar territories at the end of the war, which involved expelling the territories' large ethnic German and ethnic Ukrainian minorities. It must be emphasized here that the Polish Communists only embraced *part* of the nationalist programme of the National Democratic movement: the objective of removing perceived 'national minorities' and that of taking over new western and northern territories from Germany. A great many actions taken

16 Marcin Zaremba, *Wielka Trwoga. Polska 1944–1947: Ludowa reakcja na kryzys* (Kraków, 2012).

17 Tomáš Staněk, *Odsun Němcu z Československa 1945–1947* (Prague, 1991); Staněk, *Verfolgung 1945: Die Stellung der Deutschen in Böhmen, Mähren und Schlesien (außerhalb der Lager und Gefängnisse)* (Vienna, 2002); Detlef Brandes, *Der Weg zur Vertreibung 1938–1945: Pläne und Entscheidungen zum 'Transfer' der Deutschen aus der Tschechoslowakei und aus Polen* (Munich, 2001); Detlef Brandes and Václav Kural (eds.), *Der Weg in die Katastrophie: Deutsch-Tschechoslowakische Beziehungen 1938–1947* (Düsseldorf, 1994); Andreas Wiedemann, *"Komm mit uns das Grenzland aufbauen!" Ansiedlung und neue Strukturen in den ehemaligen Sudetengebieten 1945–1952* (Essen, 2007); R. M. Douglas, *Orderly and Humane. The Expulsion of the Germans after the Second World War* (New Haven, 2012); Benjamin Frommer, *National Cleansing: Retribution against Nazi Collaborators in Postwar Czechoslovakia* (Cambridge, 2005); Philipp Ther and Ana Siljak (eds.), *Redrawing Nations: Ethnic Cleansing in East-Central Europe, 1944–1948* (Lanham, 2001).

by the Communist-controlled regime at the end of the Second World War of course clashed in the most overt sense with the sentiments of all Polish nationalists – most strikingly, as we shall discuss in Chapter 2, their collaboration in the Soviet Union's annexation of the entirety of prewar eastern Poland and their acquiescence towards the Kremlin's direct interference in the internal affairs of the Polish state after 1944. Notwithstanding these crucial qualifications, the Communist-led government pursued a nationalist campaign across postwar Polish territory after 1944 aimed at transforming the country into a homogeneous nation-state. This campaign had particularly drastic consequences for the new northern and western territories taken over from Germany in 1945.

The second conclusion builds directly on the first: that in Poland's new territories the mass expulsion of Germans was not the only manifestation of this nationalist campaign of ethno-national homogenization. Other important elements were the campaign to repopulate the territories with millions of new Polish inhabitants; the drive to 'culturally cleanse' these territories of all signs, symbols, institutions and organizations (such as schools and churches) associated with German national culture and to replace them with Polish cultural equivalents; and the campaign of ethnic screening and pressured cultural assimilation aimed at demonstrating that a large proportion of the residents of Poland's new territories were 'indigenous Poles' rather than Germans. Precisely what each of these elements involved will be made clear in the chapters of this book.

What the new literature has not done is demonstrate the extent to which the process of expelling Germans from Poland's new territories was influenced and controlled by the other elements of the Soviet-backed regime's nationalist campaign of ethno-national homogenization. This book is an attempt to do precisely that. It has four broad objectives. First, it seeks to demonstrate that in areas of Poland's new territories which were inhabited by homogeneously German-speaking populations before 1945 and where large concentrations of Germans remained or returned once the war was over, the regime's policy of transporting huge numbers of Polish settlers into these territories played a critical and very practical role in the expulsion of Germans. Getting underway in spring 1945, this massive influx of millions of Polish settlers helped to instigate the expulsion of Germans in late spring and early summer 1945, enhanced the scope and speed of the expulsions for around a year and a half, and then, from around the start of 1947 until the end of the decade, set the pace at which Germans were expelled. The second objective of this book is to demonstrate that in areas of Poland's new territories where many local inhabitants spoke both Polish dialects and German, the process of expelling Germans and that of repopulating these territories with Polish settlers were controlled by a third population policy: that of ethnic screening and pressured assimilation. Third, the book examines the extent to which the campaign of 'cultural cleansing' against German signs, symbols and institutions varied in intensity across Poland's new territories. Finally, the book aims to add further detail to our understanding of the fate of Jews in Poland in the aftermath of the Holocaust and to shed light on the fate of foreign displaced persons who happened to find themselves in Poland's new territories once the war was over.

This examination of the postwar ethno-national transformation of Poland's new territories joins the small wave of new studies focusing on particular localities. Where this book diverges from the current literature, however, is in examining not one but two localities, selected because they experienced very different ethno-national transformations in the immediate aftermath of the war. The first is the district of Hirschberg/Jelenia Góra. Like most other localities in Poland's new territories, this district had possessed a homogeneously German-speaking population before 1945. Populated by around 115,000 residents in the late 1930s, it was located in the region of Lower Silesia. Because it was not fully conquered by Soviet forces until the very final days of the war, Lower Silesia experienced much less damage to buildings and infrastructure and lost far fewer prewar residents through mass flight than most other areas of Poland's new territories. Indeed, over half of the German population remaining in Poland's new territories at the war's end were to be found in Lower Silesia.[18] Located in the least damaged southern area of Lower Silesia, Hirschberg/Jelenia Góra District contained at least as many German residents once the war was over as it had before the war. Therefore, the vast majority of the German residents of Hirschberg/Jelenia Góra District were uprooted through active expulsion by the Polish authorities once the war was over rather than through wartime flight and evacuation before the Polish authorities had arrived. This makes Hirschberg/Jelenia Góra District a very good case study of the interaction between two key elements of the Communist-led Polish government's nationalist campaign of ethno-national homogenization: the expulsion of Germans and the mass influx of Polish settlers.

The second locality chosen for this book is Oppeln/Opole District, inhabited by around 198,000 residents at the end of the 1930s. In contrast

[18] Włodzimierz Borodziej, 'Einleitung' [sections 3–8], in Włodzimierz Borodziej and Hans Lemberg (eds.), *"Unsere Heimat ist uns ein fremdes Land geworden..." Die Deutschen östlich von Oder und Neiße 1945–1950: Dokumente aus polnischen Archiven* (4 vols., Marburg, 2000–2004), vol. 1: *Zentrale Behörden. Wojewodschaft Allenstein* (Marburg, 2000), p. 76.

to Hirschberg/Jelenia Góra District, most inhabitants of Oppeln/Opole District before 1945 had been bilingual in German and a west Slavic dialect closely related to Polish. In this respect Oppeln/Opole District was not the norm in Poland's new territories. Yet neither was it by any means unique. Two entire regions of the new territories were inhabited by large numbers of people who were bilingual in German and regional dialects of Polish: southern East Prussia and western Upper Silesia. Precisely because of the widespread use of Polish dialects among residents of these two regions, the Communist-led authorities directed their campaign of ethnic screening and pressured assimilation primarily at these areas in the aftermath of the war. Located in western Upper Silesia and with a large number of bilingual speakers, Oppeln/Opole District offers good material for examining the interaction between the processes of expulsion, repopulation and ethnic screening in Poland's new territories in the second half of the 1940s.[19]

The book starts by examining an absolutely crucial piece of context for the events examined in this book: the policies of forced migration, ethnic cleansing and mass killing implemented or facilitated by the Nazi and Soviet occupiers of East-Central and Eastern Europe during the Second World War. Chapter 2 looks at what can broadly be described as the political backdrop to the postwar ethno-national transformation of Poland's new territories. It probes the decisions, actions and developments at home and abroad which brought massive changes to Poland's territory at the end of the war and allowed the Polish Communists to establish a full-fledged dictatorship by 1949. Chapter 3 examines events in our two districts in the final months of the war and at the war's end – including the mass flight of residents westwards, deportations to the Soviet Union and the arrival of the Polish state authorities. The fourth and fifth chapters address the expulsion of Germans and the mass influx of Polish settlers into homogeneously German-speaking areas of Poland's new territories, focusing on the case of Hirschberg/Jelenia Góra District. The sixth and seventh chapters look at the processes of ethnic screening, expulsion and repopulation in areas of Poland's new territories inhabited by a large number of bilingual Polish-dialect and German-speakers, focussing on the district of Oppeln/Opole.

Chapter 8 investigates the fate of Polish Jews who survived or evaded the Holocaust and gathered in southern areas of Poland's new territories in the aftermath of the war. It also examines what happened to the many

[19] The population figures for both districts are from Alfred Bohmann, *Menschen und Grenzen: Strukturwandel der deutschen Bevölkerung im polnischen Staats- und Verwaltungsbereich* (Köln, 1969), p. 209.

foreign displaced persons who had been brought to Poland's new territories during the war by the Nazi German authorities – forced civilian workers, foreign prisoners of war and foreign Jews.[20] Chapter 9 looks at the policies of pressured cultural assimilation which accompanied ethnic screening in Poland's new territories. Chapter 10 addresses the 'cultural cleansing' campaign which accompanied the population policies involved in the nationalist campaign in the second half of the 1940s. The book's Conclusion provides a discussion of the wave of forced migration against perceived 'national minorities', which accompanied the Communist consolidation of power in much of East-Central and Eastern Europe at the end of the war. The Conclusion seeks to place the events witnessed in Poland's new territories between 1945 and 1949 in the context of massive population movements and radical policies of ethno-national reordering seen in most of the eastern half of the continent in the five years after Soviet 'liberation' from Nazi German occupation and domination.

This book, then, is not merely about the impact of ethno-national transformation and the Communist takeover in the territories which Poland gained from Germany in 1945. Rather, it is an attempt to understand the impact of a brutal Nazi German occupation and massive post-liberation forced migrations on the whole of East-Central and Eastern Europe in the era of the Second World War. Let us start by examining the policies of occupation, expulsion and mass killing implemented or encouraged by Nazi Germany and the Soviet Union in this region during the Second World War.

[20] I use the term 'foreign' here to refer to individuals with neither Polish nor German citizenship or 'state membership'.

CHAPTER 1

Eastern Europe, 1939–44
Occupation, expulsion, killing

The wave of forced migration which gripped Poland and much of the rest of East-Central and Eastern Europe in the aftermath of the war did not come out of the blue. In the preceding five years Nazi Germany and the Soviet Union together presided over a torrent of forced migration in Poland and Eastern Europe, bringing tragedy to the lives of many millions of people. The two occupying powers set an awful precedent, demonstrating to inhabitants of the eastern half of the continent exactly how massive and rapid shifts of population could be achieved. Devastating and exploitative occupation regimes were imposed on Poland and nearby states. Localized inter-ethnic conflicts were set off and systematic mass killing – and genocide in the case of Germany – was perpetrated. The effect was that Poles and other Eastern Europeans would have few qualms about implementing brutal population policies of their own once the war was over. The Nazi and Soviet occupations of East-Central and Eastern Europe therefore formed the crucial backdrop against which the events examined in this book took place.

THE GERMAN OCCUPATION

During the interwar period, just like what the ethnic Polish minority of Germany endured at that time, ethnic Germans in Poland suffered a series of discriminatory measures aimed at inducing them either to assimilate into ethnically Polish society or to emigrate. After coming to power in Germany in 1933, Hitler's Nazi regime had paid very little attention to the difficulties faced by this German minority in Poland – despite the strong Nazi views held by most of them from the mid 1930s onwards. This only changed after spring 1939, as the Nazis, seeking a pretext to launch an unprovoked attack on Poland, began spewing out propaganda with exaggerated claims of atrocities being committed against Germans in

Poland. Vast German forces invaded Poland on 1 September 1939, crushing Polish military resistance within a few weeks. The attack, of course, had nothing to do with protecting ethnic Germans. Indeed, it had quite the opposite effect, sparking a wave of Polish violence against them. The aim of Germany's invasion, instead, was to take control of western and central Poland, as had been agreed with the Soviets at the end of August 1939 (see Chapter 2) and as part of Hitler's broader aim of securing 'Lebensraum' in the east.[1]

At the start of October 1939, the German occupiers divided in two the area of Poland they had occupied in the preceding few weeks, annexing to Germany the western territories and designating central Poland a colonial territory which they labelled the 'General Government for the occupied Polish territories' (see Map 1). From the outset, the Germans sought to eliminate the capacity of Poland to reemerge as an independent, sustainable state any time soon. In the western annexed areas, this meant dissolving all Polish state institutions, eliminating all Polish political organizations and physically destroying the social and economic elites of Polish society. In fact, the killing of Polish civilians from all social backgrounds was started in September 1939 by regular German soldiers, who carried out individual and group killings of thousands of individuals – a disproportionate number of them Jews – as they moved across Poland establishing German control in early autumn 1939. The *Wehrmacht* was followed into Poland by Operation Groups (*Einsatzgruppen*), made up of SS and police personnel, which were charged with the task of both stamping out Polish civilian resistance and killing the top stratum of Polish society, in an action known as Operation Tannenberg. Perhaps 40,000 Polish civilians were killed by the SS and police troops in the annexed territories in what remained of 1939, often with the assistance of newly created 'self-protection' militias composed of ethnically German Polish citizens. At the same time, the new German authorities set about 'cleansing' the annexed territories of all forms of Polish culture by eliminating Polish newspapers, schools, cultural institutions, signs and symbols and by Germanizing place names. The authorities created new German cultural facilities to replace the Polish ones and massively expanded the network of German secondary and primary schools in the

[1] Richard Blanke, *Orphans of Versailles: The Germans in Western Poland 1918–1939* (Kentucky, 1993), pp. 163–236; Jerzy Kochanowski, 'Schicksale der Deutschen in Zentralpolen in den Jahren 1945–1950', in Borodziej and Lemberg, *Heimat*, vol. 2 (Marburg, 2003), pp. 15–16; Gustavo Corni, 'Germans outside the Reich: From Protection to "Heim ins Reich"', in Ahonen et al., *People*, pp. 15–16; Richard J. Evans, *The Third Reich at War, 1939–1945* (London, 2008), pp. 3–9.

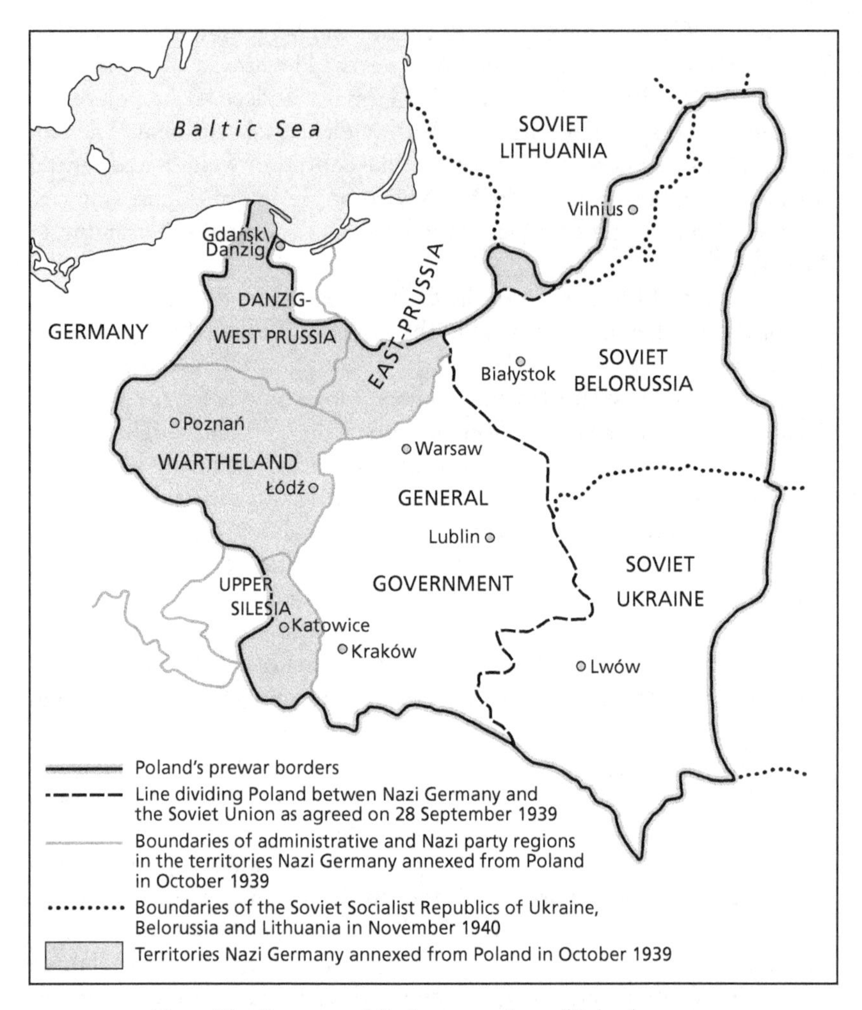

Map 1 The German and Soviet occupations of Poland, 1939–41

territories, even founding a new German university in Posen/Poznań in April 1941.[2]

[2] Czesław Łuczak, *Od Bismarcka do Hitlera. Polsko-niemieckie stosunki gospodarcze* (Poznań 1988), pp. 339–48, 369–70; Alexander B. Rossino, *Hitler Strikes Poland. Blitzkrieg, Ideology, and Atrocity* (Lawrence, Kansas, 2003), pp. 10–16, 29–30, 58–87; Richard C. Lukas, *The Forgotten Holocaust: The Poles under German Occupation 1939–1944* (2nd edn, New York 1997), pp. 2–13; Kochanowski, 'Schicksale', pp. 29–30; Catherine Epstein, *Model Nazi. Arthur Greiser and the Occupation of Western Poland* (Oxford, 2010), pp. 197–206, 234–5, 244–50, 260–2; Timothy Snyder, *Bloodlands: Europe between Hitler and Stalin* (New York, 2010), 119–23, 126–8; Andrzej Paczkowski, *The Spring Will Be Ours. Poland and the Poles from Occupation to Freedom* (Pennsylvania, 2003), pp. 51–4.

In the General Government the situation was somewhat different, but similarly horrendous for Poles and Jews. The Nazi leaders originally intended the General Government to serve two principal purposes. First, it would become a source of very cheap, tightly controlled labour. Because Poles were now supposed to serve simply as manpower, they had no need for advanced education. All universities and secondary schools were closed down, with only primary schools and some vocational schools allowed to continue operating. As in the annexed western areas of Poland, all political organizations, cultural institutions and newspapers were dissolved. The difference was that new German-controlled Polish-language newspapers were established in their place in the General Government to ensure that the subjugated Polish population heard the messages and information the Germans wished to communicate to them. Moreover, as in the annexed areas, the German occupiers wanted to get rid of Poland's intelligentsia. Thousands of Polish civilians from all social backgrounds had already been killed in central Poland during and after the German invasion. In November 1939, mass arrests of Kraków's academics took place. Then, in spring 1940, the so-called Extraordinary Pacification Action was launched, with the aim of killing the remaining educated and political elites in the General Government. This goal was by no means achieved in subsequent months. Nevertheless, several thousand were shot and several thousand more were sent to concentration camps; several thousand common criminals were also killed as part of this action.

As in the annexed territories, Polish state administration in central Poland was immediately dissolved in autumn 1939. A leading Nazi, Hans Frank, was appointed to head the General Government. A German administration, staffed with officials from Germany, was erected in Kraków – which was made the capital of the General Government rather than Warsaw. But in contrast to the annexed territories, Poles were kept on to run local urban authorities, and although many local ethnic Germans were installed as mayors in rural areas, the majority of rural mayoral positions and other local official posts in the countryside were retained by ethnic Poles. German control in the General Government throughout its existence, between 1939 and 1944, rested firmly on the use of terror, wielded principally by Heinrich Himmler's SS and police apparatus. The most trivial 'offences' by Poles became punishable with execution.

More generally, Frank's administration put in place a regime directed towards the total economic exploitation of central Poland. All Polish state property was confiscated and large amounts of private property were likewise taken into German ownership or placed under German control. The result was that the German occupiers ran all significant industrial enterprises in the General Government. Work was made compulsory for all Poles aged over 14 years and harsh working conditions were imposed. Polish access to food and other essential goods was severely rationed, quickly throwing broad swaths of the urban population into acute poverty and exposing a great many to serious malnutrition. Buying and trading on the black market became the only way of ensuring anything like adequate sustenance and income. The material situation in the countryside was not so bad at first, but deteriorated after 1941, once the Germans began systematically and coercively enforcing harsh quotas for compulsory agricultural deliveries from the farming population.[3]

The second principal purpose of the General Government was to serve as a dumping ground for the unwanted people of the annexed western areas of Poland. Nazi leaders believed that to make the annexed areas fully integrated territories of Germany they needed, in the long run, to ensure that their inhabitants were homogeneously German. As we shall discuss later, the Nazi leadership also needed to free up housing for arriving ethnic German settlers, whom they were about to begin transporting to these territories from various places in Eastern Europe and from northern Italy. This meant that the millions of Polish citizens who were not ethnically German, including some 600,000 Polish Jews, would have to be gradually removed. SS chief and Reich Commissioner for Strengthening Germandom Heinrich Himmler ordered his officials to begin organizing the expulsion of non-German Polish citizens from the annexed territories to the General Government in October 1939. According to the plans his officials subsequently compiled, a million and a half would be displaced in the first two years of the action. Disorganized violent expulsions of Polish citizens to the General Government started in autumn 1939. Then, between December 1939 and spring 1941, a series of systematic, large-scale and brutal deportations took place. Local German officials in the annexed territories played a crucial role in these deportations, because they were generally the ones who drew up the lists of Polish citizens designated for removal. SS troops, police units and ethnic German militias would descend on the targeted families, giving them often less than half an hour to pack a maximum of 30 kg luggage, before wrenching them from their homes and throwing them into collection camps. They would spend at least a few days in these

[3] Jan Tomasz Gross, *Polish Society under German Occupation: The Generalgouvernement, 1939–1944* (Princeton, New Jersey, 1979), pp. 45–116, 131–44; Robert Seidel, *Deutsche Besatzungspolitik in Polen. Der Distrikt Radom 1939–1945* (Paderborn, 2006), pp. 11–12, 34–60, 89–137, 170–207; Łuczak, *Stosunki*, pp. 344–52; Lukas, *Forgotten*, pp. 7–17, 27–37; Paczkowski, *Spring*, pp. 52–5.

camps before being transported in crammed goods trains to the General Government. No provisions were made by the German authorities in the General Government to receive these expellees, and their prospects for an adequate material existence there were bleak, to say the least.

Over 400,000 Polish citizens were uprooted to the General Government between autumn 1939 and spring 1941. The vast majority of them were non-Jewish Poles, and most were from the Wartheland region of the annexed territories. The General Government's governor, Hans Frank, had resisted these expulsions from the outset, because he objected to the use of his fiefdom as a dumping ground. His stubborn attitude combined with the changing military and economic circumstances confronting Nazi Germany to ensure that only small numbers were sent to the General Government after spring 1941. Part of the objective of these expulsions was to free up farms and other properties for ethnic German settlers transferred to the annexed territories from Eastern and South-Central Europe as part of the Nazis' 'Heim ins Reich' policy. Over three quarters of a million ethnic Germans were transported to the annexed territories from the Baltic states, Soviet-occupied Polish and Romanian territories, Nazi-allied Romania and northern Italy between 1939 and 1941 – with the aim of repopulating the 'cleansed' annexed territories of prewar western Poland. But this plan was ultimately thwarted by the insufficient number of Polish citizens expelled from the annexed territories, so that over one-third of the ethnic German settlers were still languishing in transit camps in the annexed territories as late as 1944.[4]

Because the Nazi leaders' original expectations for transferring Polish citizens to the General Government had by no means been met in the first year of the war, they were forced to accept that they would have to put up with the continued presence of the vast majority of ethnic Polish inhabitants of the annexed territories for a long time to come. This was not something they were willing to contemplate with regard to the

[4] Maria Rutowska, *Wysiedlenie ludności polskiej z Kraju Warty do Generalnego Gubernatorstwa 1939–1941* (Poznań, 2003), pp. 21–96, 148–61, 197–216; Esch, *Verhältnisse*, pp. 326–31, 336–45; Łuczak, *Stosunki*, pp. 370–7; Gross, *Polish Society*, pp. 71–3; Corni, 'Germans', pp. 16–20; Corni, 'The Implementation of the German Plans in the Occupied Eastern Territories', in Ahonen et al., *People*, pp. 26–31; Isabel Heinemann, 'Umvolkungspläne, Rassenauslese, Zwangsumsiedlungen: Die Rasseexperten der SS und die "bevölkerungspolitische Neuorderung" Europas', in Ralph Melville, Jiří Pešek and Claus Scharf (eds.), *Zwangsmigrationen im mittleren und östlichen Europa. Völkerrecht – Kozeptionen – Praxis (1938–1950)* (Mainz, 2007), pp. 207–10; Epstein, *Model Nazi*, pp. 160–6, 170–7, 191–2, 218–21; Jan Czerniakiewicz and Monika Czerniakiewicz, *Przesiedlenia ze Wchodu 1944–1959* (Warsaw, 2007), pp. 43–61; Wolfgang Benz, 'Zweifache Opfer nationalsozialistischer Bevölkerungspolitik: Die Zwangsmigration von Volksdeutschen', in Melville et al., *Zwangsmigrationen*, pp. 248–57; Ahonen and Kochanowski, "Heim ins Reich", in Ahonen et al., *People*, pp. 114–17, 119–20.

territories' Polish Jewish residents. German efforts to get rid of Polish Jews were not limited to expulsions to the General Government. The SS and police Operation Groups operating behind the German military advance in September 1939 had been charged with the task of terrorizing Jews into flight eastwards out of German-controlled territory through killings and general brutality. Their actions and the attacks on Jews by regular German troops operating in the annexed territories and the General Government helped to ensure that around 350,000 Polish Jews fled to Soviet-occupied eastern Poland and to nearby countries in the early months of the war.

But this left hundreds of thousands of Jews residing in the annexed territories at the start of 1940, something deemed unacceptable by Arthur Greiser – the Nazi governor of the largest region of the annexed territories, the Wartheland. Because Hans Frank was obstructing the expulsion of Jews to the General Government, Greiser decided that the only thing for it was to confine these Jews to ghettos. By far the largest concentration of Jews in the annexed territories resided in the city of Łódź. Greiser's authorities therefore chose to establish the first of the annexed territories' Jewish ghettos there. The construction of its walls began in February 1940. Łódź Ghetto had been completely sealed off by the start of May, by which time 162,000 Jews were already living there. In the General Government, Frank had already begun setting up ghettos and labour camps for Jews in late 1939. By November 1940 the walls of the largest and most notorious ghetto in occupied Poland had been constructed in the northwestern quarter of Warsaw. Four hundred forty-five thousand Jews were crammed together, living under terrible conditions in the Warsaw Ghetto by the start of 1941. In early 1941 there were said to be a total of around 300 ghettos in towns and cities across German-occupied Poland, where conditions were very bad and the death rate very high. Hundreds of labour camps had also been erected throughout prewar central and western Poland, where Jews suffered even worse living and working conditions.[5]

THE SOVIET OCCUPATION

Jews of course were not the principal target of the similarly repressive occupation regime put in place in eastern Poland by the Soviets between 1939 and

[5] Gustavo Corni, *Hitler's Ghettos. Voices from a Beleaguered Society 1939–1944* (London, 2003), pp. 23–31, 39–40, 119–39, 155–6, 195–210; Rossino, *Poland*, pp. 88–120; Christopher R. Browning, *The Origins of the Final Solution. The Evolution of Nazi Jewish Policy, September 1939–March 1942* (London, 2004), pp. 25–168; Esch, *Verhältnisse*, pp. 324–6, 335–43, 347–8; Saul Friedländer, *The Years of Extermination: Nazi Germany and the Jews 1939–1945* (London, 2007), pp. 26–43, 104–8, 144–58; Łuczak, *Stosunki*, pp. 358–60; Epstein, *Model Nazi*, pp. 166–70, 178–80, 237–42; Snyder, *Bloodlands*, pp. 122–3, 127, 144–6; Evans, *War*, pp. 49–64.

1941. The Red Army thrust its way into eastern Poland on 17 September 1939 after reaching an agreement with the Germans at the end of August to divide Poland in two and to allow the Soviets to assert control over the Baltic states (see Chapter 2). They immediately handed the city of Vilnius and its surrounding countryside to Lithuania, but incorporated the vast majority of eastern Poland into the Soviet Union. They formalized this annexation on 22 October 1939 by staging sham elections to two so-called People's Assemblies of Western Ukraine and Western Belorussia on 22 October 1939, which immediately requested incorporation into the Soviet Socialist Republics of Ukraine and Belorussia (see Map 1).

These annexed eastern Polish territories had an ethnically very diverse population. Perhaps 43 per cent were ethnic Poles, 33 per cent were ethnic Ukrainians, 8 per cent were Yiddish-speaking Jews, 8 per cent were ethnic Belorussians and 6 per cent were merely designated as 'locals' (*tutejsi*) in interwar censuses. A number of smaller ethnic groups also inhabited these territories, including ethnic Germans. Arriving there in the second half of September, Red Army troops had been actively welcomed by a large proportion of the local population. To a large extent this can be understood, quite simply, as a pragmatic response to the arrival of a powerful invading force. But there was an added element to this welcome, because it appears to have been mainly the ethnic Ukrainians, Jews and ethnic Belorussians who came out of their homes and onto the roads and streets to greet the arriving Soviet forces. The primary reason for this was not greater support for Communism among these ethnic groups than among ethnic Poles. Rather, what was behind it was a clear desire to see a chauvinistic and authoritarian Polish state collapse. In the previous two decades, Polish state authorities had introduced a series of discriminatory nationalist measures in eastern Poland, which included the suppression of Ukrainian and Belorussian schools, the exclusion of Jews, Ukrainians and Belorussians from high-ranking positions in the state and army, and the discriminatory application of a land reform which enabled hundreds of thousands of ethnic Poles to settle in the eastern Polish countryside. The understandable resentment these measures provoked among non-Poles was most visibly expressed by members of the large ethnic Ukrainian population. It was out of this population that a militant nationalist formation called the Organization of Ukrainian Nationalists emerged. This group carried out a number of antistate, anti-Polish terrorist attacks in the interwar period, including the assassination of Poland's Minister for the Interior in 1934.

The Soviets arrived in these territories in late September 1939 to find that the power vacuum left behind by the collapsing Polish state authorities had allowed the serious inter-ethnic tension of the 1930s to escalate into vicious fighting between ethnic groups. Mostly this involved attacks on ethnic Poles by Ukrainian nationalists and by Ukrainian and Belorussian peasant groups, as well as assaults on non-Polish locals by scattered Polish army units and local Polish armed groups. But rather than intervene to stamp out this violence, the Soviets decided to channel it into a campaign of social-revolutionary transformation. What this meant was that they actively encouraged attacks on large landowners and other local elites – something easily achieved because the vast majority of elites in these territories were ethnic Poles. They transferred control over local state administration in the countryside to what they deemed to be the least privileged sections of society. This generally meant non-Poles. At the same time, they presided over a land redistribution campaign, in which large landholdings – again mostly in the hands of ethnic Poles – were broken up and handed to local peasants.[6]

Having cemented their control, the Soviet authorities then set about Sovietizing the economy, state administration and cultural provisions in the prewar eastern Polish territories. At the end of October 1939, the two People's Assemblies launched the nationalization of banks, industry, mines, railways and trading enterprises. Even the smaller factories and businesses not taken into state ownership were brought under state administrative control. Savings were wiped out by first devaluing and then completely replacing the Polish złoty with the Soviet rouble and by confiscating all bank deposits. Having earlier authorized land redistribution as a basis for building support for their new regime, the Soviets now began applying pressure through taxes and propaganda aimed at bringing about the collectivization of agriculture. There was also an influx of officials from the Soviet Union, who took up high-level positions in state administration in these territories. All political, social, cultural and economic organizations – whether Polish, Ukrainian, Belorussian or Jewish – were closed down. Newspapers too were shut and replaced with new Soviet organs. Soviet curricula were introduced in schools and the output of theatres, cinemas and the like was brought strictly into line with rigid ideological norms. But not all the Soviets' actions were about repression and restriction. They also made efforts to open up higher education to the lower

[6] Gross, *Revolution*, pp. 17–108; Rafał Wnuk, *"Za pierwszego Sowieta". Polska konspiracja na Kresach Wschodnich II Rzeczypospolitej (wrzesień 1939–czerwiec 1941* (Warsaw, 2007), pp. 13–25, 34; Anna M. Cienciala, 'Prisoners of an Undeclared War, 23 August 1939–5 March 1940', in Anna M. Cienciala, Natalia Z. Lebedeva and Wojciech Materski (eds.), *Katyn. A Crime without Punishment* (New Haven, 2007), pp. 17–25; Alexander V. Prusin, *The Lands Between: Conflict in the East European Borderlands, 1870–1992* (Oxford, 2010), pp. 90, 105–8, 112–16, 122–33; Snyder, *Bloodlands*, pp. 123–8.

orders, introduced free medical services and sponsored the promotion of workers into managerial posts at workplaces. The network of Ukrainian- and Belorussian-language schools and the number of Yiddish-speaking teachers were also greatly increased. In this way, the Soviets introduced a regime which was at once highly authoritarian and – in certain respects at least – socially and culturally progressive.

It also appears that, in contrast to the German occupation of prewar central and western Poland, the Soviet occupation was not aimed at all-out economic exploitation. Yet it would be a mistake to believe that material motives were absent from Stalin's takeover of prewar eastern Poland. Indeed, the Soviet authorities used their control over the admittedly modest local industrial sector to gear it strongly to the needs of the Soviet Union. Moreover, they carried out massive requisitioning of goods in the early phase of the occupation, many of which were transported back to the Soviet Union to deal with the widespread shortages there. These confiscations, the state control over trade and the fact that the Soviets cut off prewar eastern Poland's businesses from their interwar markets and suppliers ensured that these territories soon started to experience the same severe shortages of goods so characteristic of the rest of the Soviet Union. For almost everybody, therefore, living standards quickly plunged. As happened in the German-controlled General Government, the black market assumed a critical role in the everyday lives of most ordinary people in Soviet-occupied eastern Poland. The pressure to collectivize farms provoked great hostility from peasants – which ensured that only a small minority of agricultural land was brought into collective farms by summer 1941. The authorities' attack on religion and on the property of churches and synagogues likewise prompted serious resentment from members of all ethnic groups.[7]

It was not only in the form of the expropriation of land and private businesses that the social and economic elites of prewar eastern Poland came under attack from the Soviet occupiers. Immediately after the Soviet conquest of these territories, the Soviet NKVD set about arresting active members of political parties, state officials, policemen, military personnel, priests and – soon enough – anybody deemed to be showing the slightest

[7] Gross, *Revolution*, pp. 125–42; Wnuk, *Sowieta*, pp. 22–8, 34; Włodzimierz Bonusiak, *Polityka ludnościowa i ekonomiczna ZSRR na okupowanych ziemiach polskich w latach 1939–1941 ("Zachodnia Ukraina" i "Zachodnia Białorus")* (Rzeszów, 2006), pp. 187–241, 250–65; Keith Sword, 'Soviet Economic Policy in the Annexed Areas', in Keith Sword (ed.), *The Soviet Takeover of the Polish Eastern Provinces, 1939–41* (London, 1991), pp. 86–99; Stanisław Ciesielski, Grzegorz Hryciuk and Aleksander Srebrakowski, *Masowe deportacje ludności w Związku Radzieckim* (Toruń, 2003), pp. 206–8; Cienciala, 'Prisoners', pp. 23–4; Prusin, *Lands Between*, pp. 132–5.

hint of 'disloyalty' or 'unreliability'. It was mainly ethnic Poles who were affected by this massive wave of arrests. But so too were many Ukrainians, Belorussians and Jews. Indeed, by summer 1941, some 110,000 residents of these territories had been arrested, of whom thousands were eventually executed and perhaps one-third sent to forced labour camps in the Soviet interior.

In addition to these people, well over 200,000 Polish prisoners of war were initially captured by the Red Army in September 1939. The vast majority of them were relatively swiftly released. But 15,000 Polish officers were taken to camps in Kozelsk and Ostashkov in Russia and Starobilsk in eastern Ukraine. Two-thirds of these officers were not professional soldiers but reservists, often with very high levels of education. Because of the political danger the Soviets believed these professional officers and highly educated reservists posed to their regime, all but a few hundred were executed in April 1940. Those from Kozelsk were shot on the edge of the Katyn Forest, where their corpses were discovered in a mass grave by the Germans in 1943 (see Chapter 2). Both mass arrests and collective killings were, therefore, employed by the Soviets in a deliberate effort to remove the upper layers of eastern Polish society during 1939–41 – much like what happened, as we have seen, in German-occupied Poland at this time.[8]

Like the Germans, moreover, the Soviets carried out a series of massive forced migrations in prewar eastern Poland in these years. As part of a 'population exchange' agreed on with Nazi Germany in autumn 1939, the Soviets sent around 180,000 ethnic Germans in 1940 to the territories Germany had annexed from Poland at the start of the war – as part of the Nazis' 'Heim ins Reich' campaign (see the preceding section). The Soviets also carried out a series of huge forcible deportations, in which specific social groups deemed 'untrustworthy' by the Soviet leadership were uprooted from prewar eastern Poland to the Soviet interior. The first deportation mainly affected military veterans, state officials, policemen, forestry guards and forestry workers. On a single night in early February 1940, in extremely cold temperatures, the NKVD pulled almost 140,000 of these people and

[8] Cienciala, 'Prisoners', pp. 23–39; Cienciala, 'Extermination, March–June 1940', in Cienciala et al., *Katyn*, pp. 121–48; Grzegorz Hryciuk, 'Victims 1939–1941: The Soviet Repressions in Eastern Poland', in Elazar Barkan, Elizabeth A. Cole and Kai Struve (eds.), *Shared History – Divided Memory. Jews and Others in Soviet-Occupied Poland, 1939–1941* (Leipzig, 2007), pp. 178–84; George Sanford, *Katyn and the Soviet Massacre of 1940. Truth, Justice and Memory* (London, 2005), pp. 1, 22–6, 29, 39–55, 75–111; N. S. Lebedeva, 'The Deportation of the Polish Population to the USSR, 1939–41', in Alfred J. Rieber (ed.), *Forced Migration in Central and Eastern Europe, 1939–1950* (London, 2000), pp. 30–1; Snyder, *Bloodlands*, pp. 125–6, 133–40; Prusin, *Lands Between*, pp. 141–3; Ciesielski, *Masowe deportacje*, p. 208; Gustavo Corni and Jerzy Kochanowski, 'Soviet Population Policy in Poland', in Ahonen et al., *People*, p. 26.

their families out of their homes, giving them perhaps half an hour to gather what luggage they could carry. They were then crammed into generally unheated goods wagons and sent by rail eastwards, on journeys lasting several weeks, receiving little or no food and water along the way. Many of the children, elderly and sick died en route before the cargo trains reached their destinations. The endpoints of these terrible journeys were 'special settlements' – forced labour facilities – in Kazakhstan and Siberia. The second deportation took place on a single night in April 1940 and targeted the families of people who were in Soviet custody, including prisoners of war. The third, in June 1940, affected mainly Polish Jewish refugees from German-occupied Poland, who had refused to accept Soviet internal passports.

In summer 1940 the Soviets moved to annex the three Baltic states of Estonia, Latvia and Lithuania as well as the prewar Romanian territories of Bessarabia and Bukovina. Almost a year then passed before the Soviets carried out a fourth massive wave of deportations, between May and June 1941. This wave started in prewar eastern Poland before sweeping northwards to the three Baltic states and southwards to Bessarabia and Bukovina. Perhaps 91,000 people in total were deported at this time, almost half of them from the Baltic states. Around a third of the approximately 34,000 Polish citizens deported in the fourth wave were ethnic Ukrainians, who the Soviets claimed were connected to the Ukrainian nationalist underground movement.

Taken as a whole, the four waves of Soviet deportation which were implemented between 1940 and 1941 principally targeted political, social, economic and administrative elites. They can therefore be understood as part of a broader campaign of 'social cleansing', which also involved mass arrests and killings and was aimed at remoulding the class structure of the occupied territories of Poland, Romania and the three Baltic states. Yet in the prewar eastern Polish territories, social and ethnic divisions were so closely intertwined that ethnic Poles were made to bear the brunt. Of the 309,000–327,000 Polish citizens deported to the Soviet interior in the four deportation waves in 1940–41, 57.5 per cent – according to Soviet documents – were ethnic Poles, 21.9 per cent were Jews, 10.4 per cent were ethnic Ukrainians and 7.6 per cent were ethnic Belorussians.[9]

[9] Ciesielski, *Masowe deportacje*, pp. 208–47, 260–70, 311–14, 320–37; Hryciuk, 'Victims', pp. 184–95; Lebedeva, 'Deportation', pp. 32–42; Pavel Polian, *Against Their Will: The History and Geography of Forced Migrations in the USSR* (Budapest and New York, 2004), pp. 115–23; Gross, *Revolution*, pp. xiv, 197–222; Prusin, *Lands Between*, pp. 135–6, 143–4; Corni and Kochanowski, 'Poland', pp. 24–6; Corni, 'Germans', p. 19; Gustavo Corni, 'Nazi Germany's Plans for Occupied Poland', in Ahonen et al., *People*, p. 21.

A NEW RACIAL ORDER, 1941–4

The Soviets were still carrying out their fourth wave of deportations when Nazi Germany attacked them on 22 June 1941. This was the biggest military offensive in history, and it brought an end not merely to the Soviet deportations, but to the entire Soviet occupation of eastern Poland, the Baltic states and northeastern Romania. It also initiated a massive radicalization of German violence in East-Central and Eastern Europe. Thrusting their way into Soviet territory in summer and autumn 1941, the Germans treated Soviet civilians with utter ruthlessness. They shot dead anyone suspected of sabotage and starved hundreds of thousands of people to death through mass food requisitioning. The German forces also showed no mercy whatsoever to the Soviet soldiers they captured during their advance. In numerous open-air prisoner-of-war camps set up across prewar western Soviet and prewar Polish territory, they deliberately starved Soviet POWs to death in late 1941 and 1942. The mortality rate in these camps was 57.5 per cent in the course of the war. A total of 2.6 million Soviet POWs died from starvation, disease or maltreatment in the camps or on their way to these camps and a further half million were simply shot dead by the Germans.[10]

Moreover, it was in what had been eastern Poland and western Soviet territory (see Maps 1 and 2) that the genocide against Europe's Jews got underway. In late June and early July 1941, the SS and German police Operation Groups deliberately triggered and participated in numerous pogroms against Jews by non-Jewish locals in prewar eastern Poland and the Baltic states – in which perhaps 20,000 Jews were killed. The minority of local Poles, Ukrainians, Belorussians, Lithuanians and Latvians who carried out these attacks on Jews were motivated above all by an anti-Semitic association of Communism with Jews. Accordingly, they saw what they were doing as 'revenge' for the Soviet atrocities committed against their compatriots during the Soviet occupation. One such atrocity by the Soviets was the mass killing of prisoners as the Germans invaded in late June 1941. With the help of local nationalist groups, whom the Germans formed into auxiliary police formations, the SS and police personnel of the Operation Groups and Order Police battalions began large-scale shootings of Jews across prewar eastern Poland, the prewar Baltic states and prewar western

[10] Christian Streit, *Keine Kameraden. Die Wehrmacht und die sowjetischen Kriegsgefangenen 1941–1945* (2nd edn, Bonn, 1991), pp. 83–109, 128–90, 244–9; Christian Gerlach, *Kalkulierte Morde. Die deutsche Wirtschafts- und Vernichtungspolitik in Weißrussland 1941 bis 1944* (Hamburg, 1999), pp. 265–92, 774–81, 788–859, 870–84; Snyder, *Bloodlands*, pp. 155–84; Barbara Stelzl-Marx, 'Forced Labourers in the Third Reich', in Ahonen et al., *People*, pp. 169–70.

Map 2 Nazi German hegemony in East-Central and Eastern Europe, 1942–4

Soviet territory in summer 1941. These shootings radicalized over time. At first only men were targeted, but within a few months entire Jewish communities were being systematically massacred. Throughout these territories, thousands of Jews were taken to the edges of towns and cities to be shot into pits. Perhaps the single best-known case occurred in Kiev at the end of September 1941 when almost all of the city's surviving Jews – over 33,771 Jewish men, women and children – were shot into the Babi Yar ravine. At least 500,000 – probably up to a million – Jews were killed in these territories in the second half of 1941.

Many ghettos for Jews had been set up in towns and cities across the prewar eastern Polish, western Soviet and Baltic territories in summer and autumn 1941. But most of these ghettos were short-lived, because the Jews forced to stay in them were quickly killed. The mass shootings of Jews continued during 1942. They claimed perhaps a million more victims in the course of that year. Shootings of Jews became increasingly regarded by the German occupiers as an antipartisan measure, and hundreds of thousands of non-Jewish civilians were also killed in supposed 'reprisals' for partisan attacks in prewar Soviet Belorussia and Ukraine in these years. In Romania, too, the military dictatorship allied to Nazi Germany carried out its own autonomous mass killings of Jews in the second half of 1941 and in 1942, murdering around 300,000 individuals.[11]

The Germans, therefore, launched their genocide against European Jews in summer 1941 in the territories occupied by the Soviets during 1939–41 and in prewar western Soviet territory. At the end of 1941, however, this policy of mass killing was extended westwards into the prewar central and western Polish territories. By this time a new method of mass slaughter had been developed. It was based on techniques utilized in the early war years for the murder of mentally ill and physically disabled Germans and Poles. This method was gassing, and it consisted of pumping exhaust fumes into sealed vans. A number of these gas vans were delivered to the Operation Groups working in the pre-1941 western Soviet borderlands in late autumn 1941 and a significant number of the Jews were subsequently killed there using gas, not guns.

But in prewar central and western Poland gas was, from the outset, the principal means of mass murder against Jews. This started in early December 1941, when the ghettos of the Wartheland began to be cleared. The Polish Jews from these ghettos were sent to a special new killing site near the village of Chełmno nad Nerem, where three gas vans had been stationed. After January 1942, the Wartheland's largest concentration of Jews, Łódź Ghetto, were poured steadily into Chełmno to be gassed. One hundred forty-five thousand mainly Polish Jews were killed at Chełmno in late 1941 and 1942, after which this facility was shut. But by this time three new killing centres, each one more efficient than Chełmno, had taken up the task of murdering Polish Jews. Bełżec, Sobibór and Treblinka were built in the eastern areas of the General Government (see Map 2). Each had its own purpose-built rail line linking it to the major ghettos of the General Government. Each used gas chambers rather than vans. The gassing of Jews started in these sites between March and July 1942 and the Jews, arriving on crammed cargo trains from ghettos across the General Government, were gassed straight away on arrival – only in exceptional cases was the gassing

[11] Peter Longerich, *Holocaust. The Nazi Persecution and Murder of the Jews* (Oxford, 2010), pp. 182–240, 242–7, 250–5, 345–56, 366; Browning, *Origins*, pp. 224–34; Jürgen Matthäus, 'Operation Barbarossa and the Onset of the Holocaust, June–December 1941', in Browning, *Origins*, pp. 244–308; Gerlach, *Morde*, pp. 521–628, 870–958; Friedländer, *Extermination*, pp. 197–201, 207–27, 232–3, 236, 240–2, 246–50, 259–62, 282–3, 323–7, 359–65, 450–1; Dennis Deletant, *Hitler's Forgotten Ally. Ion Antonescu and His Regime, Romania 1940–44* (Houndmills, Basingstoke, 2006), pp. 127–87, 205; Prusin, *Lands Between*, pp. 149–60, 169–75; Snyder, *Bloodlands*, pp. 188–208, 217–23, 228, 235–43, 250–3, 275.

not immediate. In late summer 1942, the vast majority of the Jews who had so far survived the terrible conditions of the Warsaw Ghetto were murdered in Treblinka. Bełżec, Sobibór and Treblinka each ceased operating between the end of 1942 and autumn 1943. By this time they had been used to kill perhaps 1.7 million Jews. The vast majority of them were Polish citizens from the General Government. But not all of them were, because from October 1941 onwards significant numbers of the Jews in occupied Poland's largest ghettos were foreign, having been sent there – as well as to the largest ghettos in pre-1941 western Soviet territory – from Germany and elsewhere.[12]

Two other sites were fitted with gas chambers in these years. Unlike Bełżec, Sobibór and Treblinka, these were not pure killing centres, but rather concentration camps where a large proportion of the inmates were used for labour rather than immediately killed. And many prisoners were not Jewish. The first was Majdanek, near the city of Lublin in the General Government, where gassings started in late summer 1942 and up to 120,000 Jews were killed through guns, gas, beatings, malnutrition and disease in the course of the war. The other was Auschwitz-Birkenau, located in the annexed western Polish territories. Gas chambers were built there in early 1942, and it became the main site of the genocide against European Jews once Treblinka was closed in November 1943. The gassing was done in Auschwitz-Birkenau using hydrogen cyanide rather than exhaust fumes. It started in March 1942. The majority of the just under one million Jews subsequently killed there came from outside Poland. Under one-third were Polish Jews. A third were from Western Europe, the Czech lands, Slovakia, Croatia, Belorussia and Italy. Three hundred ninety-four thousand – all killed between May and July 1944 – were Hungarian Jews.

In 1943–4, the Germans had used brutal violence to clear all remaining Jews from the ghettos of occupied Poland and pre-1941 western Soviet territory before finishing them off in the various extermination sites. One such clearance set off the famous Warsaw Ghetto Uprising in April–May 1943. Łódź was the last major ghetto in East-Central and Eastern Europe to be closed down. Almost all of its remaining inhabitants were sent to Auschwitz-Birkenau and to the briefly reopened Chełmno killing centre in summer 1944. The final phase of the Holocaust, in the final months of the war, as we shall see in Chapter 3, consisted of the SS forcing the non-Jewish and Jewish survivors of concentration camps in occupied western Poland

[12] Yitzhak Arad, *Belzec, Sobibor, Treblinka. The Operation Reinhard Death Camps* (Bloomington and Indianapolis, 1987), pp. 7–99, 119–49, 165, 370–5; Longerich, *Holocaust*, pp. 265–304, 320–6, 330–41, 343–4, 375–82, 392; Browning, *Origins*, pp. 188–93, 352–420; Friedländer, *Extermination*, pp. 234, 262–7, 283–91, 306–18, 337, 345–58, 387–95, 405, 426–47, 479–80, 486, 490–6, 529–33, 557–9; Snyder, *Bloodlands*, pp. 254–73, 310; Esch, *Verhältnisse*, pp. 349–54.

and eastern Germany to embark on terrible death marches westwards towards prewar central Germany. By the time these marches were over, the Germans had killed around 5.5 million Jews – in addition to the 300,000 killed by Antonescu's Romanian dictatorship – around 3 million of whom had been Polish citizens. Up to a million of these people had died not in gas chambers or through mass shootings but as a result of the terrible conditions, beatings and small-scale shootings at concentration camps, in ghettos, in train wagons and on forced marches. Many non-Jews were also killed in various ways at German concentration camps, including over 70,000 non-Jewish Poles at Auschwitz alone.[13]

The invasion of the Soviet Union in summer 1941, then, had heralded the start of the Holocaust. But that was not all. It also brought with it an expansion of German policies of mass population displacement. Since late 1939, hundreds of thousands of Poles had already been sent from occupied Poland to Germany to provide manual labour, mainly in agriculture. The attack on the Soviet Union then opened up prewar eastern Poland, prewar western Soviet territory and the prewar Baltic states as a vast new source of workers for Germany's factories. At first the German authorities recruited the Poles from the General Government and so-called *Ostarbeiter* (eastern workers) from further east voluntarily. But once it became widely known among the potential recruits that they would face extremely harsh and tightly controlled working and living conditions on arrival in Germany, the Germans resorted to forcible roundups. Of the roughly 4 million Poles, Soviets and other Eastern European civilians sent to Germany in the course of the war – almost 1.4 million of them from the General Government – only a fraction were recruited voluntarily. The vast majority were forcibly transported. In addition to these civilians, almost 2 million Soviet and 300,000 Polish prisoners of war were sent to Germany for forced labour in these years.[14]

Another significant mass displacement carried out by the Germans in occupied Poland happened in response to the Warsaw Uprising of August–October 1944 (see Chapter 2). The uprising had involved brutal street

[13] Longerich, *Holocaust*, pp. 280–3, 302–3, 324–9, 334–5, 343–5, 360–3, 377–410, 414–18; Friedländer, *Extermination*, pp. 235–6, 358–9, 372–8, 404–25, 480, 487, 490–4, 501–10, 520–31, 579–85, 599–602, 606–19, 630–2, 638–9, 646–51; Corni, *Ghettos*, pp. 266–9, 274–5, 283–5, 315–20; Sybille Steinbacher, *Auschwitz: A History* (London, 2005), pp. 85–126, 132–6; Snyder, *Bloodlands*, pp. 253–4, 273–6, 281–94, 310–11; Evans, *War*, pp. 294–318.

[14] Mark Spoerer, *Zwangsarbeit unter dem Hakenkreuz. Ausländische Zivilarbeiter, Kriegsgefangene und Häftlinge im Deutschen Reich und im besetzten Europa 1939–1945* (Stuttgart and Munich, 2001), pp. 35–50, 66–9, 71–5, 80, 84, 87; Ulrich Herbert, *Hitler's Foreign Workers. Enforced Foreign Labor in Germany under the Third Reich* (Cambridge, 1997), pp. 61–4, 79–87, 163–76, 192–4, 198–204, 248, 278–82, 296–8; Stelzl-Marx, 'Forced Labourers', pp. 168–81, 202; Gross, *Polish Society*, pp. 78–81; Esch, *Verhältnisse*, pp. 331–4.

fighting in which an estimated 185,000 noncombatant civilians had died, the majority of them deliberately killed by the Germans. Once the uprising was over, the Germans forced hundreds of thousands of surviving residents out of Warsaw. Around 60,000 of them were then sent to concentration camps and around 90,000 to Germany for labour. The Germans then systematically destroyed the city, building by building.[15]

Of course, labour shortages and 'reprisals' were not the only reason for mass forced displacements in occupied Poland during the later war years. German policies of national-racial engineering also continued to shift people against their will. By mid 1942, officials from Himmler's Reich Commissariat for Strengthening Germandom had come up with ambitious plans for the expulsion of some 45 million Slavs from prewar Polish and prewar western Soviet territories to make room for a vast network of new German settlements, known as the *Generalplan Ost* (General Plan East). The only significant attempt to implement these plans took the form of a pilot project carried out in the Zamość district of the General Government. In autumn 1942, Odilo Globocnik – the SS man in charge of exterminating Jews in the General Government – launched a brutal campaign against the Polish inhabitants of this ethnically mixed district. Over 300 villages were cleared of their residents – more than 100,000 people fled, were expelled eastwards or were transported to Germany for labour. The intention had been to bring in the same number of German settlers within a year. But only 13,000 volunteers could be found, and they quickly came under attack from incensed Polish partisan groups. In these highly unstable and dangerous circumstances, the project could not be continued for long. It was abandoned in August 1943. Other smaller experiments with the *Generalplan Ost* tried out in Ukraine and the Crimea region proved similarly short-lived.[16]

In annexed western Poland, too, the Nazis continued their campaign of national-racial reordering after their attack on the Soviet Union in summer 1941. But forced migration was no longer the primary means they employed. By this time an ethnic screening process was being implemented throughout Poland's annexed western territories, intended to identify those

[15] Włodzimierz Borodziej, *The Warsaw Uprising of 1944* (Madison, WI, 2006), pp. 74–82, 96–141; Snyder, *Bloodlands*, pp. 300–9; Paczkowski, *Spring*, pp. 124–7.

[16] Czesław Madajczyk, 'Vom "Generalplan Ost" zum "Generalsiedlungsplan". Forschungspolitische Erkenntnisse', in Mechtild Rössler and Sabine Schleiermacher (eds.), *Der 'Generalplan Ost'* (Berlin, 1993), pp. 12–17; Esch, *Verhältnisse*, pp. 346–59; Gustavo Corni and Jerzy Kochanowski, 'The Generalplan Ost' and 'Generalplan Ost: Implementation and Failure', in Ahonen et al., *People*, pp. 34–41; Łuczak, *Stosunki*, pp. 375–6; Pertti Ahonen and Jerzy Kochanowski, 'The Experience of Forced Migration', in Ahonen et al., *People*, pp. 121–2; Mark Mazower, *Hitler's Empire: Nazi Rule in Occupied Europe* (London, 2008), pp. 205–21.

Polish citizens living in these lands who were German or had some sort of connection with the German *Volk* (nation, ethnicity, race). This process was known as the *Deutsche Volksliste* (German Ethnicity List), and Polish citizens applied for registration on it by submitting a questionnaire in which they supplied various pieces of personal information. Those individuals whom the Nazi authorities decided to place on the list were then categorized into four ranked groups. The top two groups contained 'ethnic Germans' (*Volksdeutsche*) who were eligible for full Reich citizenship (*Reichsbürgerschaft*). Groups III and IV were for people who did not exhibit an overt cultural or linguistic connection with the German *Volk* but were nevertheless deemed 'German by descent' (*deutschstämmig*). Their lower status was reflected in the fact that they were entitled to no more than 'state membership' (*Staatsangehörigkeit*).

The process was implemented differently in the various regions of Nazi Germany's annexed territories. In the Wartheland, Gauleiter Arthur Greiser believed it possible to apply a strict understanding of German *Volk* to the screening process and his officials, correspondingly, classified only a minority of Polish citizens as Germans. The vast majority of them were placed into groups I and II. In contrast, in Danzig–West Prussia, German officials took a far more inclusive approach, placing the majority of the region's Polish citizens on the *Deutsche Volksliste*. Yet the vast majority there were assigned to groups III and IV. Similarly, in eastern Upper Silesia, as we shall see in Chapter 6, only a fraction of the population was not placed on the list during the war, not least because applying for *Deutsche Volksliste* registration was made compulsory. Across the annexed territories, around 2.8 million of the 9 million or so remaining prewar inhabitants had been placed on the *Deutsche Volksliste* by the start of 1944. Nearly two-thirds were placed into groups III and IV. The intention was that the people in these bottom two groups would subsequently be culturally 'Germanized'. This meant they would 're-learn' the culture and language of their supposed racial forefathers and thereby assimilate into the German *Volk*. The *Deutsche Volksliste* was also introduced outside the annexed territories, in the General Government and Ukraine, but on a much smaller scale.[17]

In the Czech lands, as well, between 1941 and 1943, the German occupiers implemented an ethnic screening process in which they sought to

[17] Esch, *Verhältnisse*, pp. 229–51; Corni, 'German Plans', pp. 33–4; Corni and Kochanowski, 'Failure', pp. 40–1; Zofia Boda-Krężel, *Sprawa Volkslisty na Górnym Śląsku. Koncepcje likwidacji problemu i ich realizacja* (Opole, 1978), pp. 14–33; Łempiński, *Przesiedlenie*, pp. 89–92; Kochanowski, 'Schicksale', pp. 17–26; Mazower, *Empire*, pp. 195–8.

separate out 'Germanizable' individuals from the rest of the Czech population. Like the *Deutsche Volksliste*, this involved classifying many people as 'Germanizable' whose first language was not German and who never previously viewed themselves as Germans. This screening process was seen by the German occupiers of the Czech interior as a prelude to the cultural 'Germanization' of half of the Czech-speaking population and the sterilization or expulsion eastwards of the unwanted remainder. Yet these plans, like most other grandiose proposals thought up by Nazi leaders during the war, were never fulfilled. The ethnic screening process was slowly sidelined following the assassination of its key architect, Reinhard Heydrich, in June 1942.[18]

The Germans extended their campaign of national-racial engineering into Southeastern Europe in these years. After Germany's invasion of Yugoslavia in April 1941, the German occupiers introduced measures aimed at culturally 'Germanizing' most of the population of northern Slovenia in preparation for the incorporation of this territory into Germany. These measures included prohibiting use of the Slovenian language. Nazi leaders also planned to uproot around a third of the Slovenian population to make room for German settlers and had already expelled approximately 80,000 locals to Croatia by summer 1942, before partisan attacks forced the German authorities to desist. Germany's allies and puppet regimes in the region pursued similar policies at this time. The Croatian fascist Ustaša regime launched vicious attacks on Serbs and Jews in Croatia in summer 1941. In subsequent months and years they expelled around 180,000 Serbs into German-occupied Serbia and killed at least 400,000 Serbs through mass shootings and death camps. At the same time, the Ustaša forced around a quarter of a million Serbs to convert to Catholicism and banned the Serbian Cyrillic alphabet. Perhaps 40,000 Serbs were likewise expelled from the Vojvodina region into Serbia by Germany's ally Hungary between April and December 1941. The year before, two other German allies, Romania and Bulgaria, had carried out a 'population exchange' uprooting 61,000 Bulgarians and 100,000 Romanians.[19]

[18] Volker Zimmermann, *Die Sudetendeutschen im NS-Staat: Politik und Stimmung der Bevölkerung im Reichsgau Sudetenland 1938–1945* (Essen, 1999), pp. 287–337; Chad Bryant, 'Either German or Czech: Fixing Nationality in Bohemia and Moravia, 1939–1946', *Slavic Review*, 61, 2002, 4, pp. 686–96; Tara Zahra, 'Reclaiming Children for the Nation: Germanization, National Ascription, and Democracy in the Bohemian Lands, 1900–1945', *Central European History*, 37, 2004, 4, pp. 527–33; Jeremy King, *Budweisers into Czechs and Germans: A Local History of Bohemian Politics, 1848–1948* (Princeton, New Jersey, 2002), pp. 185–7.

[19] Milan Ristović, 'Zwangsmigrationen in den Territorien Jugoslawiens im Zweiten Weltkrieg: Pläne, Realisierung, Improvisation, Folgen', in Melville et al., *Zwangsmigrationen*, pp. 311–22; Tamás Stark,

SOVIET ETHNIC CLEANSING, 1941–5

Germany's attacks on Yugoslavia and the Soviet Union in late spring and early summer 1941, then, helped both to set off the genocide against European Jews and to extend the geographical reach of Germany's broader campaign of national-racial transformation. But that was not all. The German invasion of the USSR also triggered a transformation in the scale and character of forced migrations carried out by Joseph Stalin and the Soviet leadership. The evolution of Soviet policies of forced migration extends back to the Russian Civil War of 1918–21, when the fledgling Bolshevik regime instigated mass displacements of groups associated with the White forces. But truly massive forced migrations were not carried out by the Soviets until the 1930s. The first wave took place in the early 1930s and is best characterized as a campaign of 'social cleansing'. To facilitate the comprehensive collectivization of agriculture in the main grain-growing areas of the USSR, the Soviet leadership decided to eliminate an entire social class: the better-off peasants or 'kulaks'. Between 1930 and 1933, the authorities rounded up somewhere near to 1.5 million peasants categorized as 'kulaks' – few of whom were at all wealthy in reality – and transported them on cargo trains from Ukraine and other cereal-growing areas to sparsely populated and undeveloped regions elsewhere in the vast Soviet state. They were sent in particular to the Urals, Kazakhstan and western Siberia. There they were made to live on tightly controlled labour settlements under very harsh conditions – a pattern which would be repeated in most subsequent forced displacements carried out by the Soviets.

In the mid 1930s, the character of Soviet forced migration then underwent an important change as the authorities started targeting people based on their ethnicity alone. In 1935–6, around 30,000 ethnic Finns were sent from northwestern Russia to central Asia and Siberia and over 100,000 ethnic Germans and ethnic Poles were transported from western Ukraine to Kazakhstan and eastern Ukraine. In each case, it was not the entire ethnic group which was uprooted, but rather those members who had the bad fortune to live in a clearly defined belt of land running along the western Soviet border. The first mass displacement to target an entire ethnic group happened in autumn 1937, when almost 172,000 people living in the Far East Krai in the eastern Soviet borderlands, the vast majority of them

'Hungary: Principles and Practices' and 'Romanian Plans and Practices', in Ahonen et al., *People*, pp. 51–2, 55; Klejda Mulaj, *Politics of Ethnic Cleansing: Nation-State Building and Provision of In/Security in Twentieth-Century Balkans* (Lanham, 2008), pp. 40–3; Mazower, *Empire*, pp. 203–4, 346–7; Hans Lemberg, '"Ethnische Säuberung": Ein Mittel zur Lösung von Nationalitätenproblemen?', *Aus Politik und Zeitgeschichte*, 1992, B46, p. 32.

categorized as ethnic Koreans, were loaded onto 124 cargo trains and transported westwards to Kazakhstan and Uzbekistan. Apparently no more than 700 ethnic Koreans were left behind. In each of these ethnically targeted forced migrations – and in a number of far smaller actions against other ethnic groups in the late 1930s – the apparent objective was to enhance the security of the Soviet state by clearing regions near to the state borders of individuals whose ethnicity meant, in the eyes of Stalin and other Soviet leaders, that they could not be trusted. A similarly warped and ethnically centred understanding of security lay behind the mass killing of members of a number of other perceived 'national minorities' and immigrant groups during the Great Terror of the late 1930s. These 'national' killing operations accounted for over one-third of all deaths during the Terror. Ethnic Poles suffered especially, with at least 85,000 of them being executed at this time.[20]

The years 1939–41, as we have seen, then saw a return to the 'social cleansing' of the early 1930s, now directed at the prewar eastern Polish, Baltic and northern and eastern Romanian territories. It principally targeted local political, social, economic and administrative elites rather than the upper stratum of the peasantry. The German invasion of the Soviet Union in summer 1941, however, returned ethnicity to the foreground. And it did so in a radical way, because almost all of the massive forced migrations subsequently carried out by the Soviets uprooted entire ethnic groups. The first victims of this new wave of forced migration were the ethnic Germans. As German military forces advanced eastwards into Soviet territory in summer 1941, the Soviet leadership decided it was necessary to carry out a preemptive strike against the Soviet Germans to prevent them – without any substantive grounds for suspecting the Soviet Germans had any such intentions – from assisting the German military as it moved deeper into Soviet territory. In September and October 1941, the NKVD therefore swept across the European part of the USSR, rounding up entire German-speaking communities – including the whole ethnic German population of the Volga German Autonomous Soviet Socialist Republic. They transported them in cargo trains to labour settlements in Kazakhstan and Siberia. Further actions against Soviet Germans followed in subsequent months, so that around 900,000 had been uprooted eastwards by March 1942.

[20] Polian, *Against*, pp. 59–102; Terry Martin, 'The Origins of Soviet Ethnic Cleansing', *The Journal of Modern History*, 70, December 1998, pp. 846–58; J. Otto Pohl, *Ethnic Cleansing in the USSR, 1937–1949* (Westport, Connecticut, 1999), pp. 3–5, 9–31; Ciesielski, *Masowe deportacje*, pp. 83–106, 139–68, 182–202; Nikolai Bougai, *The Deportation of Peoples in the Soviet Union* (New York, 1996), pp. 25–37, 114, 182; Snyder, *Bloodlands*, pp. 89–107, 329–30.

The *Wehrmacht* went on to occupy vast swaths of prewar western Soviet territory in 1942. But it was steadily forced out again by the Red Army from early 1943 onwards. This then became the basis for a new round of Soviet 'ethnic cleansing'. Many millions of Soviet citizens had come under German occupation in 1941–2, and a small fraction did collaborate with the occupiers. The north Caucasus had not seen any greater levels of collaboration from local ethnic groups than other German-occupied Soviet territories. Despite this, Stalin and his NKVD chief Lavrentii Beria regarded a number of the ethnic groups living there as a serious threat to state security as a result of their supposed involvement with the German occupation authorities in 1941–2. After the German retreat from the region in January 1943, Stalin and the Soviet leadership accused these groups of collaboration. This provided them with the pretext to displace them to remote central areas of the USSR. On a single day in early November 1943, 69,267 ethnic Karachais were pulled from their homes by the NKVD and transported eastwards, mainly to labour settlements in Kazakhstan and Kyrgyzstan. Over two days in the extreme cold of late December 1943, 91,919 ethnic Kalmyks were then loaded onto trains and sent to Siberia, followed by several thousand more in subsequent months.

Chechens and Ingush narrowly avoided the brutal German occupation regime in 1942, but this did not spare them from mass displacement by the Soviets. Beria was compelled by the lack of a German occupation of the area inhabited by Chechens and Ingush to accuse them of 'terrorism' rather than collaboration. But otherwise their fate was no different from that of the Kalmyks and Karachais. It took just a week, starting in late February 1944, for the NKVD to cram 478,479 Chechens and Ingush into trains and transport them to labour settlements in Kazakhstan and Kyrgyzstan. About a week later, 37,107 ethnic Balkars were sent in the same direction. In all the north Caucasian actions, virtually no registered member of the targeted ethnic groups was left behind. These were total displacements. The torrent of Soviet forced migration then spilled over onto the Crimean peninsula, where the German occupation held on through to May 1944. The Soviet authorities transported 191,914 Crimean Tatars to labour settlements in Uzbekistan and elsewhere at the end of May 1944. Finally, in November 1944 over 90,000 ethnic Turks, ethnic Kurds and Muslim Armenians were sent from the borderlands of Soviet Georgia to Uzbekistan, Kazakhstan and Kyrgyzstan.[21]

[21] Polian, *Will*, pp. 123–56; Pohl, *Cleansing*, pp. 31–54, 61–9, 73–91, 109–16, 129–33; Bougai, *Deportation*, pp. 49–55, 57–68, 71–84, 97–108, 134–48; Ciesielski, *Masowe deportacje*, pp. 355–66, 378–418, 422–31, 437–52; Alfred J. Rieber, 'Repressive Population Transfers in Central and Eastern Europe: A Historical Overview', in Rieber, *Forced Migration*, pp. 19–20; Snyder, *Bloodlands*, pp. 330–1.

Unlike most other acts of 'ethnic cleansing' carried out in East-Central and Eastern Europe during and after the Second World War, the Soviet forced migrations were not inspired by the nationalist ideal of ethno-nationally homogeneous lands. Rather, Soviet ethnic cleansing was based on a particular understanding of security which stigmatized particular ethnic groups as posing a special danger to the Soviet state. Nevertheless, the fundamental objective of all ethnic cleansing, including that implemented by the Soviets at this time, was to transform the ethnic or national order in a targeted territory. The Soviets sought to accomplish this goal not only by displacing unwanted ethnic groups, but also by repopulating the vacated territories with either ethnic Russians or another ethnic group which Stalin and the Soviet leadership believed was 'trustworthy'. Ethnic Russians, for example, were settled in the territories cleared of Volga Germans. Ethnic Ossetians, Russians and Dagestanis were brought to the territories vacated by Chechens and Ingush. Ethnic Kabardians were handed the homes of Balkars. Such repopulation policies accompanied all Soviet forced migrations at this time. Yet the Soviet authorities generally failed to entice or – as also often happened – force anywhere near enough settlers to relocate to the vacated areas. And this proved highly problematic for food production in the affected areas, because these were almost all agricultural regions.

The ethno-national reordering carried out by Stalin and Beria, moreover, did not target only people. All newspapers, schools, social organizations and cultural institutions obviously disappeared with their populations. But the Soviets also made sure that the names of villages and towns in the targeted areas were replaced in order to remove the cultural traces of the displaced groups. They were either Russified or – if the new settlers were not ethnic Russians – replaced with new place names from the regions where the new populations had previously lived. Similarly, most of the uprooted people had formerly resided in 'autonomous' administrative regions of one sort or another, and they too were abolished and renamed by the Soviet authorities in order to expunge the memory of these uprooted people. The Volga German Autonomous Soviet Socialist Republic (ASSR), the Karachai Autonomous Oblast, the Kalmyk ASSR and the Chechen-Ingush ASSR were simply eliminated. Their territories were incorporated into neighbouring administrative units. The Kabardian-Balkar ASSR was reduced to the Karbardian ASSR.

The most crucial insight to be drawn from this brief sketch of Soviet population policy before and during the war is that the 'cleansing' carried out by Moscow in the middle and late 1930s and resumed with greater intensity in late 1941 was both large-scale and unambiguously 'ethnic' in character. This helps us to explain why a regime which preached a Marxist-Leninist ideology of class struggle blind to ethnic or national differences attempted to force all Polish citizens who were not ethnic Ukrainians, ethnic Belorussians or ethnic Lithuanians to relocate to postwar Poland from the new territories of Soviet Ukraine, Belorussia and Lithuania after 1944 (see the Conclusion). It also helps us to understand why Stalin and the Soviet leadership sponsored the comprehensive ethno-national reordering of Poland in the early postwar years, which we shall discuss in this book.[22]

Another important piece of context for the events examined in this book is the evolution of the conflict between ethnic Poles and ethnic Ukrainians in prewar southeastern Poland in the course of the war. We have already discussed how the collapse of the Polish state in autumn 1939 sparked a surge of Ukrainian–Polish violence in these territories, which the Soviet occupiers redirected into a campaign against the territories' mainly ethnically Polish elites. This ethnic conflict then escalated under German occupation after summer 1941. It was exacerbated by the material shortages caused by the Germans' ruthless exploitation of these territories. Although some Ukrainian nationalists came under attack from the German occupiers, many others were recruited into auxiliary police units and consequently gained direct experience of the mass killing of Jews committed in these territories from summer 1941 onwards. As it became clear at the start of 1943 that the war had turned against Germany, the more radical wing of the Organization of Ukrainian Nationalists, the OUN-B, concluded that collaboration with the Germans was no longer the best way of pursuing their radically nationalist goals. Indeed, they believed an opportunity was emerging for the creation of an ethnically homogeneous Ukrainian nation-state which would be independent of both Germany and the Soviet Union. Crucially, they also believed that it should include not only prewar Soviet Ukrainian territory but also that of prewar southeastern Poland.

The OUN-B formed a new Ukrainian Insurgent Army at this time, which launched a massive campaign of violence against the ethnic Poles living in prewar southeastern Poland. This powerful partisan force hoped to drive all ethnic Poles westwards out of this territory. As the weakening German occupiers were forced to abandon the countryside to the Ukrainian Insurgent Army's control, the violence against ethnic Poles assumed gruesome forms. Many ethnic Poles responded to the Ukrainian attacks by forming 'self-help' units, by entering the German auxiliary police or by

[22] Polian, *Will*, pp. 124–63; Pohl, *Cleansing*, pp. 15–16, 36–7, 47, 59, 65, 76–7, 85–6, 90–1, 111–12, 133; Bougai, *Deportation*, pp. 52–3, 57–8, 73, 82–4, 109–10; Snyder, *Bloodlands*, pp. 329–31.

joining pro-Soviet partisan groups. This put them in a position to inflict violent reprisals on Ukrainian nationalists and civilians, which claimed the lives of about 10,000 ethnic Ukrainian civilians in the later war years. But the highly organized Ukrainian Insurgent Army retained the upper hand throughout these events. The Red Army reentered these territories from the east in January 1944, and by the time they had finally brought the situation back under control, some 300,000 ethnic Poles had fled or been expelled into prewar central Poland. At least 50,000 ethnic Poles had also been killed.[23]

It was against the backdrop of this vicious wartime Ukrainian-Polish violence that Poland's new Communist-led government carried out its forceful actions against ethnic Ukrainians in the postwar territories of Poland during 1945–7. We shall discuss these events in detail in the Conclusion. More broadly, the forced migration, mass killing and genocide which Hitler and Stalin presided over throughout East-Central and Eastern Europe during the war formed the crucial context in which the Communist-led wave of forced migration and campaign of ethno-national reordering examined in this book took place. This study will focus on how these events played out in Poland's new territories after 1945. But before we turn to look at these events, let us first sketch out the key political questions facing Poland in the years 1939–49.

[23] Timothy Snyder, 'The Causes of Ukrainian–Polish Ethnic Cleansing 1943', *Past and Present*, 179, May 2003, pp. 204–28; Snyder, '"To Resolve the Ukrainian Problem Once and for All". The Ethnic Cleansing of Ukrainians in Poland, 1943–1947', *Journal of Cold War Studies*, 1, 2, 1999, pp. 90–103; Ther, *Vertriebene*, pp. 73–7; Prusin, *Lands Between*, pp. 190–200.

CHAPTER 2

Poland, 1939–49
Territory and communism

TERRITORY

The nationalist campaign implemented in Poland's new territories after 1945 was underpinned by a fundamental transformation of both the politics and the territory of the country. At the end of the Second World War, Poland was essentially lifted up and moved 200 kilometres westwards by decision of the Soviet Union, Britain and the United States. At the same time, in a country where Communism had never previously enjoyed widespread support, a Communist-led government came to power and, within four years of the war ending, had installed a full-fledged Soviet-style Communist dictatorship in Poland. These two transformations – political and territorial – were inextricably intertwined. But how did they come about?

The first important step was taken already in the very first weeks of the war by the state which would emerge from the Second World War as the dominant power in Europe, the Soviet Union. In September 1939 Poland was attacked by not one European power but two. First, on 1 September, Nazi Germany invaded. Huge German forces overwhelmed the much weaker Polish army in a mere few weeks. Second, on 17 September, the Soviet Union attacked Poland from the east. Already crushed by the Germans, the Polish army was in no position to repel a second powerful enemy. That the Soviets invaded Poland shortly after the Germans was not mere opportunism. The path had been laid for both invasions by a secret clause in a 'Treaty of Non-Aggression' signed on 23 August 1939, in which the German and Soviet foreign ministers had agreed to divide Eastern Europe into 'spheres of influence'. They followed up this treaty on 28 September 1939 with an 'Agreement on Borders and Friendship' which divided Poland in two. Germany took over the western half of the country, the Soviet Union the eastern half. Moscow transferred the area around the city of Vilnius to Lithuania but retained for the USSR the vast majority of eastern Poland. The Soviets then set about formalizing their annexation by staging sham elections to the two so-called People's Assemblies of Western Ukraine and Western Belorussia on 22 October 1939, which immediately requested incorporation into the Ukrainian and Belorussian Soviet Socialist Republics. At the start of November, these territories were formally incorporated into Soviet Ukraine and Soviet Belorussia. At the end of that month, their residents were declared Soviet citizens. Less than two years later, the Soviet Union would be forced to switch sides and join the fight against Nazi Germany. Nevertheless, as we shall see, the Soviets would refuse to relinquish their claim to the eastern half of Poland throughout the war.[1]

The dual occupation of Poland by the Soviet Union and Germany ended Polish sovereignty. But Poland's prewar leadership took action to ensure that it did not terminate the Polish government. Poland's president and government ministers and the commander-in-chief of the Polish army fled to Romania on 17 September 1939. There they were swiftly taken into custody by the Romanians in response to pressure from Germany. But at the end of September, Poland's incarcerated president authorized the formation of a new government in exile. This government was set up in Paris, but was then forced by the fall of France in June 1940 to transfer to London. This remained the base of Poland's exile government for the rest of the war.

The exile government differed from the administration which had governed Poland until September 1939 not only in its foreign location but also in its political complexion. Before the war, Poland had been ruled by an authoritarian regime dominated by the country's military chief, Marshal Józef Piłsudski. After his death in 1935, the government remained in the hands of his military and civilian supporters. But the incarceration of the Piłsudskiite government in Romania in late September 1939 transformed Polish politics. At last the barrier had been removed to participation in government by Poland's main political parties – which had all been excluded from power since Józef Piłsudski's coup in 1926. Indeed, although the new president-in-exile and several members of the exile government were Piłsudskiites, the new prime minister, Władysław Sikorski, was a prominent opponent of the authoritarian regime and most ministries in the exile government were headed by leading politicians from Poland's opposition

[1] Jan Tomasz Gross, *Revolution from Abroad: The Soviet Conquest of Poland's Western Ukraine and Western Belorussia* (2nd edn, Princeton, New Jersey 2002), pp. 17–112; Wnuk, *Sowieta*, pp. 16–18, 20–23; Lebedeva, 'Deportation', pp. 29–31; Paczkowski, *Spring*, pp. 37–50.

parties – the Peasant Party, the National Party, the Polish Socialist Party and the Christian and conservative Labour Party.[2]

The chief task of the exile government was to promote Poland's interests among Germany's most powerful adversaries. Sikorski and fellow members of the exile government understood Poland's interests to lie with two fundamental objectives. The first was the goal of restoring Poland as a sovereign state in its prewar boundaries. The second was that of acquiring new territories at the expense of Germany as compensation for the latter's entirely unprovoked attack on Poland in September 1939. Already in autumn 1939 the exile government's foreign minister, August Zaleski, began lobbying Britain for Poland to be granted 'control' of the German region of East Prussia once Germany was defeated. In November 1940 Sikorski explicitly called for the incorporation of East Prussia into Poland in a memorandum to the British Foreign Office. This territorial change was aimed at eliminating the strategic threat posed to Poland by having a large area of Germany jutting into Polish territory from the north. It was also intended to hand Poland a much larger stretch of the Baltic Sea coast. The exile government's territorial demands did not remain static but continued to expand as the war went on. By spring 1941 Sikorski was advocating to the U.S. president, Franklin D. Roosevelt, the transfer to Poland of both East Prussia and western Upper Silesia.

Germany's attack on the Soviet Union on 22 June 1941 appeared to do away with one-half of the barrier to the restoration of Poland as a sovereign state. Poland's Soviet occupier was rapidly driven out of prewar eastern Poland by Germany and its allies. This appeared to open up the real prospect that the Soviets would henceforth adopt a friendly attitude towards Poland. But when Sikorski began to negotiate an agreement with the Soviets in July 1941, he soon found that Stalin was unwilling to relinquish his claim to prewar eastern Poland. Despite Soviet intransigence over this crucial issue for the Poles, Sikorski deemed it prudent to sign the agreement. This caused both the Piłsudskiites and the National Party to resign from the exile government and to go into political opposition.

At the end of 1941, Stalin then proposed to Sikorski and the British foreign minister, Anthony Eden, that in exchange for eastern Poland, the Poles should be granted not merely East Prussia but all German territories up to the Oder river. This added up to a vast area of land. Both Sikorski and Eden rejected Stalin's proposal as altogether too radical. By this stage

[2] Czesław Łuczak, *Polska i Polacy w drugiej wojnie światowej* (Poznań, 1993), pp. 39–51; Anita Prażmowska, *Britain and Poland, 1939–1943. The Betrayed Ally* (Cambridge, 1995), pp. 7–12; Paczkowski, *Spring*, pp. 38–40, 73–7.

the British had actually accepted the idea that Poland would be given German territory as compensation. But Britain felt that this should be limited to East Prussia, western Upper Silesia and the Danzig/Gdańsk area; all territories up to the Oder was out of the question. The United States, which had been brought into the war in December 1941 by Japan's attack on Pearl Harbour, was also starting to accept the need for Poland to be handed German territory. But the Americans were not yet willing in 1942 to go as far as either the Soviets or the British.

On the other hand, all three Allied powers recognized that all the proposed transfers of territory from Germany to Poland would necessitate compulsory relocations of very large numbers of Germans. This, they agreed, would be essential to ensure that postwar Poland was not left with a large ethnic German minority. The Allies were convinced that it was the presence of ethnic German minorities in Czechoslovakia and Poland which had provided Hitler with the pretext, at the end of the 1930s, first, to take over the Czech lands and, second, to unleash a war on the whole of Europe by attacking Poland. The British and Americans, more generally, had drawn the conclusion by this stage that the existence of 'national minorities' in East-Central and Eastern Europe had constituted a critical source of instability in the region, which had not been neutralized by the minority rights guarantees put in place at the end of the First World War. With these assumptions in mind, in July 1942, the British government decided to embrace 'the general principle of the transfer to Germany of German minorities in Central and South-Eastern Europe after the war in cases where this seems necessary and desirable'.[3]

Nineteen forty-three was the year when everything changed for Poland. The crucial event of 1943 was the Red Army's crushing victory over German forces at Stalingrad at the start of February. This victory was then backed up by a second devastating blow at Kursk in July and August. The military successes truly transformed the Second World War in Europe. They also demonstrated the sheer power of the Soviet military machine. This, in turn, put the Soviet Union in a position to begin dictating to Britain and America exactly what should happen to East-Central and Eastern Europe once the war was over. From this point onwards, the Western powers accepted that almost the whole eastern half of the continent would become a Soviet zone of domination after the war. Regarding Poland, the Soviets' visible strength allowed Stalin to begin pushing more forcefully for the Western Allies and

[3] Brandes, *Vertreibung*, pp. 47–9, 57–60, 107, 148–50, 156–63, 214–19, 419–20, 423–7; Łuczak, *Polska*, pp. 46–53; Anita Prażmowska, *Civil War in Poland, 1942–1948* (Basingstoke, 2004), pp. 14–23; Paczkowski, *Spring*, pp. 75–83; Borodziej, 'Einleitung', p. 51.

Poland to acknowledge Soviet claims to prewar eastern Poland. At the same time, it enabled Stalin to begin taking overt steps towards determining the character of the postwar Polish government.

By early 1943, the Soviets were clearly on the lookout for an opportunity to marginalize Poland's exile government in London. Just such an opportunity conveniently presented itself on 13 April 1943, when Nazi Germany announced the discovery of a mass grave in the Katyn Forest near Smolensk. These were the corpses of Polish army officers who had been killed by the Soviet NKVD between April and May 1940 (see Chapter 1). The Soviets responded to this discovery with the false claim that the Germans had themselves carried out the massacre after seizing the area from the Soviets in autumn 1941. The Polish exile government had evidence to the contrary and called for an investigation by the International Red Cross. Stalin retorted that by making this demand the Poles were demonstrating their pro-German sympathies. He used this as a pretext to break off diplomatic relations with the Polish exile government on 25 April 1943. He would refuse to resume official ties with the Polish exiles for the rest of the war.

Already massively weakened by these Soviet moves, the exile government lost its driving force on 4 July 1943, when the charismatic prime minister, Władysław Sikorski, died in an air crash off Gibraltar. The new exile prime minister, Stanisław Mikołajczyk, understood very well that the only way the exile government was going to have a say in defining the postwar territory and government of Poland was by reaching a compromise with the Soviets. The problem was that from 1943 onwards, Stalin no longer felt any need to give ground on the issue of Poland, and the British and Americans were no longer willing to challenge this. This state of affairs was revealed at the Teheran Conference in November and December 1943, when Churchill and Roosevelt made clear to Stalin that they would accept a 'westward shift' of Poland. This meant the incorporation into the USSR of all the territories which the Soviets had annexed from Poland in 1939 and the 'compensation' of Poland with vast new territories in the west at the cost of Germany. The Soviets also indicated at Teheran that they now wished to annex northern East Prussia for themselves, leaving Poland with only the southern area of that region (see Map 3).[4]

[4] Krystyna Kersten, *The Establishment of Communist Rule in Poland, 1943–1948* (Berkeley and Los Angeles, 1991), pp. 3–10, 14–18; Brandes, *Vertreibung*, pp. 229–41; Prażmowska, *Civil War*, pp. 47–51, 69–70; Anna M. Cienciala, 'Katyn and Its Echoes, 1940 to the Present', in Cienciala et al., *Katyn*, pp. 215–21; Sanford, *Katyn*, pp. 1–2, 124–9; Paczkowski, *Spring*, pp. 110–11; Snyder, *Bloodlands*, pp. 133–7.

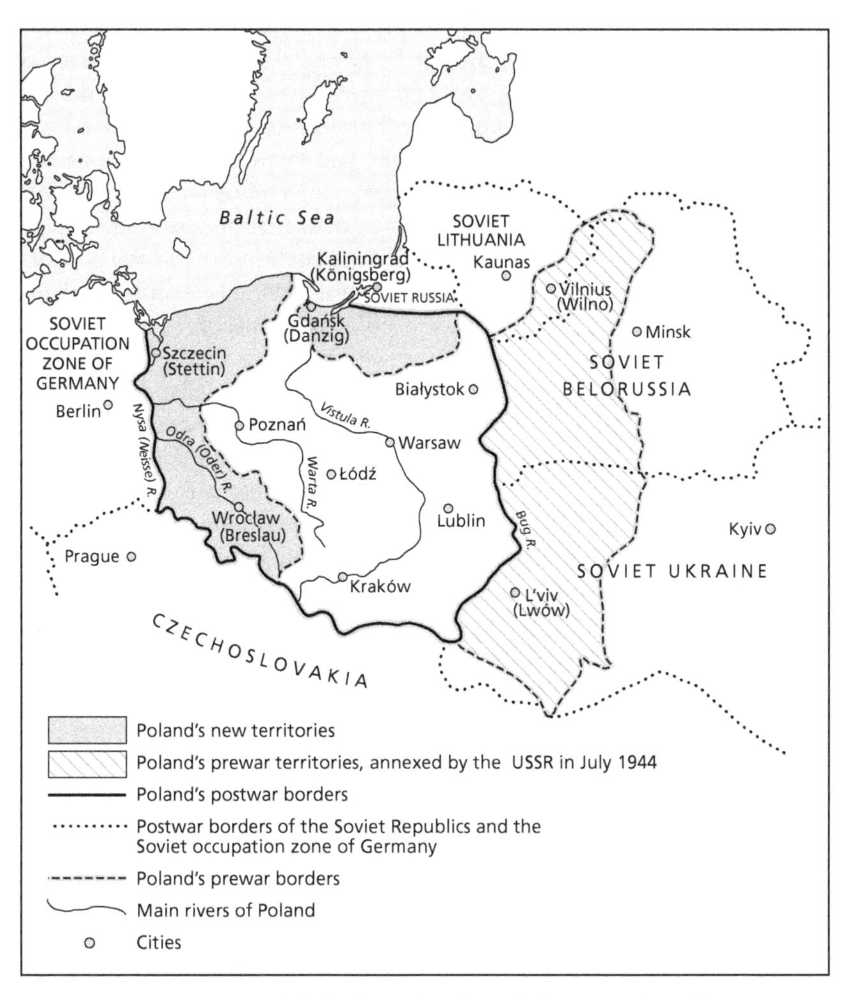

Map 3 The westward shift of Poland at the end of the Second World War

The Teheran Conference seriously weakened the Polish exile government, which was bitterly disappointed that the Western powers had not acted at the conference to put a stop to Soviet moves to take over prewar eastern Poland. But by this stage Soviet preparations to install a Communist-dominated government in Poland were already well underway. In December 1941, the Soviets had parachuted a group of Polish Communists into Poland, who then set about refounding the country's

Communist Party and attempting to build a viable base of popular support for it. The interwar Communist Party of Poland had been dissolved by Moscow in 1938. The majority of its leaders – who had misguidedly sought refuge in the USSR from political oppression in Poland – had been killed during Stalin's bloody purges of the late 1930s. During the war, the leaders of Poland's reborn Communist party, which was renamed the Polish Workers' Party (*Polska Partia Robotnicza*), at first pursued the strategy of attempting to create a broad and genuine coalition of left-wing political forces to govern Poland once the war was over. The Polish Workers' Party's leaders therefore made efforts to strike up cooperative relations with Poland's main leftist parties – each of which had its own conspiratorial cell operating in the underground in German-occupied Poland. They also attempted to foster good relations with the exile government's underground agency in Poland, the Government Delegation (*Delegatura Rządu na kraj*).

But from late 1943 onwards, under the new leadership of Władysław Gomułka, the Polish Worker's Party reluctantly abandoned this coalition strategy after recognizing that none of the main left-leaning parties, including the Polish Socialist Party, was willing to work with them. At the same time, a second circle of Polish Communist leaders, who were based in Moscow rather than Poland, had concluded that a Communist-dominated government of pliant partner parties – rather than a genuine coalition of leftist parties – was the way forward. At the end of 1943, the Moscow-based group and Gomułka's Poland-based Polish Workers' Party started setting up separate proto-governments. The Polish Workers' Party founded the 'Home National Council' (*Krajowa Rada Narodowa*); the Moscow group set up the 'Polish National Committee' (*Polski Komitet Narodowy*). Both were intended as vehicles with which a Communist-controlled government, with the outward appearance of a coalition, could – with Soviet support – be introduced into Poland once the war was over.[5]

By the end of 1943, both Poland-based and Moscow-based Polish Communist leaders were, therefore, putting into place institutional frameworks, which Stalin could deploy if and when he deemed the creation of a Communist-controlled government in Poland possible and desirable. Yet in early 1944 Winston Churchill continued to believe that this eventuality could be averted. All that was necessary was for the Polish exile government to accept the Soviet annexation of prewar eastern Poland. But Mikołajczyk knew he would never convince most members of his exile government to

[5] Kersten, *Communist Rule*, pp. 10–14, 18–22, 33–8; Prażmowska, *Civil War*, pp. 40–6, 49, 55–68, 73–4; Paczkowski, *Spring*, pp. 95–9; Fleming, *Communism*, 12–14; Borodziej, 'Einleitung', pp. 52–3.

allow this. In any case, by this time the chances of establishing in postwar Poland a government which was independent of Soviet interference had long since evaporated. The Red Army crossed into prewar Polish territory on the night of 3–4 January 1944. On 27 July, Stalin allowed the Moscow-based Polish Communists to move their new proto-government, called the Polish Committee of National Liberation (*Polski Komitet Wyzwolenia Narodowego*), to the Polish city of Lublin.

Just one organization felt it was still in a position, at this very late stage, to prevent the Soviet Union from installing a Communist government in Poland. This was not the Polish exile government in London but rather the armed underground movement in occupied Poland. A large number of resistance groups had emerged on Polish territory in the course of the war. Three were much larger and more significant than the rest. Two of them were the extreme-nationalist National Armed Forces and the Peasant Battalions. But by far the biggest was the Home Army (*Armia Krajowa*). This was a large heterogeneous organization, closely affiliated with the exile government in London and led mostly by commanders of the prewar Polish army. The Home Army had previously planned to lead a sudden uprising against the German occupation authorities throughout occupied Poland once the situation became ripe for it. But with the Soviets penetrating deep into prewar Polish territory in mid 1944, the Home Army's leaders viewed the uprising against the Germans less as a means of overthrowing the German occupation and more as way of discouraging a second Soviet occupation of Poland. A powerful uprising would demonstrate Polish strength and independence to the arriving Soviets. Home Army leaders were encouraged to believe that a signal of this sort was required by the actions of Red Army commanders in summer 1944. Despite fighting closely with Soviet forces against the Germans in prewar eastern Polish territories since spring 1944, Home Army troops and commanders had been disarmed and arrested by the Soviets in the Vilnius region in mid July. The same fate befell Home Army units in the cities of Lwów and Lublin and in many other localities east of the Vistula River over the next fortnight.

The Home Army's leadership had been delegated control over the launching of the uprising by the exile leadership in London. As the Red Army closed in on Warsaw in late July, they developed a plan for a concentrated uprising in the capital city. They were strongly convinced by the end of July that the German military was on the verge of collapsing and that the Soviets were anxious to reach German territory as quickly as possible. A Home Army–led uprising in the capital would therefore make a significant contribution to the Allied war effort by weakening German forces in prewar central Poland. But it could also count on the swift arrival of the Red Army, ensuring that it was not defeated. Believing the Red Army was about to invade Warsaw, Home Army leaders launched the Warsaw Uprising on 1 August 1944. Why the Soviets did not subsequently cross the Vistula at Warsaw to come to the aid of an uprising aimed primarily at limiting Soviet encroachments on Polish state sovereignty remains highly contested. It clearly suited Stalin's plans for Poland to see a force fighting to preserve the country's independence crushed by the Germans. But the Soviets may have been prevented from intervening primarily by circumstances beyond their control. The Germans were clearly not as weak as Home Army commanders believed they were. The Red Army had reached the limits of its supply lines by this time. And on 31 July, Soviet forces were halted by unexpectedly strong resistance from the Germans along the Vistula River. Whatever their reasons for not intervening to save the Warsaw Uprising, Soviet forces remained on the east side of the river for the rest of 1944. The Germans took until 2 October 1944 to defeat the uprising and then systematically destroyed the city and expelled its inhabitants. This crushed any last hopes that Poland would receive a postwar government independent of Soviet interference.[6]

By this stage the fate of Poland's prewar eastern territories had effectively already been determined by the Soviets and their Polish Communist partners. At the end of July 1944, the Polish Committee of National Liberation signed a secret treaty with the Soviet Union, recognizing the latter's takeover of prewar eastern Poland. Then, in September, this Polish proto-government signed population exchange agreements with the Soviet Socialist Republics of Ukraine, Belorussia and Lithuania. This paved the way for the mass relocation of hundreds of thousands of Polish citizens from prewar eastern Poland, which got underway at the end of 1944. During his visit to Moscow in October 1944, Poland's exile prime minister, Stanisław Mikołajczyk made a final attempt to reach a compromise with the Soviets over the postwar Polish–Soviet border. He also discussed the possibility of forming a cooperative relationship with the Polish Committee of National Liberation. But most members of the Polish exile government in London remained staunchly opposed to appeasing either the Soviets or the Polish Communists. This stubborn stance of most exile politicians eventually

[6] Borodziej, *Uprising*, pp. 22, 35–73, 87–95, 127–8, 139–41; Prażmowska, *Civil War*, pp. 27–36, 52–4, 69–79, 84–93, 96–7, 101–8; Jan M. Ciechanowski, *The Warsaw Rising of 1944* (Cambridge, 1974), pp. 164–280; Kersten, *Communist Rule*, pp. 22–8, 39–49, 60–75; Paczkowski, *Spring*, pp. 63–73, 83–9, 116–27; Brandes, *Vertreibung*, pp. 334–58; Antoni Czubiński, *Polska i Polacy po II wojnie światowej (1945–1989)* (Poznań, 1998), pp. 23–6.

caused Mikołajczyk to resign from his post as prime minister in November 1944. This was the final nail in the coffin of the exile government. It swiftly lost any influence it had previously enjoyed with Britain and the United States in subsequent months.

At the end of December 1944, the Soviets formally recognized the Polish Committee of National Liberation as the provisional government of Poland. It was dominated by Moscow-based Communists. Gomułka and other Poland-based Communist leaders were allowed to join this proto-government after summer 1944, but they struggled to exert the same influence as the Muscovites in the remaining months of the war. As the Polish Communists had planned, the Polish Committee of National Liberation had the superficial appearance of a multiparty coalition. But the non-Communist politicians given posts in it were all members of newly founded pro-Communist puppet parties. Two of these took the names of mainstream political parties – the Polish Socialist Party and the Peasant Party – but were actually formed from splinter groups. The third was the previously insignificant Democratic Party, formed in 1937. The Western powers refused to recognize this Communist-controlled proto-government as the provisional government of Poland. When the Allied powers met at the Yalta Conference in February 1945, the Western leaders managed to extract assurances from Stalin that when a provisional government was eventually formed, it would have a 'broader democratic basis'. But Churchill and Roosevelt did not manage to pin down exactly what this meant. Nor did they make any agreements with Stalin regarding how quickly elections would happen in Poland once the war was over. Moreover, although the two Western leaders refused to specify exactly how much territory Poland should receive from Germany in the west and north, they gave their approval at Yalta to the Soviet takeover of prewar eastern Poland.[7]

With Poland's new eastern border effectively fixed, military events started to determine Poland's new western border. On 12 January 1945, the Red Army launched a huge offensive along the Vistula River in Poland. Soviet forces reached the ruins of Warsaw on 17 January, Kraków and Łódź on 19 January, and crossed the prewar Polish–German border in many places on that day and subsequent days. Stalin had already unilaterally decided in summer 1944 that Poland's future western border would not run only along the Oder River. This would have meant a border running southwards from the Baltic Sea for around 150 kilometres and then swinging southeastwards

[7] Czubiński, *Polska*, pp. 31–42; Brandes, *Vertreibung*, pp. 355–75; Borodziej, 'Einleitung', pp. 54–6, 74; Paczkowski, *Spring*, pp. 136–41; Prażmowska, *Civil War*, pp. 73–84, 96–101, 109, 113–14, 141.

sharply just to the south of the city of Frankfurt an der Oder. Instead Stalin proposed that the new Polish–German border would run along both the Oder and western Neisse Rivers. This would give the border a fairly straight north–south path and would entail Poland acquiring much vaster German territories than the Western powers had ever been willing to contemplate in previous years (see Map 3). Already, in March 1945, the Soviets began allowing Polish civilian officials into the eastern areas of these territories to begin erecting Polish administrative authorities there. The Red Army finally conquered all German territories east of the Oder and western Neisse Rivers on 8 May 1945, the day of Germany's capitulation. Polish state authorities had arrived throughout these territories by June 1945.

This amounted to the unilateral handover of prewar eastern Germany to Poland by the Soviet Union. The Communist-controlled Polish government sought to consolidate this act of Soviet-sponsored annexation by flooding the territory with Polish settlers from March 1945 onwards, by expelling the millions of Germans living in these territories from mid June 1945 onwards, and by categorizing hundreds of thousands of local German citizens as 'indigenous Poles'. These radically nationalist population policies shall be examined in detail in this book. We shall return to them shortly.

The Soviets alone had therefore largely determined the frontiers of postwar Poland. The next task for them and their Polish Communist partners was to make sure that Poland's postwar government remained firmly under Communist control. At the end of June 1945, the Communist-controlled unelected legislative body called the Home National Council announced the creation of a Provisional Government of National Unity (*Tymczasowy Rząd Jedności Narodowej*). Britain and the United States had made concerted efforts in previous months to persuade the Soviets to allow a genuinely multiparty provisional government to be established in Poland. They had attempted to ensure that the provisional government would include leading members of Poland's main political parties and not just members of pro-Communist puppet parties. This is what the Western powers believed had been agreed with the Soviets at the Yalta Conference. Instead, the new Provisional Government of National Unity was nothing more than an expanded version of the Polish Committee of National Liberation. The Polish Workers' Party retained the key posts and almost all other positions remained in the hands of their pliant partners. The only significant way in which the Provisional Government of National Unity differed from its precursor, the Polish Committee of National Liberation, was that it included Stanisław Mikołajczyk, who was given the posts of deputy prime minister and minister of agriculture. Thereafter, his wing of the peasant movement – known after July 1945 as the Polish Peasant Party (*Polskie Stronnictwo Ludowe*) – functioned as the only legal political party in Poland which was not strongly influenced or controlled by the Polish Communists. With just one representative from the only legal party not closely affiliated with the Communists, the Provisional Government of National Unity was far from a genuine multiparty coalition. Despite this, the United States and Britain granted it formal recognition at the start of July 1945.[8]

At the Potsdam Conference, between 17 July and 2 August, the leaders of the Soviet Union, the United States and Britain took decisions of huge significance in determining the territorial and political contours of postwar Central and Eastern Europe. But for Poland the main decisions had already been made by the Soviets. Britain and the United States planned in advance of the conference to block any Soviet moves to make the Oder–western Neisse line Poland's permanent western border – on the grounds that it would require uprooting many millions of Germans. The two Western powers believed that the more German territory Poland was allowed to take over and the more Germans they expelled from it, the more vulnerable Poland would become to future German retaliation. They calculated – correctly as it turned out – that this would increase Poland's political and military dependence on the Soviet Union.

Once the Potsdam Conference was underway, Stalin and the Polish Provisional Government of National Unity's delegation claimed that almost all of the Germans living in the territory east of the Oder–western Neisse line had already fled from the territory as the Red Army arrived there in early 1945. No more than 1.5 million were said to remain. It was true that around 5 million of the approximately 9 million prewar residents of this territory had fled in the final months of the war. But the real figure for the number of German citizens remaining there at the end of the war was over 4 million. Moreover, hundreds of thousands immediately began returning to their homes in the weeks after Germany's capitulation on 8 May 1945.

The U.S. president who attended the Potsdam Conference was Harry Truman. Roosevelt had died in April. Very inconveniently, the leader of the British delegation changed towards the end of the conference; Churchill was replaced at the end of July by the newly elected Labour prime minister, Clement Attlee. Irrespective of which Western leaders participated in negotiations with the Soviets and Poles at Potsdam, they had no way

[8] Borodziej, 'Einleitung', pp. 55–73; Czubiński, *Polska*, pp. 42–3, 56–64; Prażmowska, *Civil War*, pp. 108–9, 113–14, 118–19.

of knowing exactly how many German citizens had actually fled. They were gradually worn down by the Soviet and Polish insistence that the vast majority had gone.

The decision on Poland's western border became bound up at Potsdam with Soviet pledges regarding German reparations and the Western leaders' growing belief that by opposing the Oder–western Neisse border they would strengthen Soviet influence within Poland. They also wanted to avoid providing Poland's Communist-controlled government with a pretext for delaying elections. Having agreed to the Soviet takeover of northern East Prussia earlier on in the conference, on 31 July Truman and Attlee approved the Polish takeover of all German territories up to the Oder and western Neisse Rivers. The eventual wording of the Potsdam Agreement suggested that these territories would only be placed under 'Polish administration' until a future peace conference took place. The formal peace conference would then determine the permanent fate of these territories. But the Western leaders were in no doubt at Potsdam that they were handing them to Poland on a permanent basis.

On the same day, the three Allied powers agreed to the 'transfer to Germany of German populations' from Poland, Czechoslovakia and Hungary. Expulsions of Germans and German-speakers had already taken place in Poland and Czechoslovakia before the conference (see Chapter 4 and the Conclusion). The Allied powers ordered that such 'transfers' be suspended until Allied-occupied Germany was in a position to cope with the massive influx of people caused by these expulsions. They also instructed the Poles and Czechoslovaks that when the expulsions later resumed, they be carried out in an 'orderly and humane manner'. At the Potsdam Conference, the British and Americans therefore gave their final approval to the westward shift of Poland and declared their backing for the ethnic cleansing of Germans and German-speakers from East-Central Europe.[9]

COMMUNISM

Poland's takeover of new western and northern territories and the objective of expelling Germans from the country were absolutely integral elements of the Polish Communists' effort to consolidate their hold on power in Poland. The Soviets had already levered the Communists into a controlling position in Poland by the end of the war. But the Communists believed

[9] Brandes, *Vertreibung*, pp. 401–17; Borodziej, 'Einleitung', pp. 73–6; Czubiński, *Polska*, pp. 82–3; Bernadetta Nitschke, *Vertreibung und Aussiedlung der deutschen Bevölkerung aus Polen 1945 bis 1949* (Munich, 2003), pp. 271–4.

they would not be able to sustain this position based on Soviet backing alone. They also wanted to begin implementing revolutionary changes to Poland's socioeconomic structures and considered that this would only be possible if they could build widespread popular support.

During the interwar years, the Communist Party of Poland had been a small and unpopular conspiratorial organization sitting at the very margins of Polish politics. Its lack of significant support among ordinary Poles had a lot to do with the internationalist, antinationalist ideology it had preached at that time. The Polish Communists' hard-line stance towards nationalism and patriotism had even prompted them to support Bolshevik Russia against Poland during the war of 1919–20. Against the backdrop of huge suffering at the hands of foreign occupiers during the Second World War, this antipatriotic, antinationalist position seemed even less palatable to ordinary Poles than it had appeared before the war. Tentative moves away from this stance had started already in 1935. These were continued during the war by what remained of the Polish Communist leadership after Stalin's murderous purges. But it was not until the creation of the Polish Committee of National Liberation in July 1944 that the Polish Workers' Party embraced, in certain important respects, an overtly nationalist position. To bring about this significant ideological adjustment, the Polish Workers' Party drew on the rhetoric and exclusivist ideology of the National Democratic movement. This movement had emerged in the late nineteenth century and had been dominated for most of its existence by the prominent politician and nationalist ideologue Roman Dmowski until his death in 1939. In the final months of the war, the Communists permitted the Polish Western Association – an organization very closely connected with the National Democratic movement – to begin operating openly in Poland, so that its activists could assist them in producing nationalist propaganda and conceiving of nationalist policies. At the same time, the prominent National Democratic politician, Stanisław Grabski, was brought on board to help formulate Communist policy towards Poland's 'national minorities'. He was rewarded for his collaboration by being granted the position of deputy president of the Home National Council in late June 1945.

It must be stressed that the Polish Communists made use only of certain elements of interwar Polish nationalist ideology. Polish nationalists were universally appalled by the fact that the Communists' proto-government in Lublin had helped the Soviets to annex prewar eastern Poland in July 1944 and were willing to acquiesce thereafter in Soviet interference in the government of the country. Other actions, too, made clear that the antinationalist outlook of the interwar Polish Communists had by no means been fully relinquished by the leaders of the Polish Workers' Party. But the nationalist objectives which the Polish Communists embraced were key ones: ridding Poland of its 'national minorities' and expanding westwards into German territory. These aims formed a very important part of their political programme in the period 1944–9. This partial turn towards Polish nationalism, it should be understood, was done with the permission and encouragement of Stalin and the Soviet leadership. It manifested itself in the final phase of the war mainly in nationalist rhetoric surrounding the claim that Poland had a historical right to the prewar eastern German territories because they had belonged to Poland under the Piast rulers of the medieval period. In line with this, the Communist-led government referred to this territory after 1945 as the 'Recovered Territories'.

But once the war was over, the nationalist side of the Communists' new political programme expressed itself most overtly in the implementation of a forceful campaign to transform Poland into an ethnically homogeneous nation-state 'freed' from the 'burden' of large Ukrainian, German, Belorussian and Lithuanian 'national minorities'. The loss of prewar eastern Poland in itself removed a large proportion of the Polish citizens regarded by the interwar Polish governments as members of 'national minorities'. But in the final months of the war and in the immediate postwar years, the Communist-led government carried out massive acts of forced migration which targeted hundreds of thousands of Ukrainian-speaking and German-speaking Polish citizens in Poland's prewar territories, as well as millions of German citizens in Poland's new western and northern territories. These radically nationalist actions met with very widespread approval from a Polish society whose nationalist sentiments had strengthened under the hardships and suffering of Nazi German and Soviet occupation. This play with Polish nationalism supplied Poland's fledgling Communist regime with a badly needed source of popular support. How the Polish Communists' campaign of ethno-national homogenization was applied to the new western and northern territories which Poland 'recovered' from Germany in 1945 will be examined in detail in the chapters which follow.[10]

[10] Marcin Zaremba, *Komunizm, legitymacja, nacjonalism. Nacjonalistyczna legitymacja władzy komunistycznej w Polsce* (Warsaw, 2001), pp. 72–80, 121–73; Olejnik, *Polityka*, pp. 17–40; Curp, *Clean Sweep*, pp. 10–12, 34–40; Fleming, *Communism*, pp. 1–3, 10–15, 18, 62–8, 74–5; Timothy Snyder, *The Reconstruction of Nations: Poland, Ukraine, Lithuania, Belarus, 1569–1999* (New Haven, Connecticut, 2003), pp. 179–82; Hofmann, *Nachkriegszeit*, pp. 52–9; Ther, *Vertriebene*, pp. 142–5; Krystyna Kersten, 'Forced Migration and the Transformation of Polish Society in the Postwar Period', in Ther and Siljak, *Redrawing Nations*, pp. 75, 79–81; Thum, *Breslau*, pp. 275–81; Czubiński, *Polska*, pp. 60–2.

A second important ideological adjustment made by the Polish Communists in order to build up a base of popularity was the policy of redistributive land reform. This was introduced by the Communist-controlled Polish Committee of National Liberation in September 1944 and was applied throughout Poland over the next few years. In the interwar period, the Polish Communists had declared their opposition to land redistribution and instead advocated taking all agricultural land into state ownership. But they dropped their opposition during the war, recognizing that by redistributing the land of large landowners and of ethnic Germans and German citizens to Poland's rural landless they could buy the support of Poland's vast peasant population. The policy of land reform also represented an alternative to the Soviet model of collectivizing agriculture. As such, it was part of a broader strategy on the part of the Polish Communists, in the first years of their regime, which entailed establishing a new, egalitarian socioeconomic system in Poland which could be presented to Polish society as markedly different from the Soviet one. This strategy, too, it should be emphasized, was adopted with the support of Stalin and the Soviet leadership. Another element of the strategy was the creation of a three-sector economy in which all large factories, mines, banks and trade enterprises were taken into state ownership but smaller businesses were allowed to remain in private hands and Poland's strong cooperative movement was allowed to continue expanding.

Like most other European countries, Polish society had undergone a sharp 'swing to the Left' during the Second World War, so that most sections of society and most political parties supported strong state intervention and the nationalization of industry at the end of the war. But the changes made by the Communist-controlled regime in its initial years reflected an awareness that the vast majority of Poles did not want to go the way of the Soviets. Władysław Gomułka was the greatest advocate of this cautious approach. He argued that Poland needed to go through a transitional phase between capitalism and socialism in which it would retain its 'multiparty' political system and find methods to advance socialism which would differ significantly from those used in the Soviet Union.[11]

Yet the Polish Communists were unable to rely solely on building popular support in order to secure their hold on political power in Poland. They were starting from such a low base of popularity that they and their Soviet

[11] Czubiński, *Polska*, pp. 131–3, 148–51, 204–6; Kersten, *Communist rule*, pp. 50–1, 62–3; Kenney, *Rebuilding Poland*, pp. 19–20, 29–31; Hofmann, *Nachkriegszeit*, pp. 158–60; Anita Prażmowska, *Poland: A Modern History* (London, 2010), pp. 112, 171–4; Fleming, *Communism*, pp. 55–6, 64.

sponsors recognized from the outset that the forceful suppression of political opponents would be essential. Otherwise, they recognized, their regime would not survive for long. Much of the political repression was carried out by the Soviet NKVD in the immediate post-liberation period. The NKVD continued to operate in Poland until spring 1947 and even maintained its own network of prisons and camps in the country. But alongside this foreign security organ, a powerful Polish security police apparatus was created. This organization was given the official name of the Ministry of Public Security in 1945; its regional and local cells were known as the Offices of Public Security (*Urzędy Bezpieczeństwa Publicznego*). It had many NKVD-trained personnel, including its chief, Stanisław Radkiewicz, and its main job was to identify and neutralize political opponents to the Communist-led regime. It operated independent of the Polish Communist-led government, being answerable in practice only to the NKVD.[12] Together with the various other security organs of the Communist-led regime, it engaged in a fierce struggle with a large number of armed resistance groups – many of them units of the former Home Army and National Armed Forces – which refused to lay down their arms after the war. The antigovernment activities of these armed resistance groups were especially intense in the first year or so after the war and were not entirely stamped out until 1948.

Moreover, the authorities ensured that there was little in the way of a legal political opposition in Poland. Aside from the pro-Communist partner parties, only Mikołajczyk's Polish Peasant Party and the Labour Party were given permission to function legally in the second half of 1945. The regime blocked an attempt by the mainstream socialist leadership to establish a Polish Socialist Party separate from the Communist-sponsored Polish Socialist Party, which had been created in 1944. The National Party – the party of Roman Dmowski's National Democratic movement – also applied for legalization in late 1945. But, reflecting the fact that the Polish Communists' newly discovered taste for Dmowskiite nationalism had clear limits, they refused this party permission to operate.[13]

Despite this highly restrictive political environment, the Polish Peasant Party managed to become a significant political force in Poland in the immediate postwar period. In fact, it emerged as Poland's largest political party in the first year after the war, with 800,000 members by May 1946 and corresponding levels of support from Poland's largely rural population. As

[12] The Offices of Public Security will be referred to as the 'Security Police' throughout this study.

[13] Czubiński, *Polska*, pp. 34–5, 47–55, 62–3, 74–80, 95–103, 194–8; Prażmowska, *Civil War*, pp. 119–22, 128–44, 148–58, 167, 191–3. For more on the anti-Communist armed underground after the war, see Rafał Wnuk (ed.), *Atlas polskiego podziemia niepodległościowego 1944–1956* (Warsaw, 2007).

we shall see, the Polish Peasant Party would not sustain this position for very long. But in early 1946 its leaders had reasons to be optimistic about their chances of winning the first postwar elections. The problem was that the Polish Workers' Party was not willing to hold the free and fair elections promised to the British and Americans at the Yalta Conference back in February 1945. This reflected a recognition on the part of the Communists that their ideological changes since 1944 had not boosted their popularity sufficiently for them to win genuine elections. They refused to allow elections to go ahead unless they were a simple matter of voting for or against a Communist-controlled electoral bloc of parties. This plan was thwarted by Stanisław Mikołajczyk. He had been willing to join the Communist-controlled government in June 1945, but he resisted pressure from the Communists, in late 1945 and early 1946, to bring the Polish Peasant Party into their electoral bloc. The Communist leaders therefore decided not to hold elections in 1946. Instead, they chose to stage a People's Referendum in June 1946, in which voters were asked three questions: whether they supported the abolition of Poland's upper house of parliament; whether they supported land reform and the nationalization of key branches of industry while preserving the rights of private initiative; and whether they supported the Oder–western Neisse border. Despite massive intimidation and numerous arrests against its activists by the security police apparatus, the Polish Peasant Party campaigned vigorously against answering 'yes' to the first question. These efforts proved futile. The Communist-controlled authorities rigged the results, supplying themselves with three resounding 'yeses'. The genuine results – 'no' to the first and second questions, but 'yes' to the third – were never published.[14]

The Polish Socialist Party also emerged as an important political player in the initial postwar period. With a leadership drawn from the radical left wing of Poland's Socialist movement, the Communist-sponsored Polish Socialist Party had functioned as little more than an adjunct of the Polish Workers' Party in the final phase of the war. But in summer 1945 this changed. This was because many moderate socialists started to join the party from the underground socialist movement. From this point onwards the party began pushing for greater independence from the Polish Workers' Party. As Padraic Kenney has shown, there was a good deal of tension and conflict between the Polish Socialist Party and the Polish Workers' Party in the initial postwar years, particularly at the level of workplace

[14] Czubiński, *Polska*, pp. 74–7, 151–61; Paczkowski, *Spring*, pp. 168–70, 177–83; Prażmowska, *Civil War*, pp. 191–6; Kenney, *Rebuilding Poland*, p. 45; Fleming, *Communism*, pp. 56–7.

political activism. After collaborating closely with the Communists in the struggle with the Polish Peasant Party during the referendum campaign in early summer 1946, the Socialist leadership demanded that the Communists give up their hegemonic position in the government. It called for the Communists to grant them the status of an equal partner. This, of course, the Communist leadership had no intention of doing. Tensions between the two parties continued to grow in the course of summer 1946.

What finally stifled the emerging conflict was not the Polish Workers' Party yielding to Polish Socialist Party pressure, but rather a speech given by the U.S. Secretary of State, James Byrnes, in Stuttgart in September 1946. It had become increasingly apparent to the British and Americans during 1946 that the Soviets were levering Communists into power across East-Central and Eastern Europe. This caused them to regret the decisions they had taken over Poland at the Potsdam Conference the year before. This was first given vocal expression by the former British prime minister, Winston Churchill, in March 1946. In his famous 'Sinews of Peace' speech, Churchill spoke about an 'iron curtain' being constructed across Europe. He also, rather hypocritically, condemned the 'Russian-dominated Polish government' for its takeover of German territory and expulsion of Germans. After a summer of international tensions over the postwar fate of Germany, Byrnes on 6 September 1946 delivered a similar speech in Stuttgart, describing the incorporation of German territory by Poland as a unilateral act by the Soviet Union which had not been authorized by the Western Allies at the Potsdam Conference. At the international level, Byrnes's statements merely added to growing tensions over Germany, which were steadily pulling the Soviets and Americans into a Cold War.

But their greatest impact was on the domestic political situation in Poland. This was because the Communists used Byrnes's speech to step up its repression and propagandistic attacks on the Polish Peasant Party. The Polish Communists presented the Polish Peasant Party at this time as an agent of the 'imperialist West'. Byrnes's speech and the Polish Workers' Party response to it, in turn, woke the Polish Socialist leadership up to the need to fall back into line. They joined the attack on the Polish Peasant Party and agreed in late September 1946 to form a unified electoral bloc with the Polish Workers' Party and its two most pliant allies, the Democratic Party and the Peasant Party. At the same time, the Polish Workers' Party helped to engineer the takeover of the Labour Party by the left-wing faction within the Labour leadership.

All of this left the Polish Workers' Party leadership finally feeling secure enough to hold parliamentary elections. An electoral campaign got underway in autumn 1946. Over the next few months, Polish Peasant Party activists were subjected to numerous arrests and violent attacks. When the elections finally took place on 19 January 1947, they were conducted in an atmosphere of serious, widespread intimidation. Once again, the Communist-controlled authorities made sure of their victory by rigging the results. The electoral bloc predictably received 80 per cent of the vote.[15]

After the elections, the Polish Workers' Party's leaders moved to cement their hegemonic political position in Poland. The new government formed after the election no longer contained a single representative from the Polish Peasant Party. Moreover, as well as all key ministries remaining in Communist hands, an unambiguously pro-Communist member of the Polish Socialist Party, Józef Cyrankiewicz, was given the post of prime minister. The Polish Peasant Party was thrown into crisis by the rigged election results and continued repression from the state's security authorities. During 1947, Polish Peasant Party leaders started to be put on trial. In late October 1947, Mikołajczyk fled the country to escape arrest. This left the Polish Peasant Party to be taken over by a left-wing faction. It was subsequently transformed into yet another satellite party of the Polish Workers' Party.

Thereafter, Poland had no legal political opposition. The illegal underground resistance forces had also been almost entirely eliminated by this stage. Meanwhile, the Polish Workers' Party moved to subordinate its main ally, the Polish Socialist Party. In May 1947, the Polish Workers' Party's Minister for Trade and Industry, Hilary Minc, launched the 'Battle for Trade'. This campaign was ostensibly aimed at doing away with 'speculation' and black market activities in Poland. But its underlying objective was to undermine the private and cooperative sectors of Poland's mixed economy. The Polish Socialist leaders opposed this campaign not only because they rejected the idea of an entirely state-controlled economy but also because the cooperative movement had always been a crucial source of support for their party. But the Socialists failed to block these measures, revealing their profound weakness by this time. The Communists continued their efforts to undermine the Socialists in the second half of 1947.[16]

[15] Kenney, *Rebuilding Poland*, pp. 29, 42–50; Czubiński, *Polska*, pp. 69, 155–61, 169–76, 181–5; Paczkowski, *Spring*, pp. 166, 173–86; Prażmowska, *Civil War*, pp. 130–7, 196–203, 205–7; Fleming, *Communism*, pp. 66–7.

[16] Czubiński, *Polska*, pp. 191–209, 222–7; Paczkowski, *Spring*, pp. 186–90; Kenney, *Rebuilding Poland*, pp. 192–3; Prażmowska, *Civil War*, pp. 194, 203–8.

At the end of September 1947, an important meeting of leading officials from the Communist parties of the Soviet Union, the states of East-Central and Eastern Europe, Italy and France took place in a small mountain resort in southwestern Poland called Szklarska Poręba. The location of this meeting was of no particular significance to the foreign Communists who attended it. But it was of importance to the Polish Communists who took part, because it was situated in the new territories Poland 'recovered' from Germany in 1945. Szklarska Poręba also has a very specific relevance for this book, because it was located in Jelenia Góra District, which is one of the two local case studies which form the focal points of our study (see Chapters 3–10).

The real international importance of the meeting in Szklarska Poręba, however, lies not in its location but in its impact on the political direction taken by the Communist regimes of East-Central and Eastern Europe at the end of the 1940s. Stalin had already decided during the war to transform the whole eastern half of the continent into a Soviet zone of domination. But he had always recognized that in each country the local Communists would need to be gradually levered into power rather than suddenly installed. In some countries, where the Communists were relatively popular, such as Czechoslovakia, this had meant forming genuine coalitions with left-leaning parties. In others, where they were not, such as Poland, this had meant creating sham coalitions controlled by the Communists. In all these countries, action had been taken to move economies in a state-controlled direction. But in none of them was an entirely state-owned and centrally planned economy put in place in the first two years after 'liberation', such as existed in the Soviet Union. Yet by 1947 Stalin had decided that a different approach was required.

This decision was taken against the backdrop of spiralling tensions with America and Britain, greatly exacerbated by the United States launching the Marshall Plan in summer 1947. For Stalin the Marshall Plan demonstrated conclusively that cooperation with the Western powers was no longer possible and that the Americans were intent on transforming the world into two conflicting camps. Stalin decided that the Communists across East-Central and Eastern Europe should now abandon their various 'national routes towards socialism' and instead take the Soviet road. This was made clear to them by the head of the Soviet delegation at the Szklarska Poręba meeting in September 1947, Andrei Zhdanov. The meeting also launched a new international Communist body called Cominform. Its purpose was to enable Moscow to 'coordinate' the Communist parties and regimes of East-Central and Eastern Europe. The Communist leaders of these countries took away the clear message from Szklarska Poręba that they should now fully embrace the Soviet model. This meant a political system which was entirely controlled by Communists – no longer hampered by Socialist allies who could not be fully relied upon – and an economy which was fully state-owned, centrally planned and dominated by heavy industry.[17]

In Poland, the Szklarska Poręba meeting had two main political consequences. First, the capacity of the Polish Socialists to at least temper and restrain the Polish Communists was entirely destroyed in the subsequent months. By March 1948, the Polish Socialist leaders had yielded entirely to Communist demands by agreeing to move rapidly towards a 'unification' of the Polish Workers' Party and Polish Socialist Party. In the course of 1948, hundreds of thousands of so-called 'rightists' – individuals deemed by the Communists to be opposed to 'unification' – were purged from the Polish Socialist Party. In December 1948, the party was formally absorbed by the Polish Workers' Party at a 'Unification Congress' which officially founded the Polish United Workers' Party.

The second main consequence of Szklarska Poręba was that it helped to bring about an overhaul of the Polish Workers' Party's leadership. The rift within the Polish Communist leadership had started already during the Second World War. In essence, it involved a split between those Polish Communist leaders who had spent most of the war in Poland and those who had spent most of it in the USSR. As this struggle crystallized in the immediate postwar period, the former faction broadly represented the position that the USSR was a much needed fraternal ally but that Poland should nevertheless preserve as much independence from the Kremlin as possible. The latter faction, on the other hand, held the view that Poland should continue to foster a very tight relationship with the Soviet Union and move towards a Soviet-style socioeconomic and political system as quickly as possible.

The leaders of these two factions – and the two leading men in Polish politics during 1945–8 – were respectively the general secretary of the Polish Workers' Party, Władysław Gomułka, and the supposedly 'non-Party' President of Poland, Bolesław Bierut. Unlike the other leading members of the hard-line faction, Bierut had spent much of war in Minsk rather than Moscow. He had returned to Poland already in summer 1943, when the seeds of his conflict with Gomułka first began to sprout. But in his political outlook he did not differ a great deal from the other hardliners. Despite

[17] Czubiński, *Polska*, pp. 219–22; Paczkowski, *Spring*, pp. 198–201.

the fact that Bierut and the Muscovites were already taking action to move Poland closer to a Soviet-style socioeconomic and political system in 1947, Gomułka still preached the need for a transitional phase between capitalism and socialism and the retention of some kind of 'multiparty' political system. Moreover, during the Szklarska Poręba meeting in September 1947, Gomułka had openly expressed reservations about the Soviets' proposal to create the Cominform 'coordinating' body. He was criticized for this attitude by the Polish Muscovites in subsequent months. Gomułka then started to express opposition to the pace at which the Polish Socialist Party was being destroyed. At a Polish Workers' Party Central Committee meeting on 3 June 1948, he even voiced his admiration for the fact that the Socialists had supported the cause of Polish independence before 1918. After 4 June, the Polish Workers' Party Politburo – the top body within the party – held meetings without Gomułka. But despite pressure from the Muscovites over the next few months he refused to recant his views.

Another international event intervened at this point. In early 1948 a conflict had erupted between Stalin and the Yugoslav Communist leader, Josip Tito. Tito had made clear to Stalin that he was intent on installing a Soviet-style socioeconomic system in Yugoslavia. But he was not willing to let the Soviets interfere directly in Yugoslav decision making. This was not something Stalin wanted to hear. At the end of June, Yugoslavia was therefore expelled from Cominform, and this was accompanied by a flood of Soviet propaganda railing against the 'nationalist deviation' which Tito was supposedly promoting within the international Communist movement. By 'nationalist deviation' the Soviets of course meant Tito's attempt to resist domination by the Soviet Union. Gomułka drew hostility from Stalin for seeking to mediate in this conflict. But Poland's Muscovites were not clear at this point whether Stalin would back them if they moved to remove Gomułka from power. Gomułka spent July and early August in the mountains in Kowary (a large village which again happened to be located in Jelenia Góra District). In his absence, at a Central Committee meeting in early July, the Muscovites attacked Gomułka for his 'rightist and nationalist deviation'. In mid August Bierut received permission from Stalin to remove Gomułka from power. At the end of August, Gomułka was forced to admit his 'errors' at a Central Committee meeting. He was then removed from his position as General Secretary of the Polish Workers' Party and replaced by Bierut. His supporters also lost their Central Committee posts. In subsequent months, tens of thousands of members were purged from all levels of the Polish Workers' Party. Gomułka made a final effort to defend his views in a speech to the 'Unification Congress' in December

1948. But his political marginalization by then was complete. In the next two years, Gomułka's associates were arrested by the regime's security police apparatus and Gomułka himself was placed under house arrest in 1951.[18]

The political transformation which took place in 1948 heralded dramatic changes to the economy and to levels of repression from the state authorities. In the early postwar years, the Polish Socialist Party had become a critical obstacle to the introduction of a Soviet-style economy. Gomułka too had acted as something of a restraining influence on this. The removal of Gomułka and the Socialists, therefore, cleared the way for the 'Stalinization' of the economy – meaning the installation in 1949 of a fully centrally planned economy under a new State Economic Planning Commission and the start of a massive expansion of state-owned heavy industry through a Six Year Plan. Similarly, the marginalization of Władysław Gomułka eliminated a powerful opponent to the collectivization of agriculture. This got underway in Poland at the end of 1948. Moreover, society as a whole was subjected to a Stalinist clampdown in 1948–9. All independent organizations, associations and trade unions were eliminated or forcibly absorbed into institutions controlled by the Polish United Workers' Party. Radkiewicz's Ministry for Public Security radically stepped up its suppression of all manifestations of political dissent. The Catholic Church, which had largely been spared from serious repression by the regime in the preceding years, was subjected to a forceful campaign aimed at cowing it into subservience. The highly repressive Stalinist stranglehold on Polish society would remain in place until October 1956, when Władysław Gomułka was finally allowed to return to power and to put in place a slightly milder form of Communist dictatorship.[19]

The 'Stalinization' of Poland's Communist regime in 1948–9 was accompanied by the toning down of nationalist rhetoric, which had featured prominently in the regime's propaganda in the early post-liberation years. This was not merely a matter of the Polish Communists turning towards more orthodox Marxist–Leninist ideological precepts. It also reflected the secure political position which Poland's Communist leaders felt they were in by the end of the 1940s. Overt appeals to populist and nationalist sentiments no longer seemed necessary to the hardliners now in charge of Poland's Communist regime. As we shall see, however, even if the rhetoric had changed, the campaign of ethno-national reordering would continue

[18] Czubiński, *Polska*, pp. 195, 204–9, 221–2, 228–33, 242–50; Paczkowski, *Spring*, pp. 201–8, 239–41; Kersten, *Communist rule*, p. 37; Prażmowska, *Civil War*, pp. 75–8, 203–4, 208–11.

[19] Paczkowski, *Spring*, pp. 211–19, 225–42, 246–55; Czubiński, *Polska*, pp. 231–2, 244–9; Prażmowska, *Poland*, pp. 176–81.

in Poland's new northern and western territories to the end of the decade.[20] The chapters of this book will look in detail at this campaign. But first let us seek to understand the circumstances in which this campaign was implemented in Poland's new territories. Let us look at the conditions on the ground in these territories in the final months of the war and the early days of the peace.

[20] Zaremba, *Komunizm*, 175–92; Olejnik, *Polityka*, pp. 44–7; Curp, *Clean Sweep*, pp. 37–8, 80–2, 86–7, 95–7, 103–6; Fleming, *Communism*, pp. 62–71; Strauchold, *Autochtoni*, pp. 184–7; Piotr Madajczyk, 'Niemcy', in Piotr Madajczyk (ed.), *Mniejszości narodowe w Polsce. Państwo i społeczeństwo polskie a mniejszości narodowe w okresach przełomów politycznych, 1944–1989* (Warsaw, 1998), pp. 82–3.

CHAPTER 3

War and peace

WAR

Following devastating German failures at Stalingrad and Kursk in 1943, the Red Army thrust Hitler's forces out of the Soviet Union and into East-Central Europe in 1944. By summer 1944 the Soviets had liberated much of Poland from German occupation and advanced as far as the Vistula River in central Poland. For several months the Red Army then halted. But at 4.35 am on 12 January 1945 it launched a huge offensive against German forces along the Vistula, triggering a massive flight by civilians living along the prewar Polish–German border. Droves of refugees started flooding out of Germany's prewar eastern provinces by train, horse-cart and foot, heading westwards and southwestwards towards central Germany and the borderlands of pre-1938 Czechoslovakia. Lying not far from Germany's prewar eastern border, Oppeln (Opole) District began to witness huge numbers of refugees passing through on their way to Lower Silesia and pre-1938 Czechoslovakia. Trains full of refugees from the east began arriving in the Oppeln railway station at this time. The Red Army was by this time closing in on the Upper Silesian part of the prewar Polish–German border. But Oppeln District's Nazi Party leader (*Kreisleiter*) continued to declare on local radio that the danger to the area was not yet acute. He issued the instruction that all residents of Oppeln town wishing to leave the town had to register first with the local police. Not until 17 January did he at last advise a 'precautionary evacuation' of the town by women, children, the elderly and the sick. Residents of the town began flooding out the area using whatever means of transport were available.[1]

[1] WR, P.J., a *Volkssturm* soldier who fought in Oppeln (Opole) town, 14.8.1951, BOD 10, 812, 103–4; WR, Paul M., Oppeln (Opole) town, 10.8.1955, BOD 1, 243, 9–11; WR, Helmut R., Carlsruhe (Pokój), 19.8.1958, BOD 1, 243, 53–61; WR, Annemarie K., Oppeln (Opole) town, 7.7.1947, BOD 2, 229, 36–47; Siebel-Achenbach, *Lower Silesia*, pp. 57–8; Hofmann, *Nachkriegszeit*, pp. 16–19; Ingo Eser, 'Die Deutschen in Oberschlesien', in Borodziej and Lemberg, *Heimat* vol. 2,

On 19 January 1945, the Red Army stormed across the prewar Polish–German border in Upper Silesia. On the same day the *Kreisleiter* and local Nazi leaders (*Ortsgruppenleiter*) finally ordered local people to evacuate every village in Oppeln District lying east of the Oder River. In certain villages, such as Malapane (Ozimek) at the eastern edge of Oppeln District, and Tauentzien (Okoły) and Blumenthal (Krzywa Góra) in the far north of the district, locals were told that their communities were about to become battle zones. Local men of 16–60 years were ordered to stay behind in these villages to fight in *Volkssturm* units. The *Volkssturm* was a makeshift military force created by Hitler in the final, desperate months of the war, recruited from men who had not been conscripted into the regular German military and generally received only minimal training before being sent into action.[2]

The local state and Nazi Party authorities generally made only meagre active efforts to evacuate local people. At the last minute, they tried to arrange trains to carry out evacuations from a number of these villages, but often these trains simply did not arrive. Some people were evacuated to the west side of the Oder River in *Wehrmacht* vehicles.[3] For the most part, then, this was a disorganized flight rather than an orchestrated evacuation. The vast majority of people who fled their homes in the snow and the extreme cold of 19 and 20 January 1945 did so by foot or horse-cart. Some travelled in large groups of villagers; others made the journey alone or in small groups.[4] Yet the villages lying east of the Oder River were by no means emptied of inhabitants in these frenzied days (see Map 4). In some villages – such as Bolko (Nowa Wieś Królewska), Blumenthal (Krzywa Góra), Tauentzien (Okoły), Carlsruhe (Pokój) and Finkenstein (Brzezie) – the majority of the population left. But in others – such as Eichhammer (Dębska Kuźnia), Bergdorf (Daniec), Burkardsdorf (Bierdzany), Döbern (Dobrzeń Wielki) and Brünne (Brynica) – most people seem to have remained in their homes.

pp. 374–5; Martin Broszat, 'Einleitende Darstellung', in Theodor Schieder et al. (eds.), *Dokumentation der Vertreibung der Deutschen aus Ost-Mitteleuropa* (5 vols., Bonn, 1953–61), vol. 1, 1: *Die Vertreibung der deutschen Bevölkerung aus den Gebieten östlich der Oder-Neiße* (Bonn, 1953), pp. 16–23E, 51–8E.

2 WRs: BOD 1, 243, 251–4; BOD 1, 243, 67–72; BOD 1, 243, 91–2; BOD 1, 243, 309–19; BOD 1, 243, 349–51; BOD 1, 243, 33–6; BOD 1, 243, 121–2; BOD 1, 243, 37–9; BOD 1, 243, 251–4. Claudia Kraft, 'Flucht, Vertreibung und Zwangsaussiedlung der Deutschen aus der Wojewodschaft Breslau (Województwo Wrocławskie) in den Jahren 1945 bis 1950. Das Jahr 1945', in Borodziej and Lemberg, *Heimat* vol. 4 (Marburg, 2004), p. 361; Siebel-Achenbach, *Lower Silesia*, p. 58.

3 WRs: BOD 1, 243, 67–72; BOD 1, 243, 271–4; BOD 1, 243, 255–6; BOD 1, 243, 75–6; BOD 1, 243, 251–4; BOD 1, 243, 53–61.

4 WRs: BOD 1, 243, 49–51; BOD 1, 243, 251–4; BOD 1, 243, 309–19; BOD 1, 243, 349–51; BOD 1, 243, 33–6; BOD 1, 243, 25–7; BOD 1, 243, 75–6; BOD 2, 229, 3–4.

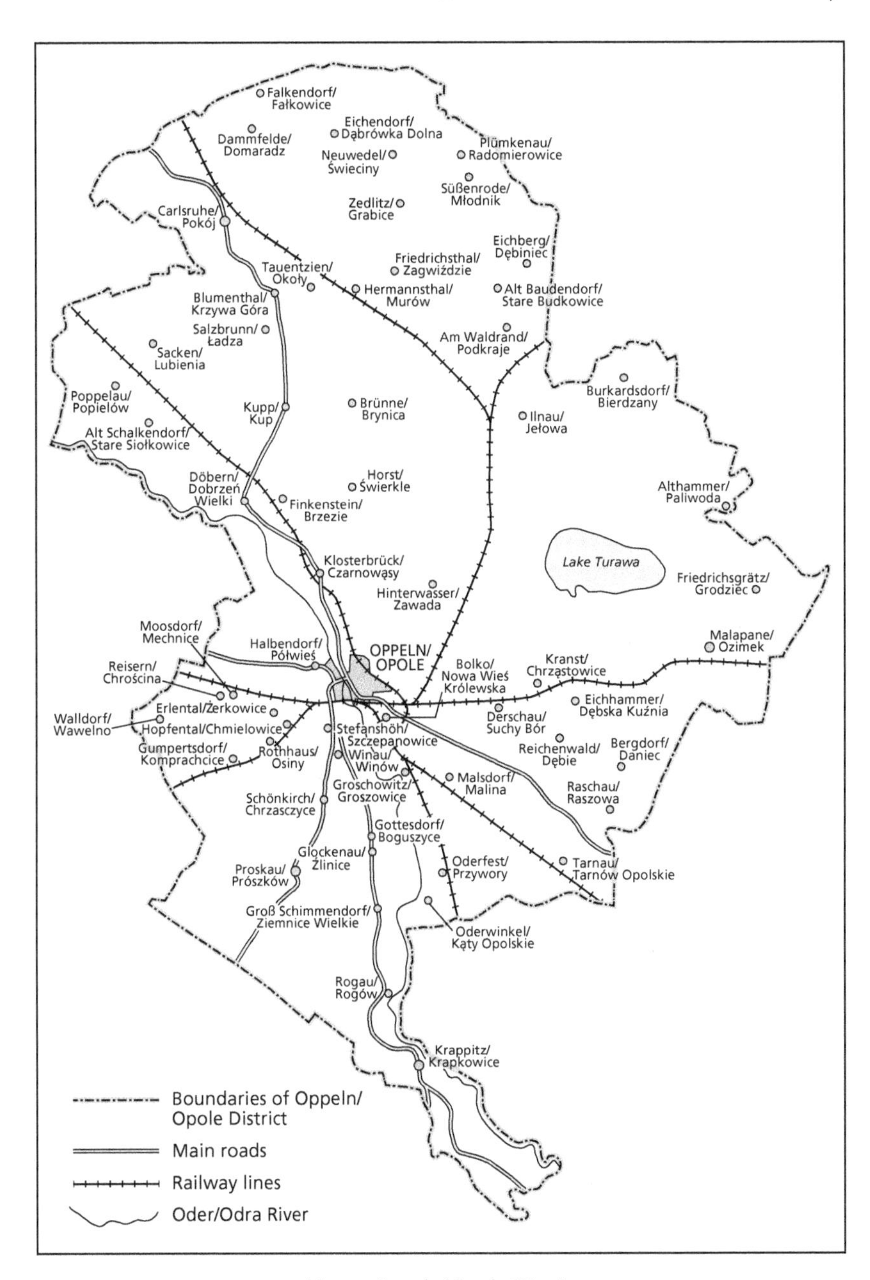

Map 4 Oppeln/Opole District

And some of the people who did flee at this time returned after just a few days.[5]

Residents of the part of Oppeln town lying on the east bank of the Oder River received a compulsory order to evacuate on 20 January 1945. A feeling of panic immediately gripped the town. Municipal buses were used to transport huge numbers of people to the west side of the river. Residents had to be packed tightly into the buses to shift such a large number of people in just a few hours. Many chose instead to make their own way across the Oder. On 21 January, the west side of the town lying on the other side of the river also received an evacuation order.[6] Residents poured out of Oppeln town westwards and southwestwards. Some people travelled on cargo trains organized by the German authorities, but most travelled by foot or horse-cart in temperatures as low as minus 20 degrees Celsius.[7] One resident of the town recalled how 'Oppeln became emptier and emptier' in these days.[8] A resident of Hopfental (Chmielowice), a village several kilometres to the west of Oppeln town, remembered the 'endless stream' of Oppeln residents moving through his village.[9] The road between Oppeln town and Neisse (Nysa), a large town located in the southwestern area of Upper Silesia, became clogged with fleeing civilians and German soldiers at this time.[10] Several residents of Oppeln District who fled the area in these days voiced anger at how late the evacuation had been ordered by local Nazi officials and at how little assistance and guidance they had provided to locals.[11] The vast majority of Oppeln town's residents left the town on 21 January 1945, only a handful of civilians choosing to remain behind.[12]

On 21 January, the retreating *Wehrmacht*, preparing for a showdown with the Red Army along the Oder River, blew up all the bridges in the

[5] WRs: BOD 1, 243, 37–9; BOD 1, 243, 33–6; BOD 1, 243, 349, 351; BOD 2, 229, 9–10; BOD 2, 229, 56; BOD 1, 243, 91–2; BOD 1, 243, 121–2; BOD 1, 243, 49–51; BOD 1, 243, 75–6; BOD 1, 243, 41–4.

[6] WR, Paul M., Oppeln (Opole) town, 10.8.1955, BOD 1, 243, 9–11; WR, P.J., a former *Volkssturm* soldier who fought in the defence of Oppeln (Opole) town, 14.8.1951, BOD 10, 812, 103–4; WR, Annemarie K., Oppeln (Opole) town, 7.7.1947, BOD 2, 229, 36–47; WR, Jakob P., Oppeln (Opole) town, September 1956, BOD 1, 243, 225–6.

[7] WR, Annemarie K., Oppeln (Opole) town, 7.7.1947, BOD 2, 229, 36–47; WR, Alfons S., Oppeln (Opole) town, 23.1.1949, BOD 2, 229, 48–52; WR, Jakob P., Oppeln (Opole) town, September 1956, BOD 1, 243, 225–6.

[8] WR, Alfons S., Oppeln (Opole) town, 23.1.1949, BOD 2, 229, 48–52.

[9] WR, Adolf R., Hopfental (Chmielowice), undated, BOD 1, 243, 193–6.

[10] WR, Annemarie K., Oppeln (Opole) town, 7.7.1947, BOD 2, 229, 36–47.

[11] WR, Paul M., Oppeln (Opole) town, 10.8.1955, BOD 1, 243, 9–11; WR, P.J., a *Volkssturm* soldier who fought in Oppeln (Opole) town, 14.8.1951, BOD 10, 812, 103–4; WR, Josef M., Malapane (Ozimek), undated, BOD 1, 243, 251–4; WR, Adolf R., Hopfental (Chmielowice), undated, BOD 1, 243, 193–6.

[12] WR, Jakob P., Oppeln (Opole) town, September 1956, BOD 1, 243, 225–6; WR, Alfons S., Oppeln (Opole) town, 23.1.1949, BOD 2, 229, 48–52.

local area, including those in Oppeln town. This prevented further civilian flight from the east side of the district.[13] Soviet forces overran villages at the northern and eastern edges of Oppeln District in the afternoon of Sunday 21 January 1945.[14] They clashed with German forces, including barely prepared *Volkssturm* units, in the district's east and northeast. Heavy fighting ensued in the village of Malapane (Ozimek) and around the village of Plümkenau (Radomierowice).[15] On 22–3 January, the Soviets thrust their way across the Oder River. It was only at this point that the German forces managed to halt the Soviets' advance westwards.[16]

On the evening of 23 January, Soviet forces overran the east side of Oppeln town but encountered heavy resistance from German forces on the west bank of the Oder.[17] Around a day later they managed to cross the frozen Oder River south of Oppeln town and occupied the villages on the west bank of the river there. In the days following, however, they were thrust back eastwards over the river by German reinforcements arriving from the southwest. Nevertheless, the Soviets managed to hold on to the west bank villages of Groß Schimmendorf (Ziemnice Wielkie) and Glockenau (Źlinice).[18] From 23 January onwards, local German officials and the *Wehrmacht* commanders instructed all residents of the villages lying to the west of the Oder River to evacuate. Many disobeyed, choosing not to flee. Some fled only short distances and returned home once the fighting had ceased. Others were transported or travelled to more distant places in southwestern Upper Silesia, particularly to the town of Neisse (Nysa). Many of these people returned home before the war was over. Many residents of the villages on the west bank of the Oder River initially chose not

[13] WR, Georg S., Tauentzien (Okoły), undated, BOD 1, 243, 349–51; WR, Gustav R., Blumenthal (Krzywa Góra), undated, BOD 1, 243, 33–6; WR, P.J., a former *Volkssturm* soldier who fought in the defence of Oppeln (Opole) town, 14.8.1951, BOD 10, 812, 103–4.

[14] WR, Josef M., Malapane (Ozimek), undated, BOD 1, 243, 251–4; WR, Helmut R., Carlsruhe (Pokój), 19.8.1958, BOD 1, 243, 53–61; WR, Dorothea S., Burkardsdorf (Bierdzany), 22.11. 1954, BOD 1, 243, 49–51.

[15] WRs: BOD 1, 243, 217–20; BOD 1, 243, 251–4; BOD 1, 243, 49–51; BOD 1, 243, 25–7; BOD 1, 243, 271–4; BOD 1, 243, 281–3; BOD 1, 243, 85–8.

[16] WRs: BOD 2, 229, 7–8; BOD 1, 243, 75–6; BOD 1, 243, 37–9; BOD 1, 243, 277–80; BOD 1, 243, 335–7; BOD 1, 243, 255–6.

[17] WR, Alfons S., remained in Oppeln (Opole) town after the general evacuation of civilians, 23.1.1949, BOD 2, 229, 48–52; WR, A., remained in Oppeln (Opole) town after the general evacuation of civilians, 15.7.1955, BOD 2, 229, 1–2; WR, P.J. a former *Volkssturm* soldier who fought against Soviet forces in Oppeln (Opole) town, 14.8.1951, BOD 10, 812, 103–4; WR, anonymous, a former *Volkssturm* soldier who fought against Soviet forces in Oppeln (Opole) town, undated, BOD 1, 243, 1–2.

[18] WR, M.T., Eichtal (Dąbrówka Górna), 21.1.1957, BOD 1, 243, 93–6; WR, Franz G., Rogau (Rogów), 8.9.1955, BOD 1, 243, 299–301; WR, Josef M., the part of Krappitz (Krapkowice) on the west bank of the Oder River, undated, BOD 1, 243, 227–8; WR, Herr K., Klein Schimmendorf (Ziemnice Małe), undated, BOD 1, 243, 205–8.

to flee but later changed their minds after getting a brief taste of the Soviet occupation. The *Wehrmacht* also issued compulsory evacuation orders to at least a few villages in the southwestern part of Oppeln District at this time.[19]

The military fronts then stopped still in Oppeln District along the Oder River. For many weeks, the Soviets and Germans exchanged heavy fire across the river in and around Oppeln town. But there was no further movement of the fronts in either direction.[20] On 28 February 1945, the Soviets ordered the final few remaining civilians living in the half of Oppeln town lying on the east side of the Oder River to leave the town, threatening death to anyone who chose not to comply. These people all made for villages in the surrounding countryside in the northern and eastern parts of Oppeln District.[21] Meanwhile, in the southwestern part of the district, between February and mid March 1945, local people received further evacuation orders from the *Wehrmacht* and local German state officials, but it is probable that few now left Oppeln District.[22] In mid March 1945, the Soviets made the decisive breakthrough, thrusting the *Wehrmacht* back from the Oder River and into headlong retreat westwards. German forces abandoned Oppeln District altogether on 17 March. Soviet forces reached most villages on the southwestern edge of the district on 18 March.[23]

This marked the end of the flight of residents from Oppeln District. Most of the district's inhabitants who had chosen to flee from the Red Army between January and March 1945 had already done so by the end of January. Where they travelled after leaving the district varied a lot. But it is possible to describe the general trends. Whether they made the journey by foot, horse-cart or railway, many people did not travel very far – moving southwestwards often through Falkenberg (Niemodlin) District to the towns and villages of Neisse (Nysa) District and Neustadt (Prudnik) District. Others instead travelled short distances westwards, mainly to Grottkau (Grotków) District.[24] Yet quite a number went further afield,

[19] WRs: BOD 1, 243, 299–301; BOD 1, 243, 93–6; BOD 1, 243, 205–8; BOD 1, 243, 335–7; BOD 1, 243, 227–8; BOD 1, 243, 105–15; BOD 1, 243, 193–6; 10.5.1955, BOD 1, 243, 167–9.

[20] WR, Karl B., Schönkirch (Chrzasczyce), 19.8.1955, BOD 1, 243, 335–7. WRs in file BOD 2, 299 and file BOD 1, 243.

[21] WR, A., Oppeln (Opole) town, 15.7.1955, BOD 2, 229, 1–2; WR, Frau K., Oderwinkel (Kąty Opolskie), 30.5.1959, BOD 1, 243, 277–80.

[22] WR, Karl B., Schönkirch (Chrzasczyce), 19.8.1955, BOD 1, 243, 335–7; WR, Hermann W., Rothhaus (Osiny), undated, BOD 1, 243, 303–6; WR, Magda E., Erlental (Żerkowice), 24.5.1956, BOD 1, 243, 105–15; WR, E.D., Walldorf (Wawelno), undated, BOD 1, 243, 379–80.

[23] WRs: BOD 1, 243, 381–2; BOD 1, 243, 227–8; BOD 1, 243, 299–301; BOD 1, 243, 93–6; BOD 1, 243, 303–6; BOD 1, 243, 289–93; BOD 1, 243, 379–80.

[24] WRs: BOD 1, 243, 309–19; BOD 1, 243, 379–80; BOD 1, 243, 335–7; BOD 1, 243, 299–301; BOD 1, 243, 53–61; BOD 1, 243, 227–8; BOD 1, 243, 205–8; BOD 1, 243, 9–11; BOD 1, 243, 25–7; BOD 1, 243, 75–6; BOD 1, 243, 105–15.

to the districts of Strehlen (Strzelin), Frankenstein (Ząbkowice Śląskie) and Glatz (Kłodzko) in southeastern Lower Silesia or to various districts in southwestern Lower Silesia. People evacuated from Oppeln District in *Wehrmacht* lorries were likewise generally taken to western Upper Silesia and eastern and southern Lower Silesia. Occasionally, those making their way by foot also received lifts from the retreating German military. An important factor determining where people ended up, particularly if they were not travelling in large groups, was where they happened to have relatives or friends living.[25]

Many people went still further afield, making their way to pre-1938 Czechoslovakia. One local witness described a 'great refugee stream' flowing from Upper Silesia to Czechoslovakia at this time.[26] They mainly travelled first to the town of Neisse (Nysa) – sometimes remaining there until Soviet forces advanced on the town in mid March 1945 – before moving southwards to pre-1938 Czechoslovakia. Some travelled through Lower Silesia to Czechoslovakia, often crossing the border near Glatz (Kłodzko). A number of residents of Oppeln District were transported directly to pre-1938 Czechoslovakia from Oppeln District on special 'evacuation trains' organized by the German authorities. Once in Czechoslovakia, people tended to make their way to the west of the country, particularly to the regions around Prague and Pilsen (Plzeň). Sometimes this was prompted by the arrival of Soviet forces from Slovakia at the very end of the war.[27]

Many residents of Oppeln District also fled as far as central, western and southern Germany. A large number took direct passenger trains or special 'evacuation trains' to these places before the local rail network was cut off from the rest of Germany in mid January 1945.[28] Once both normal trains and special evacuation trains had ceased departing from Oppeln railway station, some residents made their way to the parts of Silesia still connected to the rail network and travelled from there to southern, central and western Germany. As with journeys confined to Silesia, people often chose to seek refuge in these further-away destinations because they had relatives or

[25] WRs: BOD 1, 243, 349–51; BOD 1, 243, 33–6; BOD 1, 243, 255–6; BOD 1, 243, 53–61; BOD 1, 243, 299–301; BOD 1, 243, 41–4; BOD 1, 243, 281–3; BOD 1, 243, 205–8; BOD 1, 243, 277–80; BOD 1, 243, 193–6; BOD 1, 243, 251–4; BOD 1, 243, 105–15.

[26] WR, M.H., Carlsruhe (Pokój), 23.6.1952, BOD 2, 229, 9–10.

[27] WRs: BOD 2, 229, 36–47; BOD 2, 229, 3–4; BOD 2, 229, 19–29; BOD 1, 243, 299–301; BOD 1, 243, 349–51; BOD 1, 243, 277–80; BOD 1, 243, 225–6; BOD 1, 243, 303–6; BOD 2, 229, 9–10; BOD 2, 229, 30–31; BOD 2, 229, 19–29.

[28] WR, Friedrich K., Sacken (Lubienia), 24.7.1955, BOD 1, 243, 309–19; WR, Alfons S., Oppeln (Opole) town, 23.1.1949, BOD 2, 229, 48–52; WR, Franz G., Rogau (Rogów), 8.9.1955, BOD 1, 243, 299–301; WR, Maria K., Malsdorf (Malina), undated, BOD 1, 243, 255–6.

friends living there.[29] These journeys sometimes involved dramatic escapes. Josef M. and his wife, who fled Oppeln District at this time, for example, boarded a train in Lower Silesia which halted in Dresden just before the great Allied bombardment of the city on 13–14 February 1945. Only by chance did they decide not to get off the train in Dresden. Very large numbers of refugees from Silesia died in Dresden that night, along with tens of thousands of residents of the city.[30]

But what of the great many residents of Oppeln District who chose not to flee their homes? Why did they decide not to flee? Clearly, not wanting to leave their homes and farms unoccupied and unprotected was an important motivation. One resident of the village of Proskau (Prószków), for example, claimed it was primarily the village's landowners and houseowners who chose not to flee.[31] Another reason for not fleeing was the pragmatic calculation, made by many, that they were likely to suffer more by fleeing than if they placed themselves at the mercy of the Soviets. According to one resident of the village of Schönkirch (Chrzasczyce), an evacuation order issued by a German battalion commander at the end of January 1945 had little effect because the villagers had witnessed with their own eyes the misery endured by the refugees trekking through the village in the extreme cold of winter in previous days. Elderly people, in particular, realized that fleeing was not going to do them any good.[32]

Another important reason that many locals chose not to flee was connected to the particular ethno-linguistic identity of the local population. We will examine this matter in detail in Chapter 6, but it suffices to say, for now, that a large proportion of the local population spoke a regional dialect of Polish as well as German. As one resident of the village of Erlental (Żerkowice) in Oppeln District, describing her journey by foot back to Erlental after taking refuge in Grottkau (Grotków) before the war's end, wrote, 'In the villages of Walldorf [Wawelno], Reisern [Chróścina], Moosdorf [Mechnice] residents were suddenly speaking Polish. This made me feel very peculiar because I had never heard a single word of Polish spoken

[29] WR, Josef M., Malapane (Ozimek), undated, BOD 1, 243, 251–4; WR, Julius D., Koben (Chobie), 24.5.1959, BOD 1, 243, 217–20; WR, Adolf R., Hopfental (Chmielowice), undated, BOD 1, 243, 193–6.

[30] WR, Josef M., Malapane (Ozimek), undated, BOD 1, 243, 251–4.

[31] WR, Julius T., Proskau (Prószków), 14.4.1956, BOD 1, 243, 289–93; WR, Josef M., Malapane (Ozimek), undated, BOD 1, 243, 251–4; WR, Franz G., Bergdorf (Daniec), undated, BOD 1, 243, 25–7.

[32] WR, Karl B., Schönkirch (Chrzasczyce), 19.8.1955, BOD 1, 243, 335–7; WR, Maria K., Malsdorf (Malina), undated, BOD 1, 243, 255–6; WR, Friedrich K., Sacken (Lubienia), 24.7.1955, BOD 1, 243, 309–19; WR, Josef M., Krappitz (Krapkowice), undated, BOD 1, 243, 227–8.

in these villages before then.'[33] Less sceptically, a resident of Blumenthal (Krzywa Góra) recalled that, although most residents of his own village chose to flee in January 1945, inhabitants of nearby Salzbrunn (Ładza) 'had not fled, since their mother tongue is Polish'.[34] Likewise, an inhabitant of Bergdorf (Daniec) stated that 'almost all inhabitants remained in the village because they could speak Polish and could not separate themselves from their properties'.[35] Others agreed that being able to speak Polish had been an important factor causing many people not to flee.[36] Similarly, one witness pointed out that it was only the minority Roman Catholic population of his predominantly Protestant village who did not flee.[37] Another put the fact of not fleeing down to inhabitants being 'honest Upper Silesians' (presumably as opposed to Germans).[38] Correspondingly, several witnesses asserted that having an overly German identity caused many locals to flee. As one inhabitant of Malapane (Ozimek) put it, 'Nearly all German-inclined inhabitants and officials left, since even among the [bilingual] German-Polish speaking inhabitants who stayed behind, there were traitors, just as during the Polish Uprising of 1921.'[39]

This ethno-linguistic motive for not fleeing was based on the assumption that the Soviets would only take revenge for the brutal Nazi German occupation of the Soviet Union on unambiguously German people – sparing from retaliatory attacks anyone who could speak the local dialect of Polish. This assumption soon proved flawed. A former resident of the village of Erlental (Żerkowice) in Oppeln District recalled being stopped by a Soviet military patrol in March 1945 and being asked whether she was German or Polish. After answering 'German', she was told by the Soviet commander: 'Germans good, Poles pigs.'[40] The Soviets did not worry about subtle differences of linguistic and cultural identity when committing revenge acts against German citizens. People who spoke the regional Polish dialect suffered the same as those who did not. Every civilian who remained in Oppeln District as the Soviets arrived either witnessed or experienced this great wave of indiscriminate Soviet violence and robbery. Many local

33 WR, Magda E., Erlental (Żerkowice), 24.5.1956, BOD 1, 243, 105–15.

34 WR, Gustav R., Blumenthal (Krzywa Góra), undated, BOD 1, 243, 33–6.

35 WR, Franz G., Bergdorf (Daniec), undated, BOD 1, 243, 25–7.

36 WR, Josef M., Malapane (Ozimek), undated, BOD 1, 243, 251–4.

37 WR, anonymous, Finkenstein (Brzezie), 31.5.1952, BOD 2, 229, 56.

38 WR, Emil G., Brünne (Brynica), 1958, BOD 1, 243, 41–4.

39 WR, Josef M., Malapane (Ozimek), undated, BOD 1, 243, 251–4; WR, Leo H., Eichhammer (Dębska Kuźnia), 15.9.1954, BOD 1, 243, 91–2; WR, Adolf R., Hopfental (Chmielowice), undated, BOD 1, 243, 193–6; Stanisław Ossowski, 'Zagadnienia więzi regionalnej i więzi narodowej na Śląsku Opolskim', in Stanisław Ossowski, *Dzieła*, Vol. 3 (Warsaw, 1967, 6 vols., Warsaw, 1966–70), p. 296.

40 WR, Magda E., Erlental (Żerkowice), 24.5.1956, BOD 1, 243, 105–15.

witnesses claimed that the Soviets perpetrated collective and individual shootings against civilians soon after their invasion. There were many cases of brutal violence. In one extreme incident in the village of Kupp (Kup) in Oppeln District, 'the Russians' reportedly cut off the genitals of the local head of the state forestry and suffocated him by forcing them into his mouth. They then slit his wife's stomach and shot his ten-year-old son in the head. According to local witnesses, the Soviets also raped countless local women, often with extreme brutality. They systematically burnt down buildings in many of the Oppeln District's villages, particularly those in the northern and eastern parts of the district.[41] This intense wave of Soviet 'excesses' eventually died down, but it did not recede completely until a number of months after the war.[42]

A sizeable number of men from Oppeln District, probably numbering several thousand, were also seized by the Red Army in February and March 1945, either within the district's boundaries or in other parts of western Upper Silesia. They were subsequently transported deep inside the Soviet Union for forced labour. Some local witnesses claimed that most of the men of working age who remained in their villages were taken to the Soviet Union at this time. Others indicated that only a few were deported from their villages.[43] Several witnesses claimed that in their villages only the Nazi Party members were taken.[44] Some residents of Oppeln District provided first-hand accounts of deportation to the Soviet Union. Emil G. was 'taken prisoner' by the Soviets in his home village of Brünne (Brynica) on 19 February 1945. He was transported with many other local men, who had all fought with the *Volkssturm*, to Magnitogorsk in Siberia.[45] G. from the village of Falkendorf (Fałkowice) was seized by the Soviets in Kreuzburg (Kluczbork) District and taken with other men to a 'lunatic asylum' in the town of Kreuzburg, where they were kept until several thousand local men had been gathered. They were all subsequently transported

41 WR, Friedrich K., Sacken (Lubienia), 24.7.1955, BOD 1, 243, 309–19. WRs in file BOD 1, 243 and file BOD 2, 229. Ossowski, 'Zagadnienia', p. 288.

42 SiRep ODA, 20.6.1945, APK 185/4, sygn. 25, 12–14; SiRep ODA, 9.6.1945, APK 185/4, 43–47; SiRep O Chief on the period 20.8.1945–20.9.1945, APO 178, sygn. 41, 1–4; SiRep by O Chief on the period 20.9.1945–20.10.1945, APO 178, sygn. 41, 5–8; SiRep O Chief on the period 20.11.1945–20.12.1945, APO 178, sygn. 41, 10–12.

43 WRs: BOD 2, 229, 7–8; BOD 1, 243, 85–8; BOD 1, 243, 13–16; BOD 1, 243, 287–8; BOD 1, 243, 335–7; BOD 1, 243, 67–72; BOD 1, 243, 379–80; BOD 1, 243, 277–80; BOD 1, 243, 289–93; BOD 2, 229, 9–10; BOD 2, 229, 56; BOD 2, 229, 57; BOD 1, 243, 49–51; BOD 1, 243, 251–4; Eser, 'Oberschlesien', p. 376.

44 WR, Helmut R., Carlsruhe (Pokój), 10.8.1958, BOD 1, 243, 53–61; WR, Franz G., undated, BOD 1, 243, 25–7; WR, Georg K., Eichtal (Dąbrówka Górna), 24.10.1957, BOD 1, 243, 174–81; WR, Günther M., Bolko (Nowa Wieś Królewska), undated, BOD 1, 243, 37–9.

45 WR, Emil G., Brünne (Brynica), 1958, BOD 1, 243, 41–4.

to Dnepropetrovsk in Ukraine.[46] Friedrich K., 56 years old at the time, was seized by the Soviets in the town of Neustadt (Prudnik) in late March 1945 and marched eastwards across Upper Silesia with many others. They were loaded onto a cargo train in the town of Beuthen (Bytom) and transported to the Soviet Union. He recalled, 'The journey started on 18 April and we landed in a camp for Silesians near the city of [Kursk in Ukraine]... on 10 May [1945]. Many died along the way. There were 2400 people in the train, including women and girls. We were exposed to hunger, thirst and lice. After three months of life in the camp, only 930 of the original 2400 people were still alive.'[47] It is likely that a large proportion of the residents of Oppeln District who were transported to the Soviet Union died during the journeys or in camps once they had arrived. The conditions throughout this ordeal were extremely harsh and hazardous.[48]

Although some Soviet forces had been held up along part of the Oder River until mid March 1945, others had succeeded in conquering most of Upper and Lower Silesia by mid February. Soviet forces had also encircled Silesia's largest city, Breslau (Wrocław), which had been declared a 'fortress' by the German high command. German forces continued fighting in Breslau until the very end of the war. By the end of February 1945, the Soviets had driven German forces into the Sudeten mountain range, running along Lower Silesia's southern border. They then halted, not pursuing the Germans southwards into these mountains until right at the end of the war. It was in the western stretch of the Sudeten foothills and mountains that the town of Hirschberg (Jelenia Góra) was located. And it was there that Karl Hanke, the regional Nazi leader (*Gauleiter*) and regional governor, temporarily relocated Lower Silesia's regional administration from Breslau in the final months of the war.[49]

Refugees fleeing from the lowlands of Upper Silesia and Lower Silesia began flooding into Hirschberg District from January 1945 onwards. Some of them moved immediately onwards over the mountains into the borderlands of the western half of pre-1938 Czechoslovakia (referred to as 'the Sudetenland' by the ethnic Germans living there).[50] Those who

46 WR, Herr G., Falkendorf (Fałkowice), 8.4.1959, BOD 1, 243, 121–2.

47 WR, Friedrich K., Sacken (Lubienia), 24.7.1955, BOD 1, 243, 309–19.

48 Madajczyk, *Przyłączenie*, p. 202. WRs: BOD 1, 243, 13–16; BOD 1, 243, 287–8; BOD 1, 243, 289–93; BOD 1, 243, 251–4; BOD 2, 229, 56; BOD 2, 229, 57; BOD 1, 243, 91–2; BOD 2, 229, 9–10.

49 Siebel-Achenbach, *Lower Silesia*, pp. 57–67; Hofmann, *Nachkriegszeit*, pp. 16–19; Borodziej, 'Einleitung', pp. 57, 62; Broszat, 'Einleitende Darstellung', pp. 54E–59E.

50 WRs: BOD 2, 188, 122–37; BOD 2, 188, 169–74; BOD 1, 207, 259; BOD 1, 207, 17–18; BOD 1, 207, 237–8; BOD 1, 207, 81–2; BOD 1, 207, 127–30; BOD 1, 207, 21–4; BOD 1, 207, 97–9; BOD 1, 207, 171–5; BOD 1, 207, 43–4.

stayed in Hirschberg District for a while added to the large number of bomb evacuees who had arrived there earlier on in the war from the parts of Germany experiencing heavy Allied air bombardment.[51] Around late February 1945, Nazi officials in Hirschberg District issued evacuation orders to local women, children and elderly people as well as to all refugees who had previously fled there from further east.[52] Most refugees obeyed these orders, but most locals chose not to.[53] The authorities supplied special trains to evacuate the refugees and the local women, children and old and sick people to 'the Sudetenland'. Many were taken just a few kilometres inside pre-1938 Czechoslovakia, stopping in the nearby mountain village of Polaun (Polubný). But some were transported all the way to Bavaria in southern Germany.[54] Many of the local women and children evacuated to pre-1938 Czechoslovakia at this time returned before the war's end.[55]

It was in the final days of the war that some of Hirschberg District's residents finally came face to face with Germany's genocide against European Jews. The main part of Groß-Rosen Concentration Camp was located not far from Hirschberg District, between the towns of Jauer (Jawor) and Striegau (Strzegom). A subcamp of Groß-Rosen was actually located right next to Hirschberg town, in the village of Bad Warmbrunn (Cieplice Śląskie) (see Map 5). Tens of thousands of mainly Hungarian and Polish Jews were brought to the Groß-Rosen camp network in the course of the war. Many of the Jews evacuated from Auschwitz-Birkenau shortly before the Red Army arrived there in January 1945 were also transferred to the Groß-Rosen camp network by the German authorities. When the Red Army finally started to move into southern Lower Silesia in early May 1945, 20,000 inmates from the camp network were transported away in coal wagons or driven southwestwards on foot marches.[56] The German inhabitants of Hirschberg

[51] WR, Ursula R., Schreiberhau (Szklarska Poręba), 10.3.1954, BOD 2, 188, 122–37; WR, Johannes S., Giersdorf (Podgórzyn), 6.4.1951, BOD 2, 188, 169–74.

[52] WRs: BOD 2, 188, 169–74; BOD 1, 207, 57–8; BOD 1, 207, 7–9; BOD 1, 207, 81–2; BOD 1, 207, 259; BOD 2, 188, 122–37; BOD 1, 207, 179–82; BOD 2, 188, 122–37.

[53] WR, Johannes S., Giersdorf (Podgórzyn) 6.4.1951, BOD 2, 188, 169–74; WR, Alfred E., Kupferberg (Miedzianka), undated, BOD 1, 207, 127–30.

[54] WRs: BOD 1, 207, 179–82; BOD 1, 207, 127–30); BOD 2, 188, 169–74; BOD 1, 207, 57–8; BOD 1, 207, 17–18; BOD 1, 207, 115–21; BOD 1, 207, 81–2; BOD 1, 207, 259; BOD 1, 207, 29–32; BOD 1, 207, 7–9; BOD 2, 188, 318–32; BOD 1, 207, 171–5; BOD 1, 207, 43–4.

[55] WR, Alfred E., Kupferberg (Miedzianka), undated. BOD 1, 207, 127–30; WR, Richard K., Eichberg (Dąbrowica), undated, BOD 1, 207, 57–8; WR, Oskar S., Berbisdorf (Dziwiszów), undated, BOD 1, 207, 29–32; WR, Adolph G., Bärndorf (Gruszków), 21.9.1952, BOD 2, 188, 7–9).

[56] Borodziej, 'Einleitung', pp. 38–41; Hofmann, *Nachkriegszeit*, pp. 340–1; Łuczak, *Stosunki*, pp. 358–63; Benz, 'Der Generalplan Ost', pp. 39–41. 'Verzeichnis der Konzentrationslager und ihrer Außenkommandos gemäß § 42 Abs. 2 BEG', http://www.gesetze-im-internet.de/begdv_6/anlage_6.html [last accessed 23.3.2013]. WR, Willi O., Bad Warmbrunn (Cieplice Śląskie), 2.10.1953, BOD 1, 207, 255–6.

Map 5 Hirschberg/Jelenia Góra District

District witnessed this mass evacuation. A resident of Schreiberhau (Szklarska Poręba), for example, recalled seeing a large group of concentration camp inmates being marched towards 'the Sudetenland' by SS guards at this time. Fifteen inmates had died of exhaustion just before reaching Schreiberhau. The guards simply left them on the road where they had fallen.[57] A resident of Giersdorf (Podgórzyn) described a similar scene, witnessed shortly before Germany's capitulation:

> One of the final, terrible images of those days was a column of Jewish concentration camp prisoners, which was marched under strict guard . . . westwards: A silent column of misery. Helpless, elderly and sick people as well as small children sat on a few wagons, each being pulled with ropes by a dozen prisoners. The rest followed on foot, dragging their bundles of possessions, most of them barefoot, with looks of exhausted worry.[58]

Roads in Hirschberg District and in the rest of southern Lower Silesia became crammed with German refugees in the final days of the war. Evacuation orders, now applying to all local citizens, were issued by officials in many of the district's villages, but in most villages, only a minority of the residents obeyed.[59] In some of the district's villages locals chose to flee into nearby forests. The Soviets would later wrongly take these people to be anti-Soviet partisans.[60] Only in a small number of villages did a large proportion of the local population evacuate. Likewise, the population of Hirschberg town poured out southwards just before the Red Army's arrival. Witnessing this scene from the nearby village of Bad Warmbrunn (Cieplice Śląskie), one local described this stream of refugees as 'a messy tangle of automobiles, cyclists, pedestrians, horse-carts and mothers with children'.[61]

Most local people who fled at this time, however, did not even manage to cross Hirschberg District's boundaries. They had returned to their homes within days. This was mainly because the roads were so jammed with people and vehicles that it became nearly impossible to escape the area. The road from Hirschberg town through Schreiberhau (Szklarska Poręba)

[57] WR, O., Schreiberhau (Szklarska Poręba), 17.9.1953, BOD 1, 207, 179–82.
[58] WR, Johannes S., Giersdorf (Podgórzyn), 6.4.1951, BOD 2, 188, 169–74.
[59] WRs: BOD 1, 207, 155; BOD 1, 207, 13–14; BOD 1, 207, 239–42; BOD 1, 207, 81–2; BOD 1, 207, 237–8; BOD 1, 207, 17–18; BOD 1, 207, 29–32; BOD 1, 207, 57–8; BOD 1, 207, 115–21; BOD 1, 207, 21–4; BOD 1, 207, 43–4; BOD 1, 207, 171–5; BOD 1, 207, 89–92; BOD 1, 207, 35.
[60] WR, A.Z., Reibnitz (Rybnica), 2.10.1953, BOD 1, 207, 155; WR, Oskar S., Berbisdorf (Dziwiszów), undated, BOD 1, 207, 29–32.
[61] WR, Paul W., Bad Warmbrunn (Cieplice Śląskie), undated, BOD 2, 188, 318–32. WRs in file BOD 1, 207 and file BOD 2, 188.

and over the mountains to the city of Reichenberg (Liberec), in the pre-1938 western Czechoslovak borderlands, was one of the main escape routes for the whole of Silesia. Around the large village of Schreiberhau the road became so clogged that many local people had no choice but to turn back home.[62] Some turned around, having already got beyond Schreiberhau, because they were 'run down' by the Soviet forces.[63] Only a minority of local people therefore actually made it into pre-1938 Czechoslovakia.[64] Among them was a family from the village of Lomnitz (Łomnica). They set off for Prague in a motor vehicle shortly before the Soviet invasion and managed to reach the Czech capital by 9 May 1945.[65] Many local Nazi Party officials probably also succeeded in forcing their way through the mass of refugees into pre-1938 Czechoslovakia in those final moments of the war, spurred on by the fear of reprisals for German atrocities from the Red Army.[66] The fact that only very few people left Hirschberg District in the last phase of the war reflected what happened in southern Lower Silesia as a whole. But it contrasted with northern Lower Silesia, where a huge number of civilians chose to flee and many places were virtually depopulated by the end of the war.[67]

Soviet forces crossed Hirschberg District's northern frontier in the late afternoon or early evening of 8 May 1945. This was the day of Germany's unconditional capitulation. Red Army units crossed the Bober-Katzbach (Kaczawskie) mountains and invaded Hirschberg District from the north-east. The numerous *Wehrmacht* and *Waffen-SS* units, which had been quartered in many of the district's villages since early spring 1945, had already retreated southwards in the days and hours before the Soviet invasion. In an effort to obstruct the Soviet advance, they blew up the bridges over the river Bober (Bóbr) as they made their way southwest-wards into pre-1938 Czechoslovakia. They destroyed the great viaduct on the Hirschberg–Görlitz railway at around 6 pm on 8 May 1945. Residents of Bad Warmbrunn (Cieplice Śląskie) witnessed the 'hopeless flight' of the

62 WR, Emil L., Boberröhrsdorf (Siedlęcin), 19.2.1954, BOD 1, 207, 35; WR, A.H., Grunau (Jeżów Sudecki), undated, BOD 1, 207, 81–2; WR, Paul W., Bad Warmbrunn (Cieplice Śląskie), undated, BOD 2, 188, 318–32; WR, O., Schreiberhau (Szklarska Poręba), 17.9.1953, BOD 1, 207, 179–82.

63 WR, Elisabeth W., Kammerswaldau (Komarno), 4.7.1954, BOD 1, 207, 107–10; WR, Richard K., Eichberg (Dąbrowica), undated, BOD 1, 207, 57–8.

64 WR, Gerhard F., Hirschberg (Jelenia Góra) town, 24.3.1950, BOD 1, 207, 7–9; WR, Reinhold K., Altkemnitz (Stara Kamienica), 4.4.1953, BOD 1, 207, 13–14; WR, Elisabeth W., Kammerswaldau (Komarno), 4.7.1954, BOD 1, 207, 107–10.

65 WR, Ludwig F., Lomnitz (Łomnica), 31.1.1951, BOD 2, 188, 30–1.

66 WR, O., Schreiberhau (Szklarska Poręba), 17.9.1953, BOD 1, 207, 179–82.

67 Kraft, 'Wrocławskie', p. 362.

last of these German troops, who had been covering the German retreat. They heard explosions from near and far as the bridges exploded.[68]

Most German forces were already out of the district by the time the Soviets arrived. There was no fighting as the Soviets occupied villages in the north of Hirschberg District on the evening of 8 May. The Soviets sent a barrage of missiles southwards into the Riesengebirge (Karkonosze) Mountains aimed at the retreating German units. Approaching Hirschberg town from the northeast, they fired missiles at the town. A unit of Latvian SS were waiting for them in Straupitz (Strupice) at the northeastern edge of Hirschberg town ready to resist. As Soviet tanks and infantry, followed by heavy artillery, reached Straupitz midway through the evening on 8 May, intense local fighting ensued. This was the only fighting Hirschberg District experienced in the entire Second World War. It was over by midnight. That night Soviet forces occupied Hirschberg town.

Soviet units then advanced further southwards, reaching Bad Warmbrunn (Cieplice Śląskie) on the morning of 9 May 1945 and occupying villages further to the south in the course of the day. Meanwhile, more Red Army units entered Hirschberg District from the east, occupying villages in the eastern area of the district. On 9 May, Soviet forces also occupied the western part of the district, arriving from a northwesterly direction. Thus Soviet forces had conquered nearly the entire district by the end of 9 May. They reached the village of Krummhübel (Karpacz), high up in the mountains at the district's southern frontier – the frontier with pre-1938 Czechoslovakia – on 10 May 1945. This marked the end of the flight of civilians from Hirschberg District.[69]

As in Oppeln District and the rest of Germany's prewar eastern provinces, a huge wave of robbery and violence accompanied the Soviet invasion of Hirschberg District. In fact the robbery and looting by Red Army troops was probably more intense there than in Oppeln District, although the violence seems to have been a good deal less severe. Local witnesses claimed that a lot of local people were killed by Soviet troops shortly after their arrival, but there was none of the collective shooting of civilians witnessed by some in Oppeln District. As in Oppeln District, countless women were

[68] WR, Paul W., Bad Warmbrunn (Cieplice Śląskie), undated, BOD 2, 188, 318–32.

[69] WRs: BOD 2, 188, 169–74; BOD 1, 207, 81–2; BOD 1, 207, 35; BOD 1, 207, 29–32; BOD 1, 207, 235–6; BOD 2, 188, 14–17; BOD 1, 207, 7–9; BOD 2, 188, 24–9; BOD 2, 188, 318–32; BOD 1, 207, 243–9; BOD 1, 207, 237–8; BOD 2, 188, 169–74; BOD 1, 207, 151–2; BOD 2, 188, 122–37; BOD 2, 188, 175–97; BOD 1, 207, 179–82; BOD 1, 207, 183–95; BOD 1, 207, 97–9; BOD 2, 188, 269–76; BOD 1, 207, 127–30; BOD 1, 207, 239–42; BOD 1, 205, 159–62; BOD 1, 207, 43–4; BOD 1, 207, 57–8; BOD 1, 207, 21–4; BOD 1, 207, 17–18; BOD 2, 188, 287–91; BOD 1, 207, 155; BOD 1, 207, 133–8; BOD 1, 207, 13–14; BOD 1, 207, 115–21.

also raped by Soviet soldiers, often very brutally.[70] In one extreme case, a woman is said to have broken her back while jumping out of a window in an attempt to escape her Soviet attacker. Despite her grave injuries the Soviet soldier carried her back inside her house and raped her.[71] As in Oppeln District, Soviet 'excesses' soon calmed considerably, but the robbery and violence took months to disappear completely.[72]

PEACE

Based on a secret border agreement signed by the Polish Committee of National Liberation with the Soviets on the night of 26–7 July 1944, the Red Army began to hand over control of conquered prewar eastern German territory to Polish civilian officials several months before the war was over. Most parts of Germany's prewar eastern provinces remained under the direct control of Red Army commanders until the end of the war, but certain eastern areas, including districts of western Upper Silesia, were already placed in Polish civilian hands before the war was over. Yet giving administrative control to civilian officials appointed by Poland's Communist-controlled government did not signify the withdrawal of Soviet forces. Indeed, hundreds of thousands of Soviet troops remained stationed in this territory for a number of months after the war. Both before the end of the war and afterwards, Red Army commanders and troops based in Germany's prewar eastern provinces felt entitled to intervene in any issue they came across. Power struggles between Polish civilian officials and Soviet military commanders therefore became common in localities throughout these provinces at the end of the war. They persisted for several months after the war and manifested themselves at times even in armed clashes.[73]

The erection of Polish state administration in the prewar eastern German territories, both before and after Germany's capitulation, started with the sending of 'operational groups' (*grupy operacyjne*) of Polish civilian officials from prewar Poland into the prewar eastern German territories to begin setting up local Polish authorities there. In mid March 1945,

[70] WRs in file BOD 2, 188 and file BOD 1, 207.

[71] WR, Christian-Friedrich, Jannowitz (Janowice Wielkie), May 1946, BOD 2, 188, 269–76.

[72] WRs in file BOD 2, 188 and file BOD 1, 207. Rep by JG Chief, 6.[8].1945, APJG 123/II, sygn. 18, 3–26; Rep by JG Chief, 3.10.1945, APJG 123/II, sygn. 18, 127–32; Rep by JG Chief, 6.11.1945, APJG 123/II, sygn. 18, 109–15; Rep by JG Chief, 5.12.1945, APJG 123/II, sygn. 18, 185–200; Rep by JG Chief, 5. 1.1946, APJG 123/II, sygn. 18, 206–14.

[73] Borodziej, 'Einleitung', pp. 60–2; Kraft, 'Wrocławskie', pp. 370–3; Hofmann, *Nachkriegszeit*, pp. 70–6.

Poland's Soviet-sponsored government announced that these territories were to be divided into four 'administrative regions' (*okręgi administracyjne*): East Prussia – Masuria; Szczecin – West Pomerania; Lower Silesia; and Opole Silesia. The new Region of Opole Silesia (*Okręg Śląsk Opolski*), which encompassed the part of Upper Silesia which remained in Germany in 1922 (i.e., western Upper Silesia; see Chapter 6), was placed under the control of the newly appointed Regional Governor (*Wojewoda*) of neighbouring eastern Upper Silesia. Unlike western Upper Silesia, eastern Upper Silesia had been part of Poland between 1922 and 1939. The official name of eastern Upper Silesia at that time had been Silesia Voivodship (*Województwo Śląskie*). Already, from March 1945 onwards, eastern and western Upper Silesia were treated, in most respects, as a single administrative region, but this was not formalized until May 1946, when western Upper Silesia was officially incorporated into Silesia Voivodship as part of the Polish government's decision to extend the administrative structure of prewar Poland to all parts of Poland's new western and northern territories. From this point onwards, the whole of Upper Silesia (i.e., eastern and western Upper Silesia) was officially referred to as Silesia Voivodship (see Map 6).[74]

The Regional Governor of Silesia Voivodship, appointed in March 1945, was General Aleksander Zawadzki. He was ill-qualified for this role, having no experience of working in state administration. What qualified him was the fact that he was a member of the Polish Workers' Party's Politburo, a leading activist for the Communist Party of Poland in the interwar period and a military general in the Soviet-controlled Polish Army in the final phase of the Second World War.[75]

An organizational headquarters for the 'operational groups' due to be sent into western Upper Silesia was established in Silesia Voivodship's capital city, Katowice, in February 1945. The 'operational groups' – consisting of both administrative officials and Citizens' Militia personnel (*Milicja Obywatelska*, i.e., postwar Poland's equivalent of the ordinary police) – were sent out from Katowice into the districts of western Upper Silesia from 20 March 1945 onwards. One of them arrived in Oppeln District in late March 1945. It immediately set about installing new village and commune

[74] Because this study covers the period before and after the creation of the Silesia Voivodship in May 1946, when referring to *both* eastern and western Upper Silesia, I will use the term 'Upper Silesia' throughout the book.

[75] Eser, 'Oberschlesien', p. 381; Hofmann, *Nachkriegszeit*, pp. 65–6; Borodziej, 'Einleitung', p. 62; Świder, *Entgermanisierung*, pp. 54–5; Magierska, *Ziemie*, pp. 84–6, 88–9; Order of the Council of Ministers, 29 May 1946, Dziennik Ustaw Nr. 28, Poz. 177, http://isap.sejm.gov.pl/DetailsServlet?id=WDU19460280177 [last accessed 23.3.2013].

Map 6 Poland's new territories, 1946

mayors (*sołtysi* and *wójtowie*) in localities throughout the district.[76] These new mayors were selected from among the local Polish-dialect-speaking population, but of course not at random. They were mainly persons able to show to the arriving central Polish officials that they had been pro-Polish sympathizers and activists before 1939. Opole District's first postwar Chief

[76] For an explanation of the structure and character of state administration below the level of the voivodships, please see the 'Note on local state administration in Poland's new territories after 1945' on p. 86.

Official (*Starosta*), Dr Piechaczek, was himself a native of western Upper Silesia, who had engaged in pro-Polish activities in the region before 1939. Yet the 'operational group' also gave many local state administrative posts to individuals from central Poland and almost exclusively used young men from central Poland to staff the local Citizens' Militia. As in the rest of western Upper Silesia, the proportion of official posts filled by outsiders from central Poland would be steadily increased over the next year, as the Communist-led authorities gradually lost faith in the 'loyalty' of the local Polish-dialect-speaking population.[77]

It took somewhat longer to establish Polish state administration in Lower Silesia, because a large area of this region was not actually conquered by the Soviets until Germany's capitulation on 8 May 1945. In mid April 1945, officials arrived as an 'operational group' in the Lower Silesian town of Trebnitz/Trzebnica to begin setting up a regional administration for the new Region of Lower Silesia (*Okręg Dolny Śląsk*). Stanisław Piaskowski was appointed the region's first governor. He was a member of the Polish Socialist Party who in 1936 had been temporarily ousted from the party for advocating collaboration with the Communists. Lower Silesia's fledgling Regional Administration was moved to Liegnitz/Legnica in June 1945 and then, in November, relocated once more to the city of Wrocław. This city remained the capital of Lower Silesia from that point onwards. In May 1946, the Region of Lower Silesia was officially renamed Wrocław Voivodship (*Województwo Wrocławskie*) and Piaskowski was given the official title of *Wojewoda* (Regional Governor).[78]

Having a member of the Polish Socialist Party at the head of regional state administration in Lower Silesia appeared in 1945 to place the Socialists in a powerful position in this region. But Piaskowski was no ordinary Socialist, but rather one with pro-Communist sympathies, as he had demonstrated before the war. Moreover, what power the Polish Socialists derived from having a leading member as Regional Governor of this large region was

[77] WRs: BOD 2, 229, 1–2; BOD 1, 243, 379–80; BOD 1, 243, 105–15; BOD 1, 243, 335–7; BOD 1, 243, 277–80; BOD 1, 243, 33–6; BOD 1, 243, 25–7; BOD 1, 243, 13–16; BOD 1, 243, 271–4; BOD 1, 243, 67–72; BOD 1, 243, 289–93; BOD 1, 243, 299–301; BOD 1, 243, 121–2. Hofmann, *Nachkriegszeit*, pp. 66–7; Eser, 'Oberschlesien', p. 381; Philipp Ther, 'Die einheimische Bevölkerung des Oppelner Schlesiens nach dem Zweiten Weltkrieg. Die Entstehung einer deutschen Minderheit', *Geschichte und Gesellschaft*, 26, 2000, pp. 422–3, 430–1; Madajczyk, *Przyłączenie*, p. 176; Magierska, *Ziemie*, pp. 98–104; Strauchold, *Autochtoni*, p. 83; Kowalski, *Powrót*, p. 305.

[78] Because this study covers the period before and after the creation of the Wrocław Voivodship in May 1946, I will refer to this region as 'Lower Silesia' throughout the book. Likewise, the term 'Regional Administration' will be used to refer to both the *Urząd Pełnomocnika Rządu R.P. na Okręg Administracyjny Dolnego Śląsku* and the *Urząd Wojewódzki Wrocławski*, as it officially became known after May 1946.

more than counterbalanced by the fact that the Polish Workers' Party had control of the powerful Security Police (*Urzędy Bezpieczeństwa Publicznego*) and the Citizens' Militia throughout Poland. Moreover, the Polish Workers' Party was at this time steadily tightening its control over the administration of Poland's new western and northern territories. The creation of a new Ministry for Recovered Territories in November 1945, headed by none other than the General Secretary of the Polish Workers' Party, Władysław Gomułka, confirmed the party's monopoly on power throughout these territories.[79]

The first Polish state officials to reach Hirschberg/Jelenia Góra District arrived as an 'operational group' in a lorry from Trebnitz/Trzebnica on 19 May 1945. One member of the group later recalled that they had been '[f]oreign, ignorant of the territory and its conditions, and surrounded by the enemy'.[80] The 'operational group' was headed by Wojciech Tabaka, who became the district's first Polish Chief Official (*Starosta*). He and his officials arrived to find that the Red Army had set up military bases throughout the district. The Soviets had a district headquarters in Hirschberg/Jelenia Góra town and local bases in the villages of Schmiedeberg/Kowary, Bad Warmbrunn/Cieplice Śląskie, Krummhübel/Karpacz, Schreiberhau/Szklarska Poręba and Petersdorf/Piechowice. The new Polish state officials of the district also discovered that the Soviets were allowing German officials to continue running local administration in the district. This included keeping Germans on in local mayoral posts in the district's villages. The Polish 'operational group' swiftly got to work replacing these German village mayors with Poles. But because, even once Polish settlers began to flow into the district in large numbers in summer 1945, the district faced a shortage of qualified Polish administrative officials, the new Polish authorities were compelled to continue employing Germans for the everyday tasks of local administration for at least a year after the war. At the same time, they were forced to give posts in the state administrative authorities and in the Citizens' Militia to entirely unqualified and untrained Polish settlers. Some Polish forced labourers who had been transported to Lower Silesia by the Nazi German authorities during the war (see Chapter 1) even received official posts in Jelenia Góra District at this time. The lack of qualified state officials was not a problem unique to Jelenia Góra District.

[79] Borodziej, 'Einleitung', pp. 59–61; Hofmann, *Nachkriegszeit*, pp. 65–70; Kraft, 'Wrocławskie', pp. 370–3; Magierska, *Ziemie*, pp. 86–7, 90–3; Order of the Council of Ministers, 29 May 1946, Dziennik Ustaw Nr. 28, Poz. 177, http://isap.sejm.gov.pl/DetailsServlet?id=WDU19460280177 [last accessed 23.3.2013]; Rep by head JGTA, 3.6.1946, APJG 130, sygn. 46, 53–5.

[80] Rep by head JGTA, 3.6.1946, APJG 130, sygn. 46, 53–5.

Indeed, because of the actions taken by Poland's Nazi German occupiers to destroy educated elites during the war, this was a statewide problem in Poland in the immediate postwar period.

In this fashion, the Polish 'operational group', in summer 1945, set up a District Administration (*Starostwo*) and a Town Administration (*Zarząd Miejski*) in the newly renamed town of Jelenia Góra and – more slowly and falteringly – established local commune administrations (*zarządy gminy*) and Citizens' Militia stations in the villages of Jelenia Góra District in summer 1945.* Yet because Soviet bases and troops did not yet withdraw from the district, there remained two competing sources of authority there. This situation of dual Soviet–Polish control persisted for a number of months after the arrival of the first Polish 'operational group'. This had important consequences for the German residents of Jelenia Góra District, as we shall discuss in Chapter 4. It was a situation replicated in many other districts in Poland's new territories in the immediate postwar period.[81]

CHAOS AND LAWLESSNESS

The erection of Polish state administration in our two districts took place in circumstances of general flux and chaos throughout Germany's prewar eastern provinces – and in fact throughout postwar Polish territory at the end of the Second World War. A very large proportion of the residents of

* **Note on local state administration in Poland's new territories after 1945**
In the case of both Jelenia Góra District and Opole District, the District Administration (*Starostwo*) was in control of state administration in the large rural areas of the two districts (*powiaty*), whereas the Town Administration (*Zarząd Miejski*) had responsibility for state administration in Jelenia Góra town and Opole town. However, in both districts, the responsibilities of the District Administration and the Town Administration were not entirely separate and the former was able to influence and, to a certain extent, control the actions of the latter. In both districts, the District Administration and the Town Administration were each headed by a single individual whose respective official titles, for most of the period examined in this study, were District Chief Official (*Starosta*) and Town President. The rural areas of both districts were divided into a large number of rural communes (*gminy*), each of which was run by a commune administration (*zarząd gminy*) headed by a commune mayor (*wójt*). The rural communes, in turn, were each divided into several villages (*gromady*) which were each run by a village mayor (*sołtys*). In addition, both districts contained a few large villages, which were not placed within rural communes and were each run by a municipal mayor (*burmistrz*).

81 Rep by JG Chief, 6.[8].1945, APJG 123/II, sygn. 18, 3–26; MoRep JG Chief, 3.10.1945, APJG 123/II, sygn. 18, 127–32; MoRep JG Chief, 6.11.1945, APJG 123/II, sygn. 18, 109–15; Rep by head JGTA, 3.6.1946, APJG 130, sygn. 46, 53–5; WR, Adolph G., Fischbach (Karpniki), undated, BOD 1, 207, 21–4; WR, Paul H., Bad Warmbrunn (Cieplice Śląskie), 10.9.1958, BOD 1, 207, 243–9; WR, Paul W., Bad Warmbrunn, undated, BOD 2, 188, 318–32; WR, Ursula R., Schreiberhau (Szklarska Poręba), 10.3.1954, BOD 2, 188, 122–37; WR, Robert W., Ludwigsdorf (Chromiec), undated, BOD 1, 207, 133–8; Kraft, 'Wrocławskie', pp. 365, 370–3; Hofmann, *Nachkriegszeit*, pp. 67–9, 71–2; Jan Ryszard Sielezin, 'Polityka polskich władz wobec ludności niemieckiej na terenie kotliny jeleniogórskiej w 1945 r.', *Śląski Kwartalnik Historyczny Sobótka* 55, 2000, pp. 68–71; Magierska, *Ziemie*, pp. 100–4.

these prewar eastern German provinces who had taken flight in the final months of the war, flowed back from their places of refuge in the weeks and months after the war. In the newly renamed district of Opole, the new Polish state authorities reported in late May 1945 'an ever growing inflow of the local people who were evacuated by the Germans [at the end of the war]'. Polish officials commented a month later that the '[t]he influx of germans [*sic*] into the district strengthens by the day'.[82] Likewise, in Jelenia Góra District, a large stream of people could be witnessed returning from Czechoslovakia in the early summer of 1945. They reached the district exhausted, having trekked over the Sudeten Mountains. Only a small proportion of these arrivals were residents of Jelenia Góra District; most were refugees passing through on their way home to the Silesian lowlands. A small number of locals were also transported to Silesia by the postwar Czechoslovak authorities as part of the Prague government's campaign, going on since May 1945, to 'cleanse' the country of ethnic Germans and German citizens. The family of Ludwig F. from the village of Lomnitz/Łomnica in Jelenia Góra District, for example, were interned in a camp in Czechoslovakia for about two weeks at the end of the war. He and his family were then placed on a cargo train and transported to western Lower Silesia. From there they apparently 'begged their way back' to Lomnitz/Łomnica.[83] But the stream of returnees from Czechoslovakia soon petered out, in part because by late summer 1945 Jelenia Góra District's new Polish state authorities were taking active measures to prevent Germans from crossing the Polish-Czechoslovak border into the district.[84]

Conditions of chaos and lawlessness prevailed in Poland's new western and northern territories in the initial months after the war. The acts of robbery and violence by the very large number of Soviet troops stationed in these territories in the immediate postwar period played a central role in this and persisted for a number of months after Germany's capitulation. Soviet attacks on local civilians were also widespread in the prewar Polish

[82] Rep by ODA S-PD, 29.5.1945, APK 185/4, sygn. 21, 208–9; Rep by ODA S-PD, 20.6.1945. APK 185/4 25, 12–14.

[83] WR, Ludwig F., Lomnitz (Łomnica), 31.1.1951, BOD 2, 188, 30–31. WRs in file BOD 1, 207 and file BOD 2, 188. Kraft, 'Wrocławskie', p. 362.

[84] MoRep JG Chief, 5.2.1946, APJG 123/II, sygn. 19, 30–37; SiRep JGTA's Settlement Department, 18.6.1947, APJG 130, sygn. 47, 219–21; Rep for the Commissar for Repatriation Issues in Wrocław by JGTA, 26.1.1946, APW 331/VI, sygn. 360, 2–3; SiRep JG Chief, 31.3.1947, APW 331/VI, sygn. 51, 10–12; SiRep JG Chief, 30.4.1947, APW 331/VI, sygn. 51, 18–19; SiRep JG DepChief, 31.5.1947, APW 331/VI, sygn. 51, 20–1; SiRep JG Chief, 2.11.1948, APW 331/VI, sygn. 51, 77–8; SiRep JG Chief, 3.12.1948, APW 331/VI, sygn. 51, 79–81; SiRep JG Chief, 27.12.1948, APW 331/VI, sygn. 51, 82–6; SiRep JG Chief, 31.1.1949, APJG 123/II, sygn. 20, 240–4; SiRep JG Chief, early March 1949, APW 331/VI, sygn. 51, 98–100; Sielezin, 'Polityka polskich władz', p. 70.

territories – against Poles. These acts of violence and robbery, then, were by no means motivated purely by the desire to take revenge for German atrocities in the Soviet Union. But it has to be said that the Soviet attacks on civilians were significantly more frequent in Poland's new territories than in its prewar territories.

Just as important for creating conditions of apparent anarchy in Poland's new territories was the fact that many of the first Poles to arrive there at the end of the war had come not to settle but to loot. As Marcin Zaremba has shown, in order to understand not only this looting but also the widespread acts of criminality and violence by Poles throughout Poland at this time, it is crucial to understand the immense social and psychological damage done to Polish society by the Nazi German occupation. Nazi Germany's murderous and reckless exploitation of the country had traumatized, demoralized and severely impoverished huge swaths of Polish society. This left some Poles with few moral inhibitions about engaging in criminal and sometimes violent acts – acts which before the war they would not have contemplated doing. Of course, the great majority of inhabitants of postwar Poland did not engage in these kinds of activities. But for some, looting and robbery seemed the only route open to improve the extremely difficult situation they found themselves in. In addition to these people, there were also long-term criminals, who decided to make use of the anarchic conditions prevailing in Poland, and especially the new territories, to enrich themselves.

Looting happened across postwar Polish territory, but was particularly widespread in the new territories. Many Poles, including officials, did not believe that these territories would remain in Polish hands for long; they believed that the window of opportunity to get something out of them would remain open only very briefly. Looting by individuals and gangs arriving from central Poland was witnessed in both of our districts at the end of the war – as it was in localities throughout Poland's new territories. But it appears to have been considerably more widespread and persistent in Hirschberg/Jelenia Góra District than in Oppeln/Opole District. This may have had something to do with the fact that the former was a homogeneously ethnically German district, whereas the latter was inhabited by a large number of bilingual Polish-dialect-speakers (see Chapter 6).[85] For local Germans it was very difficult to tell the difference between genuine settlers and looters. As one German witness from Jelenia Góra District

[85] Zaremba, *Trwoga*, pp. 87–140, 154–96, 295–313; Ther, *Vertriebene*, pp. 126–30; Hofmann, *Nachkriegszeit*, pp. 76–80, 104–8; Eser, 'Oberschlesien', p. 382. WRs in: file BOD 1, 207; file BOD 1, 243; file BOD 2, 188; file BOD 2, 229.

put it, 'the first Poles... moved in robbing and looting'.[86] Jelenia Góra District's first Polish Chief Official himself remarked in August 1945 that the district had experienced an 'inflow of elements who came here not for honest work but to loot'. They had come to the district simply 'to look around, steal something and leave'.[87]

As happened throughout Poland's new western and northern territories, the looters tended to transport their booty back to central Poland as quickly as possible. Ursula R. from Niederschreiberhau/Szklarska Poręba Dolna in Jelenia Góra District claimed that the Poles often moved into a German's home, surveyed it from top to bottom, packed up all the desirable items and transported them back to central Poland in a lorry. They then returned with other Poles who wanted to do the same.[88] Ursula R.'s one-time lodger, the newly appointed Polish village mayor (*sołtys*) of Szklarska Poręba Dolna, Leon M., likewise noted at a meeting with other local Polish officials in October 1945 that it was very common for Poles to move into farms, houses and guesthouses in the local area and then pack up the contents 'and take the loot off to Central Poland'.[89] Throughout Poland's new territories, the Polish state authorities made efforts to put a stop to these activities. But it was not until February 1946 that the Ministry for Recovered Territories actually prohibited the transportation of movable property from the new territories to central Poland. A crucial obstacle to solving this problem, moreover, was the fact that many local officials themselves took part in these activities. In localities throughout the new territories, the Citizens' Militia, staffed by poorly paid, untrained, often very young recruits from central Poland, quickly became infamous for its corruption and criminality. In fact, Citizens' Militia personnel were just as notorious for dishonesty and abuse in the prewar Polish territories in the early postwar period. Many of the first Polish village mayors appointed in Poland's new territories – also inexperienced, poorly paid and in possession of substantial amounts of unchecked responsibility – likewise proved willing to abuse their positions.[90] In fact, despite the attitude he expressed

86 WR, Paul H., Bad Warmbrunn (Cieplice Śląskie), 10.9.1958, BOD 1, 207, 243–9.

87 Rep by JG Chief, 6.[8].1945, APJG 123/II, sygn. 18, 3–26; Rep by JG Chief, 3.10.1945, APJG 123/II, sygn. 18, 127–32.

88 WR, Ursula R., Niederschreiberhau (Szklarska Poręba Dolna), 10.3.1954, BOD 2, 188, 122–137. WRs: BOD 2, 188, 109–11; BOD 2, 188, 277–83; BOD 2, 188, 175–97; BOD 2, 188, 198–203; BOD 2, 188, 95–102; BOD 1, 207, 33–8. Hofmann, *Nachkriegszeit*, pp. 104–8.

89 Rep on a meeting at the mayoral office in Szklarska Poręba which took place on 24.10.1945, APJG 143, sygn. 65, 38–40; WR, Ursula R., 10.3.1954, BOD 2, 188, 122–37.

90 Zaremba, *Trwoga*, pp. 263–72; Ther, *Vertriebene*, pp. 126–30; Hofmann, *Nachkriegszeit*, pp. 104–8; Eser, 'Oberschlesien', p. 382.

in his official report cited previously, the new village mayor of Szklarska Poręba Dolna, Leon M., appears to have been one of them.[91]

Moreover, the whole of postwar Polish territory was gripped by severe shortages and material hardship at the end of the war. The Soviets exacerbated the terrible economic problems facing Poland by transporting large amounts of industrial equipment out of Poland's new territories back to the Soviet Union at this time. Both of our districts witnessed these Soviet confiscations. Many areas of the new territories had also experienced very destructive fighting in the final phase of the war. Indeed, several cities in Poland's new territories were lying in ruins. This included the city located nearest to our two districts: Breslau/Wrocław. Many towns and villages across the new territories were in the same state. As we have seen, Hirschberg/Jelenia Góra District – like the whole of southern Lower Silesia – was largely spared any wartime destruction. But the buildings and infrastructure of Oppeln/Opole town and a number of the villages in the surrounding countryside of Oppeln/Opole District had been heavily damaged in the fighting of the final months of the war.[92] One Pole from Kraków, who spent a year in the area at this time, claimed that as late as 1947 there was still a burnt-out German tank lying in a field next to the village in Opole District where he lived.[93]

These, then, were the general circumstances prevailing in Poland's new territories in summer 1945. Polish state administration was still in a fragile and precarious state. Corruption and criminality was widespread among the territories' new state officials and Citizens' Militia personnel. A very large Soviet occupation force remained in the territories. Soviet troops often seemed beyond the control of their Red Army commanders. Lawlessness prevailed. Arriving Polish settlers were struggling to overcome the traumas they had experienced under Nazi German occupation. Huge numbers of people were moving across the territories in different directions. Serious

[91] WR, Ursula R., Niederschreiberhau (Szklarska Poręba Dolna), 10.3.1954, BOD 2, 188, 122–37.

[92] SiRep ODA, 29.5.1945, APK 185/4, sygn. 21, 208–9; Rep by ODA, 5.6.1945, APK 185/4 sygn. 22, 49–51; Rep by ODA, 20.6.1945, APK 185/4, sygn. 25, 12–14; SiRep ODA, 9.8.1945, APK 185/4, sygn. 27/1, 43–7; Rep by head JGTA, 3.6.1946, APJG 130, sygn. 46, 53–5. Reports from 1945–6 in file APO 178, 41, file APJG 123/II, 18 and file APJG 123/II, 19. WR in: file BOD 1, 243; file BOD 2, 229; file BOD 1, 207; file BOD 2, 188. Zaremba, *Trwoga*, pp. 96–8, 202; see also the photos of Szczecin and Gdańsk between p. 288 and p. 289. Hofmann, *Nachkriegszeit*, pp. 68–70, 76–80, 104–5, 119–26; Ther, 'Die einheimische Bevölkerung', pp. 422–3; Kraft, 'Wrocławskie', pp. 364–8, 371–3; Madajczyk, *Przyłączenie*, pp. 178–83; Eser, 'Oberschlesien', pp. 376, 381–2.

[93] Jan Stadniczenko, 'Rok szkolny 1947/1948 na wsi opolskiej', in Z. Dulczewski and A. Kwilecki (eds.), *Pamiętniki osadników ziem odzyskanych*, Vol. 2 (Poznań, 1970).

shortages of essential goods were gripping. Many cities, towns and villages were lying in rubble. These were the highly unpropitious circumstances in which the Communist-led government attempted to enact a radical ethno-national transformation in Poland's new territories in 1945. Let us turn to examine it.

CHAPTER 4

Expulsion

DISORGANIZED EXPULSION

Around six million German citizens and German-speakers are estimated to have fled from the postwar territories of Poland as the Red Army arrived in 1944 and early 1945. A little more than a million subsequently returned. Almost five million therefore abandoned these territories permanently before the Communist-led Polish authorities took over control of the territories and began active expulsion of the German citizens living there. The majority of the just over eight million German citizens and ethnic Germans who left the postwar territories of Poland between 1944 and 1949 were therefore not uprooted by deliberate acts of forced migration carried out by the Polish state authorities after Soviet 'liberation'. Rather they were displaced by the massive wartime flight and evacuation of civilians – before both the Soviet 'liberation' and the arrival of Polish state authorities.[1]

There was a small amount of overlap between the wartime flight and postwar expulsions. Germans continued to leave areas of the prewar eastern German provinces in the final phase of the war, even after they had been conquered by the Red Army. The Polish state officials arriving in these provinces from spring 1945 onwards began to encourage and facilitate these departures in the final weeks of the war. Whether this should be viewed as the start of the postwar expulsions or the end of the wartime flight is open to interpretation. Nevertheless, the wartime flight and postwar expulsions were, in the main, separate processes and had distinct causes. This is an important point, because West German writers in the Cold War era tended to conflate the two processes. This enabled them to exaggerate the levels of chaos, suffering and violence involved in the acts of deliberate forced migration imposed by the Polish state authorities once the war was over.

[1] Nitschke, *Vertreibung*, pp. 274–80; Borodziej, 'Einleitung', p. 76.

Furthermore, because Soviet revenge attacks on civilians played a large role in causing Germans to take flight in the final months and days of the war, the conflation of wartime flight with postwar expulsion also encourages us to overestimate the role revenge motives played in the latter. The desire to retaliate for the Nazi German occupation of Poland clearly did play a part in the Polish authorities' postwar expulsions of German citizens and ethnic Germans. But it is important to understand that, insofar as the postwar expulsions were a response to the Nazi German occupation, they were, in most cases, not the result of knee-jerk acts of retaliation. Rather, they should be understood as a very specific response to the Nazi German occupation, which articulated itself in a nationalist campaign of forced migration. This campaign was pursued by the new Communist-controlled government of Poland throughout postwar Polish territory between 1944 and 1949. It was supported by almost all legal and illegal political groups in the country and by the majority of ethnically Polish society. It involved not only the uprooting of German citizens and ethnic Germans, but also the expulsion of ethnic Ukrainians and various other transformative processes aimed at turning Poland into a homogeneous nation-state.

The postwar expulsion of Germans by Poland's Communist-led government played a somewhat more important role in the ethno-national transformation of southern Lower Silesia than in most other areas of Poland's new territories. The reason for this is that no more than a fraction of the population fled this area as the Red Army arrived there in early May 1945. What this meant was that almost all the Germans uprooted from southern Lower Silesia at the end of the war were displaced as a result of deliberate enforcement of migration by the new Polish authorities rather than by wartime flight. And the reason so few fled from this area in the final phase of the war was that the Red Army – as we saw in Chapter 3 – did not arrive in southern Lower Silesia until the very end of the war. For example, Soviet forces arrived in the southern Lower Silesian district of Hirschberg/Jelenia Góra on 8 May 1945. This was the final day of fighting in Europe and the day of Germany's unconditional surrender. The vast majority of the residents of this district stayed within the district's administrative boundaries as the Soviet forces invaded. They were still living there when the first Polish state officials arrived as an 'operational group' on 19 May 1945.[2]

The postwar expulsion of Germans from Poland's new western and northern territories took place in the midst of a tussle for control between the fledgling Polish civilian authorities of these provinces and the large

[2] WRs in file BOD 1, 207 and file BOD 2, 188. Rep by head JGTA, 3.6.1946, APJG 130, sygn. 46, 53–5; Kraft, 'Wrocławskie', p. 362.

Soviet forces based in the local area. In the renamed district of Jelenia Góra, the local Soviet commander was Major Smirnov. His headquarters were located in Jelenia Góra town. He seems to have caused problems for the new Polish Chief Official of Jelenia Góra District from the very outset. Notably, he is said to have protected the district's German population from certain repressive measures taken by the Polish state authorities in the early postwar period. Polish officials also believed that Germans tended to contact local Soviet bases for assistance when faced with discriminatory orders issued by the district's new Polish village mayors.[3] According to local Polish state officials, instances of Soviet soldiers acting in defence of the Germans were very widespread at the end of summer 1945. And it was not only Polish officials who saw it this way. Local Germans supported this claim in the first-hand accounts which they wrote some years later. A German from the village of Giersdorf/Podgórzyn in Jelenia Góra District, for example, explained that a fierce 'ethnic hatred' (*Nationalitätenhaß*) existed between the Russians and the Poles. He claimed that the Russians often protected the Germans and that they did so not out of sympathy for the Germans but rather out of 'hatred for Poles'.[4]

In certain areas of Poland's new territories, the arriving Polish officials started to carry out small-scale expulsions against Germans already in late spring 1945 – that is, before the war was over. But government-led large-scale expulsions did not begin until over a month after Germany's capitulation. In mid June 1945 the Communist-controlled Polish Army's High Command instructed its soldiers to begin expelling all Germans living next to the Odra–Nysa Line – Poland's postwar western border – westwards into what would soon become the Soviet Occupation Zone of Germany.[5] In Jelenia Góra District, it was soldiers from the Polish Second Army's 10th Infantry Division who began expelling Germans from their villages in mid June 1945. The Germans were marched westwards by the Polish soldiers towards the Odra–Nysa Line, which was 70 kilometres away. The soldiers' actions quickly inspired similar expulsions by local Polish administrative officials and Citizens' Militia personnel who, having just arrived in the area, began to copy the violent, uncompromising methods of the Polish soldiers.[6]

[3] Rep by JG Chief, 6.[8].1945, APJG 123/II, sygn. 18, 3–26.

[4] Rep by JGDA S-PD, 3.9.1945, APJG 123/II, sygn. 18, 86–8; WR, A.W., Giersdorf (Podgórzyn), 5.6.1951, BOD 2, 188, 333–6.

[5] Nitschke, *Vertreibung*, pp. 169–87; Hofmann, *Nachkriegszeit*, pp. 189–94; Borodziej, 'Einleitung', pp. 62–8.

[6] WRs in file BOD 1, 207 and file BOD 2, 188. Bronisław Pasierb, 'Problemy repolonizacyjne rejonu jeleniogórskiego w latach 1945–1948', *Rocznik Jeleniogórski* 4, 1966, pp. 29–30.

Throughout Poland's new territories, the summer expulsions had a similarly violent and disorganized character. This phase of the postwar expulsions was clearly marked by revenge motives. Polish soldiers, administrative officials and Citizens' Militia personnel were finally getting the opportunity to do to Germans that which had been done to so many of their compatriots under Nazi German occupation in the past five years. Moreover, although the expulsion plans emanated from the Communist-controlled government in Warsaw, it was really the local army commanders and local officials who were in control of events. This meant that the implementation of these expulsions varied a great deal across Poland's new territories. They therefore did not necessarily reflect, by way of outcome, the original goals of the government.[7]

The chaos and disorder which characterized the expulsions are made clear by many of the first-hand accounts of them later written by German residents of the district. According to one such account, the inhabitants of the village of Rohrlach/Trzcińsko in Jelenia Góra District were expelled by Polish soldiers on 25 June 1945. Just over half of them, around 400 villagers, managed to escape into local forests immediately after their expulsion from the village. But the rest were forced to trek through the villages of Boberstein/Bobrów and Lomnitz/Łomnica, and then through Jelenia Góra town and the village of Reibnitz/Rybnica (see Map 5). They were subsequently marched out of the district and all the way to the town of Görlitz/Zgorzelec at the border of the Soviet Occupation Zone of Germany. Three villagers were reportedly shot dead along the way.[8] According to another account, the villagers of Bärndorf/Gruszków were forced out of their homes by Polish administrative officials and Citizens' Militia personnel in mid July 1945 and 'driven off like livestock'. They were marched westwards towards the Soviet Zone. But having arrived in the village of Marklisssa/Leśna, south of the town of Lauban/Lubań in western Lower Silesia, a number of villagers escaped and immediately began the journey back to Bärndorf/Gruszków. The other villagers were marched onwards into the Soviet Zone.[9] Witnesses from other villages in the district gave similar accounts of these expulsions.[10]

The tension and conflicts between local Polish officials and Soviet commanders clearly had a significant impact on these expulsions. Many of the

[7] Borodziej, 'Einleitung', pp. 67–73; Hofmann, *Nachkriegszeit*, pp. 189–99.

[8] WR, Oswald H., Rohrlach (Trzcińsko), undated, BOD 1, 207, 159–62.

[9] WR, Adolph G., Bärndorf (Gruszków), undated, BOD 1, 207, 21–4.

[10] WR, Hans T., Schmiedeberg (Kowary), late 1949, BOD 2, 188, 287–91; WR, Christian-Friedrich, Jannowitz (Janowice Wielkie), May 1946, BOD 2, 188, 269–76; WR, A.W., Giersdorf (Podgórzyn), 5.6.1951, BOD 2, 188, 333–6.

expulsions carried out in Jelenia Góra District were prevented by Soviet troops. The same was witnessed in many other districts in Poland's new territories.[11] The inhabitants of the villages of Waltersdorf/Mniszków and Jannowitz/Janowice Wielkie in Jelenia Góra District, for example, were violently expelled by Citizens' Militia personnel on 20 June 1945 and marched through the village of Rohrlach/Trzcińsko. The Poles apparently fired bullets over their heads as they marched. The Germans were halted in this village for some time so that the Citizens' Militia personnel could seize their valuables. They were then driven onwards to the village of Fischbach/Karpniki. But on arrival in this village, a Soviet 'assault unit' intervened, disarming the Citizens' Militia officers and instructing the Germans to return home.[12] Likewise, the villagers of Bärndorf/Gruszków managed to prevent an expulsion by the Citizens' Militia in late June 1945 simply by telephoning the local Soviet base in Schmiedeberg/Kowary. This phone call resulted in the swift arrival of a Soviet unit in combat vehicles, which reportedly arrested the Poles.[13]

One common feature of not only the expulsions carried out in Jelenia Góra District but also those undertaken in many other localities in Poland's new territories in summer 1945 was the ransacking and burglary of homes. This took place once the Germans had been driven out of their villages.[14] But in other respects there was a good deal of variation from village to village in how the expulsions were implemented in Jelenia Góra District. Not every village in the district appears to have experienced an expulsion, whereas some villages suffered two or even three.[15] In certain of the district's villages, the expulsions carried out by local Polish civilian officials were directed not at all German residents but only at the Nazi Party members among them. These expulsions seem to have been labelled 'Hitler marches' by the Polish officials. Robert W. claimed that he was given a special document by the local Polish administration in the village of Ludwigsdorf/Chromiec which

[11] WR, A.W., Giersdorf (Podgórzyn), 5.6.1951, BOD 2, 188, 333–6; WR, Paul H., Bad Warmbrunn (Cieplice Śląskie), 10.9.1958, BOD 1, 207, 243–9; WR, Robert W., Ludwigsdorf (Chromiec), undated, BOD 1, 207, 133–8; Pasierb, 'Problemy', p. 30.

[12] WR, Ewald S., Waltersdorf (Mniszków), 1957–8, BOD 1, 207, 239–42; WR, Christian-Friedrich, Jannowitz (Janowice Wielkie), May 1946, BOD 2, 188, 269–76.

[13] WR, Adolph G. undated, BOD 1, 207, 21–4.

[14] WR, Adolph G., Bärndorf (Gruszków), undated, BOD 1, 207, 21–4; WR, Christian-Friedrich, Jannowitz (Janowice Wielkie), May 1946, BOD 2, 188, 269–76; WR, Ewald S., Waltersdorf (Mniszków), 1957–8, BOD 1, 207, 239–42; WR, Hans T., Schmiedeberg (Kowary), late 1949, BOD 2, 188, 287–91; WR, A.W., Giersdorf (Podgórzyn), 5.6.1951, BOD 2, 188, 333–6; Hofmann, *Nachkriegszeit*, pp. 193, 197; Kraft, 'Wrocławskie', p. 382.

[15] WR, Adolf G., Bärndorf (Gruszków), undated, BOD 1, 207, 21–4; WR, Ewald S., Waltersdorf (Mniszków), 1957–8. BOD 1, 207, 239–42; WR, Christian-Friedrich, Jannowitz (Janowice Wielkie), May 1946, BOD 2, 188, 269–76; WR, Oswald H., Rohrlach (Trzcińsko), undated, BOD 1, 207, 159–62.

exempted him from a 'Hitler march', because he could prove he had never belonged to the Nazi Party.[16]

Because of the disorganized character of the summer expulsions and the frequent interventions made by the Soviet forces, many Germans living in Jelenia Góra District did not experience expulsions at all at this time. Moreover, most of those who did were able to return quickly to their homes. The German population of Jelenia Góra District was, therefore, left largely intact by these expulsions. Very few Germans were permanently uprooted. Once the expulsions were over, a government official travelled around southern Lower Silesia and reported the following:

> In those parts of Lower Silesia lying at the foot of the Sudeten Mountains something very interesting is happening. In the immediate vicinity of the towns of Jelenia Góra, Kłodzko and certain other places, the number of Germans living there is growing by the day. The German population is 20 percent larger than its prewar size. This is a side-effect of the displacement of Germans from Czechoslovakia. [The Czechoslovak authorities] simply drive the Germans up to the border [with Poland] and then just leave them to decide where to go next.

The rising number of Germans in the local area was probably more a result of local residents voluntarily returning to the region from Czechoslovakia and from other places where they had taken refuge during the wartime flight than of expulsions carried out by the Czechoslovak authorities. Nevertheless, this statement clearly demonstrated that the summer expulsions did not significantly reduce the size of the German population of Jelenia Góra District and nearby districts. Lower Silesia's Regional Governor, Stanisław Piaskowski, himself described the summer expulsions as a 'complete failure'.

Throughout Poland's new territories, these government-ordered summer expulsions, which had got underway in mid June 1945, had finished by the end of July. Their impact on Poland's new territories as a whole was somewhat more significant than that on southern Lower Silesia. Around 300,000–400,000 Germans in total are estimated to have been forced across the Odra–Nysa Line by these expulsions. Nevertheless, millions of Germans remained in the new territories at the end of July 1945.[17]

[16] WR, Richard S., Arnsdorf (Miłków), 30.11.1953, BOD 1, 207, 17–18; WR, Robert W., Ludwigsdorf (Chromiec), undated, BOD 1, 207, 133–8.

[17] The government official's description is cited in Nitschke, *Vertreibung*, p. 185. Rep by JG Chief, 6.[8].1945, APJG 123/II, sygn. 18, 3–26. WRs in file BOD 1, 207 and file BOD 2, 188. Borodziej, 'Einleitung', pp. 67–73, 76; Nitschke, *Vertreibung*, pp. 184–5, 275; Kraft, 'Wrocławskie', p. 382; Hofmann, *Nachkriegszeit*, pp. 189–94; Stanisław Jankowiak, 'Flucht, Vertreibung und Zwangsaussiedlung der Deutschen aus der Wojewodschaft Breslau (Województwo Wrocławskie)

What is usually left out of histories of these events – or mentioned only in passing as part of the general context – is that they happened against the backdrop of a massive influx of Polish settlers into Poland's new western and northern territories. Moreover, in localities throughout these territories, the arrival of hundreds of thousands of Polish settlers from spring 1945 onwards played a significant role in instigating the expulsions. This was clearly witnessed in Jelenia Góra District where, as we shall discuss in Chapter 5, thousands of Polish settlers started to arrive in June 1945, transported there on cargo trains by the Communist-led government's State Repatriation Office (*Państwowy Urząd Repatriacyjny*). The mass inflow of settlers placed acute pressure on the district's already scarce housing and resources. This gave impetus to the soldiers' expulsions, which had been ordered from Warsaw, but also helped to mobilize local Polish administrative officials and local Citizens' Militia personnel into carrying out their own expulsions against Germans in the district. The same was witnessed in many other localities in Poland's new territories.[18]

At ground level, then, the policy of flooding these territories with Polish settlers and that of expelling the territories' German residents were clearly intertwined with one another in a very practical sense. But they were also carried out in pursuit of precisely the same overall objective. By transporting millions of Polish settlers to Poland's new territories and simultaneously displacing the millions of remaining German residents to Allied-occupied Germany, the Communist-led government in Warsaw hoped to influence the decisions made by the Allied powers about postwar territorial changes in East-Central Europe once the war was over. With the full backing of Stalin and the Soviet leadership, the Polish government aimed to transform the ethnic makeup of Poland's new territories and to present this as a fait accompli to the Western powers when they met with the Soviets for a peace conference after the war. This should be understood as tightly bound up with the Polish Communists' domestic efforts to consolidate their hold on power and to marginalize their political opponents (see Chapter 2). Communist leaders presented their party to ethnically Polish society as the only political force in the country capable of securing and maintaining control over Poland's new territories in the long term.

in den Jahren 1945 bis 1950. Die Jahre 1946–1950', in Borodziej and Lemberg, *Heimat* vol. 4, p. 402; Bohmann, *Menschen*, p. 209. One Polish historian claimed in the 1960s that approximately 80,000 Germans were expelled by Polish soldiers from the Jelenia Góra area between June and July 1945. But this figure is implausibly high and it is clear that, even if so many were expelled, most soon returned to their homes. Pasierb, 'Problemy', pp. 29–30.

[18] Hofmann, *Nachkriegszeit*, p. 189.

A less important 'strategic' objective also underpinned the Communist-led governments' disorganized expulsions against German citizens in summer 1945. The government originally planned to create a zone of military settlement along the east side of the Odra–Nysa Line by settling demobilized soldiers in the vacated homes of the Germans expelled by the Polish Army. Several localities in Poland's new territories did eventually contain large concentrations of demobilized Polish soldiers as a result of the army's summer expulsions and military settlement campaign. Yet the campaign ultimately failed. This was mainly because the number of Polish military settlers who proved willing to take up residence in most areas of these territories – including Jelenia Góra District – was meagre.[19]

VOLUNTARY MIGRATION

Despite the relative lack of success of the Communist-led Polish government's disorganized expulsions against Germans in summer 1945, at the Potsdam Conference in August 1945 the Polish Communists and their Soviet sponsors achieved two fundamental objectives. The Allied powers not only granted Poland control of all territories to the east of the Odra–Nysa Line but also consented to the 'transfer' to Germany of all Germans remaining in these territories. However, they also ordered Poland temporarily to cease expelling Germans from them.[20]

Throughout Poland's new western and northern territories, the Polish authorities therefore had to find alternative 'solutions' to their so-called 'German problem'. In Jelenia Góra District, the authorities' response was what they called 'concentrating' the German population. This often meant evicting them from their homes and forcing them to move in with other Germans or relocate to crowded ghetto-like areas in the district. One of these areas was a neighbourhood of Jelenia Góra town. Thirty-six thousand Germans were said to be living in this part of the town by August 1945, a number exceeding the entire prewar population of the town. Another was a former middle-class housing estate on the edge of the village of Rybnica. Arno M. and his family were forced by local Polish officials to relocate there

[19] Hofmann, *Nachkriegszeit*, pp. 110–15, 134–5, 157–9, 163, 192–3; Borodziej, 'Einleitung', pp. 55–68; Włodzimierz Borodziej, Stanisław Ciesielski and Jerzy Kochanowski, 'Wstęp', in Ciesielski (ed.), *Przesiedlenie*, pp. 12–35, 40–5; Kraft, 'Wrocławskie', pp. 380–1; Pasierb, *Migracja*, p. 90; Jerzy Kochanowski, 'Towards a Nationally Homogeneous State: Poland 1944–6', in Ahonen et al., *People*, pp. 96–9; Thum, *Breslau*, pp. 109–11; Aleksander Pietraszko, 'Osadnik Wojskowy', in Dulczewski and Kwilecki, *Pamiętniki*, pp. 290–301; Adam Jaroszewski, 'Na turoszowskiej budowie', in Anna Kotlarska (ed.), *Pamiętniki mieszkańców Dolnego Śląska* (Wrocław, 1978), pp. 66–72.

[20] Hofmann, *Nachkriegszeit*, p. 211.

from Cieplice Śląskie towards the end of 1945. They arrived to find it very crowded with German families. Germans were also frequently allowed to remain in their own homes on the condition that they gave up most of the rooms for Polish settlers to live in. This meant that many local Germans lived together with Polish settlers under very cramped conditions. Similar 'concentrating' practices were adopted by Polish state officials in districts across Poland's new territories.[21]

But these measures were viewed by local state officials and the Communist-led government as merely temporary solutions. Because of the problems being created in many localities in Poland's new territories by the policy of transporting huge numbers of Polish settlers there, the government decided it needed to circumvent the Allies' suspension of 'transfers'. It concluded that this could be done by encouraging German residents of Poland's new territories to migrate to Allied-occupied Germany 'voluntarily'. Accordingly, in summer 1945, the government advised the new territories' local officials to 'make difficult' the lives of Germans to such a degree that even 'the most stubborn enemies of Polishness [would] lose the courage' to remain there.[22]

This policy had a profound impact on the lives of the millions of Germans remaining in Poland's new territories. The practice of 'concentrating' Germans can be viewed as part of it. Material circumstances were very tough for both Poles and Germans in the new territories after the war. But specific discriminatory measures targeting Germans caused them to undergo collective pauperization in the second half of 1945. These included forcing them to pay higher prices for fuel, food and accommodation and giving them much lower wages for work than Polish settlers. Many Germans were ruthlessly exploited as manual labourers. Some received only food as payment. Occasionally they received no payment at all. At the same time, all German property was declared state-owned. German farms and workshops were placed under the 'administration' of Polish settlers. Germans were unable to access savings in banks. And German Reichsmarks had to be exchanged for Polish złotys at an extortionate rate. In

[21] Rep by JG Chief, 6.[8].1945, APJG 123/II, sygn. 18, 3–26; Rep by JG Chief, 3.10.1945, APJG 123/II, sygn. 18, 127–32; Rep by JGDA S-PD, 3.9.1945, APJG 123/II, sygn. 18, 86–8; Rep by JG Chief, 6.11.1945, APJG 123/II, sygn. 18, 109–15; Rep by JG Chief, 5.12.1945, APJG 123/II, sygn. 18, 185–200; Rep by JG Chief, 5.1.1946, APJG 123/II, sygn. 18, 206–14; Rep by JG Chief, 5.2.1946, APJG 123/II, sygn. 19, 30–37. WR, Arno M., Bad Warmbrunn (Cieplice Śląskie), 26.6.1959, BOD 2, 188, 95–102. WRs: BOD 2, 188, 32–4; BOD 2 188, 24–9; BOD 1, 207, 29–32; BOD 1, 207, 21–4; BOD 2, 188, 14–17; BOD 1, 207, 239–42; BOD 2, 188, 318–32; BOD 1, 207, 235–6; BOD 1, 207, 183–95; BOD 2, 188, 169–74. Pasierb, *Migracja*, p. 31; Sielezin, 'Polityka polskich władz', p. 76; Bohmann, *Menschen*, p. 209; Nitschke, *Vertreibung*, p. 121; Kraft, 'Wrocławskie', p. 377.

[22] Hofmann, *Nachkriegszeit*, pp. 187–91; Kraft, 'Wrocławskie', pp. 384–5; Borodziej, 'Einleitung', p. 99; Pasierb, *Migracja*, pp. 95–6.

Jelenia Góra District, the impoverished German residents resorted to selling almost all possessions to Polish settlers at whatever prices they could get. One formerly wealthy German inhabitant of the district later admitted, 'For the first time in my long life I came to know what hunger was.'[23]

As happened in localities throughout Poland's new territories, many Germans in Jelenia Góra District experienced harassment, violence and robbery at the hands of Poles, especially from Citizens' Militia personnel. This was facilitated by the fact that many Germans were forced to wear white armbands on their left arms until at least the end of 1945.[24] A number of Germans provided first-hand accounts of violence they endured at the hands of Citizens' Militia personnel in Jelenia Góra District. Many testified to having been 'arrested' on spurious grounds and placed in makeshift cells, usually cellars. They were subjected there to brutal treatment. Some German witnesses claimed they watched fatal abuse of other Germans while in the custody of the Citizens' Militia.[25] One of the most notorious makeshift Citizens' Militia prisons in Jelenia Góra District was set up under a former gynaecological clinic in Jelenia Góra town. Christian-Friedrich from the village of Jannowitz/Janowice Wielkie was imprisoned there in 1945. He apparently witnessed the deaths of several fellow inmates. He saw one man die from being punched and kicked repeatedly in the abdomen. The man's corpse was reportedly left to lie in the cell for some time before it was finally removed by the Polish guards.[26]

Some Germans living in Jelenia Góra District were also subjected to unambiguous forced labour. For example, several locals later gave first-hand accounts of being transported to a nearby part of Czechoslovakia in late 1945, where they were forced to spend months carrying out tree felling and other hard labour in a forest there.[27] A forced labour camp

[23] WR, Liesbeth E., Hirschberg (Jelenia Góra) town, 14.10.1952, BOD 2 188, 24–9. WRs in file BOD 2, 188 and file BOD 1, 207. Kraft, 'Wrocławskie', pp. 376–8; Borodziej, 'Einleitung', p. 99; Nitschke, *Vertreibung*, pp. 95–108.

[24] Rep by JGDA S-PD, 3.9.1945, APJG 123/II, sygn. 18, 86–8. WRs: BOD 2, 188, 14–17; BOD 2 188, 24–9; BOD 1, 207, 243–9; BOD 1, 207, 7–9; BOD 1, 207, 81–2; BOD 2, 188, 122–37; BOD 1, 207, 89–92; BOD 1, 207, 133–8; BOD 2, 188, 175–97. Hofmann, *Nachkriegszeit*, pp. 191, 200–1; Kraft, 'Wrocławskie', p. 377; Nitschke, *Vertreibung*, pp. 97–9.

[25] WRs in file BOD 1, 207 and file BOD 2, 188.

[26] WR, Liesbeth E., Hirschberg (Jelenia Góra) town, 14.10.1952, BOD 2 188, 24–9; WR, Gerhard F., Hirschberg (Jelenia Góra) town, 24.3.1950, BOD 1, 207, 7–9; WR, Christian-Friedrich, Jannowitz (Janowice Wielkie), May 1946, BOD 2, 188, 269–76; WR, Jürgen M., Hirschberg (Jelenia Góra) town, 29.7.1951, BOD 2, 188, 105–7.

[27] WR, Ludwig F., Lomnitz (Łomnica), 31.1.1951, BOD 2, 188, 30–1; WR, Gustav H., Krummhübel (Karpacz), 14.3.1950, BOD 1, 207, 115–21; WR, Arnsdorf (Miłków), 30.11.1953, BOD 1, 207, 17–18; WR, Arno M., Bad Warmbrunn (Cieplice Śląskie), 26.6.1959, BOD 2, 188, 95–102; WR, Walter S.-G., Niederschreiberhau (Szklarska Poręba Dolna), 10.1.1948, BOD 2, 188, 175–97.

was set up in Jelenia Góra District in winter 1945, located high up in the mountains between the villages of Jakuszyce and Orle (see Map 5). Jelenia Góra District's Chief Official later described this camp in the following way: 'Last winter, over a distance of 7 km between Szklarska Poręba and the Czech border, snow reached 3.5 metres in depth. An average of about 500 Germans worked there clearing the road – something I will not be able to do this year using Polish labour.'[28] According to German witnesses, almost all Germans taken to this camp were women and girls. They were forced to spend a number of days or even weeks at this camp. They suffered temperatures as low as minus 20 degrees Celsius. They were compelled to work long and exhausting shifts clearing snow from a road. They slept in bare, only partly heated buildings. They were given small amounts of food and often had completely inadequate clothing.[29]

Germans endured similarly harsh treatment at the hands of the Polish state authorities in localities throughout Poland's new territories. It quickly accomplished its principal objective: escalating the number of Germans 'voluntarily' leaving these territories for Allied-occupied Germany. At the same time, in many places local officials sought to facilitate these migrations by issuing the Germans special 'travel passes'. Jelenia Góra District Administration (*Starostwo*) set up what it called a 'passport and travel passes office' in August 1945. By the start of September it had 'already sent over a thousand Germans out of the district with passes to reach the west within 18 days'. The passes contained a statement requesting all Polish officials 'to provide the stated person with assistance during the journey'.[30] In certain parts of Poland's new territories, the authorities went further than merely issuing passes in the assistance they provided to the Germans who wanted to leave. They actually supplied the Germans with the means of transport to undertake these journeys. Indeed, a significant minority of the Germans who 'voluntarily' migrated from Poland to Allied-occupied Germany in the second half of 1945 travelled part or all of the way on trains and lorries organized by local Polish administrative officials. From Jelenia Góra District, for example, some Germans appear to have travelled to the Soviet Zone at this time on lorries provided by the local officials.[31]

[28] SiRep JG Chief, 2.11.1946, APJG 123/II, sygn. 19, 401–5.

[29] WRs: BOD 2, 188, 122–37; BOD 2, 188, 139–48; BOD 2, 188, 198–203; BOD 2, 188, 39–42; BOD 1, 207, 183–95; BOD 1, 207, 178–82; BOD 1, 207, 151–2; BOD 2, 188, 318–32; BOD 2, 188, 175–97; BOD 1, 207, 7–9.

[30] SiRep JGDA S-PD, 3.9.1945, APJG 123/II, sygn. 18, 86–8; Pasierb, 'Problemy', p. 32; Pasierb, *Migracja*, p. 97; Hofmann, *Nachkriegszeit*, p. 191.

[31] Nitschke, *Vertreibung*, pp. 187–98; WR, Hans T., Schmiedeberg (Kowary), late 1949, BOD 2, 188, 287–91.

Thousands of Germans left Jelenia Góra District individually and in groups – by foot, horse-drawn cart, lorry and even passenger train – in the second half of 1945. Only a minority bothered to attain 'travel passes' from Jelenia Góra District Administration before leaving in the direction of the Soviet Zone. Unlike the summer expulsions, these 'voluntary' migrations had a significant impact on the size of Jelenia Góra District's German population. The number of Germans living in the town of Jelenia Góra declined from approximately 35,000 to 19,589 between October 1945 and the end of January 1946. A similar sudden drop in the size of the German population was witnessed in Jelenia Góra District's countryside as well. In the whole of Poland's new territories, 550,000–600,000 Germans left for Germany in the final months of 1945.[32]

MASS TRANSPORTATION

Pressured and assisted 'voluntary' migration does not, in fact, account for all of the 550,000–600,000 Germans who relocated from Poland to postwar German territory in the final months of 1945. The problem of overcrowding in many localities in Poland's new territories – particularly in southern Lower Silesia and western Upper Silesia – continued to worsen at this time. It resulted from the massive and sustained influx of Polish settlers into Poland's new territories in the second half of 1945. This caused Polish officials to turn once again to more direct methods of expelling Germans from Polish territory. With the backing of the Communist-controlled Polish government and the agreement of Soviet officials, local state authorities in Lower Silesia, Upper Silesia and the Gdańsk region ignored the Allies' temporary ban on deportations to Germany and transported tens of thousands of Germans to the Soviet Zone on cargo trains between October and December 1945.[33]

Yet in most localities in Poland's new territories – including most localities in Lower Silesia, Upper Silesia and the Gdańsk region – forcible large-scale transportations of Germans did not take place in 1945. Jelenia Góra District was one of these. This was much to the annoyance of the

[32] MoRep JG Chief, 3.10.1945, APJG 123/II, sygn. 18, 127–32; Rep by the deputy head of JGTA for the Lower Silesian Commissar for Repatriation Issues in Wrocław, 26.1.1946, APW 331/VI, sygn. 360, 2–3; SiRep head JGTA, 6.12.1945, APW 331/VI, sygn. 28, 116–31; MoRep JG Chief, 3.10.1945, APJG 123/II, sygn. 18, 127–32; Rep by JG Chief for the Lower Silesian Commissar for Repatriation Issues in Wrocław, 30.1.1946, APW 331/VI, sygn. 359, 10–11. WRs in file BOD 1, 207 and file BOD 2, 188. Borodziej, 'Einleitung', pp. 76, 100; Nitschke, *Vertreibung*, p. 200.

[33] Nitschke, *Vertreibung*, pp. 197–201; Borodziej, 'Einleitung', p. 100; Hofmann, *Nachkriegszeit*, pp. 214–17.

district's Chief Official, who expended a lot of energy in the final months of 1945 trying to persuade his superiors in Lower Silesia's Regional Administration to carry out a mass expulsion of Germans from the district. In September 1945, for example, he urged the Regional Governor, Piaskowski, to utilize the existing railway connection between Jelenia Góra town and the city of Dresden, in the Soviet Zone, in order to transport 50,000 of the district's Germans westwards in just 10–12 days. He insisted that '[t]he displacement of germans [*sic*] from this district is exceptionally urgent because the inflow of Poles is already large and if the displacement is carried out any later, weather conditions will become a great obstacle'.[34] Neither this plan nor his pleas in subsequent months elicited the desired response from Wrocław.[35] Others, too, issued similar calls for the mass forced migration of Germans to get underway in Jelenia Góra District. The local branch of the Polish Socialist Party, for example, held a large rally in Jelenia Góra's municipal theatre on 7 February 1946, apparently attended by around 2,000 Polish settlers. Its goal was to 'bring forward' the 'displacement of Germans across the Nysa river'. The rally participants reportedly passed a resolution declaring that 'the whole of the German nation must suffer the consequences for the crimes it committed, [because] allowing Germans to remain in the Polish state threatens the security of our country and our economic interests'.[36]

In the early months of 1946, Polish settlers continued streaming into Poland's new territories in very large numbers – most of them transported there on the State Repatriation Office's cargo trains. As a consequence, by spring 1946 many localities in these territories had become extremely crowded. In Jelenia Góra District, there were probably as many Polish settlers living there as Germans by this time. The Germans meanwhile still numbered around 90,000. Thus, the district's overall population vastly exceeded its prewar number of 115,000.[37] The escalating levels of overcrowding – evident in many districts in Poland's new territories in early

[34] Ltr to Lower Silesia's Regional Governor, Stanisław Piaskowski, in Legnica, 10.9.1945, APW 331/VI, sygn. 359, 5–6; SiRep JGDA S-PD, 3.9.1945, APJG 123/II, sygn. 18, 86–8.

[35] MoRep JG Chief, 5.12.1945, APJG 123/II, sygn. 18, 185–200; MoRep JG Chief, 5.1.1946, APJG 123/II, sygn. 18, 206–14; Ltr to Lower Silesia's Regional Governor, Stanisław Piaskowski, 7.1.1946, APW 331/VI, sygn. 359, 7; Ltr from JG Chief to Lower Silesian Commissar for Repatriation Issues in Wrocław, 30.1.1946, APW 331/VI, sygn. 359, 10–11; MoRep JG Chief, 5.2.1946, APJG 123/II, sygn. 19, 30–37; MoRep JG Chief, 2.3.1946, APJG 123/II, sygn. 19, 73–6; MoRep JG Chief, 1.4.1946, APJG 123/II, sygn. 19, 118–21.

[36] SiRep head JGTA, 2.3.1946, APW 331/VI, sygn. 31, 7–23; Hofmann, *Nachkriegszeit*, p. 214.

[37] Rep by JG Chief, 3.7.1946, APJG 123/II, sygn. 19, 250–52; Records of Jelenia Góra's local bureau of the SRO, APW 345, sygn. 1305, 64–70; Rep by JG Chief, June 1946 APJG 123/II, sygn. 19, 245–9; Bohmann, *Menschen*, p. 209.

1946, but particularly in southern Lower Silesia and western Upper Silesia – no doubt added much impetus to efforts being made by representatives of the Polish government in Berlin at this time to convince the British authorities to start accepting huge numbers of Germans into the British Occupation Zone of Germany. In February 1946, the Communist-led government finally gained the agreement it was looking for from the British. Within days, the government launched a huge operation to transport hundreds of thousands of Germans to the British Zone in cargo trains. The Polish government referred to this operation as the 'displacement action' (*akcja wysiedleńcza*); the British referred to it as 'Operation Swallow'. It differed a great deal from the mass transportations carried out in autumn 1945. This time the transportations were orchestrated and planned by the central government in Warsaw. The 'displacement action' was also implemented throughout the new territories and not just in certain cities and towns. In short, it targeted the entire German population remaining in Poland's new territories.[38]

Cargo trains began to set off almost immediately from Lower Silesia's main city, Wrocław, in early spring 1946. The first departed for the British Zone on 19 February 1946. But it took months for the 'displacement action' to get underway in other parts of the region, including in Jelenia Góra District. Nevertheless the start of the operation had an immediate impact even on the localities where the 'displacement action' had not yet begun, because it became the principal route taken by Germans living in these localities to migrate 'voluntarily' to Allied-occupied Germany. German residents of Jelenia Góra District, for example, would travel westwards by foot or passenger train, from late February 1946 onwards, to a 'delivery point' which had been set up as part of the 'displacement action' (see the following on the purpose of the 'delivery point'). This 'delivery point' was located in the small western Lower Silesian town of Kaławsk (today called Węgliniec). On reaching Kaławsk, the residents found they could board cargo trains which were arriving, already crammed with German expellees, from areas in the new territories where the 'displacement action' was already underway, and travel in these trains to the British Zone.[39]

[38] Nitschke, *Vertreibung*, pp. 206–7; Borodziej, 'Einleitung' pp. 101–4; Hofmann, *Nachkriegszeit*, pp. 219–24.

[39] WR, Oskar S., Schreiberhau (Szklarska Poręba) 9.2.1953, BOD 2, 188, 198–203; WR, Hans T., Schmiedeberg (Kowary), late 1949, BOD 2, 188, 287–91; WR, Christian-Friedrich, Jannowitz (Janowice Wielkie), May 1946, BOD 2, 188, 269–76; WR, Paul W., Bad Warmbrunn (Cieplice Śląskie), undated, BOD 2, 188, 318–32; Hofmann, *Nachkriegszeit*, pp. 222–3, 232; Pasierb, *Migracja*, pp. 98, 119; Nitschke, *Vertreibung*, p. 218.

Hans T. and his wife relocated to the British Zone in this manner in April 1946. Before finally reaching the 'delivery point' in Kaławsk, they made three failed attempts to travel there by lorry from their home in the large village of Kowary in Jelenia Góra District. In the first two attempts, the lorries were organized by fellow Germans. In the third effort, the vehicle was supplied by Kowary's Polish state administration and the Germans were each charged 650 Reichsmarks for the journey. For reasons unknown to Hans T., the lorry used for this third attempt failed even to make it out of Kowary before the journey was called off. The Germans were given back only 350 Reichmarks from their original fee. So Hans T. and his wife decided that their next attempt to leave Kowary would be by foot. They set off on 17 April 1946 and trekked westwards for a day. They then took a passenger train from a village station to the western Lower Silesian town of Lubań and travelled from there, again by passenger train, to Kaławsk. On 19 April they boarded a 'refugee train' which had arrived in Kaławsk's 'delivery point' from the eastern Lower Silesian town of Ząbkowice Śląskie and were transported to Lower Saxony in western Germany.[40]

It was around this time that Lower Silesia's Commissar for Repatriation Issues, Roman Fundowicz, visited Jelenia Góra town. He did so to discuss the start of the 'displacement action' in Jelenia Góra District with the district's Chief Official and other officials. A detailed plan was subsequently drawn up for the 'first phase' of the district's 'displacement action'.[41] In the next few weeks, local state officials put up posters in the district's villages informing residents that the 'displacement action' was about to begin. These notices cited a British statement announcing that the 'German population in Poland' would be 'absorbed in the west'.[42]

In overall charge of the 'displacement action' throughout Poland's new territories was the Communist-led government's State Repatriation Office. It set up a so-called 'collection point' next to the railway on Łomnicka Street, at the eastern edge of Jelenia Góra town, at some point in May. Germans from villages throughout Jelenia Góra District were to be gathered there and loaded onto cargo trains for transportation to the British Zone. This 'collection point' was nothing more than a rudimentary camp

[40] WR, Hans T., Schmiedeberg (Kowary), late 1949, BOD 2, 188, 287–91.

[41] Plan for the first phase of the displacement of Germans from Jelenia Góra District, [10].4.1946, sent from JGDA to LSRA, APW 331/VI, sygn. 359, 103–5; Pasierb, 'Problemy', p. 35.

[42] SiRep JGDA head S-PD, 3.6.1946, APJG 123/II, sygn. 19, 242–3; WR, Robert W., Ludwigsdorf (Chromiec), undated, BOD 1, 207, 133–8; WR, Adolf G., Bärndorf (Gruszków), undated, BOD 1, 207, 21–4; WR, Adolf G., Bärndorf (Gruszków), 21.9.1952, BOD 2, 188, 7–9; WR, Karl M., Jannowitz (Janowice Wielkie), undated, BOD 1, 207, 97–9.

composed of bare wooden huts. It was established on the site of a former Reich Labour Service camp from the Nazi period.[43]

The 'displacement action' finally got underway in Jelenia Góra District on 23 May 1946 when the first cargo train was sent off from Jelenia Góra's 'collection point' to the British Zone. In the first week of the action, Germans were brought to the camp on Łomnicka Street almost exclusively from the town of Jelenia Góra. Liesbeth E. recalled being marched there in the first days of the action in a long column of residents from the former Kaiser Friedrich Street in Hirschberg/Jelenia Góra town.[44] But within days, committees of administrative officials and armed Citizens' Militia personnel, wearing red and white armbands, started turning up at Germans' homes in villages throughout the district. They issued deportation orders to the Germans and usually gave them no more than 24 hours – and sometimes as little as 20 minutes – to prepare to leave their homes for the last time. They rarely allowed the Germans to take with them any more than 20 kilograms of luggage. They also often seized items from the baggage before the Germans departed from their villages.[45] In the large village of Szklarska Poręba, there were reportedly instances of Polish gangs coming at night to Germans' homes to steal their conveniently packed luggage, having been tipped off by corrupt state officials about which Germans were to be transported the next day.[46]

In most cases the Germans seem to have been taken from the district's villages to the collection camp on Łomnicka Street in groups of just over 30 individuals. Local Germans who had been working for the district's Polish commune administrations often assisted the Polish committees in selecting which Germans would make up each contingent. Many were marched all

43 Ltr from JG Chief to the Lower Silesian Commissar for Repatriation Issues in Wrocław, 5.6.1946, APW 331/VI, sygn. 359, 51; Ltr from the head of Jelenia Góra's local bureau of the SRO to the regional headquarters of the SRO in Wrocław, 3.10.1947, APW 345, sygn. 1305, 8; WR, Adolph G., Bärndorf (Gruszków), undated, BOD 1, 207, 21–4; WR, Walter F., Zillerthal-Erdmannsdorf (Mysłakowice), 17.3.1952, BOD 1, 207, 259; WR, Robert W., Ludwigsdorf (Chromiec), undated. BOD 1, 207, 133–8; WR, Reinhold K., Altkemnitz (Stara Kamienica), 4.4.1953, BOD 1, 207, 13–14; WR, Walter S.-G., Niederschreiberhau (Szklarska Poręba Dolna), 10.1.1948, BOD 2, 188, 175–97.

44 Documents for transport no. 1 from Jelenia Góra, 23.5.1946, APW 345, sygn. 1306, 2–8; Ltr from JG Chief to the Lower Silesian Commissar for Repatriation Issues in Wrocław, 5.6.1946, APW 331/VI, sygn. 359, 51; Figures on Jelenia Góra town's German population compiled by JGTA, 5.7.1946, APJG 130, sygn. 251, 165; WR, Liesbeth E., Hirschberg (Jelenia Góra) town, 14.10.1952, BOD 2, 188, 24–9; Pasierb, 'Problemy', pp. 35–7.

45 SiRep JGDA head S-PD, 3.6.1946, APJG 123/II, sygn. 19, 242–3. WRs: BOD 1, 207, 133–8; BOD 1, 207, 97–9; BOD 1, 207, 29–32; BOD 2, 188, 175–97; BOD 2, 188, 122–37; BOD 2, 188, 14–17; BOD 2, 188, 169–74; BOD 1, 207, 21–4; BOD 2, 188, 7–9; BOD 1, 207, 127–30; BOD 2, 188, 24–9; BOD 1, 207, 43–4. Jankowiak, 'Wrocławskie', p. 413.

46 WR, Ilse R., Schreiberhau (Szklarska Poręba), September 1946, BOD 2, 188, 139–48; WR, Ursula R., Niederschreiberhau (Szklarska Poręba Dolna), 10.3.1954, BOD 2, 188, 122–37.

the way to the camp from their villages. This often entailed very long treks, weighed down by heavy luggage. Other Germans were crammed onto horse-carts for this trip to the camp or transported there on passenger trains and trams.[47] The moment a group of villagers set off for the camp may often have been marked by a collective gathering of the remaining villagers. One example happened in the village of Ludwigsdorf/Chromiec. Robert W. recalled the sadness expressed before he and over 30 other villagers were marched off to the collection camp in Jelenia Góra town on 6 June 1946: 'The whole village was gathered for our departure. We sang a farewell song.'[48]

On arrival at the collection camp on Łomnicka Street, the Germans were subjected to a thorough 'customs inspection'. One of the bare huts functioned as a makeshift 'customs office'. The Germans were made to queue up outside this hut and slowly file through it with their luggage. The Polish officials performing these inspections often confiscated items of luggage. The government put in place tight restrictions on the quantity and type of luggage the Germans were permitted to 'export' from Poland. According to the government's regulations, the Germans were allowed to take only as much luggage as they could physically carry. They were also forbidden to bring specific objects of value with them, such as radios, cameras and artwork. Yet many of the confiscations made by local 'customs officials' were not in line with the regulations. The temptation to seize items for personal enrichment often proved far too great for the poorly paid Polish officials working in the camp. Similar abuses by Polish officials were witnessed at 'collection points' across Poland's new territories. Furthermore, because of British concerns about inflation in the British Zone, the amount of currency Germans were allowed to take with them was greatly restricted. One thousand Reichsmarks was permitted per person from June 1946 onwards and any amount of Reichsmarks which exceeded this limit was confiscated by the Polish state authorities.[49]

Many Germans were loaded onto the cargo trains within hours of arriving at Jelenia Góra's collection camp on Łomnicka Street. Others were forced to spend the night or even several nights there. Adolph G. claimed that he and fellow locals from the village of Bärndorf/Gruszków suffered

[47] WRs: BOD 1, 207, 171–5; BOD 1, 207, 127–30; BOD 1, 207, 133–8; BOD 1, 207, 21–4; BOD 2, 188, 7–9; BOD 1, 207, 29–32; BOD 1, 207, 43–4; BOD 1, 207, 159–62; BOD, 207, 239–42; BOD 1, 207, 97–9; BOD 1, 207, 243–9; BOD 2, 188, 175–97.

[48] WR, Robert W., Ludwigsdorf (Chromiec), undated, BOD 1, 207, 133–8.

[49] WRs: BOD 2, 188, 175–97; BOD 2, 188, 169–74; BOD 2, 188, 14–17; BOD 1, 207, 127–30; BOD 1, 207, 43–4; BOD 1 207, 239–42; BOD 1, 207, 133–8; BOD 1, 207, 29–32. Hofmann, *Nachkriegszeit*, pp. 223–5, 230; Jankowiak, 'Wrocławskie', pp. 413–14.

three days at the camp at the start of June 1946 before their train finally departed. They received no food at all during this time.[50] The Polish authorities let the collection camp become extremely crowded in early summer 1946. As a result, some Germans were forced to spend the nights in the open.[51] Each cargo wagon was crammed with 30 to 35 Germans and sometimes even more than that. The journeys were therefore intensely uncomfortable. Usually these were the same 30 to 35 villagers who had been taken to the camp together; each wagon therefore seemed to represent a different village of the district.[52]

From Jelenia Góra's collection camp the cargo trains first travelled eastwards to the village of Marciszów, before turning northwards to the town of Legnica and then westwards to the 'delivery point' in Kaławsk. This short journey took a surprisingly long time. Walter S.-G. from Niederschreiberhau/Szklarska Poręba Dolna claimed that it took five days for his train merely to reach Kaławsk. He recalled his journey on a cargo train, which departed from the Łomnicka Street camp on 19 June 1946:

> We rolled along for five days in terrible confinement, barely able to sit, basically unable to sleep, without hot or cold water . . . The hours and days in the clattering goods wagons dragged on and on . . . Small children cried and wept, day and night . . . . It was unbearable. Some spread themselves out. Others barely had space to sit. Everywhere that symbol of our times made itself apparent: Egoism . . . At one point the train stopped between a small station and a village. We [were able to get out of the wagon briefly, so] collected . . . some bits of wood and coal to light a fire. This was the first chance in the entire journey to cook something warm to eat . . . [The wagon had a] sliding door which could not be fully shut so that especially at night a strong draught of cold air was let in.[53]

The trains halted for some time at the 'delivery point' in Kaławsk before travelling onwards. A British Military Mission had been stationed there

[50] WR, Adolph G., Bärndorf (Gruszków), undated, BOD 1, 207, 21–4; WR, Adolph G., Bärndorf (Gruszków), 21.9.1952, BOD 2, 188, 7–9. WRs: BOD 2, 188, 14–17; BOD 2, 188, 169–74; BOD 1, 207, 133–8; BOD 2, 188, 24–9; BOD 2, 188, 175–97.

[51] WR, Oskar S., Berbisdorf (Dziwiszów), undated, BOD 1, 207, 29–32; Jankowiak, 'Wrocławskie', pp. 412–13.

[52] Ltr from JG Chief to the Lower Silesian Commissar for Repatriation Issues in Wrocław, 5.6.1946, APW 331/VI, sygn. 359, 51. Documents for transport no. 23 compiled by Jelenia Góra's local bureau of the SRO, 14.6.1946, APW 345, sygn. 1328; Documents compiled by Jelenia Góra's local bureau of the SRO for the trains departing in 1946–47, APW 345, sygn. 1306–73; Figures on the transportation of Germans from Jelenia Góra's 'Collection Point' compiled by Jelenia Góra's local bureau of the SRO, APW 345, sygn. 1305, 64–70; Customs clearance certificate for transport no. 1 from Jelenia Góra District, 23.5.1946, APW 345, sygn. 1306, 2. WRs: BOD 2, 188, 175–97; BOD 2, 188, 24–9; BOD 2, 188, 14–17; BOD 1 207, 239–42; BOD 1, 207, 243–9; BOD 2, 188, 169–74. Hofmann, *Nachkriegszeit*, p. 224.

[53] WR, Walter S.-G., Niederschreiberhau (Szklarska Poręba Dolna), 10.1.1948, BOD 2, 188, 175–97.

to inspect the trains and their human cargo. The Germans were doused in the insecticide DDT at the 'delivery point' before being allowed to reboard the trains. From Kaławsk the cargo trains crossed the nearby border with the Soviet Zone and travelled across the zone to reception camps located just inside the British Zone. Most Germans from Jelenia Góra District appear to have been taken to a reception camp in the village of Mariental near Helmstedt. According to Richard B. from Hirschberg/Jelenia Góra town, who was transported from the Łomnicka Street collection camp in late May 1946, this journey took 14 days in total. These were therefore long journeys and the Germans received very little food to sustain them along the way. Each wagon was generally given just a few loaves of bread and some salted herrings to share out. This forced the Germans to get by on the limited amount of food they had been permitted by local Polish officials to bring with them from their homes. The Germans had been wrongly informed by these officials that three days' rations would suffice. We shall discuss what happened to the German expellees after they left the British Zone's reception camps and how they coped with starting a new life in western Germany in the Conclusion.[54]

The 'first phase' of Jelenia Góra District's 'displacement action' was carried out between 23 May and 30 June 1946. A huge number of Germans were transported to the British Zone from Jelenia Góra District during this period. In the final week of May alone, 12,626 were sent off from Jelenia Góra's collection camp to the British Zone. All but 1,000 of them were residents of the town of Jelenia Góra. This meant that the town's German population plummeted from approximately 19,000 to 7,199 between 23 May and 1 June 1946. In the following month, a total of almost 45,000 Germans were transported to the British Zone. This time all but 1,800 of them came from the district's countryside rather than Jelenia Góra town. The vast majority of the Germans transported in both May and June 1946 – probably over three-quarters of them in total – were women and children. Most local German men still alive after the war had not yet returned home from Allied prisoner-of-war camps. In total, 34 cargo trains departed from the 'collection point' on Łomnicka Street in the 'first phase' of the 'displacement action', transporting over 57,000 Germans to the British Zone. In little more than a month, therefore, Jelenia Góra District's remaining German population had been reduced in size by

[54] WR, Richard B., Hirschberg (Jelenia Góra) town, 15.7.1952, BOD 2, 188, 14–17. WRs: BOD 1, 207, 133–8; BOD 2, 188, 169–74; BOD 1, 207, 127–30; BOD 2, 188, 175–97; BOD 1, 207, 21–4; BOD 2, 188, 7–9; BOD 2, 188, 24–9. Jankowiak, 'Wrocławskie', p. 414; Hofmann, *Nachkriegszeit*, pp. 222–4.

60 per cent. The district's Chief Official remarked that Germans were 'no longer visible on the canvas of everyday life'.[55]

As we shall discuss in Chapter 5, this transformed general living conditions for the Polish settlers who had recently come to live in Jelenia Góra District. On the other hand, the district's population remained much larger than its prewar size, and in summer 1946 the district's Chief Official continued pleading with his superiors in Lower Silesia's Regional Administration in Wrocław to cease sending cargo trains carrying Polish settlers to the district. Similar overcrowding faced by officials in many other localities in Poland's new territories kept the pressure on Poland's government to sustain the massive scope of the 'displacement action' throughout 1946. This was despite the fact that Germans were, by this time, increasingly in the minority in these places.

From July 1946 onwards, the government's State Repatriation Office began sending cargo trains to the Soviet Occupation Zone after the Communist-led government's representatives reached an agreement with the Soviet Zone's officials in Berlin. As a result, despite the fact that the British Zone's authorities reduced the number of Germans they were willing to accept in summer 1946, the Polish authorities were able to continue sending huge numbers of Germans westwards in summer and autumn 1946.[56] Yet Jelenia Góra District's own 'displacement action' remained on hold for several months after June 1946. There were still over 25,000 Germans living in the district in early autumn 1946 and local officials yearned for the 'displacement action' to restart. In October 1946, preparations for the 'second phase of the repatriation of Germans' from Jelenia Góra District finally got underway. The cargo trains began departing again at the start of November.[57]

[55] Ltr from JG Chief to the Lower Silesian Commissar for Repatriation Issues in Wrocław, 5.6.1946, APW 331/VI, sygn. 359, 51; Figures on the size of the German population from November 1945 to July 1946, compiled by JGTA, 5.7.1946, APJG, 130, sygn. 251, 165; Figures compiled by Jelenia Góra's local bureau of the SRO, APW 345, sygn. 1305, 3; SiRep JG Chief, 3.7.1946, APJG 123/II, sygn. 19, 250–52; SiRep JGDA head S-PD, 1.7.1946, APJG 123/II, sygn. 19, 273–4; Rep by JGDA head S-PD, 30.7.1946, APW 331/VI, sygn. 34, 35–7; Figures compiled by Jelenia Góra's local bureau of the SRO, APW 345, sygn. 1305, 64–70; WR, Christian-Friedrich, Jannowitz (Janowice Wielkie), May 1946, BOD 2, 188, 269–76; Jankowiak, 'Wrocławskie', pp. 417–18; Pasierb, 'Problemy', p. 37; Pasierb, *Migracja*, p. 135.

[56] Rep by JG Chief, 3.7.1946, APJG 123/II, sygn. 19, 250–52; SiRep JG Chief, 3.3.1947, APJG 123/II, sygn. 21, 33–8; Hofmann, *Nachkriegszeit*, pp. 224–5; Pasierb, *Migracja*, pp. 113, 116, Nitschke, *Vertreibung*, pp. 223–6.

[57] Rep by JGDA head S-PD, 29.8.1946, APJG 123/II, sygn. 19, 355; Rep by JGDA head S-PD, 31.10.1946, APJG 123/II, sygn. 19, 410–11; Note from JG Chief to the Lower Silesian Commissar for Repatriation Issues, Fundowicz, 11.10.1946, APW 331/VI, sygn. 359, 59; Rep by JG Chief, 2.11.1946, APJG 123/II, sygn. 19, 401–5.

Journeys to the Soviet Zone from districts throughout Poland's new territories took place under extremely harsh weather conditions in the final months of 1946. The winter of 1946–7 was a particularly brutal one. Already in early November 1946 it was snowing. This was when Johannes F. from Hirschberg/Jelenia Góra town was transported. He and his family were forced to endure a terrible night without shelter in this weather at the collection camp on Łomnicka Street before their train finally departed. They were loaded onto a cattle wagon which was supplied with only 'pathetic' amounts of food and fuel for the journey to the Soviet Zone.[58] The weather obviously got much worse as the winter properly set in. The fact that food rations remained meagre and the cargo wagons were draughty and barely heated greatly exacerbated the Germans' ordeal. Some of the Germans transported from Jelenia Góra at this time may even have travelled on completely unheated wagons, because fuel and heating stoves were often stolen from cargo trains before they were sent back from Germany. The Polish authorities took a ruthless attitude by refusing to reduce the scope of the 'displacement action' in response to these thefts. Several trains arrived in both the British and Soviet Zones from Poland's new territories in December 1946 with the corpses of Germans who had frozen to death along the way. This finally caused both British and Soviet officials to reject further deportations to their zones at the start of January 1947. In subsequent days, they only accepted those trains which had already been prepared for the journeys.[59]

From Jelenia Góra District's 'collection point' 12 cargo trains departed for the Soviet Zone during the 'second phase' of the district's 'displacement action' between November 1946 and January 1947. Not all of the Germans on these trains were from Jelenia Góra District. Many 'collection points' in Poland's new territories were closed down in early autumn 1946. After this, Jelenia Góra's 'collection point' functioned as a place to gather and transport not only Germans from Jelenia Góra District but also those from neighbouring Lwówek Śląski District, Złotoryja District, Kamienna Góra District and Jawor District. Nevertheless, these trains reduced the number of Germans living in Jelenia Góra District to fewer than 12,000.[60]

58 WR, Johannes F., Hirschberg (Jelenia Góra) town, 19.12.1949, BOD 2, 188, 32–4.

59 Hofmann, *Nachkriegszeit*, pp. 235–7; Jankowiak, 'Wrocławskie', pp. 419–20; WR, Robert W., Ludwigsdorf (Chromiec), undated, BOD 1, 207, 133–8; WR, Johannes F., Hirschberg (Jelenia Góra) town, 19.12.1949, BOD 2, 188, 32–4.

60 Rep by JG Chief, 4.12.1946, APW 331/VI, sygn. 38, 100–101; Figures compiled by Jelenia Góra's local bureau of the SRO, APW 345, 1305, 64–70; SiRep JG Chief, 2.1.1947, APW 331/VI, sygn. 39, 15–17; Rep by JG Chief, 1.2.1947, APW 331/VI, sygn. 51, 1–4; Pasierb, 'Problemy', pp. 30, 40; Pasierb, *Migracja*, pp. 117, 136–7; Hofmann, *Nachkriegszeit*, pp. 225–6; Jankowiak, 'Wrocławskie', p. 407.

Interestingly, a small number of Jewish Germans were transported to postwar German territory in the 'second phase'. Shortly before the local Polish authorities got this phase underway, a leading official at Jelenia Góra District Administration sent a letter to Lower Silesia's Regional Administration in Wrocław asking two questions: Should 'German citizens of Jewish descent' be displaced from the district? And if so, should they undergo 'voluntary displacement' or 'forced displacement like the Germans'?

Lower Silesia's Commissar for Repatriation Issues in Wrocław, Roman Fundowicz, was apparently flummoxed by these questions. He forwarded the enquiry to the Main Delegate for Repatriation Issues at the Ministry for Recovered Territories, Józef Jaroszek. The latter's response was brief: 'I must stress that it is our task to repatriate the German population.'[61] This answer seemed ambiguous. But if we take into account the treatment German Jews generally received in Poland's new territories at this time, his meaning was clear: No differentiation should be made between non-Jewish and Jewish Germans. Both needed to be displaced from Poland in order to achieve the Communist-controlled government's goal of Polish ethno-national homogeneity in Poland's new territories. The government did not feel that either the Germans who had suffered as political opponents of the Nazi regime before 1945 or Jewish Germans should be spared from expulsion after the war. With few exceptions, all surviving Jewish Germans were therefore transported to the British and Soviet Zones after 1946.

At one point, midway through 1947, the Ministry for Recovered Territories considered changing Poland's policy towards Jewish Germans. It considered granting Jewish Germans the right to stay in Poland as long as they could prove their Jewish descent and had previously demonstrated a 'loyal attitude' towards the Polish nation. But nothing ultimately came of this proposal. As Andreas Hofmann has eloquently written: 'The surviving German Jewish [residents of the prewar eastern German provinces], who like the overwhelming majority of German Jews had until 1933 viewed themselves, in the first place, as members of the German nation, suddenly found themselves after 1945 once again sharing the fate of the German people.'[62] The expulsion of Jewish Germans from Poland's new territories, then, is a striking symbol of the fact that the primary objective of

[61] Letters from JGDA head S-PD (11.9.1946), from Lower Silesia's Commissar for Repatriation Issues in Wrocław, Roman Fundowicz (30.9.1946), and from the Main Delegate for Repatriation Issues at the Ministry for Recovered Territories, Józef Jaroszek (30.10.1946), APW 331/VI, sygn. 359, 64.

[62] Hofmann, *Nachkriegszeit*, pp. 371–7. Although it is true that some Polish Jews managed to convince the Polish authorities that they were in fact German Jews in order to board cargo trains to Allied-occupied Germany (see Fleming, *Communism*, pp. 49–50), it is not the case that all German Jews

the forced migration of Germans was not revenge for Nazi German crimes but rather the ethno-national homogenization of these territories. '[T]he German element', declared Jelenia Góra District's Chief Official in January 1947, 'is being conclusively eradicated.'[63]

GERMAN LABOUR

To restate our argument thus far, the forced migration of Germans from Poland's new territories after the Second World War was tied tightly together with the simultaneous policy of systematically repopulating these territories with Polish settlers. Not only were both processes the product of the Communist-led Polish government's postwar campaign of ethno-national homogenization, but also the policy of repopulating Poland's new territories with Polish settlers played an important practical role in instigating and sustaining the pace of the expulsion of Germans in the second half of 1945 and throughout 1946.

At around the start of 1947, however, the role the repopulation process played in the expulsion process changed. It continued to help determine the pace of the forced migration of Germans but now acted as both brake and accelerator on the process. This resulted from the fact that the policies of expelling Germans and resettling Poles were locked tightly together not only by the ideological goal of establishing Polish ethno-national homogeneity in Poland's new territories but also by a more pragmatic factor: the need to preserve the pool of skilled labour in these territories. By 1946 the Polish government had recognized that if they were to rid the new territories of all Germans at once, industrial production would quickly collapse. There would not be enough skilled workers to sustain the territories' factories and workshops. The Polish authorities could rapidly expel all unskilled Germans from the new territories without harming the local economy. But Germans with important skills needed to be kept back until Polish settlers with equivalent training and qualifications arrived to replace them. In this crucial respect, the arrival of Polish settlers set the speed at which the remaining phases of the 'displacement action' were implemented.

The need to preserve the new territories' supply of skilled German workers was reflected in the plans and proposals for mass transportation which Jelenia Góra District's Chief Official sent to Lower Silesia's Regional

living in Lower Silesia before 1945 were gone by the end of the war, as recently stated, for example, by Ewa Waszkiewicz, 'A History of Jewish Settlement in Lower Silesia, 1945–1950', *Polin: Studies in Polish Jewry*, 23, 2011, p. 507.

[63] SiRep JG Chief, 2.1.1947, APW 331/VI, sygn. 39, 15–17.

Administration in Wrocław in autumn 1945 and early 1946. In his September 1945 plan, for example, he called for the transportation of only 65 per cent of the district's Germans at first, because the remaining 35 per cent were 'experts, scientists and other specialists who are needed for the time being for normal life to continue developing'. Similarly, his so-called coordinated resettlement plan which he presented to Lower Silesia's Regional Administration at the end of January 1946 proposed three phases of mass transportation. In the first phase 'unemployed' and 'burdensome' Germans would be displaced. In the second phase the unskilled and low-skilled 60 per cent of the German labour force would go. In the third phase most of the remainder would be transported. But 'specialist workers' (and their families) would be kept back in the district for an undetermined period of time.[64]

Poland's Communist-controlled government in Warsaw set out four phases for the 'displacement action' in early 1946. In the first phase, all Germans who were unable to work would be transported to Allied-occupied Germany. The government estimated that these people made up around 50 per cent of postwar Poland's entire remaining German population. In the second phase, the Germans employed by private businesses would be transported. These people were estimated at 25 per cent of all remaining Germans. In the third phase, the low- and medium-skilled workers employed by state-run factories and workplaces would go. This would leave behind only workers with specialist expertise (and their dependent relatives), who were said to constitute only around 10 per cent of the remaining German population. The government envisaged that the last category of Germans would not be transported until a much later fourth phase of the action.[65]

With the need to preserve the new territories' resources of skilled labour in mind, the government ordered all state and private employers in January 1946 to compile lists of the Germans working for them whom they regarded as indispensable for their businesses. Based on this information, Germans were issued one of three types of coloured 'labour certificates'. Those categorized as unskilled or low-skilled workers received white labour certificates. Medium-skilled workers received blue certificates. Highly skilled workers received red ones. As the Polish authorities implemented this process in

[64] Ltr from JG Chief to Lower Silesia's Regional Governor, Stanisław Piaskowski in Legnica, 10.9.1945, APW 331/VI, sygn. 359, 5–6; Ltr from JG Chief to Lower Silesian Commissar for Repatriation Issues in Wrocław, 30.1.1946, APW 331/VI, sygn. 359, 10–11.

[65] Jankowiak, 'Wrocławskie', p. 406; Hofmann, *Nachkriegszeit*, pp. 220–1; MoRep JG Chief, 5.2.1946, APJG 123/II, sygn. 19, 30–37.

Jelenia Góra District, the lists first needed to be approved by officials at either the District Administration (*Starostwo*) or the Town Administration (*Zarząd Miejski*). After this the district's labour office could issue the Germans the particular coloured labour certificates which corresponded with their specific levels of qualifications and training.[66]

Crucially, each certificate, whatever its colour, was supposed to protect its holder from eviction from a home, internment in a camp and expulsion to Germany. In principle, none of these things could happen until the holder's certificate was formally revoked by state administrative officials. But in practice the treatment of certificate holders diverged considerably from the regulations. In Jelenia Góra District, for example, possession of a certificate offered Germans only partial protection from eviction from their homes. In fact, the district's authorities removed many certificate holders from their homes at this time to free this accommodation up for arriving Polish settlers. They also forced many certificate holders to live together with Polish settlers in their own homes. These practices probably affected low-skilled white-certificate and medium-skilled blue-certificate holders far more than they did the holders of red certificates – who do seem to have been spared from evictions in the main.[67]

Poland's Communist-led government expected all state and private employers to replace white- and blue-certificate holders with Polish workers as quickly as possible. This would mean that their labour certificates could be revoked and they could be expelled to Germany. But to achieve this, the state authorities often had to subject Polish employers to considerable pressure. Both state-run and private enterprises often proved very reluctant to release their low-skilled German workers for displacement to Germany, in part because the Germans were more experienced in their jobs than arriving Polish settlers. Even more important was the fact that German workers did not have to be paid as much as Poles. This partly explains why in July 1946 Jelenia Góra District's Chief Official wrote to his superiors in Lower Silesia's Regional Administration with the request that they cease transporting eastern Polish 'repatriates' to the district on the specific ground that there were not a sufficient number of jobs for them there.[68]

[66] Ltr from JG Chief to Lower Silesia's Commissar for Repatriation Issues, 30.1.1946, APW 331/VI, sygn. 359, 10–11; Hofmann, *Nachkriegszeit*, pp. 244–5.

[67] Ltr from JG Chief to Lower Silesia's Commissar for Repatriation Issues, 30.1.1946, APW 331/VI, sygn. 359, 10–11; Rep by the deputy head of JGTA for the Commissar for Repatriation Issues in Wrocław, 26.1.1946, APW 331/VI, sygn. 360, 2–3; MoRep JG Chief, 5.2.1946, APJG 123/II, sygn. 19, 30–37; MoRep JG Chief, 2.3.1946, APJG 123/II, sygn. 19, 73–6; Hofmann, *Nachkriegszeit*, pp. 244–5.

[68] Hofmann, *Nachkriegszeit*, pp. 247–8; Jankowiak, 'Wrocławskie', p. 425; Ltr from the clerk of the public electricity plant in Szklarska Poręba to the Ministry for Recovered Territories,

Individual Polish settler-farmers were also unhappy about losing their German workers through expulsion. At the start of June 1946, the local German farmer, Robert W. from Ludwigsdorf/Chromiec, registered himself and his family for the second contingent of 30 villagers to be sent to Jelenia Góra's 'collection point' on Łomnicka Street for transportation to the British Zone. But before Robert W.'s family could be sent to the camp, he had been removed from the 'displacement list' by the Polish farmer he worked for, on the farm he had previously owned. The farmer evidently did not want to lose the labour and local farming expertise which Robert W. had so far been providing for him.[69]

The Ministry for Recovered Territories stepped up its pressure on the new territories' local state officials in the summer of 1946 to make sure that all unskilled and low-skilled German workers were removed from at least private employment. The ministry was particularly keen to have Germans removed from 'visible' workplaces, by which it meant shops, restaurants and the like. In Jelenia Góra District, posters were put up in every village in August 1946 displaying an order which prohibited the employment of Germans in hotels, restaurants and similar businesses. In October 1946, just before the 'second phase' of the 'displacement action' started in Jelenia Góra District, the district's Chief Official reported that Germans were no longer being employed in shops, restaurants and hotels. A large number, however, were apparently still working in factories, on state farms and in 'public works' such as road maintenance.[70]

The ministry also took action at this time to tighten Poland's grip on the most highly skilled workers among the remaining German population of the new territories. In July 1946 it introduced new green labour certificates for specialist German workers 'of statewide economic importance'. Those skilled workers who did not receive the new green certificates – and instead kept their blue or red certificates – were now described as having skills of only 'regional importance'. The new territories' local state officials were warned that green-certificate holders should not, under any

2.8.1946, APW 331/VI, sygn. 359, 96; Ltr from the director of the State Hospital in Cieplice to LSRA's Health Department, 2.11.1946, APW 331/VI, sygn. 359, 100; SiRep JGDA S-PD, 3.6.1946, APJG 123/II, sygn. 19, 242–3; MoRep JG Chief, 3.7.1946, APJG 123/II, sygn. 19, 250–52.

69 WR, Robert W., Ludwigsdorf (Chromiec), undated, BOD 1, 207, 133–8.

70 Note from JG Chief to the Lower Silesia Commissar for Repatriation Issues in Wrocław, 11.10.1946, concerning the implementation of Regional Governor Piaskowski's order of 25.7.1946, APW 331/VI, sygn. 359, 59; Rep by JGDA S-PD, 29.8.1946, APJG 123/II, sygn. 19, 355; SiRep JG Chief, 2.11.1946, APJG 123/II, sygn. 19, 401–5; Hofmann, *Nachkriegszeit*, pp. 248–52; Jankowiak, 'Wrocławskie', p. 403.

circumstances, be transported to Germany without the ministry first granting permission.[71]

One Polish settler who migrated to Jelenia Góra District from the Vilnius region (incorporated into Soviet Lithuania in July 1944) in 1946 gave a first-hand account of the process of replacing skilled German workers with equivalently skilled Poles:

> The war had put my studies of mathematical and natural sciences on hold. I had some experience of office work [having worked for some time at a Tax Office in the town of Święciany in the Vilnius region]. After a long discussion with my wife, we decided [that she would take over the running of our new farm in Karpacz in Jelenia Góra District and] I would go to work elsewhere, helping her on the farm in my free time. On 11 December 1946 I replaced the last German employee at the paper factory in Karpacz in the position of accountant. I took over his desk. He told me he had worked there for 35 years. He would soon leave for the Vaterland. Two paper machines were already running again [having stopped operating in the final phase of the war] and were now being run by two of our specialists. One was in the hands of Stanisław Żyła. The other was under the control of Owsik, an old paper maker [*papiernik*] from Landwarów near Vilnius.[72]

So in the course of 1946 a government-imposed hierarchy of skills had determined which Germans were transported to the British and Soviet Zones from Poland's new territories and which ones were kept back. This was clearly in evidence in Jelenia Góra District, where it was essentially only unskilled and low-skilled white-certificate holders and what the district's Chief Official termed 'the most burdensome element' who were transported to Allied-occupied Germany during 1946. By 'the most burdensome element', the district's Chief official explained he meant single mothers with children, elderly individuals and 'cripples'. Most of the roughly 12,000 Germans remaining in Jelenia Góra District by the start of 1947 were therefore blue-, red- and green-certificate holders (and their dependant relatives). All subsequent phases of the 'displacement action' were aimed, above all, at weaning Polish employers off the cheap skilled German labour they had become used to since 1945.[73]

The 'displacement action' recommenced across Poland's new territories in April 1947 after the signing of a new agreement between Polish and

[71] Hofmann, *Nachkriegszeit*, pp. 248–52; Jankowiak, 'Wrocławskie', p. 403.

[72] Stanisław Czepułkowski, 'W Karpaczu', in Kotlarska, *Pamiętniki*, pp. 281, 291.

[73] MoRep JG Chief, 5.2.1946, APJG 123/II, sygn. 19, 30–7; Rep by JGDA head S-PD, 1.7.1946, APJG 123/II, sygn. 19, 273–4; SiRep JG Chief 2.11.1946, APJG 123/II, sygn. 19, 401–5; SiRep JG Chief, 2.1.1947, APW 331/VI, sygn. 39, 15–17; Figures compiled by JGTA, 1.1.1947, APJG 130, sygn. 251, 218. WR, Robert W., Ludwigsdorf (Chromiec), undated, BOD 1, 207, 133–8. Jankowiak, 'Wrocławskie', pp. 417–18; Hofmann, *Nachkriegszeit*, pp. 229, 245.

Soviet officials.[74] In Jelenia Góra District, the authorities began preparing for the 'third phase' of the 'displacement action' in late March by registering all remaining Germans.[75] Starting in late April 1947, nine trains departed for the Soviet Zone from the Łomnicka Street collection camp in the first three months of the 'third phase'.[76]

Throughout Poland's new territories, the conditions which Germans experienced improved a great deal when the 'displacement action' resumed in spring 1947. The journeys were still extremely unpleasant and still involved very cramped cargo wagons. But the Polish authorities provided larger food rations than in 1946 and higher levels of medical supervision at the 'collection points' and in the trains. Officials also took a more lenient attitude when inspecting the food provisions Germans had brought with them from home. In addition, Poland's Communist-controlled government made efforts to reduce the scope for abuse and corruption by local state officials during 1947. For example, the government ordered local state authorities to take action to prevent 'informal committees' from carrying out unauthorized 'luggage inspections' in villages before Germans were sent off to the 'collection points'.[77] These practices, however, were by no means completely stamped out in 1947. The Deputy Chief Official of Jelenia Góra District reported in June, for example, that 'some local mayors arbitrarily seize belongings [from Germans] and allow destruction and looting to go on by not securing the homes of the people who have been displaced'. In the weeks after this, he fired a number of officials from local 'displacement committees' because of the 'abuses' they had been committing.[78]

In the first three months of Jelenia Góra District's 'third phase', the authorities constantly stepped up the pressure on local factories to replace skilled German workers with Polish settlers. In May 1947, Lower Silesia's Regional Governor, Stanisław Piaskowski, went further, cancelling all blue and red labour certificates. In July, Piaskowski's Regional Administration then ordered a clampdown on the green certificates, instructing local officials to cancel any of them which they saw as 'unnecessary'. Jelenia Góra District's authorities responded to Wrocław's order by appointing

[74] Hofmann, *Nachkriegszeit*, pp. 225, 237–8; Jankowiak, 'Wrocławskie', pp. 420–1; Pasierb, *Migracja*, p. 119; Nitschke *Vertreibung*, pp. 239–42.

[75] Rep by JGDA head S-PD, 31.5.1947, APJG 123/II, sygn. 21, 134.

[76] SiRep JG Chief, 30.4.1947, APW 331/VI, sygn. 51, 18–19; Rep by JGDA S-PD, 30.4.1947, APW 331/VI, sygn. 51, 17; SiRep JG DepChief, 31.5.1947, APW 331/VI, sygn. 51, 20–21; Pasierb, *Migracja*, pp. 119–20, 137; Jankowiak, 'Wrocławskie', pp. 422–3; Borodziej, 'Einleitung', p. 105.

[77] Jankowiak, 'Wrocławskie', pp. 421, 423; Hofmann, *Nachkriegszeit*, pp. 225, 238; Nitschke, *Vertreibung*, pp. 239–40.

[78] SiRep JG DepChief, 5.[7].1947, APJG 123/II, sygn. 21, 167–8 and 198; Rep by JG DepChief for LSRA S-PD, 31.7.1947, APJG 123/II, sygn. 21, 199–201.

special 'screening committees' to assess the necessity of each individual green certificate. These committees reportedly found 'that a large number of germans [*sic*] holding green work certificates can be replaced by Polish workers and . . . are not . . . remarkably qualified'. Local village mayors in the district were subsequently ordered to send to the collection camp on Łomnicka Street every German whom the committees had designated as 'replaceable'.[79] On the other hand, Jelenia Góra's District Administration did not take kindly to local 'displacement committees' and village mayors attempting to displace German workers who had not been categorized as 'replaceable' by the 'screening committees'. The District Administration intervened on a number of occasions in early summer 1947 to prevent this from happening.[80]

Between July and October 1947, a further six cargo trains departed from Jelenia Góra's collection camp for the Soviet Zone. The last left at 2.25 am on 2 October 1947. On 3 October, an official from Jelenia Góra's local headquarters of the State Repatriation Office sent a letter to his superiors in Wrocław asking what was to be done with Jelenia Góra's 'collection point' on Łomnicka Street now that the 'repatriation' of Germans had 'finished'. He must have received a response almost immediately, because over the next few days the collection camp was closed down. A total of around 23,000 Germans were transported to the Soviet Zone from the camp on 15 trains during the 'third phase', implemented between April and October 1947. Less than half of them had been residents of Jelenia Góra District. Jelenia Góra's 'collection point' by June 1947 was one of only six 'collection points' still operating in Lower Silesia. The 'third phase' of Jelenia Góra District's 'displacement action' had reduced the district's German population from around 12,000 to only 2,377. Of this very small number of remaining Germans, only 302 lived in the town of Jelenia Góra.[81] As one district official put it, 'The district

[79] SiRep JG Chief, 1.3.1947, APW 331/VI, sygn. 51, 5–6; SiRep JG Chief, 31.3.1947, APW 331/VI, sygn. 51, 10–12; SiRep JG Chief, 30.4.1947, APW 331/VI, sygn. 51, 18–19; Rep by JGDA head S-PD, 31.5.1947, APJG 123/II, sygn. 21, 134; Rep by JGDA S-PD, 30.4.1947, APW 331/VI, sygn. 51, 17; SiRep JG DepChief, 31.5.1947, APW 331/VI, sygn. 51, 20–21; Rep by JGDA head S-PD on the period 1.8.1947–26.9.1947, APJG 123/II, sygn. 20, 136–7; Rep by JG DepChief, 23.8.1947 on the period 1.10.1946–30.7.1947, APJG 123/II, sygn. 21, 223–9; Pasierb, *Migracja*, pp. 119–20, 137; Hofmann, *Nachkriegszeit*, pp. 225, 237–8; Jankowiak, 'Wrocławskie', pp. 407, 420–3; Nitschke, *Vertreibung*, pp. 239–42; Borodziej, 'Einleitung', p. 105.

[80] Rep by JGDA head S-PD, 31.5.1947, APJG 123/II, sygn. 21, 134; SiRep JG DepChief 5.[7].1947, APJG 123/II, sygn. 21, 167–8 and 198.

[81] Rep by JG DepChief on the period 1.10.1946–30.7.1947, 23.8.1947, APJG 123/II, sygn. 21, 223–9; SiRep JG DepChief, 4.8.1947, APJG 123/II, sygn. 21, 199–201; SiRep JG Chief, 20.9.1947, APJG 123/II, sygn. 20, 123–4; Rep by the head of the SRO's 'Collection Point' in Jelenia Góra town, 2.10.1947, APW 345, sygn. 1373, 12; Ltr from the head of Jelenia Góra's local bureau of the SRO to

of Jelenia Góra has been almost completely cleansed of its German element.'[82]

The principal reason this small number of Germans had been kept back was that, although many Polish settlers with high levels of qualification and training must have arrived in the district by this time, local factories and workshops still lacked Polish workers with all the highly specialized skills they required. This meant that the district's industry remained dependent on a hard core of very highly skilled Germans even once the 'third phase' of the 'displacement action' had ended. Jelenia Góra District's Chief Official made this point emphatically in a report to his superiors in Wrocław at this time, in which he stressed to them that the district still lacked Polish 'specialist experts'. The same was true of many other districts in Poland's new territories at this time.[83]

Yet the key goal of repopulating Jelenia Góra District with Polish settlers had been well and truly accomplished by 1948. Although Polish settlers were no longer being systematically transported to the district, the influx of Poles had continued unabated. This was much to the displeasure of the district's officials, who were still facing a serious problem of overcrowding at the start of 1948. The total size of Jelenia Góra District's population had reached approximately 132,000 by this time, exceeding its prewar size by almost 20,000.[84]

Very few of the Polish settlers arriving in Jelenia Góra District in 1948 can have possessed the highly specialized skills required by the district's factories and workshops, because only a small fraction of the remaining German population was transported to Germany in that year. In spring and summer 1948, the district's officials again made concerted efforts to persuade local factory directors to identify their 'inessential' and 'unneeded' German green-certificate holders for 'repatriation' to Germany. But these

the regional headquarters of the SRO in Wrocław, 3.10.1947, APW 345, sygn. 1305, 8; Rep on the year 1947 probably by JG Chief, undated, APJG 123/II, sygn. 21, 248–79; Rep on the year 1947 by JGTA, 10.1.[1948], APJG 130, sygn. 48, 10–21; Pasierb, *Migracja*, p. 137; Jankowiak, 'Wrocławskie', pp. 407–8, 421; Hofmann, *Nachkriegszeit*, pp. 237–8.

[82] Rep on the year 1947, probably by JG Chief, undated, APJG 123/II, sygn. 21, 248–79.

[83] Rep by JG Chief, 5.2.1946, APJG 123/II, sygn. 19, 30–7; Rep by JGDA, 1.5.1946, APJG 123/II, sygn. 19, 202–3; Rep by JG Chief, 5.1.1946, APJG 123/II, sygn. 18, 206–14; Rep by JG Chief on the third quarter of 1947, 13.11.1947, APJG 123/II, sygn. 21, 232–6.

[84] SiRep JG Chief, 3.3.1947, APJG 123/II, sygn. 21, 33–8; SiRep JG Chief, 2.4.1947, APJG 123/II, sygn. 21, 69–71; Situation reports by JG Chief, 3.5.1947, APJG 123/II, sygn. 21, 96–8; Rep on the third quarter of 1947 by JG Chief, 13.11.1947, APJG 123/II, sygn. 21, 232–6; SiRep JG DepChief, 4.[6].1947, APJG 123/II, sygn. 21, 131–3; SiRep JG DepChief, 5.[7].1947, APJG 123/II, sygn. 21, 167–8 and 198; SiRep the head of JGTA's Settlement Department, 18.6.1947, APJG 130, sygn. 47, 219–21; Rep on the year 1947 by JG Chief, undated, APJG 123/II, sygn. 21, 248–79; Rep on the year 1947 by JGTA, 10.1.[48], APJG 130, sygn. 48, 10–21; Rep by JGTA, undated, start October 1947, APJG 130, sygn. 48, 59–64; Bohmann, *Menschen*, p. 209.

endeavours were obstructed by the repeated claim made by the factory directors that there were simply not enough 'Polish experts' to replace them. In 1948, workplaces in Poland still did not have to pay highly qualified Germans as much as equivalently qualified Poles. German workers would not be placed on the same wage scale as their Polish colleagues until June 1949. Because of the determination of many Polish employers to keep hold of their valued German workers, when the 'displacement action' resumed in Jelenia Góra District in July 1948, the number transported was very small. Between July and October 1948 a total of only 767 Germans were sent to the Soviet Zone from Jelenia Góra District. All of them travelled via one of Lower Silesia's two remaining 'collection points' in Legnica and Wrocław.[85] Unrelated to the 'displacement action', around 80 Germans were also forcibly relocated from the southern area of the district to the northern area during the winter of 1948. It had been decided that having Germans living so close to the Polish–Czechoslovak border was undesirable 'for security reasons'.[86]

In 1949, even fewer highly skilled German workers were released by the district's factories and workshops. Perhaps fewer than 20 Germans were transported to Germany from Jelenia Góra District in the course of the year. They migrated to the Soviet, British and American Zones. In fact, the Germans could by this time choose their destinations. Permission merely needed to be obtained in advance from the local German authorities in the particular place in Germany where they wished to be sent. These were usually towns and villages where the Germans had relatives living.[87]

[85] SiRep JG Chief, 6.[2].1948, APW 331/VI, sygn. 51, 42–3; SiRep JG Chief, 1.3.1948, APW 331/VI, sygn. 51, 44–5; Rep on the first quarter of 1948 by JG Chief, 6.4.1948, APW 331/VI, sygn. 51, 48–52; Rep on the second quarter of 1948 by JGT Pres, start of July 1948, APW 331/VI, sygn. 50, 15–21; SiRep Jelenia Góra JG Chief, 5.5.1948. APW 331/VI, sygn. 51, 53–4; SiRep JG Chief, 1.6.1948, APW 331/VI, sygn. 51, 55–7; SiRep JG Chief, 27.6.1948, APW 331/VI, sygn. 51, 60–61; SiRep JG Chief, 4.8.1948, APW 331/VI, sygn. 51, 65–6. SiRep JG Chief, 2.9.1948, APW 331/VI, sygn. 51, 67–8; SiRep JG Chief, 2.10.1948, APW 331/VI, sygn. 51, 69–70; SiRep JG Chief, 2.11.1948, APW 331/VI, sygn. 51, 77–8; Rep on the third quarter of 1948 by JGT Pres, start of October 1948, APW 331/VI, sygn. 50, 42–8; Rep on the third quarter of 1948 by JGTA head S-PD, start of October 1948, APW 331/VI, sygn. 50, 40–41; Nitschke, *Vertreibung*, pp. 253–8; Jankowiak, 'Wrocławskie', pp. 407–8; Hofmann, *Nachkriegszeit*, p. 254.

[86] SiRep JG Chief, 2.11.1948, APW 331/VI, sygn. 51, 77–8; SiRep JG Chief, 3.12.1948, APW 331/VI, sygn. 51, 79–81; SiRep JG Chief, 27.12.1948, APW 331/VI, sygn. 51, 82–6.

[87] SiRep JG Chief, 31.1.1949, APJG 123/II, sygn. 20, 240–4; SiRep JG Chief, start March 1949, APW 331/VI, sygn. 51, 98–100; SiRep JG Chief, 6.4.1949, APW 331/VI, sygn. 51, 101–4; SiRep JG Chief, 30.4.1949, APW 331/VI, sygn. 51, 111–12; SiRep JG Chief, 31.5.1949, APW 331/VI, sygn. 51, 113–15; SiRep JG Chief, 8.7.1949, APW 331/VI, sygn. 51, 117–20; SiRep JG DepChief, 5.10.1949, APW 331/VI, sygn. 51, 160–2; Rep by JG Chief on the first quarter of 1949, 6.4.1949, APW 331/VI, sygn. 51, 105–10; Rep on the first quarter of 1949 by JTA head S-PD, undated, APW 331/VI, sygn. 50, 96–7; Nitschke, *Vertreibung*, pp. 256–7; Hofmann, *Nachkriegszeit*, p. 254.

Not all of the Germans relocated to Germany in 1949 were highly skilled workers. Sabine von S. from the village of Hermsdorf/Sobieszów, for example, had been too ill for transportation to Germany in previous years. In 1949 she received a request via the Red Cross to join her daughter, who was living in a village in the region of Hesse in the American Occupation Zone of Germany. Having attained the necessary documents from Jelenia Góra District Administration, she was transported in a cargo train eastwards to a collection camp in Głubczyce in southern Upper Silesia. She spent 14 days at this camp before finally being transported westwards to western Germany on a hospital train.[88]

How many Germans remained in Jelenia Góra District by the end of the 1940s? Eight hundred forty-three highly skilled German workers (and their dependant relatives) were still living in the district, whose 'repatriation' to Germany had been ruled out by local state officials for the foreseeable future. In addition, the district probably contained a smaller group of highly skilled German workers whom officials had designated for 'repatriation' but who had not yet been sent to Germany.[89] In localities throughout Poland's new territories, many of the highly skilled German workers kept back by the Polish state authorities in the second half of the 1940s were finally getting used to life in Poland by the end of the decade. Certain rights continued to be denied them, but conditions were not unbearable. Their wages had gradually been brought up to the level of equivalently qualified Poles by June 1949. They were often highly valued workers in their workplaces. Most were still living in the homes they had inhabited before 1945. Paul H., for example, kept hold of his own home and continued working in his old workplace, the former Füllnerwerk factory in Bad Warmbrunn/Cieplice Śląskie. He did not migrate to West Germany until 1957.[90]

Although most of the Germans who were still living in Jelenia Góra District at the end of the 1940s were highly skilled workers (and their relatives), they did not account for all of the Germans who had not yet been 'repatriated'. There were several smaller sets of Germans remaining in Jelenia Góra District for other reasons. These included a small group of Germans deemed too ill or frail to cope with the journeys to Germany.

[88] WR, Sabine von S., Hermsdorf (Sobieszów), undated, BOD 2, 188, 277–83.

[89] Rep by JG Chief on the second quarter of 1949, 6.7.1949, APW 331/VI, sygn. 51, 137–42; SiRep JG DepChief, 5.10.1949, APW 331/VI, sygn. 51, 160–2; Rep on the final quarter of 1949 by JGT Pres, 30.12.1949, APW 331/VI, sygn. 50, 141–9; Rep by JG Chief on the third quarter of 1947, 13.11.1947, APJG 123/II, sygn. 21, 232–6.

[90] WR, Paul H., Bad Warmbrunn (Cieplice Śląskie), 10.9.1958, BOD 1, 207, 243–9; WR, Albert S., Schreiberhau (Szklarska Poręba), undated, BOD 1, 207, 183–95; Jankowiak, 'Wrocławskie', p. 427; Hofmann, *Nachkriegszeit*, p. 254.

Sabine von S. had been a member of this group until her migration in 1949.[91] Another small group of Germans was made up of individuals whom local state officials had chosen not to expel because they were married to Polish citizens. Almost all of these so-called 'mixed marriages' were probably between Poles and Germans who had married at some point in the interwar period. But Walter S.-G. from Niederschreiberhau/Szklarska Poręba Dolna in Jelenia Góra District provided a more unusual example of the possible forms perceived 'mixed marriages' in Poland's new territories sometimes took. In spring 1946 he was asked by the local state administration whether he and his wife wanted to 'opt for Poland' on the grounds that his wife had been a Polish citizen for twenty years. As he explained, his wife was actually a German who had become a Polish citizen by marrying her first husband, an ethnically German Polish citizen (*Volksdeutscher*). According to Walter S.-G., her first husband had been 'killed by Poles' in September 1939.[92]

There was yet another small set of Germans remaining in the district at the end of the 1940s, whose exact number officials did not know and of whose existence officials were, in fact, only vaguely aware. These were Germans who were not officially registered with the Jelenia Góra District Administration as residents of the district. Most of them were illegally employed by Poles. When the district's authorities came across them, this was generally only by chance. Those whom officials did identify were apparently sent to work on state farms while they awaited 'repatriation' to Germany.[93]

Taking all these categories into account, a rough estimate of the total number of Germans remaining in Jelenia Góra District by the end of the 1940s would be around 1,500. It has been estimated that around 300,000 people whom the Communist-led government viewed as 'Germans' remained in the whole of postwar Poland by the end of 1949.[94]

---

91 Rep by JG Chief on the second quarter of 1949, 6.7.1949, APW 331/VI, sygn. 51, 137–42; SiRep JG DepChief, 5.10.1949, APW 331/VI, sygn. 51, 160–2; Rep on the final quarter of 1949 by JGT Pres, 30.12.1949, APW 331/VI, sygn. 50, 141–9; Rep by JG Chief on the third quarter of 1947, 13.11.1947, APJG 123/II, sygn. 21, 232–6.

92 SiRep JGDA S-PD, 3.9.1945, APJG 123/II, sygn. 18, 86–8; SiRep JGT Pres, 23.6.1949, APW 331/VI, sygn. 50, 121–5; WR, Walter S.-G., Niederschreiberhau (Szklarska Poręba Dolna), 10.1.1948, BOD 2, 188, 175–97.

93 SiRep JG DepChief, 5.10.1949, APW 331/VI, sygn. 51, 160–2; Rep by JG Chief on the first quarter of 1949, 6.4.1949, APW 331/VI, sygn. 51, 105–10; Rep on the first quarter of 1949 by JGTA head S-PD, undated, APW 331/VI, sygn. 50, 96–7; Rep by JG Chief on the third quarter of 1947, 13.11.1947, APJG 123/II, sygn. 21, 232–6; Hofmann, *Nachkriegszeit*, p. 254.

94 Nitschke, *Vertreibung*, p. 280.

In the second half of the 1940s, then, the prewar eastern German territories had played host to one of the most massive population displacements in history. The huge flight of civilians from the Red Army in the final months of the war had already reduced the number of German citizens living there by almost 5 million. But the Communist-controlled Polish authorities arrived in these territories in spring and summer 1945 to find that there were still millions of German citizens residing there. In the aftermath of the war, they carried out a systematic campaign of forced migration against most of these people. This cleared the vast majority of localities in Poland's new western and northern territories, which had contained monolingual German-speaking inhabitants before 1945, of all but a tiny number of their prewar residents by the end of the decade. This campaign of expulsion was bound up with the policy of flooding these territories with millions of Polish settlers. Both of these population policies – expulsion and repopulation – were done with the aim of incorporating these territories into the ethno-nationally homogeneous postwar Polish nation-state. But the latter policy also helped, in a very practical sense, to instigate and set the pace of the expulsion of German citizens from the homogeneously German-speaking areas of these territories. We shall turn now to examine the policy of repopulation.

CHAPTER 5

Repopulation

The Polish Communists' attempt to transform Poland from a multiethnic country into an ethno-nationally 'pure' Polish nation-state after the Second World War required a fundamental remoulding of the population of the new territories acquired from Germany. As we have seen, part of the way the Communist-led government tried to achieve this was by expelling the vast majority of the German citizens who were still living there in early summer 1945. But of no less importance to the fulfilment of the Communists' ethno-nationalist vision was the policy of deliberately and systematically repopulating the territories with Polish settlers. After all, it was not their aim to depopulate these territories, but rather to establish Polish ethno-national homogeneity there. Moreover, just as the Polish Communists' and the Soviets' desire to influence the Allies' territorial decisions at the Potsdam Conference added urgency to Polish efforts to expel Germans from these territories, so this consideration added impetus to the repopulation process. It removed any apprehensions the Communist-controlled state authorities may otherwise have had about flooding these territories with huge numbers of Polish settlers several months before the war was over and many months before local Polish state officials in these territories were anywhere near ready to receive them.[1]

MASS INFLUX

Aside from Polish soldiers and civilian officials, the first Poles to arrive in Germany's prewar eastern provinces did not go there to settle permanently. Before the war was over, large numbers of Polish looters and criminal gangs started flowing into the these provinces – particularly the areas lying nearest to the prewar Polish–German border – in search of easy booty. But their

[1] Ther, *Vertriebene*, pp. 107, 123–6, 249; Hofmann, *Nachkriegszeit*, pp. 96–7; Borodziej, 'Einleitung', p. 68.

arrival was followed almost immediately by that of genuine Polish settlers, who had every intention of making a new life in these provinces. In some eastern-lying places in the prewar eastern German territories, as we shall see in Chapter 7, Polish settlers arrived by early spring 1945, but in many places this process did not get underway until the early summer.

In Jelenia Góra District, both looters and genuine settlers started to arrive in early June 1945. The settlers had been attracted to Poland's new western and northern territories by advertisements which the government placed in newspapers in central Poland as part of its effort to bring about a rapid repopulation of these territories. Particular destinations in the new territories were advertised as attractive places to resettle. Jelenia Góra District itself appeared in an advertisement at this time. It was not exactly difficult to present this district as an appealing place to start a new life, because it was located in a beautiful alpine landscape among the Karkonosze Mountains on the northern Sudeten slopes. It had also been left almost untouched by war damage and had a good railway connection.[2] The idyllic surroundings of Jelenia Góra District were captured very well in the first impressions of one of the Polish settlers who came to live there after the war: 'I was enchanted by the beauty of the Karkonosze foothills. It was spring time, the apple trees were blossoming, the landscape was utterly peaceful, there were no traces of the war and the place really took me in. I decided to settle there with my family'.[3] Another Polish settler remembered, 'Jelenia Góra was a very clean and tidy town.... The landscape reminded me of similar scenery along the river Berezyna in the Polesie region, where I spent a holiday back in the 1930s. Something touched my heart at that time. I felt a delightful weariness and everything suddenly seemed close and familiar'.[4]

Within weeks of the first Poles arriving in Jelenia Góra District from central Poland unassisted by the authorities, the Communist-led government started actively transporting Polish settlers to the district on cargo trains organized by the State Repatriation Office. As we have seen, this mass influx of settlers played an important role in instigating and adding impetus to the first attempts by Polish soldiers and Polish civilian authorities to uproot Germans from the district through disorganized expulsions in summer 1945. The Polish settlers who arrived in Jelenia Góra District came

[2] Rep by JGTA on the period May 1945–March 1947, 10.3.1947, APJG 130, sygn. 48, 22–35; Rep by JG Chief, 3.10.1945, APJG 123/II, sygn. 18, 127–32; Rep on Jelenia Góra town since 19 May 1945 by head JGTA, 3.6.1946, APJG 130, sygn. 46, 53–5. WRs in file BOD 1, 207 and file BOD 2, 188. Hofmann, *Nachkriegszeit*, p. 103.

[3] Jaroszewski, 'Na turoszowskiej budowie'.

[4] Czepułkowski, 'W Karpaczu', pp. 287–8.

from both central Poland and the prewar eastern territories. The latter had been annexed by the Soviet Union with the help of the Polish Committee of National Liberation in July 1944 (see Chapter 2). Alongside the nationalist aim of transforming the ethno-national makeup of residents of Poland's new territories, the massive resettlement of Poles to these territories fulfilled two further purposes. First, the Communist-led government hoped that encouraging and inducing hundreds of thousands of Poles to relocate from central Poland to the new territories would help to resolve the acute problem of overpopulation which existed in many rural localities in central Poland.[5] Second, and more importantly, this was a way of providing homes to the hundreds of thousands of Poles who were being forcibly uprooted from the Soviet-annexed eastern territories at this time. Around 300,000 Poles had already fled westwards from the prewar southeastern territories of Poland in 1943–4 in order to escape the brutal violence being meted out to Poles by the Ukrainian Insurgent Army (see Chapter 1). In September 1944, Poland's Soviet-backed and Communist-controlled proto-government had agreed to carry out compulsory 'population exchanges' with the newly expanded Soviet Socialist Republics of Ukraine, Belorussia and Lithuania. As a result of this, 1.5 million Poles were forcibly transported westwards from the ceded prewar eastern Polish territories between 1944 and 1948. The vast majority of these forced migrants were relocated to Poland's new territories. The first cargo trains carrying eastern Polish forced migrants arrived in these territories by early spring 1945.[6]

These journeys were long and very arduous. The trains travelled very slowly through a country which had been reduced to ruins by heavy fighting at the start and end of the war and by Nazi Germany's vicious occupation regime. The Poles were often transported in open coal wagons to Poland's new territories, even in the extreme cold of winter. The trains took many weeks to reach their destinations. It deserves emphasis that these journeys were frequently far worse ordeals than the journeys from Poland's new territories to the British and Soviet Zones endured by Germans from 1946 onwards.[7] The eastern Polish forced migrants who arrived in Jelenia Góra District from summer 1945 onwards, for example, had 'travelled for 10–12 weeks by [cargo] train, [reaching the district] exhausted, louse-infested

[5] Rep on Jelenia Góra town since 19 May 1945 by head JGTA, 3.6.1946, APJG 130, sygn. 46, 53–5. WRs in file BOD 1, 207 and file BOD 2, 188. Hofmann, *Nachkriegszeit*, pp. 157–9, 163, 189.

[6] Borodziej et al., 'Wstęp', pp. 12–32, 40–5; Ther, *Vertriebene*, pp. 67–88; Philipp Ther, 'A Century of Forced Migration: The Origins and Consequences of "Ethnic Cleansing"', in Philipp Ther and Ana Siljak, *Redrawing Nations*, pp. 53–4; Snyder, 'Ukrainian–Polish Ethnic Cleansing', pp. 217–29.

[7] Borodziej et al., 'Wstęp', pp. 32–5; Hofmann, *Nachkriegszeit*, pp. 110–15.

and sometimes even suffering from typhus'.[8] It should also be stressed that the majority of forced migrants transported to Poland's new western and northern territories from the lost eastern Polish territories came from the southern areas gripped by the Ukrainian Insurgent Army's campaign of terror since 1943. Therefore, whereas for all eastern Polish forced migrants these painful journeys came in the wake of five extremely hard years of Soviet and Nazi German occupation, for those forced migrants from the southern areas of prewar eastern Poland it also came in the aftermath of around a year of horrendous anti-Polish violence (see Chapter 1).

As happened in many other localities in Poland's new territories at this time, the government's propaganda and massive transportation operation had a nearly instant impact on circumstances in Jelenia Góra District. By August 1945, Polish settlers already made up around 5 per cent of the district's population. Within two months, their number had increased dramatically: 35,000 Polish settlers were living in the rural areas of the district and 12,000 in the town of Jelenia Góra. Settlers already amounted to almost one-third of the overall population of the district.[9]

All these settlers needed places to live. As happened throughout Poland's new territories, many of the first Poles to arrive in the district took the matter of finding property into their own hands. They seized control of farms and homes without first seeking approval or assistance from the fledgling Polish state authorities. But by late summer 1945 officials were starting to gain some control over the process. In localities throughout the new territories, special Settlement Departments (*Referaty Osiedleńcze*) were created by each new District Administration (*Starostwo*) and Town Administration (*Zarząd Miejski*) to orchestrate the process of allotting farms and homes to arriving settlers.[10] The main problem confronting officials in certain areas of Poland's new territories was the fact that the German population was no smaller than it had been before the war. This was especially true in the case of southern Lower Silesia and western Upper Silesia; but it was also witnessed in various other areas of these territories. As we saw in Chapter 4, Jelenia Góra District's officials dealt with this, principally, by sending Polish settlers to live on farms which were still inhabited by Germans. Jelenia Góra District's Chief Official claimed in

[8] Rep by JG Chief, 6.11.1945, APJG 123/II, sygn. 18, 109–15.

[9] Rep by JG Chief, 6.[8].1945, APJG 123/II, sygn. 18, 3–26; Rep by JG Chief, 3.10.1945, APJG 123/II, sygn. 18, 127–32.

[10] Rep by JG Chief, 6.[8].1945, APJG 123/II, sygn. 18, 3–26; SiRep JG Chief, early June 1946, APJG 123/II, sygn. 19, 245–9; Rep by JGTA on the period 1.10.1946–31.12.1946, 26.2.1947, APJG 130, sygn. 48, 41–58; SiRep JG Chief, 20.9.1947, APJG 123/II, sygn. 20, 123–4; Ther, *Vertriebene*, pp. 124–6, 154; Czepułkowski, 'W Karpaczu', pp. 288–91.

October 1945, 'On every farm [in the district] lives both a Polish family and a German one.' This often meant that 10–20 individuals were living on each farm. Polish settlers were already occupying 95 per cent of all habitable farms in the rural areas of the district by this time. Only the 1–3 hectare properties were still unoccupied by Poles, and the few farms above 3 hectares which had not yet been allotted to Polish settlers were mainly in ruins.[11] By December 1945, all habitable farms, as well as almost all shops and artisanal workshops, in the rural areas of the district had been assigned to Poles.[12] Some of the Polish settlers exploited the situation in which they found themselves by forcing the Germans they were living with to perform unpaid farm work for them. With some exaggeration, the German farmer Ewald S. from the village of Waltersdorf/Mniszków recalled, 'The Poles occupied the farms . . . and became the masters. The Germans were pushed into a corner and allowed only to work and live from the scraps which fell from their masters' tables – which was mainly very little'.[13]

The same practice of moving Polish settlers in with Germans was also witnessed in the town of Jelenia Góra. But it was more common there than in the rural areas of the district for Germans to be evicted from their homes altogether and forced to live under very cramped conditions together with other Germans – particularly in a ghetto-like neighbourhood of the town which had been designated German-only. As more and more Polish settlers arrived in Jelenia Góra town, local state officials progressively reduced the number of rooms which the few Germans who continued to occupy their own homes, together with Polish settlers, were allowed to use.[14]

Despite the fact that many Germans were being permitted to continue living in their old homes along with Polish settlers, what was happening across Poland's new territories was a massive transformation in property relations. As the local German Richard W. recalled, posters were put up around Jelenia Góra town in early summer 1945 declaring that all German property now belonged to the Polish state.[15] These posters referred to a

[11] Rep by JG Chief, 6.[8].1945, APJG 123/II, sygn. 18, 3–26; Rep by JG Chief, 3.10.1945, APJG 123/II, sygn. 18, 127–32; Rep by JG Chief, 6.11.1945, APJG 123/II, sygn. 18, 109–15; Rep by JG Chief, 5.12.1945, APJG 123/II, sygn. 18, 185–200; Rep by JG Chief, 5.1.1946, APJG 123/II, sygn. 18, 206–14. WRs in file BOD 1, 207 and file BOD 2, 188.

[12] Rep by JG Chief, 5.12.1945 APJG 123/II, sygn. 18, 185–200.

[13] WR, Ewald S., Waltersdorf (Mniszków), 1957–8. BOD 1, 207, 239–42. WRs: BOD 1, 207, 43–4; BOD 1, 207, 159–62; BOD 2, 188, 122–37; BOD 1, 207, 57–8; BOD 1, 207, 21–4; BOD 2, 188, 287–91; BOD 2, 188, 109–11; BOD 2, 188, 277–83; BOD 2, 188, 318–32; BOD 2, 188, 139–48; BOD 1, 207, 29–32.

[14] Rep for the Lower Silesian Commissar for Repatriation Issues in Wrocław by the deputy head of JGTA, 26.1.1946, APW 331/VI, sygn. 360, 2–3.

[15] WR, Richard W., Hirschberg (Jelenia Góra) town, 3.7.1950, BOD 2, 188, 337–9.

decree issued by the government in early May 1945 which expropriated all Germans living in the new territories and declared their homes and land henceforth the property of the Polish state. This action was the basis for sending Polish settlers to live on German farms and forcing Germans to pay rent for property they had owned before 1945. But, more crucially, it was one of the key cornerstones for the entire ethno-national transformation which the Communist-controlled government attempted to bring about in Poland's new territories in the aftermath of the war. It underpinned both the forced migration of Germans from these territories and the repopulation of these territories with Polish settlers.

But the Communist-led Polish government viewed the expropriation of Germans not merely as a crucial part of its campaign of ethno-national homogenization in Poland's new territories, but also as a key element of the revolutionary socioeconomic transformation it wished to bring about throughout postwar Polish territory. In September 1944 the Soviet-backed proto-government had issued a decree introducing a comprehensive land reform, laying the path for the seizure of all large land estates without compensation and their redistribution to landless or land-poor peasants. The Communist-led state authorities soon began to carry this out in central Poland and intended to do the same in the new territories as they came under Polish state control. Indeed, the takeover of prewar German territory and the expropriation of German property appeared to offer the Communists a unique opportunity to impose a radically new agricultural structure on a large part of postwar Poland. The blanket expropriation of all prewar owners of land in the new territories – on the grounds that they were ethnically German – would mean that there were far fewer obstacles there than in the rest of Poland to full-blooded land reform. Yet it soon became clear to the Communist-led authorities that a fundamental alteration of land distribution in the new territories was not going to happen. Although many large land estates were quickly turned into state farms, German farms were generally simply passed into the hand of individual settlers in the new territories – without any changes in the sizes of the properties. This resulted not only from the fact that the new territories' officials only gradually gained a grip on the process of allotting property to settlers, but also from the widespread refusal of settlers to accept anything less than a whole German farm.[16]

[16] Hofmann, *Nachkriegszeit*, pp. 157–71, 175; Ther, *Vertriebene*, pp. 171–4, 188–95; WR, Richard W., Hirschberg (Jelenia Góra) town, 3.7.1950, BOD 2, 188, 337–9; WR, Sabine von S., Hermsdorf (Sobieszów), undated, BOD 2, 188, 277–83.

Many of the settlers, after all, were farmers who had been forcibly uprooted from their own farms in prewar eastern Poland. They knew that attaining adequate farms in their new surroundings would be the only form of compensation they were likely to receive from the Communist-controlled Polish state. Similarly, the settlers who voluntarily relocated to the new territories from central Poland – the 'resettlers' (*przesiedleńcy*), as the authorities called them – had only agreed to do so based on the expectation that their material assets would be improved. A very large proportion of them hoped, specifically, to attain German farms.[17] Reflecting the material motives lying behind so many settlers' decisions to relocate from central Poland to the new territories, one settler who moved from Kutno to Jelenia Góra District in 1946 recalled, 'I thought a lot about how in the west so many beautiful homes were standing empty [and so decided to resettle there]. The place I arrived in the west was Cieplice . . . a very little town, but very clean and well maintained.'[18] Another settler had similar recollections of arriving in Jelenia Góra District after the war: 'The buildings were convenient, in a good state . . . and comfortably furnished . . . We set ourselves up nicely with a detached house . . . a garden and several fruit trees.'[19]

Moreover, particularly for the forced migrants from prewar eastern Poland, the buildings, equipment and infrastructure they found in Poland's new territories were often of a much higher material standard than they were used to. The recollections of one settler from the Vilnius region, who passed through Jelenia Góra in 1946 but was later allotted a farm elsewhere in Lower Silesia, represented this well:

> When I looked around the farm, I discovered that there was a running water supply and electricity. Even the threshing machine was in a good state. [There were also] various agricultural machines including ones for mowing, seeding and raking. . . . The majority of the people who resettled to the west from behind the Bug River [that is, the lost prewar eastern Polish territories], where backwardness and darkness prevailed, had no idea of electricity and technology. Very often they did not know what particular objects and machines were actually for.[20]

This settler was not exaggerating. Many people from prewar eastern Poland had never before lived in homes with electricity and running water.[21]

The clear material motives underpinning resettlement from central Poland to the new territories did not always mean that the most respectable

[17] Ther, *Vertriebene*, pp. 219–27; Hofmann, *Nachkriegszeit*, pp. 164–5.
[18] Czepułkowski, 'W Karpaczu', pp. 286–8. [19] Jaroszewski, 'Na turoszowskiej budowie', pp. 68–9.
[20] Pietraszko, 'Osadnik Wojskowy', pp. 292, 296. [21] Ther, *Vertriebene*, p. 200.

individuals arrived. Looters aside, even many of the genuine settlers from central Poland did not seem entirely committed to leading a puritan existence in Poland's new territories. In October 1945, for example, Jelenia Góra District's Chief Official contrasted the settlers 'from behind the Bug river' (i.e., from prewar eastern Poland) and the settlers from the Poznań region with the settlers from the central provinces of Poland. He felt that the last group were 'very poor material', interested only in making 'quick gains' in the new territories. Two months later he declared that many central Polish settlers had come to the district purely 'so that they could grow wealthy at the expense of the state and their fellow citizens'.[22] Other local state officials said similar things, among them that 'a huge mass of people had arrived from every part of central Poland, including an assortment of criminals, slackers and bums who have a disgust for work and spend whole days selling clothes on the free market.'[23] Nor did these unfavourable impressions of many central Polish settlers fade as the years passed. In 1947, for example, the district's Chief Official was still declaring that whereas settlers 'from behind the Bug and San rivers' exhibited great diligence and prudence, many central Polish settlers did not: the former 'are peaceful and hard working . . . mostly peasants, whereas a lot of the resettlers [from central Poland] are profiteers and traders seeking . . . an easy life'.[24]

The massive influx of Polish settlers from both central and prewar eastern Poland in the second half of 1945 placed a huge strain on local housing and resources in Poland's new territories, particularly in southern Lower Silesia and western Upper Silesia. Officials in many localities in these territories, therefore, soon began to call on the government in Warsaw, the central headquarters of the State Repatriation Office in Łódź and the regional headquarters of the State Repatriation Office in the new territories' main cities to stop sending cargo trains to their areas. In Jelenia Góra District, for example, local State Repatriation Office officials sent repeated requests to the institution's regional headquarters in Wrocław in early autumn 1945 calling on its officials to desist from directing settler trains to the district. A 60-wagon cargo train arrived in Jelenia Góra town at this time full of settlers, who immediately had to be transported by lorry to 'less saturated' districts elsewhere in Lower Silesia. There was simply 'no space'

[22] Rep by JG Chief, 3.10.1945, APJG 123/II, sygn. 18, 127–32; Rep by JG Chief, 5.12.1945, APJG 123/II, sygn. 18, 185–200; Hofmann, *Nachkriegszeit*, p. 105.

[23] SiRep head JGTA, 2.3.1946, APW 331/VI, sygn. 31, 7–23; SiRep JGDA S-PD, 30.7.1946, APW 331/VI, sygn. 34, 35–7; Rep by head JGTA, 6.12.1945, APW 331 VI, sygn. 28, pp. 116–31.

[24] SiRep JG Chief, 2.1.1947, APW 331/VI, sygn. 39, 15–17; Rep on the third quarter of 1947 by JG Chief, 13.11.1947, APJG 123/II, sygn. 21, 232–6.

to accommodate them in Jelenia Góra District, local officials declared.[25] Likewise, in November 1945, Jelenia Góra District's Chief Official reported that 'train after train' full of 'repatriates from behind the Bug river' was arriving in the district – and because the State Repatriation Office's local bureau lacked the vehicles and fuel 'to unload them' to the less populated northern districts of Lower Silesia, the district was being forced to 'bear the whole burden'. Indeed, he doubted whether any other district in Lower Silesia was so densely populated as Jelenia Góra District.[26]

Unlike southern Lower Silesia, which had not suffered much damage during the war, northern Lower Silesia had endured a great deal of destructive fighting in the war's final months. As a direct consequence of this, southern Lower Silesia became extremely crowded in the second half of 1945, whereas the northern areas of the region remained virtually depopulated for a long period after the war.[27] In the early months of 1946, demands continued to be sent from Jelenia Góra District to the State Repatriation Office's regional headquarters in Wrocław pleading for the arrival of settler trains to cease. But these pleas continued to go unheeded. At the same time, the regional headquarters prohibited its local bureau in Jelenia Góra District from sending arriving settler trains straight onwards to northern Lower Silesia. Settlers continued to pour into the district in these months not only on these trains but also travelling to the district without any assistance from the state authorities. Reportedly, these unassissted arrivals came 'from every direction, uncontrolled'.[28]

As we saw in Chapter 4, this massive influx of Polish settlers caused Jelenia Góra District's Chief Official to plead incessantly with his superiors in Wrocław in late 1945 and early 1946 to get the mass transportation of Germans underway. Taking the Polish and German populations of the district together, there may have been as many as 180,000 people living in Jelenia Góra District by late spring 1946. This figure was vastly in excess of the district's prewar population size: 115,000.[29] Similar circumstances in the rest of southern Lower Silesia, in western Upper Silesia and in certain

[25] Rep by JG Chief, 3.10.1945, APJG 123/II, sygn. 18, 127–32; Hofmann, *Nachkriegszeit*, pp. 106, 161; Borodziej et al., 'Wstęp', pp. 17, 43–4.

[26] Rep by JG Chief, 6.11.1945, APJG 123/II, sygn. 18, 109–15.

[27] Borodziej et al., 'Wstęp', p. 43; Hofmann, *Nachkriegszeit*, pp. 116, 161.

[28] Rep by JG Chief, 5.1.1946, APJG 123/II, sygn. 18, 206–14; Rep by JG Chief, 5.2.1946, APJG 123/II, sygn. 19, 30–7; Rep by JG Chief, 5.12.1945, APJG 123/II, sygn. 18, 185–200; SiRep head JGTA, 2.3.1946, APW 331/VI, sygn. 31, 7–23; Rep by JG Chief, 2.3.1946, APJG 123/II, sygn. 19, 73–6; Rep by JG Chief, 1.4.1946, APJG 123/II, sygn. 19, 118–21; Rep by JG Chief, early June 1946, APJG 123/II, sygn. 19, 245–9.

[29] Rep by JG Chief, 3.7.1946, APJG 123/II, sygn. 19, 250–2; Records of Jelenia Góra's local bureau of the SRO, APW 345, sygn. 1305, 64–70; Bohmann, *Menschen*, p. 209.

other areas in Poland's new territories no doubt added impetus to the Polish government's efforts to persuade British officials in Berlin to allow them to begin transporting Germans to the British Zone on cargo trains (see Chapter 4).

The start of the 'displacement action' in localities throughout Poland's new territories in spring and summer 1946 transformed general living conditions for Polish settlers. In Jelenia Góra District, the first phase of the 'displacement action' in late May and June 1946 involved the expulsion of over 57,000 Germans. Some Polish settlers who had taken up residence in the district since summer 1945 regretted losing the cheap labour which Germans had so far been providing for them. But most greeted the removal of such a huge number of local Germans with unqualified relief. It allowed many of these settlers finally to take possession of whole farms, houses or flats as their permanent homes. Those who had lost almost all their property through their forced migration from Poland's lost eastern territories were obviously desperate to attain adequate living conditions in the district to start their lives anew. They were therefore very pleased to see the Germans go.[30]

On the other hand, Jelenia Góra District remained overcrowded in summer 1946. The district's officials, consequently, continued to call on their superiors in Wrocław to halt the arrival of settler trains. In early July 1946, the district's Chief Official told Wrocław that he believed the trains bringing 'repatriates' to the district should be stopped for 'at least six months'.[31] One settler who arrived from the Vilnius region at around this time described how Jelenia Góra District had, by that point, become so 'crowded [that], after very little thought, we simply decided to travel onwards'.[32]

The State Repatriation Office finally appears to have stopped sending settler trains to Jelenia Góra District at the end of summer 1946.[33] But this did not solve the problem of overpopulation. The problem was that, as the district's Chief Official reported in autumn 1946, there was still a 'constant inflow of people' to the district – individuals and families arriving from central Poland without any help from the state authorities. Settlers, he believed, were still being instructed to come here by officials in other parts of Poland. They reportedly all demanded farms upon arrival. There was no chance these demands could be met, because almost every farm

[30] Rep by JG Chief, 3.7.1946, APJG 123/II, sygn. 19, 250–2.
[31] Rep by JG Chief, 3.7.1946, APJG 123/II, sygn. 19, 250–2.
[32] Pietraszko, 'Osadnik Wojskowy', p. 292.
[33] SiRep JG Chief, 3.3.1947 APJG 123/II, sygn. 21, 33–8.

in the district had already been allotted to a settler family before early summer 1946. Many settlers who had arrived in mid 1946 were, therefore, still waiting to be allotted farms in midautumn. There was no prospect that they would receive them soon. The number of Poles residing in both Jelenia Góra town and the rural part of Jelenia Góra District by November 1946 was around 100,000 – in addition to around 25,000 remaining Germans. Around 13,000 of these Germans were transported from the district in the final two months of 1946 (see Chapter 4).[34]

THE PROPERTY QUESTION

It was around this time that the Communist-controlled government finally made a concerted effort to resolve the ambiguities still surrounding property relations in Poland's new territories. The farms, houses and businesses expropriated from Germans and handed to Polish settlers in 1945 had not actually become the property of the settlers. Rather, they remained Polish state property. The Polish settlers had merely been designated their 'users' (*użytkownicy*). But in September 1946 the government issued a settlement decree aimed at transferring these farms, houses, flats and businesses to the settlers as their private property. Yet this was by no means an instant transfer of property. The settlers had to jump through several bureaucratic hoops before the farms, houses and businesses became their property. And the slowness of this property transfer process – as we shall see – would have important consequences in later years.[35]

Moreover, what this decree did not do was enable local state officials to confiscate properties from those individuals who had seized farms, housing and business without the approval of the state authorities in early summer 1945 – the so-called 'wild settlers'. Local officials wished to be able to do this, because they wanted to provide farms and housing to the especially needy settlers who had been expelled from prewar eastern Poland but were yet to be allotted permanent accommodation in Poland's new territories.[36] Broadly, the Communist-controlled government agreed with local state officials on this issue, because in November 1946 the Ministry for Recovered Territories ordered local state authorities to grant the eastern Polish 'repatriates' (*repatrianci*) (i.e., forced migrants from prewar eastern Poland)

[34] SiRep JG Chief, 2.11.1946, APJG 123/II, sygn. 19, 401–5; Rep by JG DepChief on the period 1.10.1946–30.7.1947, 23.8.1947, APJG 123/II, sygn. 21, 223–9; SiRep JG Chief, 3.7.1946, APJG 123/II, sygn. 19, 250–2; Rep by JGTA on the period 1.10–31.12.1946, 26.2.1947, APJG 130, sygn. 48, 41–58.

[35] Ther, *Vertriebene*, pp. 223–5; Hofmann, *Nachkriegszeit*, pp. 160–3, 175–80.

[36] Ther, *Vertriebene*, pp. 219–22.

priority over the central Polish 'resettlers' when allotting any new properties which happened to become available in the new territories.[37]

The problem was that by this time farms, houses and flats in Poland's new territories were only rarely freed up for reallotment. Aside from properties made available through the forced migration of the now dwindling number of Germans, one of the only ways farms and housing became available for reallotment was when central Polish settlers decided, of their own free will, to return to central Poland. A relatively significant number of central Polish settlers did indeed become fed up with life in the new territories, relinquished their farms, houses and flats there and made their way back to central Poland in the early postwar years. This had been happening in localities across Poland's new territories since the second half of 1945. Jelenia Góra District's Chief Official tried to explain why this was. He commented in late 1945 that because many central Polish settlers had arrived in the new territories with high expectations that they would find 'the best conditions', they were often very disappointed to find shortages and overcrowding. This soon 'put them off' from the new territories.[38] Such was the amount of coming and going between the central Poland and Jelenia Góra District at this time that the district's Chief Official proposed, in early 1946, that arriving settlers from central Poland should be compelled to submit written declarations confirming that they no longer owned property in central Poland before being allowed to settle there. And if it did transpire that they still owned property in central Poland, it should be confiscated by the Polish state.[39] In the course of 1946, more and more settlers seemed to be voluntarily leaving Jelenia Góra District in order to return to central Poland.[40] This phenomenon is one of the things which distinguished central Polish 're-settlers' from the eastern Polish 'repatriates' most starkly. The latter obviously had no option of returning to their former homes.

The other way in which property became available for reallotment to homeless settlers in Poland's new territories was by the authorities actively removing central Polish settlers from their properties. It was particularly settlers living on farms who were targeted with such actions. This process got underway by the second half of 1945. Jelenia Góra District's Chief Official, for example, reported at that time that some of the

[37] Ibid., pp. 221–2; Hofmann, *Nachkriegszeit*, pp. 163–4.

[38] Rep by JG Chief, 3.10.1945, APJG 123/II, sygn. 18, 127–32; Rep by JG Chief, 6.[8].1945, APJG 123/II, sygn. 18, 3–26.

[39] Rep by JG Chief, 5.1.1946, APJG 123/II, sygn. 18, 206–14; SiRep head JGTA, 6.12.1945, APW 331/VI, sygn. 28, 119–31.

[40] SiRep JG Chief, 2.12.1946, APW 331/VI, sygn. 38, 97–9.

settlers in possession of farms in the district were proving 'unsuitable for their tasks'; they did not possess the necessary farming experience to run them. The district's authorities were therefore starting to confiscate the farms from them.[41] During 1946, a special 'screening committee' carried out the work of identifying 'unsuitable' settlers and confiscating their farms. Interestingly – given our discussion in Chapter 4 about German skilled workers – the designation 'unsuitable' also included those Polish settlers who had important industrial skills, which the state authorities felt were being 'wasted' by the fact that these people had taken up farming. The district's Chief Official remarked in November 1946 that his authorities should be permitted to remove settlers from farms not only when they lacked necessary expertise, but also when they continued to spend much of their time in central Poland. Settlers had to be 'tied to this territory', he declared. In Jelenia Góra District, the farms which became available through these forcible interventions from the local state authorities – as well as through voluntary relinquishment and return to central Poland – were almost always given to eastern Polish 'repatriates from behind the Bug river' rather than to central Polish settlers. This was fully in line with the Ministry for Recovered Territories' November 1946 order.[42]

One settler who appears to have benefited from the priority given to eastern Polish settlers was Stanisław Czepułkowski. He migrated to Jelenia Góra District from the Vilnius region in May 1946. At first he stayed in temporary accommodation in the village of Cieplice while he looked for a permanent home for his family in the district. Then after several months living in the district, he heard from a work colleague that a settler in possession of a farm in the mountain village of Karpacz – in the southern area of Jelenia Góra District – had decided to move back to the central Polish city of Łódź:

> I made use of this information and quickly submitted the necessary documents to the Settlement Department of the District Administration [*Starostwo Powiatowe*] in Jelenia Góra. I then went with my work colleague to Karpacz. But on arrival he made clear to me that he was not willing to mediate the settlement process. Instead, he just showed me the property and said 'go and sort it out with him yourself colleague'. So I went and presented myself [to the settler and said] I was interested in his farm. After some hesitation he agreed to give me the farm on the condition that I paid him something for the farming he had already done there. I agreed and on 17 December 1946 became the user [*użytkownik*] of a 3.89 hectare farm in Karpacz, at 9 Kolejowa Street (formerly 50 Zarzecze Street).[43]

[41] Rep by JG Chief, 3.10.1945, APJG 123/II, sygn. 18, 127–32.
[42] Rep by JG Chief, 5.1.1946, APJG 123/II, sygn. 18, 206–14; Rep by JG Chief, 2.11.1946, APJG 123/II, sygn. 19, 401–5; Czepułkowski, 'W Karpaczu', p. 286.
[43] Czepułkowski, 'W Karpaczu', pp. 289–90.

Despite the fact that settlers were no longer being transported to Jelenia Góra District in cargo trains by 1947, the influx of settlers continued over the course of that year. In an effort to reduce this, local officials sent requests to their superiors in Wrocław at this time, asking them not to encourage settlers to come to the district.[44] As we saw in Chapter 4, the continued inflow of settlers kept the pressure on local officials to reduce the number of skilled German workers living in the district and to displace as many of the remaining Germans as possible to the Soviet Zone. The district's Chief Official described the capacity of the district to take in more settlers at this time as 'completely exhausted'. His deputy declared that 'there is no space for new settlers' and that the district should be viewed as 'closed for settlement'.[45] Yet these declarations and requests to Wrocław brought no noticeable reduction in the number of settlers arriving. By the end of 1947 the total number of people living in Jelenia Góra District had reached almost 132,000 – over 97 per cent of whom were now Polish settlers rather than Germans. Despite the fact that almost all the district's Germans had been expelled from the district by this time, the district's overall population still exceeded its prewar size significantly.[46]

The overcrowding of the district only increased in the course of 1948, because settlers continued to arrive under their own steam. According to one official, they were still being drawn there by Jelenia Góra's 'pretty location, good climate and fame in Central Poland'.[47] A large number of forced migrants from the prewar eastern territories were still waiting to be allotted farms in Jelenia Góra District in 1948. These people, as the district's Chief Official stressed at this time, were legally entitled to farms in Poland's new territories, because they had lost farms in prewar eastern Poland. But the state authorities were only able to grant them farms when

44 SiRep JG Chief, 3.3.1947, APJG 123/II, sygn. 21, 33–8; SiRep JG Chief, 2.4.1947, APJG 123/II, sygn. 21, 69–71; SiRep JG DepChief, 3.5.1947, APJG 123/II, sygn. 21, 96–8; Rep on the third quarter of 1947 by JG Chief, 13.11.1947, APJG 123/II, sygn. 21, 232–6; Rep by JGTA, 10.3.1947, APJG 130, sygn. 48, 22–35; Rep by JGTA, 7.5.1947, APJG 130, sygn. 47, 117–21; Rep by JGTA, 6.6.1947, APJG 130, sygn. 47, 159–64.

45 SiRep JG Chief, 3.3.1947, APJG 123/II, sygn. 21, 33–8; SiRep JG DepChief, 4.[6].1947, APJG 123/II, sygn. 21, 131–3; SiRep JG DepChief, 5.[7].1947, APJG 123/II, sygn. 21, 167–8 and 198; SiRep the head of JGTA's Settlement Department, 18.6.1947, APJG 130, sygn. 47, 219–21.

46 Rep by JG Chief, 20.9.1947, APJG 123/II, sygn. 20, 123–4; Rep on the third quarter of 1947 by JG Chief, 13.11.1947, APJG 123/II, sygn. 21, 232–6; Rep on the year 1947 probably by JG Chief, undated, APJG 123/II, sygn. 21, 248–79; Rep by JGTA, early October 1947, APJG 130, sygn. 48, 59–64; Rep on the year 1947 by JGTA, 10.1.[1948], APJG 130, sygn. 48, 10–21; Bohmann, *Menschen*, p. 209.

47 Rep on the second quarter of 1948 by JGT Pres, start of July 1948, APW 331/VI, sygn. 50, 15–21; Rep on the third quarter of 1948 by JGT Pres, 30.9.1948 APW 331/VI, sygn. 50, 42–8; Rep on the third quarter of the 1948 by JG Chief, 2.10.1948, APW 331/VI, sygn. 51, 72–7; SiRep JG Chief, 3.12.1948, APW 331/VI, sygn. 51, 79–81; SiRep JG Chief, 27.12.1948, APW 331/VI, sygn. 51, 82–6.

central Polish settlers chose voluntarily to relinquish them and to return home to central Poland. The voluntary return of central Polish settlers to central Poland had never constituted a very large outflow of people. But by 1948 the district's authorities had become totally reliant on it as a means of freeing up farms and housing for needy eastern Polish settlers. They were no longer actively confiscating farms from 'inappropriate' settlers by this time.[48]

THE COMMUNIST VISION

As the process of 'Stalinization' set in in Poland in 1948, the regime's revolutionary programme of socioeconomic transformation was radicalized dramatically – impacting heavily on the situation of Polish settlers in Poland's new territories. From the outset, the regime's efforts to alter socioeconomic structures in Poland radically had been targeted primarily at Poland's countryside rather than its urban centres and industry – and particularly the countryside of Poland's new territories. We have already discussed one element of this programme of socioeconomic transformation: the land reform.[49] Another early radical measure was the creation of state farms. State farms were established throughout Poland's new territories in the aftermath of the war. One settler who arrived in Jelenia Góra town in April 1946 – shortly before the mass transportation of Germans got underway – described how he joined a state farm after hearing that a new one was looking for workers in the village of Korczakowo (later renamed Barcinek), 10 km from Jelenia Góra town:

> The employment conditions were 200 złoty per month plus farm produce and accommodation for the family . . . For the time being, I would be the only Pole working on the farm, apart from the cowman and his family. Before then the farm had been run indirectly from a station in the nearby village of Bobrowice with the assistance of a local German steward. The farm was a typical livestock one, around 200 hectares in size . . . My work mainly involved protecting the remaining possessions of the farm, sowing the fields and looking after the cowshed. Milk was the farm's only source of income. It had to be delivered to Jelenia Góra town every day. The day started at dawn when the [German] workers gathered in front of my office and the [German] steward gave me a quantitative report in a soldier-like manner. I then assigned work [to the Germans] and despatched the milkman to the town . . . Gradually more and more [Polish settlers] arrived in Korczakowo and the administrative posts on the farm were steadily filled.[50]

[48] Rep on the first quarter of 1948 by JG Chief, 6.4.1948, APW 331/VI, sygn. 51, 48–52; Rep by JG Chief on the period 1.10.1946–30.7.1947, 23.8.1947, APJG 123/II, sygn. 21, 223–9; SiRep JG Chief, 3.3.1947, APJG 123/II, sygn. 21, 33–8.

[49] Ther, *Vertriebene*, pp. 171–2.

[50] Jaroszewski, 'Na turoszowskiej budowie', pp. 68–9.

As this example illustrates, very large numbers of Germans were employed on state farms in Poland's new territories in the initial postwar years. Directors of these farms therefore strongly resisted the displacement of their German workers when the mass transportation of Germans got underway in spring 1946. But ultimately they proved unable to prevent this from happening. Nevertheless, at the start of 1947, 52,000 Germans were still being employed on state farms throughout Poland's new territories, compared to only 26,000 Poles. The state farms had great problems attracting Polish settlers as employees, because the settlers tended to want farms of their own. The ones from central Poland had often come to the new territories for that very reason. As more and more Germans were expelled from these territories, running the state farms became more and more of a struggle. This explains the dramatic change of attitude shown by Jelenia Góra District's Chief Official towards the expulsion of Germans towards the end of 1947. The Chief Official was extremely enthusiastic about expelling Germans in the first year or two after the war (see Chapter 4). But in November 1947 – when the 'third phase' of the 'displacement action' had just come to an end and there were barely more than 2000 Germans left in the district – he suddenly started to complain about the lack of unskilled German agricultural labourers remaining there.[51]

In 1948, Poland's Communist-controlled government decided to subject the county's agricultural sector to a far more radical change. Midway through that year, at a crucial international meeting of the new Cominform organization, the Communist leaders of East-Central and Eastern Europe's new People's Democracies committed themselves to the collectivization of agriculture. In Poland, two Polish Workers' Party central committee plenums took place after this meeting, in summer 1948. At them, the Polish Communist leaders took the decision to begin collectivizing farmland throughout the country. The political backdrop to this was the political marginalization of the Polish Workers' Party's General Secretary, Władysław Gomułka (see Chapter 2). His fall from power was cemented by the dissolution of the Ministry for Recovered Territories in January 1949, the ministry which he had led since autumn 1945. The process of collectivizing farms in Poland got underway in late 1948. It was not at first implemented using force, as it had been in the 1930s USSR. Nevertheless, it triggered a great deal of unease among the rural population of Poland.[52]

[51] Rep by JG Chief on the third quarter of 1947, 13.11.1947, APJG 123/II, sygn. 21, 232–6; Hofmann, *Nachkriegszeit*, pp. 168–71.

[52] Paczkowski, *Spring*, pp. 203–19; Hofmann, *Nachkriegszeit*, pp. 181–6; Ther, *Vertriebene*, pp. 154–5, 241–2.

The initial impact of collectivization on Jelenia Góra District is not exactly clear. But in late 1948 and early 1949, a particularly large number of settlers appear to have relinquished their farms in the district and returned to central Poland. It is almost certain that this had something to do with the collectivization campaign. Significantly, the district's Chief Official began to show far more concern at this time about return-migrations to central Poland than he had done in previous years. Indeed, he started to offer diverse explanations for why it was happening. In December 1948, he noted that although settlers generally claimed that the reasons they were relinquishing their farms in the district were illness or not liking the climate, the actual reason was that they were only 'farmers by chance' and just wanted 'easy profits'.[53] Some, he added a month later, had already accumulated enough money while living in Jelenia Góra District to buy land and build a house in central Poland.[54] In late January 1949 he supplemented his previous explanations with yet another one: these settlers were abandoning their farms because they were not allowed to employ labourers on them. This is very interesting because the Chief Official was referring here to another manifestation of the government's programme of socioeconomic change: the ruling contained in the September 1946 settlement decree that those settlers who took possession of individual farms were not allowed to employ paid workers on them.[55] In spring 1949, Jelenia Góra District's Chief Official was suddenly replaced – having held the position for almost four years. The new Chief Official deviated somewhat from the line taken by his predecessor, agreeing that 'the lack of labour on farms' was one reason for the return migration of settlers to central Poland. At the same time, he stressed that another reason for it was the district's harsh mountainous climate, which farmers, originally from the lowlands of central Poland, were unable to adapt to. He added that fear of possible sanctions for not carrying out spring agricultural work also caused some to leave.[56]

The district's first and second postwar Chief Officials were sensible enough not to state explicitly that a widespread fear among settlers that farms were about to be forcibly collectivized was causing a large number of them to return to central Poland. But it seems very likely this was precisely the message they were attempting to get across to their superiors at the

[53] SiRep JG Chief, 3.12.1948, APW 331/VI, sygn. 51, 79–81. This contradicted an opinion he had put forward two years earlier – see SiRep JG Chief, 2.12.1946, APW 331/VI, sygn. 38, 97–9.

[54] SiRep JG Chief, 27.12.1948, APW 331/VI, sygn. 51, 82–6.

[55] SiRep JG Chief, 31.1.1949, APJG 123/II, sygn. 20, 240–44; Hofmann, *Nachkriegszeit*, pp. 162–8.

[56] Rep by JG Chief on the first quarter of 1949, 6.4.1949, APW 331/VI, sygn. 51, 105–10; SiRep JG Chief, 7.4.1949, APW 331/VI, sygn. 51, 101–4; Rep on the third quarter of the year by JG Chief, start October 1949, APW 331/VI, sygn. 51, 154–9.

Regional Administration in Wrocław by devoting so much space in official reports to the exodus of settler-farmers from the district.

Collectivization hit Poland's new territories much harder than the rest of Poland. This stemmed from how slowly the transfer of the ownership of farms to settlers had proceeded since the issuing of the settlement decree in September 1946. By 1948 the property transfer process, initiated by that decree, had pretty much ground to a halt. By that time a mere 5 per cent of the agricultural land in Poland's new territories had passed from the Polish state into private hands. With so much land either already under state control or liable to be taken over by the state from their settler 'users' at short notice, it was possible for Poland's newly Stalinized regime to proceed with the collectivization of land in Poland's new territories much more rapidly and comprehensively than elsewhere in the country. The state authorities used various forms of economic pressure to induce farmers in the new territories to join collective farms; later, overt force was deployed. For the forced migrants from prewar eastern Poland, this was the second time in less than a decade that they confronted forcible collectivization, having experienced it for the first time during the Soviet occupation of their homelands in 1939–41 (see Chapter 1).[57]

One of the many settlers who did not respond to collectivization by leaving Jelenia Góra District recalled its introduction at the end of the 1940s:

> Soon we started to witness on our own farm the first phases of the new tendency in agriculture. The collective which I joined was made up of around 15 member farms. It was a type III collective. The area of shared cultivation amounted to around 100 hectares. The crops were the easiest part of the work to deal with because they were cultivated on the basis of top-down inspired and approved production plans. Livestock proved a more difficult issue. The selection of horses, switching over to motorization, preserving the pedigree of cattle and swine – all of these matters were long-term processes connected to investment, construction and the adaptation of stables, barns, pigsties etc.[58]

THE NATIONALIST VISION

Despite the significant exodus of settlers who relinquished their farms and returned to central Poland at the end of the 1940s, it would seem that even in 1949 the number of Polish settlers living in Jelenia Góra District grew as a result of the persistent inflow of new settlers. The number of settlers still

[57] Ther, *Vertriebene*, pp. 224–5, 241–3; Hofmann, *Nachkriegszeit*, pp. 183–4.
[58] Jaroszewski, 'Na turoszowskiej budowie', p. 71.

waiting to be allotted farms in the district increased gradually in the course of this final year of the decade.[59] The state authorities' fundamental goal of repopulating the district with Polish settlers, then, had been well and truly accomplished by the end of the 1940s. The new population of the district was almost entirely Polish; there were probably fewer than 1,500 Germans living there by 1949.

Yet this new settler population was by no means a culturally or linguistically homogeneous one. Almost all the Polish settlers now living in Jelenia Góra District were either from central Poland or from the prewar eastern territories ceded to the Soviet Union in July 1944. But a small fraction were also from Polish émigré communities abroad, who had been enticed to relocate to Poland from various foreign countries. The government launched a campaign at the end of the war to 'bring back' Polish émigrés from abroad in order to help replenish the population of Poland, after the loss of millions of its citizens through Nazi German genocide and mass killing during the war. The other purpose of this campaign was to provide the fledgling Communist regime with a much needed propaganda boost. It would put out the message that even people who had experienced other ways of running a country were buying into the Communist model. Two hundred five thousand émigrés were ultimately persuaded to relocate to Poland, coming above all from France, the British, American and French Occupation Zones of Germany, Yugoslavia and the United States. The 'repatriations' from these countries almost all took place between 1946 and 1949. Nearly three-quarters of the former émigrés were resettled in Poland's new territories.[60]

It is not exactly clear how many arriving Polish émigrés settled in Jelenia Góra District after the war, but it was certainly only a very small number. They included Adam Jaroszewski and his family, who moved there from Sarajevo after the war. Around 30,000 ethnic Poles had been living in Yugoslavia in the late 1930s – mainly the product of immigration from Poland in the late nineteenth century. At the end of the Second World War, like various other ethnic minorities living in the region, Yugoslavia's Poles

[59] SiRep JG Chief, 3.12.1948, APW 331/VI, sygn. 51, 79–81; SiRep JG Chief, 27.12.1948, APW 331/VI, sygn. 51, 82–6; SiRep JG Chief, 31.1.1949, APJG 123/II, sygn. 20, 240–4; Rep by JG Chief on the first quarter of 1949, 6.4.1949, APW 331/VI, sygn. 51, 105–10; SiRep JG Chief, 7.4.1949, APW 331/VI, sygn. 51, 101–4; SiRep JG Chief, 30.4.1949, APW 331/VI, sygn. 51, 111–12; SiRep JG Chief, 31.5.1949, APW 331/VI, sygn. 51, 113–15; SiRep JG Chief, 8.7.1949, APW 331/VI, sygn. 51, 117–20; SiRep JG DepChief, 5.10.1949, APW 331/VI, sygn. 51, 160–62; Rep by JG Chief on the third quarter of 1949, early October 1949, APW 331/VI, sygn. 51, 154–9.

[60] Hofmann, *Nachkriegszeit*, pp. 142–4.

started to come under attack from Serbian-nationalist Četnik paramilitaries. In the second half of 1945, negotiations took place between the Yugoslav Poles and Communist-controlled Polish authorities regarding the possibility of resettling to Lower Silesia. In January 1946, an agreement was reached between Poland and Yugoslavia's Communist governments and a number of 'repatriation trains' transported Yugoslav Poles directly to Lower Silesia from April 1946 onwards. Yet before these Lower Silesia-bound 'repatriation trains' set off, some Yugoslav Poles had already migrated to Poland.[61] Adam Jaroszewski, for example, described how he migrated with his family from Sarajevo to Jelenia Góra District already in the second half of 1945. The first leg of this journey seems to have entailed travelling from Sarajevo to Hungary, where they boarded a 'repatriation train' bound for Poland:

> It was the afternoon of 15 September 1945 when my family and I stepped out of a repatriation train from Hungary at Swoszowice railway station near the city of Kraków with all our possessions. The comrades we had met during the journey travelled onwards further into Poland . . . Around 15 of us got out at Swoszowice. Horse-carts were standing ready for us at the station to transport us and our things to nearby Kraków. I put my family and our belongings on one of them. There were four of us: my 25-year-old wife and me, 41 years old, as well as our two little daughters, three-year-old Monika and two-year-old Jolanta. All that we now owned consisted of two bundles of bedclothes, three shabby cases containing the rest of our things and an empty basket in which we had carried our food for the journey. [Having arrived at my aunt's apartment in Kraków, been warmly welcomed by her and eaten a modest meal together] we quickly fell asleep. Several days travelling in a troop-train cattle wagon had really taken it out of us . . . Early the next day I rushed down to the [State] Repatriation Office to announce our return and was issued with a resettlement card. [Shortly after that, I left my family with my aunt in Kraków and moved to Wrocław, where I found work helping to run a warehouse.] My duties were not restricted to Wrocław. Frequently I had to travel to Kraków to fetch goods . . . In April 1946, as part of my work, I found myself in Jelenia Góra [and] decided to resettle there with my family. [In late April I moved from Wrocław to a village in Jelenia Góra District, where I had already found employment and a place to live. Midway through May 1946] I travelled to Kraków to fetch my family.[62]

Aside from the small number of former Polish émigrés from Yugoslavia and from a number of Western countries who took up residence in the district after the war, the vast majority of the new settler population, as

[61] Ibid. pp. 144–5. [62] Jaroszewski, 'Na turoszowskiej budowie', pp. 66–8.

should be clear, were from prewar Polish territories. These people were regarded by the Communist-controlled state authorities as forming two separate groups: 'resettlers' from central Poland and 'repatriates' from prewar eastern Poland. In the town of Jelenia Góra, the latter made up around two-thirds of the population at the end of the 1940s. They also made up the majority of settlers in the rural areas of the district – perhaps a ratio of eastern Polish 'repatriates' to central Polish 'resettlers' similar to that in the town.[63] The cultural and linguistic differences between these two 'groups' were stark and the district's authorities very often described relations between them as poor. The district's Chief Official noted in 1947, for example, that settlers from central Poland had a habit of disparagingly calling the eastern Polish forced migrants 'Ukrainians', because of the different way they spoke Polish.[64] In 1949, 'sporadic cases' of 'regional antagonism' between the two 'groups' were still being reported by the district's offficials.[65]

Yet the cultural and linguistic heterogeneity of the district's settler population ran still deeper than differences between the eastern Polish 'repatriates' and the central Polish 'resettlers'. There was also considerable cultural and linguistic diversity *within* each of these 'groups'. This was particularly true of the eastern Polish forced migrants, who came from localities scattered across the absolutely vast swaths of territory ceded to the Soviet Union in July 1944. As was the case in the whole of Lower Silesia, the majority of eastern Polish forced migrants now living in Jelenia Góra District probably came from the prewar southeastern Polish territories which had been handed to Soviet Ukraine in July 1944. A much smaller number came from the territories ceded to Soviet Lithuania and Soviet Belorussia.[66] The cultural heterogeneity of the district's new settler population prompted the district's Chief Official to describe it as 'a conglomeration of the various

[63] Rep by JG Chief on the third quarter of 1947, 13.11.1947, APJG 123/II, sygn. 21, 232–6; Rep on the year 1947 by JG Chief, undated, APJG 123/II, sygn. 21, 248–79; Rep on the first quarter of 1948 by JG Chief, 6.1.1948, APW 331/VI, sygn. 51, 48–52; SiRep the head of JGTA's Settlement Department, 18.6.1947, APJG 130, sygn. 47, 219–21.

[64] SiRep JG Chief, 2.1.1947, APW 331/VI, sygn. 39, 15–17; Rep on the third quarter of 1947 by JG Chief, 13.11.1947, APJG 123/II, sygn. 21, 232–6; Rep on the first quarter of 1948, 6.4.1948 by JG Chief, APW 331/VI, sygn. 51, 48–52; Rep on the year 1947 by JG Chief, undated, APJG 123/II, sygn. 21, 248–79; SiRep JG Chief, 1.2.1947, APW 331/VI, sygn. 51, 1–4; SiRep JG Chief, 3.12.1948, APW 331/VI, sygn. 51, 79–81.

[65] Rep on the third quarter of 1949 for LSRA by JG DepChief, 3.1049, APW 331/VI, sygn. 51, 154–9; SiRep JG DepChief on the third quarter of 1949 for LSRA S-PD, 5.10.1949, APW 331/VI, sygn. 51, 160–2.

[66] Borodziej et al., 'Wstęp', p. 44; Thum, *Breslau*, pp. 159–61; Czepułkowski, 'W Karpaczu', pp. 283–300.

regions of Poland' and a 'mosaic of society deriving from different parts of Poland'.[67]

In localities throughout Poland's new territories, the same high levels of cultural and linguistic diversity were very much in evidence in the late 1940s. In every district in these territories where there was a large number of settlers, the new population came from all over prewar Polish territory as well as from abroad.[68] Moreover, adding further to the new population's heterogeneity was a significant number of 'Ukrainians'. As we shall discuss in the Conclusion, the Communist-led Polish authorities expelled around 483,000 ethnic Ukrainians from Poland to Soviet Ukraine between 1944 and 1946. But this had left around 150,000 individuals living in southeastern Poland, whom the authorities viewed as 'Ukrainians' and whom others categorized also as Lemkos, Rusyns, Russians and Belorussians. Principally in order to advance its objective of transforming Poland into a homogeneous nation-state, the Communist-led government decided to relocate these people from their homelands in postwar southeastern Poland to the new territories in late spring 1947. This plan was known as *Akcja Wisła* (Operation Vistula). It was carried out between 28 April and 31 July 1947. Polish military and security forces rounded up approximately 140,000 'Ukrainians' in southeastern Poland and transported them in cargo trains to the new territories. On arrival there they were deliberately dispersed in order to ensure swift cultural assimilation among the territories' new Polish settler communities. A maximum of two to three 'Ukrainian' families were allowed to settle in each village in the new territories. Over one-third were sent to southern East Prussia. The remainder were scattered across the other regions of the new territories. Many were sent to Lower Silesia and some may have ended up in Jelenia Góra District, because a number of Eastern Orthodox (*Prawosławny*) Church members suddenly seem to have arrived there in the second half of 1947. They numbered just over 150 in 1948. Most of them lived in Jelenia Góra town.[69] We shall return

[67] SiRep JG Chief, dated 27.12.1948, APW 331/VI, sygn. 51, 82–6; Rep on the first quarter of 1949 by JG Chief, 6.4.1949, APW 331/VI, sygn. 51, 105–10.

[68] Ther, *Vertriebene*, pp. 145, 253; Thum, *Breslau*, pp. 159–61.

[69] Marek Jasiak, 'Overcoming Ukrainian Resistance: The Deportation of Ukrainians within Poland in 1947', in Philipp Ther and Ana Siljak (eds.), *Redrawing Nations*, pp. 173–89; Orest Subtelny, 'Expulsion, Resettlement, Civil Strife: The Fate of Poland's Ukrainians, 1944–1947', in Philipp Ther and Ana Siljak (eds.), *Redrawing Nations*, pp. 166–8; Konrad Zieliński, 'To Pacify, Populate and Polonise: Territorial Transformations and the Displacement of Ethnic Minorities in Communist Poland, 1944–49', in Peter Gatrell and Nick Baron (eds.), *Warlands: Population Resettlement and State Reconstruction in the Soviet–East European Borderlands, 1945–50* (Basingstoke, 2009), pp. 197–9; Thum, *Breslau*, pp. 128–9; Rep on the third quarter of 1947 by JG Chief, 13.11.1947, AP JG 123/II,

once more to the subject of *Akcja Wisła* and the expulsions carried against ethnic Ukrainians in 1944–6 in the Conclusion.

Pointing to the cultural and linguistic diversity of the new settler population of Poland's new territories adds an important layer of complexity to the claim that the Communist-led government established a new ethnonationally homogeneous Polish society in these territories in the second half of the 1940s. Nevertheless, it cannot be disputed that the linguistically and culturally German population living in most localities of Poland's new territories before 1945 had been – almost entirely – replaced by a culturally and linguistically Polish one by the end of the 1940s, albeit a culturally and linguistically heterogeneous one. The government's twin policies of expulsion and repopulation had therefore achieved one of the Polish Communists' key nationalist goals.

But another important qualification must be added. By no means every locality in Poland's new territories was repopulated quite so comprehensively as was Jelenia Góra District. Indeed, there was a great deal of variation in the density of the settler population across the new territories at the end of the 1940s. This was determined largely by differences in the amount of damage which had been inflicted on buildings and infrastructure in the different localities by wartime Allied bombing and by ground-warfare in the final phase of the war. The uneven distribution of Polish settlers across these territories was reduced somewhat by deliberate actions taken by local Polish officials to relocate some settlers from heavily crowded areas in these territories to more sparsely populated ones during the early postwar years. Nevertheless, at the end of the decade there remained a great deal of variation in population density. Western Upper Silesia and southern Lower Silesia were the most heavily populated regions in the new territories. Many districts in these regions had populations which, like Jelenia Góra District's one, were larger at the end of the 1940s than they had been at the end of the 1930s. The fact that other areas in Poland's new territories remained sparsely populated at the end of the decade stemmed not only from uneven population distribution, but also from the fact that the number of Polish settlers who came to live in these territories in the second half of the 1940s did not actually equal the number of Germans who left them between 1944 and 1949. Over 7.5 million Germans, in total, abandoned Poland's new territories for good in the years 1944–9, either through wartime flight or through postwar expulsion. In contrast, only around 4 million Polish

sygn. 21, 232–6; SiRep JGT Pres, 31.5.1948, APW 331/VI, sygn. 50, 4–8; SiRep JG Chief, 3.12.1948, APW 331/VI, sygn. 51, 79–81.

settlers arrived to replace them between 1945 and 1949. Of these, 2.5 million were 'resettlers' from central Poland; 1.3 million were 'repatriates' from prewar eastern Poland; and just over 200,000 were former Polish émigrés from various foreign countries.[70]

———

The arrival of millions of Polish settlers between 1945 and 1949 utterly transformed the character of the prewar eastern German territories. The policy of repopulation assumed truly massive proportions in the first two years after Soviet 'liberation'. Within weeks of the first Polish looters and settlers arriving in these lands in spring 1945, the Communist-controlled authorities began transporting hundreds of thousands of settlers there from both central and prewar eastern Poland on cargo trains. This enormous influx helped to trigger and sustain the pace of the expulsion of Germans in 1945 and 1946. Thereafter the inflow decreased a great deal in size. The authorities stopped transferring settlers there from 1947 onwards. This was partly in response to complaints from local state officials in the new territories, who had been struggling to find enough housing for these settlers in their overcrowded or badly war-damaged districts. But a more modest inflow of Polish settlers continued right through to the end of the decade. Not every settler remained in these territories in the long run. Some chose to return to central Poland. The collectivization of agriculture played a role in this after 1948. But the vast majority stayed.

The arrival of millions of new residents, bringing with them their own cultural traditions and practices, made the cities, towns and villages of the new territories feel like very different places at the end of the decade from what they had been in 1945. So too did the increasingly repressive and radical policies of Poland's Communist-controlled regime. Those prewar residents of these territories who continued to live there throughout the 1940s must, very often, have struggled to comprehend what was going on around them. This was true not only of the roughly 300,000 remaining German citizens whom the authorities regarded as ethnically German (see Chapter 4), but also the much larger group of German citizens who the regime believed were 'indigenous Poles'. Let us now examine what happened to them at the end of the Second World War.

[70] Thum, *Breslau*, p. 133; Ther, *Vertriebene*, pp. 125, 216–17; Nitschke, *Vertreibung*, pp. 271–80; Hofmann, *Nachkriegszeit*, pp. 115–16, 161–2.

CHAPTER 6

Verification

In Jelenia Góra District and in most other localities in the territories which Poland acquired from Germany at the end of the Second World War, almost all residents had spoken only German and regarded themselves as Germans before 1945. In the vast majority of localities in Poland's new territories, the end of the war was the first time Polish nationalist ideas and objectives had had any discernible impact on the lives of the local inhabitants. But this was not true of all areas of Poland's new territories. In western Upper Silesia and southern East Prussia, the events which followed the Second World War represented a new phase in a fierce struggle between Polish and German nationalists. This struggle had started at the end of the nineteenth century and culminated in the upheavals and plebiscite campaigns which followed the end of the First World War. The end of the Second World War provided the circumstances for a second climax in this struggle. But this time the struggle was one-sided, and the Polish side was represented by a Communist-controlled government with the backing of the Soviet Union.

UPPER SILESIA BEFORE 1945

Upper Silesia had always represented something of a frontier province for the rulers in Berlin. The region first became part of Prussia in the mid eighteenth century. It had lost its connection with Poland four centuries earlier and had passed first to the Bohemian Kingdom and then to the Habsburg Empire before it was conquered by Prussia's Frederick the Great in 1742. At the start of the nineteenth century, its inhabitants were overwhelmingly Catholics and speakers of a regional Polish dialect, with German speakers mainly restricted to the towns of the region.[1] Under Prussian rule,

[1] Eser, 'Oberschlesien', pp. 360–1; Kraft, 'Wrocławskie', pp. 358–9; T. Hunt Tooley, *National Identity and Weimar Germany. Upper Silesia and the Eastern Border, 1918–1922* (Lincoln and London, 1997),

German became the language of both state administration and education. The introduction of popular elementary education in 1825 and the rapid industrialization of Upper Silesia in the nineteenth century gradually disseminated knowledge of German among more and more of the region's inhabitants.

Yet standard Polish also started to gain a foothold in the region in the early-mid nineteenth century. In 1822 the Prussian state authorized the use of Polish in schools and churches. In 1848 the Roman Catholic Church, backed by the Prussian state's school inspector in Upper Silesia, used its control over primary and secondary schooling in the region to introduce standard Polish as a teaching language in schools. However, this increasingly liberal stance taken by the Prussian state towards the Polish language lasted only until 1863. In that year Prussian officials reinstated German as the principal language of education in Upper Silesia. By that time knowledge of German had become a prerequisite for upward social mobility. Language and class were by the mid-late nineteenth century inextricably intertwined: the middle and upper classes of Upper Silesia spoke German, whereas the lower orders continued to use the regional Polish dialect.[2]

After founding the German Reich in 1871, Otto von Bismarck launched a secularist and nationalist campaign to undermine the Roman Catholic Church throughout the Reich and the Polish language in the eastern provinces. This campaign was known as the *Kulturkampf*, and Upper Silesia was one of its principal battlegrounds. It began with the dissolution of the Catholic Department at the Prussian Ministry of Culture in Berlin in the same year that the Reich was created. A year later, control over education in Upper Silesia was removed from the Roman Catholic Church. During the next few years, standard Polish was prohibited in the final two areas of education in Upper Silesia where the state still permitted its use: the teaching of first-year primary school pupils and religious education. In 1876 German became the only language allowed for use in the region's

pp. 6–7; Siebel-Achenbach, *Lower Silesia*, pp. 6–11; Ther, 'Die einheimische Bevölkerung', p. 411; Manfred Alexander, 'Oberschlesien im 20. Jahrhundert – eine mißverstandene Region', *Geschichte und Gesellschaft* 30, 2004, pp. 469–71.

[2] Tomasz Kamusella, *Silesia and Central European Nationalism. The Emergence of National and Ethnic Groups in Prussian Silesia and Austrian Silesia, 1848–1918* (West Lafayette, Indiana, 2007), pp. 115–19, 122, 171–3; Kamusella, *The Szlonzoks and Their Language: Between Germany, Poland and Szlonzokian Nationalism* (EUI working paper, Florence, 2003), pp. 11–13, 14–18; James E. Bjork, *Neither German nor Pole. Catholicism and National Indifference in a Central European Borderland* (Ann Arbor, Michigan, 2008), pp. 60–2; Tooley, *National Identity*, pp. 8–14; Ther, 'Die einheimische Bevölkerung', p. 411; Alexander, 'Oberschlesien', pp. 471–4; Piotr Madajczyk, 'Oberschlesien zwischen Gewalt und Frieden', in Philipp Ther and Holm Sundhaussen (eds.), *Nationalitätenkonflikte im 20. Jahrhundert: Ursachen von inter-ethnischer Gewalt im Vergleich* (Wiesbaden, 2001), pp. 148–9.

government offices. Then in 1886 the civil service was ordered to dismiss all staff who could not speak German.[3]

The Roman Catholic Church and the Catholic *Zentrum* Party condemned these German nationalist attacks on the Polish language, believing that the spread of German would facilitate the expansion of Protestantism into Catholic Upper Silesia. At the same time, the Catholic Church continued, defiantly, to provide church services in standard Polish and to teach religion to children in churches in that language. From the 1870s onwards, the Church also sponsored the creation of Catholic Polish-language newspapers. Through these actions, the Roman Catholic Church attempted to advance a Catholic universalist agenda, not a Polish nationalist one. Moreover, rather than triggering an explosion of Polish nationalist feeling among the inhabitants of Upper Silesia, the widespread alienation caused by Bismarck's *Kulturkampf* merely transferred the region politically into the hands of the Catholic *Zentrum* Party. The region remained a *Zentrum* Party stronghold through the rest of the nineteenth century.[4]

At the turn of the century, Upper Silesia's politics underwent considerable change. By the start of the twentieth century, Polish nationalism was at last playing an important role in the region's politics. It had been imported to Upper Silesia in the 1890s by activists from the Posen region. It had manifested itself at first in Polish nationalist newspapers. But around the turn of the century, a young Upper Silesian called Wojciech Korfanty seized control of the Polish nationalist movement in the region and began to funnel its energy into parliamentary politics. In the 1903 statewide elections, he made a crucial breakthrough, winning a seat in Germany's state parliament, the *Reichstag*. In 1907, his nationalist movement did even better, winning five of Upper Silesia's 12 *Reichstag* seats.[5]

The Berlin government responded to the rising tide of Polish nationalism in Upper Silesia with a new anti-Polish drive. German nationalists also moved into the region, bringing in organizations such as the *Deutscher Ostmarkenverein* and seeking to advance use of the German language through both German-language newspapers and bilingual German–Polish ones. The Polish–German nationalist struggle was therefore already very lively before the outbreak of the First World War.[6]

[3] Kamusella, *Silesia*, pp. 174–6; Kamusella, *The Szlonzoks*, p. 13; Tooley, *National Identity*, pp. 14–15.

[4] Kamusella, *Silesia*, pp. 175–81; Bjork, *Neither*, pp. 63–70; Tooley, *National Identity*, pp. 14–16; Alexander, 'Oberschlesien', pp. 479–80.

[5] Kamusella, *Silesia*, pp. 182–95, 202–3; Madajczyk, 'Oberschlesien', p. 151; Bjork, *Neither*, pp. 98–119; Tooley, *National Identity*, pp. 15–16.

[6] Kamusella, *Silesia*, pp. 195–9; Tooley, *National Identity*, pp. 14–15; Bjork, *Neither*, pp. 89–98; Kamusella, *The Szlonzoks*, pp. 12–13; Ther, 'Die einheimische Bevölkerung', pp. 413–14; Alexander, 'Oberschlesien', pp. 476–80.

But the war dramatically changed circumstances in Upper Silesia. The First World War placed wrenching demands on eastern Upper Silesia's massive coal and steel industry. It brought about a drastic deterioration in working conditions and acute food shortages. Strikes proliferated after summer 1917. Once again, local people began turning towards the Polish nationalist movement as a way to express their grievances. This movement had waned considerably in the half decade leading up to the war. But at the end of the war, it rediscovered the vitality it had enjoyed at the start of the century.

These, then, were the political and social circumstances prevailing in Upper Silesia in 1919. It was at this time that diplomatic discussions got underway among the Western powers in Paris about how the territories of East-Central and Eastern Europe should be reshaped now that Germany had been defeated and the Austro-Hungarian and Russian Empires had collapsed. One of the key questions was whether Upper Silesia should remain in Germany or be handed to the newly recreated state of Poland. Unwilling to decide one way or the other, in June 1919 the powers announced that a plebiscite would determine the region's future.[7]

This decision sparked three years of violent nationalist struggle in Upper Silesia. Three armed uprisings took place in this period. The first broke out in August 1919, launched by pro-Polish paramilitaries after several days of strikes in eastern Upper Silesia. It was quickly and forcefully put down by German armed units, mostly regular troops. But tensions remained high. The violence escalated steadily as the plebiscite campaign intensified. The following year, after a pro-German riot in Kattowitz in August 1920, Korfanty set off the second uprising. Thousands of pro-Polish armed paramilitaries took control of most of eastern Upper Silesia before Korfanty called the uprising off at the end of the month. It was not until the following spring, 20 March 1921, that the plebiscite was finally held. The results revealed strong support for Poland in the eastern area of the region. But the overall vote was won by Germany with 60 per cent. The German victory was helped by the votes of tens of thousands of Upper Silesian economic migrants, who were deliberately transported to the region from western Germany in order to boost the German vote.

Convinced that this outcome would prompt the Western powers to hand Poland only part of eastern Upper Silesia, on 2 May pro-Polish paramilitaries staged the third uprising. With the help of volunteers and supplies from Poland, pro-Polish forces, numbering tens of thousands, soon gained

[7] Tooley, *National Identity*, pp. 20–3, 45–52; Madajczyk, 'Oberschlesien', pp. 151–4; Tomasz Kamusella, 'Upper Silesia 1918–1945', in Karl Cordell (ed.), *The Politics of Ethnicity in Central Europe* (Basingstoke, 2000), pp. 94–5.

control of not only eastern Upper Silesia but also the central and western areas of the region. On 18 May 1921 government-backed German paramilitaries struck back. All-out paramilitary warfare engulfed almost the entire region. The pro-Polish forces suffered their key defeat at the Annaberg on 21 May, when they were thrust back into their eastern stronghold. Hostilities were finally brought to an end through the intervention of Western diplomats and peacekeepers in July 1921.[8]

After this, Britain and France decided that the only way to restore long-term stability to the region would be to partition it between Germany and Poland. They did so in accordance with the recommendations of a special League of Nations commission in 1922. Poland was granted the heavily industrialized area of the region. This meant the whole of eastern Upper Silesia, including the towns of Kattowitz, Tarnowitz and Königshütte. Germany kept hold of western Upper Silesia, including the towns of Gleiwitz, Beuthen, Hindenburg and Oppeln. The partition was followed by large migrations across the new border in both directions. Tens of thousands of Upper Silesia's residents relocated voluntarily to their preferred countries in the early 1920s. But the majority of the region's inhabitants remained where they were. 'National minorities' living on both sides of the new border were assured that their cultural autonomy would be protected by the provisions of a special Upper Silesian Convention. The convention was signed between Germany and Poland in Geneva in May 1922. Its protections were supposed to remain in force until 1937. Special League of Nations offices were established in the region to supervise its implementation.[9]

During the plebiscite campaign, the government of the new state of Poland had promised Upper Silesia's residents far-reaching political autonomy if they voted for Poland. The government fulfilled this promise after the region's partition by awarding eastern Upper Silesia the status of an autonomous region. This region was given the name *Województwo Śląskie* (Silesia Voivodship) and its capital became the city of Katowice (Kattowitz). The Polish government also provided Silesia Voivodship with its own parliament and constitution and its inhabitants were promised control over

[8] Tooley, *National Identity*, pp., 77–9, 182–90, 234–58; Madajczyk, 'Oberschlesien', pp. 151–6; Kamusella, 'Upper Silesia', pp. 95–7.

[9] Michał Lis, 'Mniejszość polska w niemieckiej części Górnego Śląska', in *"Wach auf, mein Herz, und denke". Zur Geschichte der Beziehungen zwischen Schlesien und Berlin-Brandenburg von 1740 bis heute* (Berlin and Opole, 1995), pp. 261–2; Ther, 'Die einheimische Bevölkerung', pp. 415–17; Kamusella, 'Upper Silesia', pp. 97–8; Tooley, *National Identity*, pp. 257–8; Maria Wanda Wanatowicz, *Historia społeczno-polityczna Górnego Śląska i Śląska Cieszyńskiego w latach 1918–1945* (Katowice, 1994), pp. 146–7.

their own affairs. But cracks quickly started to appear in this liberal edifice. From the outset, many local place names started to be replaced with Polish ones and locals came under pressure from the Polish state authorities to Polonize their surnames. The use of the eastern Upper Silesian dialect of Polish was at first tolerated in schools and in state administration. But when locals failed to show sufficient improvement in their command of standard Polish, they were gradually levered out of their posts in state administration and replaced with individuals from central Poland. Standard Polish slowly but surely became the only official language used in Silesia Voivodship. Moreover, after Józef Piłsudski's successful coup in Warsaw in 1926, eastern Upper Silesia's political elites came under attack for opposition to Piłsudski's *Sanacja* regime. In 1930 Korfanty was put on trial by Piłsudski and imprisoned in the Brest-Litovsk fortress, and in 1935 he was exiled to Czechoslovakia. In the same year, shortly before Piłsudski's death, a new constitution was introduced which withdrew much of the political autonomy given to eastern Upper Silesia in 1922. Furthermore, despite the protections guaranteed to 'national minorities' by the Upper Silesian Convention, monolingual German speakers living in Silesia Voivodship faced serious discrimination from the Polish authorities during the 1920s and 30s. This intensified acutely in the final year of the 1930s, as the threat Nazi Germany posed to Poland grew exponentially.[10]

On the other side of the 1922 border, the situation was no better. The central and western areas of Upper Silesia granted to Germany after the plebiscite were reformed by the government of the Weimar Republic into the new *Provinz Oberschlesien* (Province of Upper Silesia) with a provincial capital in Oppeln. The province lost most of its pro-Polish elites and intelligentsia in the postpartition migrations of the early 1920s. This dealt a severe blow to Polish cultural and political life there. But Polish cultural and nationalist activities were by no means snuffed out. A number of committed pro-Polish activists stayed put, grouped together after 1923 in the regional arm of the Association of Poles in Germany (*Związek Polaków w Niemczech*). This organization's headquarters was soon transferred from Beuthen to Oppeln. Also important for sustaining Polish cultural life in the *Provinz Oberschlesien* was the Polish-Catholic Schools Society (*Polsko-Katolickie Towarzystwo Szkolne*), which also had headquarters in Oppeln. After 1923, the society set up a number of Polish-language state schools. Together with the Association of Poles, it also created a network of

[10] Kamusella, 'Upper Silesia', pp. 99–101; Tooley, *National Identity*, 261–3; Ther, 'Die einheimische Bevölkerung', pp. 419–20; Linek, *Polityka*, pp. 30–3.

Polish libraries in the province. At the same time, Roman Catholic priests continued to provide church services in standard Polish. Various Polish-language newspapers continued to publish. And Polish banks and Polish cooperatives continued to operate.[11]

Yet the influence of these Polish cultural and political organizations on the *Provinz Oberschlesien*'s population should not be overestimated. Less than 1 per cent of pupils in the province attended a Polish-language state school in the interwar period. More impressive was the influence of the Polish-language newspapers – 20,000 copies were being sold in the province in the late 1920s. But even if we assume that each copy was read by a number of readers, this still represented only a minority of the overall population of the region. Moreover, pro-Polish political parties in the *Provinz Oberschlesien* fared badly in interwar elections, even before the Nazis destroyed them in the mid 1930s. Not a single pro-Polish candidate won a *Reichstag* seat there after the First World War. At the peak of their interwar success, in 1925, pro-Polish candidates in the province gained only four seats in the Prussian parliament. Furthermore, even before the Nazis came to power, official attitudes remained openly hostile to Polish language and culture. The German state authorities took measures to prevent Polish dialect speakers from purchasing land in the province and from gaining jobs in commerce and as craftsmen. They also attempted to destroy the network of Polish banks – for example, closing down the Polish *Bank Ludowy* in Oppeln in 1932. Furthermore, even before the Nazis took control in Germany, pro-Polish activists started to fall victim to violent attacks by German nationalist groups.[12]

Contrary to what one might expect, the Nazi seizure of power in 1933 brought some respite from the German state's chauvinistic, nationalistic campaign. The Nazis' hatred was at first targeted at other enemies. But this did not last long. Polish dialect speakers living in the *Provinz Oberschlesien* soon started to lose posts in the state administration. The Germanization of local Slavic place names, begun already in 1931, was radically stepped up in 1933. Locals were put under great pressure to Germanize their Slavic-sounding personal names. Polish libraries and newspaper offices were attacked by Nazi Party activists. School pupils were exposed to intense Nazi propaganda at school and in the Nazi youth organizations. Both schools and youth organizations deliberately stigmatized the regional Polish dialect, causing many young people in western Upper Silesia to lose touch with

[11] Wanatowicz, *Historia*, pp. 145–51; Lis, 'Mniejszość polska', pp. 264–8.
[12] Wanatowicz, *Historia*, pp. 149–58; Lis, 'Mniejszość polska', pp. 263–9.

the dialect in the 1930s. In 1937 the authorities started to physically remove pro-Polish political activists from the *Provinz Oberschlesien*, sending them westwards to other parts of Germany. This was part of a broader campaign to 'cleanse' Germany's borderlands of 'disloyal' elements. In 1939, the use of the Polish language in churches was banned and drastic restrictions were placed on the Polish-language press. The invasion of Poland on 1 September 1939 was accompanied by a wave of arrests of pro-Polish political activists across the province. Many were sent straight to Buchenwald Concentration Camp. All Polish cultural organizations, Polish-language newspapers and Polish schools in the *Provinz Oberschlesien* were dissolved at that time.[13]

The Nazi German authorities then turned their attention to eastern Upper Silesia. This region was swiftly conquered by the German armed forces in September 1939. Mass arrests of eastern Upper Silesia's pro-Polish activists and intelligentsia followed during the next two months. This time many were simply shot dead and the remainder sent to concentration camps. In October 1939, eastern Upper Silesia was formally reincorporated into Germany. Tens of thousands of Polish immigrants, who had moved to eastern Upper Silesia from Poland after 1922, started to be expelled eastwards into the General Government – a process which continued through to 1942. In December 1939, the German police carried out a comprehensive registration of all long-term inhabitants of eastern Upper Silesia, requiring them to specify whether they were ethnically German or Polish. The vast majority sensibly declared themselves the former. But this was only the start of the process of ethnically categorizing the population of eastern Upper Silesia.[14]

In March 1941, Nazi Germany's authorities introduced a much more systematic ethnic screening process in eastern Upper Silesia – as well as in the rest of German-occupied Poland – which they called the *Deutsche Volksliste* (German Ethnicity List). The ostensible aim of this process was to sift Germans from Poles among the local population. As we discussed in Chapter 1, those Polish citizens classed as Germans were categorized into four ranked groups. In groups I and II the Nazi authorities placed 'ethnic Germans' (*Volksdeutsche*) eligible for full Reich citizenship (*Reichsbürgerschaft*). In groups III and IV they put 'persons of German descent' (*Deutschstämmige*) entitled to no more than 'state membership' (*Staatsangehörigkeit*). Applying

[13] Wanatowicz, *Historia*, pp. 153–60, 176–8; Ther, 'Die einheimische Bevölkerung', pp. 417–19; Kamusella, 'Upper Silesia', pp. 102–5; Madajczyk, *Przyłączenie*, p. 197; Lis, 'Mniejszość polska', pp. 263–9.

[14] Wanatowicz, *Historia*, pp. 177–81; Kamusella, 'Upper Silesia', pp. 104–6; Kamusella, *The Szlonzoks*, p. 22.

for entry on the *Deutsche Volksliste* entailed filling out a questionnaire. In contrast to what happened in most other areas of German-occupied Poland, Nazi Germany's authorities made this compulsory in eastern Upper Silesia. Refusing to apply could be punished with imprisonment in a concentration camp. Local committees were appointed in each of the region's districts to determine whether an application should be accepted. The committees were composed of local Nazi Party chiefs (*Kreisleiter*) and SS members, especially members of the SS Security Service (*Sicherheitsdienst*). But few applications were ultimately rejected in eastern Upper Silesia. Crucial pragmatic considerations argued against doing so. Above all other factors, the importance Berlin attached to eastern Upper Silesia's coal and steel industry for the war effort and the growing need to make as many of the region's residents as possible available for conscription into the *Wehrmacht* encouraged a relaxed interpretation of 'German descent' and 'German ethnicity' on the part of the committees. They placed 95 per cent of eastern Upper Silesia's population on the *Deutsche Volksliste* in the course of the war, albeit 73 per cent of them in group III.[15]

NATIONAL VERIFICATION

The defeat of Nazi Germany in 1945 did not put an end to the practice of ethnic screening in East-Central Europe. Already in the early months of 1945, after the 'liberation' of all prewar Polish territory from Nazi German occupation by the Red Army, Poland's new Communist-controlled government introduced its own ethnic screening process directly aimed at dealing with the *Deutsche Volksliste*. The government called this process the 'rehabilitation action' (*akcja rehabilitacyjna*). Its purpose was to reclassify as ethnic Poles many of the people categorized as 'ethnic Germans' or 'of German descent' through Nazi Germany's *Deutsche Volksliste*. In eastern Upper Silesia, Polish officials implemented the 'rehabilitation action' in a way which recognized that – in contrast to much of the rest of the territories Nazi Germany had annexed from Poland in 1939 – the residents of this region had been given little choice but to register on the *Deutsche Volksliste*. As a result, the overwhelming majority of those residents of eastern Upper Silesia who had been placed in groups III and IV of the list during the war were 'rehabilitated' as ethnic Poles through a simple administrative process in 1945. Group II members were subjected

[15] Boda-Krężel, *Sprawa Volkslisty*, pp. 14–33; Łempiński, *Przesiedlenie*, pp. 89–92; Eser, 'Oberschlesien', pp. 371–3; Wanatowicz, *Historia*, pp. 180–1; Kamusella, 'Upper Silesia', pp. 107–10.

to a more rigorous, quasi-judicial process of ethnic screening – carried out over several years by legal courts rather than by administrative officials. But a significant proportion of group II members in eastern Upper Silesia ultimately also received positive decisions. In contrast, the 'rehabilitation' applications of local group I members were almost all rejected. Nevertheless, overall, the vast majority of eastern Upper Silesia's population were reclassified as ethnic Poles through the 'rehabilitation action' implemented by the Communist-controlled authorities in the second half of the 1940s.[16]

Yet it was not only in the territories which had belonged to Poland already before 1939 that ethnic screening was introduced by the postwar authorities in the aftermath of Germany's defeat. We have already discussed in Chapters 4 and 5 how Poland's Communist-controlled government, with Soviet support, attempted to persuade Britain and America to approve the Kremlin's handover to Poland of the German territories lying to the east of the Odra–Nysa Line – both by rapidly expelling the remaining German residents and by flooding the territories with Polish settlers. But the government also implemented a third important population policy which was, likewise, aimed at convincing the two Western powers to grant Poland permanent control of these territories. Drawing on ideas which had been advanced by Roman Dmowski's National Democratic movement for several decades, the Communist-led government believed that a sizable proportion of the German citizens living in these territories were not ethnic Germans but 'indigenous Poles' (*autochtoni*). It believed that the presence of this 'indigenous Polish population', in these territories, living principally in the regions of western Upper Silesia and southern East Prussian, was a key fact legitimizing Poland's postwar takeover of these territories. In these circumstances, ethnic screening came to be seen by the new Soviet-backed Polish government not only as a way of 'rehabilitating' former *Deutsche Volksliste* members living in Poland's old territories, but also as a means of demonstrating that very large 'indigenous Polish' communities already populated the eastern provinces of prewar Germany. An ethnic screening process would help to 'prove' that these communities existed and therefore, in the long run, greatly strengthen Poland's hold over these previously German territories.[17]

The Communist-controlled state authorities applied ethnic screening throughout the prewar eastern German territories in the five years following the war. But the first area where they introduced it was western

[16] Eser, 'Oberschlesien', pp. 391–4; Borodziej, 'Einleitung', pp. 106–7.
[17] Borodziej, 'Einleitung', p. 108; Strauchold, *Autochtoni*, pp. 8–9; Hofmann, *Nachkriegszeit*, p. 326.

Upper Silesia (the part of Upper Silesia which had remained in Germany after the 1922 partition and had been known as the *Provinz Oberschlesien* in the interwar years). It started as an initiative not of Poland's central government in Warsaw but rather of Upper Silesia's new Regional Governor (*Wojewoda*), the army general and Polish Workers' Party politburo member Aleksander Zawadzki. He began to set up an ethnic screening process in western Upper Silesia in March 1945. His officials referred to it as 'verification' (*weryfikacja*).[18]

The importance Aleksander Zawadzki attached from the outset to the 'verification action' (*akcja weryfikacyjna*) ensured that one of the first actions undertaken by the Polish state officials arriving as 'operational groups' in localities throughout western Upper Silesia from spring 1945 onwards was to set up special ethnic 'verification committees' (*komisje weryfikacyjne*) – to carry out the task of determining local people's ethno-national identity. The new Polish officials immediately instructed locals to begin submitting applications to these committees containing evidence of their Polish ethno-national identity (*narodowość polska*).[19] Based on the committees' judgements, successful applicants were issued 'temporary certificates of Polish nationality' (*tymczasowe zaświadczenia o przynależności narodowej*) by their local District Administration (*Starostwo*) or Town Administration (*Zarząd Miejski*).[20]

We will examine the 'verification action' in detail by focussing on one locality of western Upper Silesia: the newly renamed district of Opole, where the 'verification action' was introduced by arriving Polish officials in late spring 1945.[21] Opole District's officials created a large number of 'verification committees' to carry out the task of judging the ethno-national identity of local people. A single 'town verification committee' dealt with all applications from residents of the town of Opole. An entire three-tier system of 'verification committees' was set up to do the same in the district's countryside.[22] At the bottom of the three tiers stood the 'village verification committees'. There were around 90 of these operating in the district and they were the first committees to examine the 'verification'

[18] Eser, 'Oberschlesien', pp. 389–90; Kowalski, *Powrót*, pp. 296–7.

[19] Kowalski, *Powrót*, pp. 296–7, 301; Misztal, *Weryfikacja*, pp. 94, 98–9; Eser, 'Oberschlesien', pp. 388–91; Hofmann, *Nachkriegszeit*, p. 283.

[20] Kowalski, *Powrót*, pp. 296–7, 301; Eser, 'Oberschlesien', pp. 388–91; Hofmann, *Nachkriegszeit*, p. 283.

[21] SiRep ODA S-PD, 29.5.1945, APK 185/4, sygn. 21, 208–9.

[22] Rep by OTA S-PD, 24.8.1945, APO 185, sygn. 85, 3; Rep on inspection of the 'verification action' in Opole District, second half December 1945, APK 185/4, sygn. 435, 51–2; Rep by the OTA head S-PD, 20.12.1945, APO 185, sygn. 85, 11; SiRep OTA head S-PD, 21.6.1946, APO 185, sygn. 85, 33; SiRep by O Chief on the period 20.8.1945–20.9.1945, APO 178, sygn. 41, 1–4; Rep on an inspection of the 'verification action' in Opole District, second half December 1945, APK 185/4, sygn. 435, 53–6.

applications. Their job was to categorize each application as 'indisputable', 'rejected' or 'contentious' before sending it to one of the district's 21 'commune verification committees' for further inspection. The commune committees, which were each given control of the ethnic screening process in several of the district's villages, then recategorized the applications as accepted, rejected or contentious. Only those placed in the last of these three categories were subsequently sent upwards to Opole District's single 'district verification committee', standing at the top of the hierarchy, to make final decisions. Yet some of the 'contentious' applications were later sent back down again by the district committee to the commune committees for further consideration. Three special 'mobile committees' moved between Opole District's localities, helping the commune committees to reach decisions on these applications.[23] A similar hierarchy of 'verification committees' was set up in each of western Upper Silesia's districts in the course of 1945, although there was a good deal of variation in the number of committees operating in each district.[24]

In terms of how the committees were composed, the 'village verification committees' were each headed by the village mayor (*Sołtys*) or local head teacher, the commune committees by the commune mayor (*Wójt*). Each village and commune 'verification committee' operating in Opole District was supposed to contain at least three members of the 'local Polish population' (*miejscowa ludność polska*). In many of the 'village verification committees' in the district, these 'local Polish' people may even have constituted a majority of the committee members. By 'local Polish population', the authorities, at the very least, meant people from western Upper Silesia who were able to speak the local Polish dialect. However, whether they specifically meant residents of the particular villages and communes in which the 'verification committees' did their work is less clear. In any case, they are all likely to have been people who could demonstrate their Polish nationalist credentials to the state authorities by proving they had been members of pro-Polish organizations before the war – especially the Association of Poles in Germany. The remaining members of the committees were all outsiders from the old territories of Poland who had been given official administrative posts in the district after spring 1945.[25]

[23] Rep on an inspection of the 'verification action' in Opole District, second half December 1945, APK 185/4, sygn. 435, 53–6; Misztal, *Weryfikacja*, p. 88; Kowalski, *Powrót*, p. 330.

[24] Misztal, *Weryfikacja*, pp. 87–8.

[25] Rep on inspection of the 'verification action' in Opole District, second half December 1945, APK 185/4, sygn. 435, 53–6; Misztal, *Weryfikacja*, p. 91; Ther, 'Die einheimische Bevölkerung', pp. 423, 430–1; Madajczyk, *Przyłączenie*, p. 176; Strauchold, *Autochtoni*, p. 83; Kowalski, *Powrót*, p. 305.

The district and town 'verification committees', which were respectively headed by Opole District's Chief Official and Opole's Town President, had much larger and broader memberships. Closely reflecting instructions issued by the Regional Governor, Aleksander Zawadzki, in summer 1945, Opole's 'town verification committee', for example, contained representatives from the Polish Workers' Party, the Polish Socialist Party, the Polish Peasants' Party, the Democratic Party, the powerful Security Police (*Urząd Bezpieczeństwa Publicznego*), the Citizens' Militia (i.e., the equivalent of the regular police), the Committee for Former Political Prisoners, the school inspectorate, the Association of Veterans of the Silesian Uprisings and the Polish Western Association. The 'district verification committee' was similarly composed.[26] The involvement of the Polish Western Association in the 'verification action' highlights the nationalist idea underpinning this screening process. This staunchly nationalist organization, with very close links to the National Democratic movement, had been founded in Poznań in 1921. It was only out of political necessity that it had accepted close cooperation with Poland's Soviet-sponsored government after 1944. Otherwise, it would not have been given permission to come back into existence. The government granted it an important role in the 'verification action' not just in Opole District but throughout Poland's new territories.[27]

Zawadzki demanded that not only the village and commune 'verification committees', but also the district and town 'verification committees' contained representatives from the 'local Polish population'. Opole's 19-member 'town verification committee' reportedly contained as many as nine prewar residents of the town in August 1945. All of them were said either to be former members of the Association of Poles in Germany or 'trusted individuals who are very knowledgeable about the local region'. 'Trusted individuals' was the phrase the Communist-controlled authorities used to describe local people who had proven to the state officials that they had engaged in pro-Polish activism before 1945.[28] Opole District, in fact, was rather unusual in having significant numbers of 'local Polish' people represented on the 'verification committees'. Elsewhere in western Upper Silesia it was common for the committees to contain not a single prewar resident of the region.[29] Zawadzki criticized this in a circular sent out to local state officials on 24 October 1945. This circular invalidated all decisions reached by committees which did not include prewar residents

[26] Rep by OTA head S-PD, 20.12.1945, APO 185, sygn. 85, 11; Rep by OTA S-PD, 24.8.1945, APO 185, sygn. 85, 3; Hofmann, *Nachkriegszeit*, pp. 284–5; Kowalski, *Powrót*, p. 299.

[27] Hofmann, *Nachkriegszeit*, pp. 272–3; Curp, *Clean Sweep*, pp. 21–5, 39–40.

[28] Rep by OTA S-PD, 24.8.1945, APO 185, sygn. 85, 3. [29] Kowalski, *Powrót*, pp. 305–6.

of western Upper Silesia.[30] Yet given how many seats in Opole District's town and district 'verification committees' were assigned to state officials, policemen and activists from the ruling political parties – most, if not all, of whom were outsiders from central Poland – it is clear that the participation of prewar residents of the district in the 'verification' process had more to do with vesting the process with legitimacy than with giving these people a chance to influence the decisions.[31]

So how exactly did the committees reach decisions about whether a local resident was an ethnic Pole or not? In fact, they received surprisingly little guidance from Aleksander Zawadzki's Regional Administration in Katowice on what counted as evidence of Polish ethno-national identity.[32] According to the recollections of one member of Opole's 'district verification committee', they therefore devised their own criteria for determining 'Polishness'. He claimed,

> A good command of Polish was demanded as well as... facts attesting to an affiliation with the Polish nation – such as membership of the Association of Poles in Germany, subscription before the war to Polish newspapers and books, attendance of Polish minority schools, [experience of] persecution and repression at the hands of the Germans, having relatives who had participated in the plebiscite campaign or in the Silesian Uprisings, experience of excursions to Poland including pilgrimages..., Roman Catholic faith, and a loyal attitude towards Polish affairs and the Poles.[33]

This suggested that 'behavioural' criteria for Polish ethnicity – such as what organizations an individual had chosen to join before 1945 and how an individual had decided to act during the Silesian Uprisings of 1919–21 – were attributed an importance equal to that of the supposedly 'objective' criteria of language and religion. Opole's 'district verification committee' was not doing anything unique in this respect. Despite offering little in the way of detailed guidelines, Katowice did stress from the outset that the region's 'verification committees' should base their decisions about Polish ethno-national identity as much on 'behavioural' criteria as on 'objective' ones.[34]

Nevertheless, the version of proceedings presented by this former member of Opole's 'district verification committee' was highly idealized. Because western Upper Silesia's new Polish authorities wished to strengthen Poland's

[30] Hofmann, *Nachkriegszeit*, pp. 290–1; Kowalski, *Powrót*, pp. 330–1.
[31] Hofmann, *Nachkriegszeit*, p. 285. [32] Ibid., pp. 286, 300.
[33] Cited in Hofmann, *Nachkriegszeit*, pp. 285–6; Rep by OTA head S-PD, 20.12.1945, APO 185, sygn. 85, 11.
[34] Misztal, *Weryfikacja* pp. 94–6; Hofmann, *Nachkriegszeit*, pp. 274–9, 281.

claim to the region, their aim from the start was to demonstrate that a very large proportion of the region's inhabitants were ethnic Poles. To achieve this, the region's 'verification committees' simply could not afford to apply strict criteria when judging 'verification' applications. In practice, the committees were therefore often willing to 'verify' people as ethnic Poles based solely on the signatures of support they received from prewar residents of the region designated as 'trusted' by the state authorities (by which officials always meant having a proven record of interwar pro-Polish activism). And in certain localities in western Upper Silesia, very small numbers of 'trusted' prewar residents supplied signatures of support for very large numbers of applicants – people whom they rarely knew personally.[35]

This practice was clearly in line with the Regional Governor, Aleksander Zawadzki's intentions. He made it absolutely plain to the region's local state officials that he did not want the 'verification committees' to be too stringent when judging Polish ethno-national identity. For example, he complained in an October 1945 circular that too many applications were being rejected.[36] This circular may in fact have been what prompted Opole District's Chief Official, at precisely this time, to inspect the camps in the local area where people whose 'verification' applications had been rejected, or who had refused to submit applications, were being interned. He reportedly came across individuals in these camps who could 'speak Polish' and immediately ordered their release so that they could undergo 'verification' as ethnic Poles.[37]

There was another important factor influencing the specific way the 'verification action' was implemented in Opole District. There was a long-established assumption in Poland that the part of the Odra River running through western Upper Silesia could be regarded as an 'ethnic border' which divided 'Poles' to the east from 'Germans' to the west. Although part of Opole District's territory was located on the west bank of the Odra river (see Map 4), the postwar state officials seem to have viewed the whole of the district as lying 'ethnically' to the east of this border. Based on this assumption, it appears that in all western Upper Silesian districts lying to the east of the Odra River, including the whole of Opole District, the new Polish authorities implemented a far less stringent ethnic screening process than in those districts lying to the west of it. A much large proportion of local inhabitants were 'verified' as ethnic Poles in the districts on the east side of the Odra River than on the west side.

[35] Misztal, *Weryfikacja*, pp. 94–9. [36] Kowalski, *Powrót*, pp. 330–1.

[37] Rep by the chairman of VoiInspCom, second half of December 1945, APK 185/4, sygn. 435, 53–6; Nowak, *Obozy*, pp. 213–14.

In Opole District, the 'verification committees' rejected very few applications in the first year or so of the process. Of the approximately 59,000 locals who submitted applications for 'verification' in the course of 1945, around 57,000 were 'verified' as ethnic Poles. Only 1,595 applications – less than 3 per cent – were rejected. Twenty-nine per cent of Opole District's entire prewar population had therefore already been 'verified' as ethnic Poles by the end of 1945.[38]

Any prewar resident of Opole District whose 'verification' application was rejected or who refused to submit an application – as we shall discuss in Chapter 7 – was categorized as an ethnic German and therefore designated for expulsion to Allied-occupied Germany. But those individuals whose 'verification' applications were successful were fully entitled to continue living in Opole District, because they were now regarded by the authorities as 'proven' members of the 'indigenous Polish' population. Yet the problem with this was that Polish settlers from both central Poland and from the prewar eastern territories of Poland were flooding into Opole District and the rest of western Upper Silesia at this time, causing extreme overcrowding similar to that witnessed in southern Lower Silesia's districts such as Jelenia Góra. How Opole District's authorities set about dealing with this overpopulation will also be examined in Chapter 7.

RETURN MIGRATIONS

The 'verification action' continued into 1946. Opole District's prewar population by this point apparently exhibited 'utter indifference' towards it.[39] It was in the spring of 1946 that Poland's Communist-controlled government in Warsaw finally decided to take full control of the 'verification' process. As stated already, although western Upper Silesia was both the first and the main region in Poland's new territories where a 'verification action' was introduced in 1945, it was not the only one. Other 'verification actions' were introduced elsewhere in these territories in the second half of the year. The second largest in scale and scope was the one implemented in southern East Prussia, where a large proportion of local residents spoke the Masurian and Warmian dialects of Polish. The Ministry for Recovered

[38] Opole's 'district verification committee' had accepted around 53,000 applications and rejected only 1266. Opole's 'town verification committee' had accepted 3,897 applications and rejected only 329. Rep on the 'verification action' in Opole District, second half December 1945, APK 185/4, sygn. 435, 51–2; Rep by OTA S-PD, 20.12.1945, APO 185, sygn. 85, 11; SiRep O Chief on the period 20.12.1945–20.1.1946, APO 178, sygn. 41, 13–15; Bohmann, *Menschen*, p. 209.

[39] SiRep O Chief on the period 20.12.1945–20.1.1946, APO 178, sygn. 41, 13–15.

Territories sent out an order on 6 April 1946 which had two principal consequences. First, it brought the new territories' other 'verification actions' procedurally into line with western Upper Silesia's action.[40] Second, and more importantly for Opole District and the rest of western Upper Silesia, the Polish government – believing that almost everybody eligible for 'verification' in Poland's new territories had already been 'verified' as an ethnic Pole by spring 1946 – ordered the dissolution of all 'verification committees'. The ministry instructed local state officials in Poland's new territories that they should complete the dismantling of these committees by the end of the summer.[41]

The problem with the ministry's order was that in Opole District and the rest of western Upper Silesia the number of people eligible for 'verification' was not static. Quite the contrary, it was growing relatively rapidly at this time. This was because in 1946 western Upper Silesia was still witnessing a steady stream of prewar residents returning from Allied-occupied Germany after fleeing from the Red Army in the final phase of the war. In the first few postwar months, Opole District's new Polish officials had taken the view that almost all the local people who had fled Opole District to escape the Red Army at the end of the war were ethnic Germans and not 'indigenous Poles'. The district's Chief Official had suggested in summer 1945, for example, that because most local people who had fled the district were Germans, a much higher proportion of the district's prewar residents now said they were Poles than had voted for Poland in the 1921 plebiscite. Correspondingly, the district's officials believed that because most of the people who had fled were Germans, so too were the majority of the people returning from flight. Thus, one official noted in summer 1945 that 'unfortunately most of the returning immigrants are Germans who are coming back in order to wreak havoc among the calm rural population'. The decisions to flee (or not) were thus regarded by state officials in the early postwar months as a kind of preliminary phase of the ethnic screening process; they had filtered out many 'Germans' from the largely 'indigenous Polish' local population. This view was not at all unique to Opole District's authorities. It was widely held by state officials in districts throughout western Upper Silesia in the immediate aftermath of the war.[42]

[40] Borodziej, 'Einleitung', p. 109; Hofmann, *Nachkriegszeit*, pp. 284, 300–1; Kowalski, *Powrót*, pp. 298–9, 338–9; Blanke, *Polish-Speaking Germans*, pp. 279–310.

[41] Hofmann, *Nachkriegszeit*, p. 301.

[42] SiRep O Chief on the period 20.8.1945–20.9.1945, APO 178, sygn. 41, 1–4; Rep by ODA S-PD, 5.6.1945. APK 185/4, sygn. 22, 49–51; Rep by ODA S-PD, 20.6.1945. APK 185/4 25, 12–14; WR, Julius D., Koben (Chobie), 24.5.1959, BOD 1, 243, 217–20; Hofmann, *Nachkriegszeit*, p. 279.

This attitude was not entirely detached from reality. As was indicated in Chapter 3, ethno-linguistic identity did indeed play a part in some locals' decisions to flee. Nevertheless, by 1946 Opole District's state officials had clearly abandoned the assumption that all fleers were Germans. As one local official put it in March 1946, 'The people arriving from abroad . . . generally make a good impression . . . [T]hese people, like the majority of natives [*tubylcy*], should be energetically taken care of, which means giving them work and an income, as well as treating them as brothers or at least kindly.'[43] Taking care of the 'returnees' and treating them as 'brothers' – first and foremost – meant allowing them to submit 'verification' applications. Large numbers of returnees flowed into Opole District and the rest of western Upper Silesia from Allied-occupied Germany in the course of 1946. The practice was adopted at some point during that year that anybody wishing to return to western Upper Silesia from Allied-occupied Germany first had to formally apply for permission to do so from the state authorities in Poland. Opole District's authorities were subsequently required to provide Polish state officials based in Germany with information on every individual applying to return to the district. Yet, at the same time, many prewar residents continued to make their return journeys from Germany to western Upper Silesia using unofficial and illegal routes. A significant number of local men, who had served in the *Wehrmacht* during the war, also began returning to Opole District and the rest of western Upper Silesia from Allied prisoner-of-war camps in 1946. By the second half of 1946, the district's 'verification committees' were therefore almost exclusively 'verifying' recent returnees from Germany and from POW camps. Much the same was witnessed in other districts in western Upper Silesia.[44]

Despite the fact that thousands of 'verification' applications were still being submitted by the returning locals in the second half of 1946, Opole District's officials were forced to dissolve their 'verification committees'

[43] SiRep OTA head S-PD, 21.3.1946, APO 185, sygn. 85, 28.

[44] SiRep O Chief on the period 20.6.1946–20.7.1946, APO 178, sygn. 41, 34–6; Rep on an inspection of the 'verification action' in Opole District, 10–23.6.1946, APK 185/4, sygn. 436, 62–4; SiRep OTA S-PD, 21.3.1946, APO 185, sygn. 85, 28; SiRep OTA S-PD, 21.4.1946, APO 185, sygn. 85, 31; SiRep OTA S-PD, 21.5.1946, APO 185, sygn. 85, 32; SiRep OTA S-PD, 21.6.1946, APO 185, sygn. 85, 33; SiRep OTA head S-PD, 21.7.1946, APO 185, sygn. 85, 34; SiRep OTA S-PD, 21.8.1946, APO 185, sygn. 85, 35; SiRep OTA head S-PD, 21.9.1946, APO 185, sygn. 85, 39; SiRep OTA S-PD, 21.10.1946, APO 185, sygn. 85, 40; SiRep OTA S-PD, 21.11.1946, APO 185, sygn. 85, 43; SiRep OTA S-PD, 31.12.1946, APO 185, sygn. 85, 44; SiRep ODA S-PD, 31.12.1946, APK 185/4, sygn. 39, 54–54a; SiRep OTA S-PD, 21.3.1947, APO 185, sygn. 85, 51; SiRep OTA S-PD, 21.4.1947, APO 185, sygn. 85, 52; SiRep ODA S-PD, 12.8.1948, APO 178, sygn. 62, 21–3; Rep on the year 1948 by ODA S-PD, 31.12.1948, APO 178, sygn. 64, 7–8; WR, Friedrich K., Sacken (Lubienia), 24.7.1955, BOD 1, 243, 309–19; Madajczyk, *Przyłączenie*, pp. 205–6.

in the autumn, as stipulated by the Ministry for Recovered Territories' 6 April 1946 order. The district's officials responded to the gaping gap this inserted into the process by simply transferring the task of evaluating 'verification' applications to departments of local state administration. The committees operating in the rural part of Opole District handed their functions to Opole District Administration's Social-Political Department. The 'town verification committee', which was dissolved on 19 November 1946, likewise transferred its tasks to Opole Town Administration's Social-Political Department.[45] Officials in districts throughout western Upper Silesia did the same in the second half of 1946.[46] Given that by this time the majority of the region's administrative posts were filled by outsiders from central Poland rather than prewar residents of western Upper Silesia, this rather drastic procedural change meant that local involvement in implementing the 'verification' process was now very limited indeed.[47]

In 1947, prewar residents of western Upper Silesia who had been deported to the Soviet Union in early 1945 also started to arrive back in the region. Up to 90,000 people had been deported to the Soviet Union from both western and eastern Upper Silesia in the early months of 1945. This resulted from an order issued by the Soviet State Defence Committee on 3 February to mobilize all physically fit men found on conquered German territory. As we discussed in Chapter 3, many of the men seized in February and March 1945 were residents of Opole District. Throughout western and eastern Upper Silesia, the Soviets tended first to gather the residents in factories and schools before moving them into transit camps in Gleiwitz/Gliwice, Beuthen/Bytom and other towns in the region. The Soviets then crammed them into cargo wagons and sent them off eastwards – on terrible journeys lasting several weeks – to the Ural and Donbass regions, Kazakhstan and elsewhere in the depths of the Soviet Union. Wherever they landed, the deportees were made to do long, hard and exhausting forced labour under horrendous conditions. The death rate reached 50 per cent in 1945 and 1946. Polish state officials lobbied the Soviet authorities hard during 1946 in an attempt to convince them to send the Upper Silesian deportees back

45 SiRep ODA S-PD, 31.12.1946, APK 185/4, sygn. 39, 54–4a; SiRep OTA head S-PD, 21.11.1946, APO 185, sygn. 85, 43; Special SiRep by OTA head S-PD, 13.11.1946, APO 185, sygn. 85, 41–2; Rep by OTA head S-PD, 17.1.1947, APO 185, sygn. 85, 47.

46 Kowalski, *Powrót*, p. 375.

47 Ther, 'Die einheimische Bevölkerung', pp. 423, 430–1; Madajczyk, *Przyłączenie*, p. 176; Strauchold, *Autochtoni*, p. 83; Kowalski, *Powrót*, p. 305. WRs: BOD 2, 229, 1–2; BOD 1, 243, 379–80; BOD 1, 243, 105–15; BOD 1, 243, 335–7; BOD 1, 243, 277–80; BOD 1, 243, 33–6; BOD 1, 243, 25–7; BOD 1, 243, 13–16; BOD 1, 243, 271–4; BOD 1, 243, 67–72; BOD 1, 243, 289–93; BOD 1, 243, 299–301; BOD 1, 243, 121–2.

home. Opole District's own officials expressed great concern at this time about the fate of the prewar residents 'taken to Russia for labour'.[48] In early spring 1947, Polish and Soviet officials finally came to an agreement on the issue; the Soviets agreed to start sending the deportees home. In June 1947, deportees gradually started to return to Upper Silesia. Around this time, Opole District's branch of the State Repatriation Office received 100,000 złoty to support 'autochthons' (i.e., indigenous residents) who had recently 'returned from imprisonment in the Soviet Union'.

Yet not all the released deportees were sent back to western Upper Silesia. Those who told the Soviet authorities they were Germans, not Poles, were instead sent to the Soviet Occupation Zone of Germany. Irrespective of whether they arrived in the Soviet Zone or western Upper Silesia, they could count themselves very lucky to have survived the extremely harsh conditions of transportation, incarceration and forced labour. The survivors reached Upper Silesia and the Soviet Zone sick, starving and exhausted. Some died within days of reaching Central Europe.[49] One prewar resident of Opole District, for example, recalled leaving Magnitogorsk in Siberia 'completely destroyed', a 'living skeleton'. Another claimed he had weighed 80 kilograms before his deportation to Dnepropetrovsk in Soviet Ukraine but came away weighing 38 kilograms. A third wrote of his of time in the Soviet Union, 'The water there was unfit for human consumption. It contained oil and lead. After two years the first of the sick and dying were transported back . . . I was among them. It took six weeks to travel back from the Urals to Frankfurt an der Oder [at the Polish–Soviet Zone border]. [Many people] died from exhaustion along the way.'[50]

Like the locals who returned to Opole District from Germany and from POW camps, the deportees coming back from the Soviet Union had to submit 'verification' applications upon arrival in the district. Otherwise they would not have been allowed to remain there. Their 'verification' applications were added to those being submitted in 1947 by the large number of locals still returning from Allied-occupied Germany and the small number of local men continuing to arrive back from POW camps.

[48] SiRep OTA head S-PD, 21.9.1946, APO 185, sygn. 85, 39; SiRep OTA head S-PD, 21.3.1947, APO 185, sygn. 85, 51; SiRep OTA head S-PD, 21.4.1947, APO 185, sygn. 85, 52; Ewa Ochman, 'Population Displacement and Regional Reconstruction in Postwar Poland: The Case of Upper Silesia', in Gatrell and Baron, *Warlands*, pp. 213–17, 220–2; Madajczyk, *Przyłączenie*, pp. 202–4.

[49] CuRep ODA S-PD, 8.1.1948, AP Katowcie 185/4, sygn. 52, 39–40; WR, Arthur M., Derschau (Suchy Bór), 7.10.1954, BOD 1, 243, 67–72; WR, Frau K., Oderwinkel (Kąty Opolskie), 30.5.1959, BOD 1, 243, 277–80; WR, E.D., Walldorf (Wawelno), undated, BOD 1, 243, 379–80; Ochman, 'Displacement', pp. 215–16, 222–3; Madajczyk, *Przyłączenie*, pp. 202–4; Linek, *Polityka*, p. 247.

[50] WR, Emil G., Brünne (Brynica), 1958, BOD 1, 243, 41–4; WR, Herr G., Falkendorf (Fałkowice), 8.4.1959, BOD 1, 243, 121–2; WR, Friedrich K., Sacken (Lubienia), 24.7.1955, BOD 1, 243, 309–19.

Fuelled in this way by several separate return migrations – by far the biggest of which was the inflow from Germany – Opole District's authorities were still in 1947 processing large numbers of 'verification' applications. But despite this, in spring 1947 Opole Town Administration's Social-Political Department, whose principal task until that time had been running the 'verification action' in Opole town, was suddenly dissolved. Now in charge of the 'verification action' in both Opole town and the district's surrounding countryside, Opole District Administration's Social-Political Department was unable to process the very large number of applications flowing in from returnees. A large backlog of unprocessed applications therefore quickly formed.[51]

This backlog was not resolved until 1948, when the Social-Political Department transferred responsibility for issuing 'temporary certificates of Polish nationality' to local commune administrations. Also helpful for resolving this backlog was the fact that the number of returnees arriving in Opole District from Germany had decreased a great deal by 1948. But the return migration did not yet come to a complete end, and the district's 'verification action' therefore continued to tick over during 1948. It was not until 1949 that the trickle of 'verification' applications finally dried up. The 'verification action' was finished throughout western Upper Silesia in summer 1949.[52]

By this time, Opole District's authorities had managed to 'verify' a very large proportion of the district's prewar population as ethnic Poles. As

[51] By August 1947 the backlog of unprocessed applications numbered around 3000. Depiction of the General Situation for OT Pres by OTA head S-PD, 17.1.1947, APO 185, sygn. 85, 47; SiRep OTA head S-PD, 21.1.1947, APO 185, sygn. 85, 48; SiRep OTA head S-PD, 21.3.1947, APO 185, sygn. 85, 51; SiRep ODA S-PD, 1.4.1947, APO 178, sygn. 62, 7–11; SiRep ODA S-PD, 2.5.1947, APO 178, sygn. 62, 12–14; SiRep ODA S-PD, 6.6.1947, APO 178, sygn. 62, 16–18; SiRep ODA S-PD, 12.8.1947, APO 178, sygn. 62, 21–3; SiRep ODA S-PD, 30.1.1947, APO 178, sygn. 62, 2–3; SiRep ODA S-PD, 3.3.1947, APO 178, sygn. 62, 4–6; SiRep OTA S-PD, 21.4.1947, APO 185, sygn. 85, 52; Rep on the first quarter of 1948 by ODA S-PD, undated, APO 178, sygn. 65, 13–16.

[52] CuRep ODA S-PD, 2.3.1948, APO 178, sygn. 65, 7–8; SiRep ODA S-PD, 2.5.1947, APO 178, sygn. 62, 12–14; SiRep ODA S-PD, 6.6.1947, APO 178, sygn. 62, 16–18; CuRep ODA S-PD, 7.4.1948, APO 178, sygn. 65, 11–12; CuRep ODA S-PD, 6.5.1948, APO 178, sygn. 65, 23–4; CuRep ODA S-PD, 4.9.1948, APO 178, sygn. 65, 56–7; Rep by ODA S-PD on the first two quarters of 1948, APO 178, sygn. 65, 50–2; CuRep ODA S-PD, 1.6.1948, APO 178, sygn. 65, 25–6; Rep on the liquidation of the traces of German language and culture by ODA head S-PD, 31.7.1948, APO 178, sygn. 113, 64–5; CuRep ODA S-PD, 4.8.1948, APO 178, sygn. 65, 54–5; Rep by ODA S-PD on the period 1.1.1948–31.12.1948, APO 178, sygn. 64, 7–8; Rep by ODA S-PD, 5.8.1949, APO 178, sygn. 64, 36; Rep by ODA S-PD, 25.11.1949, APO 178, sygn. 64, 43; Rep by ODA S-PD, 8.3.1949, APO 178, sygn. 64, 14; SiRep O Chief on the period 20.7.1947–20.8.1947, APO 178, sygn. 42, 35–6; SiRep O Chief on the period 20.8.1947–20.9.1947, APO 178, sygn. 42, 43–5; SiRep O Chief on the period 20.9.1947–20.10.1947, APO 178, sygn. 42, 39–41; Note to USRA from ODA S-PD, 26.4.1948, APO 178, sygn. 65, 22; SiRep O Chief on the period 20.9.1948–20.10.1948, APO 178, sygn. 43, 45–6; Kowalski, *Powrót*, p. 377.

one district official put it in November 1949, the '[t]he native population has yielded to the verification process'.[53] In total, Opole District's 'verification committees' and Social-Political Departments had positively 'verified', according to one source, 139,944 individuals (including children) by 1949. This suggested that 72 per cent of the district's entire prewar population was 'verified' as ethnic Poles in the second half of the 1940s.[54] The figure for the whole of western Upper Silesia was also large: 851,454 individuals or 56 per cent of the region's entire prewar population.[55]

LOYAL CITIZENS

This massive number had been achieved, as we have seen, by avoiding a stringent approach to the 'verification' of the prewar residents of western Upper Silesia. What is striking, however, is that this apparent leniency extended to considering former Nazi Party members for 'verification' as ethnic Poles. In fact, Opole District's authorities allowed not only former Nazi Party members but even former Brown Shirts and SS men to submit 'verification' applications after the war.[56] Thirty former Nazi Party members were actually 'verified' as ethnic Poles by Opole's 'district verification committee' in the initial months of the action. This must have happened before October 1945, because Upper Silesia's Regional Governor, Zawadzki, at that time sent out an order to the region's state officials instructing them that local 'verification committees' were not authorized to positively 'verify' former Nazi Party members. He issued the instruction that the region's 'verification committees' must, henceforth, send any applications from former party members – which, for whatever reason, they did not wish to reject outright (which they were fully entitled to do) – to Upper Silesia's Regional Administration for further consideration.[57]

Opole District's authorities had been assured by many 'trusted' prewar residents in the initial postwar months that many of the former Nazi Party members living in the district 'had never concealed their Polish ethnicity

[53] Rep by ODA S-PD, 25.11.1949, APO 178, sygn. 64, 43.

[54] This figure is given by USRA, 1.7.1949, cited in Kowalski, *Powrót*, p. 381 and Misztal, *Weryfikacja*, p. 158. Other figures suggest that the number was under 130,000: Rep on the 're-Polonization action' by ODA S-PD, 21.4.1948, APO 178, sygn. 65, 17–21; Rep by ODA S-PD, 25.11.1949, APO 178, sygn. 64, 43.

[55] Misztal, *Weryfikacja*, p. 158; Bohmann, *Menschen*, p. 209; Eser, 'Oberschlesien', p. 391.

[56] SiRep O Chief on the period 20.8.1945–20.9.1945, APO 178, sygn. 41, 1–4; CuRep ODA S-PD, 4.9.1948, APO 178, sygn. 65, 56–7.

[57] Rep on the 'verification action' in Opole District, second half December 1945, APK 185/4, sygn. 435, 53–6; Kowalski, *Powrót*, pp. 330–1, 350–1.

and always used the Polish language', and had only joined the party under pressure from the Nazi authorities.[58] The famous Polish sociologist, Stanisław Ossowski, was told the same by pro-Polish locals when he visited this area in August 1945.[59] The attitude of Poland's Communist-controlled government in Warsaw towards the issue of Nazi Party members changed over time. In July 1945 it had taken an uncompromising attitude, ruling that former members of the Nazi Party and other Nazi organizations were simply ineligible for 'temporary certificates of Polish nationality'. But in April 1946 it decided, more generously, that former Nazi Party membership should not be viewed as an absolute obstacle to positive 'verification', because many people had been 'coerced' into joining.[60]

How many former Nazi Party members submitted 'verification' applications in Opole District between 1945 and 1949? Already by February 1946, 333 applications had been submitted to Opole District Administration and then forwarded to the Regional Administration in Katowice for further consideration. More arrived from former Nazi Party members after that. In late 1948 there was a sudden flood of applications from these people. One possible explanation for this is that these former Nazi Party members were more reluctant than most other prewar residents of the district to have themselves categorized as ethnic Poles, but by 1948 they had realized that only 'verification' as ethnic Poles would enable them to remain in the district and to hold onto their homes. At least 700 new 'verification' applications arrived from former members of 'the NSDAP, SA, and other Nazi organizations' between September and December 1948 alone. In all, several thousand 'verification' applications were probably submitted between 1945 and 1949 by former Nazi Party members living in Opole District. A large proportion of them were sent to the Regional Administration for further consideration. What number were ultimately 'verified' as ethnic Poles cannot be said for certain. But some definitely were. In western Upper Silesia as a whole, several thousand former Nazi Party members are estimated to have been 'verified' as ethnic Poles in the half decade after the war.[61]

[58] SiRep the ODA S-PD, 5.6.1945, APK 185/4, sygn. 22, 49–51; Rep by ODA S-PD, 20.6.1945, APK 185/4, sygn. 25, 12–14.

[59] Ossowski, 'Zagadnienia', pp. 271, 285, 296.

[60] Hofmann, *Nachkriegszeit*, pp. 284, 301; Borodziej, 'Einleitung', p. 109; Kowalski, *Powrót*, pp. 298–9, 338–9.

[61] Rep on an inspection of the 'verification action' in Opole District, 6–19.2.1946, APK 185/4, sygn. 436, 60–1; SiRep OTA S-PD, 21.5.1946, APO 185, sygn. 85, 32; Rep on an inspection of the 'verification action' in Opole District, 10–23.6.1946, APK 185/4, sygn. 436, 62–4; SiRep ODA S-PD, 2.5.1947, APO 178, sygn. 62, 12–14; CuRep ODA S-PD, 4.9.1948, APO 178, sygn. 65, 56–7; CuRep ODA S-PD, 5.11.1948, APO 178, sygn. 65, 63–5; Rep by ODA S-PD on the period 1.1.1948–31.12.1948, APO 178, sygn. 64, 7–8; Kowalski, *Powrót*, pp. 330–1, 350–2.

In practice, most of the former Nazi Party members who submitted successful applications in western Upper Silesia were able to show that their jobs would have been at risk had they not joined the Nazi Party. One successful applicant from Opole District, for example, claimed that he had been a pro-Polish activist in the plebiscite period and had joined the Nazi Party only to avoid losing his position as the local mayor of his village. Another Opole District resident also managed to convince officials that he had joined the Nazi Party – and Germanized his surname – merely to retain his job. This person included in his application a letter of support from a Special Committee for Former Concentration Camp Prisoners based in Bamberg. In the letter, the committee explained that he had been a political prisoner during the Nazi period, had fought against Nazi Germany before 1945, and had helped many Poles to escape from concentration camps during the war.[62]

Although 'verification' as an ethnic Pole allowed an individual to continue living in Poland, it did not automatically bestow permanent Polish citizenship upon them. In April 1946, the Warsaw government ruled that German citizens who had been 'verified' as ethnic Poles would have to submit a signed 'declaration of loyalty towards the Polish Nation and State' before they could gain Polish citizenship.[63] Western Upper Silesia's state authorities made concerted efforts to extract these 'declarations of loyalty' from local people in the following years. In Opole District, the locals referred to them as their 'second signature', the 'first signature' being the one given on their 'verification' applications. Locals proved far more reluctant to deliver their 'second signature' than they had been to submit 'verification' applications. The district's state officials tended to put this down to the local population's 'passivity' and 'uncertainty' about whether Polish rule would endure in the region.[64] This attitude was not unique to the prewar population of western Upper Silesia. Similar resistance to submitting 'declarations of loyalty' was encountered throughout Poland's new territories. The process of granting Polish citizenship to 'indigenous Poles' in Poland's new territories lagged far behind the 'verification action' and continued into the 1950s.[65]

[62] Misztal, *Weryfikacja*, pp. 142–4.
[63] Borodziej, 'Einleitung', p. 109; Hofmann, *Nachkriegszeit*, p. 300; Kowalski, *Powrót*, pp. 342, 370–1.
[64] SiRep OTA head S-PD, 21.7.1946, APO 185, sygn. 85, 34; SiRep OTA head S-PD, 21.8.1946, APO 185, sygn. 85, 35; SiRep OTA head S-PD, 21.9.1946. APO 185, sygn. 85, 39; SiRep OTA head S-PD, 21.10.1946, APO 185, sygn. 85, 40; Special SiRep by OTA head S-PD, 13 November 1946, APO 185, sygn. 85, 41–2; SiRep OTA head S-PD, 21.11.1946, APO 185, sygn. 85, 43; SiRep OTA head S-PD, 21.12.1946, APO 185, sygn. 85, 44; SiRep ODA S-PD, 31.12.1946, APK 185/4, sygn. 39, 54–4a.
[65] Rep by ODA S-PD on the period 1.1.1948–31.12.1948, undated, APO 178, sygn. 64, 7–8; Borodziej, 'Einleitung', p. 111; Strauchold, *Autochtoni*, 166–7.

'Verification' was not in fact the only form of ethnic screening witnessed in western Upper Silesia in the second half of the 1940s. As we discussed earlier, in neighbouring eastern Upper Silesia, the Communist-led authorities implemented a 'rehabilitation action' after the war which was aimed at dealing with Nazi Germany's own ethnic screening process, the *Deutsche Volksliste*. A number of people migrated from eastern Upper Silesia to Opole District in the early postwar months, and because they had been placed in group II of the *Deutsche Volksliste*, they were required to submit 'rehabilitation' applications to Opole's district court at this time. This was a necessary condition for their being allowed to remain in Poland and to avoid expulsion to Germany. These people were ethnically screened by Opole's district court from 1946 onwards – though it is unclear how many the court ultimately chose to 'rehabilitate' as Poles. The same must have happened in other western Upper Silesian districts at this time.[66]

UPPER SILESIAN IDENTITY

The central premise on which the 'verification action' rested was that the prewar population of western Upper Silesia was composed of two national groups, Poles and Germans. Once the Poles had been identified, the Germans could be expelled. Or, as Upper Silesia's Regional Governor, Aleksander Zawadzki, put it, '*Nie chcemy ani jednego Niemca, nie oddamy ani jednej duszy polskiej*' (We don't want a single German, nor will we give away a single Polish soul).[67]

There were clear grounds for claiming that a large proportion of western Upper Silesia's prewar population was ethno-nationally Polish. First, there were the results of German censuses carried out before the 1922 partition of Upper Silesia. In the statewide census of 1910, the majority of residents in most western Upper Silesian districts put down 'Polish' as their mother tongue. In Oppeln/Opole District, 63 per cent of residents answered 'Polish' in the census, whereas in both Gross-Strehlitz/Strzelce Opolskie District and Rosenberg/Olesno District the figure was as high as 79 per cent. The proportion of Polish speakers was found to be even higher in a census of

[66] SiRep O Chief on the period 20.8.1945–20.9.1945, APO 178, sygn. 41, 1–4; SiRep O Chief on the period 20.6.1946–20.7.1946, APO 178, sygn. 41, 34–6; SiRep O Chief on the period 20.9.1945–20.10.1945, APO 178, sygn. 41, 5–8; Population figures provided by OTA S-PD, 21.2.1946, APO 185, sygn. 85, 14–15; SiRep O Chief on the period 20.3.1946–20.4.1946, APO 178, sygn. 41, 20–3; situation reports by O Chief on the periods 20.4.1946–20.5.1946, 20.5.1946–20.6.1946, 20.6.1946–20.7.1946, APO 178, sygn. 41, 25–36.

[67] Cited in Eser, 'Oberschlesien', p. 388.

primary school children of 1911: 75 per cent in Oppeln/Opole District, 89 per cent in Gross-Strehlitz/Strzelce Opolskie District, 94 per cent in Rosenberg/Olesno District and clear majorities in most of the remaining districts of western Upper Silesia.[68]

Second, a relatively large proportion of the residents of western Upper Silesia had regularly read Polish-language newspapers in the early decades of the twentieth century. This included the Oppeln/Opole-based publication *Nowiny*.[69] Third, although the number of people categorized as Polish speakers dropped dramatically in censuses carried out in the interwar period – so that, for example, less than 1 per cent of Oppeln/Opole District's residents were found to speak Polish by the time of the 1939 census – many Catholic masses continued to be given in Polish in the region right into the 1930s, even once the Nazis came to power. As late as the mid 1930s, for example, over 70 per cent of masses given in Oppeln/Opole District's Roman Catholic churches were delivered in Polish.[70]

Yet none of this means that the postwar Communist-controlled Polish authorities were right to regard the majority of western Upper Silesia's prewar inhabitants as Poles. The authorities' belief that most locals were Poles was based principally on the claim that most of them spoke Polish. But this assertion was not beyond dispute. One former resident of the village of Eichberg/Dębiniec in Oppeln/Opole District recalled a number of years after the war, 'Pure Polish was not spoken in the region from which I came. The local Wasserpolnisch dialect... should never be regarded as Polish. [During the war] I myself was assigned the job of a guard in a camp for foreigners. There were Poles in this camp and they could not understand the Wasserpolnisch dialect whatsoever.'[71] This individual, who was living in West Germany at the time of writing this statement, clearly exaggerated the dialect's distance from standard Polish. There can be little doubt, in fact, that the Slavic vernacular spoken in western Upper Silesia

[68] As well as people whose mother tongue was said to be Polish, these figures include the much smaller proportion of the region's residents described as bilingual in Polish and German. Sarah Wambaugh, *Plebiscites since the World War. With a Collection of Official Documents* (2 vols., Washington, DC, 1933), Vol. 1, p. 250; Tooley, *National Identity*, p. 240; Bohmann, *Menschen*, pp. 192, 211, 238.

[69] Wanatowicz, *Historia*, pp. 145–60, 177–8; Lis, 'Mnieszość polska', pp. 262–9; Kamusella, 'Upper Silesia', pp. 97–101, 104; Ther, 'Die einheimische Bevölkerung', pp. 415–18; Madajczyk, *Przyłączenie*, p. 197; Linek, *Polityka*, pp. 30–3.

[70] The figure cited here from the 1939 census again includes people said to be bilingual in Polish and German. But in contrast to the 1910 census, the 1939 census also included the categories 'Upper Silesian' and 'Upper Silesian and German'. Less than 5 per cent of Oppeln District's population placed themselves in these categories in the 1939 census. The census figures are provided by Bohmann, *Menschen*, pp. 238–9. On Polish-language Roman Catholic masses, see Lis, 'Mniejszość polska', pp. 261–70.

[71] WR, Josef J., Eichberg (Dębiniec), 19.12.1954, BOD 1, 243, 13–16.

midway through the twentieth century was a dialect of Polish. Yet the type of Polish spoken in western Upper Silesia was very different to the language spoken in central Poland.

This was captured well in the recollections of another witness familiar with this region, a Polish teacher from Kraków called Jan Stadniczenko. He was sent to run a village school in a remote part of Opole District in 1947. Describing one of his first encounters with a resident of the village, he wrote with deliberate understatement, 'She did not speak Polish like the poet Adam Mickiewicz. But her Polish was a beautiful, archaic Silesian dialect.' Elsewhere he highlighted the disparity between the local dialect and the standard Polish language when referring to the difficulties he encountered teaching local children in standard Polish:

> It was a very beautiful dialect, without the number of German expressions found in the eastern Upper Silesian dialect. The problem was that our school textbooks were written [in conventional Polish] not in the [local] dialect. The people living in this village were real Silesians – and it was obvious that the language spoken by the children at school on the first day of lessons would be the same as their parents. So I knew right away that it would not be at all easy for them to understand the textbooks.[72]

The Polish sociologist Stanisław Ossowski, who visited Opole District in August 1945, described the situation in the following way:

> The older generation speaks a beautiful dialect with elegant archaisms . . . [but] German vocabulary arises when they speak about administrative and technical matters and occasionally when they speak about trade. Their command of written Polish is worse . . . The number of German words and terms proliferates among the younger generation . . . Small children do not speak any Polish [dialect] whatsoever . . . The amount of German in the local Polish dialect also varies from village to village.[73]

This dialect was in fact the product of centuries of cultural and political separation from Poland and centuries of political and cultural affiliation with the Kingdom of Bohemia, the Habsburg Empire and Prussia. It therefore had strong links with both the Czech and German languages, particularly in terms of vocabulary. It was often barely intelligible to the settlers from central and prewar eastern Poland who arrived in the region after the Second World War. It was almost always speakers of this dialect rather than of standard Polish whom the 1910 and 1911 census results

[72] Stadniczenko, 'Rok szkolny', pp. 399, 404. [73] Ossowski, 'Zagadnienia', p. 276.

were referring to in western Upper Silesia, when they categorized locals as speakers of 'Polish'.[74]

Yet it would be equally dubious to claim that most of western Upper Silesia's prewar inhabitants were ethnically German or regarded themselves as Germans. To be sure, the majority of voters in western Upper Silesia had opted for Germany in the plebiscite of 1921. They included 69 per cent of the voters in the rural part of Oppeln/Opole District and 95 per cent in Oppeln/Opole town. But the 60 per cent vote which Germany had received in the overall Upper Silesian vote had not been achieved without the German authorities transporting many tens of thousands of Upper Silesian migrant workers into the region from western Germany, a cynical act aimed at boosting the German vote. More importantly, voting for Germany in the 1921 plebiscite and regarding oneself as a German were two quite separate things. People had diverse, often very pragmatic reasons for voting for Germany. They usually had little to do with a person regarding him or herself as having a German ethno-national identity. Before the Second World War, a large proportion of western Upper Silesia's inhabitants clearly had viewed themselves as Germans. But they constituted a minority of the overall population of the region, concentrated in the region's larger towns and in the region's southwestern area, lying to the west of the Oder/Odra river. Moreover, although the postwar Communist-led authorities had been wrong to assume in the immediate postwar months that everyone who had fled the region as the Red Army invaded in January 1945 was an ethnic German, they had been right to believe that most of the people who had viewed themselves as Germans had fled.[75]

In fact, most prewar residents of western Upper Silesia, as the Polish sociologist Stanisław Ossowski discovered on his trip to Opole District in August 1945, regarded themselves neither as Germans nor as Poles. Rather, most people were 'nationally indifferent' and exhibited a collective consciousness which was rooted in the region, town or village in which they lived rather than in the German or Polish nation. According to Ossowski, most people were much more likely to identify themselves as 'Silesians' (*Ślązacy*) or 'locals' (*swojacy*) than 'Germans' or 'Poles'. They tended to

[74] Ther, 'Die einheimische Bevölkerung', p. 411; Alexander, 'Oberschlesien', pp. 467–8, 474–6; Ossowski, 'Zagadnienia', pp. 271, 275–6, 281, 287, 289; Kamusella, *Silesia*, pp. 118–24; Kamusella, *The Szlonzoks*, pp. 11–21; Tooley, *National Identity*, p. 11.

[75] Bożena Malec-Masnyk, *Plebiscyt na Górnym Śląsku (geneza i charakter)* (Opole, 1989), pp. 179–80; Tooley, *National Identity*, pp. 234–52; Ther, 'Die einheimische Bevölkerung', pp. 415–21; Lis, 'Mniejszość polska', pp. 261–2.

be bilingual in the local Polish dialect and German and could move easily between the two languages, but did not view this as contradicting their feelings of distinction from 'Germans'. In fact, when the younger generation sought to distance themselves from 'Germans', they did not do so by avoiding use of the German language. Instead, they did so by speaking the Polish dialect alongside German – outwardly demonstrating their 'bilinguality'. Ossowski also observed that the section of the prewar population which exhibited the weakest command of the local Polish dialect and the greatest propensity to use German were those who had been children in the 1930s and early 1940s, meaning they attended schools and youth organizations during the Nazi period. At the same time, Ossowski stressed that most locals regarded their attendance of Polish-language Catholic masses as a part of the religious tradition of western Upper Silesia rather than a manifestation of Polish national identity.[76]

Only a small fraction of the prewar population actively regarded itself as Polish. According to Stanisław Ossowski, that fraction comprised the small number of locals who had supported the Polish insurgents during the Silesian Uprisings of 1919–21, run local branches of the Association of Poles in Germany in the interwar period and sent their children to the small number of Polish language schools which were set up in western Upper Silesia after 1922. In short, those people who actively regarded themselves as Poles after 1945 comprised the small fraction of the prewar population which had engaged openly in pro-Polish political and cultural activism before the war. Not by coincidence, they also tended to be the people who, after Poland's incorporation of western Upper Silesia in 1945, were given local administrative and mayoral posts by the arriving Polish officials or were selected to sit on the 'verification committees' as 'trusted representatives' of the 'local Polish population'. Finally, they were generally the only prewar inhabitants of the region – other than interwar immigrants from the old territories of Poland – who spoke something akin to standard Polish. To be more exact, Ossowski stated that, through their long-term contact with people in prewar Poland, a small number of actively pro-Polish locals spoke a type of Polish 'somewhere between the dialect and standard Polish'. He also observed that a small number of young prewar residents were 'trilingual' in the local Polish dialect, German and standard Polish (*polski język literacki*) – an outcome of having been sent for

[76] Ossowski, 'Zagadnienia', pp. 271, 273–85, 287, 291–5; Stadniczenko, 'Rok szkolny', pp. 403–4, 407, 414, 425; Kamusella, *The Szlonzoks*, pp. 12–13; Ther, 'Die einheimische Bevölkerung', pp. 413–14; Alexander, 'Oberschlesien', pp. 476–80; Strauchold, *Autochtoni*, pp. 86, 95.

schooling in central Poland before the war by their actively pro-Polish parents.[77]

But if only a small fraction of the prewar western Upper Silesian population regarded itself as Polish or spoke standard Polish, why did so many people apply for 'verification' as ethnic Poles after the Second World War? In Opole District, some of the prewar residents who relocated or were expelled to Germany after 1945 claimed that most local people were 'pressured', 'blackmailed', or 'forced' into 'opting for Poland'.[78] Opole District's postwar state officials also acknowledged that a certain amount of pressure was sometimes exerted to induce people to submit 'verification' applications. One official from Opole Town Administration, for example, mentioned in a report from January 1948 'people whose verification had not been achieved without a certain amount of difficulty'.[79] But it is clear that nobody was physically forced to submit a 'verification' application. Instead, the local state authorities confronted local people with a stark choice: either submit a 'verification' application or face eviction from your home, internment in a camp and forcible transportation to Germany. As one former resident of the village of Proskau/Prószków in Opole District put it: 'Those who wished to retain their property had to opt. If you did not opt [for Poland], you had no rights.'[80] There was, then, a choice only of sorts. Any locals who wished to 'opt for Germany' were free to do so as long as they were willing to accept the severe consequences of this decision.[81]

The 'verification action' implemented in western Upper Silesia after the Second World War, therefore, did not filter Poles from Germans, as the Communist-controlled Polish authorities claimed it did. Rather, it removed individuals who openly presented themselves as Germans and individuals who were willing to lose their homes in order to avoid living in Poland from a population which largely had no feelings of 'national' affiliation. The majority of local inhabitants were understandably willing to let pragmatic considerations dictate their choice of ethno-national identity. As long as a person did not go out of his or her way to emphasize a German

[77] Ossowski, 'Zagadnienia', pp. 266–74, 280; Wanatowicz, *Historia*, pp. 147–51; Lis, 'Mniejszość polska', pp. 262–8. Rep by OTA S-PD, 24.8.1945, APO 185, sygn. 85, 3. WRs in file BOD 1, 243 and file BOD 2 229.

[78] WRs: BOD 2, 229, 3–4; BOD 1, 243, 49–51; BOD 1, 243, 67–72; BOD 1, 243, 381–2; BOD 1, 243, 25–7; BOD 1, 243, 13–16; BOD 1, 243, 37–9; BOD 1, 243, 299–301; BOD 1, 243, 225–6; BOD 1, 243, 227–8; BOD 1, 243, 13–16.

[79] SiRep OTA head S-PD, 21.1.1948, APO 185, sygn. 85, 48.

[80] WR, Rudolf T., Proskau (Prószków), undated, BOD 1, 243, 287–8.

[81] WR, Gustav R., Blumenthal (Krzywa Góra), undated, BOD 1, 243, 33–6; WR, Arthur M., Derschau (Suchy Bór), 7.10.1954, BOD 1, 243, 67–72; WR, Josef J., Horst (Świerkle), 2.8.1955, BOD 1, 243, 197–8.

ethno-national identity or 'hostility' to Poland, his or her application for 'verification' was generally successful. One extraordinary consequence of this was that close relatives were often placed in different ethno-national categories by the 'verification committees' and state officials during the 'verification' process. For example, the brother of Gustav R. from the village of Blumenthal/Krzywa Góra in Opole District submitted an application and was therefore allowed to remain there as a 'Pole'. In contrast, Gustav and the rest of his family refused and were transported to Germany as 'Germans' in August 1946.[82]

All this might point to the conclusion that the authorities of Opole District and of other western Upper Silesian districts prioritized the goal of strengthening Poland's territorial claim to the region over the goal of transforming postwar Poland into an ethno-nationally homogeneous Polish nation-state. It might be taken as suggesting that the region's state authorities 'verified' as ethnic Poles hundreds of thousands of people whom they did not actually regard as such. But this was not at all how Opole District's and western Upper Silesia's officials viewed the 'verification action'. As far as they – and, for that matter, the distinguished sociologist Stanisław Ossowski – were concerned, the people they had 'verified' as ethnic Poles were just that, ethnic Poles. But they were ethnic Poles whose 'Polish national consciousness' had not yet fully 'crystallized'. From the outset, the authorities therefore accompanied their 'verification action' with measures aimed at bringing about this 'crystallization' – or 're-Polonization' (*repolonizacja*), as they more frequently termed it. We will examine the authorities' 're-Polonization' measures in detail in Chapter 9.

Stanisław Ossowski published a refined, sophisticated study of the population of western Upper Silesia in the late 1940s. The clear implication of most of his analysis was that it was a crude simplification to understand the region's inhabitants as divided into two national groups, Poles and Germans. This plainly did not reflect the complex linguistic and cultural identities and collective self-understandings of most prewar inhabitants of the region. Yet, writing at a time when the ideology of nationalism was reaching its apotheosis in Europe, Ossowski was unable to free himself entirely from nation-centred understandings of collective identity. Rather incongruously, he therefore presented the western Upper Silesian population, at certain points in his study, as composed of two 'objective' groups,

[82] WR, Gustav R., Blumenthal (Krzywa Góra), undated, BOD 1, 243, 33–6. WRs: BOD 1, 243, 264; BOD 1, 243, 309–19; BOD 1, 243, 49–51; BOD 1, 243, 289–93; BOD 1, 243, 121–2; BOD 1, 243, 174–81.

Germans and Poles.[83] What explains this contradiction? The answer lies in the fact that Ossowski believed that 'ethnic nationality' (*narodowość*) was a social category which could be determined, principally, by the 'objective' criterion of language. Because the local Slavic dialect in western Upper Silesia was a dialect of Polish, those people who spoke it as their first language, irrespective of whether they viewed themselves as Poles or not, were 'objectively' of Polish *narodowość*. Conversely, those locals whose mother tongue was German were 'objectively' of German *narodowość*. But Ossowski made clear that this 'objective' category of 'ethnic nationality' had to be thought of as separate from how the western Upper Silesians understood themselves: the fact that some local people viewed themselves as Germans, some as Poles, but the majority as neither. The majority, he emphasized, elected to ground their collective identities in the region or local community in which they lived. But what Ossowski failed to recognize is that 'ethnic nationality' can no more be objectively determined than can regional or local identity. And because most residents of western Upper Silesia in the late 1940s saw themselves as neither Germans nor Poles, it made no sense to categorize the majority of them as either Germans or Poles.

In fact, this was the basic flaw underpinning the 'verification action' implemented in western Upper Silesia at the end of the Second World War. As we shall discuss in Chapter 9, this flaw would become very apparent to the postwar state authorities of the region in the course of time.

'INDIGENOUS POLES' OUTSIDE WESTERN UPPER SILESIA

The postwar 'verification action' was targeted principally at the two regions of Poland's new territories where a large percentage of local residents spoke dialects of Polish as well as German: western Upper Silesia and southern East Prussia. In the latter, the Communist-controlled Polish authorities encountered a lot of resistance to the 'verification action' from the local population. Officials were only able to convince a small minority of speakers of the Masurian and Warmian dialects of Polish to submit 'verification' applications in the second half of the 1940s.[84] Yet the postwar 'verification action' was not restricted to these two linguistically mixed regions of the new territories. In homogeneously German-speaking areas – the majority of the prewar eastern German territories before 1945 – it also played a

[83] Ossowski, 'Zagadnienia', pp. 255, 259–61, 263–6, 272–5, 280–83, 285, 291–4.

[84] Strauchold, *Autochtoni*, pp. 59–60, 76, 166; Blanke, *Polish-speaking Germans*, pp. 279–310; Claudia Kraft, 'Who Is a Pole, and Who Is a German? The Province of Olsztyn in 1945', in Ther and Siljak, *Redrawing Nations*, pp. 116–17.

role in early postwar events, albeit a much smaller one. Lower Silesia was one of these homogeneously German areas. Only the three northeastern districts of Lower Silesia, bordering western Upper Silesia and prewar Poland, Groß Wartenberg/Syców, Namslau/Namysłów and Brieg/Brzeg, contained a significant number of speakers of Polish dialect before the war. Indeed, Polish dialect speakers amounted to just a few tens of thousands of people in Lower Silesia as a whole, a tiny fraction of the overall population of the region.[85]

Faced with a very different population to the one inhabiting most of western Upper Silesia, Lower Silesia's Regional Administration in Wrocław showed little enthusiasm for the 'verification action' in the early postwar years. It was only under pressure from the government in Warsaw that Wrocław introduced a 'verification action' at all in 1946. In most districts in Lower Silesia it does not appear to have got underway until the Ministry for Recovered Territories issued its 6 April 1946 order. The main intention of this order, as we have seen, had been to bring the separate 'verification actions' already being carried out in several other regions in Poland's new territories procedurally into line with the western Upper Silesian action. The 'verification action' implemented in Lower Silesia, therefore, closely resembled the one in neighbouring western Upper Silesia.

In Jelenia Góra District, two 'verification committees' were set up after April 1946, one to evaluate 'verification' applications from residents of Jelenia Góra town, the second to screen applications from inhabitants of the surrounding countryside. Not unlike what happened in Opole District, the 'verification committees' in Jelenia Góra District were headed by an administrative official and included representatives from the 'District Inter-Party Liaison Committee', the Polish Western Association, the Peasant Self-Help Association, trade unions and local teachers. Officials also claimed that the committees contained 'three to five representatives from the local Polish population' – though what they meant by 'the local Polish population' in this district, which had been almost entirely German-speaking before 1945, is not at all clear. Based on the evaluations these 'verification committees' made of the applications, the District Administration's and Town Administration's respective Administrative-Legal Departments issued successful applicants with 'temporary Polish citizenship'. Conversely, unsuccessful applicants were displaced to Allied-occupied Germany with the rest of the prewar population of Jelenia Góra District. This was how the 'verification action' operated in the district only until the end of 1946.

[85] Hofmann, *Nachkriegszeit*, pp. 326–8 including footnote 161; Jankowiak, 'Wrocławskie', pp. 427–8.

Thereafter, the 'verification committees' were dissolved and the powerful Security Police became directly involved in the screening of 'verification' applications. The 'verification action' operated in much the same way in most other districts in Lower Silesia.[86]

How many people were 'verified' as 'indigenous Poles' in Jelenia Góra District between 1946 and 1949? Roughly 2,000 'verification' applications were submitted by prewar German citizens living there in these years. Of these, 1,229 succeeded in gaining 'verification' as 'indigenous Poles', sparing them from expulsion to Germany. Of the positively 'verified' people, 160 lived in Jelenia Góra town; the rest lived in the surrounding countryside of Jelenia Góra District.[87]

These 1,229 individuals constituted a surprisingly high proportion of the number of people positively 'verified' in Lower Silesia as a whole in the second half of the 1940s. Only around 17,000 individuals were 'verified' as 'indigenous Poles' in Lower Silesia between 1946 and 1949. This was a much lower figure than the number of 'indigenous Poles' the Communist-led government believed had inhabited the northeastern districts of the region – Syców District, Namysłów District and Brzeg District – before 1945. State officials had done very little to encourage local people living in these districts to apply for 'verification' in the previous few years. The majority of Polish-dialect-speakers living in Syców, Namysłów and Brzeg had never become aware of the 'verification' process and had failed to submit 'verification' applications in the early postwar years. They had been transported to Germany in the second half of the 1940s along with millions of other German citizens.[88] In Poland's new territories as a whole, just over 1 million people were 'verified' as 'indigenous Poles'

[86] SiRep JGDA head S-PD, 31.8.1946, APW 331/VI, sygn. 35, 32–4; SiRep head JGTA, 2.3.1946, APW 331/VI, sygn. 31, 7–23; Rep by JG Chief for LSRA S-PD, 1.4.1947, APW 331/VI, sygn. 51, 15–16; SiRep the deputy head of JGTA, 31.7.1946, APW 331/VI, sygn. 34, 25–7; Rep by JG Chief on the year 1947, undated, APJG 123/II, sygn. 21, 248–79; Hofmann, *Nachkriegszeit*, pp. 301, 326–31; Jankowiak, 'Wrocławskie', pp. 427–32; Strauchold, *Autochtoni*, p. 51.

[87] SiRep Jelenia Góra's Deputy Town President, 23.6.1949, APW 331/VI, sygn. 50, 121–5; SiRep the head of JGTA's Settlement Department, 18.6.1947, APJG 130, sygn. 47, 219–21; Rep by JG Chief for LSRA S-PD, 1.4.1947, APW 331/VI, sygn. 51, 15–16; Rep by JG DepChief on the period 1.10.1946–30.7.1947, 23.8.1947, APJG 123/II, sygn. 21, 223–9; SiRep JG Chief, 2.11.1948, APW 331/VI, sygn. 51, 77–8; SiRep JG Chief, 3.12.1948, APW 331/VI, sygn. 51, 79–81; SiRep JG Chief, start March 1949, APW 331/VI, sygn. 51, 98–100; SiRep Jelenia Góra's Deputy Town President, 23.6.1949, APW 331/VI, sygn. 50, 121–5; SiRep JGT Pres, 31.5.1949, APW 331/VI, sygn. 50, 119; SiRep Jelenia Góra's Deputy Town President, 23.6.1949, APW 331/VI, sygn. 50, 121–5; Rep by JGT Pres, 29.9.1949, APW 331/VI, sygn. 51, 143–51; Rep by JGT Pres, 30.12.1949, APW 331/VI, sygn. 50, 141–9; Rep on the second quarter of 1949 by JG Chief, 6.7.1949, APW 331/VI, sygn. 51, 137–42.

[88] Hofmann, *Nachkriegszeit*, pp. 326–30; Jankowiak, 'Wrocławskie', pp. 430, 432; Strauchold, *Autochtoni*, p. 166.

between 1945 and 1949. Around 85 per cent of them lived in western Upper Silesia.[89]

Who exactly were the 1,229 residents of Jelenia Góra District who were 'verified' as 'indigenous Poles' in the years 1946–9? One Polish state official clearly indicated in autumn 1945 that the district had contained no 'indigenous Poles' before 1945. He stated unequivocally that 'the Polish population to be found in the territories of our district is an immigrant one'.[90] Indeed, it is very likely that at least some of the German citizens 'verified' as 'indigenous Poles' in Jelenia Góra District were not prewar residents of the district at all but rather postwar migrants to the district from western Upper Silesia.[91] A significant percentage almost certainly also comprised Poles who had come to the district and gained German citizenship before the war as ordinary immigrants.[92]

Yet it is equally certain that, at the very least, several hundred were people whose families had lived in the district for generations, who could not speak any form of Polish, who did not regard themselves as Poles and who, at the most, had a Polish-sounding surname or a distant Polish ancestor.[93] A number of German witnesses provided anecdotal evidence of this. Paul H. from Bad Warmbrunn/Cieplice Śląskie recalled in a rather sarcastic tone, for example, that '[a] few Germans discovered... their old Polish great, great, great grandmother. They ran into the offices of the Polish authorities and told them that they wanted to become genuine, upright Poles'.[94] With a good deal less bitterness, Robert W. remembered the case of one local woman from the village of Ludwigsdorf/Chromiec who could prove her Polish descent and was therefore allowed to continue

[89] Strauchold, *Autochtoni*, pp. 165–8, 176; Nitschke, *Vertreibung*, p. 277; Misztal, *Weryfikacja*, p. 158.

[90] SiRep JGDA S-PD, 3.9.1945, APJG 123/II, sygn. 18, 86–8. Rather inexplicably, Jelenia Góra District's Chief Official contradicted this in 1947 by claiming that there had already been 2,500 'indigenous Polish people' living in the district when Polish officials first arrived there in 1945. Rep by JG Chief for the LSRA S-PD, 1.4.1947, APW 331/VI, sygn. 51, 15–16.

[91] Rep on the second quarter of 1949 by JG Chief, 6.7.1949, APW 331/VI, sygn. 51, 137–42; WR, Albert S., Schreiberhau (Szklarska Poręba), undated, BOD 1, 207, 183–95; WR, Oskar S., Berbisdorf (Dziwiszów), undated, BOD 1, 207, 29–32; WR, Walter S.-G., Niederschreiberhau (Szklarska Poręba Dolna), 10.1.1948, BOD 2, 188, 175–97.

[92] Jankowiak, 'Wrocławskie', pp. 430–1; SiRep JG Chief, 2.12.1946, APW 331/VI, sygn. 38, 96–7.

[93] SiRep JG Chief, 31.1.1949, APJG 123/II, sygn. 20, 240–44; SiRep JGDA head S-PD, 31.8.1946, APW 331/VI, sygn. 35, 32–4; SiRep JG Chief, 1.2.1947, APW 331/VI, sygn. 51, 1–4; SiRep JG DepChief, 31.5.1947, APW 331/VI, sygn. 51, 20–1; WR, Richard K., Eichberg (Dąbrowica), undated, BOD 1, 207, 57–8; WR, Willi F., Schmiedeberg (Kowary), 2.8.1955, BOD 1, 207, 171–5; WR, Paul H., Bad Warmbrunn (Cieplice Śląskie), 10.9.1958, BOD 1, 207, 243–9; WR, Gustav H., Krummhübel (Karpacz), 14.3.1950, BOD 1, 207, 115–21; WR, Alfred E., Kupferberg (Miedzianka), undated, BOD 1, 207, 127–30; Czepułkowski, 'W Karpaczu', p. 297; Jankowiak, 'Wrocławskie', pp. 429, 431–2; Hofmann, *Nachkriegszeit*, p. 329.

[94] WR, Paul H., Bad Warmbrunn (Cieplice Śląskie), 10.9.1958, BOD 1, 207, 243–9.

living in the village when the rest of the population was transported to Germany in 1946. This had happened after she had fallen in love with a Polish settler living in her home, together with her and her German husband. As a German, her husband could do nothing to prevent her affair with the settler. Despairing at his situation, he left home in spring 1946 and had been missing for some weeks before his corpse was found hanging in a forest near Ludwigsdorf/Chromiec.[95]

The Polish settler Stanisław Czepułkowski, who took up residence in the mountain village of Karpacz in the late 1940s, also made clear that at least some of the people 'verified' as 'indigenous Poles' in the local area had lived there for generations, when he wrote, 'From the autochthons I learnt of the values and advantages of these mountain localities.'[96] The district's state officials also provided evidence that German citizens, with no more than a dubious claim to being Polish, submitted 'verification' applications in Jelenia Góra District after the war. They reported a flood of 'verification' applications in late summer 1947 just as the 'third phase' of the 'displacement action' reached its conclusion. They rejected the vast majority of these applications.[97] Similarly, in summer 1946, one of the district's officials called for greater caution to be shown towards the 'verification' process, because 'Nazi germans [*sic*] [had been positively 'verified'] who did not in reality have a single trace of Polish roots' and 'got themselves re-Polonized' purely to hold on to their properties or to regain properties which they had previously lost. This official also claimed that this was provoking much resentment from Polish settlers. Several of the people positively 'verified', he added, had written 'no', using German gothic script, to all three questions in the 30 June 1946 People's Referendum – including the third question asking whether voters approved of Poland's new borders.[98]

In contrast to western Upper Silesia, then, the type of people 'verified' as 'indigenous Poles' in Jelenia Góra District probably comprised not merely prewar residents of the district, but rather an assorted mixture of monolingual German speakers, interwar Polish immigrants and postwar arrivals from western Upper Silesia. The same was very likely true of the majority of other localities in Poland's new territories, which had been homogeneously German-speaking localities before 1945.

———

95 WR, Robert W., Ludwigsdorf (Chromiec), undated, BOD 1, 207, 133–8.

96 Czepułkowski, 'W Karpaczu', p. 297.

97 SiRep JG Chief, 20.9.1947, APJG 123/II, sygn. 20, 123–4.

98 SiRep JGDA head S-PD, 30.7.1946, APW 331/VI, sygn. 34, 3–37; SiRep JGDA head S-PD, 31.8.1946, APW 331/VI, sygn. 35, 32–4; Jankowiak, 'Wrocławskie', p. 430.

The top priorities for the Communist-controlled state authorities in the majority of localities in Poland's new territories at the end of the Second World War were to accommodate the masses of arriving Polish settlers and to get rid of the remaining German residents. The 'verification action' came very low on their priority list. They did little to encourage the prewar residents of these localities to submit 'verification' applications in the second half of the 1940s.

This was in stark contrast to what happened in the two large regions in Poland's new territories which had contained linguistically mixed populations before 1945: southern East Prussia and western Upper Silesia. The authorities there were determined from the outset to ensure that a very large proportion of the locals were 'verified' as ethnically Polish and thus kept in these territories. This was principally because the Communist-led government believed that by 'proving' that a large percentage of the prewar residents of these regions were 'indigenous Poles', they would strengthen Poland's long-term claim to all the territories acquired from Germany in 1945.

In southern East Prussia, the authorities ultimately failed to convince more than a small fraction of the local Polish-dialect-speaking population to submit 'verification' applications after the war. The 'verification action' was a failure there. But in western Upper Silesia it was not. The authorities in that region proved willing to accept as an 'indigenous Pole' virtually any prewar resident of western Upper Silesia living east of the Odra River. Even Nazi Party membership did not present itself as an absolute obstacle to 'verification' as an 'indigenous Pole'. The result was that the vast majority of the region's residents who had not fled to postwar German territory in the final phase of the war were 'verified' as ethnic Poles between 1945 and 1949. Western Upper Silesia's state authorities, then, had given the 'verification action' clear precedence over accommodating Polish settlers and expelling Germans. So what exactly did the expulsion and repopulation processes look like in western Upper Silesia? Let us now address that question.

CHAPTER 7

Expellees, settlers, natives

CHAOTIC MIGRATIONS

Given that the Communist-controlled government of Poland viewed western Upper Silesia, from the outset, as populated predominantly by 'indigenous Poles', one might assume that it would have made sure that only small numbers of Polish settlers were sent there in the early postwar years. Instead, hundreds of thousands of Polish settlers began flooding into the region several months before they reached the homogeneously German-speaking areas of Poland's new territories lying further to the west. This had three broad causes. First, in the circumstances of chaos and disorder facing Poland at the end of the Second World War, the Communist-controlled government was simply not fully in control of the repopulation process. Second, the government wished to repopulate the whole of Poland's new territories with as many Polish settlers as possible, as quickly as possible. As discussed in Chapter 5, this had to do with its desire to influence the decisions reached by the Allied powers at the Potsdam Conference about postwar territorial changes in East-Central Europe. Third, western Upper Silesia became one of the main stopping points for cargo trains carrying settlers to Poland's new territories from prewar southeastern Poland and from postwar south-central Poland.

The mass influx of Polish settlers into western Upper Silesia started already in March 1945, when the first cargo trains organized by the government's State Repatriation Office began transporting Polish 'repatriates' to the region from prewar Poland's lost eastern territories. One resident of the town of Opole recalled returning home on 1 April 1945, following the end of fighting, to find that thousands of Poles had arrived from the 'territories annexed by the Russians'. At the same time as the first cargo trains began arriving from postwar Soviet territory, Poles also started to flow into western Upper Silesia from the Zagłębie Dąbrowskie region and other nearby areas. These people travelled to the region without assistance from the state authorities. By early summer 1945, the State Repatriation Office was also transporting large numbers of voluntary 'resettlers' to western Upper Silesia from the heavily populated provinces of central Poland.[1]

Many tens of thousands of Polish settlers were unloaded by the State Repatriation Office at western Upper Silesia's main railway stations at this time. The specific reason for this was that this region happened to be where the Soviet broad-gauge railway – installed by the Red Army to serve its military needs in the final phase of the war – ended. The fact that the Soviets had not laid their railway any further westwards into Poland's new territories meant that the Polish state authorities needed to use western Upper Silesia's main towns as 'reloading points'. Polish settlers arriving on broad-gauge trains from both prewar eastern Poland and central Poland were transferred at these 'reloading points' onto narrow-gauge trains for onward transportation to Lower Silesia, the Poznań region and Pomerania. But because the State Repatriation Office did not at first have access to a sufficient number of trains or motor vehicles to transport such large numbers westwards out of western Upper Silesia, there was a huge build-up of settlers in a number of the region's towns at this time. In Opole town, for example, state officials reported in early summer 1945 that 8,000–10,000 eastern and central Polish settlers were arriving per day. A large proportion of them simply could not be transported immediately westwards because of an 'acute lack of rail links, especially to the territories located west of the Odra river, and an absolute shortage of lorries'.[2] Transporting eastern Polish forced migrants westwards from western Upper Silesia was made even more difficult by the fact that many eastern Polish families reached the region with one to two tonnes of belongings and many had livestock as well. In Opole District, officials reported the additional problem that there was simply not enough fodder in the district to feed all of the settlers' arriving livestock. The same problem was probably encountered in other western Upper Silesian districts at this time.[3]

The situation in Opole town appears to have been considerably worse than in western Upper Silesia's other main towns. The State Repatriation Office set up a makeshift camp next to Opole's railway station at the

[1] Borodziej et al., 'Wstęp', p. 43; Eser, 'Oberschlesien', p. 384; Hofmann, *Nachkriegszeit*, pp. 103, 108; WR, Alfons S., Oppeln (Opole) town, 23.1.1949, BOD 2, 229, 48–52.

[2] Rep by the chairman of VoiInspCom on an inspection of Opole District, 6–19.2.1946, APK 185/4, sygn. 436, 60–1; SiRep ODA, 9.8.1945, APK 185/4, sygn. 27/1, 43–7; Hofmann, *Nachkriegszeit*, pp. 109, 115–16; Eser, 'Oberschlesien', p. 384; Ther, *Vertriebene*, pp. 122–3.

[3] Rep by the chairman of VoiInspCom on an inspection of Opole District, 6–19.2.1946, APK 185/4, sygn. 436, 60–1; Borodziej et al., 'Wstęp', pp. 35–6; Hofmann, *Nachkriegszeit*, p. 109.

end of the war to accommodate the growing mass of homeless Polish settlers. Conditions at this camp rapidly deteriorated. By midsummer 1945, 27,000 settlers were staying there and a serious epidemic had broken out. Opole District's officials noted at this time that 'thousands of repatriates are without a roof over their heads, living in terrible hygienic conditions'. By late September 1945 the number of settlers living in the camp or in 'barracks' elsewhere in Opole District had soared to 87,737 – a figure equivalent to well over two-fifths of the entire prewar population of the district.[4] In the rural part of Opole District, farms were also frequently used as temporary accommodation for settlers. The district's officials reported in summer 1945 that three or more families of 'repatriates' were frequently required to live together temporarily on a single farm.[5] The eastern Polish settlers often faced terrible material hardships on arrival in western Upper Silesia. In Opole District, for example, the Chief Official noted in autumn 1945 that large numbers of 'repatriates' 'find themselves without any means to live' and the coming winter would be a 'tragedy' for them if they did not receive aid soon. Three months later he described the 'aid campaign', which local state officials had initiated to help impoverished eastern and central Polish settlers, as 'hopeless'. Especially bad were the 'conditions in which repatriates live' and the lack of cattle fodder.[6]

Only a minority of the Polish settlers who came to western Upper Silesia in 1945 were given permanent housing in the region. Many of the farms, houses and flats which had been abandoned by their prewar occupants during the wave of wartime flight from the Red Army had already been seized in the final months of the war by those Polish settlers who had arrived in the region without the state authorities' assistance. These settlers had taken possession of farms, houses and flats without the authorities' approval and state officials described them as 'wild settlers'. In Opole District, the state authorities set up special committees towards the end of 1945, whose task was to locate any unoccupied farms and houses remaining in the district. The idea was that these properties would be allotted to the large number of settlers who wanted to become permanent residents of the district. But the committees were unable to find anywhere near

4 SiRep ODA S-PD, 20.6.1945, APK 185/4, sygn. 25, 12–14; SiRep O Chief on the period 20.8.1945–20.9.1945, APO 178, sygn. 41, 1–4; Eser, 'Oberschlesien', p. 384; Hofmann, *Nachkriegszeit*, pp. 109–10, 115–16.

5 SiRep ODA, 9.8.1945, APK 185/4, sygn. 27/1, 43–7.

6 SiRep O Chief on the period 20.9.1945–20.10.1945, APO 178, sygn. 41, 5–8; SiRep ODA, 9.8.1945, APK 185/4, sygn. 27/1, 43–7; SiRep O Chief on the period 20.11.1945–20.12.1946, APO 178, sygn. 41, 10–12; SiRep O Chief on the period 20.12.1945–20.1.1946, APO 178, sygn. 41, 13–15; SiRep O Chief on the period 20.5.1946–20.6.1946, APO 178, sygn. 41, 30–2.

enough farms and houses to meet the level of demand from settlers. The fact that, as we saw in Chapter 3, the majority of Opole town's prewar population had fled from the Red Army and not returned after the war meant that the town had greater capacity for taking in permanent settlers than the much larger rural part of Opole District, where only a minority had fled permanently. By the end of October 1945, a total of 8,854 people had been given permanent housing in Opole town, whereas only 6,005 had been permanently settled in the rural part of the district. Four months on, 14,071 Polish settlers had been allotted permanent housing in Opole town, whereas only 7,145 had been given farms and houses in the rural part of the district.[7]

In localities throughout Poland's new territories, once the first massive influx of Polish settlers was over, the only way that farms, houses and flats became available for transfer to newly arriving Polish settlers as their permanent homes was when prewar residents were forcibly evicted from them or decided 'voluntarily' to migrate to postwar Germany. As was indicated in Chapter 6, any prewar resident of western Upper Silesia whose 'verification' application was rejected or who refused to submit an application was automatically categorized as a 'German'. This meant that he or she was designated for expulsion to Germany. Opole District's Chief Official summed this up in a statement in his report from autumn 1945 that the 'verification action' was aimed at 'clearly establishing who will be verified and who must be displaced'. At the same time, as elsewhere in Poland's new territories, the 'displacement process' and the 'settlement process' were intimately intertwined in western Upper Silesia. As one of Opole District's state officials put it in summer 1945, '[t]he settlement problem in the towns and villages is highly dependent on the displacement of the remaining Germans.' In contrast to most of the rest of Poland's new territories, however, at the centre of both the 'displacement process' and the 'settlement process' in western Upper Silesia was the 'verification action'. The ethnic screening process welded the processes of expulsion and repopulation firmly together in this region. Again, this was succinctly expressed by Opole District's Chief Official when he wrote in October 1945 that the 'verification action' will make clear 'who is verified and who should be displaced. In this way,

[7] SiRep O Chief on the period 20.9.1945–20.10.1945, APO 178, sygn. 41, 5–8; SiRep O Chief on the period 20.8.1945–20.9.1945, APO 178, sygn. 41, 1–4; SiRep O Chief on the period 20.12.1945–20.11.1946, APO 178, sygn. 41, 13–15; Rep by OTA S-PD, 21.2.1946, APO 185, sygn. 85, 14–15; Rep by the chairman of VoiInspCom, second half of December 1945, APK 185/4, sygn. 435, 53–6; Rep by the chairman of VoiInspCom on an inspection of Opole District, 6–19 February 1946, APK 185/4, sygn. 436, 60–1; Hofmann, *Nachkriegszeit*, pp. 115–16; Ther, *Vertriebene*, pp. 123–6.

we will know how many repatriates we can settle [in the district] and how many repatriates will be forced to travel westwards'.[8]

Yet 'displacement' in western Upper Silesia did not at first, in the main, signify expulsion from postwar Polish territory. Disorganized expulsions aimed at uprooting local residents to postwar German territory were carried out in western Upper Silesia by the Polish Army and by local civilian authorities in the second half of June and July 1945. But they were largely restricted to areas lying to the west of the 'ethnic border' represented by the Odra River – the southwestern and southern areas of western Upper Silesia. A large proportion of the population of these areas had been monolingual German-speakers before 1945. These summer expulsions succeeded in uprooting no more than a few tens of thousands of residents of the whole region. On 18 June 1945 Upper Silesia's Regional Governor, Aleksander Zawadzki, had ordered local state officials to begin the total 'de-Germanization' of western Upper Silesia's territory. But in most of western Upper Silesia's districts, including Opole District, rather than seeking to expel 'Germans' from the region altogether, the local state authorities responded to Zawadzki's order by interning as many of them as possible in camps. The region's officials believed that this would prevent the 'Germans' from having a 'harmful influence' on the 'indigenous Poles' until the time came when they could be transported to Germany. The authorities' other objective in interning 'Germans' in camps was to free up accommodation for arriving Polish settlers. The great influx of settlers into western Upper Silesia in 1945 clearly, therefore, played a critical role in instigating the process of confining 'Germans' to camps. Opole District's officials justified the internment of 'Germans' with the simple comment that 'repatriates wait for weeks to be allocated a farm'.[9]

Internment camps were set up throughout western Upper Silesia in summer 1945. In Opole District, one state official remarked already in early June 1945 that the problem of 'Germans' remaining in, or returning to, the district 'should be solved as quickly and ruthlessly as possible by placing every German in a place of isolation'. In the weeks after this, before the Regional Governor, Aleksander Zawadzki, had himself ordered these

[8] SiRep O Chief on the period 20.9.1945–20.10.1945. APO 178, sygn. 41, 5–8; SiRep ODA, 9.8.1945, APK 185/4, sygn. 27/1, 43–7; Rep by ODA S-PD, 5.6.1945, APK 185/4, 22, 49–51; Rep by ODA S-PD, 20.6.1945. APK 185/4 sygn. 25, 12–14; WR, Arthur M., Derschau (Suchy Bór), 7.19.1954, BOD 1, 243, 67–72; WR, Rudolf T., Proskau (Prószków), undated, BOD 1, 243, 287–8; Eser, 'Oberschlesien', p. 385.

[9] SiRep ODA S-PD, 5.6.1945, APK 185/4, sygn. 22, 49–51; Eser, 'Oberschlesien', pp. 385–7; Madajczyk, *Przyłączenie*, pp. 219–20; Borodziej, 'Einleitung', pp. 68–9; Hofmann, *Nachkriegszeit*, pp. 192–8; Linek, *Polityka*, pp. 148–60; Nitschke, *Vertreibung*, pp. 172–81.

kinds of actions, the district's Citizens' Militia and Security Police began evicting the local people they regarded as 'Germans' from their homes and placing them in camps in the local area. They targeted only the rural part of Opole District at first. Similar measures do not appear to have been introduced in Opole town until the start of 1946.[10] In certain cases, whole villages were displaced to camps. These were villages which both the Polish state authorities and local people agreed had had an especially German character before 1945. Plümkenau/Radomierowice, Zedlitz/Grabice, Süßenrode/Młodnik and Neuwedel/Świeciny were a set of villages situated in the far north of Opole District (see Map 4), which were said by locals to have been founded by German settlers under Frederick the Great in the eighteenth century. Unusually for western Upper Silesia, which had overwhelmingly Roman Catholic inhabitants, the residents of these villages were nearly all Protestants. Almost all residents of the four villages were forced into camps in swift, violent actions in summer 1945. Marta D. recalled how Citizens' Militia personnel arrived in Plümkenau/Radomierowice with 15 lorries at 6.30 one morning in summer 1945. According to her account, the villagers were forcibly wrenched from their homes, given no time to collect belongings and loaded into waiting lorries. Most were then driven to a camp in another part of Opole District, after the small number of men of working age were dropped off in a separate camp in Opole town along the way.[11]

The task of confining Opole District's 'Germans' in camps was reportedly often made difficult by the very large amount of 'assistance' they received from 'the local Polish population'. Opole District's Chief Official remarked at the end of 1945 that it would only be possible to 'catch' all of the 'germans [*sic*] concealing themselves' in the district, once everyone 'verified' as a Pole had received a 'temporary certificate of Polish nationality'. This would make it easier to distinguish between 'Germans' and 'verified Poles'.[12] Corruption and abuses were also widespread among the local state officials, Citizens' Militia and Security Police personnel who carried out these expulsions. Opole District Administration, for example, accused the local Citizens' Militia of exhibiting 'dishonest tendencies' while implementing

[10] Rep by ODA S-PD, 5.6.1945, APK 185/4, 22, 49–51; SiRep O Chief, 9.8.1945, APK 185/4, sygn. 27/1, 43–7; SiRep O Chief on the period 20.8.1945–20.9.1945, APO 178, sygn. 41, 1–4; Rep by OTA head S-PD, 21.1.1946, APO 185, sygn. 85, 16; WR, Jakob P., Kranst (Chrząstowice), September 1956, BOD 1, 243, 225–6; Madajczyk, *Przyłączenie*, pp. 220–1; Eser, 'Oberschlesien', p. 387.

[11] WR, Marta D., Plümkenau (Radomierowice), 15.9.1956, BOD 1, 243, 281–3; WR, Emilie B., Neuwedel (Świeciny), 29.8.1955, BOD 1, 243, 271–4; WR, Wilhelm B., Neuwedel (Świeciny), 30.7.1955, BOD 1, 243, 275–6.

[12] SiRep O Chief on the period 20.9.1945–20.10.1945, Opole 178, sygn. 41, 5–8; SiRep O Chief on the period 20.11.1945–20.12.1945, APO 178, sygn. 41, 10–12; Rep by OTA head S-PD, 21.1.1946, APO 185, sygn. 85, 16.

expulsions in summer 1945. It also criticized local officials in the district's villages of expelling residents from their homes without permission from the District Administration.[13]

There were several camps located in and around Opole District where 'German' residents of the district were taken during 1945 and 1946. One was a labour camp in the village of Półwieś. The two main local camps were situated respectively on Kropidły Street in the centre of Opole town and some distance east of Opole town near the town of Niemodlin. Both of these camps were set up in summer 1945 and were run by the Security Police. Opole District's Chief Official referred to them in one of his reports as 'penal camps'. Their inmates were subjected to forced labour. It is an indication of the treatment and conditions which inmates endured at the two camps that by the end of December 1945, 53 inmates had already died.[14]

Yet interning 'Germans' in camps was just one of a series of anti-German discriminatory measures introduced by the Communist-controlled authorities in western Upper Silesia at the end of the war with the deliberate aim of making circumstances there bad enough so that they would start to migrate to Germany of their own volition. As we discussed in Chapter 4, the same approach of seeking to induce 'voluntary migration' through 'situational force' was taken by state officials throughout Poland's new territories at this time. In fact, it had been encouraged by Poland's central government in Warsaw in June 1945. As happened elsewhere in the new territories, town and district administrations in western Upper Silesia also issued 'Germans' with official 'passes' which were supposed to facilitate their journeys to Germany. Opole District Administration began to provide local 'Germans' with what they called 'passes for permanent emigration' in the second half of 1945.[15]

Almost as soon as the war had ended, local people began to leave western Upper Silesia and migrate to the postwar territory of Germany using

[13] SiRep ODA, 9.8.1945, APK 185/4, sygn. 27/1, 43–7; Rep by chairman of VoiInspCom on an inspection of the 'verification action' in Opole District, second half December 1945, APK 185/4, sygn. 435, 53–6.

[14] Nowak, *Obozy*, pp. 212–17; SiRep O Chief on the period 20.8.1945–20.9.1945, APO 178, sygn. 41, 1–4; Rep by ODA S-PD, 5.6.1945, APK 185/4, 22, 49–51; Rep by VoiInspCom on the 'verification action' in Opole District, second half December 1945, APK 185/4, sygn. 435, 51–2; Rep by VoiInspCom on an inspection of the 'verification action' in Opole District, second half December 1945, APK 185/4, sygn. 435, 53–6; SiRep O Chief on the period 20.9.1945–20.10.1945, APO 178, 41, 5–8; WR, M. T., Eichtal (Dąbrówka Górna), 21.1.1957, BOD 1, 243, 93–6; WR, Marta D., Plümkenau (Radomierowice), 15.9.1956, BOD 1, 243, 281–3; WR, Wilhelm B., Neuwedel (Świeciny), 30.7.1955, BOD 1, 243, 275–6.

[15] Rep by OTA head S-PD, 16.1.1946, APO 185, sygn. 85, 13; Rep by the head of the OTA S-PD, 16.1.1946, APO 185, sygn. 85, 13; WR, Alfred von A., Althammer (Paliwoda), 10.4.1951, BOD 2, 229, 3–4; WR, Marta D. Plümkenau (Radomierowice), 15.9.1956, BOD 1, 243, 281–3; Madajczyk, *Przyłączenie*, pp. 222–3; Borodziej, 'Einleitung', p. 99; Eser, 'Oberschlesien', p. 387.

whatever means were available. They were motivated not only by the state authorities' anti-German discriminatory measures, but also by the terrible security situation and the very tough material circumstances which prevailed in the region at the end of the war. In addition, they were driven to leave by the wave of attacks many of them suffered at the hands of Polish robbers and looters in spring and summer 1945 and by the poor treatment many subsequently received from hostile Polish settlers. Furthermore, many prewar residents of the region decided to leave in order to join spouses and other relatives who had not returned from Germany after the end of fighting. As one former resident of Opole District, Oskar T., put it, he and his wife were 'forced by the general situation to disappear from Carlsruhe [Pokój] for good' in the second half of 1945.

For those local people who had fled from the Red Army in the final phase of the war but had quickly returned once the fighting was over, this was the second time they had abandoned their homes in less than a year. Alfred von A. and his wife, for example, returned to the village of Althammer/Paliwoda in Opole District at the end of the war, and then 'opted for Germany' on the forms the new Polish state authorities gave them in summer 1945 (i.e., 'verification' application forms). In September 1945, Opole District's Chief Official suddenly summoned them to the District Administration in Opole town and advised them to leave the district before the end of the month. He issued them with 'documents' to facilitate their journey. Soon afterwards, they set off for Wrocław on a passenger train full of Polish settlers. On arrival they were squashed into a luggage wagon and transported to Żagań. There they were transferred onto a Soviet cargo train and, crossing the border at Forst, transported to Allied-occupied Germany.[16]

Tens of thousands of locals left western Upper Silesia on their own initiative in the second half of 1945. The number of people who had left Opole District 'voluntarily' by the end of 1945, according to official figures, was 2,435. But this number almost certainly only included individuals who had been issued with official passes by Opole District Administration rather than the total number of people who had migrated to Allied-occupied Germany unassisted in the second half of 1945. The latter clearly amounted to a much larger number of people. Opole District's state officials admitted that they actually had no idea how many local people were migrating to Germany 'surreptitiously' at this time. A very large proportion of the

[16] WR, Oskar T., Carlsruhe (Pokój), 19.6.1952, BOD 2, 229, 58–62; WR, Alfred von A., Althammer (Paliwoda), 10.4.1951, BOD 2, 229, 3–4; WR, Josef J., Horst (Świerkle), 2.8.1955, BOD 1, 243, 197–8; WR, Julius D., Koben (Chobie), 24.5.1959, BOD 1, 243, 217–20; WR, Alfons S., Oppeln (Opole) town, 23.1.1949, BOD 2, 229, 48–52; WR, A., Oppeln (Opole) town, 15.7.1955, BOD 2, 229, 1–2; Madajczyk, *Przyłączenie*, pp. 222–3, 200–2.

people who made this journey from western Upper Silesia in the first year after the war did so without the authorities' assistance, permission or knowledge. Something like 120,000 people, in total, either were forcibly expelled from western Upper Silesia or left the region 'voluntarily' in the course of 1945 after Germany's capitulation in May.[17] In February 1946, Upper Silesia's Regional Governor, Aleksander Zawadzki, prohibited the region's district and town administrations from issuing 'travel passes' to 'Germans' – a practice which had never had a proper legal basis anyway. Nevertheless, residents of western Upper Silesia continued to migrate to Germany on their own initiative throughout the first half of 1946.[18]

MAKING SPACE FOR SETTLERS

At the start of 1946, western Upper Silesia's state officials were still struggling to meet the needs of the mass of Polish settlers staying in temporary accommodation in the region while awaiting transportation to other destinations in Poland's new territories. Large numbers of Polish settlers were still arriving both from prewar eastern Poland and from central Poland. In Opole District, for example, there were said to be around 1,000 'repatriate' families – numbering several thousand individuals – staying in temporary accommodation in February 1946. Around 550 settlers were still living in the camp next to Opole's railway station. The rest were now staying temporarily with prewar residents of the district, on farms located throughout the local countryside. Apparently plans were being put in place at this time to increase the number of rail tracks at Opole's railway station. Opole District's officials claimed that this would help to prevent any future mass build-up of settlers in Opole town, because it would enable the State Repatriation Office to load three trains simultaneously with 1,200–1,300 settlers each.[19]

[17] Rep by VoiInspCom, second half December 1945, APK 185/4, sygn. 435, 51–2; Rep by VoiInspCom, second half December 1945, APK 185/4, sygn. 435, 53–6; Rep by OTA head S-PD, 16.1.1946, APO 185, sygn. 85, 13; Special SiRep by OTA S-PD, 13.11.1946, APO 185, sygn. 85, 41–2; Depiction of the General Situation for OT Pres by OTA head S-PD, 17.1.1947, APO 185, sygn. 85, 47; Madajczyk, *Przyłączenie*, pp. 222–4; Eser, 'Oberschlesien', p. 387; Nitschke, *Vertreibung*, p. 193; Banasiak, *Przesiedlenie*, pp. 39–40.

[18] Madajczyk, *Przyłączenie*, p. 223; Eser, 'Oberschlesien', pp. 384, 395, 397; SiRep OTA head S-PD, 21.6.1946, APO 185, sygn. 85, 32; SiRep ODA S-PD, 4.12.1946, APO 178, sygn. B15, 1–1a; WR, Adolf D., Oderfest (Przywory), 10.4.1951, BOD 2, 229, 7–8; WR, Gustav L., Rogau (Rogów), 3.8.1951, BOD 2, 229, 30–1.

[19] Rep by the chairman of VoiInspCom on an inspection of Opole District, 6–19.2.1946, APK 185/4, sygn. 436, 60–1; Rep on an inspection which took place 10–23.6.1946, APK 185/4, sygn. 436, 62–4; SiRep O Chief on the period 20.1.1946–20.2.1946, APO 178, sygn. 41, 16–18; Hofmann, *Nachkriegszeit*, pp. 115–16.

Opole District's officials were also still contemplating, in early 1946, what could be done to make permanent housing available to those settlers staying in temporary accommodation who had expressed a wish to become long-term residents of the district. One official suggested that three large land-estates could be 'divided up' for distribution among these settlers. Yet he acknowledged that neither this measure nor the displacement of the relatively small number of 'Germans' living in the district would produce enough property to meet the needs of the large number of settlers who wanted to remain.[20]

In most localities in western Upper Silesia, state officials were increasingly recognizing that very few of the Polish settlers living in temporary accommodation could ultimately be given permanent housing in the region. They would therefore have to be compelled to relocate to other areas of Poland's new territories. The region's authorities had already carried out relocation actions of this sort in 1945. In Opole District, for example, the authorities had transported 1,683 Polish settlers from the camp next to Opole railway station to the neighbouring western Upper Silesian districts of Niemodlin, Brzeg and Prudnik in summer 1945. But it was not until 1946 that more systematic efforts to shift Polish settlers out of western Upper Silesia got underway. In Opole District, in spring 1946, the authorities started to move Polish settlers to districts in northern Lower Silesia – an area of Poland's new territories which had remained very sparsely populated since the war. By the end of June 1946, a total of 1,153 settler families, including both eastern and central Polish settlers, along with livestock, had reportedly been compulsorily relocated from Opole District to northern Lower Silesia. At the same time, no doubt in part prompted by the threat of these official relocation actions, many Polish settlers began to leave the district on their own initiative, unassisted, in search of permanent homes in other areas of the new territories. As a result, by late October 1946 the number of settler families living in temporary accommodation in the district had diminished to 380. The same steady outflow of Polish settlers, caused by both compulsory relocation actions and voluntary migrations, was witnessed in other districts of western Upper Silesia in the course of 1946.[21]

[20] Rep by the chairman of VoiInspCom on an inspection of Opole District, 6–19.2.1946, APK 185/4, sygn. 436, 60–1.

[21] SiRep ODA, 9.8.1945, APK 185/4, sygn. 27/1, 43–7; Rep by the chairman of VoiInspCom on an inspection of Opole District, 6–19.2.1946, APK 185/4, sygn. 436, 60–1; Rep on an inspection which took place 10–23.6.1946, APK 185/4, sygn. 436, 62–4; SiRep O Chief on the period 20.12.1945–20.1.1946, APO 178, sygn. 41, 13–15; SiRep O Chief on the period 20.1.1946–20.2.1946, APO 178, sygn. 41, 16–18; Rep by OTA S-PD, 21.2.1946, APO 185, sygn. 85, 14–15; SiRep O Chief on the period

Another way that western Upper Silesia's Communist-controlled authorities sought to reduce the level of overcrowding in the region during 1946 was by forcibly removing all remaining 'Germans'. Only a relatively small minority of western Upper Silesia's prewar population were categorized as 'Germans' during the 'verification action'. Yet there was significant variation across the region. In Opole District, for example, the authorities believed that 5,776 'Germans' remained by February 1946. In contrast, in Nysa District and Prudnik District, both located in the southwestern corner of western Upper Silesia, where a large proportion of locals had been monolingual German-speakers before 1945, the numbers were said to be 20,500 and 21,526, respectively.

As we discussed in Chapter 4, on 14 February 1946, British and Polish representatives in the Allied Control Council in Berlin finally agreed on terms for the mass transportation of Germans by rail from Poland to the British Zone. In western Upper Silesia, the 'displacement action' (*akcja wysiedleńcza*) got underway on 17 May 1946, when the first cargo train carrying prewar residents of the region set off for the British Zone.[22]

But Opole District was not, at first, included in the operation, and this frustrated the district's officials a great deal. One of Opole town's officials remarked in June 1946, for example, that he and his colleagues 'long for the first transports to leave Opole. Unfortunately, however, according to the information we have received, the first transport will probably not happen until the middle of July at the earliest'. The authorities finally launched the 'displacement action' in Opole District in August 1946. It is not exactly clear how many cargo trains departed from Opole District in the course of the month, but at least two did, setting off on 11 and 12 August. Many of the locals transported to Germany at this time were people who had been placed in local camps in 1945. Others were taken to the camp in Opole town – where all 'Germans' from Opole District were eventually gathered before they were transported to Germany – just a day or two before the trains departed. Some probably arrived there on the same day as their departure. In general, people were given very short notice before they were evicted from their homes and taken to the camp. Gustav R.'s family and six other families from the village of Blumenthal/Krzywa Góra were

20.3.1946–20.4.1946, APO 178, sygn. 41, 20–3; SiRep by O Chief on the period 20.4.1946–20.5.1946, APO 178, sygn. 41, 25–7; SiRep O Chief on the period 20.7.1946–20.8.1946, APO 178, sygn. 41, 38–41; SiRep O Chief on the period 20.8.1946–20.9.1946, APO 178, sygn. 41, 43–5; SiRep O Chief on the period 20.9.1946–20.10.1946, APO 178, sygn. 41, 47–9; Kowalski, *Powrót*, p. 365; Hofmann, *Nachkriegszeit*, p. 116.

22 Rep by OTA S-PD, 21.2.1946, APO 185, sygn. 85, 14–15. Madajczyk, *Przyłączenie*, p. 228; Hofmann, *Nachkriegszeit*, pp. 222–3; Eser, 'Oberschlesien', p. 394.

transported to Opole town's camp on 9 August. They were kept there for several days, while people were collected from other villages in the local area, before they were at last placed on a cargo train and transported to Germany.[23]

From Opole town the residents were transported to a special collection camp in the town of Głubczyce in the southern area of western Upper Silesia. Głubczyce Camp was one of western Upper Silesia's main 'collection points'. 'Germans' from various western Upper Silesian districts were sent there en route to Allied-occupied Germany. The conditions in Głubczyce Camp were rudimentary, to say the least. It is not clear how long residents of Opole District remained there in August 1946 before they were sent westwards to Germany. Karl B. from the village of Schönkirch/Chrzasczyce in Opole District, who was transported to Głubczyce four months later, claimed that he was forced to spend a number of nights in this camp before he departed for Germany. But the residents brought to Głubczyce Camp in August 1946 may have only spent a few hours there before departing. Polish state officials at the camp subjected them to a thorough luggage inspection prior to departure and confiscated many items. The residents were then crammed into goods and cattle wagons, each containing up to 36 people, and transported westwards to the 'delivery point' in Kaławsk in western Lower Silesia, where a British Military Mission was stationed (see Chapter 4). From there, they were taken into the Soviet Zone and onwards to the reception camp in Mariental near Helmstedt, located just inside the British Zone. The journeys were almost certainly longer than those from Jelenia Góra District. People often had access only to very limited supplies of food along the way. A total of 2,426 'Germans' from the rural part of Opole District and 625 from Opole town were said to have been transported to the British Zone during August 1946. In some of the district's villages, the August transports were the start and finish of the 'displacement action'. From these villages no more residents were subsequently displaced.[24]

[23] SiRep OTA head S-PD, 21.5.1946, APO 185, sygn. 85, 32; SiRep O Chief on the period 20.6.1946–20.7.1946 APO 178, sygn. 41, 34–6; SiRep OTA head S-PD, 21.8.1946, APO 185, sygn. 85, 35. WR, Gustav R., Blumenthal (Krzywa Góra), undated, BOD 1, 243, 33–6. WRs: BOD 1, 243, 53–61; BOD 1, 243, 271–4; BOD 1, 243, 275–6; BOD 2, 229, 9–10; BOD 1, 243, 379–80; BOD 1, 243, 289–93; BOD 1, 243, 25–7; BOD 1, 243, 49–51; BOD 1, 243, 349–51; BOD 1, 243, 227–8. Madajczyk, *Przyłączenie*, p. 227.

[24] SiRep OTA S-PD, 21.8.1946, APO 185, sygn. 85, 35; SiRep O Chief on the period 20.7.1946–20.8.1946, APO 178, sygn. 41, 38–41. WR, Karl B., Schönkirch (Chrzasczyce), 14.8.55, BOD 1, 243, 335–7. WRs: BOD 1, 243, 271–4; BOD 1, 243, 33–6; BOD 1, 243, 379–80; BOD 1, 243, 53–61; BOD 1, 243, 349–51; BOD 1, 243, 289–93; BOD 1, 243, 49–51; BOD 1, 243, 25–7. Eser, 'Oberschlesien', p. 395; Hofmann, *Nachkriegszeit*, pp. 222–4, 229–31.

Like the earlier practice of confining local people to camps, the mass transportation of western Upper Silesia's 'German' residents to Germany was tightly bound up with the 'verification action'. As the Communist-controlled authorities had originally planned it, western Upper Silesia's 'displacement action' would target only those prewar residents whose 'verification' applications had been rejected or who refused to submit an application. To a large extent, this is precisely what happened. As Dorothea S. from the village of Burkardsdorf/Bierdzany in Opole District put it, everyone in the local area who refused to 'opt for Poland' was 'deported' to Germany in August 1946. In this respect, the 'displacement action' was based on compulsion and coercion.

Yet the same 'force of circumstances' which drove many tens of thousands of prewar residents of western Upper Silesia to leave the region 'voluntarily' in 1945 caused a significant percentage of the region's residents, who had actually been 'verified' as 'indigenous Poles', to register voluntarily for transportation to Germany from 1946 onwards. Throughout western Upper Silesia, a large number of the prewar residents who were sent on cargo trains to Germany after 17 May 1946 were therefore individuals who had previously been 'verified' as ethnic Poles. This included many of the prewar residents transported from Opole District in August 1946. Interestingly, a few of these residents had sought assurance from local state officials, before registering for displacement to Germany, that they were not going to be transported to Siberia. Opole District's 'indigenous Poles' continued to register voluntarily for transportation to Germany in subsequent months. According to an official from Opole Town Administration, some proved very impatient to leave, showing up at the town hall to ask '*kiedy już, gdzie, jak, co?*' (When will it be? Where? How? What?).[25]

Opole Town Administration appears to have come into conflict with Opole District Administration at this time over the issue of 'displacing' residents who had been 'verified' as 'indigenous Poles'. Opole town's officials felt that Opole District Administration was too reluctant to enter on the 'displacement list' people who had been 'verified' as ethnic Poles. The Town Administration believed that the District Administration was, in this way, preventing another cargo train from being sent to Germany from Opole railway station. The town officials explained that the 'natural national cleansing of the town' [*naturalne oczyszczanie miasta po względem*

[25] SiRep OTA S-PD, 21.8.1946, APO 185, sygn. 85, 35; SiRep O Chief on the period 20.8.1946–20.9.1946, APO 178, sygn. 41, 43–5; SiRep OTA S-PD, 21.9.1946, APO 185, sygn. 85, 39; WR, Dorothea S., Burkardsdorf (Bierdzany), 22.11.1954, BOD 1, 243, 49–51; Eser, 'Oberschlesien', pp. 396–7.

narodowy] required the transportation to Germany not only of 'Germans' but also of people 'verified' as ethnic Poles, who 'desire to migrate to Germany and whose emigration it is not in Poland's interests to prevent'.[26]

Nevertheless, on 9 December 1946, a cargo train set off from Opole District carrying 623 residents. Once again the residents were transported first to the collection camp in Głubczyce. But this time, after spending over a week at this camp, they were sent to the Soviet Zone rather than to the British Zone. Opole Town Administration had registered 618 of the town's residents for this train, but only 434 of them were actually transported on 9 December. The town's officials again put this down to the 'inflexibility' of Opole District Administration. On the other hand, Opole District Administration's officials were much more positive about the impact of the 9 December transport. They declared in an official report from this time that it had helped to 'solve the German problem on Opole District's terrain'.[27]

The family of Karl B., from the village of Schönkirch/Chrzasczyce in Opole District, were transported to the Soviet Zone on the 9 December train. Karl B. described their journey:

From Schönkirch we were taken to the camp in Oppeln [Opole] on 8 December 1946. From there we were transported in cattle wagons to Leobschütz [Głubczyce] where a collection camp had been erected. This was the start of a terrible ordeal for us. The winter of 1946–1947 was a very harsh one. We were put up in unheated rooms with temperatures outside of minus 20–25 degrees Celsius. We were squashed together with 40–50 others in a single room of 20–30 square metres, so that we could only sleep sitting or standing. On 21 December we were finally transported onwards in cattle wagons. There was a stove in our wagon but no fuel. We reached Görlitz [on the Poland-Soviet Zone border] on the evening of 25 December. We received food only once during this journey and that was in Kohlfurt [Kaławsk] on 24 December. Our wagon, which contained 37 people, received only two 1.5 kg loaves of bread and three salt herrings. If anyone attempted to get hold of more food on their own initiative along the way, they were beaten up by the Polish Militia. There were no opportunities to make a complaint about this. It was not possible to reach the British [Military] Commission in Kohlfurt. In the *Reichert* camp in Görlitz almost every child under three years old died as a result of this journey.[28]

[26] SiRep OTA S-PD, 21.10.1946, APO 185, sygn. 85, 40; SiRep OTA S-PD, 21.11.1946, APO 185, sygn. 85, 43; Special SiRep by OTA S-PD, 13.11.1946, APO 185, sygn. 85, 41–2; SiRep OTA S-PD, 21.11.1946, APO 185, sygn. 85, 43.

[27] SiRep ODA S-PD, 31.12.1946, APK 185/4, sygn. 39, 54–54a; SiRep OTA S-PD, 21.12.1946, APO 185, sygn. 85, 44; SiRep ODA S-PD, 4.12.1946, APO 178, sygn. B15, 1–1a; WR, Karl B., Schönkirch (Chrzasczyce), 19.8.1955, BOD 1, 243, 335–7; Hofmann, *Nachkriegszeit*, p. 224.

[28] WR, Karl B., Schönkirch (Chrzasczyce), 19.8.1955, BOD 1, 243, 335–7.

The claim that nearly all young children died was probably an exaggeration. But it is certainly true that the winter of 1946–7 was a brutal one in Central and Eastern Europe and that the goods wagons carrying Germans from Poland's new territories were often inadequately heated or not heated at all. According to Soviet sources, a number of cargo trains arrived in the Soviet Zone in late December 1946 and early January 1947 containing many cases of acute hypothermia and a number of frozen corpses. At the very least, it can be said with certainty that the residents of Opole District, who were transported to the Soviet Zone on the 9 December train, went through a very painful experience.[29]

Another cargo train was sent to Germany from Opole railway station on 14 January 1947 carrying no more than 100 residents of Opole District and probably far fewer. No further transports appear to have departed from Opole during the rest of 1947.[30]

Despite the fact that the vast majority of the prewar residents of Opole District were still living there, one settler from central Poland, allotted a farm in the district after the war, recalled the relief brought to him and other settlers by the departure of several thousand 'Germans' between August 1946 and January 1947: 'It was not until 1947, when the Germans were gone . . . that we finally knew the Western Territories were ours and that we therefore needed to get back to work'.[31]

The Communist-controlled authorities' operations aimed at 'resettling' Polish settlers from western Upper Silesia to northern Lower Silesia and to other sparsely populated areas of Poland's new territories continued during 1947. So did the voluntary migration of Polish settlers from the region to these areas. In Opole District, state officials noted in May 1947 that, given the large number of prewar residents who were returning to the district from Allied-occupied Germany at this time (see Chapter 6), this steady 'outflow' of Polish settlers was the only reason the district's population was not dramatically increasing. The district's authorities relocated quite a large number of settler families from both Opole town and the district's rural localities to other areas of Poland's new territories during 1947. They referred to these efforts as 'resolving the surplus of repatriates'. Throughout

[29] Hofmann, *Nachkriegszeit*, pp. 235–6.

[30] SiRep ODA S-PD, 31.12.1946, APK 185/4, sygn. 39, 54–54a; SiRep ODA S-PD, 30.1.1947, APO 178, sygn. 62, 2–3; Rep by OTA S-PD, 17.1.1947, APO 185, sygn. 85, 47; situation reports by ODA S-PD, 3.3.1947, 1.4.1947, 2.5.1947, 12.8.1947, APO 178, sygn. 62, 4–14 and 21–3.

[31] Extract from a settler's recollections, cited in Krystna Kersten and Tomasz Szarota (eds.), *Wieś Polska 1939–1948. Materiały Konkursowe* Vol. 1 (Warsaw, 1967), p. 651; Łempiński, *Przesiedlenie*, p. 221.

western Upper Silesia, these 'resettlement' actions appear to have ceased altogether at some point in 1948.[32]

In both 1947 and 1948, large numbers of western Upper Silesia's prewar residents continued to register voluntarily for expulsion to Germany. In addition to the motives we discussed earlier in this chapter, an increasingly significant factor causing locals to register for displacement was the dramatic political changes taking place in Poland at this time. The sham elections staged by the regime in January 1947 convinced many that Poland was becoming a full-fledged Communist dictatorship – something even more obvious after the regime's lurch towards Stalinist Soviet orthodoxy in 1948. This prompted a great many 'verified' locals to choose displacement towards the end of the decade. For example, just as the collectivization of agriculture had caused many Polish settlers to abandon the new territories and to return to central Poland in late 1948 and 1949 (see Chapter 5), so it became an important factor inducing many 'indigenous Polish' farmers to seek a way out of western Upper Silesia by relocating to Germany at this time. Of course, when the prewar residents of the region were asked by the authorities why they wished to emigrate, they were wise enough not to cite the Communists' policies as the reason.[33]

The Stalinization of Poland after 1948 was in any case just one of the important factors behind the emigration wave at the end of the decade. For the large number of 'indigenous Polish' women who found themselves alone with their children in western Upper Silesia at the end of the war, the desire to join their husbands in Germany was clearly the principal reason they registered for displacement to Germany. These were women whose husbands – former *Wehrmacht* soldiers – had been taken prisoner by the Allies at the end of the war and had refused to return to the region from Germany after the war. Deprived of the family breadwinner, a large proportion of these women, by 1948, were living in dire poverty and believed that joining their husbands in Germany was the only way to get themselves and their children out of this hopeless situation. In Opole District, state officials described the problem of 'Polish wives with children'

[32] SiRep ODA S-PD, 2.5.1947, APO 178, sygn. 62, 12–14; SiRep O Chief on the period 20.5.1947–20.6.1947, APO 178, sygn. 42, 27–8; SiRep O Chief on the period 20.7.1947–20.8.1947, APO 178, sygn. 42, 35–6; SiRep O Chief on the period 20.8.1947–20.9.1947, APO 178, sygn. 42, 39–41; SiRep O Chief on the period 20.9.1947–20.10.1947, APO 178, sygn. 42, 43–5; CuRep ODA S-PD, 11.12.1947, APK 185/4, sygn. 51, 69–69a; SiRep O Chief on the period 20.12.1947–20.1.1948, APO 178, sygn. 43, 9–12; Kowalski, *Powrót*, p. 365; Ther, *Vertriebene*, pp. 308–9.

[33] SiRep OTA head S-PD, 21.2.1947, APO 185, sygn. 85, 50; SiRep OTA head S-PD, 21.4.1947, APO 185, sygn. 85, 52; CuRep ODA S-PD, 8.1.1948, APK 185/4, sygn. 52, 39–40; CuRep ODA S-PD, 2.3.1948, APO 178, sygn. 65, 7–8; CuRep ODA S-PD, 5.11.1948, APO 178, sygn. 65, 63–5; Madajczyk, *Niemcy polscy*, pp. 75, 83; Eser, 'Oberschlesien', pp. 396–7.

who wished to join their 'German husbands' as a 'burning issue' in summer 1948.[34]

A related problem, which western Upper Silesia's Communist-led authorities made a concerted effort to resolve during 1947–8, was that of the large number of children living in the region who had become separated from their parents or whose parents had died during the war. In Opole District, for example, the state authorities set up a special committee in early 1948 to identify these parentless children. In June this committee sent a list of 47 children living in the district to Upper Silesia's Regional Administration in Katowice, recommending their 'repatriation' to Germany.[35]

Around the same time, western Upper Silesia's state authorities reached the conclusion that a lot of 'mistakes' had been made during the 'verification action'. These 'mistakes', they believed, could only be 'corrected' by 'displacing' those residents who had been 'wrongly verified' as ethnic Poles. As we shall discuss in Chapter 9, this was linked to the growing unease, expressed by many state officials in the region at this time, about the amount of German still being spoken there. Against this backdrop, Upper Silesia's Regional Administration decided to send a number of inspection committees to western Upper Silesia's districts to evaluate 'the results' of the 'verification action'. In Opole District, the committees identified 220 prewar residents who had been 'wrongly verified' as Poles and immediately registered them for displacement to Germany. The Security Police also became involved in indentifying 'wrongly verified individuals' in the district. It instructed Opole District Administration to withdraw 'temporary certificates of Polish nationality' from a number of local residents in 1947. One official from Opole District Administration commented towards the end of that year that 'many germans [*sic*] had managed to get themselves verified . . . very few [of whom] . . . own up to their [German] ethnicity'.

In early 1948, a new 'nationality-displacement committee' (*komisja narodowościowo-wysiedleńcza*) was appointed 'to catch the hostile individuals

[34] Rep by ODA S-PD on the first two quarters of the year 1948, undated, APO 178, sygn. 65, 50–2; CuRep ODA S-PD, 2.3.1948, APO 178, sygn. 65, 7–8; WR, Frau K., Oderwinkel (Kąty Opolskie), 30.5.1959, BOD 1, 243, 277–80; WR, Arthur M., Derschau (Suchy Bór), 7.10.1954, BOD 1, 243, 67–72; WR, Dorothea S., Burkardsdorf (Bierdzany), 22.11.1954, BOD 1, 243, 49–51; WR, Friedrich K., Sacken (Lubienia), 24.7.1955, BOD 1, 243, 309–19; WR, Wilhelm K., Winau (Winów), 25.3.1956, BOD 1, 243, 381–2; WR, Oskar G., Eichendorf (Dąbrówka Dolna), 16.10.1954, BOD 1, 243, 85–8; Madajczyk, *Przyłączenie*, pp. 200–2; Linek, *Polityka*, pp. 204–7, 251–2, 317.

[35] CuRep ODA S-PD, 8.1.1948, APK 185/4, sygn. 52, 39–40; CuRep ODA S-PD, 7.4.1948, APO 178, sygn. 65, 11–12; Rep by ODA S-PD on the first two quarters of 1948, [July 1948], APO 178, sygn. 65, 50–2; Eser, 'Oberschlesien', p. 396; Madajczyk, *Przyłączenie*, p. 229.

hidden by temporary certificates of Polish nationality' living in Opole District. By May the committee had designated 300 locals for 'repatriation'. Three-quarters of them had previously been 'verified' as ethnic Poles. The district's officials also noted that more residents would be earmarked for 'repatriation' once 'two German colonies' had been 'unloaded'; one of these, they specified, was the village of Krzywa Góra. By September 1948, a total of 882 prewar residents of Opole District had been earmarked for 'repatriation'. The authorities throughout western Upper Silesia undertook similar actions to identify 'wrongfully verified' individuals for expulsion to Germany in 1947 and 1948.[36]

On 8 October 1948, another train was sent from Opole railway station to Głubczyce Camp. But it did not contain all the prewar residents who had been designated for 'repatriation' in the preceding months. Only 344 individuals were sent to Głubczyce on this transport and only 101 of them were then transported onwards to Germany. The rest were sent back to Opole District. Many of them had submitted appeals in Głubczyce Camp against the 'documents cancelling certificates of Polish nationality', which they had received from officials before leaving Opole District. The decision to send these people back home from Głubczyce Camp was probably taken by a special 'verification committee' working there since 1946, whose task was to prevent the wrongful displacement of ethnically Polish individuals from western Upper Silesia.[37]

The 8 October transport was the last large group of prewar residents of Opole District to be transported to Allied-occupied Germany as part of the 'displacement action'. Transports to Germany were suspended throughout Poland's new territories at the end of October 1948. They did not resume until the following year. As happened elsewhere in these territories (see Chapter 4), small groups of people continued to be sent to Germany from western Upper Silesia during 1949. As before, many of these people registered voluntarily for transportation to Germany. Providing an interesting insight into the political atmosphere prevailing in western Upper Silesia at the end of the 1940s, one of Opole District's leading state officials remarked in 1949, 'It is my view that if it were ever to cease being so difficult to migrate

[36] SiRep ODA S-PD, 12.8.1947, APO 178, sygn. 62, 21–3; CuRep ODA S-PD, 11.12.1947, APK 185/4, sygn. 51, 69–69a; CuRep ODA S-PD, 6.5.1948, APO 178, sygn. 65, 23–4; CuRep ODA S-PD, 1.6.1948, APO 178, sygn. 65, 25–6; Rep by the municipal mayor of Krapkowice, 2.10.1948, APO 178, sygn. 66, 156; Rep by the ODA S-PD on the first two quarters of 1948, [early July 1948], APO 178, sygn. 65, 50–2; CuRep ODA S-PD, 4.8.1948, APO 178, sygn. 65, 54–5; CuRep the department, 4.9.1948, APO 178, sygn. 65, 56–7; Kowalski, *Powrót*, p. 356; Hofmann, *Nachkriegszeit*, p. 305.

[37] CuRep ODA S-PD, 5.11.1948, APO 178, sygn. 65, 63–5; CuRep ODA S-PD, 24.1.1949, APO 178, sygn. 64, 12–13; Kowalski, *Powrót*, pp. 358–9.

to Germany, if it were not bound up with numerous costs and much effort, and if it did not bring with it a certain risk – by which I mean the risk of political harassment from us – then the number of volunteers would be very large indeed.'[38]

Between 1946 and 1949 around 165,000 prewar residents of western Upper Silesia were transported to the British and Soviet Occupation Zones of Germany. This represented only a small fraction of the prewar population of the region. A disproportionate number of them came from the southwestern districts of western Upper Silesia, where – in contrast the rest of the region – most of the local population had been monolingual German-speakers before 1945. In Opole District, the proportion of prewar residents transported to the British and Soviet Zones in the years 1946–9 was very small indeed. The authorities provided conflicting figures for exactly how many were transported from the district at this time, but it may have been less than 5,000 individuals and was certainly not much more than 8,000. Either way, the number of residents sent to Germany on cargo trains in these years constituted a tiny fraction of the prewar population of Opole District.[39]

IMMIGRANTS AND NATIVES

How many Poles settled permanently in western Upper Silesia after the Second World War? Because only a minority of the region's prewar residents had fled the region permanently in the final months of the war, migrated to Germany on their own initiative in first year after the war or been transported there by the Communist-controlled authorities between May 1946 and the end of 1949, officials struggled to find permanent housing for Polish settlers in western Upper Silesia during these years. As we have seen, from spring 1946 onwards the authorities instead took action to shift Polish settlers out of the region to northern Lower Silesia and to other underpopulated areas of Poland's new territories. Nevertheless, a little over 500,000 Polish settlers were able to take up permanent residence in western Upper Silesia in the second half of the 1940s. Settlers therefore represented between one-third and two-fifths of the overall population of the region

[38] CuRep ODA S-PD, 7.1.1949, APO 178, sygn. 63, 9–10; Special Rep by ODA S-PD, 19.3.1949, APO 178, sygn. 64, 16–17; Rep on the year 1948 by ODA S-PD, undated, APO 178, sygn. 64, 7–8; Rep by ODA S-PD, 5.8.1949, APO 178, sygn. 64, 36; WR, Arthur M., Derschau (Suchy Bór), 7.10.1954, BOD 1, 243, 67–72; Nitschke, *Vertreibung*, pp. 253–8, 266, 276.

[39] Document 324, 'rep on the displacement of Germans by USRA S-PD for the Ministry for Recovered Territories, 16.4.1947', in Borodziej and Lemberg (eds.), *Niemcy* (Warsaw, 2000) vol. 2, pp. 465–6; Łempiński, *Przesiedlenie*, pp. 216–22, 259.

by the end of the 1940s. In Opole District, a little over 40,000 Polish settlers settled permanently after the Second World War. They made up perhaps three-quarters of the population of Opole town and 23 per cent of the overall population of Opole District at the end of the 1940s. This meant that in the rural part of Opole District, settlers made up only around 9 per cent of the population – forming only a small minority of residents in most of the district's villages. The same was true in most other villages in western Upper Silesia, where a large majority of the prewar population were 'verified' as 'indigenous Poles' in the five years after the war.[40]

In terms of the structure of western Upper Silesia's settler population, around 49 per cent were 'repatriates' from prewar eastern Poland, the vast majority from the territories ceded to Soviet Ukraine. A smaller proportion, perhaps 41 per cent, were 'resettlers' from central Poland. Yet – as in other regions of Poland's new territories (see Chapter 5) – not all the settlers who took up permanent residence in western Upper Silesia after the war were from prewar eastern Poland and central Poland. A large number were also Polish émigrés from abroad who had been persuaded by the Polish government to relocate to Poland from various foreign countries. In fact, these people constituted a greater proportion of the settler population in western Upper Silesia than in other areas of the new territories: perhaps as much as 10 per cent of the settler population of this region, compared to just under 5 per cent in Poland's new territories as a whole. The émigrés who settled in western Upper Silesia appear to have come primarily from Western countries and from Germany rather than from Eastern European ones. In the rural part of Opole District, 're-emigrants' from Western countries may have amounted to 16 per cent of the settler population, with the settlers from central Poland and from the ceded eastern territories each constituting a little over 40 per cent. The structure of Opole town's much larger settler population is less clear. As was the case throughout Poland's new territories, the settler population of western Upper Silesia was culturally and linguistically very diverse – with great heterogeneity apparent both *between* the different categories of settlers we have discussed and *within* them.[41]

How did western Upper Silesia's diverse settler population get along with the region's prewar residents? The locals' opinion of the settlers was tainted

[40] Rep by ODA S-PD, 21.4.1948, APO 178, sygn. 65, 17–21; Rep by ODA S-PD, 25.11.1949, APO 178, sygn. 64, 43; Ossowski, 'Zagadnienia', p. 289; Stadniczenko, 'Rok szkolny', p. 399; Eser, 'Oberschlesien', p. 384; Madajczyk, *Przyłączenie*, p. 169.

[41] Rep by ODA S-PD, 25.11.1949, APO 178, sygn. 64, 43; SiRep ODA, 9.8.1945, APK 185/4, sygn. 27/1, 43–7; SiRep O Chief on the period 20.8.1945–20.9.1945, APO 178, sygn. 41, 1–4; Eser, 'Oberschlesien', p. 384; Madajczyk, *Przyłączenie*, p. 169; Borodziej et al., 'Wstęp', p. 44.

from the outset by the behaviour of the first Poles to reach the region in spring and early summer 1945. Many of them, as we have discussed, were opportunistic robbers and looters from nearby areas rather than genuine settlers.[42] The Polish sociologist Stanisław Ossowski recorded local perceptions of these early arrivals during his trip to Opole District in August 1945:

Barely had the fighting finished when the first wave of "Poloks" [local dialect term for 'Poles'] appeared. But these Poles did not bring Silesia closer to Poland. For the inhabitants of the [village which I visited] this was just another phase of the disaster brought on them by war. A plague of agile looters suddenly appeared, who were all the more threatening insofar as they held posts in the [local] state authorities which shielded them from the terrified local population. Alongside their desire to find booty to loot, some of the arrivals from the Zagłębie Dąbrowskie region [an area located just to the east of eastern Upper Silesia] were motivated by a wish to take revenge on Silesians for the wrongs done to them during the German occupation by gendarmes who had come from Upper Silesia and had spoken the Upper Silesian dialect . . . In spring 1945 [the village] was terrorized for three months by [the newly appointed Polish] commune mayor . . . He was universally regarded by villagers as a capable and courageous man and as a good organizer. Villagers were particularly impressed by his readiness to use his revolver when confronting armed marauders. But they also remembered him as somebody prone to banditry and willing to displace the wealthiest farmers as alleged Germans in order to seize their homes . . . The fact that it was these kinds of people who represented the Polish nation to the villagers caused embarrassment and sadness among [the small minority of the village's prewar inhabitants who had been pro-Polish activists before 1945].[43]

The first Poles to arrive in the local area made a similar impression on Maria K. from the village of Malsdorf/Malina, who did not migrate from Opole District to West Germany until 1956. She claimed that these people were all from the nearby Zagłębie Dąbrowskie region and they 'threw us out of our homes, appropriated our possessions and moved into our houses'.[44]

But it was not only the Polish looters, revenge-seekers and corrupt officials who met with attitudes of distrust and hostility from the local population of western Upper Silesia. The genuine settlers, too, were often regarded with acute suspicion by the prewar residents of the region. For example, one settler from Kraków who took up residence in a remote village in Opole District after the war recalled how one of the first villagers he

[42] Madajczyk, *Przyłączenie*, pp. 172, 178–9. [43] Ossowski, 'Zagadnienia', pp. 288–9.
[44] WR, Maria K., Malsdorf (Malina), undated, BOD 1, 243, 255–6.

met appeared to 'view me as a visitor from another planet'.[45] He described another villager's impressions of the settlers:

She told me about . . . the people who had arrived in the local area from the other side of the Bug river [i.e., from prewar eastern Poland]. She was unable to get her head around the fact that these people, who in her opinion – but not only her opinion – had found paradise in their new place of residence [western Upper Silesia], felt able to express their dislike for this and that and showed general dissatisfaction.[46]

The sociologist Ossowski attempted to give his own impartial assessment of the situation:

The settlers from the Lwów region [in the southeastern territories of prewar Poland ceded to Soviet Ukraine in July 1944], who arrived in [the village which I visited in August 1945] and the neighbouring village, did not much alter the [negative] opinion which locals [had already formed about Poles in spring and early summer 1945]. Only a small number, around 12 families, settled in this village because there had only been a small number of German farms there. More arrived in the neighbouring villages. The settlers and locals came into conflict because of their contrasting cultures, differing customs and divergent farming methods . . . For the hardworking, frugal and methodical Silesians, the repatriates – who were unable to adapt to the new circumstances, were accustomed to less intensive farming on excellent soil, were bitter about having been compelled to abandon their farms and homelands [*rodzinne strony*] and had yet to drop their thoughts of returning – were foreign people whom the Silesians were unable to understand. The Silesians were shocked with how lazy and unreliable the repatriates were – which was caused or exacerbated by the hardships of war and migration.[47]

Interestingly, the perception that a significant proportion of the settlers were idle was shared by some of western Upper Silesia's state officials, who were mostly newcomers to the region from central Poland. In Opole District, for example, one official wrote in December 1946 that, although he often encountered members of Opole town's 'settler population' (*ludność napływowa*) who distinguished themselves with their work ethic, the majority showed no desire to work at all. These settlers, he claimed, often criticized the state authorities' orders and amounted to a 'mass of layabouts, profiteers and reactionary elements'.[48] Yet it has to be said that there are not many statements of this kind to be found among Opole District Administration's official reports. This was in stark contrast, as we saw in

[45] Stadniczenko, 'Rok szkolny', p. 400; Madajczyk, *Przyłączenie*, pp. 170–3.
[46] Stadniczenko, 'Rok szkolny', p. 425. [47] Ossowski, 'Zagadnienia', p. 289.
[48] SiRep ODA S-PD, 4.12.1946, APO 178, sygn. B15, 1–1a; Madajczyk, *Przyłączenie*, p. 172.

Chapter 5, with the frequent criticisms directed at central Polish settlers by Jelenia Góra District's state officials.

The feelings of suspicion and antipathy between settlers and locals in western Upper Silesia seem, in general, to have been mutual. The settler from Kraków, cited earlier, admitted in his later recollections that when he first arrived in the region, he viewed it as an 'unknown land with foreign people'.[49] Somewhat differently, Stanisław Ossowski asserted that one of the reasons many settlers felt hostile towards the prewar residents of the region was that most locals believed that Poland's takeover of the region had brought disaster rather than liberation:

> An outdoor sermon given by a Silesian priest to a large crowd of local people at a big religious festival which took place while I was staying in the village . . . spoke of the misfortune which had befallen the local population since the end of the war . . . The repatriates regarded this as a sermon for Germans delivered in Polish. All local people . . . with the exception of a young female teacher, who had witnessed the suffering of Poles during the German occupation, failed to see anything inappropriate in this sermon.[50]

Yet the key issue over which settlers and prewar residents came into conflict was neither cultural and linguistic differences nor different attitudes towards Poland's incorporation of western Upper Silesia. Instead, it was property. Many of the 'abandoned' farms, houses and flats which had been allotted to Polish settlers as permanent accommodation by western Upper Silesia's Communist-led authorities in spring and summer 1945 quickly turned out not to have been abandoned after all. The prewar residents, who returned to the region weeks, months or years after fleeing from the Red Army in early 1945, were often shocked to find their homes and businesses in the possession of Polish settlers. The only way to retrieve these properties, they soon found out, was to undergo 'verification' as ethnic Poles. As Opole District's Chief Official acknowledged in September 1945, 'It seems that after recognizing the Polish ethnicity [of some local people], we will be forced to remove a certain number of repatriates who have already been given permanent housing or have taken over craft and industrial workshops and shops, because . . . people whose Polish ethnicity has been recognized have the right to private property.'[51]

[49] Stadniczenko, 'Rok szkolny', p. 397; Madajczyk, *Przyłączenie*, pp. 170–3.

[50] Ossowski, 'Zagadnienia', pp. 290–1.

[51] SiRep O Chief on the period 20.8.1945–20.9.1945, APO 178, sygn. 41, 1–4; Hofmann, *Nachkriegszeit*, pp. 291–2, 311; Kowalski, *Powrót*, pp. 361–7.

The 'indigenous Poles' 'right to private property' was actually not quite so clear-cut as Opole District's Chief Official acknowledged with this statement. In February and May 1945, the government ruled that all property belonging to German citizens in Poland's new territories would henceforth be regarded as the property of the Polish state. It would be distributed to arriving Polish settlers as part of both the 'settlement campaign' and the policy of land reform (see Chapter 5). These rulings also appeared to expropriate the people the authorities regarded as 'indigenous Poles', because they too were German citizens. Yet from the very start of the 'verification action' onwards, the state authorities generally operated under assumption that the government's rulings on property did not concern individuals 'verified' as ethnic Poles.

This did not mean, however, that the issue of 'indigenous Poles', who had fled from Poland's new territories in the final phase of the war and who returned to find their farms, houses and flats in the hands of Polish settlers, was easy to resolve. In October 1945, Upper Silesia's Regional Governor, Aleksander Zawadzki, ruled that, once these people had been 'verified' as ethnic Poles, they had the right to retrieve their properties from the settlers. Poland's Communist-led government in Warsaw was slower to give its own ruling on this matter. But in its September 1946 decree it confirmed Zawadzki's ruling by ordering that 'verified Poles' throughout Poland's new territories had the right to retrieve their prewar property from Polish settlers.[52]

Based on these rulings, property became a source of serious tension between settlers and 'indigenous Poles' in western Upper Silesia in the second half of the 1940s. In Opole District, for example, state officials reported huge resentment caused by the removal of Polish settlers from farms whose owners had been 'verified' as ethnic Poles. 'Repatriates' were declaring that 'it would be better to be a german [*sic*] than a Pole'. In late April 1946, Opole District's officials noted the significant impact on local settlers of a recent article which had appeared in the official regional newspaper of the Polish Workers' Party, *Trybuna Robotnicza*. This article had attempted to explain the government's recent 'standardisation' of the 'verification action' (see Chapter 6). But it had reportedly raised 'false hopes' among Polish settlers that all 'verification' decisions which had so far been issued would henceforth lose their validity. As a result of this, many Polish settlers were apparently refusing to leave the farms owned by 'verified' local people. On the other hand, it came as a great relief to the many 'native people' (*tubylcza ludność*) in Opole District who had been forced to share their farms with

[52] Ther, *Vertriebene*, pp. 188–98.

settlers since 1945, when in early summer 1946 the authorities started to relocate a large number of settlers to northern Lower Silesia.[53]

In line with the rulings on property issued by both Zawadzki and the Polish government in 1945 and 1946, western Upper Silesia's state authorities generally came down on the side of the 'verified indigenous Poles' of western Upper Silesia when seeking to resolve property disputes between locals and settlers. Indeed, in Opole District, the state authorities seem to have done so in every single case. In one exceptional case, in early 1948, a group of prewar residents of the district, who had previously been classified as 'Germans' through the 'verification action', even managed to retrieve their homes from settlers. These people had been designated for displacement to Germany but were released from a camp in Gliwice after the temporary suspension of the 'displacement action'. Despite the authorities' previous decision that these people were not 'indigenous Poles', without exception they were given back their farms in Opole District on returning from the camp. According to Opole District's officials, this caused great 'resentment . . . from the settlers who had occupied the farms in the meantime. They had to be forced to hand the farms over'. It is not at all clear why the authorities felt they needed to return properties to individuals whom they had categorized as Germans; this was not at all in line the rulings on property by either Warsaw or Katowice.[54]

The Polish settlers' hostile reaction to being removed from the properties they had been allotted by the state authorities in the immediate postwar period was very understandable – especially when one considers the terrible poverty gripping Polish society at this time as a result of Nazi Germany's ruthless occupation of the country. It was all the more understandable in the case of the eastern Polish 'repatriates'. These people, after all, had been compelled to leave their farms and houses in prewar eastern Poland at the end of the war. Having lost almost everything they owned, they were obviously extremely anxious to secure permanent housing in their new places of residence. In fact, the animosity with which some Polish

[53] SiRep O Chief on the period 20.12.1945–20.1.1946, APO 178, sygn. 41, 13–15; SiRep O Chief on the period 20.3.1946–20.4.1946, APO 178, sygn. 41, 20–3; Rep by the chairman of VoiInspCom on an inspection of Opole District, 10–23.6.1946, APK 185/4, sygn. 436, 62–4; Kowalski, *Powrót*, p. 339; Strauchold, *Autochtoni*, pp. 169–72.

[54] CuRep ODA S-PD, 7.4.1948, APO 178, sygn. 65, 11–12; Special SiRep by OTA head S-PD, 13.11.1946, APO 185, sygn. 85, 41–2; SiRep O Chief on the period 20.12.1945–20.1.1946, APO 178, sygn. 41, 13–15; SiRep O Chief on the period 20.6.1946–20.7.1946, APO 178, sygn. 41, 34–6; SiRep O Chief on the period 20.7.1946–20.8.1946, APO 178, sygn. 41, 38–41; SiRep O Chief on the period 20.8.1946–20.9.1946, APO 178, sygn. 41, 43–5; SiRep O DepChief on the period 20.12.1947–20.1.1948, APO 178, sygn. 43, 9–12; WR, Günther M., Bolko (Nowa Wieś Królewska), undated, BOD 1, 243, 37–9; Ther, *Vertriebene*, pp. 307–9.

settlers responded to being removed from farms and houses in western Upper Silesia was occasionally so intense that the state authorities had great difficulty retrieving the properties from them.

Property disputes between locals and settlers persisted in Opole District through to the end of the 1940s. The district's officials commonly cited them, in their official reports, as the main or even sole reason for antagonism between the two groups. The same was reported by local state officials in the other districts of western Upper Silesia and in many other areas of Poland's new territories at this time. In fact, in southern East Prussia – the area of Poland's new territories which the Communist-controlled government viewed as having the second largest concentration of 'indigenous Poles' – the disputes between prewar residents and settlers proved even harder to resolve than in western Upper Silesia. This was because a much larger percentage of the prewar population of that region refused to undergo 'verification' as ethnic Poles after the war. Unwittingly summing up the situation in both western Upper Silesia and southern East Prussia, one of Opole District's state officials remarked in summer 1948, 'Finally resolving the matter of disputed property would be desirable because without this there can be no talk of harmonious co-existence'.[55]

Poland's Communist-controlled government had been convinced before 1945 that the majority of German citizens living in western Upper Silesia were 'indigenous Poles' and should be allowed to remain there as Polish citizens. It had known from the outset that there would be little space for Polish settlers in this region. Despite this, it sponsored a mass influx of new migrants into western Upper Silesia from Poland's lost eastern territories and from central Poland at the end of the Second World War. Partly this resulted from circumstances beyond the government's control. But it was also the product of the government's reckless desire to see the whole of Poland's new territories repopulated with Polish settlers as quickly as possible.

[55] Rep on the first two quarters of 1948 by ODA S-PD, undated, APO 178, sygn. 65, 50–2; SiRep O Chief on the period 20.6.1946–20.7.1946, APO 178, sygn. 41, 34–6; SiRep O Chief on the period 20.7.1946–20.8.1946, APO 178, sygn. 41, 38–41; SiRep O Chief on the period 20.8.1946–20.9.1946, APO 178, sygn. 41, 43–5; Special SiRep by OTA head S-PD, 13.11.1946, APO 185, sygn. 85, 41–2; SiRep ODA S-PD, 4.12.1946, APO 178, sygn. B15, 1–1a; SiRep O Chief on the period 20.9.1947–20.10.1947, APO 178, sygn. 42, 43–5; CuRep the ODA S-PD, 2.3.1948, 7.194.1948, 6.5.1948, 1.6.1948, 4.8.1948, 4.9.1948, 5.11.1948, 7.1.1949, APO 178, sygn. 65, 7–8, 11–12, 23–4, 25–6, 54–5, 56–7, 63–5 and sygn. 63, 9–10; Strauchold, *Autochtoni*, pp. 169–71; Zaremba, *Trwoga*, pp. 96–7.

What housing had been freed up in western Upper Silesia by the flight of hundreds of thousands of locals from the Red Army at the start of 1945 was quickly filled by the first waves of Polish settlers. Later arrivals were generally not so lucky. Most never received permanent homes in the region, because only a minority of western Upper Silesia's prewar residents were forcibly expelled as 'Germans' by the Communist-led authorities in the second half of the 1940s. Many Polish settlers continued living in temporary accommodation in the region for a long period after the war's end in the hope of eventually receiving permanent homes there. But most ultimately left the region of their own accord or were relocated to sparsely populated areas of Poland's new territories by the state authorities. Even many of the settlers who had attained homes in the region in spring and summer 1945 were eventually forced out of them when their prewar owners returned and were 'verified' as ethnic Poles.

Nevertheless, a large settler population had been established in western Upper Silesia by the end of the 1940s. In the western and southwestern areas of the region, Polish settlers made up the vast majority of the population at the end of the decade. But to the east of the authorities' imagined 'ethnic border' running along the Odra River – the central, northern and eastern areas of western Upper Silesia – the settlers were surrounded by a local population, which was often openly hostile to them, seemed culturally foreign and spoke a strange dialect of Polish as well as German. We shall examine the authorities' efforts to encourage these locals to adopt more conventionally Polish cultural and linguistic identities in Chapter 9. But first let us address the question of what happened to Polish Jewish Holocaust survivors and the foreign victims of Nazi German oppression who found themselves in Poland's new territories at the end of the Second World War.

CHAPTER 8

Holocaust survivors and foreigners

SURVIVORS

One of interwar Poland's perceived 'national minorities' had been almost entirely eliminated already before the Soviets established a Communist-controlled government in Poland in July 1944. Both before and after the Second World War, Poland's Jews were viewed by the Polish state authorities and by mainstream Polish society as a 'national minority'. In fact, in the interwar period they had been a socially and culturally very diverse population, partly the result of living in territories divided between the Russian, Habsburg and German Empires before 1918. There had been great divergences in the extent to which they had been assimilated within Polish society and in their levels of religiosity. This heterogeneity makes it difficult to pin down exactly how many 'Jews' had lived in interwar Poland. Yet it can roughly be estimated that at the end of the 1930s the number of Polish citizens who either had viewed themselves as religiously Jewish or had regarded Yiddish or Hebrew as their first language had been a little over three million, or 10 per cent of the overall population. A large proportion of these people had been highly assimilated within Polish society. Indeed, many important members of interwar Poland's cultural and artistic elite had been self-conscious Jews. But the majority of Poland's Jews had not been well assimilated. A significant minority had regarded Polish as their first language, but the vast majority had viewed Yiddish as their mother tongue and a tiny fraction Hebrew. Many of Poland's Jews had been secular, but the majority had not. Some had been members of the ultra-orthodox Hassidic movement.

Unlike other perceived 'national minorities' in interwar Poland, Jews had not been geographically concentrated. They had lived all over the country. Those living in the western areas, formerly part of the German Empire, had exhibited strong cultural affiliations with Germany. But the vast majority had lived in the central and eastern regions of interwar Poland, where they had been exposed to the many different cultural influences of the various ethnic groups inhabiting these territories. In three of Poland's main cities, Jews had composed a very large proportion of the overall population: around one-third of the residents of Warsaw, Łódź and Lwów. There had also been numerous small towns called *shtetls* scattered across central and eastern Poland where Jews had formed the majority of residents.[1]

This culturally rich and diverse population had been decimated by the Nazi German occupiers of Poland during the Second World War. Around three million Polish citizens had been killed between 1939 and 1945 because the Nazi German authorities had regarded them as Jews – murdered through shootings, gas chambers, beatings, starvation and exhaustion (see Chapter 1). Only around 10 per cent of Poland's Jews had survived – amounting to just a few hundred thousand individuals. Only a minority of these survivors had managed to evade death without leaving Polish territory. Some of them had succeeded in staying alive in concentration camps just long enough for the Red Army to save them in the final phase of the war. Others had managed to conceal their prewar Jewish identity by blending into non-Jewish Polish society, often with the help of altruistic Poles. But the majority of survivors had only survived by fleeing to the Soviet Union or by being involuntarily deported there in the first third of the war.[2]

Already in the second half of 1944, as Soviet forces started liberating Polish territory from German occupation, some of the Jews who had survived on Polish territory started to return to the towns and villages in which they had previously lived. When they attempted to reclaim their homes and businesses, they often met with hostility from the non-Jewish Poles, who had taken possession in their absence. Some were attacked or murdered by their former neighbours. These abhorrent attacks on members of an extremely vulnerable population over property were part of a broader wave of anti-Semitic attacks which happened in Poland at the end of the Second World War. They must be understood – as Marcin Zaremba has rightly stressed – in the context of the severe trauma, anxiety and moral collapse which the Nazi German occupation had brought on Polish society during

[1] Jerzy Tomaszewski, 'Niepodległa Rzeczpospolita', in Jerzy Tomaszewski (ed.), *Najnowsze Dzieje Żydów w Polsce: w zarysie (do 1950 roku)* (Warsaw, 1993), pp. 157–62, 175–8; Jan Tomasz Gross, *Fear: Anti-Semitism in Poland after Auschwitz. An Essay in Historical Interpretation* (Princeton, 2006), p. 4; Prażmowska, *Poland*, pp. 104–5; Czubiński, *Polska*, pp. 142–4; Paczkowski, *Spring*, pp. 18–19.

[2] Józef Adelson, 'W Polsce Zwanej Ludową', in Tomaszewski, *Najnowsze*, pp. 387–91; Gross, *Fear*, pp. 4–5; Waszkiewicz, 'Jewish Settlement', pp. 508–10; Olejnik, *Polityka*, p. 344; Zeev W. Mankowitz, *Life between Memory and Hope. The Survivors of the Holocaust in Occupied Germany* (Cambridge, 2002), pp. 17–18; Thum, *Breslau*, p. 126.

the war. They must also be viewed against the backdrop of the heightened influence of ethno-nationalism among Poles as well as the conditions of widespread lawlessness and severe poverty which the occupation had left in its wake. Anti-Communism, too, played an important role in the post-liberation attacks on Jews – based partly on the widespread, erroneous belief that most Jews had welcomed the Soviets into Poland in September 1939. This belief was itself derived from the long-standing Polish myth that Communism was the product of a hostile Jewish-led conspiracy, as encapsulated by the phrase '*Żydo-Komuna*'. Yet as David Engel has convincingly argued, it would be wrong to suggest that any more than a minority of attacks on Jews happened because the targets were actually deemed to be Communist officials or Communist sympathizers.

In terms of the perpetrators, most attacks on Jews were carried out by members of nationalist underground groups, most frequently the National Armed Forces (see Chapter 2). Some were committed by individuals or small groups with no apparent political affiliation or by large disorganized mobs. Yet it should be emphasized that although anti-Semitism was fairly widespread within Polish society at this time – as it was in many other European societies as well – a great many non-Jewish Poles viewed these attacks with revulsion. As had happened during the Nazi German occupation, many non-Jewish Poles provided help to Jews after the war and made efforts to challenge the anti-Semitic sentiments of others. Anti-Jewish attacks were particularly frequent in the period March to August 1945, culminating in a bomb attack in Rzeszów in early August, which killed 16 Jews, and in a pogrom in Kraków a few days later. In the latter incident, a Polish mob, made up of local residents, local policemen and soldiers, attacked a synagogue, seriously injured dozens of Jews and killed up to five. The wave of attacks subsided after summer 1945, but as we shall see, only temporarily.[3]

The wartime leaders of Poland's nationalist movement were open about their desire to see Jews removed from the country in the immediate aftermath of the war – and the extreme-nationalist National Armed Forces' attacks on Jews at the end of the war were clearly aimed, in part, at bringing about their exodus from the country. But although the Polish

[3] Zaremba, *Trwoga*, pp. 71–85, 555–60, 584–643; David Engel, 'Patterns of Anti-Jewish Violence in Poland, 1944–1946', *Yad Vashem Studies*, 26, 1998, pp. 59–60, 65–85; Engel, 'Marek Jan Chodakiewicz, after the Holocaust: Polish–Jewish Conflict in the Wake of World War II', *Polin: Studies in Polish Jewry*, 18, 2005, pp. 425–9; Joanna Michlic-Coren, 'Anti-Jewish Violence in Poland, 1918–1939 and 1945–1947', *Polin: Studies in Polish Jewry*, 14, 2001, pp. 40–61; Gross, *Fear*, pp. 31–47, 81–2; Fleming, *Communism*, p. 96; Adelson, 'Polsce', pp. 393–4, 400–2, 404–5; Olejnik, *Polityka*, pp. 281–3; Zieliński, 'Polonise', pp. 200–1.

Communists shared the nationalists' objective of expelling ethnic Ukrainians, ethnic Germans and other perceived 'national minorities' from Poland, they appeared to have no intention, at this time, of actively uprooting Polish Jews. In fact, as we shall discuss, the Communist-controlled authorities made efforts to assist Polish Jews in reconstructing their lives and communities in Poland in the immediate postwar years.

The government also facilitated the return to Poland of those Polish Jews who found themselves outside of the country's postwar borders at the end of the war. Of the probably no more than 100,000 Polish Jews who had managed to survive the Nazi German occupation without leaving prewar Polish territory, a significant percentage found themselves in the territories ceded in July 1944 to the Soviet Socialist Republics of Ukraine, Belorussia and Lithuania. These Polish Jews were transported to Poland's postwar territories together with non-Jewish Polish 'repatriates' from the end of 1944 onwards, as part of the Polish–Soviet population exchanges (see Chapter 2 and Conclusion). It is thought that 54,594 Polish Jews arrived from the three western Soviet republics as part of these exchanges in the early post-liberation years. The vast majority reached postwar Polish territory before August 1946. Between early February and the end of July 1946, those Polish Jews who had fled to or had been deported to the interior of the Soviet Union were also transported to Poland on cargo trains. Including 8,000 who travelled to Poland without any assistance from the Soviet and Polish state authorities, a total of 132,000 arrived in the country from the Soviet interior in these months. The vast majority of Polish Jewish 'repatriates' from both the western Soviet republics and the Soviet interior were transported directly to Poland's new territories. In the case of the latter, they were mostly sent to the region of Lower Silesia.[4]

The reason Lower Silesia became the main destination for the Polish Jewish 'repatriates' who were transported to Poland from the Soviet interior stemmed from negotiations which took place between official representatives of Poland's surviving Jewish population and the Communist-led government in early summer 1945. In the final months of the war, the nucleus of a Polish Jewish community, numbering around 7,000, had already formed in Lower Silesia as a consequence of the Red Army's liberation of Groß-Rosen Concentration Camp and its subcamps. Most of these Jews chose to remain in Lower Silesia after 1945 rather than return to their former homes in prewar Polish territory. They were aware that the towns

[4] Adelson, 'Polsce', pp. 387–8, 390, 397–9; Hofmann, *Nachkriegszeit*, pp. 345–6; Engel, 'Patterns', pp. 77–8, 80–1; Olejnik, *Polityka*, pp. 41–2, 345–6; Waszkiewicz, 'Jewish Settlement', pp. 510, 512.

and villages of central and south-central Poland had suffered much greater destruction than most places in Lower Silesia. They had also wanted to avoid the traumatic reminders of the suffering and deaths of their relatives, which their former home villages, towns and cities would contain.

In June 1945 a Jewish Regional Committee was set up to represent the Jews living in Lower Silesia. Almost as soon as it was created, it proposed the idea of establishing a permanent area of settlement for Polish Jews in Lower Silesia to the Ministry for Public Administration. The idea was supported by the Central Committee for Jews in Poland, a multiparty body set up by the Communist-controlled government in November 1944 as a vehicle for guiding the political activities of Poland's surviving Jews. The government was attracted to the Lower Silesia Jewish settlement plan for various reasons. It seemed to offer a way out of the attacks on Polish Jews in prewar Poland. It would provide places to live and work for the Jews being 'repatriated' from the Soviet Union. It would supply the fledgling state and party authorities of Lower Silesia with a pool of potential recruits, who the regime believed would be less hostile to Communism than most non-Jewish Polish settlers. Most crucially – as will be argued later – the government also viewed the Lower Silesia Jewish settlement plan as a means of advancing the ethno-national homogenization of postwar Polish territory. Towards the end of June 1945, the Ministry for Public Administration granted approval for the plan.[5]

The Polish Jewish population of Lower Silesia grew steadily in the second half of 1945. By the end of the year, it numbered around 18,000. Most of the Polish Jews who arrived in these months were probably 'repatriates' from the three western Soviet republics. But a small number may also have been Jews who decided to relocate from central Poland in order to escape the anti-Semitic attacks. Yet it was not until cargo trains began arriving from the Soviet interior in February 1946 that the size of Lower Silesia's Polish Jewish population suddenly increased exponentially. By the end of July 1946, when the 'repatriation' of Polish Jews from the Soviet interior came to an end, the number in Lower Silesia had soared to around 100,000 and they amounted to over half of all Polish Jews living in Poland. This mass influx of Polish Jews to the region led to the emergence of numerous Polish Jewish communities. The largest ones were located in the southeastern Lower Silesian towns of Dzierżoniów, Wałbrzych, Bielawa,

[5] Adelson, 'Polsce', pp. 389–95, 426–7; Bożena Szaynok, 'Jews in Lower Silesia 1945–1950', in Marcin Wodziński and Janusz Spyra (eds.), *Jews in Silesia* (Kraków, 2001), pp. 213–15; Hofmann, *Nachkriegszeit*, pp. 339–42; Waszkiewicz, 'Jewish Settlement', pp. 508–13.

Kłodzko, Ząbkowice and Świdnica, in Lower Silesia's regional capital, Wrocław, and in the western Lower Silesian town of Legnica.[6]

But there were also small Polish Jewish communities located elsewhere in the region. Jelenia Góra town, situated around 30 kilometres to the west of Wałbrzych, contained one of these small Polish Jewish communities. It may have initially been formed by Polish Jews liberated at the end of the war from a subcamp of Groß-Rosen Concentration Camp. This subcamp had been located before 1945 on the edge of Hirschberg/Jelenia Góra town, in the village of Bad Warmbrunn/Cieplice Śląskie. It is not clear how many Polish Jews were living in Jelenia Góra town in the first year after the war, but there is evidence that Polish Jews in the town in summer 1945 numbered around 100. A branch of Lower Silesia's Regional Jewish Committee was established there already in June 1945.[7]

The Lower Silesia Jewish settlement plan also impacted upon areas lying directly adjacent to the region. Yet although western Upper Silesia was located just to the east of Lower Silesia's largest Jewish communities, its Polish Jewish population was small by comparison in the first year after the war. Nevertheless, it is of some interest to us because the biggest community of Polish Jews in western Upper Silesia appears to have been in Opole town. Officially, there were 99 Polish Jews living in Opole town in late February 1946. Opole District's officials also noted repeatedly in spring and summer 1945 that 'transports of Jews are arriving from the Soviet Union'. Although many of these people would have travelled immediately onwards into Lower Silesia, it is highly probable that a significant number took up residence in Opole District.[8]

Unlike the non-Jewish Polish 'repatriates' from the Soviet Union, Polish Jewish 'repatriates' arriving in Poland's new territories after 1945 were not taken care of by the Polish government's State Repatriation Office and local state administrative authorities. Instead, the government placed full

[6] Adelson, 'Polsce', pp. 389–90, 395–9; Szaynok, 'Jews', pp. 214, 216, 218–19; Hofmann, *Nachkriegszeit*, pp. 345–8; Waszkiewicz, 'Jewish Settlement', pp. 509–10, 513; Olejnik, *Polityka*, pp. 345–6.

[7] SiRep JG Chief, 6.[8].1945, APJG 123/II, sygn. 18, 3–26; Rep by JGDA head S-PD, 29.8.1946, APJG 123/II, sygn. 19, 355; Rep by JGDA head S-PD, 30.9.1946, APJG 123/II, sygn. 19, 377; 'Verzeichnis der Konzentrationslager und ihrer Außenkommandos gemäß § 42 Abs. 2 BEG', http://www.gesetze-im-internet.de/begdv_6/anlage_6.html [last accessed 23.3.2013]; WR, Willi O., Bad Warmbrunn (Cieplice Śląskie), 2.10.1953, BOD 1, 207, 255–6; Adelson, 'Polsce', p. 391.

[8] Rep by OTA S-PD, 21.2.1946, APO 185, sygn. 85, 14–15; SiRep O Chief on the period 20.3.1946–20.4.1946, APO 178, sygn. 41, 20–3; SiRep O Chief on the period 20.4.1946–20.5.1946, APO 178, sygn. 41, 25–7; SiRep O Chief on the period 20.6.1946–20.7.1946, APO 178, sygn. 41, 34–6; SiRep O Chief on the period 20.7.1946–20.8.1946, APO 178, sygn. 41, 38–41. Situation reports by O Chief, 20.8.1946–20.9.1946 and 20.9.1946–20.10.1946, APO 178, sygn. 41, 43–5 and 47–9. Wojciech Jaworski, 'Jewish Religious Communities in Upper Silesia 1945–1970', in Wodziński and Spyra, *Jews*, pp. 249–60; Hofmann, *Nachkriegszeit*, p. 346; Olejnik, *Polityka*, p. 346.

responsibility for feeding, sheltering, and finding work and providing permanent housing for Polish Jewish 'repatriates' in the hands of the Central Committee for Jews in Poland and its subordinate Regional Jewish Committees. But the role these government-authorized Jewish Committees played in the lives of Polish Jewish 'repatriates' went far beyond merely providing welfare support for them. In fact, they were the main institutions of Jewish communal life for all of Poland's surviving Jews in the early postwar years. They received funds from the American Jewish Joint Distribution Committee for the provision of material support to Jews in Poland. The existence of the Jewish Committees enabled those Polish Jews who desired it to lead a social and cultural life which was quite separate from that of the rest of postwar Polish society. As a consequence, there was generally very little social interaction between Jewish and non-Jewish settlers in Poland's new territories in these years. In Lower Silesia, the Regional Jewish Committee had branches in 43 towns and villages by July 1946.

The Jewish Committees ran most of the Jewish schools set up or restarted in Poland from autumn 1945 onwards. The main teaching language for most of these schools was Yiddish, but a significant number also taught in Polish. A smaller number of Jewish schools were run by two further very important institutions for Polish Jewish life in early postwar Poland: Jewish political parties and the Jewish Faith Congregations. In total, 16 Jewish schools had been set up in Lower Silesia by summer 1946. The Central Committee for Jews in Poland and Jewish political parties also established a large number of Yiddish, Polish, Hebrew and bilingual newspapers in the region in the immediate postwar period.

Moreover, the Jewish Committees and Jewish political parties both played a leading role in the so-called 'productivization campaign' (*akcja produktywizacji*) in the early postwar years. This campaign, which was backed by Poland's Communist-led government, stemmed from a policy which had been pursued in the interwar period by Jewish left-wing political parties in Poland. The aim of this campaign was to transform the socio-occupational structure of the Jewish population in such a way that fewer would work in retail and trading occupations and more would earn their living from 'production jobs' in manufacturing and agriculture. In addition, a large number of Jewish cooperatives of various sorts were established as part of the 'productivization campaign'. There were 69 co-ops operating in Lower Silesia by summer 1946, amounting to over half of all Jewish cooperatives in Poland at that time.[9]

[9] Adelson, 'Polsce', pp. 391–2, 395–7, 426–72; Szaynok, 'Jews', 216–21; Waszkiewicz, 'Jewish Settlement', pp. 513–16; Olejnik, *Polityka*, pp. 361–81.

Yet this very swift emergence of a vibrant Polish Jewish community in Lower Silesia was suddenly disrupted by a serious incident elsewhere in Poland in summer 1946. On 4 July 1946, the biggest pogrom yet took place in the central Polish city of Kielce. On 1 July a local boy had gone missing and when he finally turned up two days later, he explained his absence with the dubious claim that he had been kidnapped by Jews. This became the pretext for a pogrom against local Jews, carried out by local residents, policemen and soldiers. According to official figures, 42 people were killed and around 100 wounded. The Kielce Pogrom was the culmination of a second surge of anti-Jewish attacks which had started in spring 1946. It seemed to many after 4 July that further pogroms were on the verge of happening in cities across prewar Polish territory. In order to gain control of this volatile situation, the Communist-led government quickly withdrew the local army garrison from Kielce and replaced it with an Internal Security Corps unit sent directly from Warsaw. Communist activists then organized protest rallies condemning the pogrom at factories across central Poland. On 11 July, nine perpetrators of the Kielce Pogrom were sentenced to death and three others received milder sentences. But far from bringing an end to the problems, these sentences sparked anti-Jewish protest strikes in various locations in central Poland. These strikes were only prevented from spilling over into pogroms through direct interventions by high-ranking Communist officials.[10]

In Lower Silesia, too, anti-Semites attempted to set off anti-Jewish riots in summer 1946. These acts appear to have been restricted mainly to southeastern Lower Silesia, where the bulk of the Polish Jewish community lived. But Jelenia Góra District was not left untouched. At the end of July, Jelenia Góra's Deputy Town President reported that the 'Kielce incidents' had impacted seriously on the mood of the population. He claimed that although most residents had responded 'calmly' to events since 4 July, the 'reactionary elements' had attempted to whip up a response from local residents. Stiff punishment of the culprits had reportedly soon put an end to this. The second surge of anti-Jewish attacks in postwar Poland gradually ebbed away in the second half of 1946. Taking into account all of the attacks which happened in Poland in the first few years following Soviet 'liberation', somewhere between 500 and 1,500 Polish Jews were killed.[11]

[10] Adelson, 'Polsce', pp. 402–3; Gross, *Fear*, pp. 81–117; Michlic-Coren, 'Violence', pp. 50–4, 58–60; Zaremba, *Trwoga*, pp. 606–13; Olejnik, *Polityka*, pp. 383–92.

[11] SiRep Jelenia Góra's Deputy Town President, 31.7.1946, APW 331/VI, sygn. 34, 25–7; Szaynok, 'Jews', p. 221; Hofmann, *Nachkriegszeit*, pp. 347–8; Adelson, 'Polsce', pp. 401, 403, 418; Gross, *Fear*, p. 35; Engel, 'Patterns', pp. 50, 58–9, 80–4; Engel, 'After the Holocaust', pp. 425, 428; Zaremba, *Trwoga*, p. 584; Fleming, *Communism*, pp. 96–7.

EXODUS

The Polish Communist leaders' attitude towards Poland's Jews was ambiguous. As the response to the Kielce Pogrom illustrates, the regime's leadership and the Polish Workers' Party's activists often took action to confront anti-Semitic activities in the early postwar years. Yet there were clear limits on how far the regime's leaders were willing to go. They were aware that by taking too resolute a stance against anti-Semitic sentiments, they might alienate many ordinary Poles from the regime and thereby diminish the slender support base they had managed to build up since the war. Moreover, anti-Semitic attitudes were also fairly widespread among lower-ranked party and state officials. A disproportionate number of leading posts in the party-state structure were held by Polish Jews, yet anti-Semitic sentiments even penetrated into the upper echelons of the regime. It is, in part, with this in mind that we should understand the regime's willingness to tolerate and, increasingly, facilitate the illegal emigration of Poland's Jews in the early postwar years.[12]

The most crucial impact of the Kielce Pogrom was that it helped to set off a wave of mass emigration of Polish Jews from the country. Already, in late 1944, Polish Jews had begun to emigrate from Poland, mainly with the help of the illegal *Brichah* organization, set up by Jewish partisan fighters in the final phase of the war. Before the war was over, *Brichah* (Hebrew for 'Flight') enabled several thousand Polish Jews to make their way through the devastated territories of South-eastern Europe to Palestine. But once the war was over, the main route to Palestine became Displaced Persons camps in the American and British Occupation Zones of Germany – particularly the American one. *Brichah* smuggled around 33,000 Polish Jews across Poland's new western border and the Soviet Zone and into western Germany in the second half of 1945. Over 15,000 also probably managed the same journey using the more dangerous strategy of going it alone. Despite tighter controls on Poland's borders after 1945, *Brichah* moved over 14,000 Polish Jews illegally into western Germany in the first half of 1946, in addition to several thousand who made the journey unassisted. But the Kielce Pogrom on 4 July 1946 caused the number of Jewish emigrants truly to soar. The panic it unleashed prompted influential members of Poland's Jewish community to begin lobbying the Warsaw government to lift restrictions on Jewish mass emigration from Poland. In

[12] Gross, *Fear*, pp. 120–8, 153–66; Hofmann, *Nachkriegszeit*, pp. 351–4; Adelson, 'Polsce', pp. 403–5; Fleming, *Communism*, pp. 48–9, 86–7; Zieliński, 'Polonise', pp. 200–1; Czubiński, *Polska*, pp. 144–7.

the course of July, the Minister of Defence, Marian Spychalski, agreed to open the southern border unofficially to emigration by Polish Jews.

Jews began pouring across the southern border into Czechoslovakia at crossings in the small Lower Silesian towns of Mieroszów and Kudowa. From the northern borderlands of Czechoslovakia they were able to travel by train to the American Zone. At the same time, *Brichah* continued smuggling people across Poland's western border with the Soviet Zone from the city of Szczecin. It also infiltrated Polish Jews into the cargo trains being used to expel Germans from the new territories at this time. A total of around 80,000 to 90,000 of Poland's remaining Jews made their way illegally or semi-legally to western Germany from Poland in the mass exodus which took place in the second half of 1946. Thereafter, the panic unleashed by the Kielce Pogrom at last died down and the state authorities closed the southern border again. Tens of thousands of Polish Jewish residents of Lower Silesia had emigrated in this exodus. This diminished the size of the community to around 57,000 by December 1946. It was not out of simple altruism that members of the Communist-led government had deliberately facilitated this exodus – even if it met the wishes of many Polish Jews. The regime's leaders viewed Polish Jews as a 'national minority' and regarded the mass emigration of Poland's surviving Jews, by this time, as part of the way in which it would achieve its goal of creating an ethno-nationally homogeneous Polish nation-state. Correspondingly, the regime was much more pro-active when it came to preventing non-Jewish Poles – many of whom also wanted to abandon the country at this time – from emigrating.[13]

The Kielce Pogrom also sparked a frenzy of internal migration within Poland by Polish Jews. Those still living in small towns in central Poland now decided to move to nearby cities, where there were larger Jewish communities and therefore there was greater security. This was encouraged by the Central Committee for Jews in Poland and by the numerous regional and local Jewish Committees. Many Polish Jews also chose to relocate from central Poland to the by then well-established Jewish communities of Lower Silesia. Migration from central Poland to Lower Silesia had probably already been going on since the second half of 1945. But after the Kielce Pogrom, it changed from a small stream into a large flow. At the same time, within

[13] Adelson, 'Polsce', pp. 390, 405–14, 416–17; Szaynok, 'Jews', pp. 221–2; Mankowitz, *Life*, pp. 17–22; Albert Stankowski, 'Nowe spojrzenie na statystyki dotyczące emigracji Żydów z Polski po 1944 roku', in Grzegorz Berendt, August Grabski and Albert Stankowski (eds.), *Studia z Historii Żydów w Polsce po 1945 Roku* (Warsaw, 2000), pp. 108–11; Olejnik, *Polityka*, pp. 346, 389–90; Fleming, *Communism*, pp. 48–50; Juliane Wetzel, '"Displaced Person". Ein vergessenes Kapitel der deutschen Nachkriegsgeschichte', *Aus Politik und Zeitgeschichte*, B7–8/95, pp. 34–6.

Lower Silesia, many Polish Jews relocated from small Jewish communities to the larger ones. Unlike the mass wave of emigration, this large-scale domestic migration continued throughout 1947. It caused a significant consolidation of the large Jewish communities of southeastern Lower Silesia to take place in late 1946 and 1947. The end to mass emigration in early 1947 also brought an atmosphere of renewed stability to Poland's remaining Jewish community, especially in Lower Silesia. In spring 1947, Lower Silesia still contained around half the 94,000 Polish Jews officially registered as living in Poland.[14]

The stability which set in during 1947 meant that, far from dwindling away in the aftermath of the mass exodus, Polish Jewish communal life in Lower Silesia became even livelier. During 1947 the Jewish press in the region expanded, the number of Jewish schools increased and other cultural activities flourished – including the staging of Yiddish plays and the emergence of numerous Jewish community centres. Jewish political parties also started to play a more prominent role in Jewish communal life than previously.[15] This was not witnessed only in Lower Silesia's large Jewish communities. It was also evident in the small communities, such as the one in Jelenia Góra town, where the Jewish Social-Democratic Workers' Poalej Syjon Lewica Party – a party which was both Zionist and Communist in outlook – opened a local office in May 1947. According to Polish officials, its first clear sign of activity was to put on a Yiddish play at the municipal theatre, which was attended by a 'large audience' from the 'local Jewish colony'. Similarly, in Opole town, the more moderately left-wing Hitachdut Zionist-Socialist Labour Party set up a local branch in early summer 1947.[16]

At the same time, the Communist-controlled government in Warsaw became significantly more involved in the 'productivization campaign' after the Kielce Pogrom. This was decisive in enabling the official Jewish Committees and Jewish political parties to continue expanding the network of Jewish cooperatives. By autumn 1947 the number of Jewish cooperatives in Lower Silesia had reached 100, making up over half of all Jewish cooperatives in Poland. Jewish organizations also ran special vocational schools as part of the campaign and continued to provide Jews with support to

[14] Adelson, 'Polsce', pp. 418–20; Szaynok, 'Jews', pp. 219, 222; Jan Tomasz Gross, 'Stereotypes of Polish–Jewish Relations after the War: The Special Commission of the Central Committee of Polish Jews', *Polin: Studies in Polish Jewry*, 13, 2000, p. 199; Engel, 'Patterns', pp. 81–2; Olejnik, *Polityka*, p. 390.

[15] Szaynok, 'Jews', pp. 222–5; Adelson, 'Polsce', pp. 417–20.

[16] SiRep JG DepChief, 31.5.1947, APW 331/VI, sygn. 51, 20–1; SiRep ODA S-PD, 6.6.1947, APO 178, sygn. 62, 16–18; Adelson, 'Polsce', pp. 439–42, 445.

help them establish farms in the new territories. Polish Jews had taken over 64 farms in Lower Silesia by mid 1947. Much of this activity had a distinctly idealistic and pioneering spirit to it. The head of Lower Silesia's Regional Jewish Committee later recalled that his intention in these years had been to establish a 'Yiddish homeland' in Lower Silesia. Many others viewed the Jewish settlements in Lower Silesia in a similarly romantic way. But this pioneering spirit was even stronger among those whose intention was not actually to remain in Poland. Theirs was a romantic vision directed not at Lower Silesia but at Palestine. Most of Poland's Jewish political parties were Zionist, and they viewed Lower Silesia as merely a temporary home, a place to get ready for Palestine. The umbrella youth organization of Poland's left-wing Zionist parties, Hehaluc, set up socialist work communes known as *kibbutzim* in Lower Silesia in these years. Their explicit aim was to provide young Polish Jews with vocational training for a new life in Palestine. After the outbreak of fighting between Jews and Arabs in Palestine in November 1947, special camps were also set up in Poland, with the permission of Poland's Ministry of Defence, to train Polish Jewish recruits for the Jewish military organization Hagana. One of these camps was established just 20 kilometres to the east of Jelenia Góra town.[17]

Although the mass exodus of Polish Jews from Poland was over by early spring 1947, small-scale emigration continued during the year. Greater control over the borders by the state authorities seriously restricted the scope for illegal border crossings. Only 9,315 are believed to have emigrated with the help of *Brichah* during 1947. As a consequence, legal emigration for the first time became a key route out of Poland for the country's remaining Jews. This kind of emigration, involving passports and visas, had actually gone on since late 1945, with emigrants travelling not only to Palestine but also the United States, South America and other destinations. But very few used the long-winded legal route before 1947 – perhaps only a couple of thousand people. Yet the 6,000 Polish Jews who emigrated legally during 1947 constituted two-fifths of all Jewish emigrants. And a further 6,000 emigrated legally during 1948 – amounting to almost three-quarters of all Jewish emigrants; only 2,300 were smuggled across the border illegally by *Brichah* during that year.[18]

The Polish Communists' treatment of Polish Jews had never been unambiguously benevolent. But from 1948 onwards – as the regime lurched into line with Stalinist Soviet orthodoxy – even their official policies became

[17] Adelson, 'Polsce' pp. 421, 457–62; Szaynok, 'Jews', pp. 213, 223–7.
[18] Adelson, 'Polsce', pp. 413–16; Stankowski, 'Żydów', pp. 110–14.

decidedly malevolent. The Recovered Territories Exhibition in Wrocław in 1948, a propagandistic event put on by the regime to celebrate Poland's takeover of the new territories, was originally supposed to have contained two pavilions devoted to the new territories' Polish Jewish community. But in July 1948 the regime's leaders decided that expressions of ideological and cultural diversity of this sort should no longer be encouraged. The pavilions were closed down. Then, at the start of 1949, the Jewish arm of the Polish Workers' Party took control of the Marxist pro-Communist Bund party and asserted full numerical dominance within the Central Committee for Jews in Poland. This gave the Polish Worker's Party an absolutely hegemonic political position within Poland's Jewish community. The Bund party had been the only other Jewish party – other, that is, than the Jewish branch of the Polish Workers' Party – to express consistent opposition to the emigration of Jews from Poland in the early postwar years. But this did not prevent the Polish Communists from ending its political independence. The Communists' assertion of control over the Bund party was followed in late 1949 and 1950 by the dissolution of almost all other Polish Jewish institutions. All Zionist parties were disbanded. All Jewish schools were taken into state ownership and then either merged with Polish state schools or abolished. All Jewish newspapers were closed down, the only exception being the Yiddish-language *Fołks-Sztym*, an organ of the Polish United Workers' Party. All Jewish cooperatives were dissolved. Most Jewish farms also disappeared because they were unable to sustain themselves without material support from the Jewish organizations. The suppression of Polish Jewish institutions at the end of the 1940s can partly be understood as part of the broader Stalinist clampdown on political plurality and ideological diversity in Poland after 1948. It also coincided with a change of attitude towards Zionism on the part of Poland's Communist leaders, prompted by Stalin's decision to oppose the new state of Israel, founded in May 1948. Other reasons that the regime clamped down on Polish Jewish institutions will be discussed in the following.[19]

This crackdown was accompanied by a new wave of emigration. The regime's leadership decided at this time that the most effective way of destroying Poland's Zionist political parties would be to allow and encourage Zionist Jews to emigrate. As information spread within the Polish Jewish community at the end of the 1940s that large-scale emigration was about to become possible once more – and as the regime started its suppression

[19] Adelson, pp. 421, 427, 434–9, 459, 463–5, 470–2; Szaynok, 'Jews', pp. 225–8; Hofmann, *Nachkriegszeit*, pp. 377–80; Waszkiewicz, 'Jewish Settlement', pp. 517–19; Olejnik, *Polityka*, pp. 398–412.

of Jewish institutions – a new panic took off among Poland's remaining Jews. Many believed this could be their final chance to get out of the country. Between September 1949 and the end of 1950, some 27,500 Polish Jews were granted permission to emigrate from Poland to Israel. Around 16,000 Polish Jews left Lower Silesia as part of this exodus. Together with the fact that Jews continued to migrate within Lower Silesia from small to large Jewish communities in the late 1940s, this new wave of emigration brought an end to many of the region's once numerous Jewish communities in 1949–50. Jelenia Góra town's Polish Jewish community appears to have disappeared at this time, and something similar probably happened to the one in Opole town as well. In the whole of Poland, only 60,000 to 80,000 Jews remained after 1950 – having numbered over 3 million in 1939. The majority continued to live in Lower Silesia.[20]

The Communist-led regime's treatment of Poland's Jews after the war did not fit as neatly as its treatment of other perceived 'national minorities' into its postwar campaign to transform Poland into an ethnically homogeneous nation-state. In stark contrast to the other perceived 'national minorities', Polish Jews were granted very significant cultural autonomy in the early postwar years and were given the freedom to foster a large number of independent political organizations representing a variety of political outlooks. The latter was, right from the outset, unavailable to the rest of Polish society (see Chapter 2). Moreover, unlike ethnic Germans, ethnic Ukrainians and to a lesser extent ethnic Belorussians and ethnic Lithuanians, the government did not attempt to uproot Polish Jews forcibly from the country. Yet this should not be understood as reflecting a belief on the part of most of the regime's leadership that the presence of a culturally, socially and politically autonomous Polish Jewish community in postwar Poland was in line with their objective of creating an ethnically homogeneous Polish nation-state.

Several key factors explain why, unlike other perceived 'national minorities', Polish Jews were granted extensive autonomy and were not targeted with overt expulsion in the early postwar years. First, the surviving Jewish population of Poland was small compared to the ethnic Ukrainian population and tiny relative to the ethnic German one. Second, in the first couple of postwar years – before the Cold War set in fully – the Communist-led

[20] SiRep the head of JGTA's Settlement Department, 18.6.1947, APJG 130, sygn. 47, 219–21; Rep on the third quarter of 1947 by JG Chief, 13.11.1947, APJG 123/II, sygn. 21, 232–6; SiRep JG Chief, 3.12.1948, APW 331/VI, sygn. 51, 79–81; Stankowski, 'Żydów', pp. 114–17; Szaynok, 'Jews', pp. 222, 227–8; Jaworski, 'Jewish Religious Communities', pp. 250–5, 260; Adelson, 'Polsce' pp. 421–4; Olejnik, *Polityka*, pp. 406–8.

regime was anxious not to alienate the Western powers. Actively expelling Poland's Jews would clearly have done that. Third, accusations of anti-Semitism were an important element of the propaganda attacks which the Polish Communists directed at exile politicians abroad and at legal and illegal political opponents at home in this period – something they would not have been able to do had they begun expelling Polish Jews from the country. Fourth, unlike the other perceived 'national minorities', the regime's leaders did not view Polish Jews as representing an irredentist threat, because they were not living in a territory adjacent to a state or a Soviet republic whose dominant 'nation' laid claim to them as fellow members.

The Polish Communists' support for the Jewish settlement plan in Lower Silesia should be viewed, partly, as representing for them an alternative way of bringing greater ethno-national homogeneity to the majority of Poland's postwar territories. The Communist leaders appear to have taken the view that if most of Poland's surviving Jews were concentrated into a single region of the country, the rest of Poland would become more ethno-nationally homogeneous. Likewise, the regime's leaders tolerated and facilitated illegal and semi-legal mass emigration in the early postwar years, in part because they regarded this as a way of advancing the objective of creating a homogeneous nation-state without antagonizing the Western powers. It was only once the Cold War had brought full rupture to relations with the United States and Britain that the situation changed.

Moreover, the regime's suppression of Jewish political and cultural institutions after 1948 should be understood as fulfilling two fundamental objectives for the regime. First, it brought Poland closer to Stalinist Soviet political and ideological orthodoxy by eliminating some of the country's last surviving independent political and social organizations. Second, it moved Poland closer to ethno-national homogeneity by eliminating cultural institutions and activities which were not regarded as expressions of mainstream Polish national culture. The regime did move away from the overtly nationalist rhetoric and propaganda of the early postwar years in 1948–9. But there were important ways in which the regime continued to pursue its campaign of ethno-national homogenization. The suppression of cultural autonomy for the small number of Jews remaining at the end of the 1940s was one of the final significant steps taken by the regime to complete the transformation of Poland into a fully ethno-nationally homogeneous Polish nation-state after the Second World War.[21]

[21] Hofmann, *Nachkriegszeit*, pp. 377–80; Zieliński, 'Polonise', pp. 199–201; Szaynok, 'Jews', p. 226.

FOREIGNERS

It was not only Polish and German Jews (see Chapter 4 on the latter), but also Jews of various different nationalities who were released from camps in Poland's new territories at the end of the Second World War. Alongside foreign Jews, there were also many other foreigners – individuals without Polish or German citizenship – who found themselves in these territories at the end of the war. This was because the Nazi German authorities had transported millions of foreign forced civilian workers and foreign prisoners of war to Germany during the war, including the German territories which fell to Poland in 1945. The prisoners of war came from the many different countries Nazi Germany had invaded or fought against. The forced civilian workers were transported to Germany, above all, from the Soviet Union, Poland and other Eastern European states. But large numbers were also taken from the Western and Northern European countries occupied by Germany.[22]

The evidence from Opole District and Jelenia Góra District is that there was a lot of coming and going by foreign displaced persons in the localities of Poland's new territories in the immediate aftermath of the war – as these diverse victims of Nazi Germany gradually made their way back home. Local witnesses in both Opole District and Jelenia Góra District reported the presence of foreign forced workers from the Soviet Union and elsewhere during the war. Josef M., from the village of Malapane/Ozimek in Opole District, for example, remembered that Russians, Latvians and even British prisoners of war were among the foreign labourers forced to work in the village's high-grade steel works in the war years.[23] Many of these forced workers departed from the two districts already in the final phase of the war. But some remained for some time after the war. Other foreign forced workers seem to have arrived in the two districts after the war, as they gradually made their way back home from elsewhere – either from other places in Poland's new territories or from territories further west, which were still part of Germany. Opole District's postwar Polish state officials thus reported the presence of Russians, Ukrainians, Italians, Romanians and

[22] Stelzl-Marx, 'Forced Labourers', pp. 170–5, 181–3; Evans, *War*, pp. 348–57, 364–71; Adelson, 'Polsce', p. 389; Thum, *Breslau*, p. 133.

[23] WR, Josef M., Malapane (Ozimek) in Oppeln (Opole) District, undated, BOD 1, 243, 251–4; WR, Georg S., Tauentzien (Okoły) in Oppeln (Opole) District, undated, BOD 1, 243, 349–51; WR, Oskar S., Berbisdorf (Dziwiszów) in Hirschberg (Jelenia Góra) District, undated, BOD 1, 207, 29–32; WR, Paul W., Bad Warmbrunn (Cieplice Śląskie) in Hirschberg (Jelenia Góra) District, undated, BOD 2, 188, 318–32; WR, Adolph G., Bärndorf (Gruszków) in Hirschberg (Jelenia Góra) District, undated, BOD 1, 207, 21–4; Thum, *Breslau*, p. 133.

Czechs at various times during 1945 and 1946. Most of these people appear to have left the district by the second half of 1946, although some were still said to be waiting to receive passports and visas in order to return home in summer 1946.[24] Jelenia Góra District's officials noted the presence of French and Dutch individuals, as well as Belgians and Ukrainians, in summer 1945. These people were said to be waiting for train networks to be restarted so that they could return home to their respective states. Two months later, officials indicated that only the French nationals and Belgians were still present in the district and that they were now attempting to 'remove' them 'gradually through voluntary departure'. These efforts continued through to the early months of 1946. In late 1945 and early 1946, the district's officials also reported the presence of Yugoslavs, Romanians and Latvians in Jelenia Góra District, but noted that they were gradually 'leaving' of their own accord. Then, around the start of February 1946, the district's authorities carried out a full registration of all remaining 'foreigners' in the district. After they registered all individuals they came across who fell into this category, letters were apparently sent to their consulates by the district's authorities, asking for assistance in transporting them back to their own countries. The district's officials explained in an official report that many of the foreigners wanted to return home but were inhibited by the costs involved and by difficulties attaining 'passes'. Most of these foreign displaced persons appear to have left Jelenia Góra District by the second half of 1946.[25]

At the end of the war, the Soviet authorities made concerted efforts to ensure that every Soviet citizen who had been transported to Germany during the war returned to the Soviet Union. A significant minority refused to return home. One of the main reasons for this was that they knew the Soviet authorities suspected everyone who had spent time in Nazi Germany – whether involuntarily or not – of collaboration.[26] In 1947, there

[24] SiRep ODA, 9.8.1945, APK 185/4, 27/1, 43–7; SiRep O Chief on the period 20.8.1945–20.9.1945, APO 178, sygn. 41, 1–4; SiRep O Chief on the period 20.9.1945–20.10.1945, APO 178, sygn. 41, 5–8; Population figures provided by OTA S-PD, 21.2.1946, APO 185, sygn. 85, 14–15; SiRep O Chief on the period 20.3.1946–20.4.1946, APO 178, sygn. 41, 20–3; SiRep O Chief on the period 20.4.1946–20.5.1946, APO 178, sygn. 41, 25–7; SiRep O Chief on the period 20.5.1946–20.6.1946, APO 178, sygn. 41, 30–2; SiRep O Chief on the period 20.6.1946–20.7.1946, APO 178, sygn. 41, 34–6; Thum, *Breslau*, p. 133.

[25] Rep by JG Chief, 6.[8].1945, APJG 123/II, sygn. 18, 3–26; Rep by JGDA S-PD, 3.9.1945, APJG 123/II, sygn. 18, 86–8; MoRep JG Chief, 3.10.1945, APJG 123/II, sygn. 18, 127–32; SiRep JG Chief, 5.12.1945, APJG 123/II, sygn. 18, 185–200; SiRep head JGTA, 6.12.1945, APW 331/VI, sygn. 28, 77–92; SiRep JG Chief, 5.1.1946, APJG 123/II, sygn. 18, 206–14; SiRep JG Chief, 5.2.1946, APJG 123/II, sygn. 19, 30–7.

[26] Stelzl-Marx, 'Forced Labourers', pp. 182–91; Nick Baron, 'Remaking Soviet Society: The Filtration of Returnees from Nazi Germany, 1944–49', in Gatrell and Baron, *Warlands*, pp. 93–6.

were therefore still a significant number of Soviet citizens not only in Allied-occupied Germany but also in Poland's new territories. In Opole District, the District Administration took action to repatriate these people to the Soviet Union from the end of 1946 onwards. One individual of 'Soviet nationality' (*narodowość sowiecka*) was reportedly already 'displaced' to the Soviet Union at the end of December 1946. But thereafter there remained at least 23 Soviet citizens who had been transported to the district as forced labourers by the Nazi German authorities during the war and were now requesting Polish citizenship. In addition to these people, officials noted that two Russians were living in the district who had arrived there as prisoners of war in the First World War and had been treated as 'stateless persons' by the German authorities in the interwar period. In May 1947, a 'Polish–Soviet Commission' arrived in Opole District from Katowice to determine who, among the Soviet citizens living there, would be awarded Polish citizenship and who would be designated for repatriation to the Soviet Union. The commission gave these people a month to gather the necessary documents together 'to prove they are ethnically Polish' or face repatriation to the Soviet Union. The commission ended up earmarking only four of the Soviet citizens for repatriation. And it appears that the authorities failed even to repatriate that small number in the course of summer 1947.[27]

In Jelenia Góra District, there remained a similar number of Soviet citizens in 1947. But the local state authorities there were more successful in their efforts to repatriate these people. In mid March 1947, 20 Soviet citizens, who had been 'residing illegally' in the district since the war, were repatriated to the Soviet Union. They were transported from the district with food provisions for a seven-day journey.[28]

As indicated by the example of the stateless Russians in Opole District, not all of the perceived foreigners who found themselves in Poland's new territories after the Second World War had been transported there by the Nazi German authorities. In Jelenia Góra District, there appear to have been a small number of Italian and Austrian citizens living there since before the war – presumably regular immigrants who had moved to this area of what was then Germany entirely voluntarily in the interwar years.

[27] SiRep ODA S-PD, 31.12.1946, AP Katowcie 185/4, sygn. 39, 54–54a; SiRep ODA S-PD, 2.5.1947, APO, 178, sygn. 62, 12–14; SiRep ODA S-PD, 6.6.1947, APO 178, sygn. 62, 16–18; SiRep O Chief on the period 21.5.1947–20.6.1947, APO 178, sygn. 42, 27–8; SiRep ODA S-PD, 12.8.1947, APO 178, sygn. 62, 21–3; Rep by ODA head S-PD, 5.8.1949, APO 178, sygn. 64, 36.

[28] SiRep JG Chief, 31.3.1947, APW 331/VI, sygn. 51, 10–12; MoRep the District Social-Political Department, 31.347, APJG, 123/II, sygn. 21, 68.

Moreover, the district also contained a relatively large number of long-term 'Czech' residents. The district's officials indicated that this 'Czech' population comprised several hundred individuals after the war. In the second half of 1945, the district's authorities tried to bring about their 'voluntary departure' to Czechoslovakia, and around a dozen 'Czech families' were reported to have left the district by the end of 1945. Yet the authorities had no intention of forcibly expelling ethnic Czechs to Czechoslovakia. In fact, in early autumn 1946, Jelenia Góra District's officials reported that because some Czechs living in the district had recently been granted Czechoslovak citizenship, their homes, which had earlier been seized from them when they had been deemed to be Germans, now had to be returned to them. Interestingly, the authorities reported having to do the same for some residents who had recently been granted Austrian citizenship. The problem of distinguishing between 'Czechs' and 'Germans' did not end there. A 'mixed Polish–Czechoslovak verification committee' subjected a significant number of the district's residents to ethnic screening in the second half of 1947. By September, the committee had apparently refused Czechoslovak citizenship to around 130 individuals. The authorities thereafter referred to these people as 'former Czechs' and designated them all for 'repatriation' to Germany. Some of the 'former Czechs' sought help from the Czechoslovak Embassy at this time, in the hope of preventing their expulsion to Germany. But this appears to have failed. How many people were granted Czechoslovak citizenship by this committee and therefore allowed to continue living in the district after the end of the decade is unclear.[29]

The frenzy of population movement which had taken place in Poland's new territories in the second half of the 1940s, then, had not involved only Germans and non-Jewish Poles. Polish Jews and foreigners – many of them victims of Nazi German concentration camps and forced labour – also made their way across these territories in the early postwar years, looking for new homes or attempting to return home. At the same time, many members of established immigrant communities living in these territories

[29] Rep by JG Chief, 6.[8].1945, APJG 123/II, sygn. 18, 3–26; Rep by JGDA S-PD, 3.9.1945, APJG 123/II, sygn. 18, 86–8; MoRep JG Chief, 3.10.1945, APJG 123/II, sygn. 18, 127–32; SiRep JG Chief, 5.12.1945, APJG 123/II, sygn. 18, 185–200; SiRep JG Chief, 5.1.1946, APJG 123/II, sygn. 18, 206–14; SiRep JGDA head S-PD, 30.9.1946, APW 331/VI, sygn. 36, 24–5; SiRep the head of JGTA's Settlement Department, 18.6.1947, APJG 130, sygn. 47, 219–21; SiRep the JG DepChief, 31.7.1947, APW 331/VI, sygn. 51, 26–7; Rep by JGDA head S-PD, 26.9.1947, APJG 123/II, sygn. 20, 136–7; Wiedemann, *Grenzland*, pp. 260–3.

emigrated at this time, after finding that the cities, towns and villages in which they had lived had become part of a foreign Communist-led state. The Polish Jews, foreign Jews, foreign forced workers and foreign immigrants were not forcibly expelled from Poland's new territories after the war. But the majority of them had left these territories and migrated to other countries by the end of the 1940s.

An important factor underpinning their exodus was the Communist-controlled government's campaign to transform Poland into an ethno-nationally homogeneous nation-state. It had become obvious to most Polish Jews and most foreigners with a legal basis to remain in Poland after the war that there would be no place for them in the ethnically 'pure' Polish nation-state of the postwar era. Their emigration was, therefore, not forced, but neither was it entirely voluntary. Let us now turn our attention to a population which was neither expelled nor pressured to emigrate from Poland's new territories in the second half of the 1940s: the 'verified indigenous Poles'.

CHAPTER 9

Assimilation

In theory, the 'verification action' implemented in western Upper Silesia at the end of the war was aimed at sifting Poles from Germans. In practice, it filtered out only the minority of individuals who actively presented themselves as Germans or were overtly hostile to Polish society or to living in Poland from a population which largely held no feelings of 'national' affiliation. Yet, as we discussed in Chapter 6, western Upper Silesia's Communist-controlled state authorities did not believe that they were 'verifying' hundreds of thousands of people as ethnic Poles who were not in fact ethnic Poles. Rather, they were convinced that these were 'indigenous Poles' whose 'Polish national consciousness' had simply not yet fully 'crystallized'. They therefore accompanied their 'verification action' with measures aimed at culturally and linguistically assimilating these 'indigenous Poles' into mainstream Polish society. They referred to these measures as 're-Polonization' (*repolonizacja*).

'Re-Polonization' took on particular significance in western Upper Silesia because the vast majority of the people living in Poland's new territories who were 'verified' as ethnic Poles in the second half of the 1940s resided in that region. But because the 'verification action' was not limited to western Upper Silesia, neither was the policy of 're-Polonization'. Wherever the authorities introduced 're-Polonization' measures in Poland's new territories, their goal was the same: to ensure that the 'verification' of a large minority of the territories' prewar population as 'indigenous Poles' did not undermine the government's objective of transforming Poland into an ethno-nationally homogeneous nation-state.[1] In this chapter we shall look in detail at the 're-Polonization action' (*akcja repolonizacyjna*) implemented in western Upper Silesia in the early postwar years, before turning, in the final section of the chapter, to examining its application to the rest of Poland's new territories.

[1] Strauchold, *Autochtoni*, pp. 70–1, 75–6, 85–7, 93–7; Madajczyk, *Przyłączenie*, pp. 185–9.

LANGUAGE AND IDENTITY

Western Upper Silesia's Communist-led authorities launched the 're-Polonization action' in the region in early autumn 1945. At its core were 're-Polonization courses' (*kursy repolonizacyjne*). These were largely voluntary. They were aimed principally at adults among the 'indigenous population' (*ludność autochtoniczna*). They were run mainly by state schools with the support of the Ministry of Education and the region's town and district administrations. The primary purpose of these courses was to teach standard Polish to a local population which mainly spoke a distinct regional dialect of the language (see Chapter 6). But they also included lessons on Polish history, Polish geography and often even vocational subjects such as bookkeeping. A number of 're-Polonization courses' were started in western Upper Silesia in early autumn 1945 as the first postwar academic year got underway. Thereafter the state authorities attempted to set up or facilitate the setting up of new courses in as many of western Upper Silesia's towns and villages as possible. The number of 're-Polonization courses' therefore increased steadily over the next several years. In Opole District, for example, a total of 34 courses were run in the academic year of 1945–6, attended by 1,325 students from both Opole town and the rural part of Opole District. A further eight courses had been started by December 1946. From the very outset a new 'Gymnasium for Adults' in Opole town functioned as one of the main institutions providing 're-Polonization courses' in the whole of western Upper Silesia.[2]

Yet the region's authorities regarded 're-Polonization courses' as only one of the means through which they would bring about the cultural assimilation of the 'indigenous Poles'. 'Re-Polonization' would also be a matter of exposing the 'autochthons' (i.e., indigenous residents) to Polish language and culture in a more general sense, including providing them with opportunities to interact with Polish settlers. As we shall discuss in Chapter 10, one of the things this implied was allowing the Polish arm of the Roman Catholic Church to take control of German Roman Catholic and Protestant churches in the region. But it also meant setting up in towns and villages throughout the region Polish community centres (*domy kultury*), Polish social clubs, Polish libraries, Polish cinemas and, most importantly, Polish state schools. Despite a severe shortage of Polish teachers in the immediate postwar period, the authorities started

[2] SiRep ODA S-PD, 4.12.1946, APO 178, Sygn. B15, 1–1a; Rep on the 're-Polonization action' by ODA S-PD, 21.4.1948, APO 178, sygn. 65, 17–21; Stadniczenko, 'Rok szkolny', pp. 425–6; Madajczyk, *Przyłączenie*, pp. 196–7; Strauchold, *Autochtoni*, pp. 93–4; Linek, *Polityka*, p. 310.

to open Polish state schools in western Upper Silesia at the start of the school year in early autumn 1945. German schooling had already been prohibited in the region in February 1945. The Communist-led authorities regarded Polish state schools as an absolutely central element of the 're-Polonization' process. This was partly because they used school buildings for the 're-Polonization courses' run for the local adult population. But, more importantly, the authorities believed that normal school education for children was an integral element of the 're-Polonization' process. By attending Polish school lessons, 'indigenous children' would inevitably become instilled with conventional Polish language and culture. At the same time, Polish language tuition could be provided to children during normal school hours.

Throughout western Upper Silesia, the Communist-led authorities viewed the 're-Polonization' of children and teenagers as especially important because they recognized that this section of the 'indigenous population' would be easier to influence than the adults. They also realized that older children and teenagers had been exposed to particularly heavy doses of Nazi propaganda before 1945 and were more likely to have no command of the regional Polish dialect. The 're-Polonization' of older children and teenagers was therefore more urgent than for the rest of the population. The problem was that 'indigenous Polish' parents proved very reluctant to send their children to Polish schools in the early postwar years. The proportion of 'indigenous' children attending school in western Upper Silesia never crossed 15 per cent in the years 1945–8.[3]

Western Upper Silesia's authorities also viewed Polish newspapers and books as playing an important role in the 're-Polonization' of 'indigenous Poles'. In Opole District, for example, officials had spoken already in summer 1945 of the need to radically increase the quantity of Polish newspapers and books available to the local population, noting that this would help to make them 'conscious' of their 'Polish nationality'. In July 1946, a new Polish newspaper called *Nowiny Opolskie* (Opole News) began publication in Opole town – named after *Nowiny*, a Polish-language newspaper published in Oppeln town in the early decades of the twentieth century. Opole District's state officials expressed hope in summer 1946 that this newspaper would 'awaken the Polish spirit' in the local population and deal a blow to 'German language and culture' there. *Nowiny Opolskie* rapidly became western Upper Silesia's main newspaper. Within a month of getting started, it was distributing to five of the region's districts and

[3] Madajczyk, *Przyłączenie*, pp. 174, 197–8; Strauchold, *Autochtoni*, pp. 93–7, 101; Linek, *Polityka*, pp 218, 335; SiRep ODA S-PD, 4.12.1946, APO 178, sygn. B15, 1–1a.

producing 15,000 copies per issue. Opole District's Chief Official expressed the view, in August 1946, that the newspaper needed to be reduced in price from its current five złoty and turned into a daily. Nevertheless, he approved of the fact that it 'displays outstandingly anti-German tendencies and raises serious historical matters'.[4]

But the state authorities' initial confidence that the prewar population of western Upper Silesia had an 'uncrystallized' Polish ethno-national identity which could be 're-Polonized' with relatively little effort soon started to unravel. As we discussed in Chapter 3, most of the new Polish state officials sent into western Upper Silesia from early spring 1945 onwards were from central Poland, and they seriously struggled to grasp the complicated cultural dynamics at work in the region. They were genuinely shocked by the amount of German which continued to be spoken there after the war – a great deal of it, as soon became clear, by individuals who had been 'verified' as ethnic Poles. In Opole District, for example, the Chief Official noted in October 1945 that it was really only the Polish settlers in the village of Opolska Nowa Wieś who spoke Polish. Most of the local population spoke German. Two months later, he added, 'It is a very strange phenomenon that members of the local population [of Opole District], who partially know the Polish language, nevertheless use German.' By spring 1946, it had apparently become clear that a significant section of the 'verified population' in Opole District was 'failing to Polonize' and that efforts to 'Polonize the segment . . . possessing a low level of Polish consciousness' were achieving almost nothing. One official from Opole Town Administration even remarked at this time that a lot of people who had been 'verified' as Poles and were 'categorically of our blood . . . harm not only Polish language and thought but also healthy thought in general'. The same levels of consternation were expressed by local state officials in western Upper Silesia's other districts.[5]

Across the region, officials showed particular concern about the linguistic shortcomings of 'indigenous children'. Almost all the teachers working in western Upper Silesia's schools after the war were from prewar Poland. State officials were often alarmed at the level of hostility many

[4] SiRep ODA, 9.8.1945, APK 185/4, sygn. 27/1, 43–7; SiRep O Chief on the period 20.8.1945–20.9.1945, APO 178, sygn. 41, 1–4; SiRep O Chief on the period 20.9.1945–20.10.1945, APO 178, sygn. 41, 5–8; SiRep O Chief on the period 20.6.1946–20.7.1946, APO 178, sygn. 41, 34–6; SiRep OTA head S-PD, 21.746, APO 185, sygn. 85, 34; SiRep O Chief on the period 20.7.1946–20.8.1946, APO 178, sygn. 41, 38–41; Strauchold, *Autochtoni*, pp. 100–2; Lis, 'Mniejszość polska', p. 267.

[5] SiRep O Chief on the period 20.11.1945–20.12.1945, APO 178, sygn. 41, 10–12; SiRep O Chief on the period 20.9.1945–20.10.1945, APO 178, sygn. 41, 5–8; SiRep OTA head S-PD, 21.4.1946, APO 185, sygn. 85, 31; SiRep OTA head S-PD, 21.5.1946, APO 185, sygn. 85, 32; SiRep OTA head S-PD, 21.6.1946, APO 185, sygn. 85, 33; Linek, *Polityka*, pp. 200–4, 222; Strauchold, *Autochtoni*, pp. 91–3.

of these teachers showed towards 'indigenous Polish' children. The teachers mainly chastised children for speaking German. But they sometimes also took offence at their pupils' use of the regional Polish dialect. In Opole District, state officials noted that the lack of 'native teachers' (*nauczyciele tubylcy*) meant that 'native' children had to be taught by 'non-native Polish repatriates' without 'proper interpreters', so that they struggled to keep up in lessons and results were 'poor'.[6]

Yet this can be looked at from the opposite perspective as well. The Polish teacher from Kraków, Jan Stadniczenko, who arrived in a village in Opole District around this time, recalled the difficulties he encountered teaching standard Polish to local children in the primary school he ran in the village:

> I very much enjoyed seeing the interest with which the children looked through their first Polish textbooks and how they tried to read them. But my fears were soon met because the children found it extremely difficult to read [these books] . . . The Polish textbooks . . . were not at all suited to teaching the Polish language in the circumstances existing in the recovered territories . . . [Teaching Polish to children] in western Upper Silesia [*Opolszczyzna*] was a real challenge. The toil involved in getting the children to learn and digest material from a few classes in a short time fell entirely on my shoulders as their teacher. And getting results from the classes depended on me finding a way through the textbook's labyrinth . . . The teaching programme [compiled by the state education authorities] envisaged taking just one school year [to teach the children standard Polish]. But my early experiences showed me that one year was just not going to be enough.[7]

Western Upper Silesia's Communist-led authorities, moreover, increasingly interpreted the speaking of German by 'indigenous Poles' not merely as a matter of convenience but as one of wilful subversion. The Regional Governor of Silesia Voivodship, Aleksander Zawadzki, had actually prohibited use of German in western Upper Silesia at the start 1945, before Polish officials had even begun arriving there. But it seems not to have been until 1946 that town and district administrations began to take action to punish people caught speaking German in public. In Opole town, for example, it was only in summer 1946 that officials launched a concerted action to 'eliminate' the 'German jabber' being spoken in streets and squares.[8]

[6] Special SiRep by OTA head S-PD, 13.11.1946, APO 185, sygn. 85, 41–2; Strauchold, *Autochtoni*, pp. 94–7, 99–100; Madajczyk, *Przyłączenie*, p. 197.
[7] Stadniczenko, 'Rok szkolny', p. 406.
[8] SiRep OTA head S-PD, 21.8.1946, APO 185, sygn. 85, 35; Linek, *Polityka*, pp. 217–22.

Yet it was not only public speaking of German which western Upper Silesia's authorities interpreted as subversive. Already in early summer 1945, Opole District's officials reported that particular members of the prewar population were 'stirring up' other locals, encouraging them to believe that Poland had 'no established borders and no Polish government'. Rumours were also being spread 'that the Germans will soon return and will then square accounts with those who feel so drawn to all things Polish'. These views were also transmitted in written form. At the end of 1945, a number of 'hostile leaflets written in German' were found in the village of Dąbrówka Dolna in Opole District, thought to have been produced by 'local verified citizens'. Throughout western Upper Silesia, the state authorities read into these kinds of activities the actions of highly organized and dangerous pro-German groups. Opole District's Chief Official referred repeatedly at this time to the involvement of 'secret organisations' in the production and distribution of 'hostile leaflets', claiming that '[t]alk of the existence of the secret organisation "Wehrwolf" is insistent'. In early 1946 two 'Wehrwolf' gangs were reportedly uncovered in Opole District, composed of both recognized Germans and 'verified people'. In June, the Chief Official remarked that '[t]he ever stronger and more impudent activities of secret and hostile elements instil in us fear'. References to the subversive 'German underground' movement and 'Wehrwolf' groups were very common among western Upper Silesia's state officials at this time. Yet it is not at all certain that they always believed in what they were reporting. Local state officials clearly exploited the concept of a subversive German underground movement, at least in part, to justify incarcerating 'Germans' in camps and to excuse any failings to their superiors.[9]

The region's state authorities found evidence of subversive attitudes among 'indigenous Poles' in their voting behaviour as well. On 30 June 1946, Poland's Communist-controlled government staged a statewide People's Referendum. It posed three simple questions to Poland's population (see Chapter 2). The third question asked voters whether they approved of Poland's new western borders. Characteristically, the fledgling Communist regime falsified the results for public consumption. But according to the

[9] SiRep ODA, 5.6.1945, APK 185/4, sygn. 22, 49–51; SiRep ODA S-PD, 29.5.1945, APK 185/4, sygn. 21, pp. 208–9; SiRep ODA, 9.8.1945, APK185/4, sygn. 27/1, 43–7; SiRep O Chief on the period 20.9.1945–20.10.1945, APO 178, sygn. 41, 5–8; SiRep O Chief on the period 20.11.1945–20.12.1945, APO 178, sygn. 41, 10–12; SiRep O Chief on the period 20.12.1945–20.1.1946, APO 178, sygn. 41, 13–15; SiRep O Chief on the period 20.1.1946–20.2.1946, APO 178, sygn. 41, 16–18; SiRep O Chief on the period 20.3.1946–20.4.1946, APO 178, sygn. 41, 20–23; SiRep O Chief on the period 20.4.1946–20.5.1946, APO 178, sygn. 41, 25–7; SiRep O Chief on the period 20.5.1946–20.6.1946, APO 178, sygn. 41, 30–2; Linek, *Polityka*, pp. 208–12.

real results, 63.4 per cent of voters from the rural part of Opole District answered 'no' to the third question, indicating that they did not approve of the new western border. Similar levels of 'no' voting were recorded elsewhere in western Upper Silesia. The authorities' attitude towards these voters was reflected in an article published in *Nowiny Opolskie* shortly after the referendum, which described the 'no' voters as 'Germans passing themselves off as Poles'.[10]

Two international events in 1946 were viewed by western Upper Silesia's state authorities as having given further impetus to 'hostile' activities in the region. On 5 March 1946, Winston Churchill delivered his 'Sinews of Peace' speech in Fulton, Missouri, in which he famously declared that 'an iron curtain has descended across the Continent'. Ignoring his own very substantial share of responsibility in the forced migrations and territorial changes which occurred at the end of the Second World War, he hypocritically declared that '[t]he Russian-dominated Polish government has been encouraged to make enormous and wrongful inroads upon Germany and mass expulsions of millions of Germans on a scale grievous and undreamed-of are now taking place'. This was followed by a speech in Stuttgart on 6 September 1946 by the United States' Secretary of State, James Byrnes. In his speech, Byrnes described the takeover of German territory by Poland in 1945 as a unilateral act by the Soviet Union which had not been authorized by the Western Allies at the Potsdam Conference. Both speeches were taken by western Upper Silesia's state authorities as having fuelled subversive attitudes among the region's 'indigenous population'. In Opole District, for example, the Chief Official spoke of a 'panic' which had gripped the district's population as a result of 'the speeches of various gentlemen from the West'. Byrnes' speech was even said to have inspired 'autochthons' in the village of Popielów in Opole District to pass a resolution calling for the abolition of the local Citizens' Militia and the sacking of the local commune mayor. Villagers had demanded that these posts be filled instead by 'autochthons' and that 'immigrants' from central Poland 'go back to where they came from'.[11]

[10] SiRep O Chief on the period 20.5.1946–20.6.1946, APO 178, sygn. 41, 30–2; Madajczyk, *Przyłączenie*, p. 211; Linek, *Polityka*, p. 209 including footnote 486; Siebel-Achenbach, *Lower Silesia*, pp. 215–16.

[11] Winston Churchill, 'Sinews of Peace', 5.3.1946, http://www.winstonchurchill.org/learn/speeches/speeches-of-winston-churchill/120-the-sinews-of-peace [last accessed 23.3.2013]; James Byrnes, 'Restatement of Policy on Germany', 6.9.1946, http://usa.usembassy.de/etexts/ga4-460906.htm [last accessed 23.3.2013]; Linek, *Polityka*, pp. 212–14; Siebel-Achenbach, *Lower Silesia*, pp. 252–3.

THE PENAL APPROACH

During 1947, western Upper Silesia's Communist-led authorities stepped up their efforts to bring an end to use of the German language by the local residents. Across the region, district and town administrations began to introduce fines for speaking German in public. In Opole District, it was the Citizens' Militia which, in many cases, was first to respond to these 'violations' by compiling 'penal reports' 'in the presence of witnesses'. Based on these 'penal reports', Opole District Administration's Penal-Administrative Department imposed fines on the culprits. It was not until early summer 1947 that Upper Silesia's Regional Governor, Aleksander Zawadzki, formally endorsed the use of fines to deter what he called 'sporadic' use of German. He spoke to the Chief Officials of Upper Silesia's districts at this time of growing signs of 'German arrogance' in the region, instructing them to treat speaking German as an 'act of provocation'. Opole District's Chief Official responded by ordering his officials to 'destroy the German language with utter ruthlessness'. It was, in fact, not only the Citizens' Militia and administrative authorities that took action in this period to suppress German speaking in the region; their efforts were supplemented by those of local branches of the much-feared Security Police.[12]

In August 1947, Zawadzki called for a radical intensification of the campaign against what he saw as a 'resurgence of German language and culture' in western Upper Silesia, demanding that action be taken against all 'manifestations of German language and culture' (*przejawy niemczyzny*). He stressed that 'the speaking of German in both public and private . . . must be viewed as proof of German ethnicity'. He declared that pro-German, anti-Polish statements and activities must no longer be tolerated. He placed a series of new sanctions at the disposal of the region's district and town administrations to bring an end to these things. Among the new potential punishments were fines of up to 30,000 złoty and the power to send people to a special labour camp in Gliwice. Yet Zawadzki did not believe that punishment by the state authorities would suffice. He therefore aimed his anti-German appeal at society as a whole, giving it wide publicity in the official press.[13] Western Upper Silesia's district and town administrations sought to respond to Zawadzki's appeal by mobilizing local party activists and Communist-led social organizations in late summer and early

[12] SiRep O Chief on the period 20.5.1947–20.6.1947, APO 178, sygn. 42, 27–8; SiRep ODA S-PD, 12.8.1947, APO 178, sygn. 62, 21–3; Linek, *Polityka*, pp. 217–18, 247, 253–4.

[13] Linek, *Polityka*, pp. 261–4.

autumn 1947. In Opole District, for example, the Chief Official held several meetings with local commune mayors, the Citizens' Militia and local state officials to discuss the 'campaign against manifestations of German language and culture' at this time. He also claimed to the Regional Administration in Katowice that he was endeavouring to get political parties, official youth organizations and schools fully engaged in this campaign.[14]

Yet officials throughout western Upper Silesia were, by this time, fully aware that stamping out German speaking and 'hostile' attitudes entirely was going to be an uphill struggle. One of Opole District's officials gave a rather disheartening assessment of the situation in late summer 1947:

> The re-Polonization of the district has been held back significantly. Heavy fines for using German have not had the desired effect and in some villages, such as Królewska Nowa Wieś and Zagwiździe, there is now more German being spoken than when [Polish] authorities took up administration there. The reason for this is the arrival of large numbers of local youth from abroad [returning from Germany] who are unable to speak Polish or who find it more comfortable to use German.[15]

It was not just the apparent rise in speaking German which Opole District's officials connected with the return of local people from Germany. They also claimed that most of 'the local youth' arriving from Germany exhibited behaviour which was 'directly hostile to Poland'. Throughout western Upper Silesia, state officials made similar claims about these returning prewar residents. In fact, the region's officials were still seeing 'hostile' activities everywhere. In Opole District, for example, officials treated very seriously the discovery of German graffiti painted on an indoor wall at a school in Krapkowice, in summer 1947, containing the statement '*Polen raus nach Polen, hier ist Deutschland*' (Poles go back to Poland, this is Germany). Around the same time, 'unknown culprits' broke into a nursery school in Gosławice in Opole District, robbing it and tearing down the Polish state emblem from one of the walls, after which they 'performed physiological activities on it'. Simple acts of teenage vandalism of this sort tended to be presented by state officials throughout western Upper Silesia as sinister, hostile and linked to a dangerous pro-German underground movement.[16]

'Hostile rumours', too, were still regarded as a serious problem in western Upper Silesia. In Opole District, for example, one official noted at the end

[14] Rep on the 're-Polonization action' by ODA S-PD, 21.4.1948, APO 178, sygn. 65, 17–21; CuRep ODA S-PD, 11.12.1947, APK 185/4, sygn. 51, 69–69a; Linek, *Polityka*, pp. 265–6.

[15] SiRep ODA S-PD, 12.8.1947, APO 178, sygn. 62, 21–3.

[16] SiRep ODA S-PD, 6.6.1947, APO 178, sygn. 62, 16–18; Linek, *Polityka*, pp. 247, 261–4, 306, 315.

of 1947 that '[a] certain unaware section of Polish society inadvertently collaborates with German propagandists by prophesying the imminent outbreak of war and border changes'. These 'uncertainties', he believed, were exacerbated by the 'deliberations' going on in London. By this he must have meant the meeting of the Council of Foreign Ministers which took place in London at this time. What is ironic about this is that this diplomatic meeting should have reduced uncertainties about Poland's western frontiers rather than exacerbated them. Indeed, it was a discussion at the meeting on 27 November 1947 which definitively ended American and British hopes that they might convince the Soviets to accept a revision of the territorial changes which had taken place in Poland at the end of the war.[17]

Despite the difficulties they were encountering, western Upper Silesia's Communist-controlled authorities still seemed, at this time, to have faith in the idea that the region's 'indigenous Poles' could, with time, be 're-Polonized'. Across the region, the state authorities were still seeking to extend the scope and reach of the 're-Polonization action' in 1947. In Opole town, for example, a new 'gymnasium for indigenous youth' was opened in that year with the aim of providing more 're-Polonization courses' for young adults. The town's officials hoped that this would help to tackle the problem that many young 'autochthons' wanted to migrate to Germany simply because their Polish was not good enough for them to attain work in the region. The number of 're-Polonization courses' run in western Upper Silesia was still on the increase at this time. In Opole District, for example, new 're-Polonization courses' were launched in the district's larger workplaces in 1947. A total of 48 're-Polonization courses' were provided in the district in the academic year 1946–7, attended by 2,035 students. The following academic year, 72 're-Polonization courses' were run in Opole District, attended by 3,320 students. Five of the courses were run in Opole town, but the rest in the district's villages.[18]

Our teacher from Kraków, Jan Stadniczenko, described his experience of setting up a 're-Polonization course' in one of Opole District's villages at this time:

> Having recovered from illness, I started a re-Polonization course for adults in the village. The villagers were going to learn Polish and I would receive an extra 3000 [złoty from the state education authorities]. Attendance was quite high,

[17] CuRep ODA S-PD, 11.12.1947, APK 185/4, sygn. 51, 69–69a; Siebel-Achenbach, *Lower Silesia*, p. 264.

[18] SiRep OTA head S-PD, 21.2.1947, APO 185, sygn. 85, 50; CuRep ODA S-PD, 11.12.1947, APK 185/4, sygn. 51, 69–69a; Rep on the 're-Polonization action' by ODA S-PD, 21.4.1948, APO 178, sygn. 65, 17–21; Madajczyk, *Przyłączenie*, p. 196; Strauchold, *Autochtoni*, pp. 179–85.

but with a significant preponderance of girls. I was very nervous at first because I was finally coming into direct contact with the generation who had emerged from the care of [the Nazi girls' organization] the *Bund Deutscher Mädel.* On the other hand, the girls were pretty, shapely and very sociable . . . I was often forced to explain the texts we were reading in German. But I felt this was the easiest way of consolidating the material we were going through . . . Perhaps my course brought something new to the dull and monotonous life of this small village on the Odra river . . . Over time attendance of the re-Polonization course declined before stabilizing towards the end of it. Those who dropped out were mainly people who had sought diversion from the dullness of everyday life but did not end up finding it on the course . . . Around 30–40 percent were lost along the way. I also noticed as soon as the course started that I could not find, among the people who had registered for the course, the relatives of children who showed a lack of familiarity with our language at the village school . . . A few of the participants were individuals who had gained work in offices and institutions outside the village as white collar workers. Without a doubt, the course was helpful for them. The course also fulfilled its function because a significant proportion of the young villagers were able to converse freely in Polish after attending it.[19]

Yet western Upper Silesia's state officials held firm to the belief that 're-Polonization' would not be achieved through 're-Polonization courses' alone. In Opole District, for example, one official remarked at this time that young local people would benefit from being placed, at their workplaces, among 'individuals who have come here from deep inside Poland', because they usually had no acquaintances able to speak 'literary Polish'. Opole District's Chief Official instructed his officials in summer 1947 'to draw [the indigenous Poles] into work, bring them into relationships, induce them to use correct Polish and treat them in such a way that they feel like our brothers'. Similarly, one official stressed, in early 1948, that the district's authorities understood the term 're-Polonization' in the 'broadest sense', applying it 'to every sphere of life'. There were now 25 community centres located in villages throughout the rural part of the district and these, according to this official, were playing a central role in the 're-Polonization process'. A new radio station, *Polskie Radio Wrocław*, also contributed to the process by broadcasting 'radio re-Polonization courses' to western Upper Silesia.[20]

Despite the efforts western Upper Silesia's Communist-controlled authorities were therefore still putting into the 're-Polonization' of the

[19] Stadniczenko, 'Rok szkolny', pp. 409, 412, 425–6.

[20] SiRep OTA head S-PD, 21.4.1947, APO 185, sygn. 85, 52; SiRep O Chief on the period 21.5.1947–20.6.1947, APO 178, sygn. 42, 27–8; CuRep ODA S-PD, 11.12.1947, APK 185/4, sygn. 51, 69–69a; CuRep ODA S-PD, 8.1.1948, APK 185/4, sygn. 52, 39–40; Rep on the 're-Polonization action' by ODA S-PD, 21.4.1948, APO 178, sygn. 65, 17–21; Strauchold, *Autochtoni*, pp. 175, 179–88.

prewar population, they had not yet registered any letup in the amount of German being spoken in the region. Officials throughout the region were constantly coming across people speaking German in public. Yet only small numbers were actually punished by the state administrative authorities for this. In Opole District, for example, the Citizens' Militia submitted a total of only 155 'penal reports' to Opole District Administration between 1 January and 31 July 1948, only 16 of which had, by that time, resulted in fines, amounting to 50,500 złoty altogether. By 1948, the problem of German speaking was apparently starting to take on another more sinister feature: '[B]y becoming intimate with the local population, the children of immigrants, and sometimes even [adult] repatriates, are beginning to acquire the German language or particular [German] expressions. This will be difficult to root out in the future.' Cases were even reported to the district's officials of Polish settlers conversing with the local population in German at work. Officials viewed this as very damaging to the process of 're-Polonizing' locals. The settlers who did this were motivated 'purely by vanity'. They would receive 'stern reprimands' initially and then fines if they continued to speak German.[21]

One of Opole District's officials offered the opinion at this time that prewar residents spoke German 'more out of convenience than any hostile goals' and the problem would best be solved through 're-Polonization courses' rather than fines. But most of the rest of western Upper Silesia's officials were clearly losing faith in the 're-Polonization courses' by summer 1948. As state officials across the region admitted, any success the 're-Polonization courses' had so far enjoyed applied only to the younger generation. Trying to put a positive spin on this, one of Opole District's officials reported in summer 1948 that '[t]he [indigenous] youth are now using the Polish language, speaking it ever better and increasingly fluently. One meets more and more of them who speak Polish correctly', and they 'incline towards the current reality [i.e., the Communist system] increasingly readily'. In contrast, however, 'older society' only engaged with 're-Polonization' 'perfunctorily and unwillingly', because they were still 'firmly gripped' by the 'German language' and still strongly exhibited 'the influences of Germanism'.[22]

[21] Rep on the 're-Polonization action' by ODA S-PD, 21.4.1948, APO 178, sygn. 65, 17–21; CuRep ODA S-PD, 2.3.1948, APO 178, sygn. 65, 7–8; Rep on the first two quarters of 1948 by ODA S-PD, undated, APO 178, sygn. 65, 50–2; Rep on the liquidation of traces of German language and culture by ODA S-PD, 31.7.1948, APO 178, sygn. 113, 64–5; Linek, *Polityka*, pp. 300–10.

[22] CuRep ODA S-PD, 4.8.1948, APO 178, sygn. 65, 54–5; CuRep ODA S-PD, 4.9.1948, APO 178, sygn. 65, 56–7; CuRep ODA S-PD, 2.3.1948, APO 178, sygn. 65, 7–8; Rep on the 're-Polonization action' by ODA S-PD, 21.4.1948, APO 178, sygn. 65, 17–21; Strauchold, *Autochtoni*, pp. 174, 177–87.

Nor did western Upper Silesia's officials feel that 'hostile attitudes' among prewar residents were diminishing. Yet rather than seeking out the underlying causes of these sentiments, the region's officials generally sought to explain them away as the product of malevolent external influences. After the resumption of postal contact between western Upper Silesia and Allied-occupied Germany in 1946, the letters local people received from relatives and acquaintances living in Germany were often cited by western Upper Silesia's state officials as a major source of subversive ideas among the locals. Opole District's officials, for example, reported in June 1948 that '[a] lot of verified families have relatives and acquaintances in Germany and, through the letters they exchange, anti-Polish propaganda is filtering through'. Many of the letters the region's prewar residents received from Germany in the late 1940s probably did contain expressions of anti-Polish sentiment. But the state authorities were no doubt equally disturbed by the simple fact that the letters were written in German by people who had been classified as ethnic Poles.[23]

Western Upper Silesia's officials also tended to believe that signs of weakness on their part contributed to subversive attitudes among local residents. In 1948, for example, a number of Opole District's residents were sent to a special camp in Gliwice for deportation to Germany, but were then sent back to the district by officials at the camp who did not think they should be deported (see Chapter 7). Opole District's officials claimed that '[p]ro-German feelings had strengthened and the use of the German language had increased the moment these Germans . . . had been released from the camp in Gliwice'.[24]

Western Upper Silesia's Communist-controlled authorities also continued to believe that international events exacerbated the 'hostile' attitudes of many prewar residents. In Opole District, for example, officials spoke repeatedly in late 1948 and early 1949 of the subversive ideas feeding off the 'tense international situation' caused by the Berlin blockade and airlift. '[T]he tale about the third war is particularly well cultivated in the minds of the pro-German locals – and there are a large number of them', one official wrote at this time. 'False rumours about an imminent war' were said to be rife, as was talk of new border changes. These subversive ideas had reportedly sown great anxiety within broad swaths of the district's population, causing some people to start buying up stocks of soap, flour,

[23] CuRep ODA S-PD, 1.6.1948, APO 178, sygn. 65, 25–6; Special Rep by ODA S-PD, 19.3.1949, APO 178, sygn. 64, 16–17; Linek, *Polityka*, pp. 214–16, 313–14.

[24] CuRep ODA S-PD, 7.4.1948, APO 178, sygn. 65, 11–12; Linek, *Polityka*, pp. 256–7; Nowak, *Obozy*, pp. 174–8.

sugar and other basic provisions in preparation for the coming war. The district's officials believed that these 'hostile and subversive' ideas would only cease when the international situation had been definitively 'settled' by a peace treaty signed with a 'democratic German government'.[25]

Western Upper Silesia's state authorities steadily lost interest in the 're-Polonization action' in 1948–9, as new Stalinist ideological imperatives gained ascendancy throughout Poland. Nevertheless, they continued to implement the action through to the end of the decade. In Opole District, for example, new 're-Polonization courses' were set up in villages which had previously not had them during the academic year of 1948–9. So too were new libraries. More and more 'native youth' (*młodzież rodzima*) in the district were also said to be finally attending secondary school.[26] Towards the end of 1949, an official from Opole District Administration claimed that the four years of 're-Polonization' – which he emphasized had been a truly multifaceted campaign involving 're-Polonization courses', schools, the district's network of libraries, community centres and the presence of the settler population – had achieved 'satisfactory results'. It was true, he went on, that the 'older generation' of local people 'often preserve influences from German language and culture and are less willing and less capable of accepting Polish culture' than the 'native youth'. But the latter section of local society had been educated in a 'thoroughly Polish spirit', each becoming 'a new person in the revolutionary spirit, in the spirit of progress and socialism'.[27] Yet these statements were clearly aimed just as much at demonstrating this official's political and ideological reliability to his superiors in Poland's party-state hierarchy as they were at providing an accurate description of the outcome of the 're-Polonization action' in western Upper Silesia.

The reality was quite different. Throughout the region, only a minority of the 'verified' locals had attended 're-Polonization courses' since autumn 1945. Even individuals whom the authorities had specifically targeted with pressure to attend the courses had often refused. Opole District's officials, for example, noted in 1949 that 'there are, of course, still people who refuse

[25] Rep on the first half of 1948 by ODA S-PD, early July 1948, APO 178, sygn. 65, 50–2; Special Rep by ODA S-PD, 19.3.1949, APO 178, sygn. 64, 16–17; Rep by ODA S-PD, 8.3.1949, APO 178, sygn. 64, 14; CuRep ODA S-PD, 4.8.1948, APO 178, sygn. 65, 54–5; SiRep the municipal mayor of Krapkowice, 2.10.1948, APO 178, sygn. 66, 156; CuRep ODA S-PD, 5.11.1948, APO 178, sygn. 65, 63–5; Linek, *Polityka*, pp. 299, 307.

[26] CuRep ODA S-PD, 5.11.1948, APO 178, sygn. 65, 63–5; Rep by ODA S-PD, 7.1.1949, APO 178, sygn. 63, 9–10; CuRep ODA S-PD, 24.1.1949, APO 178, sygn. 64, 12–13; Strauchold, *Autochtoni*, pp. 184–91.

[27] Rep by ODA S-PD, 25.11.1949, APO 178, sygn. 64, 43.

to take part in the re-Polonization courses despite repeated summonses by school directors'. More generally, only the most impressionable section of western Upper Silesia's prewar population – children and teenagers – had exhibited any progress in learning how to speak and write standard Polish. The German language was very widely spoken among the region's inhabitants. And even the small fraction of the local population who had engaged in pro-Polish activism before 1945 had generally lost their enthusiasm for the Polish nation by the end of the 1940s.[28]

One of Opole District's officials acknowledged the extent of the problem very candidly in 1949:

There are very few families among the local population who do not teach their children German. This is connected to rumours about the return of the Germans to the Western Territories [i.e., Germany's re-incorporation of these territories]. The German language and German radio can still be heard in homes. Fighting this phenomenon is simply not possible, not only because of the insufficient number of Security Police in the district but also because this is a mass phenomenon . . . It is known that these people once used Polish when the Polish language was prohibited, and now, conversely, despite the fact that they are Poles and they can speak Polish, they speak German. Quite clearly, that is the nature of the "autochthons" [sic]. Only time can change it!'[29]

Underpinning the failure of the 're-Polonization action' across western Upper Silesia was a complete misapprehension of local cultural identity on the part of the region's Polish state authorities, which we discussed in Chapter 6. Many of the actions and attitudes which state officials interpreted as 'subversive' and 'hostile' towards Poland and Poles were really just a product of feelings of local solidarity and local cultural distinctiveness. For example, in October 1945, Opole District's officials construed as 'pro-German' the fact that locals were 'deliberately hiding and concealing' large numbers of 'Germans' to prevent them from being evicted from their homes and interned in camps. But the locals' real motivation was clearly the desire to protect other locals who were their neighbours, friends or relatives. Local solidarity manifested itself in other ways too. Officials complained in December 1946 that the district's prewar residents who had been appointed as village and commune mayors at the end of the war tended to see the purpose of their role as 'guarding the interests of the indigenous population'.[30] This claim was supported by the recollections of

[28] Rep by ODA S-PD, 25.11.1949, APO 178, sygn. 64, 43; Rep by ODA S-PD, 7.1.1949, APO 178, sygn. 63, 9–10; Ossowski, 'Zagadnienia', pp. 288–9; Linek, *Polityka*, p. 318.

[29] Special Rep by the ODA head S-PD, 19.3.1949, APO 178, sygn. 64, 16–17.

[30] SiRep O Chief on the period 20.9.1945–20.10.1945, APO178, sygn.41, 5–8; SiRep ODA S-PD, 4.12.1946, APO 178, sygn. B15, 1–1a; SiRep ODA S-PD, 3.3.1947, APO 178, sygn. 62, 4–6.

a former resident of the village of Tauentzien/Okoły in Opole District, Georg S., who remembered being told in June 1946 by the postwar village mayor – a prewar resident of the village who had been given his post on the grounds that he could speak the local Polish dialect – that he had only accepted the post because it enabled him to protect the interests of other long-term inhabitants of the village. Other witnesses made similar claims.[31]

These feelings of local solidarity and local cultural distinctiveness had existed long before the Communist-controlled Polish authorities arrived in western Upper Silesia in spring 1945. But it is clear that these sentiments were strengthened, not diminished, by events in western Upper Silesia from spring 1945 onwards. As we discussed in Chapter 7, local people were antagonized and intimidated by the wave of violence and robbery they suffered at the hands of Polish looters and corrupt officials in spring and summer 1945. They were also alienated by the hostile attitudes which many ordinary Polish settlers exhibited towards them – resulting from conflicts over property, perceptions of cultural foreignness and difficulties in understanding very different dialects of Polish. Polish settlers often referred to the prewar residents by their derogatory term for Germans: 'szwaby'. Correspondingly, the locals often claimed that the settlers from the ceded eastern territories were speaking not Polish but Ukrainian or Russian – a claim which the Polish sociologist Stanisław Ossowski also heard when visiting the region in August 1945. At the same time, the locals' feelings of alienation were strongly exacerbated by the Polish state authorities' aggressive nationalist policies towards them – especially the expulsion of local 'Germans' and the policy of pressuring those not expelled to 're-Polonize' by learning standard Polish and by adopting mainstream Polish cultural norms.[32]

The feelings of antipathy towards Poland and towards Polish society and culture among local people manifested themselves in two broad ways. First, as Stanisław Ossowski witnessed in late summer 1945, the feelings of distance and separation which many local people had previously felt towards 'Germans' and towards viewing themselves as 'Germans' started to disappear. In this respect, the Polish state authorities may very well have

[31] WR, Georg S., Tauentzien (Okoły), undated, BOD 1, 243, 349–51; WR, Georg K., Hinterwasser (Zawada), 24.10.1957, BOD 1, 243, 174–81; WR, Julius T., Proskau (Prószków), 14.4.1956, BOD 1, 243, 289–93.

[32] SiRep OTA head S-PD, 21.11.1946, APO 185, sygn. 85, 43; Ossowski, 'Zagadnienia', pp. 288–90; Linek, *Polityka*, pp. 270–2, 222, 201; Ther, 'Die einheimische Bevölkerung', pp. 424, 427–9, 431–7; Strauchold, *Autochtoni*, pp. 169–78.

been correct that some of the cases of German being spoken in public which they witnessed, were done out of defiance rather than out of necessity or convenience.[33] Second, local people's sense that their collective identity was rooted in the particular region, town or village in which they lived and not in either the German or Polish nation appeared to intensify. As one official from Opole District Administration remarked in 1948, '[l]ocal people, without meaning to, often stress that they are not Poles but Silesians. They use the term "Pole" only to describe the immigrant population . . . So they feel and they emphasize their separate identity'. He described this as 'local patriotism' (*patriotyzm dzielnicowy*) and commented that the locals often declared that they would 'never marry a Pole'.[34] The director of the new State Grammar School for Adults, opened in Opole town in 1947, spoke in similar terms of the 'somewhat too well developed feeling of Silesian identity among the native youth'.[35] Opole District's officials also noted at this time that the prewar population of the district had 'closed in on itself' and 'fenced itself off' from the rest of society. Thus, whereas Polish settlers participated readily in public events and social activities, the locals generally avoided them. Likewise, it was only really the settlers who were willing to join political parties. The same was reported by local state officials across western Upper Silesia at this time.[36]

Precisely the same strategies of seeking refuge in the local and in the private had been witnessed in western Upper Silesia during the Nazi period as a response to similarly aggressive nationalist policies on the part of the Nazi German authorities. Just as Nazi German policies before 1945 had failed dismally to 're-Germanize' the dialect-speaking population of western Upper Silesia, so the postwar Polish policies of 'verification' and 're-Polonization' had precisely the opposite effect to the one intended. As the former Deputy Regional Governor of Upper Silesia, Arkadiusz Bożek – himself a native of Upper Silesia – remarked in 1950: 'The Germans must now be laughing at us because what they failed to accomplish in seven centuries . . . we will achieve in just seven years, the eradication of Polishness in these territories right down to the roots'.[37]

[33] Linek, *Polityka*, pp. 270–2, 222, 201; Ossowski, 'Zagadnienia', p. 290.

[34] CuRep ODA S-PD, 5.11.1948, APO 178, sygn. 65, 63–5; Ossowski, 'Zagadnienia', p. 298.

[35] Cited in Strauchold, *Autochtoni*, pp. 182–3.

[36] CuRep ODA S-PD, 7.4.1948, APO 178, sygn. 65, 11–12; CuRep ODA S-PD, 6.5.1948, APO 178, sygn. 65, 23–4; Rep by ODA S-PD on the first half of 1948, early July 1948, APO 178, sygn. 65, 50–2; CuRep ODA S-PD, 4.8.1948, APO 178, sygn. 65, 54–5; CuRep ODA S-PD, 4.9.1948, APO 178, sygn. 65, 56–7; Ther, 'Die einheimische Bevölkerung', pp. 431–7.

[37] Cited in Ther, 'Die einheimische Bevölkerung', p. 433. See ibid., pp. 417–20, for Nazi German policies in Upper Silesia.

NAMES

When the new Communist-led Polish authorities of western Upper Silesia first arrived in the region in spring 1945, it was not only the local dialect, linguistic habits and problematic attitudes of the region's 'indigenous Poles' which seemed to signal that they were not unequivocally Polish. Their names did too. For a start, the vast majority of local people possessed forenames which sounded typically German to the region's new state officials from central Poland: names such as Gustav, Friedrich, Günther, Dorothea and Emilie. But the surnames of many local people also alarmed these officials – because a large proportion of the local population had surnames which sounded just as German as their forenames; names such as Schönfelder, Becker, Engler or Leibner. Arriving from central Poland, the officials assumed that these people had almost all Germanized their surnames in the Nazi period. And it was true that some locals had replaced their surnames with typically German ones after 1933, often in response to coercive pressure from the Nazi German authorities. But this was actually only the case with a small fraction of the locals. Most locals with German-sounding surnames were from families which had possessed these names since well before the Nazi period.

Less of a problem for Polish officials – though, as we shall see, by no means viewed by them as entirely unproblematic – was the fact that the majority of the prewar inhabitants of western Upper Silesia had surnames which sounded more Polish than German but nevertheless did not seem entirely Polish. These were surnames typical of the region of western Upper Silesia, names such as Kowol, Nowok, Kamuzela, Dambowy and Poliwoda. They differed from their Polish equivalents, Kowal, Nowak, Kamizela and Dębowy, in both spelling and sound and were often viewed by Polish officials from central Poland as merely misspelled Polish surnames.[38] Our teacher from Kraków, Jan Stadniczenko, was just as baffled as the officials from the region's state administrative authorities by the names of local people. He started grappling with the issue of local surnames almost as soon as he arrived in a remote village in Opole District to run the village school:

[I visited the village's graveyard the day after my arrival and] read from the gravestones surnames such as Dombietz, Adamietz, Kalinsky, Wolnik and Czop . . . Of course there were also names like Schönfelder and Leibner but the other surnames

[38] Linek, *Polityka*, pp. 29–31, 223–4, 226–8, 230–32, 321, 329–32; Ther, 'Die einheimische Bevölkerung', p. 417; Stadniczenko, 'Rok szkolny', pp. 402–3.

were very much in the majority and looked much more familiar and Polish [*swojsko*]. Well, I thought to myself, it can't be so bad in this village, the relatives of Wolnik and Czop are sure to speak Polish . . . [That evening after supper at a villager's house] the neighbours came round with their small son Peter. Peter greeted me like he knew me and very soon started calling me 'teacher, sir' [*pan ucíciel*] or more often *Onkel Lehrer*. These neighbours had the surname Schönfelder and their command of Polish was worse than poor, a fact which I linked to their surname.[39]

Western Upper Silesia's state authorities do not seem to have taken quite the same view as Jan Stadniczenko. Having a German-sounding surname was not an obstacle to being 'verified' as an ethnic Pole in the region. Moreover, unlike our teacher from Kraków, the authorities did not view the typically Silesian surnames as entirely unproblematic, as we shall see in the following.

Western Upper Silesia's authorities recognized from the outset that some sort of name-changing campaign would have to take place. But it took quite some time for them to introduce name changing into the broader 're-Polonization action'. A key reason for this was the fact that there was actually no legal basis for changing the personal names of individuals who did not have Polish citizenship. As discussed in Chapter 6, it only became possible for 'verified Poles' living in Poland's new territories to attain Polish citizenship from April 1946 onwards. This, in turn, was what finally made it possible for them to change their names. Upper Silesia's Regional Governor, Aleksander Zawadzki, attempted to initiate a name-changing campaign in western Upper Silesia in late spring 1946. There was actually something of a precedent for him to draw on. In the 1920s and 1930s, the Polish authorities of eastern Upper Silesia – the part of Upper Silesia which had fallen to Poland in 1922 – had succeeded in persuading a considerable number of people to Polonize their surnames. But Zawadzki proved unable to mobilize western Upper Silesia's local state officials into action in the course of 1946. Very few residents of Opole District and the rest of western Upper Silesia therefore submitted name-change applications during that year.[40]

The situation changed in 1947. Perhaps this resulted, in part, from a change of attitude from local state officials towards the name-changing campaign. For example, an official from Opole Town Administration called for a major 'campaign to de-Germanize surnames' in early 1947, stating that '[t]he active spirit of German language and culture lives on

[39] Stadniczenko, 'Rok szkolny', pp. 402–3.

[40] Linek, *Polityka*, pp. 31–2, 224–35; Rep on the liquidation of the traces of German language and culture by ODA S-PD, 31.7.1948, APO 178, sygn. 113, 64–5.

in the huge mass of foreign names'.[41] The same view was clearly held by Aleksander Zawadzki, because in summer 1947 he instigated a large-scale name-changing campaign across the region in conjunction with his intensification of the campaign against 'German language and culture', which we discussed previously. In August 1947, Zawadzki relaunched the name-changing campaign by instructing the region's officials that 'surnames and first names must be unwaveringly Polonized'.[42] Opole District Administration responded within days by ordering all registry offices in Opole District to cease entering forenames and surnames 'which sound German' into their registers and to encourage local people 'in an uncompromising fashion' to submit applications 'to replace German surnames and first names with Polish ones'. It left open what 'uncompromising methods' registry officials should employ, but suggested that they might wish to exploit the fact that they conducted marriages for local people to deliver 'encouragement'.[43]

At the start of September, Zawadzki intervened to facilitate the process by abolishing the fees charged to people for changing their names and doing away with the obligation people were under to announce their name changes publicly. Zawadzki told western Upper Silesia's state officials at this time that if local people were proving reluctant to change their names, they should 'make every effort to impel them to start proceedings and, if they refused, to report this to the relevant District Administration or Town President'.[44] In Opole District, the District Administration ordered local commune mayors in October 1947 to develop 'propaganda' in conjunction with the regime-controlled social organizations, political parties, teachers and village mayors aimed at 'encouraging and inducing [local people] to replace their German first names and surnames with Polish ones'.[45]

Zawadzki was particularly anxious to ensure that state officials did not themselves have German names. He reminded the region's Town Presidents and District Chief Officials in October 1947 that their officials should be setting an example to the rest of the population. He stressed that very soon not a single official should have a German first name or surname or a 'surname with offending spelling'. By the latter he clearly meant typically Silesian surnames.[46] Opole District's Chief Official responded at

[41] SiRep OTA head S-PD, 21.1.1947, APO 185, sygn. 85, 48; SiRep OTA head S-PD, 21.2.1947, APO 185, sygn. 85, 50.
[42] Linek, *Polityka*, pp. 233–5, 320.
[43] Rep on the 're-Polonization action' by ODA S-PD, 21.4.1948, APO 178, sygn. 65, 17–21; Linek, *Polityka*, pp. 264, 320.
[44] Linek, *Polityka*, p. 321.
[45] Rep on the 're-Polonization action' by ODA S-PD, 21.4.1948, APO 178, sygn. 65, 17–21.
[46] Linek, *Polityka*, pp. 326–7.

the end of October by issuing an instruction to all employees of the District Administration that any of them who had a German surname or forename must immediately submit an application to replace it with a Polish one.[47]

The region's state authorities were equally concerned about the number of children in the region who had German names. In Opole town, for example, special 'information meetings' were held in two secondary schools at the end of October 1947 to inform parents and caregivers about the need to replace children's German surnames with Polish ones. The prominent interwar Upper Silesian pro-Polish activist, Jan Wawrzynek, gave speeches at these meetings. They were obviously regarded by the Communists as high in propaganda value, because on 4 November an article about them appeared in the Communist-controlled Katowice newspaper *Dziennik Zachodni* (Western Daily).[48]

These and similar actions implemented elsewhere in western Upper Silesia greatly increased the number of name-change applications the state authorities received across the region. In Opole District, for example, the number of applications submitted by locals increased by many times after August 1947. The district's officials declared towards the end of that year that '[t]he matter of changing surnames and Polonizing first names is currently the top issue in the field of re-Polonization'.[49] But despite Zawadzki's best efforts to facilitate the process, the procedure remained cumbersome and officials took quite a while to process each application. This meant that officials could not execute the name changes as fast as the name-change applications flowed in. In Opole District, most applications were processed by the district's own officials, but some, perhaps trickier cases had to be sent on to Upper Silesia's Regional Administration in Katowice for examination. This was probably the procedure followed throughout western Upper Silesia.[50]

Zawadzki was keen to ensure not only that as many of western Upper Silesia's inhabitants as possible altered their personal names, but also that they received the right names. With regard to forenames, the Regional Administration in Katowice therefore provided lists of approved names to assist officials in the region's localities. At the end of 1947 it then revised these lists with the help of the Silesian Institute (*Instytut Śląski*) in Katowice. There were four such lists. The first list contained 'recommended'

[47] Rep on the 're-Polonization action' by ODA S-PD, 21.4.1948, APO 178, sygn. 65, 17–21.
[48] Rep on the 're-Polonization action' by ODA S-PD, 21.4.1948, APO 178, sygn. 65, 17–21; Linek, *Polityka*, p. 337.
[49] CuRep ODA S-PD, 11.12.1947, APK 185/4, sygn. 51, 69–69a; Linek, *Polityka*, pp. 332–3.
[50] CuRep ODA S-PD, 8.1.1948, APK 185/4, sygn. 52, 39–40; Linek, *Polityka*, pp. 320, 334.

forenames, the names most widely given to children in Poland. The second contained 'acceptable' first names, only infrequently given to children in Poland. The third consisted of 'Slavic' forenames, also designated as acceptable. The fourth list contained names most widely given to children in Germany. Registry office officials were prohibited from entering names from this fourth list in their births register. They were also instructed to encourage people possessing them to change them.[51] There do not seem to have been similar lists of approved surnames. But Upper Silesia's Regional Administration did offer some guidance: 'Although the Regional Administration places no obstacles in the way of individuals wishing to take on native Silesian surnames like Nowok, Kowol etc., we are of the opinion that nothing stands in the way of people taking names which sound correct and grammatical, like Kowal and Nowak'.[52] Opole District Administration's officials themselves referred to this as 'adjusting corrupted spellings to fit with Polish spelling rules'.[53]

During 1948, western Upper Silesia's Communist-controlled authorities steadily stepped up the pressure on the region's population to submit name-change applications. Even Polish settlers who had German-sounding surnames started to come under pressure to change them. Yet Zawadzki stressed that those settlers who shared surnames with individuals who had made important contributions to Poland's national history and culture should feel no obligation to change them. In Opole District, Polish settlers with German-sounding surnames not surprisingly proved 'very reluctant' to change them.[54]

The principal target of the name-changing campaign, the prewar residents of western Upper Silesia, came under growing pressure to change their names in 1948. In Opole District, for example, the District Administration ruled in March 1948 that people applying for 'verification' as ethnic Poles who had German forenames or surnames would not receive a 'temporary certificate of Polish nationality' until they submitted a name-change application.[55] But to the annoyance of Opole District's officials, this did not have the desired effect. They did not know exactly why this was, but speculated that it was because many locals feared the consequences of Polonizing their names were western Upper Silesia later to be reincorporated

[51] Linek, *Polityka*, pp. 329–30. [52] Cited by Linek, *Polityka*, p. 332.

[53] CuRep ODA S-PD, 8.1.1948, APK 185/4, sygn. 52, 39–40.

[54] Linek, *Polityka*, p. 330; Rep on the 're-Polonization action' by ODA S-PD, 21.4.1948, APO 178, sygn. 65, 17–21.

[55] CuRep ODA S-PD, 2.3.1948, APO 178, sygn. 65, 7–8; CuRep ODA S-PD, 7.4.1948, APO 178, sygn. 65, 11–12; Linek, *Polityka*, pp. 319, 324, 332–4.

into Germany. One of the district's officials remarked around this time, 'Although receiving a certificate of Polish nationality has been made conditional upon [submitting a name-change application] these people prefer to forgo the certificates altogether rather than change their surnames.'[56] Opole District's local commune administrations continued this policy of attempting to 'force' name changes after they took over from the District Administration the task of issuing 'temporary certificates of Polish nationality' midway through 1948 (see Chapter 6).[57] Opole District Administration was even willing to intervene at people's workplaces in order to bring about a name change or to punish the lack of one. For example, it sent a note to the state sawmill in Murów around this time demanding that a particular worker be fired because he had not submitted an application to change his name.[58]

Despite such tactics, Opole District Administration reported in March 1949 that people who had already submitted name-change applications were actually starting to retract them, 'declaring in writing' that they now wished to retain their German names. But officials had already devised a new method for dealing with such cases – and with instances of people refusing altogether to submit applications. It sent them repeated summonses to appear at the premises of Opole District Administration, issuing a new one every few days until they got so fed up with coming there that they either submitted an application or reversed their retraction. If, however, they failed to respond to one of the summonses, this became a 'pretext' for an 'administrative penalty'. As one of the district's officials reported with a hint of smugness, 'This system has proven effective in practice'.[59]

Across western Upper Silesia, local state officials employed similar methods, finally prompting the Ministry of Public Administration in Warsaw to send a letter to Upper Silesia's Regional Administration in Katowice in March 1949 asserting that no decrees or ministerial orders had permitted officials to use compulsion in name changing. Yet it took until November 1949 before Upper Silesia's Regional Administration finally ordered the region's district and town administrations to cease applying 'administrative pressure' to people and to carry out only voluntary name changes.[60]

How many people in western Upper Silesia had been persuaded to change their names by the end of the 1940s? This question cannot be

[56] Rep on the 're-Polonization action' by ODA S-PD, 21.4.1948, APO 178, sygn. 65, 17–21; CuRep ODA S-PD, 7.4.1948, APO 178, sygn. 65, 11–12.
[57] Rep on the liquidation of the traces of German language and culture by ODA S-PD, 31.7.1948. APO 178, sygn. 113, 64–5; Linek, *Polityka*, p. 224.
[58] Linek, *Polityka*, p. 341. [59] Special Rep by ODA S-PD, 19.3.1949, APO 178, sygn. 64, 16–17.
[60] Linek, *Polityka*, pp. 340–2.

answered precisely. By the start of 1948, 5,360 residents of Opole District were said by the state authorities to have changed their names. The figure for the whole of Upper Silesia (i.e., the entire Silesia Voivodship, including both western and eastern Upper Silesia) was 99,408. Of the name changes which occurred in Opole District, the majority, 3,800, had been 'spelling corrections' of surnames, meaning the Polonization of typically western Upper Silesian surnames. Only 1,200 were full replacements of first names and 360 were full replacements of surnames. In contrast, in the whole of Upper Silesia, the largest proportion, 42,928, were full replacements of first names, with only 17,164 'spelling corrections' of surnames and 39,316 full replacements of surnames. It is unclear how many name changes were carried out in 1948 and 1949. But an informed guess would suggest that the figures probably doubled in that period, meaning that around 10,000 name changes ultimately happened in Opole District and perhaps 200,000 in the whole of Upper Silesia. Both figures represented a relatively small minority of the prewar population. In that respect, despite the huge pressure the Communist-controlled authorities had brought to bear on this population, the name-changing campaign had failed. In that regard, it did not differ from the rest of the 're-Polonization action' implemented in western Upper Silesia in the second half of the 1940s.[61]

INDIGENOUS POLES

It was not only in western Upper Silesia that the new Polish state authorities introduced a 're-Polonization action' after the Second World War. The other large-scale 're-Polonization action' in Poland's new territories was implemented in southern East Prussia. This region was inhabited by a large number of speakers of the Masurian and Warmian dialects of Polish. In the view of Poland's Communist-controlled government, it contained the second largest concentration of 'indigenous Poles' in the new territories. As in western Upper Silesia, the 're-Polonization action' got underway in southern East Prussia in autumn 1945. But the action was implemented differently in southern East Prussia to how it was carried out in western Upper Silesia. In the latter region, it was the regional administrative and educational officials who were in control of the 're-Polonization action'. In contrast, in southern East Prussia, the state administrative authorities handed over responsibility for implementing the action, to a large extent,

[61] Rep by ODA S-PD, 7.1.1949, APO 178, sygn. 63, 9–10; Rep on the liquidation of the traces of German language and culture by ODA S-PD, 31.7.1948. APO 178, sygn. 113, 64–5; Linek, *Polityka*, pp. 319, 327, 332–5, 341.

to the Polish Western Association. As noted in Chapters 2 and 6, the Polish Western Association was a nationalist organization which Communist leaders had allowed to come back into existence in 1944 in order to help them produce nationalist propaganda and implement nationalist policies in Poland's new territories.[62]

The research which has so far been done on the 're-Polonization action' implemented in Poland's new territories after the Second World War has understandably focused on western Upper Silesia and southern East Prussia. After all, the action had the greatest significance in these two linguistically mixed regions. Yet 're-Polonization' measures were also eventually introduced in areas which had been almost entirely German-speaking before 1945. This was because, as we discussed in Chapter 6, in these areas too, small numbers of prewar residents were 'verified' as ethnic Poles after the war. As in western Upper Silesia and southern East Prussia, the state authorities in these formerly German-speaking localities also wanted to ensure that the locals 'verified' as ethnic Poles were culturally assimilated into mainstream Polish society.

Let us examine what the 're-Polonization action' looked like in the previously German-speaking areas of Poland's new territories at ground level, by focusing on its implementation in Jelenia Góra District. The extent to which the initiative for introducing 're-Polonization' measures in the districts and towns of Lower Silesia came from the government in Warsaw, the Polish Western Association, the Regional Administration in Wrocław or Lower Silesia's various district and town administrations remains unclear. But 're-Polonization' measures started to be introduced in Jelenia Góra District towards the end of 1946. The district's Chief Official noted at that time that 'in the eyes of every Pole, an autochthon is merely a german [*sic*]'. 'Polish society' therefore treats 'autochthons' with 'reserve' and 'suspicion'. To deal with this, 'evening courses' were being run for 'autochthons' in local schools to teach them the Polish language, to foster in them 'the feeling of being a Pole' and to 'document' for them 'the return of these territories to the Motherland'. Jelenia Góra District's officials also sought to involve 'autochthons' in 'social activities' and organized for Polish settlers lectures and 'awareness talks' about 'autochthons'.[63]

As in the rest of Poland's new territories outside of western Upper Silesia, it was the Polish Western Association which ran the 're-Polonization

[62] Strauchold, *Autochtoni*, pp. 93–7, 184–5, 188.

[63] SiRep JG Chief, 2.12.1946, APW 331/VI, sygn. 38, 96–7; SiRep JG Chief, 2.1.1947, APW 331/VI, sygn. 39, 15–17; SiRep JG Chief, 1.2.1947, APW 331/VI, sygn. 51, 1–4; SiRep JG Chief, 1.3.1947, APW 331/VI, sygn. 51, 5–6.

courses' in Jelenia Góra District. The declared purpose of these courses was to give the 'indigenous Poles' command of their 'mother tongue', to educate them generally about the 'regained Fatherland' and to help them gain employment in the district's factories and workshops. They were set up in several villages in the district from late 1946 onwards. For example, a 're-Polonization course' was run by the Polish Western Association in the village of Cieplice between autumn 1948 and early summer 1949. It was attended by 52 residents of the local area. For most of the period studied here, no course appears to have been provided for the small number of 'indigenous Poles' living in Jelenia Góra town. But the association continued to set up new courses in the district during 1949. Midway through that year, with help from the state education authorities, it finally opened courses in Jelenia Góra town. Around this time, the association also held a general gathering for the district's 'autochthons' to discuss 're-Polonization issues'. It reportedly handed out questionnaires at this meeting aimed at finding out how many 'autochthons' had attended 'Polish language instruction' in the past few years, how many still needed 'instruction' and how many of their children actually went to school.[64]

Officials in Jelenia Góra District saw the 're-Polonization action' as aimed at 'erasing the differences existing between the autochthons and the settler population'. But this goal did not prove easy to accomplish. It was reported at least a year into the action that the 'native population' (*ludność tubylcza*) and the 'immigrants' were still 'showing reserve' towards one another.[65] By February 1948 the situation was little changed. 'Resettlers' were acting very 'distrustfully' towards the 'natives' (*tuziemcy*), whereas the 'natives' were 'withdrawing into their own tight circle and refusing to interact with their neighbours, the resettlers'.[66] Part of the reason for this appears to have been disputes over property between Polish settlers and 'indigenous Poles' similar to those witnessed in western Upper Silesia at this time. But property disputes seem to have played a more minor role in conflicts between settlers and 'autochthons' in Jelenia Góra District than

[64] SiRep JG Chief, 30.4.1947, APW 331/VI, sygn. 51, 18–19; SiRep JG Chief, 3.12.1947, APW 331/VI, sygn. 51, 37–8; SiRep JGT Pres, 29.4.1948, APW 331/VI, sygn. 50, 1–3; SiRep JG Chief, 8.7.1949, APW 331/VI, sygn. 51, 117–20; SiRep JG Chief, 30.4.1949, APW 331/VI, sygn. 50, 107–11; SiRep JG Chief, 7.4.1949, APW 331/VI, sygn. 51, 101–4; Rep on the first quarter of 1949 by JG Chief, 6.4.1949, APW 331/VI, sygn. 51, 105–10; SiRep Jelenia Góra's Deputy Town President, 23.6.1949, APW 331/VI, sygn. 50, 121–5; Rep on the second quarter of 1949 by JG Chief, 6.749, APW 331/VI, sygn. 51, 137–42; Strauchold, *Autochtoni*, p. 94.

[65] SiRep JG Chief, 30.4.1947, APW 331/VI, sygn. 51, 18–19; SiRep JG Chief, 3.12.1947, APW 331/VI, sygn. 51, 37–8.

[66] SiRep JG Chief, 3.12.1947, APW 331/VI, sygn. 51, 37–8; SiRep JG Chief, 6.[2].1948, APW 331/VI, sygn. 51, 42–3.

they did in the districts of western Upper Silesia.[67] Jelenia Góra's Town President believed that the main reason 'verified Poles' chose to keep their distance from settlers was 'an inexact knowledge of Polish' and the fact that too little was being done to 'instil in them a Polish spirit', draw them into social and cultural activities and allow them to make greater use of their 'citizenship rights on an equal footing with the settler population'.[68]

At the start of 1949, Jelenia Góra District's Chief Official went as far as to describe relations between settlers and 'autochthons' as amounting to a 'complete lack of coexistence' between the two populations. Unlike Jelenia Góra's Town President, he believed the settlers were chiefly to blame for this, because it was their 'psychosis' which caused them to regard 'autochthons' as 'Polish but "not purely Polish"' and to treat them as 'second class citizens'.[69] A few months later the district received a new Chief Official and, thinking along the same lines as his predecessor, he suggested that both the 'native population' (*ludność rodzima*) and the 'settler population' needed to be made aware of the 'national community' to which they both belonged in order to bring about 'close cooperation' and 'unification' between them.[70]

Nevertheless, Jelenia Góra District's state officials did feel they had some limited grounds for optimism. The district's new Chief Official noted in early summer 1949 that although older 'native people' had only a 'weak' knowledge of Polish, showed little interest in learning Polish and made almost no progress with the language, young 'autochthons' participated readily in the courses, made systematic use of the district's libraries and were gaining a 'good command of the language'. He claimed that there had therefore been 'visible improvements' in the 'native population's feeling of Polishness' and their ability to express themselves in their 'mother tongue'.[71] A few months later another official from Jelenia Góra District Administration described a similarly mixed picture. Young 'native people' seemed to be assimilating well as a result of the 're-Polonization courses'

[67] SiRep JG Chief, 1.2.1947, APW 331/VI, sygn. 51, 1–4; SiRep JG Chief, 1.3.1947, APW 331/VI, sygn. 51, 5–6; SiRep JG Chief, 31.3.1947, APW 331/VI, sygn. 51, 10–12; SiRep JG Chief, 30.4.1947, APW 331/VI, sygn. 51, 18–19; SiRep JG DepChief, 31.5.1947, APW 331/VI, sygn. 51, 20–1.

[68] SiRep JGT Pres, 29.4.1948, APW 331/VI, sygn. 50, 1–3; SiRep JG Chief, 1.3.1948, APW 331/VI, sygn. 51, 44–5; SiRep JG Chief, 5.5.1948, APW 331/VI, sygn. 51, 53–4; SiRep JG Chief, 2.11.1948, APW 331/VI, sygn. 51, 77–8.

[69] SiRep JG Chief, 31.1.1949, APJG 123/II, sygn. 20, 240–44; SiRep JG Chief, start March 1949, APW 331/VI, sygn. 51, 98–100.

[70] The phase he used was 'wspólnota pod względem narodowym'. SiRep JG Chief, 7.4.1949, APW 331/VI, sygn. 51, 101–4; Rep on the first quarter of 1949 by JG Chief, 6.4.1949, APW 331/VI, sygn. 51, 105–10.

[71] SiRep JG Chief, 31.5.1949, APW 331/VI, sygn. 51, 113–15; SiRep JGT Pres, 30.4.1949, APW 331/VI, sygn. 50, 107–11; SiRep JG Chief, 30.4.1949, APW 331/VI, sygn. 51, 111–12; SiRep JG Chief, 8.7.1949, APW 331/VI, sygn. 51, 117–20.

and the fact that 'natives' and 'newcomers' shared workplaces. However, 'bringing about a complete eradication of the differences between the native population and the immigrant population is difficult' mainly because of 'the language difficulties of the native population as well as the lack of family bonds between the population groups'. The settlers' attitude towards 'autochthons' also remained a key hindrance, because 'in the opinion of the majority of the inhabitants of this district, the terms autochthon and native population are always associated with the word "German" or at least someone who has been "remade" into a Pole'.[72]

These comments by Jelenia Góra District's officials suggest that the situation for 'indigenous Poles' there had many similarities to the one in western Upper Silesia. But as we saw in Chapter 6, in stark contrast with most districts in western Upper Silesia, only a tiny fraction of Jelenia Góra District's prewar population were 'verified' as 'indigenous Poles' and allowed to continue living there. Unlike the 'autochthons' in most of western Upper Silesia, those living in Jelenia Góra District and most of the rest of Poland's new territories were completely surrounded by Polish settlers – both at their workplaces and in the villages and towns in which they lived. And given the fact that by 1949 many 'autochthons' of a working age had experienced several years of immersion in the new Polish settler communities, Jelenia Góra District's new Chief Official may well not have been putting too rosy a tint on things when he described the linguistic progress being made by younger 'autochthons' as considerable. Younger 'autochthons' very likely were starting to get to grips with the Polish language by the end of the 1940s. They were probably proving somewhat more willing to assimilate into Polish settler society than were most 'indigenous Poles' in western Upper Silesia.

And yet the fact that many 'autochthons' in Jelenia Góra District were still not feeling particularly well assimilated, even in the mid 1950s, is made clear by an account provided by the Polish settler Stanisław Czepułkowski. Describing a meeting he chaired as first secretary of the village branch of the Polish United Workers' Party, which took place shortly after the political upheavals in Poland in 1956, he stated, 'Every resident of Karpacz wanted to see positive changes in the village... Autochthons also came to the meeting. At first they were timid, just watching and sitting there quietly... [but] I did manage to get them to speak to the gathering.'[73]

[72] SiRep JG DepChief on the third quarter of 1949 for LSRA S-PD, 5.10.1949, APW 331/VI, sygn. 51, 160–2; Rep on the third quarter of 1949 for LSRA's General Department by JG DepChief, 3.10.1949, APW 331/VI, sygn. 51, 154–9.

[73] Czepułkowski, 'W Karpaczu', p. 295.

As in western Upper Silesia, 're-Polonization' in Jelenia Góra District was not just about language but also about names. A name-changing campaign, aimed specifically at the district's 'autochthons', does not seem to have got underway there until 1948. Forty name-change applications had been submitted to Jelenia Góra District Administration in the previous year. But they had not been submitted by 'autochthons', but rather by 'individuals of Polish and Jewish origin who had used false surnames during the [Nazi German] occupation'.[74] The 'campaign to re-Polonize the forenames and surnames of autochthons' was launched in Jelenia Góra District in summer 1948, probably in response to an order from the Ministry for Recovered Territories. Jelenia Góra's District Administration and Town Administration both began to summon 'autochthons with German-sounding names' to their premises to persuade them to submit name-change applications. Applicants apparently needed to be in possession of various documents in order for their applications to be processed, though it is unclear what specific documents these were. Unlike the procedure in western Upper Silesia, all applications received by Jelenia Góra's District Administration and Town Administration had to be forwarded to Lower Silesia's Regional Administration in Wrocław to obtain formal authorization for the name changes. By autumn 1949 the district's authorities had received a total of 74 applications from 'autochthons' living in the rural part of the district and at least 70 – and possibly around 100 – from 'autochthons' living in Jelenia Góra town. It is very likely that almost all of these applications resulted in name changes. But this meant that only a minority of the roughly 1000 'verified indigenous Poles' living in Jelenia Góra District after the war changed their names in the late 1940s. The district's new Chief Official explained in 1949 that the campaign had simply not met with 'appropriate understanding' from the 'native population'. This, he added, had not been helped by the fact that the Polish Western Association had not engaged in it energetically enough.[75]

In localities across Poland's new territories, the same unsatisfactory results were witnessed from the name-changing campaign. The 'verified

[74] Rep on the year 1947 by JG Chief, undated, APJG 123/II, sygn. 21, 248–79.

[75] Rep on the first quarter of 1949 by JG Chief, 6.4.1949, APW 331/VI, sygn. 51, 105–10; SiRep JG Chief on the month February 1948, March 1948, APW 331/VI, sygn. 51, 98–100; Rep on the second quarter of 1948 by JGTA head S-PD, undated, APW 331/VI, sygn. 50, 13–14; Rep on the third quarter of 1948 by JGTA head S-PD, undated, APW331/VI, sygn. 50, 40–1; Rep on the final quarter of 1948 by JGTA head S-PD, undated, APW 331/VI, sygn. 50, 66–7; SiRep JG Chief, 27.12.1948, APW 331/VI, sygn. 51, 82–6; SiRep JG Chief, 31.149, APJG 123/II, sygn. 20, 240–4; Rep on the third quarter of 1949 by JG DepChief, 3.10.1949, APW 331/VI, sygn. 51, 154–9; Linek, *Polityka*, p. 324.

Poles' of southern East Prussia proved even more resistant to changing their surnames and forenames than the residents of western Upper Silesia. In fact, the campaign can be said to have failed dismally there. Throughout Poland's new territories, perhaps a little over 265,000 individuals agreed to change their names in the second half of the 1940s, the vast bulk of them residents of western Upper Silesia.[76]

Other aspects of the 're-Polonization action' also faced greater problems in southern East Prussia than in western Upper Silesia. The authorities of southern East Prussia, like those of western Upper Silesia, believed that the 're-Polonization' of the Masurian and Warmian dialect-speaking populations would be brought about through a combination of 're-Polonization courses', Polish community centres, Polish social clubs, Polish libraries, Polish newspapers and, most importantly, Polish state schools. All these facilities and provisions would provide 'autochthons' with exposure to conventional Polish culture and the opportunity to interact with Polish settlers. But 'indigenous Polish' parents in southern East Prussia proved even more reluctant to send their children to Polish state schools than their counterparts in western Upper Silesia. Only 3 per cent of 'indigenous children' attended school in that region in the period 1945–48, compared to 15 per cent in western Upper Silesia. Well under 3,000 school pupils are estimated to have attended Polish-language courses at schools in southern East Prussia in these years. The 're-Polonization courses' for adults met with similar rejection from the region's older 'autochthons'. Moreover, state officials in southern East Prussia appear to have been even more troubled than those in western Upper Silesia by the extent to which the Polish-dialect-speaking locals continued to speak German, expressed hostile views about Poland and Poles, grounded their collective identities in the region, town and village in which they lived – rather than the Polish nation – and conflicted with Polish settlers over property and other issues. By summer 1948, the Ministry for Recovered Territories was clearly aware that the 're-Polonization action' was failing throughout Poland's new territories.[77]

Yet it was not only the lack of progress in 'crystallizing' the 'Polish national consciousness' of 'indigenous Poles' in Poland's new territories which ultimately brought an end to the 're-Polonization action'. It also resulted from a fundamental change in the priorities of the state authorities in Poland's new territories during 1948–9, as the regime brought itself into line with the political and ideological imperatives of Stalinist Soviet

[76] Strauchold, *Autochtoni*, pp. 87–8, 177; Linek, *Polityka*, p. 335.
[77] Strauchold, *Autochtoni*, pp. 75–87, 91–124, 169–91.

orthodoxy. One of the ways this expressed itself was in the fact that conventional Marxist-Leninist concepts started to take clear precedence over nationalist rhetoric in the regime's propaganda. It also manifested itself in the fact that the staunchly nationalist Polish Western Association steadily lost the political influence it had enjoyed in the early postwar years. With regard to the 're-Polonization action', in 1948 the Ministry for Recovered Territories – which itself was disbanded in January 1949 as part of the Stalinist political changes – reduced the financial support it had previously provided to the Polish Western Association for running 're-Polonization courses' in Poland's new territories. From the end of 1948 onwards, the state authorities in the new territories started to pay at least as much attention to the attitudes 'indigenous Poles' exhibited towards the Communist regime and towards Communist ideology as to their ability to speak standard Polish and to their levels of Polish national consciousness. By the start of 1949, the 're-Polonization action' had already become a matter of very marginal importance, both for the decision-makers in Warsaw and for the local state officials on the ground in Poland's new territories. By the end of the decade, the authorities throughout these territories had simply stopped implementing it.[78]

The attempt to instil Polish national culture in the roughly one million German citizens whom Poland's Communist-led authorities 'verified' as ethnic Poles after the war formed a fundamental element of the government's broader nationalist campaign in the second half of the 1940s. The authorities regarded 're-Polonization' as a crucial adjunct to the 'verification action' in Poland's new territories. This was because they recognized that the vast majority of the German citizens they were 'verifying' as 'indigenous Poles' did not regard themselves as Poles, frequently had German-sounding names, often spoke German and could not express themselves in standard Polish. The authorities attempted to bring about the 're-Polonization' of these people in a number of ways: by encouraging school attendance, by running special courses, by expanding the opportunities to interact with Polish settlers, by inducing changes to personal names, by prohibiting the use of German in public and by various other means. They hoped that this mixture of measures would bring about an accelerated cultural, linguistic and social assimilation of the 'indigenous Poles' within a matter of a mere few years.

[78] Strauchold, *Autochtoni*, pp. 184–7, 189–91; Madajczyk, 'Niemcy', pp. 82–3.

By the end of the 1940s, however, these hopes had been dashed. They had proven totally unrealistic. Moreover, in western Upper Silesia and southern East Prussia – the two regions where the authorities' attributed greatest significance to the 're-Polonization action' – the government's nationalist policies actually succeeded in making Polish-dialect-speakers feel more distanced from Polish culture and society than they had felt before 1945. We shall discuss the consequences of this failure to assimilate and integrate 'verified' former German citizens in the final section of Chapter 10. But first let us examine what can broadly be described as the 'cultural cleansing' of Poland's new territories in the second half of the 1940s.

CHAPTER 10

Culture, religion, society

Poland's postwar Communist-led authorities believed that in order to transform Poland into a homogeneously Polish nation-state it was necessary to replace or 're-Polonize' the inhabitants of Poland's new territories. But their nationalist 'cleansing' of these territories between 1945 and 1949 was not limited to population policies. Indeed, they attempted to enact in these territories a far-reaching cultural transformation in which all expressions of German national culture would be removed and, where necessary, replaced with culturally Polish equivalents. This campaign of 'cultural cleansing' came to embrace almost everything. It targeted anything that could be viewed as a culturally German institution, organization or facility. This meant schools, churches, libraries, community centres, newspapers, cinemas, theatres, museums, social clubs, leisure organizations and artistic groups. It also included almost all physical manifestations of German culture: signs, notices, monuments, writing painted on buildings, books, tickets and many more things. In this way the authorities attempted to ensure that Poland's new territories had a cultural appearance and a cultural infrastructure which was purely Polish. They hoped that this would enable these formerly German territories to become an integral part of the postwar ethno-nationally homogeneous Polish nation-state.

CULTURAL TRACES

The authorities viewed the eradication of the physical 'traces' and 'remnants' of German national culture from Poland's new territories as an end in itself. But they also regarded it as important for the psychological impact it would have on the new territories' postwar inhabitants – both the settlers and the 'indigenous Poles'. They hoped it would reduce the prevalent perception among Polish settlers that these were foreign lands, alleviate their fears that these territories would soon be reincorporated into Germany and gradually help them to feel rooted there. At the same time, they believed it would facilitate the 're-Polonization' of the 'indigenous Poles' by helping them to recognize the villages, towns and cities they lived in as Polish, not German.

The earliest actions to remove the physical remnants of German culture from these territories were taken by officials in the region the authorities believed had the largest concentration of 'indigenous Poles', western Upper Silesia. Already, in March 1945, Upper Silesia's Regional Governor, Aleksander Zawadzki, ordered western Upper Silesia's new Polish officials to begin eradicating all forms of German writing on public display in the region. The Polish state officials arriving in localities throughout the region as 'operational groups' at this time quickly set about implementing this order. They tended to focus initially on the German writing painted and inscribed on the exteriors of buildings, the German inscriptions found on monuments and the region's innumerable German street and road signs. In Opole District, for example, the new Polish authorities started the process in April 1945 by removing German writing from the walls of Opole's town hall building and by dismantling the monument to Frederick the Great standing in front of it. During May and June they reportedly focused their efforts on replacing all German road signs and eliminating all 'prusso-Hitlerist monuments'. Opole District's officials declared at this time that, as a result of the swiftness with which 'the district is being de-Germanized, [it is probable that] everything which is German will very soon have vanished from the district'.[1]

The changing of road signs went hand in hand with the changing of place names. Some places in western Upper Silesia had already received new Polish names by March 1945. From the outset the Silesian Institute (*Instytut Śląski*) in Katowice played a central role in coming up with new Polish names for the region's towns and villages. But a fair degree of local discretion was also involved. Local state officials often introduced their own names for villages without reference to the Institute. In mid June 1945, Upper Silesia's Regional Governor instructed western Upper Silesia's district and town administrations that they had only until 15 July to introduce Polish names for all villages within the areas under their control. After that date any deliberate use of German place names by residents would become punishable with internment in a camp. In Opole District, new Polish names had already been fixed for a number of the

[1] Rep by ODA S-PD, 29.5.1945, APK 185/4, sygn. 21, 208–9; Linek, *Polityka*, pp. 235–8.

villages by the start of June 1945 and very likely for all of them by early July.[2]

Throughout western Upper Silesia, a significant minority of the new Polish names given to villages in 1945 did not last for much more than a year. This resulted from the creation of a new 'Committee for Establishing Place Names' in Warsaw at the start of 1946. Between that time and 1950, this committee worked together with the Silesian Institute in Katowice to review all the new Polish names given to places in 1945 and to alter or replace those they deemed unsuitable. A number of villages in Opole District, therefore, received their second postwar names after 1946. By way of illustration, the village of Plümkenau was originally renamed Blimkinow in 1945 but was later given the new name of Radomierowice.[3]

In order to arrive at new Polish names for the towns and villages of western Upper Silesia after the war, administrative officials and the experts of the Silesian Institute and the Committee for Establishing Place Names almost always looked to the western Slavic names which these places had possessed before the Nazis came to power in the 1930s. In the mid 1930s, the Nazi German authorities had replaced most of the western Slavic names of the towns and villages of western Upper Silesia with German ones (see Chapter 6). After 1945, most of the new Polish names introduced in this region by Polish state officials and experts were merely Polonized versions of the original western Slavic place names. For example, the village of Jaschkowitz in Opole District had been renamed Johannsdorf by the Nazis in 1936. After the war it became Jaśkowice, a Polonized version of the pre-1936 name. In the minority of cases where the Nazi German authorities had not Germanized the names of villages in the mid 1930s, the officials and experts also Polonized their names after the war (e.g., Proskau to Prószków). Only very rarely did the officials and experts deem it unnecessary to Polonize the original name of a village (e.g., Podkraje became Am Waldrand in 1936 and then simply returned to Podkraje after the war).[4]

[2] Rep by ODA, 5.6.1945, APK 185/4, sygn. 22, 49–51; Świder, *Entgermanisierung*, pp. 217–19; Linek, *Polityka*, p. 238; Nitschke, *Vertreibung*, p. 153.

[3] Rep by ODA, 5.6.1945, APK 185/4, sygn. 22, 49–51; SiRep O Chief on the period 20.12.1945–20.1.1946, APO 178, sygn. 41, 13–15; SiRep O Chief on the period 20.1.1946–20.2.1946, APO 178, sygn. 41, 16–18; SiRep ODA S-PD, 1.4.1947, APO 178, sygn. 62, 7–11; Rep on the 're-Polonization action' by ODA S-PD, 21.4.1948, APO 178, sygn. 65, 17–21; WR, Marta D., Plümkenau (Radomierowice), 15.9.1956, BOD 1, 243, 281–3; Świder, *Entgermanisierung*, pp. 218–19.

[4] A. Wegener (ed.), *Historisches Ortschaftsverzeichnis. Reihe historischer Ortschaftsverzeichnisse für ehemals zu Deutschland gehörige Gebiete – Zeitraum 1914 bis 1945* (14 vols., Frankfurt am Main, 1994–7), Vol. I: *Oberschlesien* (Frankfurt am Main, 1994); Linek, *Polityka*, pp. 28–30; Świder, *Entgermanisierung*, p. 219, footnote 750; Ther, 'Die einheimische Bevölkerung', p. 417; Lis, 'Mniejszość polska', p. 263.

Similarly, in order to replace German street signs with Polish ones, western Upper Silesia's officials needed to rename streets and squares. Officials began considering new names for Opole town's streets and squares already in mid April 1945. This was perhaps slightly earlier than elsewhere in western Upper Silesia. Around that time, Zawadzki provided a set of guidelines for renaming streets and squares in the towns and villages of the region. These stipulated that the main roads should be named after important events in Poland's national history; the ordinary streets should be named after pro-Polish Upper Silesian activists and insurgents; and the roads leading out of towns and villages should be named after the places to which they led. He also specified that squares should be named after the monuments which officials intended to build there, names such as 'Liberation Square'. Interestingly, he also stated that translations of German street names should be avoided. Many examples can be cited of how these guidelines were applied in Opole District. But to quote just one, the large street of Sedanstraße, situated near the centre of Opole town, was renamed Ulica Grunwaldzka after the famous Battle of Grunwald of 1410, a key event in Poland's national history.[5]

The order which Zawadzki issued in mid June 1945, giving western Upper Silesia's district and town administrations only until 15 July to change all place names, stipulated the same deadline for removing all 'German traces' (*ślady niemieckie*) from the region. He specified what he meant by this: German writing on the external walls of shops, cafes, restaurants and private homes; German road and street signs; German anti-aircraft defences; and German public notices and posters. Nowhere in the region was it possible to keep to this deadline, given the sheer quantity of such objects. Nevertheless, the following month he extended the campaign to the region's churches, ordering the Roman Catholic Church to eradicate all German inscriptions from church walls, parish buildings and cemeteries. The Church's leaders in the region at first resisted this demand. But Zawadzki maintained his pressure on them. In December 1946 the Catholic Administrator Apostolic for western Upper Silesia, Bolesław Kominek, consented to the removal of all German inscriptions from churches and roadside crosses. Yet despite Zawadzki's efforts to maintain the intensity and extend the scope of his campaign against all remnants of German culture, secular and religious, it clearly became a peripheral issue for local state officials throughout western Upper Silesia after summer 1945, losing

[5] WR, Alfons S., Oppeln (Opole) town, 23.1.1949, BOD 2, 229, 48–52; Linek, *Polityka*, pp. 237–8; Świder, *Entgermanisierung*, p. 218; Nitschke, *Vertreibung*, pp. 153–4, footnote 113.

almost all momentum. By then numerous road and street signs had already been removed or replaced. A lot of German writing had already been eradicated from the exterior walls of buildings. And many German monuments had already been altered or dismantled. For the next year and a half the campaign crawled along at a far slower pace.[6]

It was not until 1947 that Zawadzki was able to inject renewed vigour into the campaign. This found expression in articles in Upper Silesia's newspapers in early 1947. They pointed repeatedly to the continued existence of numerous 'German remnants' (*niemieckie pozostałości*) in the form of German labels on shop products, German menus in restaurants, German beer bottles, German beer mats and much more besides. Along the same lines, in April 1947, Zawadzki asked the Warsaw government to begin applying pressure to the postal and railway authorities to get them to cease using German tickets and forms and finally to replace them with Polish ones. Interestingly, one of Zawadzki's officials in Upper Silesia's Regional Administration in Katowice expressed reservation about this at this time. He pointed out that German forms and tickets were still in such widespread use in the region that it would simply be impossible suddenly to stop using them.[7]

Then in mid August 1947, Zawadzki decided to step up the campaign radically. This was partly in response to an order from the Ministry for Recovered Territories in late June 1947 (see the next section). But, as always, Zawadzki was acting principally on his own initiative. As we shall see, he would also take the campaign much further than officials in other regions in Poland's new territories. In mid August he ordered western Upper Silesia's district and town administrations to radicalize their efforts to 'liquidate all remaining inscriptions from both public and private places, in homes, on paintings, ornaments, dishes etc.'. To assist them with this task, he placed a series of sanctions and fines at their disposal for the punishment of those people who refused to erase 'German remnants' from their homes and businesses. This was part of a broader intensification in Zawadzki's anti-German campaign, the other elements of which we discussed in Chapter 9. In October 1947, he ordered the region's authorities to set up 'civic inspection committees' whose task it would be to inspect shops, cafes, restaurants and private homes for German writing on external walls, signs, advertisements, packaging and items such as plates, ashtrays and beer mats. Those individuals found in possession of items with German text, who refused

[6] Linek, *Polityka*, pp. 238–43; Madajczyk, *Przyłączenie*, p. 198.
[7] Linek, *Polityka*, pp. 257–8; Madajczyk, *Przyłączenie*, p. 198.

to get rid of either the text or the item, would henceforth be subjected to a fine or one of the other penalties.[8]

In Opole District, these orders had a clear impact on the approach taken by local officials towards this campaign. One of Opole District's officials later remarked that the campaign had only really taken on 'concrete form' in August 1947. Between August and October 1947, Opole District Administration made efforts to ensure that local mayors and other local officials were fully engaged in the effort to eradicate 'German remnants' from the district and to 'give a Polish face to the district'. A number of 'civic inspection committees' were appointed in autumn 1947 which set about combing through the district for the numerous 'remaining traces of the German language'.[9]

By spring 1948 there were around 21 'civic inspection committees' operating in the rural part of Opole District and four working in Opole town. They inspected shops, cafes, bars, restaurants, pastry outlets and factories. They looked for such items as German advertisements, German beer mats, ashtrays bearing German text and 'all ornaments, original paintings and printed pictures of the German type'. According to the district's officials, the committees only inspected private homes if 'there was a suspicion that they still had a German character' – meaning there were still German inscriptions on external walls, stairs, letter boxes, doorbells and household items such as towels and salt and flour boxes. In February 1948, Opole District's Chief Official ordered his own officials to cover up German text on the files, ring binders and other office equipment they were using. A few months later, the district's shops and cooperatives were instructed to get rid of all German weights and scales. Opole District's village and commune mayors were then given a deadline of 22 July 1948 to 'liquidate all remnants of the German language'.[10] At the end of July, Opole District's officials claimed to have eradicated 95 per cent of the German writing painted or inscribed on the exteriors of buildings, 98 per cent on both the outside and inside walls of churches and 'all' German writing in cafes, bars, restaurants, shops and cooperatives, and to have achieved 'good results' in their efforts to eradicate German from weights, scales and tills. They claimed that the

[8] Linek, *Polityka*, pp. 261–4, 269–70, 274–5, 345.

[9] SiRep O Chief on the period 21.5.1947–21.6.1947, APO 178, sygn. 42, 27–8; Rep on the liquidation of the traces of German language and culture, by ODA S-PD, 31.7.1948, APO 178, sygn. 113, 64–5; Rep on the 're-Polonization action' by ODA S-PD, 19.4.1948, APO 178, sygn. 65, 17–21; CuRep ODA S-PD, 11.12.1947, APK 185/4, sygn. 51, 69–69a.

[10] Rep on the 're-Polonization action' by ODA S-PD, 21.4.1948, APO 178, sygn. 65, 17–21; Rep on the first half of 1948 by ODA S-PD, undated, APO 178, sygn. 65, 50–2; WR, Arthur M., Derschau (Suchy Bór), 7.10.1954, BOD 1, 243, 67–72; Linek, *Polityka*, p. 357.

only reason the campaign had not been 100 per cent successful was the size of the district and the density of its population. But another reason, not given by the officials, was clearly the fact that the range of items they viewed as 'German remnants' was constantly expanding. In August 1948, for example, housing block managers in Opole town were ordered to start removing German safety labels from electric meters.[11]

One particular element of this extraordinary attempt to eliminate every physical remnant of German national culture left in western Upper Silesia received a disproportionate amount of attention from the region's state authorities from late summer 1947 onwards. Zawadzki signalled quite plainly in late August 1947 that the region's officials should now abandon any inhibitions they may previously have had towards removing German writing from gravestones. He commented that it was 'disagreeable that Polish families tolerate German inscriptions on gravestones'. In October he instructed the 'civic inspection committees' to start applying pressure on the Roman Catholic Church's priests and officials to get them finally to remove German inscriptions from gravestones, memorials and other objects on Church grounds. But the Church proved resistant to this pressure. The committees and local state officials found, with time, that it was far easier to pass the responsibility and cost of changing gravestones on to the families of the buried individuals.[12]

In Opole District, the authorities devoted a great deal of attention to what they called the 'de-Germanization of cemeteries' during 1948. One of the district's official described it as the 'most difficult aspect' of the 'fight against manifestations of the German language'. He noted that 'in most communities, local people themselves remove the plaques containing German inscriptions from graves of their own relatives'. But if the graves were not being looked after by relatives, the plaques were removed by the local commune administrations. Opole District's Chief Official set the district's commune mayors the deadline of 15 March 1948 to eradicate all German inscriptions from gravestones in the villages under their control. But the sheer number of graves in the district made this deadline totally unrealistic. Local commune administrations also complained that they were inhibited by the costs involved in eradicating inscriptions from headstones and removing headstones from graves because relatives were often found to be living in Germany and therefore no longer present to foot the bill.

[11] Rep on the liquidation of traces of German language and culture, 31.7.1948, APO 178, sygn. 113, 64–5; Linek, *Polityka*, pp. 358–9.

[12] Linek, *Polityka*, pp. 261–4, 274–5, 345.

Similar complaints were made by local state officials elsewhere in western Upper Silesia at this time.[13]

Yet it was not only the costs involved which caused difficulties for the administrative officials in charge of 'de-Germanizing' the region's cemeteries. Throughout western Upper Silesia, state officials encountered serious practical problems with the removal German inscriptions from headstones. In Opole District, for example, officials described the inscriptions on gravestones as the 'most difficult type' of 'German remnant' to remove. This was apparently because 80 per cent were made from marble or granite. One of the district's officials admitted in late spring 1948 that the authorities had actually only managed to remove 'a fraction' of the inscriptions from gravestones. He also reported, 'In some communities attempts have been made to cover up these inscriptions with clay, plaster and cement. But this method has now been prohibited because, once these materials have set, they tend just to fracture and fall out.'[14] Little progress was made in subsequent months and in summer 1948 Opole's Town President took the extreme measure of ordering his officials to 'raze to the ground' Opole town's municipal cemeteries. It is unclear whether or not this order was actually followed. But western Upper Silesia's state authorities did sometimes remove headstones from the ground. When they did so, they generally sold them to willing buyers who wanted their stone. Opole town's officials claimed in 1948 that the money gained from selling gravestones was going to be used to finance a plaque in memory of 'the heroes who had fallen in the struggle for our freedom'.[15]

The Communist-controlled authorities' efforts to 'de-Germanize' gravestones and monuments in western Upper Silesia understandably provoked huge hostility from local people. Some residents of Opole District, who later became citizens of West Germany, remembered these events with great emotion and bitterness. Friedrich K. from the village of Sacken/Lubienia in Opole District described it as 'outrageous' that the dead were not 'allowed to rest in peace' and that the village's 'beautiful memorial' to the 57 local soldiers who had died fighting for Germany in the First World War was dismantled. Marta D. from the village of Plümkenau/Radomierowice claimed that local gravestones were 'desecrated', 'knocked over' and 'destroyed' by the authorities. Adolf D. from Oderfest/Przywory alleged that when local

[13] CuRep ODA S-PD, 8.3.1948, APO 178, sygn. 65, 7–8; CuRep ODA S-PD, 8.1.1948, APK 185/4, sygn. 52, 39–40; CuRep ODA S-PD, 7.4.1948, APO 178, sygn. 65, 11–12; Linek, *Polityka*, pp. 351–5.

[14] Rep on the 're-Polonization action' by ODA S-PD, 21.4.1948, APO 178, sygn. 65, 17–21.

[15] Rep on the liquidation of traces of German language and culture by ODA S-PD, 31.7.1948, APO 178, sygn. 113, 64–5; Linek, *Polityka*, pp. 349, 352–3.

villagers refused to remove 'German gravestones' from the cemeteries, the gravestones were confiscated by officials and the graves destroyed. He also made the rather less plausible claim that the villagers were then forced to buy back the confiscated gravestones and replace the German inscriptions on them with Polish ones. Arthur M. from the village of Derschau/Suchy Bór asserted that local villagers took action to protect the gravestones by removing them from cemeteries and hiding them in their homes. This claim was supported by Opole District Administration, which reported such activities by residents in various local villages in 1948. Similar acts of defiance by 'indigenous Poles' were noted by local state officials in other western Upper Silesian districts as this time.[16]

The authorities' campaign to eradicate all physical remnants of German culture from western Upper Silesia gradually petered out after summer 1948. Despite this, in late autumn 1949, one of Opole District's officials commented that local officials still hoped that the 'remaining traces' could be 'ruthlessly' eradicated. He also described the campaign as only '90 percent complete'. But these comments did not signal that the campaign was still in full swing in Opole District in late 1949. Quite the contrary, the district's officials by this point had long since ceased implementing it in any serious way. Rather, these comments reflected the fact that the goal of eliminating all 'German traces' from the district had never been an achievable one. They showed that, even at the end of the decade, there was still a huge amount of German material culture on show in Opole District. The same was true of all other districts in western Upper Silesia. It had never been realistic to attempt to eliminate all German material culture from the region. There was simply too much of it.[17]

OTHER REMNANTS

What measures were taken to eradicate the physical remnants of German culture outside of western Upper Silesia? At the end of June 1945, the Ministry for Public Administration sent out a circular to the new Polish state officials throughout Poland's new territories, ordering them to make sure that all physical remnants of German culture were quickly

[16] WR, Friedrich K., Sacken (Lubienia), 24.7.1955, BOD 1, 243, 309–19; WR, Marta D., Plümkenau (Radomierowice), 15.9.1956, BOD 1, 243, 281–3; WR, Adolf D., Oderfest (Przywory), 10.4.1951, BOD 2, 229, 7–8; WR, Arthur M., Derschau (Suchy Bór), 7.10.1954, BOD 1, 243, 67–72. WRs: BOD 1, 243, 255–6; BOD 1, 243, 227–8; BOD 1, 243, 287–8; BOD 1, 243, 379–80. Linek, *Polityka*, pp. 354–5.

[17] Rep by ODA S-PD, 25.11.1949, APO 178, sygn. 64, 43; Rep by O Chief, 12.5.1949, APO 178, sygn. 64, 24–5; SiRep the municipal mayor of Krapkowice, 2.10.1948, APO 178, sygn. 66, 156; Linek, *Polityka*, pp. 345–63.

removed.[18] But in many localities in the new territories – including those in western Upper Silesia (see the preceding) – these actions got underway before the ministry issued its order. The early measures were principally the product of decisions made by regional, district and town administrations rather than a response to instructions or pressure from the Communist-controlled government in Warsaw.

In Jelenia Góra District, for example, the process was initiated around the middle of June 1945. It targeted only the town of Jelenia Góra at first, but during the summer was widened to include the villages of the district as well. In Jelenia Góra town, it was the Town Administration's Construction Department which took charge of the initial efforts to 'liquidate' German signs, advertisements and monuments. But arriving Polish settlers apparently also played a role.[19] According to one Polish witness, the settlers

> threw themselves into work . . . They immediately altered the external appearance of the town. Houses and shops were decorated in Polish flags and on the streets there was Polish life, Polish language, Polish singing. And soon after that, German street names, road signs, monuments, notices and adverts all disappeared.[20]

The process of changing place names also got underway in Jelenia Góra District at this time. The district's officials changed the name of the town and district from Hirschberg to Jelenia Góra as soon as they arrived as an 'operational group' in late May 1945. But by late July 1945 only three of the district's villages had received new Polish names. These were Bad Warmbrunn, Jannowitz and Lomnitz. They were renamed Cieplice, Janowice and Łomnica, respectively. It took until the start of 1946 for the authorities to come up with new Polish names for the rest of the district's villages and also to cease using the German names to refer to these places.[21] As in western Upper Silesia, a significant minority of the district's villages were then renamed for a second time by the Committee for Establishing Place Names in Warsaw after 1946. An example of this is the village of Giersdorf in Jelenia Góra District, which was originally given the new Polish name of Popławy but was subsequently renamed Podgórzyn by the Committee.[22]

[18] Linek, *Polityka*, pp. 236–7.

[19] Rep by JGTA, 10.3.1947, APJG 130, sygn. 48, 22–35; Rep by JG Chief, 3.6.1946, APJG 130, sygn. 46, 53–5.

[20] Rep by JG Chief, 3.6.1946, APJG 130, sygn. 46, 53–5.

[21] SiRep JG Chief, 6.[8].1945, APJG123/II, sygn.18, 3–26; MoRep JGDA S-PD, 3.9.1945, APJG 123/II, sygn. 18, 86–8; Rep by JG Chief, 5.12.1945, APJG 123/II, sygn. 18, 185–200; MoRep JG Chief, 5.1.1946, APJG 123/II, sygn. 18, 206–14.

[22] SiRep JG Chief, 5.2.1946, APJG 123/II, sygn. 19, 30–7; SiRep JG Chief, 2.3.1946, APJG 123/II, sygn. 19, 73–6; SiRep JG Chief, 1.4.1946, APJG 123/II, sygn. 19, 118–21; WR, Johannes S., Giersdorf (Podgórzyn), 6.4.1951, BOD 2, 188, 169–74; Ivo Łaborewicz, 'Wykaz zespołów archiwalnych

Despite the fact that, in contrast to western Upper Silesia, only a small number of villages in Jelenia Góra District had names which appeared to have Slavic origins, the officials and experts who came up with new Polish names for local villages after the war generally tried to use the pre-1945 names as a basis. This meant either that they translated part or the entirety of the pre-1945 name (Jelenia Góra was itself a straight translation of Hirschberg, meaning 'deer mountain'); or, more commonly, that they created or found a new Polish name which was similar in look or sound to the pre-1945 names (e.g., Buchwald became Bukowiec). Only a minority of the new Polish names of the district's villages had no apparent connection with the pre-1945 name (e.g., Ludwigsdorf became Chromiec). This appears to have broadly reflected what happened in the changing of place names in most other localities in Poland's new territories in the early postwar years.[23]

Similar priciples for choosing new Polish names for streets and squares were applied in Jelenia Góra District to those in the rest of Poland's new territories – including western Upper Silesia. Thus, the main streets of Jelenia Góra town were named after important events and significant figures in Poland's national history: names such as Ulica Grunwaldzka (after the Battle of Grunwald), Ulica 3 Maja (after the 3 May 1791 Constitution), Ulica Daszyńskiego (after Ignacy Daszyński), Ulica Konopnickiej (after Maria Konopnicka), and, perhaps most notably of all, Ulica M. Stalina (Marshal Stalin Street!).[24]

German witnesses recalled these early measures taken to remove the remnants of German culture from Jelenia Góra District in summer 1945 very vividly. Ursula R., who was still living in the village of Niederschreiberhau/Szklarska Poręba Dolna in summer 1945, wrote:

> One day, to our astonishment, Polish inscriptions were put up next to the German ones on the town hall in Oberschreiberhau. At the end of July it was ordered that all inscriptions on houses, shops and street signs be removed. But it is difficult to describe how surprised – or, rather, horrified – we were to discover that the sign at the railway station no longer read "Nieder-Schreiberhau" but rather bore the unpronounceable and unintelligible words Dolna Szklarska Poreba [*sic*]. Still today I do not know what that means or who invented it.[25]

przechowywanych w archiwum państwowym we Wrocławiu oddział w Jeleniej Górze', *Rocznik Jeleniogórski* 32, 2000, pp. 93–5; Świder, *Entgermanisierung*, pp. 218–19.

[23] Łaborewicz, 'Wykaz zespołów archiwalnych', pp. 93–5; Świder, *Entgermanisierung*, p. 219, footnote 750.

[24] Rep by JGTA, October 1947, APJG 130, sygn. 48, 59–64.

[25] WR, Ursula R., Niederschreiberhau (Szklarska Poręba Dolna), 10.3.1954, BOD 2, 188, 122–37.

Another German witness claimed that these measures finally convinced Germans in Jelenia Góra District that the local area was becoming part of Poland. Local Germans apparently abandoned all hope that Germany would keep hold of these territories when 'all local place names began to be Polonized at the start of July, displaying their membership in the Polish state on every road sign'.[26]

As in western Upper Silesia, after this initial flurry of activity in Jelenia Góra District, aimed at eliminating only the most visible physical remnants of German culture – signs, monuments, advertisements and the writing on buildings' exteriors – the campaign lost momentum. In fact, unlike what happened in western Upper Silesia, the campaign probably ground to a complete halt in Jelenia Góra District after summer 1945. This total loss of impetus was probably also witnessed in most other localities in Poland's new territories in these months. The principal reason for this was that most areas of these territories were not under the control of a Regional Governor as fanatically intent on keeping the anti-German purge going as was Aleksander Zawadzki. In fact, the example being set by Zawadzki's struggle to eradicate all things German in western Upper Silesia was probably what inspired the Ministry for Recovered Territories to send out its order in late June 1947 instructing all Regional Governors in the new territories to set about eradicating every last 'trace of German language' from their voivodships. But the fact that, outside of western Upper Silesia, the renewal of the campaign was the product of direct pressure from a government ministry, rather than the product of decisions made on the ground by regional, district and town administrations, meant that the new territories' state officials generally failed to get behind it. Having already eliminated the most visible instances of German material culture in the course of 1945, they did not generally see the need to take the campaign any further.[27]

In Jelenia Góra District, for example, the local state authorities simply ignored the ministry's order. Indeed, the district's Chief Official declared in late autumn 1947 that 'the district has [already] taken on a purely Polish character. There are essentially no traces of the German language anywhere and where cases do arise they are removed immediately'. In December he claimed that 'neither Jelenia Góra town nor the surrounding countryside

[26] WR, Frau Dr Ilse R., Schreiberhau (Szklarska Poręba), September 1946, BOD 2, 188, 139–48; WR, Johannes S., Giersdorf (Podgórzyn), 6.4.1951, BOD 2, 188, 169–74; WR, Hans T., Schmiedeberg (Kowary), late 1949, BOD 2, 188, 287–91; WR, Robert W., Ludwigsdorf/(Chromiec), undated, BOD 1, 207, 33–8.

[27] Linek, *Polityka*, pp. 269–72; Świder, *Entgermanisierung*, pp. 213–14, 237–8, 250–54; Nitschke, *Vertreibung*, pp. 148–50.

contain even the tiniest trace of the previous presence of the germans [*sic*]. The inscriptions which used to be spotted occasionally have already been completely removed'.[28] In fact it was not until around the start of April 1948 that Jelenia Góra District's officials finally decided to resume the campaign. The district's Chief Official instructed local commune administrations at this time to issue 'administrative penalties' (i.e., fines) to every individual who did not comply with requests to remove 'remnants of the German language' from their homes. This was very likely a response to renewed pressure from the Ministry for Recovered Territories, because shortly afterwards, in late April 1948, the ministry sent out a new order instructing officials in the new territories to 'eliminate the German language', 'remove German inscriptions' and 'destroy all manifestations and traces of Hitlerist and Germanizing ideology'. In subsequent months, Jelenia Góra District's authorities did seem to step up their activity on this front. They fined a number of residents for not removing German material culture from their properties when requested to do so. During the summer the local Citizens' Militia took action to remove 'German inscriptions and other remnants' which local residents, despite receiving fines, had refused to eliminate. Around the same time, Jelenia Góra Town Administration prohibited the use of all packaging and paper containing 'German print'.[29]

Yet, in contrast to what happened in western Upper Silesia, the removal of inscriptions from gravestones does not appear to have entered into the campaign against the physical remnants of German culture in Jelenia Góra District. Several German witnesses did later report that local gravestones had been damaged in these years. Willi F., for example, claimed that graves in the local area were 'ruined' and parts of local cemeteries levelled. Sabine von S. alleged that 'the Poles wreaked havoc' in the local cemeteries, removing the 'best monuments', breaking open tombs and searching the corpses for gold and jewellery.[30] But these were probably a matter of

[28] Rep on the third quarter of 1947 by JG Chief, 13.11.1947, APJG 123/II, sygn. 21, 232–6; SiRep JG Chief, 3.12.1947, APW 331/VI, sygn. 51, 37–8.

[29] SiRep JG Chief, 31.12.1947, APW 331/VI, sygn. 51, 39–41; SiRep JG Chief, 6.[2].1948, APW 331/VI, sygn. 51, 42–3; Rep on the first quarter of 1948 by JG Chief, 6.4.1948, APW 331/VI, sygn. 51, 48–52; SiRep JGT Pres, 31.5.1948, APW 331/VI, sygn. 50, 4–8; SiRep JG Chief, 1.6.1948, APW 331/VI, sygn. 51, 55–7; SiRep JG Chief on the month June 1948, 27.7.1948, APW 331/VI, sygn. 51, 60–1; Rep on the second quarter of 1948 by JGT Pres, undated, APW 331/VI, sygn. 50, 15–21; Rep on the second quarter of 1948, by JGTA head S-PD, undated, APW 331/VI, sygn. 50, 13–14; Rep on the second quarter of 1948 by JGT Pres, undated, APW 331/VI, sygn. 50, 15–21; Linek, *Polityka*, pp. 278–9.

[30] WR, Sabine von S., Hermsdorf (Sobieszów), undated, BOD 2, 188, 277–83; WR, Willi F., Schmiedeberg (Kowary), 2.8.1955, BOD 1, 207, 171–5; WR, Paul H., Bad Warmbrunn (Cieplice Śląskie), 10.9.1958, BOD 1, 207, 243–9; WR, Oskar S., Berbisdorf (Dziwiszów), undated, BOD 1, 207, 29–32.

sporadic attacks carried out by opportunistic looters and revenge-seekers rather than the product of an official campaign.

After the brief initial phase of active engagement with the campaign against German material culture in spring and summer 1948, Jelenia Góra District's state authorities allowed it to peter out once more.[31] The same was witnessed in most other localities in Poland's new territories at this time. The general pattern throughout these territories had been an early burst of frenzied official actions to remove the most visible physical remnants of German culture. This phase had lasted only until the end of 1945. In most places, officials failed to respond in any serious way to the pressure to restart these activities which came from the Ministry for Recovered Territories in summer 1947. What actions they did take had dwindled away again by late 1948. Only western Upper Silesia broke with this general pattern to any significant extent. Only there did the Regional Governor see a need to maintain the campaign against 'traces' of German culture throughout the second half of the 1940s and to radicalize it dramatically in late summer 1947.

But why did Zawadzki believe it necessary to take the campaign to the extremes we have discussed in this chapter? This cannot be explained by Zawadzki's greater anti-German fanaticism alone. There was an added factor present in western Upper Silesia which was not significant in any other region in Poland new territories outside of southern East Prussia: the large prewar population regarded as 'indigenous Poles'. Zawadzki clearly viewed it as critical to the cultural 're-Polonization' of these 'autochthons' that they recognized the environment they inhabited as Polish. He felt that to achieve this, it was necessary to eliminate the German language from every single object in the region and not merely from signs, monuments and the external walls of buildings. This explains the very comprehensive character of the campaign in western Upper Silesia. Yet the campaign had precisely the opposite effect to the one Zawadzki desired. Far from contributing to the assimilation of the 'indigenous Poles', the efforts to eliminate German material culture – and particularly the actions taken against gravestones – contributed in a crucial way to the profound alienation of this population, which we discussed in Chapter 9.[32]

[31] SiRep JG Chief, 4.8.1948, APW 331/VI, sygn. 51, 65–6; SiRep JG Chief, 2.9.1948, APW 331/VI, sygn. 51, 67–8; Rep by JGDA S-PD on the period 1.7.1948–30.9.1948, 30.9.1948, APW 331/VI, sygn. 51, 71; Rep on the third quarter of 1948 by JGTA head S-PD, APW 331/VI, sygn. 50, 40–1; Rep on the third quarter of 1948 by JGTA, 30.9.1948, APW331/VI, sygn. 50, 42–8.

[32] Strauchold, *Autochtoni*, pp. 174–8; Linek, *Polityka*, pp. 354, 363; Nitschke, *Vertreibung*, p. 150.

CULTURAL LIFE

Poland's Communist-led government attempted to wipe out German national culture throughout Poland's new territories after 1945 in a very broad sense. The arrival of Polish state officials as 'operational groups' in spring and early summer 1945 brought an immediate end to almost all main institutions of German cultural life in Poland's new territories. All German political, social, leisure and artistic organizations, all newspapers and almost all other German cultural provisions and facilities were instantly extinguished. One partial exception was the German Communist Party, whose members, with Soviet support, started an anti-fascist movement in the new territories after the war. This movement became particularly active in Lower Silesia and had branches in Wrocław and various other towns in the region, including Jelenia Góra. But it was viewed with acute suspicion by the Polish state authorities and was prevented from engaging in political activism. The authorities allowed it to meet some of the welfare needs of the German population. They also permitted it to organize voluntary transport to Germany after summer 1945 and to provide some organizational help for the 'displacement action' after spring 1946. But otherwise its activities were kept very limited. In fact, the only German organizations which the Polish authorities explicitly permitted to continue functioning after summer 1945 were the German churches (see the following).[33]

The German educational system was also dissolved. German schools and universities located in these territories had already ceased functioning in the final phase of the war. But the arrival of Polish state authorities after spring 1945 prevented them from reopening once the war was over. In June 1945, Poland's Ministry of Education explicitly prohibited the running of German schools in the new territories. Much to the annoyance of the state authorities, however, unofficial German schooling reemerged. In Jelenia Góra District, for example, officials received evidence that two illegal German schools were being run in the village of Cieplice Śląskie in autumn 1945. Officials in many other localities in Poland's new territories reported similar activities. Despite the makeshift character of these schools, the authorities viewed them with serious concern, because they appeared to indicate that the Germans were regaining confidence after the humiliations of military defeat, Soviet occupation and the Polish takeover. This seemed to suggest that the remaining German population of the new territories

[33] Kraft, 'Wrocławskie', pp. 385–9; Nitschke, *Vertreibung*, pp. 112–13; Pasierb, 'Problemy', pp. 25–6; Sielezin, 'Polityka polskich władz', pp. 72–4.

was starting to reconstruct the social and cultural structures which would allow them to continue living there. The unease the illegal German schools caused the authorities soon resulted in a circular sent out to the new territories' officials by the Ministry for Recovered Territories in January 1946, instructing them that German teachers should be 'prioritized' for 'repatriation' to Germany once the 'displacement action' got underway.[34] In Jelenia Góra District, this is precisely what happened. On 1 June 1946, the Lower Silesian Commissar for Repatriation Issues sent a letter to the district's Chief Official containing a list of 45 German teachers known to be living there. The letter ordered him to 'repatriate' the teachers, along with their families, before all other remaining Germans and then to give their homes to arriving Polish teachers.[35]

In western Upper Silesia, in addition to German organizations, schools, newspapers and the like, the state authorities also tried to eradicate German books. In summer 1945, the authorities in a number of the region's districts started to call on the prewar population to hand in their German books. In Opole District, for example, the School Inspectorate's officials started gathering German books from around July 1945 onwards. At this stage, this amounted to sporadic, separate initiatives. In September 1945 Zawadzki instructed the region's administrative authorities to start doing the same. But this did not yet spark a systematic regionwide campaign to collect German books.[36]

This changed in late August 1947 when, as we have seen, Zawadzki dramatically escalated his crackdown on the German language in western Upper Silesia. Zawadzki declared at this time that reading German books was a sign of 'sympathy for Germans'. He ordered the region's officials to set about eliminating them from western Upper Silesia altogether. From autumn 1947 onwards, the new 'civic inspection committees' were brought into the campaign and German books became one of the main items they looked for as they combed through the region's cafes, restaurants and homes. Officials were instructed that the only German books which could be spared from confiscation were academic ones.[37] In Opole District, the District Administration issued an order at the end of 1947 calling on the district's commune mayors and 'civic inspection committees' to engage fully

[34] Documents 207 and 221, in Borodziej and Lemberg, *Niemcy*, vol. 4 (Warsaw, 2001); Documents 98 and 108, in Borodziej and Lemberg, *Niemcy*, vol. 1 (Warsaw, 2000); Borodziej, 'Einleitung', footnote 291, p. 112; Kraft, 'Wrocławskie', pp. 385–9; WR, Robert W., Ludwigsdorf (Chromiec), undated, BOD 1, 207, 133–8.

[35] Note from the Lower Silesian Commissar for Repatriation Issues in Wrocław to JG Chief, 1.6.1946, APW 331/VI, sygn. 359, 50.

[36] Linek, *Polityka*, pp. 243–4.

[37] Linek, *Polityka*, pp. 258, 262, 345

with the campaign against German books. But the mayors and committees struggled in subsequent months to find the large quantities of books they had expected to come across in the district's villages. In April 1948, Opole District Administration noted, 'According to reports sent from the district's localities, German books were destroyed by their owners even before an order to collect them was issued. In some rural communes literally only a dozen German books have been collected. This raises the suspicion that the books are being concealed.'[38]

In late April 1948 Zawadzki stepped up his campaign to 'cleanse this territory of the German book'. He ordered the region's district administrations to appoint 'district classification committees' (*powiatowe komisje klasyfikacyjne*) to carry out the task of categorizing the confiscated books. This was required because, although Zawadzki intended to scrap all literary fiction, 'propaganda' and 'worthless literature', he stipulated that specialist and academic works needed to be preserved and transferred to 'specialist institutions' and libraries. Midway through 1948, Zawadzki's Regional Administration in Katowice revised the categories. Alongside the academic and specialist works, they instructed that German books printed before 1800, Nazi journalism, Nazi propaganda and German books about Poland should also be preserved. Significantly, the Regional Administration no longer wanted all German literary fiction to be destroyed. Indeed, it provided a list of specific authors whose works were not to be scrapped. It included, among others, Thomas Mann, Heinrich Mann, Gerhart Hauptmann, Erich Maria Remarque and Stefan Zweig.[39]

In Opole District, a 'special committee for sorting and classifying collected German books' was created at the start of May 1948. A separate 'classification committee' was set up for books collected from Opole town in September. A total of 6,000 books had been received from the district's rural localities by the end of July and an unknown number from the town of Opole. The books were kept in a 'specially designated store room' in the basement of Opole District Administration's premises, which was reportedly placed under the supervision of librarians. An entire German library was transferred to this 'general collection' from one of the district's villages in summer 1948. It is not clear how many German books were ultimately collected in Opole District by the end of the decade, but it is safe to assume that the eventual figure represented a tiny fraction of the number of German books present in the district at the end of the war. In

[38] CuRep ODA S-PD, 8.1.1948, APK 185/4, sygn. 52, 39–40; Rep on the 're-Polonization action' by ODA S-PD, 21.4.1948, APO 178, sygn. 65, 17–21.

[39] Linek, *Polityka*, pp. 276, 346–7.

most cases, this was not because the books had been destroyed or looted but rather because prewar residents of the district simply refused to hand them over and deliberately hid them from the authorities. As the mayor of the rural commune of Kup in Opole District explained, the locals tended to do this because they were unable to read Polish. The schools they had attended had been German ones; German was therefore their only reading language. In western Upper Silesia as a whole, it is also unclear how many German books were eventually collected by the state authorities by the end of the 1940s. But, again, it appears to have been a tiny fraction of the quantity originally expected by the authorities. Opole District's first 'classification committee' had not yet started to categorize the books at the end of July 1948 and it is not, in fact, clear when either this committee or the town committee actually began their work. It is also not known what proportion of books were eventually scrapped. Throughout western Upper Silesia, the books which were scrapped were eventually sold to paper factories for the production of recycled paper. In 1949, Upper Silesia's Regional Administration set up a 'Re-Polonization Fund' into which the proceeds from selling both scrapped books and gravestones were transferred. By this time, the region's authorities had pretty much stopped collecting books; the action had gradually petered out with the rest of the campaign against German material culture from the end of summer 1948 onwards.[40]

Unlike what occurred in western Upper Silesia, but probably reflecting what happened in most other districts in Poland's new territories, there do not appear to have been any systematic efforts made to eliminate German books in Jelenia Góra District. Instead, the actions taken against German books in this district were probably restricted to sporadic initiatives by the new Polish village or commune mayors in the immediate postwar months. Several German witnesses recalled local measures of this sort taken in summer and early autumn 1945. Ursula R., for example, recalled the local mayor putting up notices in the large rural community of Szklarska Poręba in October 1945, which instructed German residents to hand over all German books and newspapers. She claimed that although these notices were written in German, they failed to stipulate where the books should be delivered. Local Germans therefore ignored them.[41] The reason no

[40] CuRep ODA S-PD, 6.5.1948, APO 178, sygn. 65, 23–4; Rep on the first half of 1948 by ODA S-PD, undated, APO 178, sygn. 65, 50–2; Rep on the liquidation of traces of German language and culture by ODA S-PD, 31.7.1948, APO 178, sygn. 113, 64–5; Linek, *Polityka*, pp. 347–9.

[41] WR, Ursula R., Schreiberhau (Szklarska Poręba), 10.3.1954, BOD 2, 188, 122–37; WR, A.H., Grunau (Jeżów Sudecki), undated, BOD 1, 207, 81–2; WR, Robert W., Ludwigsdorf (Chromiec), undated, BOD 1, 207, 133–8.

systematic campaign was launched by the local state authorities in Jelenia Góra District is probably best explained, once again, by the lack of a large population they regarded as 'indigenous Poles'. Unlike western Upper Silesia's officials, the authorities in Jelenia Góra District – and in all the other districts in Poland's new territories which had been inhabited almost exclusively by monolingual German-speakers before 1945 – had no reason to believe that any more than a tiny fraction of the postwar population might wish to continue reading German books. After all, almost all the residents of these districts at the end of the 1940s were Polish settlers.

For rather different reasons, Jelenia Góra District's authorities were concerned about the presence of German writers in the district after the war. More specifically, they were concerned about the presence of the corpse of one particular very distinguished German writer. For many years, the Nobel Prize winning playwright and novelist Gerhart Hauptmann had lived in a villa in the picturesque rural village of Agnetendorf/Jagniątków in Hirschberg/Jelenia Góra District. On 6 June 1946 this elderly intellectual passed away, still surrounded by the seven German writers whom he had drawn to the village in the preceding years. This confronted Jelenia Góra District's postwar Polish state authorities with the problem of transporting Gerhart Hauptmann's corpse, his widow, his intellectual followers, his followers' families and all their possessions to Germany. The possessions included several entire libraries. The frenzy of correspondence which subsequently ensued reached to the very top of the Polish regime. In the course of June 1946, letters passed between Jelenia Góra District's Chief Official, Lower Silesia's Regional Governor, the Polish Military Mission in Berlin and the First Secretary of the Polish Workers' Party himself, Władysław Gomułka.

The delay in dealing with this matter meant that Hauptmann's corpse was left unburied in a coffin in his villa for a number of weeks. The Polish Military Mission in Berlin stressed to Gomułka at this time that the Soviet authorities in Berlin had instructed them that it was imperative that Hauptmann's corpse, his possessions, his widow, and the seven writers' families be transported in an absolutely orderly fashion. Each of them should be allowed to take their possessions, furnishings and libraries with them. The mission also emphasized that the Western powers were taking a keen interest in the matter. Poland's international prestige was at stake. The 'repatriation' finally took place in early July 1946 with no apparent hitches. The special treatment which Hauptmann's books received in western Upper Silesia after 1947 (see earlier) was therefore eclipsed by the level of special treatment his corpse, wife, followers and followers' families received in

Jelenia Góra District in summer 1946. Being forced to leave their homes must have been very painful. But at least they were not crammed into a cargo wagon with at least 30 other individuals and forced to spend two weeks in transit (see Chapter 4).[42]

THE ROMAN CATHOLIC CHURCH

After the Polish state administrative authorities, the Polish Workers' Party, the Citizens' Militia and the Security Police, the most important institution involved in the postwar ethno-national transformation of Poland's new territories was the Roman Catholic Church. Parallel to – and independently of – the Polish state authorities' takeover of administration in these territories, the leadership of the Polish arm of the Roman Catholic Church moved to assume control of the Church in the new territories in summer 1945. In August 1945, Poland's Roman Catholic Archbishop, August Hlond, persuaded the German Roman Catholic bishops, whose dioceses were located in the new territories, to renounce control over them. A few weeks later he replaced them with five Polish clerics who, although they were given the powers of bishops, each received the title of Apostolic Administrator. The reason for this was that the changes had not been authorized by the Vatican. The Communist-led government, despite the Polish Communists' ideological aversion to religion, endorsed what was effectively a territorial annexation by the Polish Roman Catholic Church. This was because they regarded the Church as crucial for the success of Poland's takeover of the territories to the east of the Odra–Nysa Line. There were two reasons for this. First, the regime believed that the Church could play an important role in the cultural 're-Polonization' of the people they regarded as 'indigenous Poles', because most of these people were Roman Catholics. Second, they recognized that if Roman Catholic churches were not established throughout Poland's new territories – which had overwhelmingly contained Protestant churches before 1945 – many Polish settlers would refuse to remain there.[43]

[42] Document 241, 'pismo Pełnomocnika Rządu RP na Obwód 29 do Pełnomocnika Rządu RP na Dolny Śląsk w sprawie opuszczenia Polski przez wdowę po Gerhardzie Hauptmanie, 4.7.1946', Document 242, 'raport Polskiej Misji Wojskowej w Berlinie do Władysława Gomułki w sprawie wyjazdu z Dolnego Śląska niemieckich intelektualistów, 5.7.1946', Document 243, 'sprawozdanie z konferencji zorganizowanej w UW Wrocławskim w sprawie wysiedlenia Niemców z Wrocławia, 8.7.1946', in Borodziej and Lemberg, *Niemcy*, vol. 4, pp. 365–9. WR, Ursula R., Niederschreiberhau/(Szklarska Poręba Dolna), 10.3.1954, BOD 2, 188, 122–37.

[43] Strauchold, *Autochtoni*, pp. 76–8; Świder, *Entgermanisierung*, pp. 257–9; Nitschke, *Vertreibung*, pp. 157–8.

As the region in Poland's new territories with both the largest concentration of Roman Catholics before 1945 and the largest number of people deemed by the Communist-controlled authorities to be 'indigenous Poles', it was western Upper Silesia above all where officials attempted to involve the Roman Catholic Church in the 're-Polonization action'. Yet Aleksander Zawadzki believed that in order for the Church to play this role, it would be essential to thoroughly de-Germanize it. In July 1945 he therefore prohibited the use of German in churches and called for 'ethnically dubious' priests to be removed from their posts. This order had a serious impact on the Roman Catholic Church in western Upper Silesia. From summer 1945 onwards, priests who were unable to speak the local Polish dialect were gradually eased out of their positions. In the town of Opole, for example, only three Catholic priests are said to have held onto their posts in the second half of 1945. In Opole District, the Chief Official may have issued his own order prohibiting the use of German in church services a little before Zawadzki had done so.

In Opole town, priests from the large Jesuit church residence later recalled having found it very difficult to adhere to this order, because only two of them were able to speak either the local Polish dialect or standard Polish. Recognizing that they had no future in Poland and believing that they could prevent the Polish state from taking ownership of the Jesuit residence if they handed it over to Polish Jesuits from Kraków, all of Opole town's Jesuits migrated to Germany voluntarily in August 1945. They travelled there in several groups.[44]

Despite the important role the Communist-controlled authorities had envisaged for the Roman Catholic Church in the 're-Polonization action' in western Upper Silesia, the Church responded for the most part with acquiescence rather than active support for their nationalist campaign. The new Apostolic Administrator for western Upper Silesia, Dr Bolesław Kominek, appointed in September 1945, broadly agreed with Zawadzki that the German language needed to be driven out of the Church in the region. But it soon became clear that he would not go as far as Zawadzki wanted.[45] More importantly, many local priests, who had retained their positions because they were regarded by the state authorities as 'indigenous Poles', were clearly hostile to his anti-German measures. This manifested

[44] Świder, *Entgermanisierung*, pp. 222, 257–60; Madajczyk, *Przyłączenie*, pp. 224–5; WR, Alfons S., Oppeln (Opole) town, 23.1.1949, BOD 2, 229, 48–52; WR, A., Oppeln (Opole) town, 15.7.1955, BOD 2, 229, 1–2.

[45] Significantly, Bolesław Kominek, two decades later, would be one of the initiators of the Polish Bishops' letter of reconciliation sent to German Bishops in 1965. See the Introduction.

itself, first and foremost, in instances of local priests resisting pressure to remove German inscriptions from church property and particularly from gravestones. Such cases were witnessed throughout western Upper Silesia at this time (as discussed previously).

The region's authorities also found that many local priests refused to comply with the ban on using the German language in church services. This soon led to the accusation that the Roman Catholic Church was deliberately protecting German priests. From 1946 onwards, Zawadzki put increasing pressure on Kominek to dismiss priests who allowed German to be used in their churches. He also demanded that the region's state officials subject priests to ethnic screening outside the parameters of the 'verification action'. This would ensure that all German priests were identified and displaced to Germany. But although Kominek showed a good deal of willingness to cooperate with Zawadzki in other aspects of his anti-German campaign, he proved reluctant to collaborate in the expulsion of local priests. Around 200 priests are estimated to have left voluntarily or been displaced to Germany between 1945 and 1947. But few were actually forced out of their positions by the Church in the second half of the 1940s.[46]

Part of the reason for this was the outrage the removal of rural priests provoked from the prewar population of western Upper Silesia. One instance of this, for example, happened in Opole District in 1947. Upper Silesia's Regional Administration in Katowice received reports at this time that a priest, whose church was located in the village of Czarnowąsy in Opole District, was allowing his parishioners to use German prayer books, speak German in church and give their children prohibited German names. Katowice demanded an explanation from Opole District Administration around the end of the year. Katowice clearly wanted the priest removed from his post. But the priest's entire congregation seems to have leapt to his defence to protect him from the state authorities and it seems likely that, as a result, he did not lose his position.[47]

From late 1947 onwards, Zawadzki applied strong pressure to Roman Catholic churches throughout western Upper Silesia to cease using German prayer and hymn books and to replace them with Polish ones. In April 1948 Kominek agreed to start collecting all German books from churches in the region. But because Zawadzki failed to fulfil his promise to Kominek to supply the region's churches with Polish prayer and hymn books as replacements, they did not desist from using the German ones. In Opole

[46] Linek, *Polityka*, pp. 110–35, 241, 287–98; Świder, *Entgermanisierung*, pp. 259–72; Madajczyk, *Przyłączenie*, pp. 174, 225–6; Strauchold, *Autochtoni*, p. 78; Nitschke, *Vertreibung*, pp. 158–60.

[47] Linek, *Polityka*, p. 293; Madajczyk, *Przyłączenie*, pp. 225–6.

District, for example, the majority of congregations were still said to be using German prayer books in spring 1949.[48]

The Roman Catholic Church in western Upper Silesia, therefore, never became the tool for 're-Polonization' that the Polish state authorities had hoped it would become when they first arrived in the region in spring 1945. This was because, on the one hand, the Church had refused to engage properly in the authorities' efforts to de-Germanize the region. On the other hand, the Communist-controlled authorities had, from the outset, held deep suspicions about many of the region's priests and this had ultimately dissuaded them from trying to incorporate the Church fully in the 're-Polonization action'. Moreover, the measures taken by the authorities to de-Germanize the Catholic Church had been yet another respect in which their actions had proven counterproductive. They had actively alienated rather than promoted the assimilation of western Upper Silesia's so-called indigenous Poles.[49]

DE-PROTESTANTIZATION

Outside of western Upper Silesia, the role Poland's Communist-controlled authorities envisaged for the Roman Catholic Church in the postwar ethno-national transformation of Poland's new territories was very different. Only western Upper Silesia and certain districts in southern East Prussia had been predominantly Roman Catholic before 1945. The vast majority of the new territories had been overwhelmingly Protestant. Leaving aside the complex case of the Protestant Masurian-dialect speakers of southern East Prussia for the moment (see the following), the state authorities believed that in most localities in the new territories, a comprehensive process of de-Protestantization and Catholicization was necessary. This would be essential to ensure that the many devout Roman Catholics among the Polish settler population would be willing to remain in these territories on a permanent basis.

Unlike almost all other German organizations and institutions, the German Protestant (*evangelisch*) churches were allowed to continue functioning legally in Poland's new territories after the war. The state authorities decided it was in their interest to allow the Protestant churches to carry on meeting the religious needs of the German population. But the authorities

[48] Linek, *Polityka*, pp. 296, 349–50; Special Rep by ODA S-PD, 19.3.1949, APO 178, sygn. 64, 16–17.

[49] Świder, *Entgermanisierung*, pp. 260–72; Strauchold, *Autochtoni*, p. 78; Madajczyk, *Przyłączenie*, pp. 225–6; Linek, *Polityka*, pp. 294–7.

viewed this very much as a purely temporary concession, which would last only as long as a large number of Germans remained in these territories. They clearly viewed this as a way of helping to keep this subjugated population passive and under control.[50] Many German Protestant pastors had fled from the new territories with millions of other Germans in the final months of the war. But there were still enough of them left there after the war for the German Protestant churches to continue functioning in areas where there were still large numbers of Germans. The Polish state authorities even permitted German Protestant pastors to provide religious teaching to German children. This soon became a source of tension between the German Protestant churches and the Polish authorities, because the authorities received reports in the early postwar months that many German pastors were exploiting this concession to provide normal school teaching to the children. This, as we have discussed, was not permitted. It was therefore not only professional school teachers but also German Protestant clerics who were accused by the authorities of running illegal German schools in the new territories in the immediate postwar period.

Outside of western Upper Silesia and part of southern East Prussia, only a small minority of inhabitants of these territories had been members of the Roman Catholic Church before 1945. The vast majority had been Protestants. Nevertheless, in localities where a large number of Germans remained after the war, the German arm of the Roman Catholic Church also attempted to resume religious services and to provide help to German Catholics in the early postwar period. Yet the German Roman Catholic Church was too small to play a significant role in the social life of the remaining German population after the war. And this was not helped by the relatively hostile relationship the German Catholic clergy had with the leadership of the Polish Roman Catholic Church in this period. This was a product of the latter's effective annexation of German dioceses in the new territories in August 1945. In stark contrast, the small Polish Protestant Church (*Kościół Ewangelicko-Augsburski*) proved very keen to assist the German Protestant clergy. Indeed, the Communist-controlled authorities viewed the relationship between the German and Polish Protestants as rather too close. They accused the Polish Protestants of helping the Germans to provide illegal schooling and even of appointing German pastors to posts in the Polish Protestant Church.[51]

[50] Kraft, 'Wrocławskie', pp. 387–8; WR, the German Protestant pastor Johannes S., Giersdorf (Podgórzyn), 6.4.1951, BOD 2, 188, 169–74.

[51] Kraft, 'Wrocławskie', pp. 387–8.

We can turn once again to the example of Jelenia Góra District to examine what the process of de-Protestantization and Catholicization looked like on the ground in the areas of Poland's new territories which had been predominantly Protestant before 1945. As Polish settlers arrived in Jelenia Góra District, from early summer 1945 onwards, Roman Catholic parishes were gradually set up to provide religious services for them. This created a situation in which the Polish Roman Catholic Church functioned alongside the German Protestant churches in Jelenia Góra District. This lasted for over a year after the arrival of the first Polish settlers in the district. The same was witnessed in localities across Poland's new territories which still contained large numbers of Germans.[52]

This situation came to an abrupt end in Jelenia Góra District in summer 1946 with the start of the mass transportation of Germans. The evidence from Jelenia Góra District suggests that, as the start of the 'displacement action' approached in early 1946, the state authorities decided to prioritize the expulsion not only of German teachers, but also of German Protestant pastors. Presumably this was because the authorities had realized that the pastors, like the teachers, were helping to sustain German social and cultural life in the new territories in a way which went beyond merely meeting the religious needs of the remaining German population. At the start of July 1946, Jelenia Góra District Administration prepared a list of remaining German Protestant pastors and church personnel designated for displacement from the district as a matter of priority. These people were all transported to Germany in the course of July. They appear to have been sent first to Wrocław. From there they were probably transported to Germany with a large number of German Protestant clerics from other localities in Lower Silesia. It seems that, as far as the district's administrative authorities were concerned, there were no active German Protestant pastors remaining in Jelenia Góra District after July 1946. In Poland's new territories as a whole, the German Protestant churches appear to have ceased all religious and other activities by autumn 1946. It formally handed over its responsibilities to the Polish Protestant Church at that time.[53]

The recollections of Johannes S., a German Protestant pastor living in the village of Podgórzyn in Jelenia Góra District, provides evidence that the Polish state authorities had not originally intended to prioritize the

[52] SiRep JG Chief, 3.10.1945, APJG 123/II, sygn. 18, 127–32; SiRep JG Chief, 5.12.1945, APJG 123/II, sygn. 18, 185–200; SiRep JG Chief, 5.1.1946, APJG 123/II, sygn. 18, 206–14; SiRep JG Chief, 5.2.1946, APJG 123/II, sygn. 19, 30–37; SiRep JG Chief, 2.3.1946, APJG 123/II, sygn. 19, 73–6.

[53] SiRep JGDA S-PD, 1.7.1946, APJG 123/II, sygn. 19, 273–4; SiRep JGDA head S-PD, 30.7.1946, APW 331/VI, sygn. 34, 35–7; Kraft, 'Wrocławskie', p. 389.

displacement of German clerics and only later changed their minds about this. He claimed that he and fellow pastors in the local area had previously been assured by the authorities that they would not be 'deported' until August or September 1946. This would have allowed them to continue providing religious services for the remaining German population until only a small fraction of Germans remained in the local area. Instead, a Polish committee, headed by a Polish Roman Catholic priest from the nearby village of Sobieszów, reportedly appeared at his parish-house in Podgórzyn on 27 June 1946 to inform him of his imminent expulsion. The committee demanded that Johannes S. hand over his church and leave the house. While his wife and daughter packed some belongings, he was forced to show the committee around the church and to hand over the keys. The family were then escorted to the collection camp on Łominicka Street in Jelenia Góra town on a passenger train (see Chapter 4). They were then transported to Germany.[54]

The property of the German Protestant churches, like all other German property in Poland's new territories, had been taken into Polish state ownership in May 1945. But the evidence from Jelenia Góra District indicates that, although the Roman Catholic Church was already serving the religious needs of Polish settlers in the new territories from summer 1945 onwards, it was not until the German Protestant clerics actually left or were displaced from Poland's new territories that the state authorities formally placed most of the German Protestant churches' property under the sole control of the Roman Catholic Church. In the rural areas of Jelenia Góra District, almost all the churches appear to have been handed over to the Roman Catholic Church in the course of July 1946. The same very likely happened at this time in Jelenia Góra town. The Catholicization of Jelenia Góra District had, in essence, already been completed by the end of July 1946.[55]

Yet the story is not quite that simple, because not quite all German Protestant churches were transferred to the Roman Catholic Church. One of the churches in the rural part of Jelenia Góra District, in fact, was assigned in summer 1946 to the separate Old Catholic Church. Nor were Roman and Old Catholics the only religious groups which began

[54] WR, the German Protestant pastor Johannes S., Giersdorf (Podgórzyn), 6.4.1951, BOD 2, 188, 169–74.

[55] SiRep JG Chief, 3.10.1945, APJG 123/II, sygn. 18, 127–32; SiRep JG Chief, 5.12.1945, APJG 123/II, sygn. 18, 185–200; SiRep JG Chief, 5.1.1946, APJG 123/II, sygn. 18, 206–14; SiRep JG Chief, 5.2.1946, APJG 123/II, sygn. 19, 30–37; SiRep JG Chief, 2.3.1946, APJG 123/II, sygn. 19, 73–6; SiRep JGDA S-PD, 30.7.1946, APW 331/VI, sygn. 34, 35–7; Nitschke, *Vertreibung*, p. 161.

operating in the district after the war. The Polish Protestant Church formally registered with Jelenia Góra District Administration in summer 1946 and the number of other religious organizations with branches in the district proliferated during the next year. In early 1947, the district's state officials listed the religious groups represented in Jelenia Góra District, in order of size, as the Roman Catholic Church, the Old Catholic Church, the Protestant Church, Judaism, the Jehovah's Witnesses and the Methodist Church. By autumn 1947, the Eastern Orthodox Church had been added to the list and by early summer 1948, the Polish Evangelical Christian Church and the Seventh Day Adventists as well. The explanation for this proliferation is that small religious groups in Poland had recognized that, with so many Polish settlers in Poland's new territories facing disorienting circumstances and requiring material aid, there was an excellent opportunity to gain new followers. Yet the religious diversity in the district should not be overstated. None of these religious groups had anywhere near the number of followers of the Roman Catholic Church. Whereas the latter had many tens of thousands of adherents in Jelenia Góra District, the Old Catholic Church and Protestant Church each had little more than 1,000 members. All other Christian groups were just a fraction of that size and the district's Jewish population (as we discussed in Chapter 8) had abandoned the district by the start of the 1950s.

The religious complexion of the district by end of the 1940s, therefore, may not have been entirely uniform, but it clearly was overwhelmingly Roman Catholic. The Communist-led state authorities facilitated the same process of Roman Catholicization in almost all other previously Protestant areas in Poland's new territories in the early postwar years. The one important but only partial exception to this general pattern, as we shall discuss, was the area of southern East Prussia inhabited by the Protestant Masurian-dialect speakers.[56]

The case of the Polish Protestant Church is worth dwelling on for the moment because it says a lot about where religion figured in the Communist-controlled authorities' conception of German and Polish

[56] SiRep JGDA S-PD, 30.7.1946, APW 331/VI, sygn. 34, 35–7; SiRep JG Chief, 1.3.1947, APW 331/VI, sygn. 51, 5–6; SiRep JG Chief, 31.3.1947, APW 331/VI, sygn. 51, 10–12; SiRep JG Chief, 30.4.1947, APW331/VI, sygn. 51, 18–19; SiRep the head of JGTA's Settlement Department, 18.6.1947, APJG 130, sygn. 47, 219–21; Rep on the third quarter of 1947 by JG Chief, 13.11.1947, APJG 123/II, sygn. 21, 232–6; Rep on the first quarter of 1948, by JG Chief, 6.4.1948, APW 331/VI, sygn. 51, 48–52; SiRep JG Chief, 5.5.1948, APW 331/VI, sygn. 51, 53–4; SiRep JGT Pres, 31.5.1948, APW 331/VI, sygn. 50, 4–8; SiRep JG Chief, 3.12.1948, APW 331/VI, sygn. 51, 79–81; Nitschke, *Vertreibung*, pp. 160–1; Strauchold, *Autochtoni*, p. 77.

national identities. Most of the property of the German Roman Catholic Church – not only in western Upper Silesia but throughout Poland's new territories – passed automatically into the hands of the Polish Roman Catholic Church in the early postwar years. In stark contrast, there was no chance that the Polish Protestant Church would automatically receive the property of the German *Protestant* churches. This was because, in the immediate aftermath of the war, the state authorities tended to equate 'Protestant' with 'German' and 'de-Germanization' with 'de-Protestantization'. As we have seen, almost all German Protestant property was therefore transferred by the state authorities to the Polish Roman Catholic Church during 1946. It was only from around autumn 1946 onwards that the authorities softened their stance on the activities of the Polish Protestant Church in Poland's new territories.

This was clearly witnessed in Jelenia Góra District. After officially registering with Jelenia Góra District Administration in summer 1946, the Polish Protestant Church applied to be given one of the churches in the rural part of district. This was swiftly rejected by the district's authorities. Tellingly, the district's authorities referred to all the district's churches at this time as 'post-Protestant' (*poewangelicki*). Yet by the end of the summer the district's officials were reporting that the Polish Protestants were entangled in a 'battle between Churches for assets'. In autumn 1946, the authorities yielded by granting them 'temporary' – and probably shared – use of a church in Cieplice Śląskie. In Jelenia Góra town, too, a struggle between the Polish Protestant Church and the Roman Catholic Church erupted over control of a church located on Panieńska Street in autumn 1946. It is probable that the Polish Protestants did not succeed in taking over the latter church. But they do seem to have taken sole control of one church in the rural part of the district by 1948.[57]

The Polish Protestant Church's struggle against the prejudices and hostility of the Communist-controlled state authorities was played out in

[57] SiRep JGDA S-PD, 30.7.1946, APW 331/VI, sygn. 34, 35–7; SiRep JGDA head S-PD, 31.8.1946, APW 331/VI, sygn. 35, 32–4; Rep by JGDA head S-PD, 30.9.1946, APJG 123/II, sygn. 19, 377; Rep by JGDA head S-PD, 31.10.1946, APJG 123/II, sygn. 19, 410–11; SiRep JG Chief, 1.2.1947, APW 331/VI, sygn. 51, 1–4; SiRep JG Chief, 31.3.1947, APW 331/VI, sygn. 51, 10–12; SiRep JGDA S-PD, 26.9.1947, APJG 123/II, sygn. 20, 136–7; Rep by JGDA S-PD, 31.3.1947, APJG, 123/II, sygn. 21, 68; SiRep JG DepChief, 31.5.1947, APW 331/VI, sygn. 51, 20–1; Rep on the third quarter of 1947 by JG Chief, 13.11.1947, APJG 123/II, sygn. 21, 232–6; SiRep JG Chief, 30.4.1947, APW 331/VI, sygn. 51, 18–19; SiRep JG Chief, 3.12.1947, APW 331/VI, sygn.51, 37–8; Rep by JG Chief on the period 20.11.1947–30.1.1948, APJG 123/II, sygn. 20, 226–7; SiRep JG Chief, 3.12.1948, APW 331/VI, sygn. 51, 79–81; Nitschke, *Vertreibung*, pp. 160–4.

localities across Poland's new territories after the war. Only in southern East Prussia was the treatment of Protestants more nuanced. We have discussed how in the vast majority of Poland's new territories the postwar state authorities broadly equated 'de-Germanization' with 'de-Protestanization'. In the overwhelmingly Roman Catholic region of western Upper Silesia, inhabitants of predominantly Protestant villages were often therefore regarded by the state authorities automatically as Germans purely because of their religious identities. In Opole District, for example, in the small minority of villages which had overwhelmingly Protestant residents in 1945, almost all villagers were expelled in summer 1945, without, it would seem, being given any opportunity to undergo 'verification' as ethnic Poles (see Chapter 7).

But in southern East Prussia the situation was different. Although this region was regarded by the Communist-led government as having the second largest concentration of 'indigenous Poles' in Poland's new territories, the majority of these people, who spoke the Masurian dialect of Polish as well as German, were Protestants. Because of this, the government envisaged that the Polish Protestant Church would play a role in the 're-Polonization' of 'autochthons' in this region. The Church itself, keen to expand into this area, voiced its support for the 're-Polonization' of the Masurians. The state authorities even provided the Church with funding to assist with its activities in Masuria. Yet the Church's use of standard Polish in church services alienated the Masurian-dialect-speaking population. The local population felt that their regionally distinct Protestant traditions and practices were under threat from the Polish Protestant Church. This prevented the Polish Protestant Church from becoming a vehicle for 're-Polonization' in the region. At the same time, like everywhere else in Poland's new territories, a large proportion of the German Protestant churches' property in this area was handed over to the Roman Catholic Church in these years. The Roman Catholic Church, together with the local state officials, placed the Masurian-dialect-speaking population under considerable pressure to convert to Catholicism at this time. The equation of 'Catholics' with 'Poles' therefore also played a role in how the Masurians were treated in these years. All of this contributed significantly to the hostility felt by most Masurian-dialect speakers living in southern East Prussia towards Poland and Polish society.[58]

[58] Strauchold, *Autochtoni*, pp. 76–81; Blanke, *Polish-Speaking Germans*, pp. 290–1, 296; Nitschke, *Vertreibung*, pp. 160–3.

The regime's attitude towards the Roman Catholic Church changed dramatically from late 1947 onwards, as it started to make Stalinist moves towards gaining control of the only institution which had thus far managed to preserve its independence. In western Upper Silesia, this Stalinist clampdown on the Church soon brought an end to Zawadzki's efforts to bring the Church on board with the 're-Polonization' of 'autochthons' and the removal of German material culture from the region's churches.[59]

Throughout Poland, the Roman Catholic Church started to come under attack at this time. In Poland's new territories there was something bitterly ironic about this. The Communist-controlled authorities had, after all, spent the previous few years deliberately Catholicizing most localities in these territories. What happened in Jelenia Góra District in the final two years of the decade was typical of most other localities in Poland's new territories in this regard. From December 1947 onwards, the district's Chief Official began to claim that the Roman Catholic Church was directing a 'hostile campaign' against the 'current reality', issuing orders 'from the pulpit' to 'smite' the 'current system', attacking 'secular society' and obstructing the realization of 'the government's programme'. Despite having facilitated the transfer of German Protestant property to the Roman Catholic Church in the early postwar years, in 1949 the district's authorities began to seize much of it back. Then, following the new line taken by the regime's Stalinist leadership in Warsaw, the district's branch of the Polish United Workers' Party launched a campaign of anti-Vatican propaganda. The district's authorities began to attack particular priests for their 'hostile stances' towards the regime. By the end of 1949, the district's officials were reporting to their superiors in Wrocław that they had gained the full compliance of the district's Roman Catholic priests.[60] Thus, having promoted the Roman Catholicization of Poland's new territories in the early postwar years – when it had helped with achieving their nationalist objectives to do so – the Communist authorities set about attempting to reverse this process. They attempted to de-Catholicize these territories once more at

[59] Linek, *Polityka*, pp. 287–91; Świder, *Entgermanisierung*, pp. 260, 269–71; Strauchold, *Autochtoni*, pp. 76–7.

[60] SiRep JG Chief, 3.12.1947, APW 331/VI, sygn. 51, 37–8; SiRep JG Chief, 31.12.1947, APW 331/VI, sygn. 51, 39–41; SiRep JG Chief, start March 1949, APW 331/VI, sygn. 51, 98–100; Rep on the first quarter of 1949 by JG Chief, 6.4.1949, APW 331/VI, sygn. 51, 105–10; Rep on the first quarter of 1949 by JGT Pres, 31.3.1949, APW 331/VI, sygn. 50, 98–106; Rep on the third quarter of 1949 by JG Chief, 3.10.1949, APW 331/VI, sygn. 51, 154–9; SiRep JG DepChief, 5.10.1949, APW 331/VI, sygn. 51, 160–2; Prażmowska, *Poland*, pp. 179–80.

the end of the 1940s. This new objective would prove immeasurably more difficult to achieve.

BELONGING AND NOT BELONGING

In order to accomplish the objective of making the postwar inhabitants of Poland's new territories feel that they were living in a culturally Polish environment, the Commmunist-controlled authorities recognized that they needed not only to allow the Polish Roman Catholic Church to expand into these territories but also to set up Polish state schools, libraries, community centres, newspapers, cinemas, theatres, museums and other cultural provisions. As we discussed in Chapter 9, these educational and cultural provisions were viewed by the authorities as playing an important role in the 're-Polonization' of 'indigenous Poles'. But clearly, the 're-Polonization' of 'autochthons' was only a secondary reason for introducing these facilities to these territories. In most areas of Poland's new territories, where 'indigenous Poles' formed no more than a tiny fraction of the postwar population, these facilities were aimed almost entirely at settlers alone. The authorities knew that in order to convince especially those settlers who had moved to the new territories voluntarily from central Poland to remain there on a permanent basis, they needed not merely to provide them with places to live and worship, but also to ensure that their children could attend school and that they could access a range of Polish cultural facilities. With this in mind, getting these educational and cultural provisions up and running in Poland's new territories became an important priority for the state authorities soon after the war.

The first Polish state schools were opened in localities throughout Poland's new territories by the second half of 1945. In Jelenia Góra District, for example, a number of Polish state schools were already set up for settler children by the start of the first postwar academic year, in autumn 1945. One of the district's officials noted at that time that more schools would be opened in the district as more settlers arrived. A full network of Polish state schools was established in Jelenia Góra District in the course of the next two years. A Polish newspaper called *Głos Pogranicza* (Voice of the Borderland) also began publishing in the district in late summer 1945. It appears to have closed down at some point during the next year, but the district's officials made efforts, over the next several years, to ensure that regional Polish newspapers reached as many villages in the district as possible. From autumn 1945 onwards, they also set up or facilitated the setting up of Polish libraries and community centres in villages throughout the district. The local state authorities did the same in districts throughout Poland's new territories in these early postwar years.[61]

Moreover, Poland's Communist-controlled government was quick to introduce Polish higher education into these territories. Many of the survivors of the occupation among the academics of interwar Poland's third largest university, the Jan Kazimierz University in Lwów, relocated collectively to Wrocław in 1945. This enabled the state authorities to open the new University of Wrocław as early as September 1945. This was followed in 1946 and 1947 by the transfer from Lwów to Wrocław of the Ossolineum Institute, with a large part of its hugely important collection of Polish literature and art.[62]

The authorities' principal objective in introducing educational institutions, social facilities and cultural resources in Poland's new territories was to ensure that the settlers, who made up the vast majority of the territories' postwar population, would feel they could lay down roots in these territories. The authorities also appear to have believed that settlers would not feel truly rooted to these territories until they viewed one another as members of the same community; that is, until a sense of shared identity emerged among them. One of Jelenia Góra District's officials communicated this idea quite well when he spoke in early autumn 1945 of the importance of bringing settlers recruited 'from every part of Poland' together in the 'hope for a better tomorrow in the newly acquired territories' by 'strengthening' their consciousness of sharing a 'Polish spirit' with one another.[63] Going on the account of Adam Jaroszewski, a settler and former soldier, who took up residence in the small village of Twardów (later Górzyniec) in Jelenia Góra District after the war, there were early signs in the late 1940s that a

[61] Rep by JGDA S-PD, 3.9.1945, APJG 123/II, sygn. 18, 86–8; Rep by JG Chief, 6.[8].1945, APJG 123/II, sygn. 18, 3–26; SiRep head JGTA, 2.11.1945, APW 331/VI, sygn. 28, 77–92; SiRep JG Chief, 5.1.1946, APJG 123/II, sygn. 18, 206–14; SiRep JG Chief, 3.7.1946, APJG 123/II, sygn. 19, 250–2; SiRep JG Chief, 2.12.1946, APW 331/VI, sygn. 38, 97–9; SiRep JG Chief, 2.1.1947, APW 331/VI, sygn. 39, 15–17; SiRep JG DepChief, 31.5.1947, APW 331/VI, sygn. 51, 20–2; SiRep the head of JGTA's Settlement Department, 18.6.1947, APJG 130, sygn. 47, 219–21; SiRep JG DepChief, 5.[7].1947, APJG 123/II, sygn. 21, 167–8 and 198; Strauchold, *Autochtoni*, pp. 93–103; Magierska, *Ziemie*, pp. 234–71.

[62] Krzystof Ruchniewicz, 'Von Lemberg nach Breslau – eine Universität zwischen Tradition und Neubestimmung', *Orbis Linguarum*, 21, 2002, pp. 9–17; Thum, *Breslau*, pp. 227–8, 394–8; Norman Davies and Roger Moorhouse, *Microcosm. Portrait of a Central European City* (London, 2002), p. 429.

[63] SiRep JGDA S-PD, 3.9.1945, APJG 123/II, sygn. 18, 86–8; SiRep JG Chief, 5.2.1946, APJG 123/II, sygn. 19, 30–7; Strauchold, *Autochtoni*, p. 188; Joanna Nowosielska-Sobel, '"Czy istnieje Polak sudecki?". Z problemów kształtowanie się tożsamości zbiorowej ludności Dolnego Śląska na przykładzie Ziemi Jeleniogórskiej w latach 60. XX wieku', in Joanna Nowosielska-Sobel and Grzegorz Strauchold (eds.), *Dolnoślazacy? Kształtowanie tożsamości mieszkańców Dolnego Śląska po II wojnie światowej* (Wrocław, 2007), pp. 21, 28.

feeling of community and shared identity was starting to surface among local settlers:

> [On moving to Twardów in 1947] [w]e found ourselves in a fully Polish environment . . . every farm was in the hands of Poles, mainly repatriates from behind the Bug river. We formed good relations with these neighbours. Based on a willingness to help one another, we created a new society . . . Among the settlers . . . were a lot of demobilized soldiers and together we decided to get involved with the Association of Military Settlers which was already active elsewhere in the Recovered Territories. We established a branch of this association with an office in the neighbouring village of Piechowice and I was elected chairman . . . Our branch developed rapidly . . . becoming the first cultural facility in the local area and we soon opened a social centre with a library and newspaper room.[64]

In Jelenia Góra District, officials also appear to have believed that they could foster the local settlers' feelings of rootedness in these territories and their sense of sharing an identity by helping to establish an artistic community there. The district's authorities thus assisted many Polish writers and poets to relocate to the picturesque territories of Jelenia Góra District in the early postwar years. They included Edward Kozikowski, Jan Sztaudynger and Jan Koprowski. In May 1947, Jelenia Góra District's Chief Official helped to organize the First Rally of Polish Writers of the Sudeten Lands. This gave birth to a new organization called the Ideological Group of Writers of the Sudeten Lands. Significantly, this organization saw its principal purpose as helping to 'form a uniform [*jednolity*] type of Pole adapted to the character and needs of the Sudeten Lands'. Both the writers involved in these activities and the district's state officials supporting them regarded what they were doing as contributing to the emergence of an integrated Polish society in Poland's new territories. But to the regime's leaders in Warsaw, their rhetoric smacked of regional separatism. Jelenia Góra District's Chief Official and the poet Kozikowski were even summoned to Warsaw to explain themselves in 1947. Yet it was the regime's measures to limit artistic freedom throughout Poland which eventually brought an end to Jelenia Góra District's Polish artistic community. The Stalinist regime imposed more repressive controls on the arts at the end of the 1940s, which caused most local writers to abandon the district for Warsaw and other more established, more secure artistic communities at this time.[65]

Although there were early signs that a feeling of shared community was starting to surface among settlers in the new territories already at the end

[64] Jaroszewski, 'Na turoszowskiej budowie', pp. 69–70.
[65] Nowosielska-Sobel, 'Polak sudecki', pp. 26–9.

of the 1940s, it was not until the first postwar generation to be born in these territories started to reach adulthood, in the mid 1960s, that the culturally and socially fractured character of the original settler population finally started to fade into the background. Moreover, the arrival of the second generation of settler children – the children produced by the first generation of settlers' children who were born in Poland's new territories – appeared to symbolize the fact that the Polish settlers were at last feeling firmly rooted to these territories. In Jelenia Góra town, the arrival of 'the first child of the second generation' on 3 December 1963 was even marked with an official reception for the parents at Jelenia Góra town's People's Council.[66]

In contrast, most German citizens who had been 'verified' as ethnic Poles in the early postwar years never reconciled themselves to life in Poland's new territories. Although the Communist regime largely abandoned overtly nationalist rhetoric in its propaganda at the end of the 1940s, the party-state authorities continued their suppression of any attempt by the 'indigenous Poles' in western Upper Silesia and in southern East Prussian to maintain German or non-Polish regional collective identities. They also kept in place their ban on use of German in public by 'autochthons'. Most 'indigenous Poles' continued to feel profoundly alienated by these measures, which – together with the fact that they wanted to escape from a dictatorship, improve their material circumstances and join their families – ensured that many thousands continued to apply for emigration to West Germany in the early 1950s.[67]

The Polish Communists' original hope that the 'verified Poles' would embrace membership of the new Polish society of the 'recovered territories', therefore, continued to founder in the 1950s. One large group of people whom the authorities had not, in 1945, intended to include in this society were the several hundred thousand residents who were officially registered as Germans (see Chapter 4). They were concentrated mainly in the regions of Lower Silesia and western Pomerania. To a certain extent – as we shall see – their fate after 1950 overlapped with that of the million or so remaining 'autochthons'. But in important respects the authorities continued to treat the registered Germans very differently to the 'autochthons'. Unlike the latter, the Germans did not receive the right to attain Polish citizenship in the late 1940s and 1950s. The Polish state authorities regarded them as stateless persons during these years. On the other hand, unlike the

[66] Ibid., pp. 21–6.

[67] Madajczyk, 'Niemcy', pp. 82–7; Ther, 'Die einheimische Bevölkerung', p. 437; Blanke, *Polish-Speaking Germans*, pp. 301–2.

'autochthons', acknowledged Germans were gradually allowed their own separate cultural provisions. This started in 1949, when the state authorities permitted the creation of German sports clubs. In 1950 the Ministry of Education then ordered the opening of German-language schools in Lower Silesia and western Pomerania. These schools soon became the centre of German cultural and social life in Poland for both adults and children. In 1951 the regime went a step further by formally guaranteeing Germans the right to maintain their own culture. As a consequence, several German-language newspapers emerged in the early 1950s – although their editors were always careful to stick well within the regime's strict ideological parameters. Moreover, between 1949 and 1951 the authorities issued several rulings stipulating that Germans received the same wages, workers' rights and social benefits as Poles. Only their pensions, based on the work they had done before 1945, continued to be denied to them after that point.

The Communist leadership's attitude towards Germans had thus liberalized dramatically since the second half of the 1940s. The leaders were clearly moving steadily over to the view that this skilled population should be enticed to remain in Poland on a permanent basis. Yet the emergence of a Soviet-style Communist dictatorship in Poland, the experience of everyday discrimination and a general aversion to living in a Polish state meant that few registered Germans had any such intention. Many tens of thousands therefore applied for emigration to West and East Germany in the early 1950s. The authorities permitted an estimated 100,000 people to emigrate between 1949 and 1954. Most of the emigrants were people the authorities recognized as Germans. But a significant number were also 'autochthons' and former '*Volksdeutsche*' (Polish citizens who had been placed on the *Deutsche Volksliste* during the Nazi German occupation of Poland but were 'rehabilitated' after the war; see Chapter 6). The authorities mainly granted the latter two groups permission to emigrate only insofar as they could prove that they had families in West and East Germany.[68]

The brief political thaw in Poland after October 1956 brought further changes to the Communist regime's policies towards both 'autochthons' and registered Germans. For the first time, it momentarily became possible to publish criticisms of the authorities' treatment of the 'indigenous Poles' in the early postwar years. The regime itself admitted at this time that it had made mistakes in its earlier policies towards the 'autochthons'. At the same time, Poland's Communist leadership provided greater scope for emigration to West Germany by both 'autochthons' and Germans, by

[68] Madajczyk, 'Niemcy', pp. 69, 77–81, 84, 87, 89.

signing a new family reunification agreement with the Federal Republic in 1956. But contrary to the authorities' original intentions, subsequent migrations were not restricted to those who could prove they had family in West Germany. This was partly because many local officials were open to bribes. The authorities managed to prevent 'autochthons' from joining the wave of emigration by registered Germans only until mid 1957. After this time, many of them too relocated to West and East Germany. The economic boom in West Germany ensured that the exodus of the late 1950s was a large one. Forty-seven thousand 'autochthons' migrated from western Upper Silesia and 38,000 from southern East Prussia in 1957–9. The vast majority of them travelled to West Germany. But the registered Germans formed the bulk of the 253,130 individuals who left Poland for West and East Germany between 1956 and 1959.

This wave of emigration ran counter to the efforts made by the authorities since 1956 to increase the level of cultural provision available to the acknowledged Germans. In the late 1950s the authorities allowed the Germans to set up their own cultural organizations and encouraged them to increase the number of German-language newspapers and German-language schools in existence in Poland. They also guaranteed the people they recognized as Germans political representation in Poland's undemocratic state parliament (*Sejm*). These actions were aimed primarily at persuading skilled German workers to remain in Poland. Nevertheless, almost all registered Germans departed from Poland in the late 1950s. Most schools and newspapers disappeared with them. For example, the number of German-language schools plummeted from 126 in 1957 to just 10 in late 1958. Only a few thousand registered Germans remained in Poland after 1959, when the family reunification agreement expired. In 1962 the regime finally made it possible for them to gain Polish citizenship – a move it probably should have made much sooner, given the fact that during the 1950s it was trying to convince most of these people to remain in Poland.[69]

Despite the mass emigration of 'indigenous Poles' in the late 1950s, there were still an estimated 560,000 living in western Upper Silesia (Opole Voivodship) in 1960, making up 61 per cent of the region's population. Meanwhile, 65,000 'autochthons' remained in southern East Prussia (Olsztyn Voivodship), amounting to 7 per cent of the region's population. A large proportion of these people regarded themselves not as Poles but Germans. But the regime refused to accept the existence of a German

[69] Madajczyk, 'Niemcy', pp. 88–97; Ther, 'Die einheimische Bevölkerung', p. 437; Blanke, *Polish-Speaking Germans*, pp. 302–4.

minority in western Upper Silesia and southern East Prussia in the 1960s. Unlike the small number of people the authorities recognized as Germans who remained in Poland, the 'autochthons' were still not allowed to establish German cultural organizations or to attend German-language schools. Local state authorities in western Upper Silesia actually suggested introducing new measures aimed at suppressing German culture and promoting Polish culture among the 'indigenous Poles' in the early 1960s – a proposal very reminiscent of the policies implemented in the region in the second half of the 1940s. However, it was rejected by the Interior Ministry. In part, this may have been because the regime's leadership felt that the assimilation of the 'autochthons' was actually beginning to make significant progress by the 1960s. Relations between 'autochthons' and settlers had improved markedly since the late 1940s. The first postwar generation of 'autochthons' – which came to adulthood in the mid 1960s – grew up speaking standard Polish at school and a significant proportion of them married the children of settlers. There was little or no intergroup tension within this new generation of 'autochthons' and 'settlers', for whom the very categories of 'autochthon' and 'settler' were ceasing to make any sense.[70]

Yet the emigration of 'indigenous Poles' had by no means ended. Applications for family reunification were accepted on a case-by-case basis by the central authorities in Warsaw after 1959 and there were also other ways to convince the authorities to grant permission for relocation to West and East Germany. Around 100,000 therefore migrated to the two German states in the course of the 1960s. Of these, 18,000 travelled from southern East Prussia and most of the rest departed from western and eastern Upper Silesia. The improvement in relations between the Federal Republic and Poland after 1970 opened up new official routes for emigration. As a result, another 100,000 or so – perhaps somewhat more – were able to relocate to West Germany in the course of the 1970s. Of these, 59,000 travelled from western Upper Silesia. In the 1980s, the migration movement decreased a good deal, but it by no means ceased. A large proportion of the tens of thousands of people who left Poland for West Germany in the course of the decade did so using tourist visas. Many were motivated to leave by the regime's crushing of Solidarity and its declaration of martial law in December 1981 – and, in fact, the same had been witnessed during the regime's crises of the 1960s and 1970s. By 1989, the 'indigenous Poles' and their descendants made up only around 2 per cent of the population of southern

[70] Madajczyk, 'Niemcy', pp. 97–103; Ther, 'Die einheimische Bevölkerung', p. 437; Blanke, *Polish-Speaking Germans*, p. 305.

East Prussia and only around one-third of the population of western Upper Silesia.[71]

The political breakthroughs made by Solidarity during the 1980s at last allowed remaining members of the 'indigenous population' to begin pushing against the nationalist prejudices which had underpinned the regime's treatment of them since 1945. The brief period of relative freedom opened up by Solidarity between August 1980 and the end of 1981 was only the second time in the history of the regime that public criticism of the Communist-controlled authorities' treatment of 'indigenous Poles' in Upper Silesia, Masuria and Warmia became possible. As expectations gathered that political changes were once more on the cards in Poland, in the late 1980s, members of the 'indigenous population' cautiously began to set up unofficial 'German minority' organizations. As the regime then crumbled in 1989, the leadership took the pragmatic decision to make it legal for individuals who were not officially registered as Germans to set up 'German minority' organizations; the number of these organizations subsequently proliferated in western Upper Silesia.

After the collapse of Communism in Poland in 1989, 'German minority' candidates won seats in local council elections in the early 1990s, mainly in western Upper Silesia. In the parliamentary elections which took place in October 1991, 'German minority' candidates gained 7 of the 460 seats in the *Sejm* (lower house of the Polish state parliament) and 2 of the 100 seats in the *Senat* (upper house of the state parliament). In 1993 the Polish government decided to give them a helping hand by exempting 'national minority' lists from the 5 per cent election threshold required for entry into the *Sejm*. The centre of gravity of this 'German minority' movement was, and is, western Upper Silesia – where, despite continued migration to Germany after 1989, a large number of 'autochthons' and their descendants are still living. At the same time, a new Silesian national and autonomist movement has taken off in the region since the late 1990s. It pushes for recognition of Silesians as a 'national minority' and of the Silesian vernacular as a separate language. This movement competes with the 'German minority' activists in Upper Silesia for the 'national' loyalties of the region's 'indigenous' inhabitants.

Despite the fact, then, that for decades the descendents of 'autochthons' – under the influence of Polish education, mass media and everyday interaction with Poles – have grown up as linguistically and culturally assimilated

[71] Madajczyk, 'Niemcy', pp. 97, 104–8; Blanke, *Polish-Speaking Germans*, pp. 304–9; Ther, 'Die einheimische Bevölkerung', p. 437.

members of Polish society, politics in the region has once more become characterized by competing nationalisms. This stems directly from the profound alienation felt by many 'autochthons' and their descendants as a result of the aggressive Polish nationalist policies targeted at them in the immediate postwar years. It is also a product of the inability of the Communist regime, in subsequent decades, to relinquish their nationalist prejudices.[72]

The Communist-controlled government of Poland had taken the view in 1945 that in order to incorporate the country's new territories into the postwar Polish nation-state, they needed to purge them of all manifestations of German culture – all signs, symbols and institutions. An ethnically homogeneous Polish nation-state needed to have cultural, educational and religious institutions and a physical appearance which was uniformly Polish. Taken to its logical conclusion – as it was by Aleksander Zawadzki in western Upper Silesia – this goal was never fully achievable. Nevertheless, in a broad sense, the authorities undoubtedly managed in the second half of the 1940s to make the new territories feel like a culturally Polish environment. This was very important for the Polish settlers who came to live there after the war. It helped them to adjust to life in these formerly foreign territories and to begin psychologically laying down roots there. By the time the first generation of 'settlers' born in these territories began to reach adulthood and to have children of their own, these roots were starting to penetrate deep into the soil.

The authorities' policies of 'cultural cleansing' had a rather different impact on the German citizens living in these territories who were 'verified' as 'indigenous Poles' after the war. The authorities believed that by replacing the German signs, symbols and institutions in Poland's new territories with Polish ones, this would help with the cultural 're-Polonization' of these people. Instead, it played a role in their estrangement from Polish culture and society. The majority emigrated in the course of the Communist era. Even many of those who did not leave never fully embraced membership in the Polish national community. The continuing appeal of 'German' and 'Silesian' identities among many of their descendants living in western Upper Silesia today is one manifestation of that. With regard to the people recognized as Germans, the authorities proved willing in the 1950s to put

[72] Madajczyk, *Niemcy Polscy*, pp. 337–43; Madajczyk, 'Niemcy', pp. 108–9; Blanke, *Polish-Speaking Germans*, pp. 305–7; Ther, 'Die einheimische Bevölkerung', p. 437; Klaus Bachmann, 'Jak skłócić Niemców z Polakami', *Gazeta Wyborcza* (Warsaw), 11 September 2006, p. 23.

aside their early postwar policies of 'cultural cleansing' by allowing this population to establish new German educational and cultural institutions. But this failed to convince most of them to stay. Almost all of them had left by the end of that decade.

The 'cleansing' of material culture and cultural institutions was one element of a multifaceted campaign of ethno-national homogenization pursued by the Polish Communists in Poland's new territories in the second half of the 1940s. This campaign, in turn, was but one episode in a wave of forced migration instigated by Communist-dominated and Communist-controlled governments throughout much of East-Central and Eastern Europe in the aftermath of the Soviet 'liberation' of these countries in 1944. In our final chapter we shall, therefore, step back from Poland's new territories and examine this broader picture.

CONCLUSION

Eastern Europe, 1944–9
Communism, nationalism, expulsion

It was not only in Poland that Communist leaders embraced the key nationalist goal of an ethnically homogeneous nation-state at the end of the Second World War. In Czechoslovakia, the new leftist coalition – which was dominated and, after 1946, led by Communists – carried out massive acts of forced migration in pursuit of this goal. As in Poland, the Czechoslovak Communists embraced this goal in order to boost their popularity, to facilitate their takeover of political power and to reduce potential opposition to the radical socioeconomic transformations they wished to bring about. They knew this would appeal to a society whose nationalist sentiments had been heightened by the humiliations and traumas of the Nazi German occupation. Similarly, in Yugoslavia, Romania and Hungary the Communists attempted to bolster their political position by sponsoring the expulsion of 'national minorities' at the end of the war. And in several of the western republics of the Soviet Union, the authorities carried out large-scale expulsions aimed at ethno-nationally homogenizing the new western territories of their republics and – at least in part – at helping to increase popular support for the local Communist leaderships. So what did this Communist-led wave of forced migration in East-Central and Eastern Europe look like outside of Poland's new territories?

THE WESTERN SOVIET REPUBLICS

The Red Army thrust Germany's once mighty military back across the western Soviet Union in 1943 and early 1944. This sparked a massive flight westwards of hundreds of thousands of people from the western and southwestern Soviet borderlands and from the territories of Poland, Romania and the three Baltic states which had been occupied by the Soviets in 1939–41. Among those who fled at this time were the ethnic Germans who had chosen not to relocate from these territories as part of the Nazi 'Heim ins Reich' campaign of the early war years. Members of the various north Caucasian and Baltic ethnic groups, ethnic Ukrainians, ethnic Poles, ethnic Romanians and others also fled at this time.

On the night of 3–4 January 1944, Stalin's forces crossed into prewar Polish territory from the east for the second time since the start of the war. They conquered the whole of prewar eastern Poland, the prewar Baltic states and the prewar Romanian regions of northern Bukovina and Bessarabia by summer 1944. The Soviets immediately resumed the radical restructuring of society and the economy started in 1939. But unlike what had happened in these territories during the first Soviet occupation in 1939–41, the Soviets now faced a number of highly organized armed resistance groups. Among the Baltic and Belorussian insurgents, the Lithuanians offered particularly vigorous opposition to the second Soviet takeover. But it was the Ukrainian Insurgent Army – still in the midst of a campaign of brutal violence against ethnic Poles in prewar southeastern Poland – which presented the fiercest challenge to Soviet rule at this stage.

The Soviets responded to these guerrilla formations with devastating force. Mass arrests were accompanied by vicious pacification campaigns in which over 110,000 insurgents and suspected supporters of insurgents were probably killed by May 1946. The Soviets also employed another familiar method from their first occupation of these territories: mass deportation. As the Soviet leadership saw it, mass deportations served two main purposes. The first was the crushing of anti-Soviet underground movements. The second was the removal of social groups which the Soviet leaders believed were likely to reject the Sovietization of the economy and society – especially so-called 'kulaks'. In prewar southeastern Poland, mass displacements to the Soviet interior started in March 1944. At least 182,000 people, suspected of having connections with the Ukrainian Insurgent Army or the Organization of Ukrainian Nationalists, had been deported eastwards on cargo trains by 1948. Likewise, well over 200,000 'nationalists', 'kulaks' and others were transported eastwards from the Baltic states between summer 1945 and spring 1949.[1]

Ethnic Poles, too, were targeted with forced migration by the Soviets at the end of the Second World War. For Stalin and his fellow leaders, the motives for uprooting Poles from these territories were essentially twofold.

[1] Prusin, *Lands Between*, pp. 202–21; Polian, *Will*, pp. 156–7, 166–8; Amir Weiner, 'Nature, Nurture, and Memory in a Socialist Utopia: Delineating the Soviet Socio-Ethnic Body in the Age of Socialism', *The American Historical Review*, 104, 4, Oct. 1999, pp. 1137–8, including note 93; Tamás Stark, 'The Fate of the Defeated Nations in the Carpatho-Danubian Basin', in Ahonen et al., *People*, pp. 70–1; Douglas, *Germans*, pp. 60–3; Kochanowski, 'Nationally Homogeneous', p. 99; Rieber, 'Repressive', p. 21; Corni, 'Germans', pp. 18–19.

Map 7 Postwar East-Central and Eastern Europe

First, the Kremlin viewed the ethnic Poles living there as a relatively cohesive group which was particularly opposed to the new Soviet order and to the socioeconomic changes the Soviets wished to implement there. Second, the Soviet leadership wanted to undermine Poland's claim to these territories and thereby to strengthen the respective claims of the Soviet Socialist Republics of Ukraine, Belorussia and Lithuania (see Map 7). In the latter respect, Stalin and other Soviet leaders seemed to be embracing the nationalist ideal of homogeneous nation-states. This was because the only reason that the removal of ethnic Poles from these prewar Polish territories would strengthen the claims of Soviet Ukraine, Soviet Belorussia and Soviet Lithuania to them was that it would make them ethno-nationally homogeneous Ukrainian, Belorussian and Lithuanian territories. But, as we will see, the Kremlin only pursued the objective of ethno-national homogeneity in the three western Soviet republics tactically and half-heartedly.

Irrespective of this, the Soviet policy of removing ethnic Poles from the republics' new territories was fully in line with the wishes of certain radical nationalist groups based there. Indeed, as we saw in Chapter 1, the Ukrainian nationalists since 1943 had been pursuing a deliberate policy of mass murder and violent expulsion against the ethnic Poles living in prewar south-eastern Poland. They had killed at least 50,000 and caused around 300,000 to abandon these territories by summer 1944. Hundreds of thousands of ethnic Poles had also been displaced from these territories or killed by the German and Soviet armies and security organs in the course of the war. As a result, only around two million of the roughly four million ethnically Polish residents of prewar eastern Poland remained there by summer 1944.[2]

At the end of July 1944, Poland's Soviet-backed Communist proto-government, based in Lublin, signed an agreement with the Kremlin, accepting the USSR's annexation of prewar eastern Poland. Then in September 1944 it signed three population exchange agreements with the governments of Soviet Ukraine, Soviet Belorussia and Soviet Lithuania. These agreements laid the path for the expulsion of most remaining ethnic Poles and surviving Polish Jews from the new western territories of the three western Soviet republics. That the Kremlin presided over all three agreements is clear; their wording was almost identical. But it should be emphasized that the Ukrainian, Belorussian and Lithuanian Communist leaderships actively supported the policy of uprooting ethnic Poles and Polish Jews from their respective republics and were in charge of its implementation. The Polish Communist leadership, too, was fully behind the exchanges – underpinned by its newfound taste for nationalism. To be sure, as was stressed in Chapter 2, the Polish Communists had no desire to embrace Polish nationalist ideology in its entirety. They took from it only the goals of expelling perceived 'national minorities' and expanding

[2] Snyder, *Reconstruction*, pp. 182–5; Czerniakiewicz, *Przesiedlenia*, pp. 67–9; Kochanowski, 'Nationally Homogeneous', pp. 96–9; Prusin, *Lands Between*, pp. 219–20.

westwards and northwards into prewar German territory. The Polish Communists broke decisively with Polish nationalist tradition in helping the USSR to annex prewar eastern Poland. Their turn towards nationalism was, then, a partial one. Yet it explains their approval for the population exchanges with the USSR, since the Polish Communists viewed the population exchanges as a means of removing three of interwar Poland's 'national minorities': the ethnic Ukrainians, ethnic Belorussians and ethnic Lithuanians. They also saw the exchanges as helping to fulfil the nationalist goal of reducing the number of ethnic Poles living beyond the frontiers of the postwar Polish nation-state.[3] We shall return to the Polish side of the population exchanges in the next section of this chapter.

The agreements stipulated that any resident of the new western territories of Soviet Ukraine, Soviet Belorussia and Soviet Lithuania who had been a Polish citizen before 17 September 1939 and was not ethnically Ukrainian, ethnically Belorussian or ethnically Lithuanian was entitled to register for 'evacuation' to Poland. In principle, then, these were to be entirely voluntary migrations. Anyone who wished to remain in the Soviet Union could do so. On the other hand, the agreements applied only to the new territories of the three western Soviet republics. Ethnically Polish residents of the prewar territories of Soviet Ukraine, Soviet Belorussia and Soviet Lithuania would not in principle be allowed to register. The agreements stated that those eligible Polish citizens living in the new territories who did choose to migrate to Poland would be entitled to take with them two tonnes of movable property as well as any livestock they possessed. Buildings and land would be subjected to valuation by the authorities so that properties of equal value could be allotted to the migrants on arrival in their new places of residence.

The Soviet and Polish authorities envisaged that the process would get underway immediately and that it would take a mere few weeks to register all volunteers and a mere few months to transport them all to Poland. The whole process would be completed by late spring 1945. After the signing of the agreements, contingents of newly appointed Polish state officials were sent to each of the three western Soviet republics to assist the Soviet authorities with registering and 'evacuating' the Polish citizens. The Soviet republics agreed to supply the trains for journeys. In October 1944 the Polish State Repatriation Office was created; it was in charge of directing

[3] Borodziej et al., 'Wstęp', pp. 13–14; Ther, *Vertriebene*, pp. 45–9; Snyder, 'Ukrainian Problem', pp. 100–1; Snyder, *Reconstruction*, pp. 186–7; Theodore R. Weeks, 'Population Politics in Vilnius 1944–1947: A Case Study of Socialist-Sponsored Ethnic Cleansing', *Post-Soviet Affairs*, 2007, 23, 1, pp. 77–8, 87; Kochanowski, 'Nationally Homogeneous', pp. 96–100.

the transports to their final destinations in postwar Polish territory and also ran transit and reception camps for arriving Polish migrants.[4]

The reality of the 'evacuations' was very different to the vision of a well-organized, efficient process presented in the Polish–Soviet exchange agreements. In all three republics, the process took longer to get going than originally planned. Moreover, once underway, it took years to complete rather than months. Local Soviet officials frequently prevented the migrants from taking their full entitlement of luggage with them. During the journeys, the migrants had to cope with a great deal of corruption from Soviet and Polish officials. The journeys took place on cargo trains, frequently lasted for many weeks and happened in ill-equipped, often unheated and frequently uncovered cargo wagons. In the extreme cold of the Eastern European winter this obviously had horrendous consequences. Conditions in transit and reception camps in Poland's remaining prewar territories and in its new territories were often similarly terrible. The migrants also encountered difficulties acquiring property in their new places of residence of a size and value equal to their former homes, farms and businesses. In many cases this was because they had been unable to attain from the Soviet authorities, before leaving the Soviet republics, the official documents detailing the property they were leaving behind.[5]

The 'evacuations' of Polish citizens from the USSR were implemented differently in each of the western Soviet republics. In Soviet Ukraine, they can be viewed as a continuation of the expulsions carried out by the Ukrainian Insurgent Army since 1943, inasmuch as a good deal of intimidation and coercion was involved. The Soviet Ukrainian authorities wanted to remove the ethnic Poles from the new western territories as rapidly and as comprehensively as possible. The mass arrests launched against specific privileged and educated sections of society in late 1944 targeted ethnic Poles disproportionately and were probably aimed partly at pressuring them to register for transportation to Poland. Other forms of pressure and intimidation were also applied by the Soviet Ukrainian officials, including threats that those ethnic Poles who did not register would instead be sent eastwards to the Soviet interior. At the same time, the Ukrainian Insurgent Army continued its attacks on Polish villages. The NKVD units based in

[4] Borodziej et al., 'Wstęp', pp. 14–17; Ther, *Vertriebene*, pp. 46–8; Weeks, 'Vilnius', pp. 81–3; Kochanowski, 'Nationally Homogeneous', pp. 96–7, 101; Snyder, *Reconstruction*, pp. 183, 188; Kataryna Stadnik, 'Ukrainian–Polish Population Transfers, 1944–46: Moving in Opposite Directions', in Gatrell and Baron, *Warlands*, pp. 171–2.

[5] Borodziej et al., 'Wstęp', pp. 17–21, 45–7; Ther, *Vertriebene*, pp. 77–82; Ahonen and Kochanowski, 'Experience', pp. 129–32.

these territories appear to have turned a blind eye to these assaults. They may even, in some instances, have collaborated in them.

The new western territories taken over by Soviet Ukraine had been ethnically very diverse. In many villages more than one language was spoken and many residents habitually spoke more than one language or were married to individuals whose first language differed from their own. It might be expected that nationally minded authorities would find it difficult in these circumstances to sift 'Poles' from 'Ukrainians'. Fortunately for the postwar Soviet Ukrainian authorities, both the Soviet and Nazi German wartime occupiers of these territories had obliged their inhabitants to choose a national group for compulsory identity documents. This meant that decisions reached about one's identity to cope with particular wartime circumstances had a very serious impact on one's postwar fate. The first cargo trains carrying Polish citizens from Soviet Ukraine's new western territories to postwar Poland were sent off in early December 1944. This was several months later than originally planned.[6]

In the Lithuanian and Belorussian Soviet Socialist Republics, the authorities' approach was rather different. The Soviet Lithuanian leaders decided to remove only that part of the Polish-speaking population which exhibited a high level of Polish national consciousness. In essence, this meant urban Poles. In particular, it meant residents of Vilnius, a city where ethnic Poles constituted over 91 per cent of the population at the end of 1944. Unlike in Soviet Ukraine, the Soviet Lithuanian authorities did not employ methods of direct violence and intimidation in order to bring about the removal of urban Poles. Instead, they relied largely on more subtle forms of pressure. As in Soviet Ukraine, arrests targeted ethnic Poles disproportionately at this time and may well have been aimed, in part, at inducing registration for 'evacuation'. But, in the main, Polish speakers were prompted to register for transfer to Poland merely by their desire not to live in a 'foreign' state – and particularly one with such shortages and repression as the Soviet Union. The Lithuanian authorities regarded rural Polish speakers as much less nationally conscious than their urban counterparts. They took the view that removing them would therefore harm agricultural production without making the territories much more ethno-nationally Lithuanian. In fact, it was common for Lithuanian officials actively to prevent rural Polish speakers from registering for transfer.

[6] Snyder, *Reconstruction*, pp. 158–9, 168–93, 205–10; Ther, *Vertriebene*, pp. 73–84; Borodziej et al., 'Wstęp', pp. 18, 26–8; Subtelny, 'Resettlement', in Ther and Siljak, *Redrawing Nations*, p. 156; Stadnik, 'Transfers', pp. 171–2; Ahonen and Kochanowski, 'Experience', p. 130.

This led to conflicts with the Polish officials working in Lithuania. The latter encouraged local Polish speakers to migrate to Poland and tried to ensure that the Lithuanian authorities were not able obstruct this. They even attempted to convince the Lithuanian authorities to include in the 'evacuation' not only ethnic Poles who had lived in Lithuania's new territories but also those who had lived in the republic's prewar territories before September 1939. This was not part of the original exchange agreement signed in September 1944 and the Lithuanian authorities rejected the proposal. Nevertheless, in all three western Soviet republics a significant but unknown number of people, who had not lived in Polish territory before the war, did manage to board the 'evacuation trains'. The approach taken by the Soviet Belorussian authorities was similar to that of Lithuania's officials. In Belorussia, too, it was urban Poles who were the principal targets and the Belorussian authorities deliberately obstructed the outflow of rural Polish speakers. In order to justify their policy of preventing rural Polish speakers from boarding trains to Poland, both the Belorussian and Lithuanian authorities made use of the fact that national identities in the linguistically mixed borderlands between Poland and Russia were never clear-cut.[7]

Cargo trains carrying Polish citizens to Poland finally started to depart from the new western territories of Soviet Lithuania and Soviet Belorussia in early 1945. The process was largely over in all three western Soviet republics by July 1946 – although a relatively small number of cargo trains also travelled to Poland in the second half of 1946 and in 1947. Between the end of 1944 and 1947 a total of over 780,000 Polish citizens were transported to Poland from Soviet Ukraine, around 274,000 from Soviet Belorussia and approximately 197,000 from Soviet Lithuania. In each case, registered ethnic Poles made up over 90 per cent of the migrants – 98 per cent in the Belorussian case – with Polish Jews forming the bulk of the remainder. The fact that different objectives underpinned the 'evacuations' in each of the three Soviet republics had a clear impact on numbers. Because the Soviet Ukrainian authorities aimed to bring about a comprehensive expulsion of all ethnic Poles from Ukraine's new territories, 90 per cent of the people who registered – or were forced to register – were transported to Poland. Outside of Soviet Ukraine, a comparably comprehensive displacement of ethnic Poles was carried out only in the city of Vilnius. In

[7] Borodziej et al., 'Wstęp', pp. 18–21, 23–6, 30–2; Weeks, 'Vilnius', pp. 80–91; Snyder, *Reconstruction*, pp. 88–9, 92–5; Kochanowski, 'Nationally Homogeneous', p. 102; Czerniakiewicz, *Przesiedlenia*, pp. 72–94, 111–12, 115–16; Ahonen and Kochanowski, 'Experience', pp. 129–30.

contrast, because the Soviet Belorussian and Soviet Lithuanian authorities deliberately obstructed the migration of rural Polish speakers, only 55 per cent of the people who registered for 'evacuation' in Soviet Belorussia and 50 per cent of those who registered in Soviet Lithuania were transported to Poland.

These were not the only ethnic Poles and Polish Jews transported to Poland from the USSR at this time. In July 1945 an agreement was signed between the Soviet and Polish governments arranging for the repatriation of Polish citizens who had been forcibly deported or who had fled to the Soviet interior in the course of the war. Based on this agreement, an estimated 220,000 Polish citizens were transported to Poland from the prewar territories of the USSR in the early postwar years. Furthermore, outside the parameters of these official relocations, a further 200,000 people are estimated to have crossed into Poland from the three western Soviet republics without the assistance or permission of the Soviet and Polish authorities in the early post-liberation years. And taking into account the roughly 300,000 people driven out of postwar Soviet Ukrainian territory by the Ukrainian Insurgent Army in 1943–4, we arrive at a total of around 1.8 million individuals uprooted from the Soviet Union to postwar Poland in the period 1943–8. The vast majority of them were ultimately resettled in Poland's new western and northern territories.[8]

In the new territories of all three western Soviet republics, the displacement of ethnic Poles and Polish Jews was accompanied by policies of 'cultural cleansing' similar to those described in this book with regard to Poland's new territories. The first Soviet occupation of prewar eastern Poland in 1939–41 had already seen a campaign of cultural de-Polonization. Polish street names and place names had been changed, Polish signs and symbols had been removed and Polish schools had been replaced with Ukrainian, Belorussian and Lithuanian ones. In late 1944 this campaign was essentially relaunched in the three western Soviet republics. It targeted any surviving Polish signs, symbols and schools. At the same time, the Stefan Batory University in Vilnius – which had been one of Poland's most important universities in the interwar period and which was closed down during the first Soviet occupation – was reopened as a Lithuanian institution after the war. The other great university of prewar eastern Poland, the Jan Kazimierz University in Lwów, was similarly Ukrainianized at the end of the war. It became the Ivan Franko University in what was now the Ukrainian city of L'viv. As we discussed in Chapter 10, most of its

[8] Borodziej et al., 'Wstęp', pp. 44, 48–50; Kochanowski, 'Nationally Homogeneous', pp. 97–103; Czerniakiewicz, *Przesiedlenia*, pp. 69–72, 105–10, 113–14, 117; Weeks, 'Vilnius', pp. 84–93; Ther, 'Century', pp. 53–4; Snyder, 'Ukrainian Problem', pp. 102–4, including footnote 48.

Polish academics took up new positions in the largest city in Poland's new territories, Wrocław.[9]

POSTWAR EASTERN POLAND

The Polish Communists viewed the population exchange agreements signed with Soviet Ukraine, Soviet Belorussia and Soviet Lithuania in September 1944 as an opportunity to move Poland decisively closer to the nationalist ideal of a homogeneous Polish nation-state, 'cleansed' of 'national minorities'. The vast majority of the ethnic Ukrainians, ethnic Belorussians, ethnic Lithuanians and other ethnic non-Poles who had lived before the war in central and eastern Poland had been removed simply by moving Poland's eastern borders two hundred kilometres westwards in July 1944. But hundreds of thousands remained within Poland's postwar boundaries. The ethnic Ukrainians were the prime target for removal by the Communist-controlled Polish government. There were two reasons for this. First, they were by far the largest non-Polish ethnic group inhabiting postwar eastern Poland. Second, the violent interethnic conflict which had raged between ethnic Ukrainians and ethnic Poles in prewar southeastern Poland since midway through the war had convinced the Polish Communist and Soviet leaders that these two nationalities could no longer live side by side.

The population exchange agreements stipulated the same regulations for the 'evacuation' of ethnic Ukrainians, ethnic Belorussians and ethnic Lithuanians from Poland as for the displacement of Polish citizens from the three western Soviet republics. In principle, the process would be entirely voluntary; two tonnes of movable property could be taken by each family; and fixed property left behind would be compensated with farms, houses and flats in the Soviet Union. According to the original plans, the whole process would be completed in not much more than half a year. Also mirroring the arrangements made in the three Soviet republics, Soviet officials were sent to Poland in autumn 1944 in order to work together with Polish officials in carrying out the registrations and 'evacuations'.[10]

As in the Soviet Union, the reality of implementing the 'evacuations' on postwar Polish territory diverged a great deal from what had been

[9] Prusin, *Lands Between*, pp. 130–3, 213, 220; Snyder, *Reconstruction*, pp. 89, 93–5; Adam Redzik, 'Szkic dzieja Uniwersytetu Lwoskiego w latach 1939–1946', *Visnyk L'vivs'kovo Universitetu*, 2007, pp. 588–90.

[10] Stadnik, 'Transfers', pp. 171–2, 178–9; Subtelny, 'Resettlement', pp. 155–7; Snyder, *Reconstruction*, pp. 179–87; Snyder, 'Ukrainian Problem', pp. 100–2, 107; Jasiak, 'Resistance', pp. 174–5; Olejnik, *Polityka*, pp. 273–4; Kochanowski, 'Nationally Homogeneous', pp. 97–100.

stipulated in the agreements. It got off to a relatively good start. The ethnic Ukrainians began to be transported from postwar southeastern Poland to Soviet Ukraine in midautumn 1944. The migrations appear to have been genuinely voluntary at first. Those who volunteered were motivated predominantly by hatred towards a Polish state which had shown so much nationalist disdain for ethnic Ukrainians in the interwar decades. Sheer ignorance of the very difficult material conditions prevailing in the Soviet Union at this time also played an important role. But information filtering back to Poland from the early volunteers about serious shortages, ruined properties and all-round harsh circumstances caused registrations to drop away abruptly in early 1945.

Poland's Communist-controlled authorities therefore resorted to coercion. They imposed extra taxes and labour obligations on ethnic Ukrainians. Poland's internal security organs and army also began to attack ethnic Ukrainian villages, arresting or killing civilians who refused to register for 'evacuation'. Separately, the National Armed Forces – an extreme nationalist partisan group which had emerged in the wartime underground – inflicted brutal attacks on ethnic Ukrainian villages. A new branch of the Ukrainian Insurgent Army emerged on the western side of the new Polish–Soviet border to resist the Polish attacks and 'evacuations'. Its recruits were mainly locals who had had no previous involvement with the Ukrainian Insurgent Army. It urged ethnic Ukrainians to reject resettlement and carried out sabotage attacks in order to obstruct the process, including blowing up rail tracks. It also inflicted reprisal massacres on ethnic Polish villages, burning down whole settlements.

The violence spiralled during 1945. By late summer 1945 it had become clear to the Polish authorities that that even terrorizing people into registering for 'evacuation' through brutal attacks was not achieving the desired results. So the Communist-led Polish government ordered three divisions of the Polish Army – already present in postwar southeastern Poland as part of efforts to crush the Ukrainian Insurgent Army – to start expelling the ethnic Ukrainians. Polish soldiers began swooping on villages, giving families just a few hours to pack and attacking those who resisted. The villagers were generally taken to the nearest large railway station, loaded onto cargo trains and sent off eastwards, with little food and often in open wagons. The journeys lasted weeks. The following year, between April and June 1946, the three army divisions, together with Poland's internal security organs, carried out a massive action against ethnic Ukrainians known as Operation Rzeszów. Its aim was to remove the hundreds of thousands of remaining ethnic Ukrainians and to wipe out the Ukrainian Insurgent

Army's strongholds in postwar southeastern Poland. As on the eastern side of the new Polish–Soviet border, on the western side the Polish authorities accompanied the uprooting of ethnic Ukrainians with 'cultural cleansing' measures, such as closing down Ukrainian-language schools, dissolving Ukrainian cultural organizations and dismantling Uniate and Orthodox churches.[11]

Like the territory on the Soviet side of the new border, the areas on the Polish side, where the Communist-led Polish authorities were violently attempting to apply their vision of nationalist simplicity, were culturally diverse. In postwar southeastern Poland, many villages had until this time had linguistically mixed populations. Moreover, a large proportion of the people classed as 'Ukrainians' by the postwar Polish state authorities did not regard themselves as Ukrainians. In fact, many of the people whom Polish officials categorized as 'Ukrainians' were regarded by others as Lemkos, Russians, Rusyns and Belorussians. The Polish state authorities responded to this cultural complexity, like all good nationalists, by ignoring it. Indeed, like their Soviet counterparts in the three western Soviet republics, they resorted to using the national designations contained in wartime Nazi German identity documents to distinguish between 'Ukrainians' and 'Poles'. Between November 1944 and June 1946 a total of around 483,000 people were transported as 'Ukrainians' from Poland to the Ukrainian Soviet Socialist Republic, over half of them in Operation Rzeszów of April–July 1946. In fact, the figure was as high as 494,000 if we include individuals who were first expelled to Soviet Belorussia but who quickly relocated to Soviet Ukraine.

In stark contrast, the ethnic Lithuanians and ethnic Belorussians remaining in Poland after the redrawing of borders were a low priority for the Communist-controlled Polish authorities. This was because the remaining ethnic Lithuanians were few in number and the ethnic Belorussians, as the Polish authorities saw things, had little in the way of a national consciousness. Only around 36,000 ethnic Belorussians and less than a thousand ethnic Lithuanians were transported to the Belorussian and Lithuanian republics in these years. This should not be understood, however, as indicating that the Polish authorities were more tolerant towards Belorussian and Lithuanian culture than towards Ukrainian culture. Indeed, they expected remaining ethnic Belorussians and ethnic Lithuanians to assimilate culturally into Polish society quickly. They therefore suppressed the

[11] Subtelny, 'Resettlement', pp. 158–63; Olejnik, *Polityka*, pp. 274–91; Snyder, 'Ukrainian Problem', 104–8; Snyder, *Reconstruction*, pp. 191–4; Stadnik, 'Transfers', pp. 172–9; Jasiak, 'Resistance', pp. 177–81; Zieliński, 'Polonise', p. 197; Kochanowski, 'Nationally Homogeneous', p. 100.

Belorussian and Lithuanian languages and cultures in the early postwar years; this included liquidating Belorussian and Lithuanian schools.[12]

One might have expected that all the people uprooted from Poland as Ukrainians, Belorussians and Lithuanians at this time would have been given new homes in the new territories of the three western Soviet republics. After all, homes were being vacated in these territories by the 'evacuation' of ethnic Poles and Polish Jews at this time. But in the Ukrainian case, not all of them were given homes there. Instead, around one-third of the registered Ukrainians were transported not to Soviet Ukraine's new western territories but to its prewar territories, where they tended to be placed on collective farms rather than given individual properties. The majority of them did quickly relocate to the republic's new western territories, believing that material conditions would be better there and wanting to live nearer to their homelands. But this had not been the authorities' original intention. Moreover, even taking into account this spontaneous movement westwards, the number of migrants who took up residence in Soviet Ukraine's new territories by the end of the 1940s represented only around three-fifths of the number of ethnic Poles and Polish Jews who were uprooted. In Soviet Belorussia's and Soviet Lithuania's new territories, the gap in population was even greater, because the number of migrants arriving from Poland represented a tiny fraction of the number of ethnic Poles and Polish Jews expelled.

In all three western Soviet republics, the authorities tried to fill this gap not only with local residents and people from the prewar territories of the western Soviet republics but also with ethnic Russians and others from the Soviet interior. This said a great deal about Stalin's commitment to the objective of creating ethno-national homogeneity in the three western Soviet republics. By organizing the removal of ethnic Poles and Polish Jews from the new territories of the republics, he had shown himself partially committed to this objective. But by repopulating them partly with settlers who were not ethnically Ukrainian, ethnically Belorussian and ethnically Lithuanian, he had made clear that he was not fully committed to it. In fact, this had already been made plain by the fact that the exchange agreements

[12] Olejnik, *Polityka*, pp. 261–3, 498–517, 538–50; Jan Pisuliński, *Przesiedlenie ludności ukraińskiej z Polski do USRR w latach 1944–1947* (Rzeszów, 2009), pp. 504–8; Snyder, *Reconstruction*, pp. 189–94; Snyder, 'Ukrainian Problem', p. 108; Subtelny, 'Resettlement', pp. 156–8, 160–5; Stadnik, 'Transfers', pp. 171, 176, 182; Stanisław Ciesielski, 'Kresy Wschodnie II Rzeczypospolitej i problemy identyfikacji narodowej' in Stanisław Ciesielski (ed.), *Przemiany Narodowościowe na Kresach Wschodnich II Rzeczypospolitej* (Toruń, 2003), pp. 50–1; Zieliński, 'Polonise', pp. 197–9; Kochanowski, 'Nationally Homogeneous', p. 100, including note 145; Joseph Schechtman, *Postwar Population Transfers in Europe 1945–1955* (Philadelphia, 1962), p. 167.

only applied to people living in the three republics' new territories and not to the many ethnic Poles who lived in their prewar territories.[13]

Stalin also presided over population exchanges with two other neighbouring states from which he seized territories at this time. At the end of the war, the USSR annexed Transcarpathia (Ruthenia) from Czechoslovakia and reannexed northern Bukovina and Bessarabia from Romania. Agreements were signed with Bucharest and Prague in 1945 and 1946, which organized the transfer of ethnic Czechs and ethnic Slovaks from Transcarpathia to Czecholovakia, ethnic Romanians from northern Bukovina and Bessarabia to Romania, and ethnic Ukrainians, ethnic Russians and ethnic Ruthenians from both Czechoslovakia and Romania to the USSR. But compared to the Polish–Soviet exchanges, these were small population shifts. They each involved thousands of people rather than hundreds of thousands.[14]

For Poland's postwar Communist-led government, the Polish–Soviet exchanges had not actually accomplished their principal purpose: getting rid of the ethnic Ukrainians. As far the government was concerned, there were still around 150,000 to 200,000 ethnic Ukrainians living in Poland at the start of 1947. It was actually a great simplification for the government to describe all of these people as 'Ukrainians'; others regarded most of them as ethnic Lemkos. But the important thing for the government was that they were not ethnic Poles. Because the population exchange with Soviet Ukraine was over by 1947, these people could no longer be displaced eastwards. So a plan was developed to scatter them across the new western and northern territories of Poland, where they would have little choice but to adopt the Polish language and culture of the territories' new settler population. This act of forcible relocation would be presented as aimed at definitively wiping out the violent and subversive activities of the Ukrainian Insurgent Army in southeastern Poland. It had the full backing of Moscow and significant direct involvement from Soviet officials.

With plans already well developed, the action was given a helping hand when the Ukrainian Insurgent Army killed a Polish Army general, Karol Świerczewski, on 28 March 1947. This provided a convenient pretext for *Akcja Wisła* (Operation Vistula), which was launched on 28 April 1947. It was carried out by around 20,000 men from the Polish Army and internal security organs in much the same way as Operation Rzeszów the

[13] Snyder, *Reconstruction*, pp. 92–5, 182–6, 203–4; Pisuliński, *Przesiedlenie*, pp. 512–34; Subtelny, 'Resettlement', pp. 157–9, 164–6; Stadnik, 'Transfers', p. 176; Jasiak, 'Resistance', pp. 177–8; Schechtman, *Postwar*, pp. 167–8; Prusin, *Lands Between*, pp. 212–13.

[14] Stark, 'Fate', pp. 74–5, 84; Prusin, *Lands Between*, p. 220; Schechtman, *Postwar*, pp. 43–7.

previous year. The troops would suddenly descend on a village, segregate the 'Ukrainians' from the 'Poles' using Nazi German identity documents, then give the 'Ukrainians' a few hours to pack before loading them onto cargo trains for transportation to Poland's new western and northern territories. The operation involved great brutality. Anyone who resisted was beaten up or killed. Houses were often burned down in order to force the 'Ukrainians' to leave. The operation was over by the end of July 1947. By that point around 140,000 people had been uprooted from southeastern Poland. The Polish authorities deliberately dispersed them throughout Poland's new territories, as they had planned. Although the original intention had been to replace all the 'Ukrainians' uprooted in both the Polish–Ukrainian population exchange and *Akcja Wisła* with ethnic Poles, this only happened to a limited extent. Indeed, whole areas of postwar southeastern Poland remained depopulated in subsequent decades.[15]

YUGOSLAVIA, HUNGARY, ROMANIA

As the Red Army reached Southeastern and East-Central Europe in summer and autumn 1944, it set off new waves of mass flight. The streams of refugees heading westwards and northwestwards were now made up overwhelmingly of ethnic Germans and ethnic Hungarians. These were people who rightly calculated that their ethno-linguistic identity would provoke reprisals from Soviet forces. Many Red Army soldiers were eager to take revenge for the German-led invasion of the Soviet Union in June 1941 – in which Hungary had participated – and the devastating occupation regime which Germany had subsequently imposed on large areas of the Soviet Union. In autumn 1944 perhaps 400,000 ethnic Hungarians and 8,000 ethnic Germans fled Romania and around 150,000 ethnic Germans and tens of thousands of ethnic Hungarians abandoned Vojvodina in northern Yugoslavia. The Red Army's advance then halted in Southeastern Europe in late autumn 1944. But it resumed at the start of 1945, once more triggering the flight of many tens of thousands of ethnic Germans from Yugoslav territories. Some 300,000 had abandoned Yugoslavia by late spring 1945. From Hungary, around 300,000 Hungarian civilians, half a million Hungarian soldiers and

[15] Jasiak, 'Resistance', pp. 183–9; Roman Drozd, 'Geneza i Przebieg akcji "Wisła"', in Roman Drozd (ed.), *Ukraińcy w najnowszych dziejach Polski 1918–1989. Tom II: Akcja "Wisła"* (Warsaw, 2005), pp. 24–44; Olejnik, *Polityka*, pp. 263–5, 291–316; Subtelny, 'Resettlement', pp. 166–8; Snyder, *Reconstruction*, pp. 195–200, 206–7; Zieliński, 'Polonise', pp. 197–8; Bartosz Nabrdalik, 'South-Eastern Poland between 1939 and the Final Soviet Frontier Demarcation in 1951 – The Destruction of an Ethnic Mosaic', *Journal of Slavic Military Studies*, 21, 2008, pp. 32–7.

perhaps 60,000 ethnic Germans fled westwards in the early months of 1945. The majority of the ethnic Hungarians who fled Eastern and Southeastern Europe for Hungary and Germany after autumn 1944 returned to their homes shortly after the war. Most ethnic Germans, on the other hand, never returned to their Eastern and Southeastern European homelands.[16]

For those ethnic Germans and ethnic Hungarians who were unwilling or unable to take flight from Romania, Hungary and Yugoslavia at this time, the trauma was only just beginning. As soon as the Soviets arrived in these countries in autumn 1944 they launched sporadic round-ups of ethnic Germans. From the end of 1944 onwards, the Soviets began systematically gathering up ethnic Germans in each of these countries, loading them onto cargo trains and sending them to the USSR for forced labour. In the Hungarian case, a combination of chaotic circumstances and the desire to secure as much forced labour as possible for the Soviet Union meant that it was mostly ethnic Hungarians rather than ethnic Germans who were transported eastwards as 'Germans' at this time. Not including the hundreds of thousands of people deported eastwards as prisoners of war, perhaps 200,000 Hungarian citizens, 70,000 Romanian citizens and over 20,000 Yugoslav citizens were forcibly deported as 'Germans' to the Soviet Union in late 1944 and early 1945.[17]

But deportation to the Soviet Union was just one of the terrible fates experienced by those ethnic Germans and ethnic Hungarians who had not fled these countries in summer and autumn 1944. In Romania, several thousand ethnic Germans and ethnic Hungarians were interned in camps on Romanian territory and hundreds more were killed by Romanian paramilitary forces in late 1944. The situation was far worse in Yugoslavia. In the final months of 1944 and early 1945, Josip Broz Tito's new Communist regime pursued a campaign of retaliatory violence and murder against ethnic Germans and ethnic Hungarians, killing tens of thousands. In midautumn 1944, the Yugoslav Communists formally expropriated ethnic Germans and began interning both ethnic Germans and ethnic Hungarians

[16] Stark, 'Fate', pp. 71–3; Douglas, *Germans*, pp. 61–4; Ristović, 'Zwangsmigrationen', pp. 325–6; John R. Schindler, 'Yugoslavia's First Ethnic Cleansing: The Expulsion of Danubian Germans, 1944–46', in Steven Béla Várdy and T. Hunt Tooley (eds.), *Ethnic Cleansing in Twentieth-Century Europe* (New York, 2003), p. 365; János Angi, 'The Expulsion of the Germans from Hungary after World War II', in Várdy and Tooley, *Cleansing*, p. 377.

[17] Stark, 'Fate', pp. 75–7; Tamás Stark, 'Ethnic Cleansing and Collective Punishment: Soviet Policy towards Prisoners of War and Civilian Internees in the Carpathian Basin', in Várdy and Tooley, *Cleansing*, pp. 494–501; Nicolae Harsányi, 'The Deportation of the Germans from Romania to the Soviet Union, 1945–1949', in Várdy and Tooley, *Cleansing*, pp. 386–90; Schindler, 'Cleansing', pp. 367–8; Agnes Huszár Várdy, 'Forgotten Victims of World War II: Hungarian Women in Soviet Forced Labour', in Várdy and Tooley, *Cleansing*, pp. 506–15.

in camps on Yugoslav territory. Around 150,000 ethnic Germans and probably tens of thousands of ethnic Hungarians were thrown into these horrendous Yugoslav camps at the end of the war – where disease, exhaustion and maltreatment killed perhaps one-third of them. Finally, between late spring 1945 and early summer 1946, the ethnic German population of Yugoslavia, together with tens of thousands of ethnic Hungarians, was violently expelled by the Yugoslav Communist forces into Hungary. The region of Vojvodina, where the vast majority of Yugoslavia's half a million ethnic Germans had lived until summer 1944, was gradually repopulated in subsequent years by ethnic Serb and Montenegrin settlers.[18]

As in Yugoslavia, around half a million ethnic Germans had lived in Hungary before the war. Around two-fifths of them fled in the mass flights of autumn 1944 and early 1945. As an ally of Nazi Germany during the war, which – unlike Romania – had been unable to switch to the Soviet side in summer 1944, there was no real will for revenge against ethnic Germans within Hungarian society at the end of the war. Nevertheless, in part as a response to pressure from the Soviets, the new Hungarian government began interning ethnic Germans in camps in January 1945. The postwar coalition government remained divided at first on whether to take this one step further by expelling the ethnic German minority from the country. But by summer 1945 the two pro-expulsion parties in this four-party coalition, the Communist Party and the National Peasant Party, had gained the upper hand on this matter. In August 1945 the Allied powers at the Potsdam Conference included Hungary in the set of countries from which Germans were to be 'transferred'. Between January 1946 and June 1948, around 185,000 ethnic Germans were, therefore, transported from Hungary to the American and Soviet occupation Zones of Germany.[19]

CZECHOSLOVAKIA AND WESTERN POLAND

As the Red Army rolled further into East-Central Europe in the second half of 1944, its troops encountered more and more Germans, triggering ever greater waves of mass flight westwards. When Soviet forces

[18] Schindler, 'Cleansing', pp. 363–70; Zoran Janjetović, 'Die Vertreibung der deutschen und der ungarischen Bevölkerung der Vojvodina am Ende des Zweiten Weltkriegs', in Melville et al. (eds.), *Zwangsmigrationen*, pp. 412–20; Ristović, 'Zwangmigrationen', pp. 323–7; Stark, 'Fate', pp. 77–9; Douglas, *Germans*, pp. 110–13, 122–3, 134–6, 142, 145–6, 150–6; Klejda, *Balkans*, pp. 43–4.

[19] Ágnes Tóth, 'Die Annahme der Kollektivschuldthese und die Bestrafung der deutschen Minderheit in Ungarn 1945–1946', in Melville et al., *Zwangsmigrationen*, pp. 393–405; Stark, 'Fate', pp. 79–86; Douglas, *Germans*, pp. 136, 167–8, 207–17; Angi, 'Expulsion', pp. 376–80.

crossed into Slovakia in late August 1944 to support an uprising against Jozef Tiso's German-allied Slovak regime, ethnic Germans abandoned Slovakia en masse, with over 100,000 fleeing into the western half of prewar Czechoslovakia by January 1945.

But it was further to the north that the really massive population shifts got going. The Red Army was already threatening prewar German territory by this time. In the German enclave of East Prussia – a vast region jutting into prewar Poland from the north and cut off from the rest of prewar Germany during the interwar period by the 'Polish corridor' – the first torrent of mass flight got underway in October 1944. Meanwhile, to East Prussia's south, ethnic Germans and German citizens were already making their way westwards from areas of prewar central Poland lying to the east of the Vistula River. In the course of the war the Polish territories which had been occupied or annexed by Germany in 1939 had accumulated a very large number of German-speaking civilians. Not only were there around 670,000 Polish citizens who had declared themselves ethnic Germans in interwar Polish censuses, but there were also over 700,000 ethnic German 'Heim ins Reich' settlers from Eastern Europe and Italy (see Chapter 1) and a further 750,000 German citizens bought to prewar Poland to work for the German occupation authorities. The vast majority of the ethnic Germans and German citizens living in areas of prewar Poland lying to the east of the Vistula River fled westwards between March and August 1944. After this the Soviets halted their advance along the Vistula for the rest of 1944. The Red Army then launched a new offensive on 12 January 1945 and crossed into prewar German territory at various points along the prewar German–Polish border in late January. The Soviet forces invaded East Prussia and prewar Germany's contiguous eastern regions at this time (see Chapter 3).

This Soviet offensive triggered a gigantic new flight wave in mid January, encompassing East Prussia, the prewar Polish territories lying to the west of the Vistula River and the entirety of prewar eastern Germany. In the snow and freezing temperatures of an East-Central European winter, these were terrible conditions for fleeing. People left using whatever means were available. Many of those seeking to escape East Prussia and other territories along the Baltic Sea coast attempted to board makeshift refugee ships to northern Germany. Around a quarter of these ships were sunk en route by the Soviet navy. Others fled by foot, horse-cart or – while the railways were still running – passenger train. The refugees were overwhelmingly women, children and elderly people. Young and middle-aged men had been conscripted into the Germany military. Tens of thousands died from exhaustion or succumbed to the elements during these perilous journeys.

The Soviets perpetrated terrible revenge attacks, including many rapes, against German civilians who did not flee or whom they caught up with. Much of the responsibility for the chaos and suffering which Germans experienced in these final months of the war lay with the Nazi German authorities. For propaganda reasons, the Nazis had deliberately delayed full-scale evacuations. A total of around 6 million German citizens and ethnic Germans are believed to have fled prewar eastern Germany and prewar central and western Poland by the time Germany capitulated on 8 May 1945.

In addition to this, as in Romania, Hungary and Yugoslavia, the Soviets deported a large number of civilians to the Soviet Union from prewar eastern Germany as they conquered these territories in spring 1945. As one of the first German territories taken by the Soviets and a region with a large concentration of industrial and mining workers, Upper Silesia experienced considerably more deportations than elsewhere in prewar eastern Germany. East Prussia too – because it of its eastern location – appears to have suffered more deportations than other regions, but not as many as Upper Silesia. Up to 90,000 residents of both western and eastern Upper Silesia – almost all of them men – were deported to the USSR in February and March 1945. By the end of the war there were therefore only around 5 million German citizens and members of interwar Poland's registered ethnic German minority remaining in the postwar Polish territories. Perhaps only around 200,000 remained in prewar Polish territory. The overwhelming majority found themselves in Poland's new territories – around half of them in the southern region of Lower Silesia.[20]

In contrast, no more than a few tens of thousands of ethnic Germans fled prewar Czechoslovakia before Prague fell to the Soviets on 9 May 1945. There were still around 3.2 million ethnic Germans in prewar Czechoslovak territory at the war's end, the overwhelming majority of them in the historically German-speaking borderlands which surrounded the Czech-speaking interior of the western half of the country. Hundreds of thousands of German citizens and German-speaking refugees from other countries in East-Central and Eastern Europe also found themselves in prewar Czechoslovakia at this time. The leftist parties, which came together with

[20] The figure of around 5 million includes the just over one million German citizens who were later 'verified' as ethnic Poles. Nitschke, *Vertreibung*, pp. 65–89, 272–4, 277–9; Borodziej, 'Einleitung', pp. 57, 76; Kochanowski, 'Zentralpolen', pp. 26–7, 34–8; Stark, 'Fate', pp. 73, 80; Ochman, 'Displacement', pp. 213–17; Blanke, *Polish-Speaking Germans*, p. 282; Pertti Ahonen and Rainer Schulze, 'The Expulsion of Germans from Poland and Czechoslovakia', in Ahonen et al., *People*, pp. 87–8; Polian, *Will*, p. 266.

the Czechoslovak Communist Party in the Slovak town of Košice in early April 1945 to form Czechoslovakia's postwar coalition government, were united in their support for the transformation of this multiethnic country into an ethnically homogeneous nation-state. This coalition was already dominated by Communists and pro-Communists in terms of the number and type of positions held; it would be led by them too after the May 1946 elections. On 5 April 1945 the coalition issued a political programme, which indicated that ethnic Germans and ethnic Hungarians would be deprived of both their property and their Czechoslovak citizenship and then expelled from the country. Although the Košice programme suggested that only 'collaborators' and Nazis would be targeted, the many decrees issued by the non-Communist early postwar president, Edvard Beneš, and the speeches he and various other leading Czech politicians gave in subsequent weeks and months, made clear that all ethnic Germans and ethnic Hungarians would be affected.

At the same time, the Soviet 'liberation' from Nazi German occupation triggered a wave of spontaneous retaliatory violence against ethnic Germans by ordinary Czechs and by members of Czechoslovakia's emerging postwar authorities. Among the numerous brutal attacks on ethnic Germans which took place in summer 1945 were two big massacres in Aussig/Ústí nad Labem and Prerau/Přerov. In summer 1945 the new Czechoslovak authorities began closing down German-language schools, forcing ethnic Germans and German citizens to wear armbands, restricting the movements of ethnic Germans and reducing their food rations. Ethnic Germans and German citizens were placed in camps and prisons from early summer 1945 onwards – around 153,000 were in camps and prisons at the end of October 1945 – where they endured horrendous conditions, abuse and forced labour. Already in May 1945, soldiers of the reconstituted Czechoslovak Army and members of the new Communist-controlled security organs and paramilitary units began carrying out violent disorganized expulsions against ethnic Germans throughout the borderlands of western Czechoslovakia. Ethnic Germans and German citizens were either marched by foot over the western borders into Germany and Austria or transported there on cargo trains. The Czechoslovak authorities took some time to cease actively expelling ethnic Germans in accordance with the temporary ban placed on 'transfers' by the Allied powers at the Potsdam Conference in early August 1945 (see Chapter 2). But by autumn 1945 they had moved over to a policy of inducing 'voluntary' migration through discriminatory measures – much like what was witnessed in Poland's new territories at that time. By the end of 1945 between 800,000 and one million ethnic Germans and German citizens had already been uprooted to Germany and Austria from Czechoslovakia.[21]

The strong anti-German rhetoric emanating from Czechoslovakia and the actions being taken there to uproot ethnic Germans since May 1945 probably helped to convince Poland's Soviet-backed regime to take similar actions of their own. All of Poland's main political parties, from left to right, had embraced the objective of expelling Germans from the country in the course of the war (see Chapter 2). But the Czechoslovak expulsions may have been what actually induced action on the part of the new Communist-led Polish government. As should be clear from earlier chapters, however, the circumstances in Poland were rather different. Unlike Czechoslovakia, Poland had been handed entirely new territories by the Soviet Union in early 1945, and the Communist-led government believed that the way to convince the Western Allies to grant definitive approval for this unilateral Soviet act was to transform the population of these territories. As discussed in Chapters 4–7, they attempted to do so by flooding the new territories with Polish settlers from prewar eastern Poland and from central Poland, by expelling the Germans living there and by demonstrating that a large percentage of the territories' residents were 'indigenous Poles'. By embarking on the policy of moving millions of Polish settlers into the new territories already in early spring 1945, the Communist-led government set in motion a campaign which would inevitably lead to mass expulsions of Germans. Indeed, the pressure on housing caused by this huge influx of settlers prompted the new local Polish state authorities in certain places in Poland's new territories to carry out the first, small-scale expulsions of Germans into postwar German territory already in late spring 1945. But in contrast to what was already happening in Czechoslovakia at this time, these were infrequent, isolated actions in Poland at that stage. The Warsaw government's campaign to expel a large proportion of the German population into Allied-occupied Germany did not get underway, as we discussed in Chapter 4, until mid June 1945.

[21] Tomás Staněk, 'Vertreibung und Aussiedlung der Deutschen aus der Tschechoslowakei', in Brandes and Kural, *Katastrophe*, pp. 176–81; Eagle Glassheim, 'The Mechanics of Ethnic Cleansing: The Expulsion of Germans from Czechoslovakia, 1945–1947', in Ther and Siljak, *Redrawing Nations*, pp. 202–9; Wiedemann, *Grenzland*, pp. 42–64, 240–3; Douglas, *Germans*, pp. 95–108, 113–22, 128–52; King, *Budweisers*, pp. 189–200; Bryant, 'Nationality', pp. 696–700; Ahonen and Schulze, 'Expulsion', pp. 87–93; Mary Heimann, *Czechoslovakia: The State that Failed* (New Haven and London, 2009), pp. 145–7.

The original plan was for the Soviet-sponsored Polish Army to clear Germans from a relatively narrow strip of land running along the eastern side of Poland's future western border. But the new Polish state administrative and security organs of these territories also got involved in the expulsions of the second half of June and July 1945. As a consequence of this, these chaotic and disorganized expulsions rapidly encompassed vast swaths of the new territories and nearby parts of Poland's prewar territories. Yet it tended only to be in areas lying directly adjacent to the Odra–Nysa Line that Germans were actually moved across Poland's future western border into Allied-occupied Germany. A very large proportion of the Germans who experienced expulsions at this time were able to return quickly to their homes, so that only around 300,000–400,000 were actually uprooted from postwar Polish territory in this first phase of the expulsion.[22]

Even harsher than violent expulsion, the experience of incarceration was among the very worst things Germans endured in Poland at the end of the war. In the prewar territories of Poland, those ethnic Germans and German citizens who had not already fled began to be placed in camps and prisons together with political opponents of the Communist-controlled regime from the start of 1945 onwards. Some of these facilities were recently liberated Nazi camps, including the former concentration and extermination sites of Auschwitz and Majdanek. Others were newly created establishments. The practice of interning Germans and ethnic Germans in camps was extended into Poland's new territories in spring and summer 1945. This was prompted above all else by the need to free up housing there for arriving Polish settlers. The concentration of Germans into ghetto-like areas within towns was another strategy employed by the Polish authorities in many places in order to supply accommodation for arriving settlers. The incarceration of German citizens and ethnic Germans, their legal and actual expropriation, the compulsion to work for little or no money, the

[22] Nitschke, *Vertreibung*, pp. 169–87; Borodziej, 'Einleitung', pp. 63–73; Stanisław Jankowiak, 'Die Deutschen in Großpolen und im Lebuser Land (Ostbrandenburg) in den Jahren 1945–1950', in Borodziej and Lemberg, *Heimat* vol. 3: *Wojewodschatf Posen. Wojewodschaft Stettin (Hinterpommern)* (Marburg, 2003), pp. 35–8; Katrin Steffen, 'Flucht, Vertreibung und Zwangsaussiedlung der Deutschen aus der Wojewodschaft Stettin (Województwo Szczecińskie) in den Jahren 1945–1950', in Borodziej and Lemberg, *Heimat* vol. 3, pp. 304–8; Kraft, 'Wrocławskie', pp. 380–4; Claudia Kraft, 'Flucht Vertreibung und Zwangsaussiedlung der Deutschen aus der Wojewodschaft Allenstein (Województwo Olsztyńskie) in den Jahren 1945 bis 1950', in Borodziej and Lemberg, *Heimat* vol. 1, pp. 453–4; Ingo Eser and Witold Stankowski, 'Die Deutschen in Wojewodschaften Pommerellen und Danzig', in Borodziej and Lemberg, *Heimat* vol. 4, p. 60; Eser, 'Oberschlesien', pp. 385–7; Kochanowski, 'Zentralpolen', p. 43.

numerous other official discriminatory measures, the hostility of Polish settlers, the near anarchic conditions in the new territories and the rapid pauperization of the German population – all these factors combined to bring about a mass 'voluntary' outflow of German citizens and ethnic Germans from postwar Poland in the second half of 1945. This continued after the Allied powers suspended 'transfers' at the Potsdam Conference in August 1945.

But the second half of 1945 also saw the resumption of active expulsions. In various places in Poland's new territories, the Polish authorities sent a small number of cargo trains carrying Germans to the Soviet Zone during autumn and early winter 1945. The Soviet Zone's authorities had given the Polish authorities their explicit permission for this and were therefore complicit in the latter's breaking of the Potsdam moratorium on 'transfers'. Taking into account the summer expulsions, the 'voluntary' migrations and these autumn transports, a total of around one million German citizens and ethnic Germans were actively uprooted from postwar Polish territory between mid June 1945 and the end of that year.[23]

SCREENING, EXPULSION, REPOPULATION

The uprooting of German citizens from Poland's new territories, as we discussed in Chapter 6, was intertwined with an ethnic screening process known as the 'verification action', which was primarily targeted at the regions of western Upper Silesia and southern East Prussia. Poland's Communist-controlled authorities used it to categorize just over one million German citizens as ethnic Poles in the second half of the 1940s – over 851,000 of them in western Upper Silesia.

The second ethnic screening process introduced in postwar Poland was the 'rehabilitation action'. We examined this process earlier with regard to eastern Upper Silesia (see Chapter 6). But in fact the authorities introduced it throughout postwar Poland. They targeted it at all Polish citizens who had been placed on the *Deutsche Volksliste* (German Ethnicity List) by the Nazi German authorities during the war. Less than a quarter of the roughly 2.8 million Polish citizens who had registered on the *Deutsche Volksliste* in the war years had previously declared themselves ethnic Germans in

[23] Nitschke, *Vertreibung*, pp. 115–22, 181–4, 187–203, 275–6; Borodziej, 'Einleitung', pp. 76–101; Kochanowski, 'Zentralpolen', pp. 47, 50–62; Eser and Stankowski, 'Pommerellen und Danzig', pp. 44–8, 58–61; Kraft, 'Wrocławskie', pp. 375–7, 384–5, 393–6; Jankowiak, 'Großpolen', pp. 48–54; Steffen, 'Stettin', pp. 294–5, 297–8, 304, 307–11; Eser, 'Oberschlesien', pp. 385–8; Kraft, 'Allenstein', pp. 453–9, 461.

Poland's interwar censuses. Many of them had been compelled by the Nazi German authorities to register on the list. Most were swiftly 'rehabilitated' by the Communist-led Polish authorities through a simple administrative procedure in the immediate postwar period. But hundreds of thousands had to undergo thorough screening by judicial courts. And in prewar central Poland, the courts tended to reject more 'rehabilitation' applications than they accepted. A large minority of the people placed on the *Deutsche Volksliste* – including hundreds of thousands of people who had declared themselves ethnic Germans already in Poland's interwar censuses – had already fled Poland in the final phase of the war. Most of those who stayed behind had their Polish citizenship reinstated through the 'rehabilitation action' after the war. But several hundreds of thousand did not, so that they were earmarked, as we shall see, for transportation to Germany in the early postwar years.[24]

Ethnic screening was also deemed necessary by the Communist-dominated postwar authorities of Czechoslovakia. The Czechoslovak ethnic screening process was more vague and uncertain than that witnessed in Poland – not least because President Beneš's decrees kept on shifting the official definition of a 'German'. Initially it appeared that anyone who had taken on German state membership (*Staatsangehörigkeit*), either in the annexed borderlands after November 1938 or in the so-called Protectorate after March 1939, should be considered a German and therefore expelled from the country. But the Prague government soon recognized that many 'ethnic Czechs' had taken on German state membership 'under duress'. A key element of the government's confusion stemmed from the fact that, much as in Upper Silesia and in southern East Prussia, in large parts of western Czechoslovakia, particularly the borderlands surrounding the Czech interior, Czech–German bilingualism and so-called mixed marriages were widespread. The 'national identity' of local residents therefore often appeared very unclear to Czechoslovak state officials.

The Czechoslovak government responded to this ethno-national ambiguity by putting in place a system whereby people who claimed to be ethnic Czechs, but whom the local authorities, for whatever reason, took to be ethnic Germans, could make their case to local commissions. In the chaotic, frantic and violent atmosphere of the immediate postwar period, it can be assumed that only a relatively small number of people were actually given the opportunity to undergo ethnic screening by these commissions

[24] Strauchold, *Autochtoni*, pp. 47–70, 165–9; Borodziej, 'Einleitung', pp. 106–11; Nitschke, *Vertreibung*, pp. 123–48; Kochanowski, 'Zentralpolen', pp. 46–51, 62–6; Misztal, *Weryfikacja*, p. 158.

before being expelled from the country. It must also be presumed that the state officials, soldiers and other organs carrying out the expulsions on the ground generally made their own decisions about the ethno-national identity of the individuals they were expelling. Nevertheless, the local commissions recategorized tens of thousands of people as ethnic Czechs, in the early postwar years, who had taken on German state membership in the German-annexed borderlands and the Protectorate during the Nazi years. These people were all given back their Czechoslovak citizenship and thus spared from expulsion to Germany.[25]

In both Poland and Czechoslovakia, the Potsdam Conference of summer 1945 laid the path for the systematic, centrally orchestrated mass transportation of German citizens and ethnic Germans in cargo trains to Allied-occupied Germany. In Czechoslovakia, this got underway in January 1946 and very much resembled the process in Poland, examined in Chapters 4 and 7. The ethnic Germans and German citizens in Czechoslovakia were entitled to take with them more luggage than were German citizens and ethnic Germans in Poland: 50 kilograms rather than merely as much luggage as they could carry. But in most other respects the process was the same in Czechoslovakia as it was in Poland; that is, it involved crammed goods wagons, terrible collection camps, insufficient food and water, and the high probability of having the bulk of one's luggage seized by corrupt officials or opportunistic gangs along the way.

One important way in which the Czechoslovak process differed from the Polish one was that the cargo trains were sent to the American and Soviet Zones of occupied Germany rather than to the British and Soviet Zones. Based on an agreement reached with the U.S. Zone's authorities in January 1946, cargo trains started to travel westwards from Czechoslovakia already in that month and continued to be sent there during most of the rest of 1946. Only in June 1946 were the Czechoslovak authorities able to start sending them to the Soviet Zone as well. After November 1946, the Soviet Zone became the sole destination for expulsion transports from Czechoslovakia because the Americans refused to accept any more trains. Much as in Poland, the Czechoslovak authorities deliberately held back highly skilled workers during the mass transportation of ethnic Germans and German citizens. They also struggled to gain the release of less skilled

[25] King, *Budweisers*, pp. 175–80, 194–202; Bryant, 'Nationality', pp. 687–91, 697–700; Zahra, 'Reclaiming', pp. 528–9, 538–9; Benjamin Frommer, 'To Prosecute or to Expel? Czechoslovak Retribution and the "Transfer" of Sudeten Germans', in Ther and Siljak, *Redrawing Nations*, p. 227; Zimmerman, *Sudetendeutschen*, pp. 279–87; Staněk, 'Vertreibung', pp. 168–9, 176, 183–4; Douglas, *Germans*, pp. 101–3.

workers from Czech employers eager to keep hold of cheap German labour. By the end of 1946, an estimated 1,859,641 ethnic Germans and German citizens had been transported to the American and Soviet Zones since the start of the year; around two-thirds of them had been sent to the American Zone. The mass transportation process was then halted by the Soviet and American Zones' authorities. It never resumed as a large-scale action. Only around 50,000 ethnic Germans were sent to Allied-occupied Germany in the years 1947–49. Thus, the mass transportation of ethnic Germans and German citizens finished almost a year earlier in Czechoslovakia than in Poland.

Another way in which the processes in Czechoslovakia and Poland contrasted was that gaining official categorization as an 'anti-Fascist' was a viable way to avoid expulsion in the former but not the latter. Of course, much as with the ethnic screening process, many people with plausible claims to being 'anti-Fascists' were expelled from Czechoslovakia without getting the chance to make their case to the Czechoslovak authorities. But around 96,000 individuals acknowledged by the Czechoslovak state authorities as 'anti-Fascists' were transported to Germany under special regulations during 1946. And around 20,000 such people remained in the country once the mass transportation of ethnic Germans and German citizens was over. In total, around 183,000 people who were recognized by the Czechoslovak authorities as 'Germans' were still living in Czechoslovakia in 1949, the vast majority in the western half of the country. Most of these people were – much as in Poland – either 'irreplaceable workers' and their families or people married to ethnic Czechs. Almost 3 million ethnic Germans and German citizens had been forcibly expelled from Czechoslovakia since May 1945.[26]

We have already examined the mass transportation of German citizens and ethnic Germans from Poland's new territories in great detail in Chapters 4 and 7. The vast majority of people uprooted from postwar Polish territory between 1946 and 1949 were residents of Poland's new territories. But not all of them were. Some were expelled from the territories which had already been part of Poland before the war. Most of the 'Germans' residing on prewar Polish territory in 1944 – whether German citizens, Polish citizens who had described themselves as ethnic Germans in interwar censuses or ethnically German 'Heim ins Reich' settlers – had already fled prewar Poland by the end of the war. Others were uprooted

[26] Staněk, 'Vertreibung', pp. 179–83; Wiedemann, *Grenzland*, pp. 244–5; Douglas, *Germans*, pp. 185–93, 198–9, 203–4, 222–3; Glassheim, 'Cleansing', pp. 208–9; Zahra, 'Reclaiming', p. 539.

by expulsions and 'voluntary' migrations in the second half of 1945. But some remained at the end of 1945. In addition to these people, there were around 2 million Polish citizens, who had never declared themselves ethnic Germans in interwar censuses but who had been placed on the *Deutsche Volksliste* during the war. The vast majority of them were still living in prewar Poland at the end of the 1945. Those of them who refused to submit 'rehabilitation' applications or whose applications were rejected by the Polish state authorities – insofar as they were not regarded as 'essential' workers – were automatically designated for transportation to Germany in 1946.

As of 1946, four of Poland's voivodships (administrative regions) contained both new Polish territories and prewar Polish territories: the Silesia Voivodship (i.e., Upper Silesia), the Poznań Voivodship, the Gdańsk Voivodship and the Białystok Voivodship (see Map 6). In the prewar Polish areas of these voivodships, German citizens and ethnic Germans were simply swept into the 'displacement action' implemented in Poland's new territories from spring 1946 onwards. In contrast, the mass transportation of German citizens and ethnic Germans from the voivodships which were composed exclusively of prewar Polish territories did not get underway until 1947.

Throughout postwar Poland – new territories and old – an estimated 2.6 million German citizens, ethnically German prewar Polish citizens and ethnically German 'Heim ins Reich' settlers were transported to the British and Soviet Zones on cargo trains between 1946 and 1949. Added to the number expelled, transported or induced to migrate in the second half of 1945, the total number of German citizens and ethnic Germans who were deliberately uprooted from postwar Poland between mid June 1945 and the end of 1949 was 3.6 million. The vast majority of them were German citizens who had lived in German territory before the war.[27]

The systematic repopulation of Poland's new territories with Polish settlers has already been discussed at length in Chapters 5 and 7. Over 7.5 million German citizens fled or were expelled from Poland's new territories between 1945 and 1949, but only around 4 million Polish settlers were permanently settled there in this period. The new territories were, therefore, not fully repopulated in the second half of the 1940s. This had two main causes. First, there had been a shortage of volunteers for resettlement in central Poland and in Polish émigré communities abroad. Second, many localities in Poland's new territories were far from attractive places to start

[27] Nitschke, *Vertreibung*, pp. 227–32, 243–9, 272–7; Borodziej, 'Einleitung', pp. 101–7; Kochanowski, 'Zentralpolen', pp. 62–72; Jankowiak, 'Großpolen', pp. 54–64; Eser and Stankowski, 'Pommerellen und Danzig', pp. 61–5; Eser, 'Oberschlesien', pp. 394–8.

a new life because of the extensive damage done to buildings and infrastructure there. The 4 million Polish settlers were therefore very unevenly distributed across these territories. A particularly large concentration of settlers lived in Lower Silesia at the end of the 1940s, because the southern areas of this region had endured virtually no damage during the war. In terms of their origins, 2.5 million settlers were from central Poland, 1.3 million were from prewar eastern Poland and just over 200,000 were from Polish émigré communities located in various foreign countries.[28]

A similar repopulation process was witnessed in western Czechoslovakia's borderlands in these years. One crucial respect in which the repopulation of these borderlands resembled the repopulation process in Poland's new territories was that it, too, was intimately intertwined with the process of expelling ethnic Germans. This was because, as in Poland's new territories, the expulsion of ethnic Germans from western Czechoslovakia was not a simple case of taking revenge for Nazi Germany's occupation and atrocities. Rather it was part of the Communist-dominated Czechoslovak government's broader nationalist campaign aimed at transforming the country into an ethnically homogeneous nation-state. To achieve this objective, the government felt it needed not only to 'cleanse' western Czechoslovakia's borderlands of millions of German-speakers, but also to repopulate them with ethnic Czechs.

In fact, the process of repopulating the western Czechoslovak borderlands bore a very close resemblance to that of repopulating Poland's new territories. As in the Polish case, it was not a matter of first clearing the ethnic Germans out and then bringing the ethnic Czechs in. Rather, the two processes happened simultaneously and therefore impacted upon one another. As in Poland's new territories, some of the earliest ethnic Czechs to arrive in the western Czechoslovak borderlands were looters and robbers rather than settlers. As in Poland's new territories, many of the first genuine settlers to arrive there were ethnic Czechs from the districts located right next to the borderlands – people who travelled there without the assistance of the authorities. As in the Polish case, an entire institutional structure was put in place by the Prague government in 1945 to coordinate the resettlement process. And as in Poland's new territories, once the Czechoslovak authorities got control of the resettlement process, they tied it up with a statewide land reform. This meant that the government viewed the redistribution of the agricultural land seized from ethnic Germans in the early postwar years as serving two purposes: first, it provided land to

[28] Thum, *Breslau*, p. 133; Ther, *Vertriebene*, pp. 125, 216–17; Nitschke, *Vertreibung*, pp. 271–80.

landless or land-poor peasants; second, it ensured that the borderlands were repopulated by ethnic Czechs.

An important difference between the Czechoslovak and Polish repopulation processes, however, was that the former did not actually get underway before the expulsion of ethnic Germans and German citizens from Czechoslovakia. Thus, in contrast to what happened in Poland's new territories, the influx of settlers into the western Czechoslovak borderlands did not have the same effect of helping to instigate the expulsion of Germans. On the other hand, it had an identical impact in adding very significant impetus to the expulsion process – reinforcing the scope and speed with which it was carried out. Another important point of contrast was that the Czechoslovak authorities did not immediately begin transporting ethnic Czechs to the borderlands, but rather relied initially on advertisements and propaganda to bring about the desired influx of settlers. Ethnic Czechs began flowing into the borderlands already in May 1945. But it was not until September 1945 that the authorities started actively transporting ethnic Czechs to western Czechoslovakia's borderlands. Before these transports got underway, a significant minority of the ethnic Czechs who arrived there were former residents of the borderlands; 200,000 ethnic Czechs had fled to the Czech interior after Nazi Germany's annexation of these territories in November 1938.[29]

But these former residents ultimately formed a very small fraction of the people who repopulated the western Czechoslovak borderlands in the second half of the 1940s. By 1949 there were around 1.8 million settlers living in the borderlands. Most were ethnic Czechs from the Czech interior, the vast majority of whom arrived there in the first two years after the war. Around 150,000 were ethnic Slovaks, who voluntarily relocated from the Slovak half of the state at this time. The rest were ethnically Czech and ethnically Slovak 're-migrants' from abroad. This was another way in which the Czechoslovak case looked very similar to the Polish one. Like the Polish government, the Czechoslovak authorities originally planned that a large proportion of the new settlers would come from abroad – from various Czech and Slovak émigré communities in Central and Eastern Europe and the United States of America. The Czechoslovak authorities produced advertisements and propaganda to entice these émigrés to 'return' to Czechoslovakia. But they ultimately only persuaded around 200,000 people to board the special 're-migration' trains they provided.

[29] Wiedemann, *Grenzland*, pp. 39–116, 235–40; Schechtmann, *Postwar*, pp. 99–122; Stark, 'Fate', pp. 80, 83–4.

These people came from Hungary, Soviet Ukraine, Romania, Yugoslavia, Bulgaria, Poland, France, Austria and Germany.[30]

The ethnically Slovak 're-migrants' from Hungary arrived in the borderlands as part of a population exchange between Czechoslovakia and Hungary. Czechoslovakia's leftist, Communist-dominated coalition had made clear in its Košice programme in April 1945 that it felt that, in order to transform the country into an ethnically homogeneous nation-state, it needed to expel not only ethnic Germans but also ethnic Hungarians. Around 600,000 ethnic Hungarians lived in Czechoslovakia at the end of the Second World War. They were concentrated in southern Slovakia. An estimated half a million ethnic Slovaks meanwhile lived in Hungary. After the war, the Czechoslovak government proposed to its Hungarian counterpart that their two countries exchange their respective Slovak and Hungarian 'national minorities'. Budapest was not enthusiastic about the idea. But it eventually signed an agreement with Prague in February 1947 and the exchange was carried out between April 1947 and April 1948.

In Hungary, the relocations were largely voluntary. In the main, only those ethnic Slovaks who wanted to leave did so. In contrast, in southern Slovakia the Czechoslovak authorities pursued a campaign of forcible expulsion. But despite their uncompromising methods, they managed to uproot only around 68,000 ethnic Hungarians to Hungary by April 1948 – far fewer than originally planned. Many Hungarian speakers avoided displacement from southern Slovakia by undergoing 're-Slovakization', meaning the Czechoslovak authorities recategorized them as ethnic Slovaks. At the same time, the Czechoslovak authorities persuaded only around 73,000 ethnic Slovaks to relocate to Czechoslovakia. The initial intention had been to give these people the homes vacated by ethnic Hungarians in southern Slovakia. But because the authorities expelled only a relatively small number of ethnic Hungarians, they decided to resettle some of the arriving ethnic Slovaks in the western Czechoslovak borderlands. Around 10,000–15,000 of them were sent there.

Furthermore – in an action which had clear parallels with *Akcja Wisła* (Operation Vistula) in Poland – over 40,000 ethnic Hungarians were forcibly resettled from southern Slovakia to the western Czechoslovak borderlands in late 1946 and early 1947. They were deliberately scattered throughout the western Czechoslovak borderlands in an effort to facilitate their de-Magyarization. But unlike the victims of *Akcja Wisła*, almost all

[30] Wiedemann, *Grenzland*, pp. 235–40, 248–76; Schechtman, *Postwar*, pp. 122–6; Stark, 'Fate', pp. 83–4.

these people were able to return to their homes in southern Slovakia at the end of the 1940s.[31]

A final important resemblance to what happened in Poland's new territories at the end of the war was that the Czechoslovak authorities accompanied their expulsion and repopulation policies in western Czechoslovakia's borderlands with a systematic campaign of 'cultural cleansing'. This was at first merely a matter of removing German-language signs, closing down German-language schools and changing German place names. But exactly as happened in western Upper Silesia, the campaign soon radicalized into an attempt to eliminate every single word of German from the borderlands, including books and gravestones. At the same time, from summer 1945 onwards, Czech state schools and various kinds of Czech cultural, social and leisure organizations were opened in the borderlands. After 1946 the authorities made concerted efforts to expand the range of Czech – and, to a much lesser extent, Slovak – cultural facilities on offer to the new settler population, including libraries, theatres and cinemas.[32]

One other territory should be mentioned in this connection. Not all the German territories lying to the east of the Oder–Neisse Line were incorporated into Poland in 1945. The northern half of East Prussia, containing Immanuel Kant's birthplace, the city of Königsberg, was taken over by Soviet Russia rather than Poland (see Map 3). The aim was to provide Russia with a winter seaport on the Baltic Sea coast. Perhaps only around 10 per cent of the 1.25 million German citizens who had lived in this territory before the war did not take flight from the Red Army in early 1945. Once the war was over, they endured similarly harsh treatment from the new Soviet authorities of northern East Prussia as did residents of the rest of prewar eastern Germany from the Communist-controlled Polish authorities. Yet one important difference was that the Soviet authorities did not immediately make an effort to move new settlers into northern East Prussia. This meant that the territory remained very sparsely populated for at least a year after the end of hostilities. This, in turn, caused its economy to collapse and the German population to experience severe hardship. Malnutrition and disease are estimated to have claimed the lives of 30 per cent of the remaining German population by November 1946.

[31] Róbert Barta, 'The Hungarian–Slovak Population Exchange and Forced Resettlement in 1947', in Várdy and Tooley, *Cleansing*, pp. 565–73; Edward Chászár, 'Ethnic Cleansing in Slovakia: The Plight of the Hungarian Minority', in Várdy and Tooley, *Cleansing*, pp. 560–2; Wiedemann, *Grenzland*, pp. 267–8, 283–6; Stark, 'Fate', pp. 80–4.

[32] Wiedemann, *Grenzland*, pp. 88–9, 347–68; Staněk, 'Vertreibung', p. 180; King, *Budweisers*, p. 202.

Moreover, in stark contrast to what the Communist-led Polish authorities did in the territories to the west and south of northern East Prussia, the Soviets at first actively prevented the remaining German population from leaving. Whereas the Polish authorities decided to compel only the highly skilled part of the working German population to remain in Poland's new territories, the Soviets wished to exploit the labour of the entire remaining German population, irrespective of skills. Some Germans did manage to cross covertly into postwar Polish territory in the immediate postwar period. From there they were able to travel through Poland to postwar German territory. But not many did. It was not until 1947 that the Soviet authorities began allowing small numbers of Germans to migrate legally from northern East Prussia to the Soviet Occupation Zone of Germany. Then in October 1947 the Soviet leadership in Moscow finally took the decision to expel the remaining German population. Between then and October 1948 they sent 97,284 Germans to the Soviet Zone on 48 cargo trains in three successive waves.

As in Czechoslovakia and Poland, this mass expulsion of Germans was bound up with a process of repopulation, because it was not until a significant number of Soviet settlers had arrived in northern East Prussia that Moscow took the decision to expel the German population. Soviet settlers began arriving under their own steam not long after the war, very often motivated to relocate to this foreign territory by the immense destruction done to their homelands by the Nazi German occupiers. It was only in August 1946 that the authorities began actively transporting Soviet settlers to this territory in large numbers. Four hundred thousand had arrived by 1950. The expulsion and repopulation processes – in line with earlier Soviet policies – were not driven by the objective of creating ethno-national homogeneity there. The settlers were not from a single 'national group'. Rather, as well as ethnic Russians, the settlers included ethnic Belorussians and probably other non-Russian ethnic groups as well. Nevertheless, accompanying the socioeconomic Sovietization of northern East Prussia, a 'cultural cleansing' process was implemented, aimed at Russifying the territory. This included changing the name of Königsberg to Kaliningrad and Russifying all other place names as well as all signs, cultural institutions, newspapers and monuments. In subsequent years, the badly damaged city of Kaliningrad received an entire Soviet-style cityscape.[33]

[33] Per Brodersen, *Die Stadt im Westen. Wie Königsberg Kaliningrad wurde* (Göttingen, 2008), pp. 45–53, 73–83; Stefan Berger, 'How to Be Russian with a Difference? Kaliningrad and Its German Past', *Geopolitics*, 2010, 15, 2, pp. 347–9; Polian, *Will*, pp. 163–4; Broszat, 'Einleitende Darstellung', pp. 88E–95E, 151E–152E.

POSTWAR GERMANY

One question we have not yet addressed is what impact Nazi population policies and postwar population movements had on postwar Germany itself. One of the most important consequences was that at the moment of Germany's capitulation in May 1945, the postwar territory of Germany contained around 9 million people categorized by the Western Allies as 'Displaced Persons' (DPs). This did not include the German and German-speaking refugees and expellees who arrived from East-Central and Eastern Europe from late 1944 onwards. But otherwise 'Displaced Persons' was an all-embracing category. It designated all foreigners not deemed to be of German ethnicity and all surviving Jews *including* German citizens. The overwhelming majority of DPs were in fact foreign civilian workers and foreign prisoners of war who had been transported to Germany for forced labour during the war, mainly from occupied East-Central and Eastern Europe and the Soviet Union (see Chapter 1). By early autumn 1945, the great bulk of these people had already been repatriated to their Eastern and Western European home countries, often against their will in the former case. As we discussed in Chapter 8, some of these people found themselves in territories falling to Poland in 1945, and they often had to make their way back home without the assistance of the Allied powers or their home states after the war.

A significant minority of the DPs on postwar German territory were Jews. It was only from summer 1945 onwards that German Jews no longer formed the majority of the Jewish DPs in Germany. What seemed to be a rising tide of anti-Semitic feeling in East-Central and Eastern Europe after Soviet 'liberation' caused hundreds of thousands of Jews to begin flowing into Allied-occupied Germany from the eastern half of the continent at this time. By summer 1946 the stream had turned into a flood, as Jews sought to escape violent anti-Semitic attacks (see Chapter 8). Because Eastern European Jews generally viewed the U.S. Zone's authorities as having more favourable policies towards Jewish DPs than the other Allies – the Americans, for example, allowed the establishment of separate Jewish DP camps – most headed to that zone rather than to the British, French or Soviet ones. Indeed, in the early postwar years, the U.S. Zone came to be seen by Eastern European Jews as the main staging post for emigration from Europe. Yet Jewish emigration was initially blocked by the highly restrictive immigration laws of the United States and other Western countries and by Britain's efforts to prevent migration to Palestine. This changed in 1948, when the foundation of Israel and the liberalization of U.S. immigration laws triggered the mass exodus of foreign and German Jews from postwar Germany. Very few Jews remained in Germany after the 1940s.[34]

What about the German and German-speaking refugees and expellees who arrived in postwar Germany from Poland, Czechoslovakia and the rest of East-Central and Eastern Europe? Around 12 million such people were uprooted from the eastern half of the continent to the shrunken occupied territory of Germany through flight and expulsion between 1944 and 1949. The vast majority came from the postwar territories of Poland and Czechoslovakia. But hundreds of thousands also arrived from Yugoslavia, Romania and Hungary. Smaller numbers came from other parts of Eastern Europe as well. This was a vast influx of people which by 1950 amounted to 20 per cent of the population of the new state of the German Democratic Republic and 16 per cent of that of the much larger Federal Republic of Germany.

The moment the war came to an end in Europe on 8 May 1945, postwar Germany faced a situation of widespread devastation and serious shortages. To say the least, these were not favourable circumstances for receiving millions of new inhabitants. The Soviet Zone was hit much harder than the rest of Germany's diminished territory by this massive influx of German and German-speaking migrants, for the simple reason that it was adjacent to both Poland and Czechoslovakia. The arrival of millions of people in the Soviet Zone from early 1945 onwards caused a desperate situation to emerge. Pervasive malnutrition and disease quickly transformed into massive epidemics of typhus, dysentery and tuberculosis. At the same time, huge numbers flooded into the U.S. Zone from Czechoslovakia and into the British Zone from the Soviet Zone. In the chaos and shortages of 1945 and early 1946, the Soviet, British, American and local German authorities could do little more with these refugees and expellees than to direct them away from the badly damaged cities and into the villages and small towns of their zones. They did so because there was more accommodation and food available in rural localities than in the ruined urban areas. This meant that in the Soviet Zone the refugees and expellees were concentrated mainly in the agricultural region of Mecklenburg-Vorpommern, whereas in the British and American Zones they were mostly steered towards the rural states of Bavaria, Lower Saxony and Schleswig-Holstein.[35]

[34] Magarete Myers Feinstein, *Holocaust Survivors in Postwar Germany, 1945–1957* (Cambridge, 2010), pp. 1–63; Wetzel, 'Displaced Persons', pp. 34–7; Mankowitz, *Life*, pp. 11–22; Constantin Goschler, 'Wiedergutmachung', in Wolfgang Benz (ed.), *Deutschland unter allierter Besatzung 1945–1949/55* (Berlin, 1999), p. 201.

[35] Ian Connor, *Refugees and Expellees in Post-war Germany* (Manchester, 2007), pp. 18–20, 25–6, 29–31, 64–5, 197–9; Andreas Kossert, *Kalte Heimat. Die Geschichte der deutschen Vertriebenen nach 1945*

Throughout Allied-occupied Germany, local Germans in the villages and small towns where the refugees and expellees arrived after 1945 were at first fairly sympathetic towards their plight. But local sympathy crumbled once it became clear that the newcomers' stay would not be temporary. Local antipathy towards the refugees and expellees grew steadily as the latter became increasingly willing to demand a greater share of the scarce local resources and improvements in living and working conditions. A crucial factor in the hostility which locals showed towards the refugees and expellees was that the former were very often compelled by the authorities to allow the newcomers to live together with them in their homes. This of course meant sharing their kitchens, bathrooms and other facilities. Throughout Allied-occupied Germany, only a minority of the refugees and expellees were accommodated in refugee camps. It was very common for them to be accommodated on private farms. The fact that local farmers tended to make them work for their keep soon became another point of friction – because many refugees and expellees quickly became fed up with farm work, started to complain about it and sought alternative jobs. More generally, the locals viewed the newcomers as a drain on local resources at a time of serious shortages. Moreover, the very evident cultural differences between the migrants and the locals also fuelled tensions. Even the refugees and expellees who arrived from the prewar German territories rather than from foreign countries used different dialects of German and maintained cultural traditions dissimilar to those of the prewar residents of the postwar German territories.[36]

But the intolerance which local rural Germans showed towards the refugees and expellees was actually the least of their problems. These migrants had lost almost everything – their property, possessions and savings – through their flight or expulsion from East-Central and Eastern

(Munich, 2008), pp. 47–67; Michael Schwartz, *Vertriebene und "Umsiedlerpolitik": Integrationskonflikte in den deutschen Nachkriegs-Gesellschaften und die Assimilationsstrategien in der SBZ/DDR 1945–1961* (Munich, 2004), pp. 47–55; Schwartz, 'Refugees and Expellees in the Soviet Zone of Germany: Political and Social Problems of Their Integration', in Rieber, *Forced Migration*, pp. 148–51; Philipp Ther, 'The Integration of Expellees in Germany and Poland after World War II: A Historical Reassessment', *Slavic Review*, 55, 4, 1996, pp. 779, 788–90; Ther, 'Expellee Policy in the Soviet-Occupied Zone and the GDR: 1945–1953', in David Rock and Stefan Wolff (eds.), *Coming Home to Germany? The Integration of Ethnic Germans from Central and Eastern Europe in the Federal Republic* (New York and Oxford, 2002), pp. 56, 59–60; Rainer Schulze, 'Growing Discontent: Relations between Natives and Refugee Populations in a Rural District in Western Germany after the Second World War', *German History*, 7, 3, 1989, pp. 333–6; Pertti Ahonen, *After the Expulsion: West Germany and Eastern Europe, 1945–1990* (Oxford, 2003), pp. 20–1, 24.

[36] Schulze, 'Relations', pp. 336–45; Connor, *Refugees*, pp. 30–5, 58–85, 209–13; Kossert, *Kalte Heimat*, pp. 71–86; Schwartz, 'Refugees', pp. 151–2; Ther, 'Policy', p. 63.

Europe. Integrating them successfully into postwar German society was therefore dependent on improving their dire material circumstances. It was actually the Soviet Zone's Soviet and local German authorities who recognized this first. They introduced a radical land reform in summer 1945, which entailed expropriating and redistributing property from all large landowners. The refugees and expellees were deliberately prioritized as recipients of this redistributed land. By 1950 they made up 43 per cent of all beneficiaries. At the same time, the authorities took radical action to increase the amount of housing available to the newcomers by confiscating property from rural elites and from former Nazi Party officials and activists. After 1946, they also began to seize 'superfluous' property from other residents of the Soviet Zone.

But by the end of the 1940s, it had become clear that these redistributive measures were not sufficient to place the refugees and expellees on anywhere near an equal material footing with the prewar population of East Germany. The land reform was a particular disaster for the refugees and expellees because they lacked the financial capital to keep the farms running and there was a shortage of machinery and buildings in the Soviet Zone's countryside. The authorities attempted to rectify the latter problem through a rural building programme after 1947. But its main impact was to delay the much-needed reconstruction of East Germany's ruined towns and cities. Special loans programmes introduced in the early 1950s did little to improve the material situation of the refugees and expellees any further. The loans programmes were, in any case, stopped in 1952 as the regime took a sudden turn towards Stalinist Soviet orthodoxy in its economic policies.[37]

In the Western Zones, the refugees and expellees were pretty much left to their own devices in rebuilding their economic lives in the early postwar years. Help was not at first forthcoming from the British, American and local German authorities. Those few migrants who managed to make some progress in this regard were slapped back down by the 1948 currency reform, which hit the refugees and expellees far harder than the rest of western German society. It was not until the end of the 1940s that the authorities at last decided to take action to help these people. In August 1949 the new Federal Republic of Germany's government introduced an Immediate Help Law, which provided the poorest refugees and expellees with much-needed aid. Far more radical was the 1952 Burden Sharing Law (*Lastenausleichsgesetz*), which placed a special tax on the property owned

[37] Schwartz, *Umsiedlerpolitik*, pp. 625–1116; Schwartz, 'Refugees', 152–67; Ther, 'Policy', pp. 62–8, 72–3; Ther, 'Integration', pp. 793–5; Connor, *Refugees*, pp. 23–4, 214–19; Kossert, *Kalte Heimat*, pp. 197–206.

by indigenous West Germans and then used the funds this generated to compensate the refugees and expellees for the property they had left behind in East-Central and Eastern Europe. Most people did not actually receive compensation until the late 1950s, but the Burden Sharing Law had an immediate psychological impact by explicitly acknowledging that the refugees and expellees had borne the main brunt of the backlash against Germany at the end of the Second World War. At the same time, in the early 1950s, the West German government began to relocate refugees and expellees from rural areas – where most of them were living – to urban areas, where more jobs were available. Some refugees and expellees had already made this move on their own initiative in the late 1940s. But in the early 1950s the West German authorities helped hundreds of thousands more of them to relocate to industrial areas, particularly to North Rhine–Westphalia. The economic integration of the refugees and expellees was then given a massive boost by the dramatic recovery of the West German economy in the mid 1950s.[38]

In terms of the broader social and political integration of the refugees and expellees, the approach taken by the Soviet and German authorities of the Soviet Zone and the German Democratic Republic amounted to little more than the suppression of all forms of collective identity and political organization. From the outset, the term 'resettler' (*Umsiedler*) was used in the Soviet Zone to describe the refugees and expellees in order to avoid any suggestion that these people had been forcibly uprooted from their homelands by the comradely regimes of East-Central and Eastern Europe. At the same time, the refugees and expellees were strictly prohibited from establishing their own separate political and cultural organizations. This ban remained in place throughout the existence of the GDR. When in 1950 the refugees and expellees expressed opposition to the GDR's official recognition of Poland's western border – the Oder–Neisse Line – they were simply ignored. From 1948 onwards, the Soviet and German authorities effectively gave up on the problem of actively helping the refugees and expellees to integrate in any political or social sense. Even the sanitized term of 'resettler' was phased out by the regime after 1948. From then until the collapse of the GDR in 1990, the refugees and expellees were expected simply to blend seamlessly into East German society.[39]

[38] Connor, *Refugees*, pp. 25–8, 35–48, 139–49, 184–6; Kossert, *Kalte Heimat*, pp. 92–109; Ahonen, *Expulsion*, 54–5, 61–2, 67; Ther, 'Integration', p. 791; Schulze, 'Relations', pp. 346–7.

[39] Schwartz, *Umsiedlerpolitik*, pp. 3–6, 1165–87; Schwartz, 'Refugees', pp. 149–51, 167–9; Ther, 'Policy', pp. 60, 68–74; Ther, 'Integration', pp. 782, 790, 795–6; Kossert, *Kalte Heimat*, 215–26; Connor, *Refugees*, pp. 219–25.

The situation in West Germany was very different. As in the Soviet Zone, refugee and expellee organizations were banned at first by the Allies in the Western Zones. But this ban was lifted in 1948 and expellee associations and 'homeland societies' quickly proliferated. These organizations were by no means representative of all the refugees and expellees living in West Germany. Most of these migrants never became dues-paying members, the organizations' leaders were generally more right-wing than the average refugee or expellee and a disproportionate number of the leaders had Nazi pasts. Nevertheless, by the start of the 1950s the expellee movement had developed into an important force in West German politics. All three main political parties – the Christian Democrats, the Social Democrats and the Free Democrats – made concerted efforts to woo this expellee lobby in the early 1950s. They did so by giving expellee activists high-ranking posts in their parties, by supporting the creation of a special ministry for refugee and expellee affairs and by backing the lobby's main political goals. In the early postwar years the lobby's main political objective was to persuade the government to grant far-reaching compensation to the refugees and expellees for the property and assets they had lost through flight or expulsion. This goal was achieved with the 1952 Burden Sharing Law. After that, the expellee movement's primary goal was to bring about the restoration of Germany's prewar 1937 territories (prior to Germany's annexation of Austria). All three of Germany's main political parties publicly backed this revisionist agenda, although they each stopped short of supporting the more extreme demand for the handover of the 'Sudetenland' to Germany, made by part of the expellee lobby. These efforts by the mainstream political parties had the consequence of bringing down the expellee movement's own short-lived political party, the Union of the Homeland-Expellees and Disenfranchised, in 1957. It also nipped in the bud any possibility that that the refugees and expellees – as a very large, impoverished and expropriated group – would turn towards political extremism.[40]

But this should not lead us to the conclusion that the integration of the refugees and expellees in West Germany was entirely successful. The social and economic inequality of these people, when compared with the pre-1945 residents of the Federal Republic's territory, persisted until at least the 1970s. Many continued to feel like 'outsiders' in West German communities beyond that time. Much like the Polish settlers in Poland's

[40] Ahonen, *Expulsion*, pp. 28–115; Ahonen, 'Domestic Constraints on West German *Ostpolitik*: The Role of the Expellee Organizations in the Adenauer Era', *Central European History*, 31, 1/2, 1998, pp. 32–53; Connor, *Refugees*, pp. 100–31, 150–62, 177–91; Kossert, *Kalte Heimat*, pp. 139–55, 165–76, 181–4; Schulze, 'Relations', pp. 346–7.

new territories (see Chapter 10), it was only really the next generation of 'refugees and expellees' – people who were born and brought up in West Germany – who, as they reached adulthood, started to feel properly embedded in West German society. The dividing lines between newcomers and locals only faded as the older generation gradually died off in the 1970s, 1980s and 1990s.

Moreover, because the mainstream political parties in West Germany pandered for so long to the revisionist territorial goals of the expellee movement, this placed a significant obstacle in the way of relations with East-Central and Eastern European counties, especially Poland and Czechoslovakia. Not until 1969 was this barrier finally lifted – with Willy Brandt's new *Ostpolitik*, which aimed to improve relations with the Soviet Union and East-Central Europe. Brandt's policy quickly bore fruit with the signing of treaties with the USSR and Poland in Moscow and Warsaw in 1970. These treaties described all European borders as 'inviolable' and officially recognized Poland's western border with the GDR. Then in 1972 Brandt's social-liberal coalition government renounced claims to any Czechoslovak territories in a treaty signed with Prague. These moves – and the broader political, social and generational changes witnessed in West Germany in the late 1960s and 1970s – finally thrust the expellee movement to the margins of West German politics and society. In the mid 1980s the movement appeared to regain some political influence under the conservative chancellorship of Helmut Kohl. But this was only superficially so. Any hopes which the expellee lobby's leaders may have had that territorial revisionism could return to the mainstream political agenda were definitively dashed in early autumn 1990. The 'Two Plus Four' Treaty, signed between the two Germanys and the four victorious Allied powers in September 1990, definitively designated the Oder–Neisse Line the border between Poland and the unified Germany.[41]

COMMUNISM AND NATIONALISM AFTER NAZISM

What happened in East-Central and Eastern Europe in the immediate aftermath of the Second World War was therefore not merely the collapse of a vicious and destructive German occupation regime and the drawing of an 'iron curtain' right through the middle of the continent by Soviet-sponsored governments. An immense and violent torrent of forced

[41] Ahonen, *Expulsion*, pp. 155–265; Connor, *Refugees*, pp. 2, 139–49, 162–9; Kossert, *Kalte Heimat*, pp. 126–35, 154–5, 165–84; Schulze, 'Relations', pp. 347–8.

migration also took place, which lasted for several years after the military hostilities had ceased. It impacted very profoundly on most countries in Central and Eastern Europe, including Germany itself. It had consequences which reverberated throughout the second half of the twentieth century. It involved the almost total expulsion of Germans and German-speakers from the eastern half of the continent.

What Germans and German-speakers experienced in East-Central and Eastern Europe at the end of the Second World War was not merely a knee-jerk act of revenge. Rather, it was one important element of a wider response to the collapse of Nazi Germany's wartime hegemony over the eastern half of the continent. This response articulated itself in a wave of expulsions against a number of different perceived 'national minorities' – not only Germans and German-speakers but also ethnic Ukrainians, ethnic Poles, Polish Jews, ethnic Hungarians, ethnic Belorussians and others.

In the territories Poland gained from Germany at the end of the war, the postwar expulsion of Germans by the new Communist-controlled authorities was part of a broader nationalist campaign aimed at bringing Polish ethno-national homogeneity to these territories. This campaign involved various nationalist population policies, which were linked together not only by their shared objective but also in a very practical sense. In those new Polish territories which had been homogeneously German-speaking before 1945, the mass influx of Polish settlers from spring 1945 onwards helped to instigate and reinforce the scope and speed of the expulsion of Germans from mid June 1945 onwards. This was of course most apparent in those areas of these territories where there were still large concentrations of Germans at the end of the war – areas which had been least affected by military fighting and where large numbers of Germans did not flee or returned very quickly after the hostilities ended. It was especially evident in Lower Silesia, where around half of all German citizens remaining in postwar Polish territory were living by the end of the war. From 1947 onwards, the inflow of Polish settlers then set the pace of the expulsion of remaining Germans from Poland's new territories, because the bulk of these Germans were highly skilled workers and their families, and they were only displaced when equivalently skilled Polish workers arrived to replace them. In this very practical sense, then, the nationalist population policies of expulsion and repopulation remained tightly locked together in Poland's new territories until the end of the 1940s.

At the same time, in the large areas of these territories, where a large proportion of German citizens spoke dialects of Polish as well as German and where the Communist-led Polish government intended from the outset to demonstrate that a very large 'indigenous Polish' population was living, both the expulsion and repopulation processes were tied together with the ethnic screening process known as the 'verification action'. The two principal such regions were western Upper Silesia and southern East Prussia. Whereas in the latter the postwar Polish state authorities failed to persuade many local residents to accept categorization as ethnic Poles, in the former they ultimately 'verified' the majority positively. This restricted both the number of German citizens expelled from western Upper Silesia and the amount of housing freed up for arriving Polish settlers. Ethnic screening therefore controlled expulsion and repopulation in this region. Moreover, throughout Poland's new territories, the three population policies of expulsion, repopulation and screening were underpinned by an accompanying process of 'cultural cleansing'; the signs, symbols, newspapers, books, schools, churches and institutions which the Polish authorities associated with German national culture were purged and replaced with Polish national-cultural equivalents.

As we have seen, similar policies were pursued by Communist-controlled and Communist-dominated regimes in much of the rest of East-Central and Eastern Europe at this time. Almost everywhere in the eastern half of the continent where expulsion occurred – not only after the war but also during it – it was accompanied by policies of repopulation and 'cultural cleansing'. Likewise, the cultural and linguistic complexity of East-Central and Eastern Europe ensured that it was not only in Poland's new territories where attempts were made to impose ethno-national simplicity on populations with multilinguistic and subnational identities through policies of ethnic screening and pressured assimilation. The parallels with events in Poland's new territories were particularly evident in postwar Czechoslovakia.

But this was not a simple matter of resemblances. There were direct and practical linkages between events in Poland's new territories and the voluntary and forced population movements going on in other nearby states at this time. For a start, the great torrent of ethnic German refugees fleeing from the Red Army, arriving in Poland's new territories from late 1944 onwards from elsewhere in East-Central and Eastern Europe, helped to set off the mass flight of Germans from these territories in early 1945. This permanently uprooted almost 5 million residents from these territories even before the Communist-led Polish authorities had arrived there. The forced migration of ethnic Poles from Soviet-annexed eastern Poland, likewise, helped to trigger the expulsion of Germans from postwar western Poland. This was because the eastern Poles started to be transported to Poland's new western territories already in spring 1945, when millions of Germans were still living there. The uprooting of eastern Poles was, in turn, entwined with the expulsion of ethnic Ukrainians from postwar eastern Polish territory because both formed part of a reciprocal population exchange. And the displacement of eastern Poles was interlocked with the population movements which took place in prewar Soviet territory because ethnic Russians and others were transported from the Soviet Union to Soviet-annexed prewar eastern Poland to repopulate it. Some of the Polish citizens transported to Poland from prewar eastern Poland at this time were Jews; they formed a large proportion of the people who would – often after several years of living in Poland's new territories – move onwards into Allied-occupied Germany en route to emigration from Europe at the end of the 1940s.

The practical linkages between ostensibly separate population movements and acts of expulsion did not end there. The start of the expulsion of ethnic Germans from Czechoslovakia in May 1945 not only, very likely, helped to galvanize the Polish Communist leadership into taking similar actions of their own on Polish territory, but also had an impact on the ground in Poland's new territories. This was because some ethnic Germans were actually expelled from Czechoslovakia into these territories rather than into postwar German territory. Events in Czechoslovakia, meanwhile, were interlinked with processes elsewhere in East-Central and Eastern Europe, because the campaigns of expulsion and repopulation in Czechoslovakia were connected to population exchanges with both Hungary and the Soviet Union. The fate of postwar Germany was also intimately interwoven with the mass population movements going on in the eastern half of the continent at the end of the war. Hundreds of thousands of Jews arrived in postwar Germany from East-Central and Eastern Europe at this time, particularly from Poland. Millions of Germans and German-speakers also flooded into postwar Germany from the east, forming a large percentage of the postwar population of both postwar German states. At the same time, millions of former forced labourers and former prisoners of war migrated in the opposite direction, flowing eastwards out of postwar German territory towards their East-Central and Eastern European home countries. These were just some of the most obvious transnational linkages evident in the frenzy of post-liberation population movement that took place in the eastern half of the continent during the years 1944–9. Others could be cited.

The Communist-led wave of forced migration which swept across East-Central and Eastern Europe after summer 1944 finally ebbed in 1948. It lost momentum entirely in the following year. Nevertheless, 1948–9 was a time of renewed transformation of a different sort – as Stalinist orthodoxy was embraced throughout East-Central and Eastern Europe, with the partial exception of Yugoslavia. By the end of 1948 overtly nationalist rhetoric and objectives had largely disappeared from official propaganda in Poland and Czechoslovakia. By 1949 the torrent of forced migration against perceived 'national minorities' was over. It had taken off across much of the eastern half of the continent as a spontaneous response to the end of Nazi Germany's occupation or domination of these countries. It had been steered and exploited by new Soviet-backed, Communist-controlled and Communist-dominated regimes in the early postwar years in order to consolidate their hold on political power and to ease their implementation of radical socioeconomic transformations. East-Central and Eastern Europe's Communist regimes would repeatedly make overt use of nationalist rhetoric and anti-minority measures as a means of preserving their shaky grip on power in the course of the postwar era. But in 1949 the era of massive forced migration against perceived 'national minorities' had finished. It would not return until the collapse of the Soviet Union and Yugoslavia at the start of the 1990s.

Bibliography

ARCHIVAL SOURCES

Archiwum Państwowe we Wrocławiu Oddział w Jeleniej Górze (APJG)
[State Archive in Wrocław, Department in Jelenia Góra, Poland]

APJG 123/II	Starostwo Powiatowe w Jeleniej Górze z lat 1945–50
APJG 130	Zarząd Miejski w Jeleniej Górze 1945–50
APJG 141	Akta Gminy Sobiszów
APJG 142	Akta Gminy Stara Kamienica
APJG 143	Akta Gminy Szklarska Poręba

Archiwum Państwowe w Katowicach (APK)
[State Archive in Katowice, Poland]

APK 185/4	Urząd Wojewódzki Śląski w Katowicach 1945–50. Wydział Społeczno-Polityczny

Archiwum Państwowe w Opolu (APO)
[State Archive in Opole, Poland]

APO 178	Starostwo Powiatowe w Opolu 1945–50
APO 185	Zarząd Miejski w Opolu
APO 332	Powiatowy i Miejski Urząd Informacji i Propagandy z lat 1945–7
APO 343	Państwowy Urząd Repatriacyjny. Powiatowy Urząd w Opolu

Archiwum Państwowe we Wrocławiu (APW)
[State Archive in Wrocław, Poland]

APW 331/VI	Urząd Wojewódzki Wrocławski (331/III). Wydział Społeczno-polityczny z lat 1945–50 (VI)
APW 345	Państwowy Urząd Repatriacyjny we Wrocławiu i oddziały powiatowe 1945–51. P.O. Jelenia Góra

Bundesarchiv, Bayreuth (BOD)
[Federal Archive, Bayreuth, Germany]

BOD 1, 207 Ost-Dokumentation 1: Fragebogenberichte zur Dokumentation der Vertreibung der Deutschen aus Ostmitteleuropa.
207 Kreis Hirschberg

BOD 1, 243 Ost-Dokumentation 1: Fragebogenberichte zur Dokumentation der Vertreibung der Deutschen aus Ostmitteleuropa.
243 Kreis Oppeln

BOD 2, 188 Ost-Dokumentation 2: Erlebnisberichte zur Dokumentation der Vertreibung der Deutschen aus Ost-Mittel-Europa.
188 Kreis Hirschberg

BOD 2, 229 Ost-Dokumentation 2: Erlebnisberichte zur Dokumentation der Vertreibung der Deutschen aus Ost-Mittel-Europa.
229 Kreis Oppeln

BOD 10, 812 Ost-Dokumentation 10, 812: Berichte über Verwaltung und Wirtschaft in den Gebieten östlich von Oder und Neiße

PUBLISHED PRIMARY SOURCES

Włodzimierz Borodziej and Hans Lemberg (eds.), *Niemcy w Polsce 1945–1950. Wybór Dokumentów* (4 vols., Warsaw, 2000–2001)
Volume 1: *Władze i instytucje centralne. Województwo olsztyńskie* (Warsaw, 2000)
Volume 2: *Polska centralna. Województwo śląskie* (Warsaw, 2000)
Volume 3: *Województwo poznańskie i szczecińskie* (Warsaw, 2001)
Volume 4: Daniel Boćkowski (ed.), *Pomorze Gdańskie i Dolny Śląsk* (Warsaw, 2001)

Włodzimierz Borodziej and Hans Lemberg (eds.), *"Unsere Heimat ist uns ein fremdes Land geworden . . ." Die Deutschen östlich von Oder und Neiße 1945–1950: Dokumente aus polnischen Archiven* (4 vols., Marburg, 2000–2004)
Volume 1: *Zentrale Behörden. Wojewodschaft Allenstein* (Marburg, 2000)
Volume 2: *Zentralpolen. Wojewodschaft Schlesien (Oberschlesien)* (Marburg, 2003)
Volume 3: *Wojewodschaft Posen. Wojewodschaft Stettin (Hinterpommern)* (Marburg, 2004)
Volume 4: *Wojewodschaften Pommerellen und Danzig (Westpreußen). Wojewodschaft Breslau (Niederschlesien)* (Marburg, 2004)

Stanisław Czepułkowski, 'W Karpaczu', in Anna Kotlarska (ed.), *Pamiętniki mieszkańców Dolnego Śląska* (Wrocław, 1978), pp. 283–300

Z. Dulczewksi and A. Kwilecki (eds.), *Pamiętniki osadników ziem odzyskanych* Vol. 2 (Poznań, 1970)

Adam Jaroszewski, 'Na turoszowskiej budowie', in Anna Kotlarska (ed.), *Pamiętniki mieszkańców Dolnego Śląska* (Wrocław, 1978), pp. 66–92

Krystna Kersten and Tomasz Szarota (eds.), *Wieś Polska 1939–1948. Materiały Konkursowe* Vol. 1 (Warsaw, 1967)

Anna Kotlarska (ed.), *Pamiętniki mieszkańców Dolnego Śląska* (Wrocław, 1978)

Stanisław Ossowski, 'Zagadnienia więzi regionalnej i więzi narodowej na Śląsku Opolskim', in Stanisław Ossowski, *Dzieła* Vol. 3 (Warsaw, 1967), pp. 252–300

Aleksander Pietraszko, 'Osadnik Wojskowy', in Z. Dulczewksi and A. Kwilecki (eds.) *Pamiętniki osadników ziem odzyskanych* Vol. 2 (Poznań, 1970), pp. 291–301

Theodor Schieder et al. (eds.), *Dokumentation der Vertreibung der Deutschen aus Ost-Mitteleuropa* (5 vols., Bonn, 1953–61)

Volume 1, 1–2: *Die Vertreibung der deutschen Bevölkerung aus den Gebieten östlich der Oder–Neiße* (Bonn, 1953)

Volume 1, 3: *Die Vertreibung der deutschen Bevölkerung aus den Gebieten östlich der Oder–Neiße. Polnische Gesetze und Verordnungen 1944–1955* (Bonn, 1960)

Jan Stadniczenko, 'Rok szkolny 1947/1948 na wsi opolskiej', in Z. Dulczewksi and A. Kwilecki (eds.), *Pamiętniki osadników ziem odzyskanych*, Vol. 2 (Poznań, 1970), pp. 396–430

INTERNET PRIMARY SOURCES

James Byrnes, 'Restatement of Policy on Germany', 6.9.1946, http://usa.usembassy.de/etexts/ga4-460906.htm [last accessed 23.3.2013]

Order of the Council of Ministers, 29 May 1946, Dziennik Ustaw Nr. 28, Poz. 177, http://isap.sejm.gov.pl/DetailsServlet?id=WDU19460280177 [last accessed 23.3.2013]

'Verzeichnis der Konzentrationslager und ihrer Außenkommandos gemäß § 42 Abs. 2 BEG', http://www.gesetze-im-internet.de/begdv_6/anlage_6.html [last accessed 23.3.2013]

Winston Churchill, 'Sinews of Peace', 5.3.1946, http://www.winstonchurchill.org/learn/speeches/speeches-of-winston-churchill/120-the-sinews-of-peace [last accessed 23.3.2013]

BOOKS AND ARTICLES

Józef Adelson, 'W Polsce Zwanej Ludową', in Jerzy Tomaszewski (ed.), *Najnowsze Dzieje Żydów w Polsce: w zarysie (do 1950 roku)* (Warsaw, 1993), pp. 387–477

Pertti Ahonen, 'Domestic Constraints on West German *Ostpolitik*: The Role of the Expellee Organizations in the Adenauer Era', *Central European History*, 31, 1998, 1/2, pp. 31–63

After the Expulsion: West Germany and Eastern Europe, 1945–1990 (Oxford, 2003)

Pertti Ahonen, Gustavo Corni, Jerzy Kochanowski, Rainer Schulze, Tamás Stark and Barbara Stelzl-Marx, *People on the Move: Forced Population Movements in Europe in the Second World War and Its Aftermath* (Oxford, 2008)

Pertti Ahonen and Jerzy Kochanowski, 'The Experience of Forced Migration', including 'The "Heim ins Reich" Programme and Its Impact', in Pertti Ahonen, Gustavo Corni, Jerzy Kochanowski, Rainer Schulze, Tamás Stark and Barbara Stelzl-Marx, *People on the Move: Forced Population Movements in Europe in the Second World War and Its Aftermath* (Oxford, 2008), pp. 111–42

Pertti Ahonen and Rainer Schulze, 'The Expulsion of Germans from Poland and Czechoslovakia', in Pertti Ahonen, Gustavo Corni, Jerzy Kochanowski,

Rainer Schulze, Tamás Stark and Barbara Stelzl-Marx, *People on the Move: Forced Population Movements in Europe in the Second World War and Its Aftermath* (Oxford, 2008), pp. 86–96

Manfred Alexander, 'Oberschlesien im 20. Jahrhundert – eine mißverstandene Region', *Geschichte und Gesellschaft* 30, 2004, pp. 465–89

János Angi, 'The Expulsion of the Germans from Hungary after World War II', in Steven Béla Várdy and T. Hunt Tooley (eds.), *Ethnic Cleansing in Twentieth-Century Europe* (New York, 2003), pp. 373–84

Yitzhak Arad, *Belzec, Sobibor, Treblinka. The Operation Reinhard Death Camps* (Bloomington and Indianapolis, 1987)

Klaus Bachmann, 'Jak skłócić Niemców z Polakami', *Gazeta Wyborcza* (Warsaw), 11 September 2006, p. 23

Klaus Bachmann and Jerzy Kranz (eds.), *Przeprosić za wypędzenie? O wysiedleniu Niemców po II wojnie światowej* (Kraków, 1997)

Joachim Bahlcke (ed.), *Schlesien und die Schlesier* (Munich, 1996)

Stefan Banasiak, *Działalność osadnicza Państwowego Urzędu Repatriacyjnego na Ziemiach Odzyskanych w latach 1945–1947* (Poznań, 1963)

Osadnictwo na ziemiach zachodnich i północnych w latach 1945–1950 (Warsaw, 1965)

Przesiedlenie Niemców z Polski w latach 1945–50 (unpublished manuscript, Uniwersytet Łódzki, 1968)

Nick Baron, 'Remaking Soviet Society: The Filtration of Returnees from Nazi Germany, 1944–49', in Peter Gatrell and Nick Baron (eds.), *Warlands: Population Resettlement and State Reconstruction in the Soviet-East European Borderlands, 1945–50* (Basingstoke, 2009), pp. 89–116

Róbert Barta, 'The Hungarian–Slovak Population Exchange and Forced Resettlement in 1947', in Steven Béla Várdy and T. Hunt Tooley (eds.), *Ethnic Cleansing in Twentieth-Century Europe* (New York, 2003), pp. 565–74

Gerd Becker, *Vertreibung und Aussiedlung der Deutschen aus Polen und den ehemals deutschen Ostgebieten. Vorgeschichte, Ursachen und Abläufe* (Doctoral dissertation, Justus-Liebig-Universität Gießen, 1988)

Mathias Beer, 'Im Spannungsfeld von Politik und Zeitgeschichte. Das Großforschungsprojekt "Dokumentation der Vertreibung der Deutschen aus Ost-Mitteleuropa"', *Vierteljahrshefte für Zeitgeschichte*, 46, 1998, pp. 345–89

'Der »Neuanfang« der Zeitgeschichte nach 1945. Zum Verhältnis von nationalsozialistischer Umsiedlungs- und Vernichtungspolitik und der Vertreibung der Deutschen aus Ostmitteleuropa', in Winfried Schulze and Otto Gerhard Oerle (eds.), *Deutsche Historiker im Nationalsozialismus* (Frankfurt am Main, 1999), pp. 274–301

'"Ein der wissenschaftlichen Forschung sich aufdrängender historischer Zusammenhang". Von den deutschen Schwierigkeiten, "Flucht und Vertreibung" zu kontextualisieren', *Zeitschrift für Geschichtswissenschaft*, 51, 2003, 1, pp. 59–64

Leszek Belzyt, *Między Polską i Niemczami. Weryfikacja narodowościowa i jej następstwa na Warmii Mazurach i Powiślu w latach 1945–1960* (Toruń, 1996)

Wolfgang Benz, 'Zweifache Opfer nationalsozialistischer Bevölkerungspolitik: Die Zwangsmigration von Volksdeutschen', in Ralph Melville, Jiří Pešek, and Claus Scharf (eds.), *Zwangsmigrationen im mittleren und östlichen Europa. Völkerrecht – Kozeptionen – Praxis (1938–1950)* (Mainz, 2007), pp. 247–58

Wolfgang Benz (ed.), *Die Vertreibung der Deutschen aus dem Osten. Ursachen, Ereignisse, Folgen* (Frankfurt am Main, 1985)

Stefan Berger, 'How to Be Russian with a Difference? Kaliningrad and Its German Past', *Geopolitics*, 15, 2010, 2, pp. 345–66

Tadeusz Białecki, *Przesiedlenie ludności niemieckiej z Pomorza Zachodniego po II wojnie światowej* (Poznań, 1969)

James E. Bjork, *Neither German nor Pole. Catholicism and National Indifference in a Central European Borderland* (Ann Arbor, Michigan, 2008)

Richard Blanke, *Orphans of Versailles: The Germans in Western Poland 1918–1939* (Lexington, Kentucky, 1993)

Polish-Speaking Germans? Language and National Identity among the Masurians since 1871 (Cologne, 2001)

Zofia Boda-Krężel, *Sprawa Volkslisty na Górnym Śląsku. Koncepcje likwidacji problemu i ich realizacja* (Opole, 1978)

Alfred Bohmann, *Menschen und Grenzen: Strukturwandel der deutschen Bevölkerung im polnischen Staats- und Verwaltungsbereich* (Köln, 1969)

Włodzimierz Bonusiak, *Polityka ludnościowa i ekonomiczna ZSRR na okupowanych ziemiach polskich w latach 1939–1941 ("Zachodnia Ukraina" i "Zachodnia Białorus")* (Rzeszów, 2006)

Włodzimierz Borodziej, 'Historiografia Polska o "wypędzeniu" Niemców', *Studia i Materiały*, 2, 1996, pp. 249–69

'Einleitung' [sections 3–8], in Włodzimierz Borodziej and Hans Lemberg (eds.), *"Unsere Heimat ist uns ein fremdes Land geworden..." Die Deutschen östlich von Oder und Neiße 1945–1950: Dokumente aus polnischen Archiven* (4 vols., Marburg, 2000–2004), Vol. 1: *Zentrale Behörden. Wojewodschaft Allenstein* (Marburg, 2000), pp. 37–114

The Warsaw Uprising of 1944 (Madison, Wisconsin, 2006)

Włodzimierz Borodziej, Stanisław Ciesielski and Jerzy Kochanowski, 'Wstęp' in Stanisław Ciesielski (ed.), *Przesiedlenie ludności polskiej z kresów wschodnich do Polski 1944–1947* (Warsaw, 1999), pp. 5–51

Włodzimierz Borodziej and Artur Hajnicz (eds.), *Kompleks wypędzenia* (Kraków, 1998)

Włodzimierz Borodziej and Hans Lemberg (eds.), *Niemcy w Polsce 1945–1950. Wybór Dokumentów* (4 vols., Warsaw, 2000–2001)

Nikolai Bougai, *The Deportation of Peoples in the Soviet Union* (New York, 1996)

Detlef Brandes, *Der Weg zur Vertreibung 1938–1945: Pläne und Entscheidungen zum 'Transfer' der Deutschen aus der Tschechoslowakei und aus Polen* (Munich, 2001)

Detlef Brandes and Václav Kural (eds.), *Der Weg in die Katastrophe: Deutsch–Tschechoslowakische Beziehungen 1938–1947* (Düsseldorf, 1994)

Per Brodersen, *Die Stadt im Westen. Wie Königsberg Kaliningrad wurde* (Göttingen, 2008)

Martin Broszat, 'Einleitende Darstellung', in Theodor Schieder et al. (eds.), *Dokumentation der Vertreibung der Deutschen aus Ost-Mitteleuropa* (5 vols., Bonn, 1953–61), Vol. 1, 1: *Die Vertreibung der deutschen Bevölkerung aus den Gebieten östlich der Oder-Neiße* (Bonn, 1953), pp. 1E–158E

'Massendokumentation als Methode zeitgeschichtlicher Forschung', *Vierteljahrshefte für Zeitgeschichte* 2, 1954, pp. 202–13

Christopher R. Browning, *The Origins of the Final Solution. The Evolution of Nazi Jewish Policy, September 1939–March 1942* (London, 2004)

Micha Brumlik, *Wer Sturm sät. Die Vertreibung der Deutschen* (Berlin, 2005)

Chad Bryant, 'Either German or Czech: Fixing Nationality in Bohemia and Moravia, 1939–1946', *Slavic Review*, 61, 2002, 4, pp. 683–706

Edward Chászár, 'Ethnic Cleansing in Slovakia: The Plight of the Hungarian Minority', in Steven Béla Várdy and T. Hunt Tooley (eds.), *Ethnic Cleansing in Twentieth-Century Europe* (New York, 2003), pp. 559–64

Jan M. Ciechanowski, *The Warsaw Rising of 1944* (Cambridge, 1974)

Anna M. Cienciala, 'Prisoners of an Undeclared War, 23 August 1939–5 March 1940', in Anna M. Cienciala, Natalia Z. Lebedeva and Wojciech Materski (eds.), *Katyn. A Crime without Punishment* (New Haven, Connecticut, 2007), pp. 1–39

'Extermination, March–June 1940', in Anna M. Cienciala, Natalia Z. Lebedeva and Wojciech Materski (eds.), *Katyn. A Crime without Punishment* (New Haven, Connecticut, 2007), pp. 121–48

'Katyn and Its Echoes, 1940 to the Present', in Anna M. Cienciala, Natalia Z. Lebedeva and Wojciech Materski (eds.), *Katyn. A Crime without Punishment* (New Haven, Connecticut, 2007), pp. 206–64

Stanisław Ciesielski (ed.), *Przesiedlenie ludności polskiej z kresów wschodnich do Polski 1944–1947* (Warsaw, 1999)

'Kresy Wschodnie II Rzeczypospolitej i problemy identyfikacji narodowej', in Stanisław Ciesielski (ed.), *Przemiany Narodowościowe na Kresach Wschodnich II Rzeczypospolitej* (Toruń, 2003), pp. 9–51

Stanisław Ciesielski, Grzegorz Hryciuk and Aleksander Srebrakowski, *Masowe deportacje ludności w Związku Radzieckim* (Toruń, 2003)

Ian Connor, *Refugees and Expellees in Post-war Germany* (Manchester, 2007)

Norbert Conrads (ed.), *Deutsche Geschichte im Osten Europas. Schlesien* (Berlin, 1994)

Karl Cordell (ed.), *The Politics of Ethnicity in Central Europe* (Basingstoke, 2000)

Gustavo Corni, *Hitler's Ghettos. Voices from a Beleaguered Society 1939–1944* (London, 2003)

'Germans outside the Reich: From Protection to "Heim ins Reich"', in Pertti Ahonen, Gustavo Corni, Jerzy Kochanowski, Rainer Schulze, Tamás Stark and Barbara Stelzl-Marx, *People on the Move: Forced Population Movements in Europe in the Second World War and Its Aftermath* (Oxford, 2008), pp. 14–20

'Nazi Germany's Plans for Occupied Poland', in Pertti Ahonen, Gustavo Corni, Jerzy Kochanowski, Rainer Schulze, Tamás Stark and Barbara Stelzl-Marx, *People on the Move: Forced Population Movements in Europe in the Second World War and its Aftermath* (Oxford, 2008), pp. 20–3

'The Implementation of the German Plans in the Occupied Eastern Territories', in Pertti Ahonen, Gustavo Corni, Jerzy Kochanowski, Rainer Schulze, Tamás Stark and Barbara Stelzl-Marx, *People on the Move: Forced Population Movements in Europe in the Second World War and Its Aftermath* (Oxford, 2008), pp. 26–34

Gustavo Corni and Jerzy Kochanowski, 'Soviet Population Policy in Poland', in Pertti Ahonen, Gustavo Corni, Jerzy Kochanowski, Rainer Schulze, Tamás Stark and Barbara Stelzl-Marx, *People on the Move: Forced Population Movements in Europe in the Second World War and Its Aftermath* (Oxford, 2008), pp. 23–6

'The Generalplan Ost' and 'Generalplan Ost: Implementation and Failure', in Pertti Ahonen, Gustavo Corni, Jerzy Kochanowski, Rainer Schulze, Tamás Stark and Barbara Stelzl-Marx, *People on the Move: Forced Population Movements in Europe in the Second World War and Its Aftermath* (Oxford, 2008), pp. 34–42

T. David Curp, *A Clean Sweep? The Politics of Ethnic Cleansing in Western Poland, 1945–1960* (Rochester, New York, 2006)

Marek Czapliński (ed.), *Historia Śląska* (Wrocław, 2002)

Stefan Czech, 'Powiat i Miasto Opole w pierwszych latach po wyzwoleniu', *Śląskie Studia* 9, 1965, pp. 131–79

Jan Czerniakiewicz, *Repatriacja ludności polskiej z ZSRR 1944–1948* (Warsaw, 1987)

Jan Czerniakiewicz and Monika Czerniakiewicz, *Przesiedlenia ze Wschodu 1944–1959* (Warsaw, 2007)

Antoni Czubiński, *Polska i Polacy po II wojnie światowej (1945–1989)* (Poznań, 1998)

Jürgen Danyel and Philipp Ther (eds.), *Flucht und Vertreibung in europäischer Perspektive, special issue of Zeitschrift für Geschichtswissenschaft*, 2003, 1

Norman Davies and Roger Moorhouse, *Microcosm. Portrait of a Central European City* (London, 2002)

Dennis Deletant, *Hitler's Forgotten Ally. Ion Antonescu and His Regime, Romania 1940–44* (Basingstoke, 2006)

Andrew Demshuk, *The Lost German East: Forced Migration and the Politics of Memory, 1945–1970* (Cambridge, 2012)

Alfred-Maurice de Zayas, *Nemesis at Potsdam: Anglo-Americans and the Expulsion of the Germans. Background, Execution, Consequences* (London, 1977)

The German Expellees: Victims in War and Peace (Basingstoke and London, 1993)

Henryk Dominiczak, *Proces zasiedlenia województwa zielenogórskiego w latach 1945–1950* (Zielona Góra, 1975)

R. M. Douglas, *Orderly and Humane. The Expulsion of the Germans after the Second World War* (New Haven, Connecticut, 2012)

Roman Drozd, 'Geneza i Przebieg akcji "Wisła"', in Roman Drozd (ed.), *Ukraińcy w najnowszych dziejach Polski 1918–1989. Tom II: Akcja "Wisła"* (Warsaw, 2005), pp. 23–44

David Engel, 'Marek Jan Chodakiewicz, after the Holocaust: Polish–Jewish Conflict in the Wake of World War II', *Polin: Studies in Polish Jewry*, 18, 2005, pp. 424–9

'Patterns of Anti-Jewish Violence in Poland, 1944–1946', *Yad Vashem Studies*, 26, 1998, pp. 43–85

Catherine Epstein, *Model Nazi. Arthur Greiser and the Occupation of Western Poland* (Oxford, 2010)

Michael G. Esch, "*Gesunde Verhältnisse": Deutsche und polnische Bevölkerungspolitik in Ostmitteleuropa 1939–1950* (Marburg, 1998)

Ingo Eser, 'Die Deutschen in Oberschlesien', in Włodzimierz Borodziej and Hans Lemberg (eds.), *"Unsere Heimat ist uns ein fremdes Land geworden..." Die Deutschen östlich von Oder und Neiße 1945–1950: Dokumente aus polnischen Archiven* (4 vols., Marburg, 2000–2004), Vol. 2: *Zentralpolen. Wojewodschaft Schlesien (Oberschlesien)* (Marburg, 2003), pp. 355–99

Ingo Eser and Witold Stankowski, 'Die Deutschen in Wojewodschaften Pommerellen und Danzig', in Włodzimierz Borodziej and Hans Lemberg (eds.), *"Unsere Heimat ist uns ein fremdes Land geworden..." Die Deutschen östlich von Oder und Neiße 1945–1950: Dokumente aus polnischen Archiven* (4 vols., Marburg, 2000–2004), Vol. 4: *Wojewodschaften Pommerellen und Danzig (Westpreußen). Wojewodschaft Breslau (Niederschlesien)* (Marburg, 2004), pp. 3–67

Heinz Esser, *Die Hölle von Lamsdorf. Dokumentation über ein polnisches Vernichtungslager* (2nd ed., Bonn, 1971)

Richard J. Evans, *The Third Reich at War, 1939–1945* (London, 2008)

Bernd Faulenbach 'Die Vertreibung der Deutschen aus den Gebieten jenseits von Oder und Neiße: Zur wissenschaftlichen und öffentlichen Diskussion in Deutschland', *Aus Politik und Zeitgeschichte*, B51–2, 2002, pp. 44–54

Magarete Myers Feinstein, *Holocaust Survivors in Postwar Germany, 1945–1957* (Cambridge, 2010)

Michael Fleming, *Communism, Nationalism and Ethnicity in Poland, 1944–1950* (Abingdon, 2010)

Matthew Frank, *Expelling the Germans: British Opinion and Post-1945 Population Transfer in Context* (Oxford, 2007)

K. E. Franzen, *Hitlers letzte Opfer* (Berlin, 2001)

Ute Frevert, 'Geschichtsvergessenheit und Geschichtsvergessenheit revisited. Der jüngste Erinnerungsboom in der Kritik', *Aus Politik und Zeitgeschichte* B40–41, 2003, pp. 6–13

Saul Friedländer, *The Years of Extermination: Nazi Germany and the Jews 1939–1945* (London, 2007)

Benjamin Frommer, 'To Prosecute or to Expel? Czechoslovak Retribution and the "Transfer" of Sudeten Germans', in Philipp Ther and Ana Siljak (eds.), *Redrawing Nations: Ethnic Cleansing in East-Central Europe, 1944–1948* (Lanham, 2001), pp. 221–40

National Cleansing: Retribution against Nazi Collaborators in Postwar Czechoslovakia (Cambridge, 2005)

Peter Gatrell and Nick Baron (eds.), *Warlands: Population Resettlement and State Reconstruction in the Soviet–East European Borderlands, 1945–50* (Basingstoke, 2009)

W. Geiszczyński, *Państwowy Urząd Repatriacyjny w osadnictwie na Warmii i Mazurach 1945–1950* (Olsztyn, 1999)

Christian Gerlach, *Kalkulierte Morde. Die deutsche Wirtschafts- und Vernichtungspolitik in Weißrussland 1941 bis 1944* (Hamburg, 1999)

Eagle Glassheim, 'The Mechanics of Ethnic Cleansing: The Expulsion of Germans from Czechoslovakia, 1945–1947', in Philipp Ther and Ana Siljak (eds.), *Redrawing Nations: Ethnic Cleansing in East-Central Europe, 1944–1948* (Lanham, 2001), pp. 197–219

Constantin Goschler, 'Wiedergutmachung', in Wolfgang Benz (ed.), *Deutschland unter allierter Besatzung 1945–1949/55* (Berlin, 1999), pp. 201–6

Jan Tomasz Gross, *Polish Society under German Occupation: The Generalgouvernement, 1939–1944* (Princeton, New Jersey, 1979)

'Stereotypes of Polish–Jewish Relations after the War: The Special Commission of the Central Committee of Polish Jews', *Polin: Studies in Polish Jewry*, 13, 2000, pp. 195–205

Revolution from Abroad: The Soviet Conquest of Poland's Western Ukraine and Western Belorussia (2nd edn, Princeton, New Jersey, 2002)

Fear: Anti-Semitism in Poland after Auschwitz. An Essay in Historical Interpretation (Princeton, New Jersey, 2006)

Eva Hahn and Hans Henning, *Die Vertreibung im deutschen Erinnern: Legenden, Mythos, Geschichte* (Paderborn, 2010)

Nicolae Harsányi 'The Deportation of the Germans from Romania to the Soviet Union, 1945–1949', in Steven Béla Várdy and T. Hunt Tooley (eds.), *Ethnic Cleansing in Twentieth-Century Europe* (New York, 2003), pp. 385–92

Mary Heimann, *Czechoslovakia: The State That Failed* (New Haven, Connecticut and London, 2009)

Isabel Heinemann, 'Umvolkungspläne, Rassenauslese, Zwangsumsiedlungen: Die Rasseexperten der SS und die "bevölkerungspolitische Neuorderung" Europas', in Ralph Melville, Jiří Pešek and Claus Scharf (eds.), *Zwangsmigrationen im mittleren und östlichen Europa. Völkerrecht – Kozeptionen – Praxis (1938–1950)* (Mainz, 2007), pp. 203–18

Ulrich Herbert, *Hitler's Foreign Workers. Enforced Foreign Labor in Germany under the Third Reich* (Cambridge, 1997)

Andreas R. Hofmann, *Die Nachkriegszeit in Schlesien. Gesellschafts- und Bevölkerungspolitik in den polnischen Siedlungsgebieten 1945–1948* (Köln, 2000)

Grzegorz Hryciuk, 'Victims 1939–1941: The Soviet Repressions in Eastern Poland', in Elazar Barkan, Elizabeth A. Cole and Kai Struve (eds.), *Shared History – Divided Memory. Jews and Others in Soviet-Occupied Poland, 1939–1941* (Leipzig, 2007), pp. 173–200

Bohdan Jałowiecki and Jan Przewłocki (eds.), *Stosunki polsko-niemieckie. Integracja i rozwój ziem zachodnich i północnych* (Katowice, 1980)

Zoran Janjetović, 'Die Vertreibung der deutschen und der ungarischen Bevölkerung der Vojvodina am Ende des Zweiten Weltkriegs', in Ralph Melville, Jiří Pešek and Claus Scharf (eds.), *Zwangsmigrationen im mittleren und östlichen Europa. Völkerrecht – Kozeptionen – Praxis (1938–1950)* (Mainz, 2007), pp. 407–20

Stanisław Jankowiak, 'Die Deutschen in Großpolen und im Lebuser Land (Ostbrandenburg) in den Jahren 1945–1950', in Włodzimierz Borodziej and Hans Lemberg (eds.), *"Unsere Heimat ist uns ein fremdes Land geworden..." Die Deutschen östlich von Oder und Neiße 1945–1950: Dokumente aus polnischen Archiven* (4 vols., Marburg, 2000–2004), Vol. 3: *Wojewodschaft Posen. Wojewodschaft Stettin (Hinterpommern)* (Marburg, 2003), pp. 3–64

'Flucht, Vertreibung und Zwangsaussiedlung der Deutschen aus der Wojewodschaft Breslau (Województwo Wrocławskie) in den Jahren 1945 bis 1950. Die Jahre 1946–1950' in Włodzimierz Borodziej and Hans Lemberg (eds.), *"Unsere Heimat ist uns ein fremdes Land geworden..." Die Deutschen östlich von Oder und Neiße 1945–1950: Dokumente aus polnischen Archiven* (4 vols., Marburg, 2000–2004), Vol. 4: *Wojewodschaften Pommerellen und Danzig (Westpreußen). Wojewodschaft Breslau (Niederschlesien)* (Marburg, 2004), pp. 401–32

Wysiedlenie i emigracja ludności niemieckiej w polityce władz polskich w latach 1945–1970 (Warsaw, 2005)

Marek Jasiak, 'Overcoming Ukrainian Resistance: The Deportation of Ukrainians within Poland in 1947', in Philipp Ther and Ana Siljak (eds.), *Redrawing Nations: Ethnic Cleansing in East-Central Europe, 1944–1948* (Lanham, 2001), pp. 173–94

Rudolf Jaworski and Marian Wojciechowski (eds.), *Polacy i Niemcy między wojnami. Status mniejszości i walka graniczna. Reporty władz polskich i niemieckich z lat 1920–1939* (München, 1997)

Wojciech Jaworski, 'Jewish Religious Communities in Upper Silesia 1945–1970', in Marcin Wodziński and Janusz Spyra (eds.), *Jews in Silesia* (Kraków, 2001), pp. 247–63

Karol Jonca, *Polityka narodowościowa Trzeciej Rzeszy na Śląsku Opolskim (1933–1940)* (Opole, 1970)

(ed.), *Wysiedlenie Niemców i osadnictwo ludności polskiej na obszarze Krzyżowa-Świdnica (Kreisau-Schweidnitz) w latach 1945–1948. Wybór dokumentów* (Wrocław, 1997)

Tomasz Kamusella, 'Upper Silesia 1918–1945', in Karl Cordell (ed.), *The Politics of Ethnicity in Central Europe* (Basingstoke, 2000), pp. 92–112

The Szlonzoks and Their Language: Between Germany, Poland and Szlonzokian Nationalism (EUI working paper, Florence, 2003)

Silesia and Central European Nationalism. The Emergence of National and Ethnic Groups in Prussian Silesia and Austrian Silesia, 1848–1918 (West Lafayette, Indiana, 2007)

Johannes Kaps (ed.), *Die Tragödie Schlesiens 1945/46 in Dokumenten. Unter besonderer Berücksichtigung des Erzbistums Breslau* (Munich, 1952–3)

Padraic Kenney, *Rebuilding Poland: Workers and Communists, 1945–1950* (Ithaca, New York and London, 1997)

Krystyna Kersten, *Repatriacja ludności polskiej po II wojnie światowej* (Warsaw, 1974)

The Establishment of Communist Rule in Poland, 1943–1948 (Berkeley and Los Angeles, 1991)

'Forced Migration and the Transformation of Polish Society in the Postwar Period', in Philipp Ther and Ana Siljak (eds.), *Redrawing Nations: Ethnic Cleansing in East-Central Europe, 1944–1948* (Lanham, 2001), pp. 75–86

Jeremy King, *Budweisers into Czechs and Germans: A Local History of Bohemian Politics, 1848–1948* (Princeton, New Jersey, 2002)

Matthias Kneip, *Die deutsche Sprache in Oberschlesien. Untersuchungen zur politischen Rolle der deutschen Sprache als Minderheitensprache in den Jahren 1921–1998* (Dortmund, 1999)

Jerzy Kochanowski, *W polskiej niewoli. Niemieccy jeńcy wojenni w Polsce 1945–1950* (Warsaw, 2001)

'Schicksale der Deutschen in Zentralpolen in den Jahren 1945–1950', in Włodzimierz Borodziej and Hans Lemberg (eds.), *"Unsere Heimat ist uns ein fremdes Land geworden . . ." Die Deutschen östlich von Oder und Neiße 1945–1950: Dokumente aus polnischen Archiven* (4 vols., Marburg, 2000–2004), Vol. 2: *Zentralpolen. Wojewodschaft Schlesien (Oberschlesien)* (Marburg, 2003), pp. 3–76

'Towards a Nationally Homogeneous State: Poland 1944–6', in Pertti Ahonen, Gustavo Corni, Jerzy Kochanowski, Rainer Schulze, Tamás Stark and Barbara Stelzl-Marx, *People on the Move: Forced Population Movements in Europe in the Second World War and Its Aftermath* (Oxford, 2008), pp. 96–103

'Memory and Commemoration of Flight and Expulsion in Poland', in Pertti Ahonen, Gustavo Corni, Jerzy Kochanowski, Rainer Schulze, Tamás Stark and Barbara Stelzl-Marx, *People on the Move: Forced Population Movements in Europe in the Second World War and Its Aftermath* (Oxford, 2008), pp. 155–65

Sylwester Koczkowski, *Osadnictwo polskie w Szczecinie 1945–1950* (Poznań, 1963)

Elżbeta Kościk, *Osadnictwo wiejskie w południowych powiatach Dolnego Śląska w latach 1945–1949* (Wrocław, 1992)

Leszek Kosiński, *Procesy ludnościowe na Ziemiach Odzyskanych w latach 1945–1960* (Warsaw, 1963)

Andreas Kossert, *Preußen, Deutsche oder Polen? Die Masuren im Spannungsfeld des ethnischen Nationalismus 1870–1956* (Wiesbaden, 2001)

Kalte Heimat. Die Geschichte der deutschen Vertriebenen nach 1945 (Munich, 2008)

Zbigniew Kowalski, *Powrót Śląska Opolskiego do Polski. Organizacja władzy ludowej i regulacja problemów narodowościowych w latach 1945–1948* (Opole, 1983)

Claudia Kraft, 'Flucht, Vertreibung und Zwangsaussiedlung der Deutschen aus der Wojewodschaft Allenstein (Województwo Olsztyńskie) in den Jahren 1945 bis 1950', in Włodzimierz Borodziej and Hans Lemberg (eds.), *"Unsere Heimat ist uns ein fremdes Land geworden . . ." Die Deutschen östlich von Oder und Neiße 1945–1950: Dokumente aus polnischen Archiven* (4 vols., Marburg, 2000–2004), Vol. 1: *Zentrale Behörden. Wojewodschaft Allenstein* (Marburg, 2000), pp. 433–80

'Who Is a Pole, and Who Is a German? The Province of Olsztyn in 1945', in Philipp Ther and Ana Siljak (eds.), *Redrawing Nations: Ethnic Cleansing in East-Central Europe, 1944–1948* (Lanham, 2001), pp. 107–20

'Flucht, Vertreibung und Zwangsaussiedlung der Deutschen aus der Wojewodschaft Breslau (Województwo Wrocławskie) in den Jahren 1945 bis 1950. Das Jahr 1945', in Włodzimierz Borodziej and Hans Lemberg (eds.), *"Unsere Heimat ist uns ein fremdes Land geworden..." Die Deutschen östlich von Oder und Neiße 1945–1950: Dokumente aus polnischen Archiven* (4 vols., Marburg, 2000–2004), Vol. 4: *Wojewodschaften Pommerellen und Danzig (Westpreußen). Wojewodschaft Breslau (Niederschlesien)* (Marburg, 2004), pp. 357–99

Vincen Kroll and Heinrich Smikalla, 'Einleitende Darstellung', in Theodor Schieder et al. (eds.), *Dokumentation der Vertreibung der Deutschen aus Ost-Mitteleuropa* (5 vols., Bonn, 1953–61), Vol. 4: *Die Vertreibung der deutschen Bevölkerung aus der Tschechoslowakei* (Bonn, 1957)

Adam Krzemiński, 'Die schwierige deutsch-polnische Vergangenheitspolitik', *Aus Politik und Zeitgeschichte*, B40–41, 2003, pp. 3–5

'Poczet rewanżystów', *Polityka* 37, 16 September 2006, 2571, pp. 60–2

Ivo Łaborewicz, 'Wykaz zespołów archiwalnych przechowywanych w archiwum państwowym we Wrocławiu oddział w Jeleniej Górze', *Rocznik Jeleniogórski* 32, 2000, pp. 91–118

Stanisław Łach, *Osadnictwo wiejskie na ziemiach zachodnich i północnych Polski w latach 1945–1950* (Słupsk, 1983)

N. S. Lebedeva, 'The Deportation of the Polish Population to the USSR, 1939–41', in Alfred J. Rieber (ed.), *Forced Migration in Central and Eastern Europe, 1939–1950* (London, 2000), pp. 28–45

Hans Lemberg, '"Ethnische Säuberung": Ein Mittel zur Lösung von Nationalitätenproblemen?', *Aus Politik und Zeitgeschichte*, 1992, B46, pp. 27–38

Zdzisław Łempiński, *Przesiedlenie ludności niemieckiej z województwa śląsko-dąbrowskiego w latach 1945–1950* (Katowice, 1979)

Sebastian Ligarski and Jakub Tyszkiewicz (eds.), *Dziennik wydarzeń punktu zborczego w Dzierżoniowie z lat 1946–1947* (Wrocław, 2004)

Bernard Linek, *"Odniemczanie" województwa śląskiego w latach 1945–1950: w świetle materiałów wojewódzkich* (Opole, 1997)

Polityka antyniemiecka na Górnym Śląsku w latach 1945–1950 (Opole, 2000)

Jan Józef Lipski, *Powiedzić sobie wszystko... Eseje o sąsiedztwie polsko-niemieckim* (Gliwice, 1996)

Michał Lis, *Ludność rodzima na Śląsku Opolskim po II wojnie światowej (1945–1993)* (Opole, 1993)

'Mniejszość polska w niemieckiej części Górnego Śląska', in *"Wach auf, mein Herz, und denke". Zur Geschichte der Beziehungen zwischen Schlesien und Berlin-Brandenburg von 1740 bis heute* (Berlin and Opole, 1995), pp. 261–70

Sprawozdania sytuacyjne starostów powiatowych (prezydentów miast) – jako źródło wiedzy o roku 1945 na śląsku opolskim' *Studia Śląskie*, LX, 2001, pp. 241–51

Peter Longerich, *Holocaust. The Nazi Persecution and Murder of the Jews* (Oxford, 2010)

Józef Lubojański, *Polska ludność rodzima na ziemiach zachodnich i północnych. Dzieje polskiej granicy zachodniej* (Warsaw, 1960)

Czesław Łuczak, *Od Bismarcka do Hitlera. Polsko-niemieckie stosunki gospodarcze* (Poznań 1988)

Polska i Polacy w drugiej wojnie światowej (Poznań, 1993)

Richard C. Lukas, *The Forgotten Holocaust: The Poles under German Occupation 1939–1944* (2nd edn, New York 1997)

Czesław Madajczyk, 'Vom "Generalplan Ost" zum "Generalsiedlungsplan". Forschungspolitische Erkenntnisse', in Mechtild Rössler and Sabine Schleiermacher (eds.), *Der "Generalplan Ost"* (Berlin, 1993), pp. 12–19

Piotr Madajczyk, *Przyłączenie Śląska Opolskiego do Polski 1945–1948* (Warsaw, 1996)

'Niemcy', in Piotr Madajczyk (ed.), *Mniejszości narodowe w Polsce. Państwo i społeczeństwo polskie a mniejszości narodowe w okresach przełomów politycznych, 1944–1989* (Warsaw, 1998), pp. 66–109

Niemcy polscy 1944–1989 (Warsaw, 2001)

'Oberschlesien zwischen Gewalt und Frieden', in Philipp Ther and Holm Sundhaussen (eds.), *Nationalitätenkonflikte im 20. Jahrhundert: Ursachen von inter-ethnischer Gewalt im Vergleich* (Wiesbaden, 2001), pp. 147–62

'Część Druga. Studium Przypadku: Powiat Kozielski 1945–1948', in Piotr Madajczyk and Danuta Berlińska, *Polska jako państwo narodowe. Historia i Pamięć* (Warsaw and Opole, 2008), pp. 375–568

Piotr Madajczyk and Danuta Berlińska, *Polska jako państwo narodowe. Historia i Pamięć* (Warsaw and Opole, 2008)

Anna Magierska, *Ziemie zachodnie i północne w 1945 roku. Kształtowanie się podstaw polityki integracyjnej państwa polskiego* (Warsaw, 1978)

Bożena Malec-Masnyk, *Plebiscyt na Górnym Śląsku (geneza i charakter)* (Opole, 1989)

Zeev W. Mankowitz, *Life between Memory and Hope. The Survivors of the Holocaust in Occupied Germany* (Cambridge, 2002)

Gilad Margalit, *Guilt, Suffering and Memory: Germany Remembers Its Dead of World War II* (Bloomington, Indiana, 2010)

Terry Martin, 'The Origins of Soviet Ethnic Cleansing', *The Journal of Modern History*, 70, December 1998, 4, pp. 813–61

Jürgen Matthäus, 'Operation Barbarossa and the Onset of the Holocaust, June–December 1941', in Christopher R. Browning, *The Origins of the Final Solution. The Evolution of Nazi Jewish Policy, September 1939–March 1942* (London, 2004), pp. 244–308

Mark Mazower, *Hitler's Empire: Nazi Rule in Occupied Europe* (London, 2008)

Joanna Michlic-Coren, 'Anti-Jewish Violence in Poland, 1918–1939 and 1945–1947', *Polin: Studies in Polish Jewry*, 14, 2001, pp. 34–61

Jan Misztal, *Weryfikacja narodowościowa na Śląsku Opolskim 1945–1950* (Opole, 1984)
Weryfikacja narodowościowa na Ziemiach Odzyskanych (Warsaw, 1990)
Robert G. Moeller, *War Stories: The Search for a Usable Past in the Federal Republic of Germany* (Berkeley and Los Angeles, 2001)
'Remembering the War in a Nation of Victims', in Hanna Schissler (ed.), *The Miracle Years. A Cultural History of West Germany, 1949–1968* (Oxford, 2001), pp. 83–109
Klejda Mulaj, *Politics of Ethnic Cleansing: Nation-State Building and Provision of In/Security in Twentieth-Century Balkans* (Lanham, 2008)
Jan Musekamp, *Zwischen Stettin und Szczecin: Metamorphosen einer Stadt von 1945 bis 2005* (Wiesbaden, 2010)
Bartosz Nabrdalik, 'South-Eastern Poland between 1939 and the Final Soviet Frontier Demarcation in 1951 – The Destruction of an Ethnic Mosaic', *Journal of Slavic Military Studies*, 21, 1, 2008, pp. 17–37
Norman M. Naimark, *Fires of Hatred. Ethnic Cleansing in Twentieth-Century Europe* (Cambridge, Massachusetts, 2001)
Heinz Nawratil, *Vertreibungsverbrechen an Deutschen. Tatbestand, Motive, Bewältigung* (Munich, 1982)
Bernadetta Nitschke, *Wysiedlenie ludności niemieckiej z Polski w latach 1945–1949* (Zielona Góra, 1999)
Vertreibung und Aussiedlung der deutschen Bevölkerung aus Polen 1945 bis 1949 (Munich, 2003)
Edmund Nowak, *Cien Łambinowic* (Opole, 1991)
Obozy na Śląsku Opolskim w systemie powojennych obozów w Polsce (1945–1950). Historia i implikacja (Opole, 2002)
Joanna Nowosielska-Sobel, '"Czy istnieje Polak sudecki?". Z problemów kształtowanie się tożsamości zbiorowej ludności Dolnego Śląska na przykładzie Ziemi Jeleniogórskiej w latach 60. XX wieku', in Joanna Nowosielska-Sobel and Grzegorz Strauchold (eds.), *Dolnoślazacy? Kształtowanie tożsamości mieszkańców Dolnego Śląska po II wojnie światowej* (Wrocław, 2007), pp. 21–43
Ewa Ochman, 'Population Displacement and Regional Reconstruction in Postwar Poland: The Case of Upper Silesia', in Peter Gatrell and Nick Baron (eds.), *Warlands: Population Resettlement and State Reconstruction in the Soviet-East European Borderlands, 1945–50* (Basingstoke, 2009), pp. 210–28
Beata Ociepka, *Deportacja, wysiedlenie, przesiedlenia – powojenne migracje z Polski i do Polski* (Poznań, 2001)
Arkadiusz Ogrodowczyk, *Nad Odrą i Bałtykiem. Osadnictwo wojskowe na zachodnich i północnich ziemiach Polski po drugiej wojnie światowej* (Warsaw, 1979)
Leszek Olejnik, *Polityka Narodowościowa Polski w latach 1944–1960* (Łódź, 2003)
Losy volksdeutschów w Polsce po II wojnie światowej (Warsaw, 2006)
Hubert Orłowski and Andrzej Sakson, *Utracona ojczyzna. Przymusowe wysiedlenia, deportacja i przesiedlenia jako wspólne doświadczenie* (Poznań, 1996)

Czesław Osękowski, *Społeczeństwo Polski zachodniej i północnej w latach 1945–1956. Procesy integracji i dezintegracji* (Zielona Góra, 1994)
Andrzej Paczkowski, *The Spring Will Be Ours. Poland and the Poles from Occupation to Freedom* (University Park, Pennsylvania, 2003)
Kazimierz Paschenda, *Einführung und Bedeutung der Deutschen Volksliste in Oberschlesien 1941–1944* (Magisterarbeit, Johann Wolfgang Goethe-Universität, Frankfurt am Main, 1998)
Bronisław Pasierb, 'Problemy repolonizacyjne rejonu jeleniogórskiego w latach 1945–1948', *Rocznik Jeleniogórski*, 4, 1966, pp. 19–42
Migracja ludności niemieckiej z Dolnego Śląska w latach 1944–1947 (Wrocław, Warsaw, Kraków, 1969)
Thomas Petersen, *Flucht und Vertreibung aus Sicht der deutschen, polnischen und tschechischen Bevölkerung* (Bonn, 2005)
Jan Pisuliński, *Przesiedlenie ludności ukraińskiej z Polski do USRR w latach 1944–1947* (Rzeszów, 2009)
J. Otto Pohl, *Ethnic Cleansing in the USSR, 1937–1949* (Westport, Connecticut, 1999)
Pavel Polian, *Against Their Will: The History and Geography of Forced Migrations in the USSR* (Budapest and New York, 2004)
Anita Prażmowska, *Britain and Poland, 1939–1943. The Betrayed Ally* (Cambridge, 1995)
Civil War in Poland, 1942–1948 (Basingstoke, 2004)
Poland: A Modern History (London, 2010)
Alexander V. Prusin, *The Lands Between: Conflict in the East European Borderlands, 1870–1992* (Oxford, 2010)
Adam Redzik, 'Szkic dzieja Uniwersytetu Lwoskiego w latach 1939–1946', *Visnyk L'vivs'kovo Universitetu*, 2007, pp. 577–92
Gerhard Reichling, *Die deutschen Vertriebenen in Zahlen. Teil 1: Umsiedler, Verschleppte, Vertriebene, Aussiedler 1940–1985* (Bonn, 1986)
Alfred J. Rieber (ed.), *Forced Migration in Central and Eastern Europe, 1939–1950* (London, 2000)
'Repressive Population Transfers in Central and Eastern Europe: A Historical Overview', in Alfred J. Rieber (ed.), *Forced Migration in Central and Eastern Europe, 1939–1950* (London, 2000), pp. 1–27
Milan Ristović, 'Zwangsmigrationen in den Territorien Jugoslawiens im Zweiten Weltkrieg: Pläne, Realisierung, Improvisation, Folgen', in Ralph Melville, Jiří Pešek and Claus Scharf (eds.), *Zwangsmigrationen im mittleren und östlichen Europa. Völkerrecht – Kozeptionen – Praxis (1938–1950)* (Mainz, 2007), pp. 309–30
Joachim Rogall, 'Zweiter Weltkrieg, Flucht, Eroberung, Vertreibung', in Joachim Bahlcke (ed.), *Schlesien und die Schlesier* (Munich, 1996), pp. 156–70
Zenon Romanow, *Ludność niemiecka na ziemiach zachodnich w latach 1945–1947* (Słupsk, 1992)
Polityka władz polskich wobec ludności rodzimej ziem zachodnich i północnych w latach 1945–1960 (Słupsk, 1999)

Alexander B. Rossino, *Hitler Strikes Poland. Blitzkrieg, Ideology, and Atrocity* (Lawrence, Kansas, 2003)

Krzysztof Ruchniewicz, 'Das Problem der Zwangsaussiedlung der Deutschen aus polnischer und deutscher Sicht in Vergangenheit und Gegenwart', *Berichte und Forschungen: Jahrbuch des Bundesinstituts für Kultur und Geschichte der Deutschen im östlichen Europa*, 10, 2002, pp. 7–26

'Von Lemberg nach Breslau – eine Universität zwischen Tradition und Neubestimmung', *Orbis Linguarum*, 21, 2002, pp. 9–17

Maria Rutowska, *Wysiedlenie ludności polskiej z Kraju Warty do Generalnego Gubernatorstwa 1939–1941* (Poznań, 2003)

Andrzej Sakson, *Mazury – społeczność pogranicza* (Poznań, 1990)

Stosunki narodowościowe na Warmii i Mazurach 1945–1997 (Poznań, 1998)

George Sanford, *Katyn and the Soviet Massacre of 1940. Truth, Justice and Memory* (London, 2005)

Joseph Schechtman, *Postwar Population Transfers in Europe 1945–1955* (Philadelphia, 1962)

Theodor Schieder, 'Die Vertreibung der Deutschen aus dem Osten als wissenschaftliches Problem', *Vierteljahrshefte für Zeitgeschichte*, 8, 1, 1960, pp. 1–16

John R. Schindler, 'Yugoslavia's First Ethnic Cleansing: The Expulsion of Danubian Germans, 1944–46', in Steven Béla Várdy and T. Hunt Tooley (eds.), *Ethnic Cleansing in Twentieth-Century Europe* (New York, 2003), pp. 359–72

Helmut Schmitz (ed.), *A Nation of Victims? Representations of German Wartime Suffering from 1945 to the Present* (Amsterdam and New York, 2007)

Rainer Schulze, 'Growing Discontent: Relations between Natives and Refugee Populations in a Rural District in Western Germany after the Second World War', *German History*, 7, 3, 1989, pp. 332–49

'Memory and Commemoration of Flight and Expulsion in Germany', in Pertti Ahonen, Gustavo Corni, Jerzy Kochanowski, Rainer Schulze, Tamás Stark and Barbara Stelzl-Marx, *People on the Move: Forced Population Movements in Europe in the Second World War and Its Aftermath* (Oxford, 2008), pp. 145–55

Michael Schwartz, 'Vertreibung und Vergangenheitspolitik: Ein Versuch über geteilte deutsche Nachkriegsidentitäten', *Deutschland Archiv: Zeitschrift für das vereinigte Deutschland*, 30, 2, 1997, pp. 177–95

'Refugees and Expellees in the Soviet Zone of Germany: Political and Social Problems of Their Integration, 1945–1950', in Alfred J. Rieber (ed.), *Forced Migration in Central and Eastern Europe, 1939–1950* (London, 2000), pp. 148–74

'Tabu und Erinnerung. Zur Vertriebenen-Problematik in Politik und literarischer Öffentlichkeit der DDR', *Zeitschrift für Geschichtswissenschaft*, 2003, 1, pp. 85–101

Vertriebene und "Umsiedlerpolitik": Integrationskonflikte in den deutschen Nachkriegs-Gesellschaften und die Assimilationsstrategien in der SBZ/DDR 1945–1961 (Munich, 2004)

Robert Seidel, *Deutsche Besatzungspolitik in Polen. Der Distrikt Radom 1939–1945* (Paderborn, 2006)

Hugo Service, 'Sifting Poles from Germans? Ethnic Cleansing and Ethnic Screening in Upper Silesia, 1945–1949', *Slavonic and East European Review*, 88, 4, 2010, pp. 652–80

'Reinterpreting the Expulsion of Germans from Poland, 1945–9', *Journal of Contemporary History*, 47, 3, 2012, pp. 528–50

Sebastian Siebel-Achenbach, *Lower Silesia from Nazi Germany to Communist Poland* (Basingstoke and London, 1994)

Jan Ryszard Sielezin, 'Polityka polskich władz wobec ludności niemieckiej na terenie kotliny jeleniogórskiej w 1945 r.', *Śląski Kwartalnik Historyczny Sobótka*, 55, 2000, pp. 67–90

K. Skubiszewski, *Wysiedlenie Niemców po II wojnie światowej* (Warsaw, 1968)

Timothy Snyder, '"To Resolve the Ukrainian Problem Once and for All". The Ethnic Cleansing of Ukrainians in Poland, 1943–1947', *Journal of Cold War Studies*, 1, 2, 1999, pp. 86–120

The Reconstruction of Nations: Poland, Ukraine, Lithuania, Belarus, 1569–1999 (New Haven, Connecticut, 2003)

'The Causes of Ukrainian–Polish Ethnic Cleansing 1943', *Past and Present*, 179, May 2003, pp. 197–234

Bloodlands: Europe between Hitler and Stalin (New York, 2010)

Mark Spoerer, *Zwangsarbeit unter dem Hakenkreuz. Ausländische Zivilarbeiter, Kriegsgefangene und Häftlinge im Deutschen Reich und im besetzten Europa 1939–1945* (Stuttgart and Munich, 2001)

Kataryna Stadnik,'Ukrainian–Polish Population Transfers, 1944–46: Moving in Opposite Directions', in Peter Gatrell and Nick Baron (eds.), *Warlands: Population Resettlement and State Reconstruction in the Soviet–East European Borderlands, 1945–50* (Basingstoke, 2009), pp. 165–87

Tomáš Staněk, *Odsun Němcu z Československa 1945–1947* (Prague, 1991)

'Vertreibung und Aussiedlung der Deutschen aus der Tschechoslowakei', in Detlef Brandes and Václav Kural (eds.), *Der Weg in die Katastrophe: Deutsch–Tschechoslowakische Beziehungen 1938–1947* (Düsseldorf, 1994), pp. 165–86

Verfolgung 1945: Die Stellung der Deutschen in Böhmen, Mähren und Schlesien (außerhalb der Lager und Gefängnisse) (Vienna, 2002)

Albert Stankowski, 'Nowe spojrzenie na statystyki dotyczące emigracji Żydów z Polski po 1944 roku', in Grzegorz Berendt, August Grabski and Albert Stankowski (eds.), *Studia z Historii Żydów w Polsce po 1945 Roku* (Warsaw, 2000), pp. 103–51

Witold Stankowski, *Obozy i inne miejsca odosobnienia dla niemieckiej ludności cywilnej w Polsce w latach 1945–1950* (Bydgoszcz, 2002)

'Obozy i miejsca odosobnienia dla Niemców w Polsce w latach 1945–1950', *Przegląd Zachodni*, 4, 2003, pp. 25–47

Tamás Stark, 'Ethnic Cleansing and Collective Punishment: Soviet Policy towards Prisoners of War and Civilian Internees in the Carpathian Basin', in Steven

Béla Várdy and T. Hunt Tooley (eds.), *Ethnic Cleansing in Twentieth-Century Europe* (New York, 2003), pp. 489–502
'Hungary: Principles and Practices' and 'Romanian Plans and Practices', in Pertti Ahonen, Gustavo Corni, Jerzy Kochanowski, Rainer Schulze, Tamás Stark and Barbara Stelzl-Marx, *People on the Move: Forced Population Movements in Europe in the Second World War and Its Aftermath* (Oxford, 2008), pp. 48–53
'The Fate of the Defeated Nations in the Carpatho-Danubian Basin', in Pertti Ahonen, Gustavo Corni, Jerzy Kochanowski, Rainer Schulze, Tamás Stark and Barbara Stelzl-Marx, *People on the Move: Forced Population Movements in Europe in the Second World War and Its Aftermath* (Oxford, 2008), pp. 69–86
Katrin Steffen, 'Flucht, Vertreibung und Zwangsaussiedlung der Deutschen aus der Wojewodschaft Stettin (Województwo Szczecińskie) in den Jahren 1945–1950', in Włodzimierz Borodziej and Hans Lemberg (eds.), *"Unsere Heimat ist uns ein fremdes Land geworden..." Die Deutschen östlich von Oder und Neiße 1945–1950: Dokumente aus polnischen Archiven* (4 vols., Marburg, 2000–2004), Vol. 3: *Wojewodschaft Posen. Wojewodschaft Stettin (Hinterpommern)* (Marburg, 2003), pp. 269–344
Sybille Steinbacher, *Auschwitz: A History* (London, 2005)
Barbara Stelzl-Marx, 'Forced Labourers in the Third Reich', in Pertti Ahonen, Gustavo Corni, Jerzy Kochanowski, Rainer Schulze, Tamás Stark and Barbara Stelzl-Marx, *People on the Move: Forced Population Movements in Europe in the Second World War and Its Aftermath* (Oxford, 2008), pp. 167–98
Grzegorz Strauchold, *Polska ludność rodzima ziem zachodnich i północnych. Opinie nie tylko publiczne lat 1944–1948* (Olsztyn, 1995)
Autochtoni polscy, niemieccy czy... Od nacjonalizmu do komunizmu (1945–1999) (Toruń, 2001)
Myśl zachodnia i jej realizacja w Polsce Ludowej w latach 1945–1957 (Toruń, 2003)
Christian Streit, *Keine Kameraden. Die Wehrmacht und die sowjetischen Kriegsgefangenen 1941–1945* (2nd edn, Bonn, 1991)
Kai Struve and Philipp Ther (eds.), *Nationen und ihre Grenzen. Identitätswandel in Oberschlesien in der Neuzeit* (Marburg, 2002)
Orest Subtelny, 'Expulsion, Resettlement, Civil Strife: The Fate of Poland's Ukrainians, 1944–1947', in Philipp Ther and Ana Siljak (eds.), *Redrawing Nations: Ethnic Cleansing in East-Central Europe, 1944–1948* (Lanham, 2001), pp. 155–72
Dorota Sula, *Działalność przesiedleńczo-repatriacyjna Państwowego Urzędu Repatriacyjnego w latach 1944–1951* (Lublin, 2002)
Małgorzata Świder, *Die sogenannte Entgermanisierung im Oppelner Schlesien in den Jahren 1945–1950* (Lauf a.d. Pegnitz, 2002)
Keith Sword, 'Soviet Economic Policy in the Annexed Areas', in Keith Sword (ed.), *The Soviet Takeover of the Polish Eastern Provinces, 1939–41* (London, 1991), pp. 86–101
Tomasz Szarota, *Osadnictwo miejskie na Dolnym Śląsku w latach 1945–1948* (Wrocław, 1969)

Bożena Szaynok, 'Jews in Lower Silesia 1945–1950', in Marcin Wodziński and Janusz Spyra (eds.), *Jews in Silesia* (Kraków, 2001), pp. 213–28

Philipp Ther, 'The Integration of Expellees in Germany and Poland after World War II: A Historical Reassessment', *Slavic Review*, 55, 1996, 4, pp. 779–805

'Die Vertriebenenproblematik in Brandenburg und im Oppelner Schlesien 1945–1952. Ausgewählte Aspekte einer vergleichenden Landesgeschichte', *Zeitschrift für Ostmitteleuropa-Forschung*, 46, 1997, 4, pp. 513–34

Deutsche und polnische Vertriebene. Gesellschaft und Vertriebenenpolitik in der SBZ/DDR und in Polen 1945–1956 (Göttingen, 1998)

'A Century of Forced Migration: The Origins and Consequences of "Ethnic Cleansing"', in Philipp Ther and Ana Siljak (eds.), *Redrawing Nations: Ethnic Cleansing in East-Central Europe, 1944–1948* (Lanham, 2001), pp. 43–72

'Die einheimische Bevölkerung des Oppelner Schlesiens nach dem Zweiten Weltkrieg. Die Entstehung einer deutschen Minderheit', *Geschichte und Gesellschaft*, 26, 2000, pp. 407–38

'Expellee Policy in the Soviet-Occupied Zone and the GDR: 1945–1953', in David Rock and Stefan Wolff (eds.), *Coming Home to Germany? The Integration of Ethnic Germans from Central and Eastern Europe in the Federal Republic* (New York and Oxford, 2002), pp. 56–76

Philipp Ther and Ana Siljak (eds.), *Redrawing Nations: Ethnic Cleansing in East-Central Europe, 1944–1948* (Lanham, 2001)

Gregor Thum, *Die fremde Stadt. Breslau 1945* (Berlin, 2003)

Jerzy Tomaszewski, 'Niepodległa Rzeczpospolita', in Jerzy Tomaszewski (ed.), *Najnowsze Dzieje Żydów w Polsce: w zarysie (do 1950 roku)* (Warsaw, 1993), pp. 143–272

T. Hunt Tooley, *National Identity and Weimar Germany. Upper Silesia and the Eastern Border, 1918–1922* (Lincoln and London, 1997)

Ágnes Tóth, 'Die Annahme der Kollektivschuldthese und die Bestrafung der deutschen Minderheit in Ungarn 1945–1946', in Ralph Melville, Jiří Pešek and Claus Scharf (eds.), *Zwangsmigrationen im mittleren und östlichen Europa. Völkerrecht – Kozeptionen – Praxis (1938–1950)* (Mainz, 2007), pp. 393–406

Jakub Tyszkiewicz, *Sto wielkich dni Wrocławia. Wystawa Ziem Odzyskanych we Wrocławiu a propaganda polityczna ziem zachodnich i północnych w latach 1945–1948* (Wrocław, 1997)

Od upadku Festung Breslau do Stalinowskiego Wrocławia. Kalendarium 1945–1950 (Warsaw and Wrocław, 2000)

Thomas Urban, *Der Verlust. Die Vertreibung der Deutschen und Polen im 20. Jahrhundert* (Munich, 2004)

Agnes Huszár Várdy, 'Forgotten Victims of World War II: Hungarian Women in Soviet Forced Labour', in Steven Béla Várdy and T. Hunt Tooley (eds.), *Ethnic Cleansing in Twentieth-Century Europe* (New York, 2003), pp. 503–16

Steven Béla Várdy and T. Hunt Tooley (eds.), *Ethnic Cleansing in Twentieth-Century Europe* (New York, 2003)

Sarah Wambaugh, *Plebiscites since the World War. With a Collection of Official Documents* (2 vols., Washington, DC, 1933)
Maria Wanda Wanatowicz, *Historia społeczno-polityczna Górnego Śląska i Śląska Cieszyńskiego w latach 1918–1945* (Katowice, 1994)
Ewa Waszkiewicz, 'A History of Jewish Settlement in Lower Silesia, 1945–1950', *Polin: Studies in Polish Jewry*, 23, 2011, pp. 507–19
Theodore R. Weeks, 'Population Politics in Vilnius 1944–1947: A Case Study of Socialist-Sponsored Ethnic Cleansing', *Post-Soviet Affairs*, 23, 2007, 1, pp. 76–95
A. Wegener (ed.), *Historisches Ortschaftsverzeichnis. Reihe historischer Ortschaftsverzeichnisse für ehemals zu Deutschland gehörige Gebiete – Zeitraum 1914 bis 1945* (14 vols., Frankfurt am Main, 1994–1997), Vol. I: *Oberschlesien* (Frankfurt am Main, 1994)
Amir Weiner, 'Nature, Nurture, and Memory in a Socialist Utopia: Delineating the Soviet Socio-Ethnic Body in the Age of Socialism', *The American Historical Review*, 104, 4, Oct. 1999, pp. 1114–55
Juliane Wetzel, '"Displaced Person". Ein vergessenes Kapitel der deutschen Nachkriegsgeschichte', *Aus Politik und Zeitgeschichte*, B7–8/95, pp. 34–9
Andreas Wiedemann, *"Komm mit uns das Grenzland aufbauen!" Ansiedlung und neue Strukturen in den ehemaligen Sudetengebieten 1945–1952* (Essen, 2007)
Manfred Wille, Johannes Hofmann and Wolfgang Meinicke (eds.), *Sie hatten alles verloren. Flüchtlinge und Vertriebene in der sowjetischen Besatzungszone Deutschlands* (Wiesbaden, 1993)
Rafał Wnuk, *"Za pierwszego Sowieta". Polska konspiracja na Kresach Wschodnich II Rzeczypospolitej (wrzesień 1939–czerwiec 1941)* (Warsaw, 2007)
Rafal Wnuk (ed.), *Atlas polskiego podziemia niepodległościowego 1944–1956* (Warsaw, 2007)
Edmund Wojnowski, *Warmia i Mazury w latach 1945–1947. Życie polityczne* (Olsztyn, 1970)
Wojciech Wrzesiński, *Dolny Śląsk: Monografia historyczna* (Wrocław, 2006)
Tara Zahra, 'Reclaiming Children for the Nation: Germanization, National Ascription, and Democracy in the Bohemian Lands, 1900–1945', *Central European History*, 37, 2004, 4, pp. 501–43
Marcin Zaremba, *Komunizm, legitymacja, nacjonalism. Nacjonalistyczna legitymacja władzy komunistycznej w Polsce* (Warsaw, 2001)
Wielka Trwoga. Polska 1944–1947: Ludowa reakcja na kryzys (Kraków, 2012)
Konrad Zieliński, 'To Pacify, Populate and Polonise: Territorial Transformations and the Displacement of Ethnic Minorities in Communist Poland, 1944–49', in Peter Gatrell and Nick Baron (eds.), *Warlands: Population Resettlement and State Reconstruction in the Soviet–East European Borderlands, 1945–50* (Basingstoke, 2009), pp. 188–209
Volker Zimmermann, *Die Sudetendeutschen im NS-Staat: Politik und Stimmung der Bevölkerung im Reichsgau Sudetenland 1938–1945* (Essen, 1999)

Stanisław Żyromski, *Przesiedlenie ludności niemieckiej z województwa olsztyńskiego poza granice Polski w latach 1945–1950* (Olsztyn, 1969)

Vertreibung und Vertreibungsverbrechen 1945–1948. Bericht des Bundesarchivs vom 28. Mai 1974. Archivalien und ausgewählte Erlebnisberichte (Bonn, 1989)

Index

CPSIA information can be obtained
at www.ICGtesting.com
Printed in the USA
LVHW08s2329160918
590346LV00025B/571/P